A World Without Walls

Freedom, Development, Free Trade and Global Governance

Mike Moore's reflection on his time as Director-General of the World Trade Organization is an important addition to the great globalisation debate. Moore explains how a boy who left school at fourteen to work in a slaughterhouse came to head an organisation charged with bringing rules and order to the world's trading system. Arriving at the WTO shortly before the ill-fated Seattle meeting, Moore sought to reform the Organization, addressing the concerns of poorer countries and engaging in open debate with the often hostile non-governmental organisations (NGOs). He successfully negotiated ten new members into the WTO, including the world's most populous nation, China, and he gives an insider's view of how these negotiations were navigated. He is proud that in November 2001, at the meeting in Doha, these nations promised their commitment to a new round of trade talks with a focus on development. Moore rebuts the attacks against the WTO, and argues that the WTO's promise of rules-based free trade offers the best hope for lifting millions of the world's poorest citizens out of poverty. *A World Without Walls* examines our interdependent world which is now just beginning to integrate and offers refreshing perspectives on an emerging global civil society and the challenges of corporate and global governance.

MIKE MOORE, the Director-General of the World Trade Organization from 1999 to 2002, is a former New Zealand Prime Minister, Trade Minister, Foreign Minister and Deputy Finance Minister. He has been honoured and recognised by over a dozen governments and universities in the Americas, Africa, the Pacific and Europe. He is also the author of *A Brief History of the Future, Children of the Poor, Fighting for New Zealand* and *The Added Value Economy*, amongst other books.

A World Without Walls

Freedom, Development, Free Trade and Global Governance

Mike Moore

CAMBRIDGE
UNIVERSITY PRESS

PUBLISHED BY THE PRESS SYNDICATE OF THE UNIVERSITY OF CAMBRIDGE
The Pitt Building, Trumpington Street, Cambridge CB2 1RP, United Kingdom

CAMBRIDGE UNIVERSITY PRESS
The Edinburgh Building, Cambridge CB2 2RU, UK
40 West 20th Street, New York, NY 10011-4211, USA
477 Williamstown Road, Port Melbourne, VIC 3207, Australia
Ruiz de Alarcón 13, 28014 Madrid, Spain
Dock House, The Waterfront, Cape Town 8001, South Africa

http://www.cambridge.org

© Mike Moore 2003

First published 2003
Reprinted 2003

Printed in the United States of America

Typeface Plantin 10/12 pt   *System* LaTeX 2$_\varepsilon$ [TB]

A catalogue record for this book is available from the British Library

ISBN 0 521 82701 9 hardback

George Bernard Shaw said that reasonable people don't make change, that all human progress is based on unreasonable people. This book is dedicated to those unreasonable people who demand and work for peace and progress.

Contents

Part Three: Citizens, corporates and a new deal for global governance

Figures

Tables

Acknowledgements

Any book is in the end only a reflection of all the author's influences, personalities encountered, books and articles read, and personal and professional experiences. I have learned a great deal from many people – politicians, public servants, academics, businessmen, authors and NGOs – whose work and ideas I have devoured over the years. I owe a special debt to colleagues, staff and ambassadors at the World Trade Organization, for their experience and advice – some of which I even took.

In particular, I want to thank David Porter for his editorial guidance, and Intan Hamdan and Katie Waters, for research assistance. Jagdish Bhagwati, Clemens Boonekamp, Tim Groser, Patrick Low, Diarmid Martin, Patrick Rata, George Soros, Peter Watson and Ernesto Zedillo took the time to read drafts of this book and comment. Paulette Planchette, Ursula Stephenson and Susan Conn mastered the art of transcribing my handwriting. As always, thanks to my wife Yvonne, who has for many years put up with me getting up at 5 am and scribbling down ideas on yellow legal pads. My thanks also to Chris Harrison at Cambridge University Press for shepherding this book through to publication. However, as is always the case, in politics or authorship, the final responsibility is mine and any errors are mine alone.

All books are works in progress. *A World Without Walls*[*] was several years in the making and draws in part upon material researched for articles and speeches I prepared and published during my term at the WTO. I have also advanced and developed some of the ideas I first canvassed in an earlier book, *A Brief History of the Future*. I hope this effort pushes, probes and promotes a wider debate on these issues that are so important for our common global future.

MIKE MOORE,
Geneva, August 2002

[*] The phrase 'world without walls' is not new – it has been used by many people, although I believe that I first read it in The Reith Lecture delivered by President Clinton.

1 Introduction: The making of an internationalist

How does a dyed-in-the-wool lifelong New Zealand Labour activist become an unabashed advocate of the advantages of globalisation? There is no contradiction between a lifelong adherence to the principles of internationalism and worker solidarity, and believing in the worldwide benefits of the free flow of trade and ideas.

I started working at fourteen, helping slaughter thousands of animals a day in one of the meat works that provided seasonal employment in Moerewa, a poor, small town in rural New Zealand. I hated the violence – not just the killing, but the brutality of the environment. Why be efficient? When you did well, you just worked your way faster out of a job.

At an early age, I learned to despise power, privilege and the bullying that goes with it, perhaps because I spent some time in a boarding school for children from 'difficult circumstances'. My mother, widowed with three boys under twelve, came from a family where Labour was a religion not an ideology, and where memories of the Great Depression of the 1930s lingered long. We were tribal in our loyalty to Labour.

For poor New Zealanders, buried away at the bottom of the world in that faraway pre-Internet age, Wall Street had little to do with our memories of the Depression, which destroyed many families that had for generations broken in hard countryside with bullock and axe. As a Labour politician of the time described it, these toiling workers lost their farms while 'wiping the sweat from their brows with the slack of their guts'. We grew up convinced it was the Conservative government in New Zealand that had caused the Great Depression, not Wall Street, and that Labour rescued our nation, as F. D. Roosevelt was to do for the USA. A photo of Labour's first Prime Minister, Michael Joseph Savage, hung on our wall. A saint, I was told. I didn't join the Labour party, I was born into it.

I grew up a rural-town boy from a small country who, lightly touched by polio and with a leg in a brace, came to the grim early realisation he could never aspire to the great New Zealand dream of becoming a rugby All Black. Instead, I devoured books and settled on the lowlier ambition, in Kiwi terms, of becoming a politician. After becoming the youngest-ever politician elected to the Parliament, at twenty-three, I quickly became the youngest-ever defeated, at the next election. But I eventually went on to help the 1984 Labour government forge the dramatic market-opening market reforms that drew the attention of economists worldwide, serving as Trade and Foreign Minister, Deputy Finance Minister and holding several other portfolios. This experience deepened my interest in the major issues of trade and globalisation that have since come to play such a significant role in world development and security. My most enjoyable portfolio, though, was as Minister for the America Cup, which saw the launch of the most expensive fleet since the Greeks invaded Troy to rescue Helen. Kiwi Black Magic eventually won the cup, and the rights to host an event that netted millions in additional tourist revenues for New Zealand and kick-started a high-tech boat-building industry.

My formative years were as a young idealist MP in a very marginal seat, watching the first Labour government in more than a decade fall apart under the pressure of the oil crisis in the early 1970s, extravagant election promises and a populist opposition National Party. I had cheered on budget night when my youthful heroes in the Cabinet tried to ban inflation in housing prices with a 90 per cent speculation tax. I was ecstatic when my government decided to ban inflation on household products by insisting companies label all products with a maximum retail price – until I visited factories in my electorate that withdrew product lines, and saw for myself that the policies didn't work. Labour was heavily defeated, I lost my seat, and I began to think through economic alternatives to how we had handled the crises, many of them of our own making.

Robert Muldoon, a populist leader, became New Zealand Prime Minister. We called him right wing, but in fact he was Peronist. His response to the oil crisis and every other problem was even more control and huge taxpayer-backed doomed 'think-big' Sukarno/Soviet-type projects to make New Zealand independent of world prices, such as a gas-to-gasoline plant. He was, as Lenin suggested when he launched the New Economic Policy, aiming to control the 'commanding heights of the economy', a policy advanced by Harold Wilson, Nehru and many other leaders of that generation.

It was a different age. They were of a generation that had seen how the world had mobilised resources to win a war. They wanted to control and mobilise the nation's resources managed from the centre to grow and win in peacetime. This view was not restricted to the democratic left. Richard Nixon decided to ban inflation and introduced wage and price controls in the USA. Edward Health sought similar remedies in the UK.

On the opposition benches following the election in 1978, a group of Labour MPs began to think and write about a different approach.

When the New Zealand economy had deteriorated to the extent that the conservative National Party government could no longer come up with a budget, things fell apart. In July 1984, Muldoon called a snap election and lost.

A week after that election, *The Economist* wrote:

> In a country with 3.2 million people and 70 million sheep, [Muldoon's] slogan was, 'Think Big'. Sir Robert preferred to borrow abroad rather than devalue, saddling New Zealand with foreign debts equal to 45 per cent of its GDP, proportionally more than Brazil has. Since Sir Robert became Prime Minister in 1975, New Zealand's GDP has grown by only 0.75 per cent a year, the slowest of the 24 countries belonging to the Organisation for Economic Cooperation and Development (OECD). New Zealanders can count themselves lucky they were rich to begin with. If theirs had been a developing country, the Muldoon treatment would have made it one of the world's disasters. Like those Third World leaders who have fouled up their economies, Sir Robert was fond of dismissing criticism by claiming he was 'on the side of the people'. The people have now had their say. Other populists please note.[1]

Labour was elected on a slogan of 'Bringing New Zealand together'. We were New Labour when Tony Blair was still at university, pioneering reforms that are still drawn upon and written about worldwide. However, in 1984 we weren't acting out of principle or idealism, but desperation. Other options were foreclosed. If we'd been a developing country, the International Monetary Fund (IMF) would have come in. Instead we were 'rich' – but deeply in debt. Within a generation of enjoying the highest living standard in the world, we were almost at the bottom of the OECD table. Radical surgery was needed.

In a short time after taking office, we:
- abolished billions of dollars in subsidies to agriculture, our most competitive products
- abolished central control of the sale of meat
- floated the dollar
- gave statutory independence to the Central Bank, based on a contract with the Governor (replicated by UK Chancellor Gordon Brown)
- paid down the debt by privatisation – debt servicing was costing 19 cents in every dollar, more than our public investment in education
- substantially increased our real investment in education and health
- abolished several hundred local government units
- reformed the waterfront, from it taking sometimes thirteen or fourteen days to turn a ship around to thirty hours
- abolished dozens of sales taxes and introduced a general sales tax (GST) of 10 per cent; brought both personal taxes, which formerly peaked at 66 per cent, and company tax, at nearly 50 per cent, down to a common 33 per cent

- introduced a family support payment system to protect low income earners from the initial costs of introducing the GST
- opened up immigration
- put a hated surcharge on pensioners who earned above a certain level
- reformed the public service.

We were pioneers: *The World Bank Development Report, 1997*, judged the New Zealand experiment as follows: 'There is a growing trend to set up focussed, performance-based public agencies with more clarity of purpose and greater managerial accountability for outputs or outcomes. New Zealand provides the most dramatic example among the high income countries. It broke up its conglomerate ministries into focussed business units, headed by chief executives on fixed-term, output-based contracts, with the authority to hire and fire and to bargain collectively.'[2]

But change is traumatic, especially in a small country, and the reforms were not popular. As the then New Zealand Central Bank Governor Don Brash observed: 'Perhaps [media commentator Lindsay] Perigo was right when he said that New Zealand was 'a country reformed by Hayekians, run by pragmatists and populated by socialists.' My own hunch is that, probably in common with the citizens of other Western countries, New Zealanders accept that socialism does not work in the economy, but remain wedded to the welfare state and a Fabian notion of 'fairness'.'[3]

None of us had read much of F. A. Hayek at that time, but a few had studied Karl Popper, whose seminal book *The Open Society and its Enemies* was written while Popper was living in New Zealand.

The initial internal contradictions eventually got too much for the Labour Party in government, and it imploded in fatal factionalism. Australian Labour, which was not as radical and did not face the same critical economic conditions, managed to resolve its internal party contradictions much better when it was in power across the Tasman. I argued in the party for a wider compact with the major players in the economy, but lost that debate.

I eventually became Prime Minister – my desperate caucus colleagues having by then given up on everyone else – when the Labour government had finally plummeted to the nadir of its popularity. In doing so, I again distinguished myself, this time by becoming the shortest-serving premier in the country's history. However, I did succeed in uniting the country – queues formed hours before the polling booths opened on election day as they voted to give me some time off. But that's democracy: the people are always right, even when they're wrong. Although I had doubled Labour's popularity in the polls, it wasn't enough to turn the tide. We had exhausted the public's patience by internal warfare, and faced a populist conservative opposition vowing to undo our reforms. To their credit, they did not do

Figure 1. New Zealand cartoonist Jim Hubbard always saw me as a panda: he summed up the standoff in the leadership struggle.

so. But at least I'd kept the Labour Party intact as the major opposition party, and I returned to Parliament to continue the fight.

Why the WTO?

I have been intimately involved with the World Trade Organization (WTO), both as a minister and as opposition spokesman on trade, since before the Uruguay Round of the General Agreement on Tariffs and Trade (GATT) in 1986. I have spent the past three years at the helm of this multilateral inter-governmental organisation. I am proud of the WTO's achievements under my leadership, in particular the successful launch of a new Trade Round, the Doha Development Agenda in 2001 – the first since the Uruquay Round in 1986 – and the accession of more than a quarter of the world's population into the membership, with the admission of Lithuania, Moldova, Oman, Jordan, Croatia, Albania, Estonia, Georgia and of course, most significantly for world trade, China and Chinese Taipei. Russia's accession is also now much closer.

Having taken part in pioneering economic reforms in a small, 'developed' country, made mistakes, observed what worked and what did not, it has been illuminating to have the opportunity to study these issues at a macro, global level, working with governments around the world as they wrestle with the key issues of trade and economic development. Over the past few years in Geneva, I've enjoyed a bird's-eye view of how and why this happens. I have reached one core conclusion, which is why I've written this book. Economies work best where there is a democratic system, a professional civil service, honest and transparent political parties, open commerce, a free and fair media, free trade unions and religious tolerance. Much of this is misunderstood and seen as a victory for the politics of the right.

The definition of left and right has always been blurred and self-serving. One definition centres on control of the economy, on how much is owned by the state or controlled by the state. That was a puerile definition, with Marxist overtones. In Marxist countries the state owned everything, in fascist countries the state controlled most things. Hitler, Mussolini, Peron and Franco all controlled their economies to a far greater extent than social democratic states like Sweden or New Zealand in the 1930s. Those who in their youth were heavily influenced by far-left thinking, many based in Paris or at the London School of Economics, from China's Deng Xiaoping to leftist Brazilian Fernando Henrique Cardoso, when in power were at the vanguard of radically reforming their economies to achieve social justice through market mechanisms.

As Deng once said, the choice was between redistributing poverty so that all were equally poor; or redistributing wealth, so that inevitably some would be rich and some poor.

Both suffered exile or imprisonment, ridicule and the contempt of colleagues. But both Deng and Cardoso were responsible for lifting millions out of poverty. When Cardoso became Finance Minister in 1993, inflation was 7,000 per cent. Within a month, under his so-called Real Plan for recovery, he brought inflation down to 10 per cent.[4] Both encouraged foreign investment, privatised costly state-owned enterprises, reformed the tax collection system and attacked corruption. Deng called it socialism with Chinese characteristics. President Cardoso talked of a regulated free market.

The WTO and globalisation have become dirty words in some circles in recent years, both blamed for everything from global poverty and human rights abuses to the destruction of indigenous cultures. But I remain an unabashed believer in internationalism, solidarity and freedom – in free trade, open markets, democracy, good governance and an active participating civil society, as the pillars of development and success. I believe that the free flow of goods and ideas promoted by bodies such as the WTO acts as a catalyst for development, and has lifted living standards worldwide and strengthened human rights. We should neither idealise nor demonise globalisation.

I described my early years and background in New Zealand's pioneering economic reforms in some detail, because it seems to confuse some commentators that a veteran labour/social democrat such as myself can also be such a passionate advocate of political and economic internationalism. There is no contradiction. Privilege, and the power that accrues through it and to it, survives and prospers best when protected by the state. By contrast, freedom and equality of opportunity acts in direct opposition to protected, powerful and privileged forces, helping break them down and redistributing power, wealth and opportunity.

As a social democrat, heading this organisation attracted me. The WTO does not act to preserve monopolies and privilege, but works to accomplish the reverse. Competition and openness is the opposite of monopolies and privilege, helping create a level playing field on which countries of the world at all stages of development can freely exchange goods and services. Protectionism and economic and political isolationism are not tenets of true social democrat thinking, but rather holdovers of colonialism and imperialism, the near collapse of capitalism in the 1920s, the Cold War stand-off and the monstrous Marxist aberration that distorted social democratic thinking.

A number of internationalists come from similar backgrounds to my own. It is no accident that officials like US Secretary of State Cordell Hull – who essentially led Franklin Roosevelt in seeking to drive internationalism through economic vehicles such as trade – was from a poor rural state and saw trade as a vehicle for peace and development. Hull once said: 'I have never faltered, and I will never falter, in my belief that enduring peace and the welfare of nations are indissolubly connected with...the maximum practicable degree of freedom in international trade.'[5]

Similarly, the thinking of the greatest British Foreign Secretary of the last century, Labour's Ernie Bevin, was moulded by his rage at the injustices he saw as he endured a poor rural upbringing. He devoted his life to trying to improve conditions for the working poor, and in doing so created both the world's largest union and Britain's largest daily newspaper. Bevin was a Christian socialist and had no time for Marxists, simply because they were undemocratic, stifled freedom and banned democratic unions and religion. His foreign policy, he said, was the freedom to be able to go to Paddington Station and from there to anywhere in the world.

And when the Mahatma Gandhi visited London in the 1930s, it was the textile and other workers who mobbed him, seeking solidarity with what he represented. The powerful ruling elite shunned, insulted and rightly feared his tactics of peaceful protest, and solidarity between classes and castes, which still inspire and are invoked wherever there is oppression.

I touch on the meaning and resonances of words such as 'internationalism' and 'solidarity' because these concepts were what mattered most to my generation, the generation that came of age in the 1960s. My generation was inspired, not by Lenin and the dictatorship of the proletariat, but rather by Lennon's 'Imagine there are no countries'. We may have been naive when, during the anti-Vietnam War and anti-apartheid struggles, we sang 'All we are saying is give peace a chance'. They were noble and idealistic sentiments, heartfelt and still felt.

Globalisation's opponents

My reason for exploring the origin of such concepts as internationalism and solidarity is simple enough. The WTO was one of the key lightning rods – especially during the 1999 Seattle Ministerial – of a well-organised movement specifically targeted against such alleged organs of global corporate dominance.

As we were corralled behind barbed wire barricades, I found myself wondering how such fine, noble, principled expressions of universal values and rights as internationalism and solidarity had become so denigrated. Globalisation as a word, a slogan, an explanation of history, all too frequently now conjures up a vision of elitism, dominance and power by the few; suppression of human rights, unbridled, unregulated capitalism and privilege. By contrast, universal values, internationalism and solidarity, were perceived as words of comfort, unity and tolerance. And yet what is globalisation, or should it be, but the implementation of just this drive to spread universal values and solidarity?

Is this just a marketing problem? What truth is there to the accusations of the aggressive protestors and NGOs – not all of whom are mad or bad – who claim everything is getting worse and that globalisation is a threat to freedom, development, indigenous peoples and local cultures. Is the world really getting worse? Are human rights in retreat? Is the environment deteriorating? Are the poor getting poorer, and the rich richer?

This book argues strongly that, while we undoubtedly have a huge distance to travel, the world is improving. In fact, on the real measurements of human progress – life expectancy, infant mortality, literacy, access to clean water, democracy, human rights – there has been enormous progress. Freedom is growing, and as it grows its benefits compound and people benefit. As individual freedoms expand, the power of the privileged and powerful contracts.

An active, constructive civil society is vital to ensure further progress. I believe that as freedoms develop in societies, the political market acts like any other in correcting itself in response to public pressure. Institution-building and an active civil society are central to this world-changing objective, and many NGOs are now bigger than some of the international government organisations (IGOs). Individual financiers such as George Soros through his foundation's networks are spending $300–500 million annually in developing countries and economies in transition worldwide. Microsoft's Bill Gates is spending more on AIDS in Southern Africa than the WHO.

It is the human condition to believe that we can always do better; that is what defines our species. Otherwise we would still be in caves, or driving Model Ts, or it would still cost a working family a year's pay to purchase the *Encyclopaedia Britannica*, instead of it coming at the price of Internet access. It is the very condition of not being satisfied, no matter what the outcome, that drives us to better results.

This constant struggle for improvement flourishes best in conditions of political and economic freedom, which are the pre-eminent preconditions for development and social justice. Freedom is growing globally, and democracy is now the best and sometimes most revolutionary option in places plagued by poverty and failure. Where freedom grows, poverty and injustice retreat. Where freedom in all its forms stalls, so does human progress.

The Doha Development Agenda agreed by the WTO in 2001 offers unprecedented opportunities for global prosperity, peace and development. In the following chapters, I will sketch out a road map that will help implement the Doha Agenda and outline some of the obstacles. I will draw on my experience in politics and world trade over many decades to examine the international architecture and the relevance of the existing international institutions. This means taking a look at the forces at work in politics, wider society, civil and uncivil society and business, and analysing how the relentless march of science and technology will continue to change everything – except perhaps our innate ability to think up new ideas.

The 'open society' still has its enemies. They have been lurking since the Reformation and the Enlightenment, in all cultures and societies throughout the ages. They opposed the Japanese Meiji openings, pulled back the great Chinese fleet that reached the Arabian Gulf almost 700 years ago, and tried to smash the new technologies in the mill towns of Britain. Extreme nationalism, protectionism and tribalism are the curses of our species and inevitably lead to a restriction of liberties, blocking the advance of human rights and the lifting of living standards and conditions.

Where ideology and theology kill discourse, freedom perishes, ideas can't flourish, investment flees, as do people, and nations fail. Many feel that science is outstripping our moral, ethical and legal capacity to cope. But debate, the competition of ideas, the tolerance of others and rational differences are a precondition for progress. Democracy and freedom are not just good ideas in themselves, but the most practical way forward to lift living standards and living styles.

The great global corporations, far from ignoring or riding roughshod over public opinion, are now terrified by it. They have great PR machines and are in most cases better employers than domestic companies in developing countries. Shareholder power and public opinion tend to force better outcomes. George Bernard Shaw said: 'Reasonable people don't make change, thus all progress is based on unreasonable people.' But they need the climate, the opportunity and the systems in place that are open to change, in order for change to be persistent and peaceful.

The professional NGO 'worriers', like Global Exchange, Focus on the Global South, Third World Network and the like, living in another reality, see a bland world of McDonalds. They tend to ignore the better reality: an exciting new world where everything from Beethoven, mass travel, cleaner water, new medicines, Pavarotti and cheaper information to Thai takeaways, are affordably available in almost every corner of the globe. Now, truly, all the knowledge, history and ideas of every culture are there for a larger percentage of the world's population than ever before, thanks to new technologies and rapidly declining costs of distribution. Drive through developing countries at night and witness the young people in cyber cafes, even when every other shop is blacked out. Mark Twain said man is the only species that can blush – or needs to. He's right. But man is also the only species motivated by hope. Globalisation is all of this.

The political marketplace keeps correcting itself as new pressures from the public force politicians to respond. Some even anticipate progress and lead the way – although if there's one lesson I've learned from more than two decades in politics, it is that it's a mistake to be right too soon. The women's movement and the environmentalists have won stunning and important victories. Thirty years ago, no country had a Minister for the Environment or a Ministry for Women's Affairs, now most do. Scrutiny, free media, engaged NGOs, responsive politicians, open economic policies – the mix works.

In Part One of this book, I begin by looking at some of the major issues of globalisation and the philosophical basis for free trade. I argue that, for a greater percentage of the world's population than ever before, the world is a better place. In Part Two, I outline the crucial role the WTO plays in the multilateral system, examine the failure of the Seattle Trade

Ministerial, and describe the strategy leading up to the launch of the Doha Development Agenda and lay out a road map that could ensure the new round is successfully concluded.

In Part Three, I analyse the increasingly important role of civil society in our media-driven age, suggest some options for business to play a more positive and socially responsible role, and discuss ways of better managing global governance – in an era of what I characterise as privatised diplomacy – to hold our international organisations more accountable to the governments and parliaments that must ultimately be their masters. Finally, I reflect upon the future challenges we face. When the Uruguay Round was launched, the Cold War imprisoned half the world in deep freeze; faxes, cellphones, the Internet and AIDS were barely visible. We could yet be undone by fallout from changes yet to come. Nothing is certain but change; and the pace of change is accelerating.

What follows are my personal perspectives and insights, given a lucky life in domestic and international politics. I hope it entertains, infuriates and helps encourage a new generation of public servants to do a better job than my own.

Part One

The bigger picture

2   What does globalisation mean?

Globalisation has joined imperialism, colonialism, capitalism and communism in becoming an all-purpose tag, which can be wielded like a club in almost any ideological direction. It is the defining political, economic and social phenomenon of the new millennium.

Most of the world's colonial regimes were liberated by the end of the twentieth century. With the collapse of the Soviet empire and communism, and the ascent of capitalism as the dominant economic force in the world, globalisation has replaced those "isms" as one of the primary galvanisers of public opinion. As, of course, is the dominant 'hyperpower', the USA, seen by many as a force for overwhelming cultural and economic imperialism, and inextricably intertwined with views on what is both bad and good about globalisation. Globalisation now conjures dark images of elite dominance, suppression of human rights and unbridled, unregulated capitalism. The final decade of the last century saw globalisation become the subject of vociferous, often violent, division and protest.

We are dealing – not with the end of history, as Francis Fukuyama proposed[1] – but rather, with the death of old ideologies. The world's political forces – democratic and despotic – have been largely cast from moulds created for a different age. Recent rightist pressures in Europe and elsewhere, fuelled by nationalistic, anti-establishment trends and immigration issues, are likely to lead to an eventual resurgence of the hard left, before a return to the rational and democratic centre. The old left is already showing signs of making a comeback in battered Latin American economies.

However, it is simplistic to see the recent success of outsiders in the European political process as a triumph of the right wing. Rather, these results might better be seen as further manifestations of the 'Age of Scepticism', in which an increasingly alienated public rewards outside forces precisely because they are seen as not being tied to an insider establishment that has failed to respond to their concerns. An ancient undercurrent of nationalism and tribalism is emerging, frustrated because power is increasingly flowing beyond the nation state. As economies and societies become more open, domestic politicians have fewer levers to pull, so their answers often fail to meet constituents' needs and expectations.

Ultimately, political differences will become, not so much a matter of left or right, but of how politicians manage, resist or encourage the various manifestations of globalisation – a force that is anyway beyond their direct control.

Globalisation, the *tsunami* of ever-more interdependent financial and trade flows, as well as of ideas and people, has been of great benefit in raising living standards around the globe. However, it has increasingly been joined by, and come into conflict with, the worldwide trend towards greater transparency, democratisation and speedy dissemination of ideas, accelerated by the splendid freedom and liberating anarchy of the Internet. While global electronic media have also played a huge role, it is the Internet that has levelled the playing field. A good web page, mailing list and strategy can turn an NGO representing a handful of the disaffected into a powerful force for resistance or change. The Internet allows the most remote, smallest player access to the economic, social and political marketplace.

The largely NGO-led phenomenon of anti-globalisation demonstrations came to public prominence when Internet-orchestrated protests spilled over from cyber space to the streets of Seattle for the WTO's ill-fated ministerial meeting in 1999. Internet-linked anti-globalisation whizz-kids put together a powerful, if awesomely contradictory, coalition of interests that shook the political establishment. (The first such Internet-linked protest was the one which killed the OECD Multilateral Agreement on Investment in 1998 (see Chapter 13).) And Seattle in turn has inspired a series of protests that are now a feature of every international gathering, from World Bank meetings to G7 summits to meetings of European leaders.

But the point here is not to debate the strengths or shortcomings of these organisations – or of NGOs – subjects I address elsewhere. Rather, it is to observe that these protests reflect a new reality: wider civil society will, quite correctly in my view, no longer tolerate being divorced from decisions that affect their lives. This is a very healthy development. Our challenge is to find creative new ways to positively facilitate the exchange between wider civil society and the international and multilateral bodies set up to manage national interaction.

US Congressional leader Tip O'Neill once noted that 'all politics is local'. Yussef Boutros Ghali, Egypt's Trade Minister, was forced to fight (successfully) in a run-off for a seat in his parliament. I cheerfully reminded him that, given a choice, most electorates would rather their MP brought home a school bus than a Nobel Prize. However, while politics

Figure 2. Protestors block the opening ceremonies at the WTO Ministerial in Seattle. Globalisation has become the subject of vociferous, often violent, division and protest. The WTO didn't need enemies; it often was its own worst enemy because of its way of working. This has changed. (Photograph by Robert Sorbo. Copyright Reuters 1999.)

are still fought locally, economics is now no longer a national, but a global issue. Governments that fail to recognise and prepare for this, not only won't get school buses – they won't be in a position to educate their up-and-coming generations to cope with this very different world.

Despite the threats it faces, the nation state, the Westphalian system, will remain the basic unit of governance. Indeed, all evidence points to an increase of national entities (see Chapter 15). It is this ever-increasing number of stakeholders in the international arena which inevitably adds to the complexity of conducting multilateral relationships – as the WTO and governments learned to their cost in Seattle in 1999.

Juan Enriquez points out the brutal truth that technology is not kind; it does not say 'please', but slams into existing systems and destroys them, while creating new ones. Countries and individuals must either surf these powerful waves of change, or get crushed trying to stop them. Governments now have to cooperate with and facilitate the new forces unleashed by the democratisation of information. How governments cooperate, humanise and share these problems and opportunities will define their relevance and success. I do not believe this is either a betrayal of national interests, or a surrender to some new 'invisible hand' of information technology and multinational corporation (MNC) dominance. As Israel's Golda Meir once said: 'International governance does not mean the end of nations, any more than an orchestra means the end of violins.' Global governance does not mean global government.

However, globalisation has ripped open a ripe seam of apprehension, rich for mining by the political opportunists who have, through the ages, blamed outside forces for internal failures, exploiting the fears of those who feel threatened by the trauma of these dramatic and accelerating changes. Everything that goes wrong in the world is now apt to be laid at the door of the forces personified by globalisation.

What do we mean by this loaded word? The *Financial Times's* Martin Wolf posed the following questions at a seminar in Norway: What is globalisation? Is it new? What does it mean for society and business? What are the challenges of globalisation? And is it reversible?

To me, the evidence suggests that for most people, in most places, the world is a better, fairer, cleaner, more democratic place because of it. As Czech President Vaclav Havel has observed: 'Globalisation by itself is morally neutral. It can be good or bad, depending on the kind of content we give it.'[2]

What is globalisation?

Perhaps it is easier to state what globalisation is not. It is not a plot hatched by faceless Davos eggheads; a ruthless MNC scenario for corporate rape and pillage; a conspiracy by the Trilateral Commission, or a plan by the WTO to create a new world order. The world is not governed – as an agitated letter-writer once informed me – by a secret cabal organised aboard the Royal Yacht Britannia.

Nor is it the Americanisation of the world: at least materially. If it is, the USA is failing dismally. Take the automotive manufacturing sector. In 1950, US car manufacturers were producing two-thirds of the world output. Over the next few years its market share of car production declined to 48 per cent in 1960, and finally to 21 per cent in 1980, when its dominance in manufacturing cars was surpassed by Japan.[3] Today, Japan maintains the number one position as the leading car manufacturer in the global economy. Of course one of the essential characteristics of globalisation – and especially of global manufacturing – is that identifying the 'national' elements in products such as cars is an increasingly complex exercise. But economies are not static. For a decade, American car-makers flatlined and worried about rust-belt erosion; books were written lamenting the US malaise and the death of the American model, and Japan was held up as the new global economic power. Then came Japan's recession and US 'new economy' resurgence on the back of the IT and Internet revolutions.

What has become better appreciated is the global impact of new international business models and the associated growth of foreign economies and their national welfare. The old international model of individual national firms, with centralised plant and equipment, exporting a finished product or products put a premium on the negotiation of the reduction of foreign tariffs in order to get the lowest entry-cost for the finished product in the foreign market. This former model was reflected, for example, in the 1993 US trade figures showing that, on average, 45.5 per cent of US imports and 32 per cent of exports, were between 'related parties' – subsidiaries or parents of home companies.[4] The nature of multinationals in the old days was to seek special privileges from governments; we will make tyres for you, if you give us a monopoly to do it, has changed. The new MNC obtains inputs from various transnational sources.

This has huge implications for international trade. Geza Feketekuty has observed that in industries which have become increasingly globalised the demand for a level playing field and common rules of the road accordingly embraces an increasing number of policies that affect relative costs of international competitors. Deeper international integration subjects many more production decisions to the influence of domestic regulatory policy. The need for 'greater coordination of microeconomic policies has become most visible in the trade context because globalisation has transformed domestic laws and regulations into potential trade barriers . . . Trade officials are therefore being forced to address an ever-expanding set of domestic policy issues that impact on international business activity'.[5] As John Jackson has noted: 'The problem of international economics today, then, is largely a problem of "managing" interdependence.'[6]

Philippe Legrain argues: 'If you are worried about corporate power, you should support globalisation. Freeing trade curbs domestic giants by exposing them to foreign competition. BT, France Telecom and Deutsche Telekom now trample on each other's turf, as do new companies, big and small, like Vodafone and Virgin. Closed domestic markets, where national champions can cosy up to government, are much more likely to be monopolised than global ones. Even though many global companies are bigger than before, they are not necessarily more powerful. It is the absence of competition, not size, that gives companies clout.'[7]

Often, anti-globalisation is synonymous with anti-Americanism. Everywhere I go in the world, the WTO is seen as an American conspiracy – except when I'm in the USA. Little credit is given to the fact that US companies account for around one-fifth of total world imports, as well as almost one-quarter of total exports. Critics of the USA and globalisation are also quick to complain when the US economy slows, imports decline and jobs are shed worldwide.

Globalisation is not a policy, but a process, which has been going on since man climbed down from trees, emerged from caves and began to organise his life, by harvesting as well as hunting, exchanging goods and ideas. It is the acceleration of international integration, spurred by a number of factors, and is now largely technology-driven. Information-driven investment – actively encouraged in countries where politicians think ahead of the game, such as Switzerland, Singapore and Costa Rica – and the dramatic lowering of transaction, transport and information costs have been the beachheads.

Pioneering management guru Peter Drucker argues: 'The world economy is not changing: it has already changed, in its foundations and in its structure, and the change is irreversible.'[8]

Perhaps the most significant trend, as Thomas Friedman has written, has been 'the democratisation of information and communications.'[9] The machinery connecting the world – both wired and wireless, by land and air – has become ever more sophisticated as transportation and communication costs implode.

Consider: between 1815 and 1900, the US railroad cut land freight rates by as much as 95 per cent, helping boost trade exponentially. The British rail system developed from a 3.2 km line in the seventeenth century to carry coal, to the age of 'railway mania' between 1830 and 1850 when some 9,650 km of rail were laid. Today, there are about 32,186 km of railway track and 2,500 stations. Following the opening of the Suez

Canal in 1869, shipping costs decreased by 30 per cent between London and Bombay. By the 1920s, shipping rates had declined 80 per cent relative to income (the same rate at which they fell in the USA over those years), and the volume of traffic soared 1,000 per cent between 1882 and 1947. As for the real revolution, air transport, some 40 per cent of the world's manufactured exports, by value, now go by air, reflecting the huge upsurge in information technology manufacturing on a globalised basis.[10]

Twenty years ago, Americans made about 200 million phone calls a day: now they make over 5 billion. Advances in telecommunications technology enable us to transmit approximately 2.5 Gbits per second across the transoceanic fibre system. In other words, one can send one and a half copies of the *Oxford English Dictionary* per second using this system. And the speed of data transmission is about to get faster. *Wired* magazine reported that a combination of two technological developments of erbium-doped fibre and solitons can deliver more than 100 Gbits per second![11] This technological advance would increase the speed of data transmission by 3,900 per cent from the present, meaning that data transmission would essentially be truly real-time, perhaps to the nanosecond, with minimal loss of information. In 1980, phone conversations travelled over copper wires, which carried less than one page of information per second. One pound of fibre-optics can shift more information than one ton of copper. Now a strand of optical fibre as thin as a human hair can transmit in a second the equivalent of 90,000 volumes of the *Encyclopaedia Britannica*. (In my youth, it took a year's pay for a working class family to purchase the *Britannica*, now it is available on the Internet or on CD for a few hour's pay.)

When one pound of fibre optics can shift as much information as a ton of copper, it has enormous implications for both cheaper and more effective distribution as well as environmental savings.

The tyranny of distance has been conquered. Those of our ancestors who left Europe for a better life in the Americas or the Australasian colonies knew, when they said a tearful goodbye to family, that that was pretty much that. Similarly, the Chinese workers who ventured after the gold mountain in far-flung parts of Asia and the USA knew they would probably never see their relatives again. The Grand Tour of Europe used to be a privilege of the well-to-do, unless of course you were a soldier in 1914 or 1939.

Their grandchildren think nothing of taking package holidays to see Aztec ruins, while the plazas and temples of Europe and Asia are full of youthful backpackers. A Singapore-based expat investment banker can spend a weekend fired up on Ecstasy howling at the moon at a beach party in Goa, and be back in his office by Monday, not much the worse for wear. Already no passports are necessary within an expanded Europe. Marco Polo earned a place in history for his travels. Today, an estimated 2 million-plus people travel across national borders everyday.[12] In 2000, the CEO of The Boeing Company, Phil Condit, forecast that by 2016, airlines will carry 3 billion people annually to their destinations.[13] In 1980, less than 300 million people took international trips. That number had doubled by the 1990s. The World Tourism Organization predicts that within 20 years – with the global population at about 7.8 billion – some 20 per cent of the world's people will make a foreign trip.[14]

There are critics who argue that globalisation is a threat to local culture, the Americanisation of popular culture and the dumbing down of values, art, literature and music. 'MTV rules,' they say. I think the opposite will become the case, as local languages, music and culture are revived. For example, there are now more people speaking Welsh and Maori – the language of indigenous New Zealanders – than a century ago. In my youth, Maori was not used in schools, and children were discouraged from speaking it. Government policy and parental influence saved the language from near extinction.

Niche radio and cable television channels and the Internet have created thousands of new individualised markets and outlets for a variety of non-mainstream music and culture. What is tourism but a celebration of other cultures, history and environments? Take the Interceltic Festival in Lorient, in Brittany, France. Almost 400,000 people assemble every August to celebrate Celtic culture. Bagpipes and music from the great Celtic diaspora arrive from all corners of the world; pipers from Uruguay, New Zealand, Cuba, the Netherlands and even Scotland share their mutual love of their culture. People are tracing their 'roots' with pride and enthusiasm. Brittany – a Celtic enclave whose Breton language is close to Welsh – had its own parliament and language until the French Revolution in 1789. It has now become a centre for this revival because enthusiastic entrepreneurs could see a commercial, and cultural, advantage in staging the event.

Those horrors of history, which created an exodus – whether it be of Armenians, Irish, Cambodians, Jews, Chinese or Hungarians – is now an inward source of investment, talent and patriotic enthusiasm. Political constituencies in the USA, Britain, France and many other developed countries were created by these flows of refugees, many succeeding in a spectacular way. Newly opened and democratic societies receive these benefits. Closed economies, such as Cuba, deny themselves the benefits of returning expatriates.

One hundred years ago, it took an average worker a full day's pay to purchase *The Times*; now it is a few minutes work – and the letterbox is full of give-away newspapers, as well as junk mail. A century ago, it took a day's pay to send ten words to London by cable; now this transaction is essentially free. Friedman writes that a three-minute call between New York and London cost the equivalent (in 1996 dollars) of $300 in 1930[15] – now this too is virtually a costless transaction in terms of overall purchasing power.

The screw, invented by the Chinese, took 1,400 years to reach the Western markets. The wheelbarrow, also invented by the Chinese, took a hundred years to reach Europe. By contrast, globalisation has enabled technological innovations to break into markets at astonishing rates. As Juan Enriquez, amongst others, has noted, it took the Internet one-fifth of the time it took the telephone to be introduced into one out of four homes in the USA.[16]

Gordon Moore's well-known law – that the amount of computing power doubles every eighteen months – is now in danger of becoming outdated. The average secretary's personal computer now has more computing power than the Manhattan Project. The chip, basically a sliver of silicon and a microscopically small wiring circuit, has changed the world. Silicon Valley, the centre and height of this revolution, generated some 250,000 millionaires. And they didn't all evaporate with the dotcom meltdown. Post 'tech-wreck', many fortunes and millions of new jobs remain. And IT industries are growing ten times faster in countries like Brazil and India than in the USA.

The following data reflects just how profound the technological revolution has been:[17]

- In 1995, 50 million personal computers were sold, compared with 35 million cars.
- Every two months, the Web doubles in size, while a home page is added online every four seconds.
- There are 320 million web pages today; there will be 3 billion within two years.
- Internet business will reach $300 billion within a decade.
- Declining prices for IT investments have helped lower global inflation.
- It took radio 38 years to reach 50 million people. It took television 13 years to reach the same audience. It took 16 years for the personal computer to reach 50 million people. And the Internet crossed the line in four years, with 1 billion users worldwide predicted by 2005. The most widely used language in the world today is neither English nor Chinese – it's the digital language of the trillions of complex 0s and 1s, which allow computers to carry out their instructions. Enriquez

forecast that by 2003, 97 per cent of data transmitted across telephone networks would be data rather than conversations between persons.[18]

Our borderless world has also spawned stateless interest and pressure groups, united in common cause. Interestingly, Al Qaeda is Arabic for database, the name originating in the database of Jihad supporters established by Osama bin Laden in 1988 to fight the Soviets in Afghanistan. Supported by Saudi weapons with US technology and intelligence, and fought by many highly motivated volunteers from the Muslim world, the war was led in the main by intellectuals with utopian ideals of a universal, globalised vision of Islamic identity. Al Qaeda remains a potent threat. Globalised, cheap, difficult to trace, impossible to stop, high-tech information and data flows offer opportunities for both good and evil. Just as doctors can share knowledge, so can terrorists and drug dealers, Technology itself is as neutral as was the printing press. That is what creates problems.

Is globalisation new?

There is nothing much new about globalisation; it's been around since long before Britain ruled the waves – and waived the rules. Historians and economists argue that the world of the late 1800s and early 1900s was more tightly integrated through trade than today. There was certainly a greater movement of people. Cotton was introduced to world trade from India as early as the 600s, and followed the trade routes to Syria, Cyprus, Sicily, Tunisia, Morocco, Spain and eventually to the Nile Valley. India was probably the world's largest exporter from 1500 to 1700. Islamic trade routes brought paper-making from China to Europe and Greek medicine back into a Europe that had lost it during the Dark Ages, note Kenneth Pomeranz and Steven Topik in *The World that Trade Created*.[19]

It took several centuries for the Europeans to break the dominance of the thriving Arab, Indian, Chinese trade networks in Asia, the Middle East and Africa, adding that the seventeenth- and eighteenth-century British East India Company is 'one of the first recognizable antecedents of today's multinational corporations'. At the same time, the Dutch, French, Danish and other European states had government-blessed monopolies on Asian imports.[20]

The French 'Sun King', Louis XIV (1638–1715) used to drink Yemen coffee, served on Chinese porcelain and sweetened with sugar from the island of São Tomé, for his soirées. To end his evening tea, he smoked Virginia tobacco. Meanwhile, some French noblemen drank the Aztec's preferred beverage, chocolate, while Englishmen favoured Indian tea. In 1840, the French diplomat Chateaubriand said of railway, telegraph and steam ships, 'Distances will disappear, it will not only be commodities which travel, but also ideas which will have wings. When fiscal and commercial barriers have been abolished between states as they have between provinces of the same state; when different countries, in daily relations, tend towards the unity of peoples; how will you be able to revive the old mode of separation?'

Harry Truman once said that the only thing new is history you haven't read. What *is* new is the accelerating speed of change, and the fact that people are now able to observe and judge changes as they take place. The very forces of information flows and openness are the same ones that have empowered critics to mount anti-globalisation Internet campaigns deploring it, an irony lost on some.

Reaction and protectionism are not new either. Britain's canal proprietors organised against the new threat from railways. Nonetheless, countries which are more open to trade grow faster than those that aren't, and so have less poverty and better jobs, hospitals and schools (see Chapter 5). Thirty years ago, Ghana had the same living standards as South Korea. Seoul changed hands four times during the Korean war; in 1945, the north had the richest, most industrialised part of the Peninsula. South Korea's GNP per capita did not reach $100 until 1963. Now South Korea is in the OECD, while its other half in the north is an economic basketcase. It repaid its IMF loan early, in 2001, and has bounced back impressively from the Asian crisis. A Taiwan factory owner who paid his workers $7.50 a month, 45 years ago, now pays them $7.50 an hour.

Malaysia in 1960 had the same income as Haiti; the Carribbean nation remains the poorest country in the Western Hemisphere. Burma's and Thailand's living standards were the same after the Second World War. Now the average Thai is twenty-five times better off. Thirty years ago, Japan had developing-country status. It may be stumbling, with major banking infrastructure problems, but it remains a technology and exporting powerhouse, with a fat cushion of savings, and is a huge importer from the developing world. The Baltic states had living standards equal to Denmark, and the Czech Republic was closer to France, before the Soviet experience and experiment. Argentina had a higher living standard than Canada or New Zealand in 1900. Guess what went wrong?

History has always been about movement, of people, ideas and products. In more primitive times, globalisation was aggressively fuelled by nationalistic and religious expansion. The Age of Discovery (i.e. of Empire) stretched, exploited and enslaved peoples worldwide. We have seen successive empires of faith, led by God's representatives on Earth, going back to before the Crusades. Those who resisted the crusaders fought with swords cast in India, from ore mined in Tanzania. When the order to mobilise for the Great War went out in 1914, the Ottoman Empire's instructions went out in fourteen languages. It is ironic that some of the most strident critics of globalisation's most modern incarnation come from some of the same churches who send missionaries into the field to globalise their faith and harvest recruits, joined by old-time Marxists, or their ideological children, who sing *The Internationale* while marching on the streets against globalisation.

The downsides of globalisation are not new either. Steel, horsepower and gunpowder allowed the tiny Spanish army of Cortez, some few hundred in number, to defeat native South American armies of tens of thousands in the sixteenth century. But it was smallpox, influenza and other diseases that wrought the most destruction. By 1618, the local population of 20 million had dropped to under 2 million. The native population in North America declined by 95 per cent in the 200 years after Columbus's arrival.[21]

Internationalism is not new. And, like nationalism, it has been promoted by villains and saints alike. At the core of all the great religions is a proposition that there is a common humanity and common rights – so long as we accept their god. The Marxist ideal of a universal proletariat united by class coming together, as well as the liberal dream of a big melting pot, have both proven illusions. Archaeologists testify to umpteen ruins and monuments built to celebrate individuals and empires who thought their power was immortal.

For the last fifty years, international politics has been dominated by the Cold War, which intellectually corrupted and distorted our vision and global institutions. It was a vital war to win, and it was won. The Cold War perverted the decolonisation process throughout the world as emerging countries were courted, their economies, politics and cultures transformed into surrogate battlegrounds. These days we are returning to more ancient rivalries between and within cultures. We have seen tribalism return with all its vicious hatreds to areas such as the Balkans and Afghanistan. Yet in both these tortured regions there is recent reason for hope.

Through the centuries, as provinces dismantled barriers within nations, economic prosperity and political power grew, not weakening the state, but strengthening it. A strong Germany arose from feuding provinces. The economic hyperpower, the USA, was created, not by fifty individual states competing with each other, but by a Union of States. The ever-growing European Union is now embarked on its own constitution-building process. The world is a safer place as a result.

Globalisation is not an aberration. The aberration was how world trade was stopped in its tracks as a response to the Great Depression which

began in late 1929. That Great Depression was made deeper, more prolonged and more lethal by the outburst of protectionism and economic
nationalism. The Smoot-Hawley Tariff legislation in the USA caused an
economic contraction of 40 per cent of its trade two years after the legislation was passed in 1930. Between 1929 and 1932, world trade volume
fell by 26 per cent and world industrial production fell by 32 per cent
because of widespread protectionism.[22]

The domino effect followed, with country after country adopting
beggar-thy-neighbour policies, including competitive devaluations of currencies. By March 1933, the volume of international trade had fallen
by 33 per cent from its 1929 level.[23] The effects of the vindictive Versailles Treaty provided further justification for future European nationalism and vicious tribalism. From all this came the twin tyrannies of the last
century – Fascism and Marxism. Both protectionist, nationalistic and
murderous.

Uniquely among species, we learn and we adapt, passing down information for others to further improve. After the Second World War the
great democracies followed exactly the opposite path from 1918. The
Marshall Plan was unique in modern history in that the victors recon-
structed the vanquished. Some of the so-called progressive left even
attacked the Marshall Plan. In the New Zealand Parliament the left
called it the Martial Plan. Their grandchildren attack the successor to
the Marshall Plan – the Secretariat of the OECD – and assail the World
Bank, accusing it of causing world poverty. Which is like accusing the
Red Cross Society of causing world wars. Clearly, this process is not new,
and neither is the reaction to it.

During the reunification ceremony in Hong Kong in 1997, I remarked
to a senior Chinese official that it was obvious China was destined to be
the other superpower. He replied that China had always been the most
powerful nation on earth. The past 200 years, he observed, had been an
exception. China had great trading ships twice the size of Columbus's
puny fleet, which sailed and traded with India, Africa and the Islamic
world. One fleet had a crew of over 20,000 men.

When China introduced the silver currency in the fifteenth century, it
impacted the then-known world. 'The Chinese traded their silks to the
British and the Dutch who bought them with Spanish pesos that had
been minted by African slaves in what is today Mexico and Bolivia and
mined by indigenous peoples recruited through adapted forms of Inca
and Aztec labor tribute.'[24] Some of this silver took the more direct route
from Mexico to China via the Philippines on Spain's Manila Galleons.

China enjoyed the benefits of magnetic compasses, drills, gunpowder,
fine silks and cloth, medicine, law and civilisation's largest irrigation

system centuries before Britons learnt that coal was a source of energy. Why did this progress stop? Why did the nation that discovered how to manufacture iron and rotate crops not remain the premier economic and organised society? Politics. A leadership battle was won by those who looked inwards and ruled rather than governed. The Middle Kingdom did not need to look elsewhere for inspiration. Economic and social chauvinism and nationalistic isolationism starved Chinese society of ideas and innovation.

The enterprising Portuguese adventurer Vasco da Gama, who in the fifteenth century became the second European to sail around the southern tip of Africa, picked up a pilot from the Kenyan coast who took him to India. Tiny Portugal and Holland in time became great trading nations. Holland is still a great trading nation, one of the world's biggest exporters of tobacco products and a great oil exporter. Yet none of these products is gathered locally. Portugal, on the other hand, retreated because inward-looking leaders and fascism pulled it back from the front line of open and curious societies.

Japan, within sixty years of the arrival of Portuguese vessels armed with a new weapon (guns), improved on those weapons and eventually owned more and better guns than any country in the world. Why did they surrender this technology until Commander Perry's gunboats forced them to do an about-turn? Because the ruling class, the samurai, were a warrior class and warfare was conducted by gentlemen who, one to one, after much grace, ritual and speeches, did battle. When peasant soldiers discovered that guns were a great equaliser, laws were passed in Japan restricting their use.

Equality and the democratisation of power are almost always resisted by those who enjoy its monopoly. Throughout history, outward-looking peoples and leaders have prospered, while inward-looking peoples and leaders have lost and their people have suffered.

What does this mean for society and business?

Production and employment

Globalisation has effected fundamental changes in the fabric of the world economy; not only by greatly facilitating financial and trade flows, but by exposing people worldwide to the consequences of global changes.

First, in the evolving post-industrial economy, production has become uncoupled from employment – growth does not always mean more jobs. But stagnation inevitably means less. Productivity has steadily been increasing in all sectors. Take agriculture: in 1948, one unit of farm labour

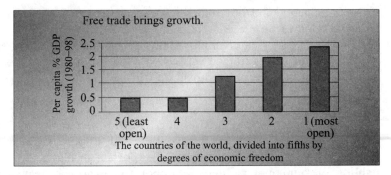

Figure 3. Relationship between free trade and growth (Source: Gwartney and Lawson et al. 2001).

in the USA produced 13 units of farm output, whereas in 1996 the same unit of farm labour produced 106 units of farm output, a percentage difference of 715 per cent. The US Department of Agriculture states that domestic agricultural output increased at an average rate of 1.89 per cent annually from 1948–96 due to productivity growth.[25]

In some industries, job-shedding is a clear prerequisite for growth – as reformist politicians have found to their personal, political cost. For example, three decades ago my own home country, New Zealand, maintained a policy of having to register meat works – as we call the slaughterhouses that are a key element in any agriculturally based economy. Twenty years ago, we had one authority with a state-sanctioned monopoly to licence meat exporters and we paid out billions of dollars in subsidies every year to produce meat that couldn't be sold, much of which came into the meat works on the hoof and went out as fertiliser.

The taxpayers paid – big time. Their hard-earned money went to solve industrial disputes, and some even to direct pay-offs to union offices. The meat workers, meat company owners and farmers were happy. However, precious taxpayers' resources were diverted from education and health to purchase political peace. And ironically, all this was put in place and maintained by conservative governments. It worked for a while, if the definition of political success is re-election. But it deep-froze the forces of change and progress.

Finally, from 1984 to 1990, this uneconomic system was dismantled by a Labour government. Innovation, which was crowded out by state subsidies, has returned to this important New Zealand industry, which is now highly competitive internationally, selling air-freighted customised meat cuts around the world. Globalisation and our newly open economic policy were blamed by populist politicians of both the right and the left in New Zealand, and our reforming government became increasingly hated. It is hard to argue the merits of Joseph Schumpeter's principles of Creative Destruction to unemployed fifty-year-old meat workers. But the argument must be made. You can save old jobs for a while at the cost of new jobs, but in the end you finish up with neither the old jobs nor the new ones.

This is a familiar pattern in terms of technology transfer, the globalisation of products and reduction of costs. But the technology first had to be invented, exported and in turn imported. Imports are seen as less worthy than exports. Being Minister of Exports is seen as a patriotic job, fighting for your country. But clever importers can also be great economic patriots. With a good deal, a skilful importer can increase workers' purchasing power at a stroke. Imports bring in technology, new ideas and connect us all with each other, wherever we live, whatever we do. A tariff is a tax on inputs, which costs jobs elsewhere. It's been estimated that US protectionist measures on steel in 2002 could result in ten times the job losses in consuming industries for every job saved in the steel industry.[26]

As New Zealand's Trade Minister in the 1980s, I gave out export awards to winners. Most countries do. I still regret the fact that I allowed myself to be talked out of also giving awards to smart importers. The prejudice against importers remains, and not just in New Zealand, even when the reality has changed.

We would be outraged if in peacetime individuals were conscripted and told where to work. How different is it when governments tell you how to spend your money, which products to buy? Because that's what many are doing by their protectionist policies.

A recent World Bank study showed that twenty-four developing countries, which increased their integration into the world economy over two decades ending in the late 1990s, achieved higher growth in incomes, longer life expectancy and better schooling. These countries, home to some 3 billion people, enjoyed an average 5 per cent growth rate in income per capita in the 1990s compared to 2 per cent in rich countries. Many of these countries – such as China, Hungary and Mexico – have adopted domestic policies and institutions that have enabled people to take advantage of global markets and thus sharply increased the share of trade in their GDP. These countries have been catching up with the rich ones – their annual growth rates increased from 1 per cent in the 1960s to 5 per cent in the 1990s. People in these integrating countries saw their wages rise, and the number of people in poverty declined.[27]

According to one report, China's entry into the WTO, over the longer term could create an additional 2 to 3 million job opportunities annually, but shorter term will result in an increase in unemployment, especially in agriculture and traditional industries. Labour intensive, tertiary industries and small enterprises will develop further, increasing employment elasticity, the report suggests.[28]

An important trend in labour markets in the advanced economies has been a steady shift in demand away from the less skilled towards the more skilled. This is the case however skills are defined, whether in terms of education, experience or job classification. This trend has produced dramatic rises in wage and income inequality between the more and the less skilled in some countries, as well as unemployment among the less skilled in other countries.

In the USA, for example, the wages of less-skilled workers have fallen steeply since the late 1970s, relative to those more skilled, according to an IMF report by Slaughter and Swagel.[29] They note that between 1979 and 1988 the average wage of a college graduate relative to the average wage of a high school graduate rose by 20 per cent and the average weekly earnings of males in their forties compared to those in their twenties rose by 25 per cent, reversing a trend of previous decades towards greater income equality.

The report suggests that, except in the UK, the changes in wage differentials have generally been much less marked than in the USA. Countries with smaller increases in wage inequality suffered instead from higher rates of unemployment for less-skilled workers. What seems to explain the differences in outcomes for wages and employment across countries is differences in labour market structures, according to the report. In countries with relatively flexible wages set in decentralised labour markets, such as the USA and, increasingly, the UK, the decline in relative demand for less-skilled labour has translated into lower relative wages for these workers. In contrast, in countries with relatively rigid wages set in centralised labour markets, such as France, Germany and Italy, it has meant lower relative employment.

Two other facts about these labour market trends shed some light on the impact of trade. The first is that about 70 per cent of the overall shift in US labour demand in manufacturing was a change in skill demands within industries, not across industries – from less skill-intensive to more skill-intensive. At all levels of industrial classification, the majority of US manufacturing industries during the 1980s employed relatively more high-skilled workers than in the 1970s, even though wages of these workers had risen.

The report's second finding was that income gaps have widened in a number of developing countries as well as in the advanced economies, and evidence suggests that labour demand in developing countries has also shifted toward workers with high skill levels relative to the average.

For example, trade liberalisation in Mexico in the mid- to late 1980s led to increased relative wages of high-skilled workers. The authors note that, rather than trade liberalisation boosting demand for unskilled labour and raising unskilled wages, in fact the opposite has happened in some developing countries.

Capital flows

Capital movements are now as – if not more – important than trade, in driving the world economy. In 1999, the value of capital movements around the world was approximately forty-eight times that of the daily value of world trade.[30] Goods and services represent $8 trillion of world trade a day; stocks, bonds and currency dealings represented $188 trillion a day in 2001. The Institute of International Finance estimated that net private capital flow into emerging markets in Asia increased approximately six times from 1998 to US$39 billion in 1999. The direct benefits and the spillover effects generated by that amount of investment has significant implications for the poor of the world who miss out by failing to secure investment. For example, China now enjoys one of the highest rates of foreign direct investment (FDI) in the world, receiving approximately 80 per cent of FDI flowing into East Asia.[31] The Chinese State Development Planning Commission estimated that FDI in China would reach an all-time high of some $47 billion in 2002.[32] India, by comparison, received around one-tenth of that ($4 billion in FDI in 2001). The *Herald Tribune* reported that for the first time ever China attracted more FDI than the USA, in one month. Whether this will be sustained is questionable.

Drucker observes that, although capital movements and trade in goods and services have not quite become uncoupled, the link has become loose and, worse, unpredictable. These changes, he argues, are permanent rather than cyclical. He adds: 'The volume of world money is so gigantic that its movements in and out of a currency have far greater impact than the flows of financing, trade or investment. In one day, as much of this virtual money may be traded as the entire world needs to finance trade and investment for a year.'[33]

Clearly, as many observers have noted – and events such as the 1997 Asian financial crisis, or the meltdown in Argentina in early 2002 demonstrate – forces of this magnitude are difficult for all but the most powerful nations to resist. Most of the responsibility for these collapses lies with domestic policy-makers, of course: banks that borrowed short from international investors and lent long on overvalued local assets; lack of transparency, crony capitalism and outright thievery. Governments that build on sand get washed away in the flood. The walls are now down and they can no longer hide.

Nonetheless, these trends allow both the users of financial services, and financial institutions themselves, to look to global solutions to their financial problems. Funds can now be raised and invested, currencies exchanged and financial risk positions changed around the world at the push of a button. Money is a coward, it goes where there is security, safety and transparency. It is the most poverty-stricken countries that are often the most corrupt. Who wants to invest their pension funds in a place where the rules can be changed at a general's whim? But rules, locally and globally, are necessary if finance is to be harnessed for development so that the poor do not miss out.

Friedman reported that at the height of the Cold War in 1975, total FDI represented $23 billion; by 1997, according to the World Bank, it totalled $644 billion.[34] In 1998, the volume of global merchandise trade stood at US$5.4 trillion while capital transactions were valued at $1.5 trillion per day on average, approximately seventy times that of merchandise trade.[35] The Institute for Policy Studies in Washington, DC estimates that fifty-one of the biggest economies in the world are businesses not nations.[36] Microsoft's Bill Gates's total worth exceeded the total value produced by Israelis, Malaysians or Chileans in 1999.[37] However, Gates's share of US wealth is smaller as a percentage than was Rockefeller's last century. And there is nothing new about great concentrations of wealth in the hands of individuals. Ask the royal houses of Europe.

Many see globalisation as just a business tool, or as a capitalist plot to make money by exploiting the poor. But businesses appear and disappear and fortunes are lost as the landscape changes: look at the richest people in the world and the top companies in the USA. We have seen enormous changes just in a decade; if this is plot by America's rich, they would seem to have been spectacularly unsuccessful. Examine the changes just in the 1990s (see Table 1). Contributing to the globalisation of finance has been the rapid trend towards financial market liberalisation. This has been seen in country after country freeing up their financial system. In that process, exchange controls (intended to insulate domestic markets from global influences) have been dismantled. In the increasingly integrated global capital market that has resulted, global financial firms with often complex financial and corporate structures have emerged as dominant players. These firms are to be found operating around the globe – relatively low transaction costs and the application of new technologies allow such firms to be active players in whichever of the world's financial markets they want to participate in. But financial markets tend to develop slowly, one reason why trade liberalisation usually precedes capital flow globalisation;

Table 1. *Changes among the largest US corporations, 1990–2010*

The largest US corporations		
USA in 1990	USA in 1998	USA in the next decade (industrial sectors)
American Cotton Oil	General Motors	
American Steel	Wal-Mart	Software
American Sugar Refining	Exxon	Aerospace
Continental Tobacco	Ford	Genomics
Federal Steel	General Electric	Bioinformatics
General Electric	IBM	Nanotechnology
National Lead	Citigroup	Phonotonics
Pacific Mail	AT&T	Micro materials
People's Gas	Philip Morris	Finance
Tennessee Coal & Iron	Boeing	IT
US Leather	Bank America	Robotics
US Rubber	SBC Communications	Entertainment

Source: Enriquez, *As the Future Catches you*, 2000; Enriquez, 2001.

a country needs to have a sound infrastructural foundation to avoid being damaged by rapidly moving bank balances.

Who suffers?

Globalisation and its consequences are frequently presented as examples of something evil, which must be stopped. According to these opponents, when somebody wins it must be at the expense of somebody else. By extension, some observers believe that if someone makes money, they must have taken it from someone else. An echo of 'Behind every fortune, there's a great crime.' That might have been a valid argument in colonial times, when imperial powers conferred privileges upon certain favoured subjects and companies; a time when the wealth of nations was based on raw resources and raw power.

There are still sweeping inequities around the world. And it is the case that – especially in commodities such as sugar, coffee and cotton – rich country buying power can play poor suppliers off against each other, protect their own markets, and subsidise local production, with lethal impact on the developing world farmers who lose out (see Chapter 3).

In Zambia, the clothing industry all but vanished because of trade liberalisation and the failure of local companies to adapt, declining from around 140 textile firms in 1991 to just under 8 firms today.[38] These sorts of outcomes fuel NGO and other concerns. Jon Jeter of the *International Herald Tribune* wrote of the impact of globalisation on Zambia's clothing industry: 'The expansion of global trade following the end of the Cold War has transformed Africa into a dumping ground for what the industrialised world no longer needs or wants; a deluge of secondhand clothes, used cars, old furniture and tools and weapons.'[39]

However, the reality is that while we can alleviate some of the impact on the developing world, we cannot shield poorer countries from the fact that now and in the future, the wealth of nations and companies is increasingly based on knowledge, and knowledge is limitless and mobile. As President Clinton noted in 2001, approximately 30 per cent of growth in US gross domestic income had come from the information technology sector since 1995.[40] The challenge for developing countries like Zambia is to establish the infrastructure that will allow it to attract investment, redirect resources from uncompetitive industries and put more into education and healthcare, giving current and future generations a better chance of competing in a globalised world.

The challenges of globalisation

The process of increasing globalisation has slowly impacted policymaking over the past century or so. Reports on the US War of Independence took weeks to appear in London newspapers; news from the Crimean and Boer wars took days. Now we see problems on television before ministers have been officially briefed. The acceleration and expansion of information began to change views, increasingly involving the public in foreign policy. The Vietnam War was fought out on the public's television screens, with a deeply influential impact on the government's eventual policy decisions. The grotesque attack on 11 September 2001 was seen live, as it happened, worldwide by millions.

Time magazine in 1997 convened a distinguished panel at the annual World Economic Forum in Switzerland, which predicted that the art and practice of government would never be the same. They all foresaw a new epoch of governance with inevitable changes, most still too new and too enormous to fully comprehend.[41]

As United Nations Secretary General Kofi Annan has observed: 'If you are into control, it's frightening. This thing cannot stop.'

The cost of this opening of the information floodgates is being felt particularly by governments with hitherto closed economies, which to capture the advantages of growth, need to open these economies fully to the outside world. I believe that democracy and freedom will increase, not contract, with globalisation. Open economies eventually force open political systems. Tyrants fear information; knowledge is power. The powers of governments over traditional areas of the economy are being transformed by the new logic of the Internet. While it is true to say that China, for example, is still trying to closely control Internet content, it is ultimately doomed to failure – just as at a certain point in the past decade it gave up trying to stop southern Chinese consumers from acquiring satellite television services.

Some have suggested that the information age will spell the end of the nation state. That's not the way I see it. The nation state is certainly changing, but will ultimately be both strengthened and softened by these changes, with the principle of subsidiarity becoming increasingly relevant (see Chapter 15).

As Peter Drucker has observed: 'In all probability, therefore, the nation state will survive the globalisation of the economy and the information revolution that accompanies it. But, it will be a greatly changed nation state, especially in domestic fiscal and monetary policies, foreign economic policies, control of international business, and, perhaps, in its conduct of war.'[42]

The great 'distribution' debate inside nations and between nations is increasingly about access to knowledge and education. Soaking the rich no longer works. Knowledge is the key ingredient of adding value to every product, new and old. Societies that act as meritocracies because they have open democratic access to higher education will prosper; those based on old school ties and restricted access to the skills necessary for this present future will slip behind, then perish. The class system is too costly; the class war is over in most successful countries, the people have won. New York has more Internet connections than all of Africa; Singapore more investment than all of Africa; this should teach us something.

The point of new wealth creation seems to have been missed. The real issue is whether this new wealth creation is lifting living standards, improving lifestyles and is being better shared within and between nations. I believe it is. And so do many millions of people worldwide. Recently, Environics International Ltd, in collaboration with the World Economic Forum, conducted a survey on perceptions of globalisation.[43] The outcome of the reports shows that the majority of people in nineteen out of the twenty-five countries surveyed expect that globalisation will be positive for themselves and their families. In India, for example, which adopts one of the most defensive positions in the WTO, 79 per cent of the people support globalisation, the highest of any country surveyed.

However, the same report notes that perceptions of globalisation are likely to remain volatile. It states that 13 per cent of its respondents changed their views on globalisation through the course of the survey. This suggests those surveyed have not yet solidified their perceptions of globalisation.

The young, given half a chance, have seized on opportunities wherever they have the freedom to do so. When I have flown into developing-country capitals like Phnom Penh, where electricity is scarce, and from the air at night you can hardly believe you are in a major city, what do you find while driving through the night? Young people queuing for a turn in dimly lit cyber cafes, reaching for the outside world after decades of horror and civil war, communicating through email addresses courtesy of Hotmail and Yahoo!

As Robert Conquest wrote in *Reflections on a Ravaged Century*: 'The survival of civilisation in the twentieth century was a near thing... Kierkegaard once said that the most dangerous mental faults are laziness and impatience. Laziness of mind meant unwillingness to face unfamiliar, complex and refractory realities. Impatience led to infatuation with supposedly all-explanatory theories in lieu of thought and judgement. Democratic muddle-headedness, or a resurgence of fanaticism, could destroy the present opportunity.' He adds: 'Above all, we must insist, as against the utopian concepts, that a tolerable order of things is one of a proper balance between the special and the individual: that a human being is neither an ant nor a shark.'[44]

The biggest danger to avoid is apathy and cynicism. As alluded to earlier, the current distrust of government in many democracies is fed by the misdeeds of an establishment that was once looked up to and respected. The young are told to respect their elders and traditional values. Yet if we were to examine, for example, the situation in the USA, two out of five marriages fail[45] and more children are being born out of wedlock – a majority in some western countries.[46] Church leaders have been exposed as child abusers, royals act less than regally, sports heroes abuse steroids, music icons take drugs, business leaders break the rules with impunity and politicians are perceived as lying spin-masters.

There are still heroes, be they 9-11 rescue workers, teachers in Afghanistan or moral leaders who changed the political landscape, such as Nelson Mandela and Lech Walesa. But now, greater transparency, a wider spread of democracy, increased media investigation and copious examples of blatant disregard of their responsibilities by many of those in power are fuelling a new age of scepticism. Politicians must now answer to a searching media and public. The Enron collapse and the spotlight on accounting and audit firms has spawned legislative changes. Influence-peddlers and their money created a constituency for campaign donor reform. Lower voter turnout throughout Europe begged questions that Europeans are trying to address. Sometimes there is over-correction, but attempts are made to answer the questions. The searchlight trained on leaders is wonderfully unrelenting, driving change and replacing those who don't respond.

Is globalisation reversible?

Martin Wolf, in his Norway seminar, answered his own question succinctly: 'Yes, if we go mad!' Or as Kofi Annan, the UN Secretary General, puts it: 'Arguing against globalisation is like arguing against the laws of gravity.'

Throughout history there have been local reversals. Cambodia was one of the wealthiest countries in the world in 1200. In the 1960s, Lebanon and Uganda were known respectively as the Switzerlands of the Middle East and Africa. As the Industrial Revolution began, India and China accounted for 40 per cent of world trade together; now they represent 3.4 per cent of world trade.[47]

Last century we saw great reactionary reversals, posing as revolutions after the First World War and the Great Depression. The Cold War further poisoned opportunities and openness and froze the idealism of the great institutions created after the Second World War to manage a hoped-for new age of international human rights and opportunities. The UN systems are irreplaceable for human progress and the civilised management of our differences. But they have not lived up to their architects' dreams.

Failure to launch a new Trade Round at Doha in November 2001, after the disaster at Seattle, could have given even greater impetus to regionalism, bilateralism and the nationalistic responses that always favour the powerful. That risk still exists; it always will. The WTO, and the multilateral system of which it is an essential component, was established in part to prevent the world retreating or returning to potential hostile trading blocs.

Democracy is a fragile flower in many places. Only twenty years ago colonels and command economies ruled in much of Latin America, Africa and Eastern Europe. Reactionaries still lurk out there with their dangerous populist, simplistic, racist and nationalistic solutions. Democracy has spread wider, but it has fragile roots in many countries. Ministers from Central America to Eastern Europe and the few bright spots in Africa tell me often how difficult it all is. One Central American leader bluntly told me that market access for his agricultural products into the rich, subsidised and protected markets of the north was crucial for the survival of his democratic regime. Unless he could get jobs and growth into his stagnating economy he feared the colonels would return.

The fear in Argentina following the collapse in 2002 was not economic contagion, but political contagion if the wrong people took advantage of this populist opportunity to seize power. The collapse wasn't caused by globalisation, although many pundits – as well as self-serving politicians and commentators in that country – were quick to point the finger of blame. It is always easier to blame outsiders than ourselves. If the global trading system was fair and open, then Argentina could enjoy an extra $5 billion a year from its beef exports. But in 2002, Argentina was looking ripe for yet another populist leader with all the usual sadly simplistic, uneven and impossible-to-fulfill promises. Poor people get understandably frustrated at their lack of progress, especially when they are forced to watch a mobile elite escape the consequences of their policies.

Economic failure brought on by bad and often corrupt governments is testing the people's patience to the limits. Populist leaders from the right and left, anti-establishment figures, are emerging in Latin America. Like political haemorrhoids, they pop out when the body politic is unhealthy. Nasty nationalism, normally dressed up in military uniforms or big business people, use the oldest trick in the political book. It's the fault of political insiders and outsiders. The World Bank, IMF, WTO, communists, capitalists, gringos, Masons, the Vatican. Whoever, wherever, as ever. Yet the people have a point. Living standards are not rising fast enough. There is massive injustice in the global trading system. Democracy works best on a full stomach.

At the time of writing, the market and politics in Brazil were shaking because of the election of President Luiz Inácio Lula da Silva. A trade-union and activist leader of the poor and excluded, he had run for President several times before. I put him in another class to others. His democratic credentials are impeccable. He may well be in the tradition of other trade-union-backed, democratic, honest, dedicated personalities that have broken the mould, from Australia to Poland, the UK to South Korea. Here's hoping!

Some of the strongest resentment against globalisation comes from extreme elements in the Islamic world, who see it as impious and exploitative, with some still dreaming of a religious, devout, golden age, which extends beyond the nation state.

Ideas, ideologies and theologies know no borders. The Iranian revolution, much like the Bolshevik and French revolutions, held out a dream that other countries and peoples would follow. The 'ideal' true path was, in all these cases, passively and aggressively exported. The more materialistic Marxists sought gain in their lifetime and 'mocked pie in the sky when you die', and when this utopian idea failed, disillusionment and counter-revolution set in.

But when the failure is seen as the work of God, or victory is achieved upon or through death, then policymakers have a far more deadly complex set of challenges. The irony, historically, is that the West sought common purpose with fundamentalism to win the Cold War. The impious, anti-religious Soviets and their satellites and clients from Bosnia, Central Asia, and across the Middle East to North Africa were targeted and funded by oil-rich enthusiasts purchasing US arms, guided by western technology and information. The climactic and – so far – ultimate clash was fought out in Afghanistan against the Soviets, then the Taliban. Next step, Iraq? The war on terror, like the Cold War, must be won. There will be innocent victims. Poverty is no excuse for violence, but evil people are more successful when they can feed off and get sanctuary and support in places of rampant injustice and poverty.

The words of Robert Zoellick, the US Trade Representative, to *The Washington Post* nine days after 11 September resonate: 'Trade is about more than economic efficiency. It promotes the values at the heart of this protracted struggle.' The struggle against terror is a battle for freedom and a race to lift living and education standards and realise our hope for a better alternative. This battle will be costly in treasure and in blood. But those who are not prepared to pay for liberty and freedom don't deserve it.

Some of those who oppose globalisation and the WTO, seized on 11 September to assert that it was all the USA's own fault. There are some very strange linkages and bedfellows in the anti-globalist forces. Is smashing up a McDonalds in Europe symbolically the same as burning the US flag? (Look forward to some even more bizarre and potentially dangerous coalitions in the future.) As Prime Minister of New Zealand, I was informed of extreme so-called local leftists who, once they lost their income from Moscow, approached some governments who were sworn enemies – and victors – over Russia's military. Earlier I quoted Martin Wolf's statement that globalisation will only be stopped if we are mad. There are insane and mad events in history and always will be. There will always be setbacks, but they will not prevail and are never permanent.

I refuse to believe that thousands of years of human expansion and improvement will be far reversed. Stalin and Hitler couldn't do it. The crash of 1987, the Asian crisis, the Mexican financial crisis, the Argentina collapse all tested the system. Yet the system held firm, despite dire predictions each time that we were in for another great depression. Why? Because we have learned from history. In the 1930s, there were few central banks. This time the world had Alan Greenspan and the greenback. Now we have the WTO: members had obligations that proved too costly to break. We have the World Bank and the IMF, often criticised, but essential global infrastructure to mitigate the negative aspects of rampant globalisation and market forces. Our failures have been caused by bad governance, lack of transparency and the short-sightedness and greed of business and political leaders. Progress can be stalled, we will experience new shocks in old clothing, but the historic trend line must make us optimistic.

The self-correcting advantages of democracy are very evident in the public debate on corporate governance, which erupted in 2002 as Enron, WorldCom, Adelphia and other former business giants crashed. For months, major news magazines, newspapers and television news shows featured business people, academics and politicians debating corporate malfeasance and suggesting reforms. NGOs were not silent on this issue, but they were crowded out of the debate because politicians were actively competing to air formulas for improving corporate governance.

The twenty-first century got off to a hopeful start but was shattered by the terror attacks of 11 September. The attacks exposed a tectonic fault line; a clash inside and between civilisations, with some fanatics even celebrating these horrors. Then the world community pulled itself together. We saw the launch of a new trade round at Doha, the successful Monterrey Conference on Financing for Development and the massive Earth Summit at Johannesburg, to name a few. The euro was launched without a hitch; China rejoined the world economy through WTO membership; and a constitutional conference is examining the best unified shape for that earlier most divided continent, Europe, a union that marches ever more democratically eastwards. NATO has reinvented itself from being a military union to contain the Communist Russian Empire to including at the table a new Russia and now looks at wider global regional security matters. The Middle East remains intractable; and the India–Pakistan relationship remains uneasy and dangerous. But these problems have been with us for half a century or more.

Moderates everywhere are in the majority, but we have learnt that failure to act on the problems of the world empowers extremists. Poverty is a breeding ground for all sorts of ills, from tuberculosis to political and religious intolerance. I don't believe that poverty is an excuse or rationale for any act of violence. But clearly the virus of terror is nurtured by bad governance. Does anyone believe that had the Oslo Peace Agreement been implemented, or the Clinton Plan, and if Sadat had not been murdered by extremist Muslims and Rabin by an extremist Jew, then there would have been no 9-11 attack? Osama bin Laden is part of a wealthy, educated elite with utopian goals, who envisions a different world and resorts to violence to achieve it. Such elites are more successful when they can feed off and get sanctuary and support from places where rampant injustice and poverty reign. This is not new. There are parallels: the brutality and injustice of Czarist Russia produced its Lenin; the arrogance and injustice of the French aristocracy, its revolution. Pol Pot and Hitler both took power because they were seen by desperate, disillusioned people as a solution to the problems created by the governing class. Without the great depression, massive unemployment and inflation, would Lenin or Hitler have had a constituency? Or would they have been dismissed as the eccentric crackpots they were?

What's different today? Poverty and injustice, disease, environmental degradation, terrorism and crime don't recognise national borders. These issues are globalised, they require global solutions. Failed nations don't only create problems for their own people; their pollution, dangerous ideas and diseases migrate around the world.

After 11 September there were those who predicted a return to more isolationist policies. As just one example, London School of Economics professor John Grey said: 'It inflicted a grievous blow to the beliefs that underpin global markets . . . the lesson of 11 September is that the go-go years of globalisation were an interregnum, a time of transition between epochs of conflict.' Just as the Doomsday scenario of Y2K-triggered collapse proved wrong, so were those who suggested the world would melt down in fear and chaos after 11 September. It didn't happen. The same editorial writers are writing similar stories about the coming collapse of China, Russia and Japan.

There are many good people endlessly seeking solutions for world problems. Why? Because we can no longer keep our distance from suffering. We now live the pain we see on television every night. We know the dangers of failure. Everyone is our neighbour now; their *suffering* degrades us all, and their success inspires us all. Globalisation means there is nowhere for policymakers to hide. Foreign policy has been democratised by information.

The problem for the world is to ensure access to globalisation's advantages, and to maintain rules and regulations for safety and fair play. We need to incorporate the standards and ethics we expect in our own family, community and nation into international best practices that are transparent, so the instruments of civil society can do their work of scrutiny, forcing better outcomes. I don't believe in the end of history: our history has hardly begun.

3   Food for thought

Nowhere has globalisation had more impact than on what we eat. There are many more Chinese, Thai and Indian restaurants in major cities, than there are KFCs and McDonalds. Most of the developed world can take for granted the fresh fish from Chile, tomatoes from Israel, dates from Tunisia, chilled lamb from New Zealand and beef from Uruguay arrayed on supermarket shelves.

Throughout the developed and developing world packaged food of every exotic sort is available just about anywhere, from tinned lychees to cubes of sugar. In lonely desert outposts in the midst of political chaos a working refrigerator selling Coca Cola can stand as a temple to consumerism, choice, global integration and corporate organisation. That such variety should be within the reach of so many would have stunned the ancient emperors of Rome.

There is no more graphic illustration of globalisation in all its forms – from freebooting adventurers to imperialists; to the present information and corporate-driven change; to trade-distorting subsidies that protect the rich world – than the history of food. People of just a few generations ago would be amazed if they could see the range of products available; they would also be staggered that we have such faith in food not grown by ourselves or trusted village neighbours. It is proof of the power of global markets and the confidence most of us now have in domestic and global regulators for food safety (see Chapter 14).

Merchant adventurers sailed for weeks across oceans in search of exotic and valuable materials to exchange for profit, a drive that opened up the world. Indian and Chinese merchants travelled half the world while Europe was in the Dark Ages, before humans reached New Zealand and when North America was hardly inhabited. Especially prized in the era before refrigeration were spices. The spice wars in the Dutch East Indies culminated in a military stand-off for the spice-rich island of Rum in what is now Indonesia; a face-saving exchange was arranged by the Dutch who gave the defeated British the 'worthless' island of Manhattan.

Technology was then, as now, a great force in creating prosperity and changing the world. Canning food was a military idea – as was the Internet – first used by the British navy in 1813,[1] giving sailors a variety of safe food to replace their restricted, often inadequate staple diet of salt meat and biscuits. Interestingly, it took half a century for canned food to become available to ordinary consumers because it took that long to invent the common can-opener. Originally dangerous, standards of factory food were improved both by legislation and by creative capitalists such as the Heinz dynasty, who saw the benefits of making such products available to ordinary people. Although they were sometimes opposed by nascent industries, these regulations built consumer trust and ultimately enhanced commercial reputations.

Refrigeration, like canning food, stretched supply links inside nations – thanks to the family fridge – and between nations. Refrigerated shipping in the late 1880s changed for ever the economies of nations like Argentina and New Zealand. Rich people in the seventeenth century began to use tobacco, coffee, tea and sugar, their addiction to these pleasures driving their merchants everywhere.

Food's production, storage and global distribution is a fascinating study of the best and worst aspects of globalisation over the ages. As a worst case example, take sugar, one of the first industrialised food products, the lure for some of the world's cruellest colonial exploitation. Today, sugar is an egregious example of how trade subsidies and tariffs keep developing countries poor.

Selling sweetness

Sugar cane, a tall grass, was first domesticated in India by 300 BCE, but spread slowly,[2] taking a millennium to reach China, Japan and the Middle East. The Arabs were the first great sugar cultivators; Egyptian sugar was regarded as the world's finest. The bitter Islamic conquest of the Iberian peninsula brought with it the planting of the sweet spice. Other Europeans became familiar with this new plant as they battled their way to Jerusalem during the Crusades.

The merchants of Venice used their large commercial fleet and navy, combined with forts and trading posts that dotted the Mediterranean, to dominate the European sugar trade of the Middle Ages. Sugar continued its westward march with the rise of the Ottoman Turks who, by the fifteenth century, had deprived the Venetians of their Moslem sources. The Venetians turned first to the recently reconquered areas of Sicily and Iberia. Then they joined with the Portuguese in a momentous departure that reshaped the world economy.

The Portuguese discovered Atlantic islands such as Madeira, and São Tomé off the African coast, where sugar production was revolutionised. Africans were enslaved and brought to work on sugar plantations to produce a fortune for their Portuguese lords and Italian merchants – and a hell for tens of thousands. The Portuguese decided to meet increasing European demand by expanding production further into Brazil. America became the fourth continent to be pulled into the world sugar market. It became a truly international crop, combining an Asian plant, European capital, African labour and American soil.

The Carribbean came next, the tropical French island of Haiti becoming a vast sugar plantation and slave station – in the process creating the forerunner of the modern factory. Between 1500 and 1880, some 10 million Africans were shipped across the Atlantic under appalling conditions. Most of these people were destined for sugar plantations, a large share for Haiti (which imported twice as many Africans as the USA).

'As Europe's sweet tooth grew, and cane replaced honey as the main way of satisfying it, tropical island after tropical island was deforested, covered with slave plantations, and committed so completely to export agriculture that they even imported their food. In Southeast Asian colonies, indebted or coerced peasants replaced slaves, but the results were not much better,' write Pomeranz and Topik. 'Even today, most former sugar colonies are very poor, and bear permanent ecological scars as well: Jamaica, Haiti, Cuba, north-eastern Brazil, Java, the Philippines...'

Not to mention their social scars.

Hawaii was effectively annexed by the USA because of sugar.[3] Only Taiwan – once a Dutch sugar colony – avoided the fate of other former colonies because it came again under the control of a mainland Chinese government that was less interested in creating colonial monocultures. The world economy does not only bring progress.

'Sugar which we think of as a leisure and pleasure product, an import from the balmy Caribbean lands of Manana, was actually the first industrial product and a cruel master to the hundreds of thousands of slaves who laboured to turn out sweet delights.'[4]

Sugar from sugar beet, a most inefficient source of production, was initially promoted in Europe by Napoleon when the British fleet embargoed trade. Sugar beet output has since hugely expanded.

Today, the world sugar market contains some of the largest and most blatant forms of trade protection. Having exploited these countries for generations, now the North keeps their products out of their markets and betrays the principles of free trade they expound in fine speeches. Consider the following facts:[5]

- Over 90 per cent of world sugar supplies are sold at prices above the 'world price'. Excess prices are paid for by taxes on consumers.
- On average, prices in developed countries are over double the world price.
- Forty per cent of the world production is highly subsidised.
- Japan, Western Europe and the USA are among the most protected.
- Some small exporters receive export subsidies as aid.
- Producer subsidies are paid for by taxes on consumers.
- For over 300 years, most national sugar industries have been maintained behind high trade barriers.
- Removal of price protection would see prices fall by around 65 per cent in Japan, 40 per cent in Western Europe and 25 per cent in the USA, Mexico, Indonesia and Eastern Europe, and by around 10 per cent in China and the Ukraine.

Protectionist policies distort prices and therefore economic incentives, leading to wasted resources. As import restrictions push the domestic price of a good above the world price, domestic firms produce more, while consumers reduce their overall purchases and suffer a real income loss as a result of the higher prices.

US producers, who developed their own sugar beet industry, as well as controlling vast sugar cane plantations, have benefited hugely from protectionism. The USA assists the domestic sugar industry through price supports and import restrictions in the form of a tariff-rate quota, under which sugar-exporting countries are given a tiny quantity that they can sell in the USA at the regular tariff, with exports beyond that subject to a tariff rate of nearly 150 per cent. These sugar import restrictions and price supports cost domestic users of sweeteners $1.9 billion in 1998, while benefiting domestic sugar beet and sugarcane producers to the tune of $1 billion. Moreover, 42 per cent of the total benefits to sugar growers went to just 1 per cent of all farms.[6]

For example, the family of Alfonso Fanjul single-handedly supplies the USA with about 15 per cent of its sugar cane through its land holdings in south Florida and the Dominican Republic, collecting somewhere between $52 million and $90 million in benefits from the price supports on US production and the quota rents on Dominican sugar exports, says Doug Irwin.[7]

The Chairman for Global Alliance for Sugar Trade Reform and Liberalisation, Bruce Vaughan notes: 'While we recognize that the elimination of tariffs will be achieved progressively, it is important that there is a concerted and coordinated reduction of all tariffs. In too many countries, sugar producers and marketers respond to support programmes rather than to the reality of natural market conditions.'[8]

This doesn't just hurt the poor. Robin Klay reports: 'The latest casualties of protectionist policies are the 600 employees of the Kraft-owned plant in Holland, Mich., that produces LifeSavers candy. In 2003, Kraft will move LifeSavers production to Canada. The reason? Sugar is cheaper in Canada, which imports it at the lower, freely traded world price. The United States, on the other hand, has protected its sugar industry with tariffs or quotas since 1922 . . . (It was Saginaw Congressman Joe Fordney who earned the nickname "Sugar Beet Joe" by sponsoring a bill that doubled the sugar tariff that year. Fordney was asked by another congressman, "Is it not true that if you had your way you would build a tariff wall around this country so high that it would be practically insurmountable?" Fordney at first denied it and then said, "But you know, that wouldn't be such a darned bad idea.")'[9]

The sugar programme is not just economically and politically inequitable; it prevents desperately poor sugar-producing countries from exporting to the USA. Countries such as Colombia and Guatemala are deprived of valuable foreign exchange earnings that could be spent on food, fuel and medicine. A number of observers have warned that Andean, as well as Caribbean, farmers are more likely to turn to illegal drug crops because they are being prevented from selling their sugar in the world marketplace, where they would be globally competitive were it not for rich country subsidies.

And it's not just the USA. Australian Trade Minister Mark Vaile told the IFAP Family Farmers' Summit on International Trade: 'The EU's out-of-quota tariffs for barley, sugar and beef are well over 100 per cent; their mean out-of-quota tariff on agricultural items is 45 per cent.'[10]

Even Cuba – where sugar was the country's most important source of cash for most of the twentieth century, and the industry is strongly associated with Castro's socialist revolution – has decided to severely cut back its sugar industry. 'Tall green cane plants sway in the wind throughout most corners of this island, where at least a fifth of the land has been devoted to sugar production,' reported the *International Herald Tribune* in July 2002. 'Cuban sugar is the key ingredient in another Cuban essential, rum, and sugar fields, mills and workers are fixtures in Cuban painting and literature.' But the government has decided to close half of Cuba's 156 sugar mills, mostly because the price of sugar has plunged on the 'world' market and its former guaranteed market in the Soviet Union no longer exists. Cuba is shifting production to oranges and mangoes, and has set its sights on tourism to make up lost export revenues.[11]

The crippling problems of commodities

Of course sugar isn't the only example: the story of coffee is just as tragic. Ten years ago, the industry was worth $30 billion and farmers received about $10 billion. Now the industry worldwide is worth $60 billion and farmers receive about $5.5 billion. Prices for farmers are below the prices they received in the Great Depression, and in real terms the lowest in a hundred years.

It is a sad and familiar story of the lack of coherence between international agencies, governments interfering with 'aid' that distorts the market and great companies not passing on the lower cost to consumers – an upmarket cup of coffee in Geneva still costs $3. Aid to Vietnam from Germany, the USA and France has seen Vietnam come from nowhere to become the second biggest exporter of coffee. It is an important crop for poor countries and accounts for 64 per cent of Ethiopia's exports, 60 per cent of Uganda's exports and 25 per cent of El Salvador's exports.

Half a million jobs have already been shed in Central America and Mexico. The theories of competition returning gains to consumers and free trade principles are not working here. Rich countries often have no tariffs on coffee beans, but escalate tariffs if they are processed in job-starved poor countries. President Pastrana of Colombia once told me in an emotional moment that the climate to grow coffee was exactly that necessary for heroin production. Nestor Osorio, the Executive Director of the International Coffee Organization, has stressed to me that the future sustainability of the coffee industry was at stake. 'All the more reason to celebrate the opportunities the Doha Development Agenda offers and finish this Development Round,' I replied.

Or take cotton, one of the few sectors of world trade in which Africa is internationally competitive as a producer. In 2001, US farmers harvested a record crop of 4.38 billion kilograms of cotton, aided largely by a US government cheque for $3.4 billion. West Africa is the third largest exporter of cotton, and farmers in Mali – the biggest grower in the region – posted a record harvest last year as well, of 200 million kilograms. The difference was that, without subsidies, the state cotton company lost money, largely because world prices have fallen by 66 per cent since 1995 (to $0.88 per kilo) and have fallen by 10 per cent in 2002 alone. The World Bank and the IMF estimate that removal of US subsidies could lead to a fall in production, a subsequent rise in the global price and a revenue increase of $250 million annually for the countries of West and Central Africa. But in fact subsidies for US cotton farmers are likely to increase by 16 per cent. This for a total of 25,000 farmers whose net household worth averages about $800,000.

Great injustices and contradictions still exist. That is why agriculture is such a difficult subject in trade negotiations and why the Doha Development Agenda holds out so much hope for many poor countries. The round should never conclude unless there is real reform in agriculture. It would be a tragedy if a compromise was fudged, leaving present inequities unchanged.

4   The philosophy, politics and economics of trade and freedom

The philosophical basis for the merits of free trade – a concept that goes to the roots of the WTO's charter – is the premise of the essential righteousness of universal reciprocity, which has a deeply moral basis that dates back thousands of years. Most-Favoured Nation (MFN) status – essentially that the best treatment you grant to one of your trading partners should be accorded to all – was arrived at as a matter of good governance, and is the basic principle of the WTO. But the concept goes back way before the creation of the nation state. What is good for the individual provides a principle of moral behaviour that extends beyond any one faith. It is the basis of civilised behaviour.

This fundamental reciprocity has underpinned the development of free trade and democracy. The more open and democratic the economy, the better the results for ordinary people, the more space for freedoms to keep growing. As John Stuart Mill observed: 'The great extent and rapid increase in international trade, in being the principal guarantee of the peace of the world, is the great permanent security for the uninterrupted progress of the ideas, the institutions, and the character of the human race.'[1]

Central to debate over the existence of a 'selfish gene' is the argument that people do not do things solely for the good of themselves or their group, but for the benefit of future generations. Genetic nepotism, the determination to ensure the survival of the species, is seen here as the source of ambition, industry and drive. As Matt Ridley says, none of our ancestors died celibate.

Postponing instant gratification for a better long-term outcome makes social and economic sense. It is the practical, wise basis of all investment, personal, social or governmental as well as by business.[2] Evidence of the rational basis for the emergence of moral values systems is widespread. The Ten Commandments are rational, as well as common sense. These principles applied more widely become the basis of good governance. The biblical theories of reciprocal treatment being the basis of a just life are as profound for nations as they are for individuals.

All societies have their own moral strictures, but all religions and cultures contain the concept of reciprocal treatment: you treat others as you would like to be treated yourself. Hans Küng writes of the 'Golden Rule of humanity',[3] which we find in all the great religious and ethical traditions. Note the commonality in his following formulations:

- **Confucius** (c.551–489 BCE): 'What you yourself do not want, do not do to another person.' (Analects 15.23)
- **Rabbi Hillel** (60 BCE–10 CE): 'Do not do to others what you would not want them to do to you.' (Shabbat 31a)
- **Jesus of Nazareth**: 'Whatever you want people to do to you, do also to them.' (Matthew 7.12; Luke 6.31)
- **Islam**: 'None of you is a believer as long as he does not wish his brother what he wishes himself.' (Forty Hadith of an-Nawawi, 13)
- **Jainism**: 'Human beings should be indifferent to worldly things and treat all creatures in the world as they would want to be treated themselves.' (Sutrakritanga I, II, 33)
- **Buddhism**: 'A state which is not pleasant or enjoyable for me will also not be so for him; and how can I impose on another a state which is not pleasant or enjoyable for me?.' (Samyutta Nikaya V, 353, 35–342, 2)
- **Hinduism**: 'One should not behave towards others in a way which is unpleasant for oneself: that is the essence of morality.' (Mahabharata XIII, 114,8)

Man has a spiritual dimension; he has a conscience, unlike other animals. We define someone without a conscience or insight into their own behaviour as a sociopath. Yet what is conscience? Why do we know instinctively what is basically right and wrong? Perhaps conscience is simply God whispering in our ear. Abraham Lincoln, during the Civil War, appealed to 'the better angels of our nature' in seeking conciliation between the warring sides.

Clearly, man learnt very early on the need for reciprocity: that no one can survive alone. We have coined the phrase synergy for a much more ancient adage; that one and one can make three if they cooperate and respect each other.

Adam Smith observed: 'Each animal is still obliged to support and defend itself, separately and independently, and derives no sort of advantage from that variety of talents with which nature has distinguished its fellows. Among men, on the contrary, the most dissimilar geniuses are of use to one another, the different produces of their respective talents, by the general disposition to truck, barter and exchange, being brought, as it were, into a common stock, where every man may purchase whatever part of the produce of the other men's talents he has occasion for.'[4]

The division of labour marked our species as different. The family tribe was, for thousands of years, the basic political and social unit. Over the 12,000 years of mankind's most rapid march, we separated into two types of existence: hunter–gatherers and those who domesticated animals and crops. The latter, the efficient farmers, began to grow and store food and domesticated animals, creating the first permanent villages. Here was a society that did not live by self-sufficiency, that began to trade its surplus grain or pottery: the beginnings of economic specialisation. Egyptian mummies have products from northern Europe, some even say from the Far East and North America, in their stomachs.

The compelling logic of the theory of comparative advantage

Specialisation led to the development of humankind's basic political, religious and social structures. In short, civil organisation. Increasing wealth and 'surplus' time allowed expeditions in search of riches and new technologies, ideas, crops and animals. This in turn helped refine the process of specialisation, improving living standards and creating a universe in which the ideas of others could be utilised. In 1779 David Ricardo, a rich Radical MP in Westminster, was able to popularise and document perhaps the best-established and most profound observation in political economics: the theory of comparative advantage. He showed that specialisation at the level of the group, not just the individual, was the basis of economic success.

Some wrongly assume that the logical extension of this is that the most efficient nation or company would consume the whole market, but this ignores the competitive advantage afforded by innovation, new product ranges, consumer sentiment and redirection of resources.

Ricardo's theory explained and built upon Adam Smith's *Wealth of Nations* (published in 1776), which basically suggested that people ought to be free to pursue their own interests, and that the government's duty was to establish legal titles and frameworks for commerce to grow. Justice was a public good, just as roads and parks were public goods. Smith explained: 'What is prudence in the conduct of every family, can scarce be folly in that of a great kingdom.'

There is no great mystery as to why free trade, democracy and good governance work. Economic liberty, which allows choice, rewards enterprise and allows the creators of wealth to enjoy the results of their work and risk, means a more efficient allocation of resources, labour and capital.

But as Smith famously argued in *The Theory of Moral Sentiments*: '...benevolence is inadequate for the task of building cooperation in a large society, because we are irredeemably biased in our benevolence to relatives and close friends; a society built on benevolence would be riddled with nepotism. Between strangers, the invisible hand of the market, distributing selfish ambitions, is fairer.'[5]

We might ask why it is that protectionist policies continue to work at the political level when they are obviously bad economics? Simply because the few who get the benefits can, from those benefits, reward those who confer these privileges. And those endangered when protectionism is threatened – be it displaced New Zealand carmakers, US steel workers or European fishermen facing reduced quotas – can bring loud pressure to bear on the policymakers. By contrast, the vast majority who pay the overall costs of protectionist policies seldom feel the effects in a measurable direct fashion and so are seldom motivated to protest or vote directly on the issue.

The whole thrust of civilisation has been to progress and to expand freedom, both materially and socially. But it requires the leadership of the state to insist on openness and maintain good governance so that these choices can be made in the political and commercial marketplace.

Legal, transparent, infrastructure is crucial for development

The problem for so many in poor countries is that they don't have the legal systems of property rights, access to justice and fair or efficient institutions and systems to uplift and unleash their people's talents, skills and ambitions. Hernando de Soto's landmark book, *The Mystery of Capital*, reveals the enormous hidden wealth, savings, assets and talents of those who struggle to prosper beyond the control of corrupt officials.

De Soto's team went into various developing countries and discovered that, for example, in Haiti in 1995, the value of extra-legal real estate was nearly ten times the holdings of the Haitian Government. His researchers found it took sixty-five bureaucratic steps, taking up to two years, to lease land under the government's plan for a five-year lease with the right to purchase. Yet in Haiti, the poorest nation in Latin America, the total assets of the poor are still more than 150 times greater than all the foreign investment received since independence from its former colonial overlord, France, in 1804.[6]

De Soto's Institute of Liberty and Democracy research reveals the following facts:

- Throughout Latin America, 80 per cent of all real estate was held outside the law.
- The extra-legal sectors in the developing world account for 50 to 70 per cent of all working people and are responsible for one-fifth to more than two-thirds of the total output of the Third World.
- The assets of the poor in Egypt alone are more than fifty times all the foreign investment ever recorded, including the funding of the Suez Canal and the Aswan Dam.
- In Egypt, it took seventy-seven bureaucratic procedures at thirty-one public and private agencies to acquire and legally register a lot on state-owned desert land. And this took five to fourteen years. This explains why millions of Egyptians build their homes illegally.

As Peter Watson, head of the Overseas Private Investment Corporation, has observed: 'The enterprises of the poor are very much like the corporations that cannot issue shares or bonds to obtain new investment and finance. Without such representations, their assets are dead capital.'[7]

As de Soto – who I think deserves a Nobel for this work – explains: 'Because the rights to these possessions are not adequately documented, these assets cannot be readily turned into capital, cannot be traded outside of narrow circles where people know and trust each other, cannot be used as collateral for a loan and cannot be used as shares against an investment. Contrast that to nations where property rights are established and protected by law. The single most important source of funding for new businesses in the USA is a mortgage on the entrepreneur's house.'[8]

Property law (limited liability companies, honest bureaucracy and an efficient public service), he argues, was the big advantage the West had over its competitors.

In developing and many ex-communist countries, it is more efficient to live outside the law and pay your tax not to governments to protect you and your assets, but to local gangsters and mafia. Sadly, sometimes they are more 'honest' and consistent than those, paid for by taxes, who should protect these citizens.

Brink Lindsey quotes F. A. Hayek's observation that it was no accident that the regimes which pursued economic centralisation to its furthest limits were also barbarous despotisms, that what appear the worst features of totalitarian systems are not accidental by-products, but phenomena which totalitarianism was certain sooner or later to produce.[9]

Property rights, access to honest public services, rule of law and protection of commercial activity from corruption are the key factors in development economics, rather than the industry that has been created by those who make a living out of describing the problem. The discomfiting truth of development is that the greatest threat to citizens' security, human rights and social advancement is despotic, corrupt individuals and the systems they spawn and feed off. They thrive on protectionism, cronyism, phoney capitalism and the siphoning off of international funds and local taxpayers' resources.

Post-colonial history – especially in Africa – has been scarred by a succession of bloated despots, from Uganda's Idi Amin to present-day Charles Taylor of Liberia, who have plundered at will, frequently whilst also fomenting strife with and within their neighbours. Zaire's Mobutu reportedly bought a castle in Spain and a thirty-two-bedroomed Swiss mansion, and hired Concordes to take his cronies on shopping sprees in Paris with the billions he stole of local people's money and international aid. Lindsey notes that on Independence there were almost 40,000 miles of workable roads in Zaire, on Mobutu's death just 3,000.[10]

Good governance – the establishment of honest transparent public services and responsible, accountable, replaceable politicians – is not some warm, fuzzy, liberal do-gooder theory, it is sound economics, and it works best.

Lindsey also quotes the widely cited study by economist Paulo Mauro, who tried to quantify the consequences of poor legal institutions. 'Using indices (prepared by a private business intelligence firm) that measure bureaucracy, red tape, corruption and judicial efficiency and integrity, the analysis points to a significant effect of inadequate legal systems on the amount of private investment, and thereby on the rate of economic growth. Specifically, an increase of one standard deviation in those indices (for example, a jump from Bangladesh's level of institutional quality to that of Uruguay's) would cause a jump in the investment rate of almost five percentage points, and a consequent jump in annual GDP growth [in Bangladesh] by more than half a percentage point.'[11]

As Lindsey observes: 'Nothing is more destructive to legal order than a rogue government bent on plunder. No property is safe, no agreements can be relied upon, and, consequently, no complex division of labour is possible. Economic life remains stunted and impoverished, confined to small scale, short-term activities that lie low and hide from the rapacious gaze of predatory government.'

Lindsey also makes the point that these autocratic regimes are often chronically unstable because they lack any institutional mechanism for transferring power. 'Since the stakes of gaining or losing power are so high, transitions are frequently bloody. They can also be highly disruptive: groups that flourished under the favour of the old regime are suddenly targeted for persecution under the new. Political instability thus translates into legal instability, which once again undermines the kind of large-scale, long-term investments upon which prosperity in a modern industrial society depends.'

As we saw when Indonesia's Suharto was toppled in 1998, the resort to repression can often conceal a tenuous grip on power, which can only be preserved by dishing out privileges that ultimately distort and destroy the economy. During Suharto's rule, his sons, daughters and favoured few friends reaped enormous gains from sweetheart deals on items such as cloves, cars and timber. As Lindsey comments: 'The weak but despotic government is incapable of upholding secure and stable property rights, which now are vulnerable to the depredations of multiple predators.'

But a few development economists are studying what works in practice and then applying the principle of success into a theory that can be adapted in other economies. One inspiring success story is that of Muhammad Yunus, the founder of the Grameen Bank in Bangladesh and a pioneer of microcredit. Bangladesh has been often cited by Transparency International as one of the most corrupt of nations, as the most difficult of cases and the largest of the less-developed countries.

Yunus, who tells his story in *Banker to the Poor*, studied the very poor in the village of Jobra. He relates how the local stool-makers were dependent on traders and moneylenders. Yunus explained: 'People . . . were poor not because they were stupid or lazy. They worked all day long, doing complex physical tasks. They were poor because the financial institutions in the country did not help them widen their economic base. This credit market, by default of the formal institutions, had been taken over by the local moneylenders. But if I could just lend the Jobra villagers the 27 dollars [they needed], they could sell their products to anyone.' What was required was an institution that would lend to those who had nothing. He also realised that in his society, like so many other developing countries, it was the women who understood because they had the final responsibility to feed the children. All very difficult when 85 per cent of poor, rural women are illiterate and find it difficult even to leave their homes without their husbands.[12]

The big banks talked of structural readjustment programmes; Yunus introduced an ethical cultural adjustment programme to the debate. Ninety-five per cent of Yunus's customers are women, repayment is reportedly nearly 100 per cent, and loans have gone out to over 2 million families of the rural poor in Bangladesh. Because it works, international agencies now seek to assist. His portfolio now amounts to $2.5 billion. But not many journalists turn up at press conferences announcing $25 loans.

Yunus is not alone. He and other pioneers have shown that good ideas can travel. The Overseas Private Investment Corporation (OPIC), a US

Government agency run by the able Peter Watson, assists US-sponsored foreign direct investment in the developing world. For example, Modern Africa Fund Managers, an OPIC-sponsored private equity fund for sub-Saharan Africa, invested in Flamingo Holdings, Inc. of Kenya, a leading supplier of vegetables and flowers to the European market. What began as a startup in the early 1980s now employs nearly 6,000 Kenyans in such roles as field workers, equipment operators, engineers, nurses and managers. In recent years, growth has been strong, allowing Flamingo to build schools for the surrounding communities, to sponsor and host events for its workers and families, to provide free quality health care and to pay a housing allowance to its workers. OPIC is also teaming up with the Soros Foundation and the National Urban Reconstruction Housing Agency in South Africa to facilitate the construction of approximately 150,000 housing units for impoverished South Africans, many currently dwelling in inadequate structures. Individual South Africans who qualify for low-income housing grants under national guidelines will take title to the houses.

The word 'conditionality' is hated in some development and NGO circles. But unless we ensure that the resources of overseas development aid (ODA) reaches its targets and is not stolen, what is the point? Poorly targeted aid can make the problem worse and instils resentment by tax-payers in the countries of the North, as well as feeding the disgust of the deprived in the South when it props up corrupt bureaucrats, business people and politicians. It is difficult to sell increases in aid budget to sus-picious taxpayers. Renowned psychologist Eric Fromm once wrote of the difference between what he characterised as the unconditional love of a mother and the conditional love of a father. The Monterrey Consensus reached in 2002 under the leadership of UN Secretary General Kofi Annan went a long way towards giving back credibility to development through good governance, trade and aid.

We should study what works in practice and then construct a theory that can be promoted. In the past, it has worked the other way around. I once received a New Zealand Treasury paper on restructuring an organisation and wrote on it: 'It works in practice, but will it work in theory?'

The big challenge is to build proper legal and commercial systems that can ensure that the 'market' works without corrupt and bureau-cratic inertia. The training and capacity-building systems we have put in place in the WTO to ensure the success of the Doha Development Agenda take a practical, solid step in this direction by empowering officials to better represent their national interests. Unfortunately, some still see technical assistance as paying the other guys to agree with them.

Cooperation without coercion is the basis of successful civil society

Isaiah Berlin once posed – in his famous BBC lectures – one of the most fundamental questions of humankind: 'Why should anyone obey any one else?' He went on to examine how political obedience was to be achieved. 'The philosopher, when he is in power, must create an artificial system of rewards and punishments, which will reward men whenever they do what in fact leads to greater happiness, and punish them when in fact they do that which diminishes it,' he said. 'What human motives are is totally irrelevant. It does not in the least matter whether people contribute to happiness because they are benevolent and approve of it, or from some self-interested, base, mean motive of their own. It does not matter whether people prevent human happiness because they are malignant or vicious, or because they are ignorant blunderers or idealistic fools – the damage they do will be identical in either case, and so will the good.'[13]

The will to cooperate without coercion is the basis of successful civil society. Countries, companies and individuals that litigate, sue or blacklist in frustration at the failure of another party to cooperate, are essentially acknowledging in doing so that they have failed to resolve their problem. In the USA, the costs accruing to businesses that are affected by litigation are passed along in the form of a 'litigation tax' of $1,200 per year in assorted increased costs on every US consumer, according to the US Chambers of Commerce.

In Plato's ideal republic, the citizen was so well-educated and trained as a citizen 'that no enforcement against him of particular duty, nor system of sanction, would be required, nor anti-civic act, wilful or inadvertent, be committed by him'.[14] Even Rousseau in *The Social Contract* warned against worship of the state, which he said was not the act of a free citizen, but of a subject or slave.[15]

What builds a strong civilized society? The answer is its institutions, customs and culture. That is its social capital. These in turn are based on that fundamental concept of reciprocity: the expectation that your neighbour, competitor, teacher, daughter's fiancé, the courts, the police and the suppliers of goods you purchase will do the right thing. They will display integrity and honour, based on common values. Perhaps England's greatest gift to the world – aside from what has become almost a universal business language, as well as the basis for liberal democratic systems of government – was the idea of an independent, clean and efficient public service. When leaders, researchers and international institutions write about good governance in developing – and indeed developed – countries they are being polite. What they are saying is: 'Stop The Corruption.' Where that social trust is broken, unempowered individuals retreat into smaller, mistrustful enclaves.

It is people's mutual cooperation within the accepted rules that makes for a civilised society. In *Making Democracy Work*, Robert Putnam writes: 'Networks of civic engagement facilitate communication and improve the flow of information about the trustworthiness of individuals . . . Trust and cooperation depend on reliable information about the past behaviour and present interest of potential partners, while uncertainty reinforces dilemmas of collective action. Thus, other things being equal, the greater the communication (both direct and indirect) among participants, the greater the mutual trust and the easier they will find it to cooperate.'[16]

Why should we treat people equally? Aristotle suggested that what we now call human rights, because we have codified them – the notion of right and wrong – is based on human nature. I have argued that democracy ultimately, if sometimes unequally and untidily, results in better social and economic outcomes.

The Age of Enlightenment destroyed the concept of the king's divine right to rule. But the belief that we are all put in our place as a God-given fact lingers on. A still popular English hymn asserts:

> All things bright and beautiful,
> All creatures great and small,
> All things wise and wonderful,
> The Lord God made them all.
>
> The rich man in his castle,
> The poor man at his gate,
> God made them high and lowly
> And ordered their estate.

Unfortunately, many still cling to privileges, unjustly oppress the weak, and deny their citizens a key element of progress, social mobility. The mobility of labour within societies is an important ingredient of economic and social success. Too many countries have been, or remain, bedevilled by the caste or class system. Not only is it morally repugnant, it is wasteful and inefficient. It is protectionism by race, rewarding those with power and privilege, while starving the economy of talent. The greatest social change in Great Britain over the past hundred years arose in the aftermath of the World Wars. In particular, the British decision to wage 'total war' in 1939, by conscripting labour on all fronts, advanced women in the workplace, smashed barriers and tremendously increased productivity.

Social mobility both reflects and produces change

In Britain and the USA during total war, the trade unions were not banned or their leaders murdered. British union leader Ernest Bevan was brought into the cabinet during the First World War. After the Second World War, Third Reich architect and Supply Minister Albert Speer lamented that Hitler's attitude to women working in factories, and the denial of scientific talent from the Jews and minority groups, were fatal to the Nazi war machine.

It became fashionably glib in the 1970s to blame the English disease – a shorthand for trade union attitudes that had become costly, short-sighted and undemocratic – for all Britain's problems. Partly true, but there was another side, a class system which prevented and discouraged working people from being socially mobile. Snobbery and class warfare is the white man's form of racism and caste system towards each other. Shopkeeper's daughter Margaret Thatcher and now New Labour are breaking this 'class war' and have attempted to create a society based more on merit in commerce, politics, education and the public service. The class structure denied the whole economy of potential talent. Equality of opportunity creating a society based on merit is more efficient, as well as good in itself as a principle of behaviour.

Social mobility lies behind much of the success of such New World former colonies as the USA, Canada, Australia and New Zealand. Those ex-colonies that replicated the old class systems from colonial capitals, as was the case in parts of Latin America, paid a price for excluding talented and productive members of society, and still do.

We are equal, but not the same. The struggle from a democratic point of view has been always between political and social imperatives that pit what Lawrence E. Mitchell describes as liberty versus equality. He observes: 'Equality requires interference with liberty: people are born equal in nature and in the eyes of God, but hardly so in economic and social circumstances. To improve the equality of the disadvantaged requires the state to interfere with the liberty of those more fortunate. Even so, we can for the most part see equality as a natural fact, with equality of condition as an aspiration – in this way of thinking, some measure of equality always remains.'[17]

Charles Darwin wrote: 'As man advances in civilisation, small tribes are united into larger communities. The simplest reason should tell each individual that he ought to extend his social instincts and sympathies to all the members of the same nation, though personally unknown to him. This point being once reached, there is only an artificial barrier to prevent his sympathies being extended to the men of all nations and races.'[18]

The so-called Americanisation of the system of Western values, based on the founding fathers' promise that every citizen has a right to the pursuit of happiness, is only part of the story. A significant aspect of establishing or living up to a values-based system concerns our responsibilities and duty to oneself and the community. Democracy, civil engagement and popular participation are more than the two-minute exercise of ticking a name and a party once every three years. They are about how we live our lives, build up constituencies, increase performance and target customers.

Some 170 years ago, Alexis de Tocqueville observed in his *Democracy in America* that through civic association, which depends on the art of political association, citizens are imbued with an ethic of 'self-interest, rightly understood', whereby 'enlightened regard for themselves constantly prompts them to assist one another and inclines them willingly to sacrifice a portion of their time and property to the welfare of the state'.[19] Robert D. Putnam noted: 'Social capital, as embodied in horizontal networks of civic engagement, bolsters the performance of the polity and the economy, rather than the reverse: strong society, strong economy; strong society, strong state.'[20]

Elected representation is the most basic component of civil society. Changing power without violence is not only morally right, it makes for good economics. It is no historic mistake that democratic states with free markets do better. It is no fluke of nature that democratic trade unions and free institutions are a consistent factor in a nation's economic and social success. Just as it is no accident that the historic changes in Eastern Europe in recent years began with trade unions, from the pivotal role of Solidarity in Poland, to the attempted coup in Moscow, which was ended with the threat of a general strike. For example, it was trade union leaders in South Africa, through the ANC, who fought and still fight for freedoms; and trade unionist Morgan Tsvangirai led the political opposition to Robert Mugabe in Zimbabwe.

Too often, business conspires with government against the people. And, of course, sometimes trade unions conspire with governments against the people, seeking gains for those with jobs at the expense of those who don't have jobs. But free trade unions are a basic component of a democratic economy. It is all about checks and balances, not cheques and brutal power.

The President of the new Czechoslovakia, Vaclav Havel, said that political repression in Eastern Europe had robbed those nations of a healthy civic life and worthwhile public institutions: 'Trade unions, democratic involvement and management of our health systems, public ownership of our energy system, are important to our life, our way of doing things.

Figure 4. With Czech President Vaclav Havel: one of my heroes, a playwright and politician who continues to inspire.

Eastern Europe's problems were not only problems of shortages of private investment, but because public investment and structures, from phones to roads to schools, were in disrepair.'

This unique playwright/politician, imprisoned by the Marxists, not only saw his country become independent of the Warsaw Pact, but assisted the country to peacefully break into two separate nations. Both now want to join the European Union. Yet in Prague in 2000, at a meeting of the IMF/World Bank/WTO, I watched in anger and dismay ill-informed protesters abuse Havel and demand that he apologise for the injustices of democracy.

The opposition to free trade and open societies is most nakedly evident when we examine the world's more nationalistic, tribal and racist countries. I am not suggesting that all opponents to free trade are anti-democratic. I do note some strange and contradictory alliances, however. We have seen opportunist populists like Pat Buchanan and Ralph Nader in the USA; the far right and left in Europe; neo-Nazis as well as neo-Marxists – all riding the bandwagon against globalisation and immigration.

Bill Moyers, of the Sierra Club, has commented: 'Since NAFTA was ratified, corporations have used Chapter Eleven to challenge the power of government to protect its citizens, to undermine environmental and health laws, even attack our system of justice.'[21] And for Nader, the essence of globalisation is 'a subordination of human rights, [and] democracy rights to the imperatives of global trade and investment'.[22] Which is an extravagant, headline-grabbing, fundraising hoax, because it is not true.

Which is not to denigrate the fundamental role that protest movements play in a democracy (see Chapter 13). The West has a better environmental record, not only because market forces operate more effectively than the state, but because democratic civil engagement by the people demands better results of politicians. Public officials and industrial managers in the communist East were free from public pressure and scrutiny, as are dictators in Burma and Africa, and were the colonels in Latin America.

Cooperation, reciprocity, democracy; what is good for the individual, is good for the community; what is good for the nation evolves into a good for the family of nations. Just as individuals cooperate for the wider community good, so must nations. The nation state evolved to resolve problems that individuals, tribes and feuding princes could not. Internationalism has, in turn, grown in significance as the solution to disputes and differences between nations.

Today, the true patriot and good citizen must also be an internationalist. We serve ourselves best when we serve others, and serve them well. The nation state needs the cooperation of others to progress. International rules and institutions protect and promote individual nations' interests. They enhance independence, which in a modern world is now advanced by interdependence.

The age of empire is over: the age of enlightened internationalism is hopefully nearly upon us. We are now achieving nationalist goals by means of international institutions. I see internationalism as the next step in an evolutionary process that gives voice to a wider democracy.

George Orwell's *1984* warned of 'newspeak' and 'doublespeak'; of government slogans like 'War is Peace.'[23] Iraq's Saddam Hussein must have read Orwell, because he recently told his people that if the Americans came back he would give them another thrashing. He may also have been drawing upon the theories of Joseph Goebbels, Hitler's propaganda minister, who reportedly said: 'If you tell a lie big enough and keep repeating it, people will eventually come to believe it.'

It's a pity Orwell isn't with us to give us a chapter on unelected, violent protesters who – in the name of democracy – try to stop democratic and accountable leaders from meeting. These extremists distort and cheapen the valid case of the opposition and pervert a full debate on how we can improve conditions. National rights and international rights are fraught with contradictions and dangers. Life will never conform to theories. As Sir Arthur Keith said: '[Hitler] perfected the double standard of in-group morality and out-group ferocity by calling his movement National Socialism. Socialism stood for communitarianism within the tribe, nationalism for its vicious exterior.'

The more open the society, the better the results

As noted at the outset of this chapter, the more open and democratic the economy, the better the results for ordinary people (see Chapter 5). The countries that have evolved into truly participatory democracies are notable for the absence of either civil or cross-border strife. Democracies don't just prefer making money to making war, their leaders find it much more difficult to rally support for such an essentially wasteful enterprise.

The most brutal repression of political and human rights, the worst environmental outcomes, are seen where governments seek still to control people, commerce and information – such as North Korea and Burma. Or where unrestrained and unmediated tribal instincts take over, from the Balkans to parts of Africa. Bad regimes need outside enemies to blame – look at Mugabe during the 2002 elections, still blaming white colonialists for problems caused by his own misrule, or Sukarno during *Konfrontasi* with Malaysia last century.

More open societies do better. And as nations become more open, they become more democratic and trade more frequently and freely. Over the past few decades, Chile, South Africa, Chinese Taipei, South Korea and Mexico are examples of this. Witness the enormous advances in the Baltic States, Hungary, the Czech Republic and other 'economies in transition'. That very description was coined to recognise and legitimise this evolutionary trend. Recent events in the Balkans, and with the New Partnership for African Development (NEPAD), where the Africans have outlined and are driving their own Renaissance, give us reason to hope.

The lifeblood of democracy is information. Karl Popper taught us that there is no perfection, because all decisions are based on imperfect information. Democracy has to be in place for a governed people to correct failure and replace their leaders. However, countries need what I characterise as a virtuous cycle, not only of free and fair elections, but of free and fair information, for the cycle to progressively turn.

When I first read *1984*, I feared government and big business would be able to control the information age and thus control people. I was wrong; the opposite happened. The rise of the information age, faxes, video cameras and mobile telephones helped the liberation of Eastern

Europe by showing the failures of Marxism. The people now watch *Big Brother*, not the other way around.

The Internet revolution has democratised information; we no longer need to wait for 'specialists' to spin the news or give us the party line. Technology allows people to seek unedited truth for themselves. George Soros donated faxes and copying machines to civil society organisations in Eastern Europe to help speed up their liberation from communism. It was the faxes, mobile phones and handheld video cameras that told the world about Tiananmen Square first, not the diplomatic community. It was short text messages sent by mobile phones that allowed the Philippines' citizens to mobilise the mass protests in 2001 that ousted Erap Estrada, the then president, who ended up facing corruption charges. It is the genius and freedoms generated by the new communications systems that have mobilised protest at every international gathering. Which is not at all bad and can be very healthy. Although the new age has generated an army of spin-doctors and PR consultants, the truth still comes out, eventually.

I believe that national, global and regional laws, rules, standards and norms are necessary if we are to save our environment, protect the world's stocks of migratory fish and fowl, establish open rules for trade and provide more effective political and economic security. This is an imperfect and painfully slow process.

But as international institutions like the WTO work through a multiplicity of complex issues, they are steadily building up a treasure-trove of case studies that is producing a consensus on some core issues and ideals in managing international exchanges, which will result in more common democratic and peaceful precedents. However, we must stay vigilant, otherwise rules and institutions have a stubborn habit of taking on lives of their own and subverting the intentions of their well-meaning architects.

The need for rules

Good intentions can often lead to dangerous outcomes, made more lethal by designer politics where opinion polls and focus groups are now used as instruments of policy formation, not just as marketing tools. De Tocqueville, who so admired the development of civil society and democracy in the USA, also warned against covering the surface of society with 'a network of small complicated rules, minute and uniform, through which the most original minds and most energetic characters cannot penetrate, to rise above the crowd.'[24]

Such rules, he suggested, rather than enforcing required behaviour, restrained men from acting. 'Such a power does not destroy, but it prevents existence; it does not tyrannise, but it compresses, enervates, extinguishes, and stupefies a people, till each nation is reduced to be nothing better than a flock of timid and industrious animals, of which the government is the shepherd,' he wrote. 'I have always thought that servitude of the regular, quiet and gentle kind which I have just described might be combined more easily than is commonly believed with some of the outward forms of freedom, and that it might even establish itself under the wing of the sovereignty of the people.'

This was prescient; a warning to today's politically correct who seek equality of outcome, instead of equality of opportunity. It also helps explain why so many leftist reforms of the 1960s failed and why well-meaning reformers, aiming to take the welfare state to its extreme, end up with the opposite result.

John Stuart Mill spoke of security by saying: '... the economical advantages of commerce are surpassed in importance by those of its effects, which are intellectual and moral. It is hardly possible to overrate the value, in the present low state of human improvement, of placing human beings in contact with persons dissimilar to themselves, and with modes of thought and action unlike those with which they are familiar. Commerce is now, what war once was, the principal source of this contact ... There is no nation which does not need to borrow from others, not merely particular arts or practices, but essential points of character in which its own type is inferior.'[25]

For those who think globalisation is new, listen again to Mill, Hume and Adam Smith, who have all argued that expanded commerce produced good government, and thus reduced the propensity for war, enhanced individual liberty and security, and promoted equality by lessening the 'servile dependency' of individuals on their superiors.

The effect of increased commerce on individual freedom, was, Smith said, the 'least observed advantage of commerce' and 'by far the most important of all [its] effects'. Mill also emphasised what he called additional 'indirect' gains from openness. Here he mainly had in mind the flow of information that accompanied trade. He noted that commerce enhanced the transfer of technology and the cultivation of refined tastes. More than 200 years ago, Immanuel Kant suggested in his essay *Perpetual Peace*: 'Durable peace could be built upon the tripod of representative democracy, international organisations and economic dependence.'

John Blundell, in the Institute of Economic Affairs publication *Waging the War of Ideas*,[26] quotes Roland Vaubel's *The Centralisation of Western Europe*: ' "Let trade be free and the international frontiers will cease to be problems. Trade, exchange of services, creates friends; it is controls that breed enemies. Huge amalgamations of states offer tempting

targets for the wrong type of politician." Trade does make friends and, as Bastiat said, "When goods can't cross borders, armies will." And, as [IEA founder]Arthur Seldon is always keen and quick to point out, every time we trade we are making an agreement with somebody and – in the absence of coercion – both parties walk away better off. What could be better?'[27]

With these forms of collective security integration and the globalisation of human and democratic values, it is easier to imagine a wealthier, healthier world with fewer wars. There will always be the Hitlers, Stalins, Saddam Husseins, Pol Pots and bin Ladens. How far and long we let them prosper will be the test of the new and increasingly robust internationalism.

5   Life is getting better

The world has grown old. The rainfall and sun's warmth are both diminishing, the metals are nearly exhausted.   Cyprian, 250 CE

The world is in a rush and is getting close to its end.
                                                    Archbishop Wulfstan, 1014 CE

This has been the most destructive period in the history of the natural world since the extinction of the dinosaurs 60 million years ago. If we continue without change, the economic, social and environmental costs will be catastrophic.
                                                    Jorgen Randers, WWF, 1998

The Beatles' *Getting Better* repeats the mantra, 'you have to admit it's getting better, a little better all the time...' Paul McCartney led on the writing of the song, with John Lennon contributing a typically sardonic 'it can't get much worse'. The available data suggests that both Beatles got it right.

What are the most important issues for people across the globe? Democracy, individual empowerment, life expectancy, infant mortality, access to clean water, hunger and poverty reduction, inequality, human rights, gender concerns, child labour abuse and the environment. On almost every useful measurement of the human condition, we have seen the greatest advances ever in the history of our species during the last half century, according to data collected by the UNDP and other agencies. Indeed, these advances are accelerating in most parts of the world. So let's study why some countries are doing better and others not so well.

There is always room for improvement, be it in the inner cities of New York, the urban sprawl of Mexico City or the many economies still undergoing a painful transition from their Marxist past. And of course in Africa, the saddest, most marginalised continent of all. There is still much to protest about, and injustice is still rampant in far too many places.

But let us not forget that in 1900, male life expectancy in America was 49 years. In the 1920s, the majority of US farms didn't have electricity. Or that the pollution level of the River Thames in London contributed to the cholera epidemics between 1831 and 1866, which killed over 35,000 people.[1] In 1861, it carried the typhoid disease which killed Queen Victoria's husband, Prince Albert.[2] In 1950, large stretches of the river were devoid of oxygen because of the pollution level, rendering it virtually dead.[3] Only fifty years ago, some 4,000 deaths were linked to the Great Smog of London. Now people fish and swim in the river, and pollution counts are hugely down in developed economies. For example, the US Environmental Protection Agency reported in 1997 that, since 1970, 'the total US population increased 31 percent, vehicle miles travelled increased 127 percent, and the gross domestic product (GDP) increased 114 percent. During that same period, notable reductions in air quality concentrations and emissions took place.'[4]

That urban dwellers in India and Beijing endure pollution levels similar to those in London fifty years ago is not good. But this is an evolutionary process. Despite the 'naysayers', a greater proportion of the world's population enjoys better living conditions than ever before.

Democracy

One hundred years ago there were very few democracies, as we understand the term today. Indeed, women did not get the vote in Great Britain until the 1920s and, despite constitutional rights, in practice millions worldwide – even specific groups such as the African-Americans in advanced democracies such as the USA – were forcefully denied access to their franchise well into the 1960s. Ironically, even Switzerland, headquarters of so many of the world's great multilateral institutions, did not grant the vote to women until 1971, and did not agree to join the UN until 2002. The Soviet Union had a great constitution but it was ignored. Wonderful, high-minded constitutions have been put in place by many of the evil regimes that shelter under the banner of being a 'democratic republic'.

A century ago, the great British, French, German and Ottoman Empires, dominated, and protected their commercial privileges by military might.

At the epochal peace conference in Versailles, in 1919, great power paternalism dominated. Although Woodrow Wilson launched his fourteen points of enlightenment, promoting the concept of self-determination and seeking to extend freedoms, the leaders of the day prevailed in extending their nations' control over traditional, if redrawn, spheres of imperial control. The Versailles Treaty was to prove a disaster for the great tribes of Europe, setting the scene for the next European war of 1939–45, worldwide conflict, followed by the anti-colonial struggle and the Cold War.

The post-war struggle to throw off the European handcuffs of imperialism distorted history for the next forty to sixty years or so, as the
competing ideologies of international Marxism clashed with those of
the more democratic west. These essentially European concepts strug-
gled for worldwide dominance in an era when virtually any despot was
acceptable to the West, so long as he was anti-communist. The killing
in 2002 of veteran Angolan rebel leader Jonas Savimbi, opportunist,
butcher and former beneficiary of American and South African anti-
communist sentiment and cash, provided an eerie reminder of that
Cold War era. The opposing ideological excesses – seen in such incidents as the Soviet invasion of Czechoslovakia in August 1968 – had
long since shattered any romantic notions of Marxism as a liberating
force.

Thirty years ago, most of Central America, all of South America
and half of Europe and South Africa, were under the jackboot of
military/command economies. But within two decades of the Prague
Spring, people's power had exploded in the Philippines, Indonesia, Peru
and Chile. In South Korea, Kim Dae Jung went from being the re-
viled opposition dissident of a military dictatorship to freely elected
President of a country that in 2002 triumphantly co-hosted the Football
World Cup. Chinese Tapei saw the peaceful installation of a multi-party
democracy.

Freedom has proven contagious – fed in large part by the globalisation
of information flows – not only because it is morally right, but because
it works in largely responding to the needs of the people. This process
of ever-expanding freedoms was frozen by the Cold War, but the crashing down of the Berlin Wall essentially ended the debate over whether
Communism would triumph.

Both the number of what can be characterised as democratic countries, as well as the number of people living under a form of democratic
governance, have continued to steadily increase. In 1950, according to
data compiled by Freedom House, 14.3 per cent of the world's countries
were democratic; by 2000 that had risen to 62.5 per cent. The number of
people living in democracies rose from 31 per cent to 58.2 per cent over
the same period.[5] This is not to deny that these economies and democracies are facing enormous challenges. It is their very fragility which makes
it all the more important to ensure that a rules-based multilateral system is in place and fairly administered for the benefit of all. Even in the
few remaining one-party states, freedoms are growing. To suggest that
the world is becoming less free, or that we have not made remarkable
progress over the past century, is simply not true.

Life expectancy

One key indicator of progress is life expectancy. More than 85 per cent of the world's inhabitants can expect to live for at least sixty years – more than twice as long as the average life expectancy a hundred years ago, while deaths from infectious diseases are expected to drop from 9.3 million to 6.5 million.[6] In developing countries, life expectancy has risen from about thirty years at the beginning of the twentieth century to sixty-five in 1999.[7] Life expectancy is still much higher in OECD countries and much worse in Sub-Saharan Africa. As I note elsewhere, there are huge areas of concern over AIDS in Africa, as well as the recent decline in life expectancy in the post-Soviet republics. Many developing countries are now about where developed countries were a hundred years ago. However, the trend is improving, not worsening, in most places.

One of the major challenges now facing the developed world is the difficulty of supporting an ageing population, a subject I address elsewhere in this book (see Chapter 16). Currently around one out of five persons in the developed countries is aged sixty or older; in 2050 it is estimated that nearly one out of every three persons will be aged sixty or older.[8] The proportion of the population over sixty-five in more developed regions, as fertility falls, is expected to reach almost 16 per cent by the end of this decade.[9] People are living longer, creating new challenges, but this is good. Longer life is clearly a much more benign challenge to face, than the risk of dying of typhoid fever at thirty.

The upward trend has been relatively consistent around the globe in recent years. For example, life expectancy worldwide increased overall by a further three years, from sixty-three to sixty-six years, between 1980 and 1999. In low-income countries it increased by six years to fifty-nine years; in middle-income countries it increased by three years to sixty-nine years and in high-income countries it increased by four years, from seventy-four to seventy-eight years.[10]

Between 1970–5 and 1995–2000, life expectancy at birth in developing countries increased by nine years from fifty-five to sixty-four. In the least developed countries (LDCs), the increase was from forty-four to fifty-one years. Even Sub-Saharan Africa showed improvement, with life expectancy at birth increasing by four years from forty-five to forty-nine years. Indeed, the only significant decrease has been recorded in Eastern Europe and the CIS, where life expectancy at birth decreased by one year from sixty-nine to sixty-eight years.[11]

Infant mortality rates have also significantly improved. The under-five mortality rate is the probability that a newborn baby will die before

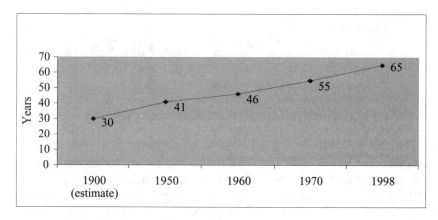

Figure 5. Average life expectancy in developing countries, 1900–98 (Source: UNDP).

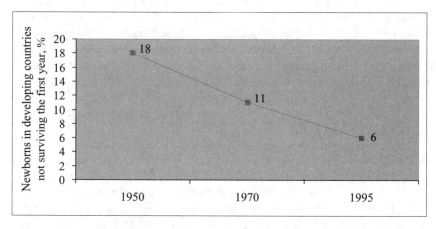

Figure 6. Infant mortality rates in developing countries, 1950–95 (Source: UNDP).

reaching age five per 1,000. Worldwide the under-five mortality rate went down from 123 to 78 from 1980 to 1999. In low-income countries, it decreased from 177 to 116. And in low- and middle-income countries it went from 135 to 85 over the same period. The largest drop was in South Asia, from 121 to 89.[12]

Sanitation and access to food

Sanitation and access to food are other good indicators of progress. Access to improved sanitation facilities (the percentage of the urban or rural population with access to at least adequate excreta disposal facilities) increased worldwide from 78 per cent to 84 per cent for the urban population and from 29 per cent to 36 per cent for the rural population from 1990 to 2000. In low-income countries, the access to improved sanitation facilities improved for the urban population from 68 per cent to 79 per cent, and for the rural population from 25 per cent to 31 per cent. In middle-income countries, this factor improved from 29 per cent to 39 per cent of the rural population, and from 75 per cent to 82 per cent of the urban population.[13]

Malthus was wrong. The Green Revolution has been victorious, Lomborg notes, adding that we now have far more food per person than we used to, even though the world's population has doubled since 1961. Production in the developing countries has tripled.[14] And enlarged international trade has played a key role in enhancing food security. Globally, the proportion of people starving in the developing world has fallen from 45 per cent in 1949, to 35 per cent in 1970, to 18 per cent in 1997 – and the UN expects that the figure will have fallen to 12 per cent by 2010.[15]

It is not just the proportion of people starving that has fallen, but the absolute number as well. While in 1971 almost 920 million people were starving, the total fell to below 792 million in 1997 (i.e. 237 million *fewer* people were starving). By 2010 it is expected to fall to 680 million.[16] Not good, but undeniably better.

The proportion of children in the developing world considered to be undernourished has fallen from 40 per cent to 30 per cent over the past fifteen years, and is expected to fall further to 24 per cent by 2020.[17] On average the developing countries have increased their food intake from 2,463 to 2,663 calories per person per day over the last decade, an increase of 8 per cent.[18] The FAO predicts that the next thirty years will see fewer malnourished people, and that all regions will experience increasing available calories per capita. The same general conclusion is reached in studies by IFPRI, USDA and the World Bank – and this increased food supply is expected to cost the poor less, not more.[19] Trade restrictions harm both the developed and developing world, since tariffs and agricultural subsidies effectively indirectly and directly increase the cost of food (and do so relatively more for working people in developed countries).

We are living longer and better. Why? Because we have made important progress in obtaining better access to clean water, medicine, sanitation and food. The greatest lift to life expectancy in London's history was the invention of the public sewerage and water system. The percentage of doctors in poor countries has doubled. Have we done enough to improve

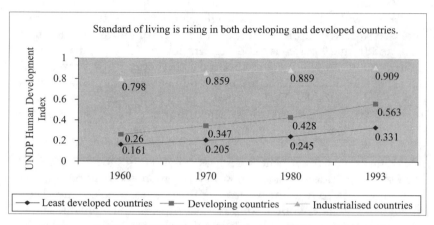

Figure 7. The UNDP Human Development Index, 1960–93 (Source: UNDP).

the lot of mankind globally? No. We never will, because no one will ever accept that the human journey is over. But we have experienced the most stunning advances in the history of our species. The World Bank predicts that if the Doha Development Trade Round is successful, it will lift over 300 million people from extreme poverty by 2015.

Johan Norberg's myth-shattering book *In Defence of Global Capitalism* states: 'Thirty years ago nearly 35 per cent of the population of the developing countries were afflicted with hunger. Today's figure is 18 per cent. Many? Yes. Too many? Of course. But the number is rapidly declining. It took the first two decades of the twentieth century for Sweden to be declared free from chronic malnutrition. In only thirty years the proportion of hungry in the world has been reduced by half, and it is expected to decline further, to 12 per cent, by 2010. There have never been so many of us on earth, and we have never had such a good supply of food.' Norberg acknowledges that the worst development has occurred in Africa south of the Sahara, where the proportion of hungry has actually increased, from 89 to 180 million people. But he adds: 'Even there, the hungry percentage of population has declined, albeit marginally, from 34 to 33 per cent. Global food production has doubled during the past half-century, and in the developing countries it has tripled.'[20]

Amartya Sen, in *Development as Freedom*, writes: 'Quite often economic insecurity can relate to the lack of democratic rights and liberties. Indeed the working of democratic political rights can even help to prevent famines and other economic disasters. Authoritarian rulers, who are themselves rarely affected by famines (or other such economic calamities) tend to lack the incentive to take timely preventive measures. Democratic governments, in contrast, have to win elections and face public criticism, and have strong incentives to undertake measures to avert famines and other such catastrophes. It is not surprising that no famine has ever taken place in the history of the world in a functioning democracy – be it economically rich (as in contemporary Western Europe or North America) or relatively poor (as in post-independence India, or Botswana, or Zimbabwe). *[Author's note: It is highly significant that Zimbabwe is reporting its first food shortages since independence following Robert Mugabe's political repression during the 2002 elections.]* Famines have tended to occur in colonial regimes governed by rulers from elsewhere (as in British India or in an Ireland administered by alienated English rulers), or in one-party states (as in the Ukraine in the 1930s, or China during 1958–61, or in Cambodia in the 1970s), or in military dictatorships (as in Ethiopia or Somalia, or some of the Sahel countries in the near past).'[21]

There is much evidence to suggest that China's leaders were reassured by their own propaganda and on statistics based more on cadres' desire not to disappoint, than on reality, while 30 million people died of starvation during the 'Great Leap Forward' between 1958 and 1961. Yet since China rejected its previous policies, it has seen the greatest material advances in its history, lifting more than 150 million people out of extreme poverty in less than twenty years by adopting more open economic reforms.

Education and literacy

Education levels have also improved. There are still huge holes: in developing countries one child in three does not complete five years of primary education.[22] But overall adult illiteracy rates in low-income countries fell from 35 per cent to 29 per cent for males aged fifteen and over between 1990 and 1999. For females aged fifteen and over they fell from 56 per cent to 48 per cent. Adult illiteracy rates in low and middle Income countries fell from 22 per cent to 18 per cent for males. Adult illiteracy rates in Sub-Saharan Africa fell by 9 percentage points from 40 per cent to 31 per cent, and for women it fell by 13 percentage points from 60 per cent to 47 per cent in the same time period. Adult illiteracy rates fell by 12 percentage points and more for women in South Asia, Sub-Saharan Africa and the Middle East and North Africa.

Youth illiteracy rates also went down. In low-income countries they went from 24 per cent to 19 per cent for males aged fifteen and over between 1990 and 1999 and 41 per cent to 31 per cent for females aged fifteen and over. For women, the fall was considerable: between 9 and

13 percentage points in South Asia, Sub-Saharan Africa and the Middle East and North Africa between 1990 and 1999.[23]

The trend is unmistakably good. Future challenges in this area will increase, simply because infant mortality rates are falling so dramatically. But distance education and new technologies have given us weapons not at the disposal of early generations. Parents everywhere, given half a chance, know that education is the key to a better future. They work and sacrifice to see their children have the opportunities they missed out on. I say parents, but it is so often the mothers: like the stream of migrant women from developing countries we see cleaning hospitals and schools, postponing their own wellbeing for their sons' and daughters' futures. Mothers are never short-termists.

It is difficult to enjoy progress if governments would rather spend money on guns than children, or are able to plunder their nations' resources. Much of the failure for slower growth in some regions remains with corrupt, decadent and sometimes insane leaders. But we are seeing encouraging signs of progress.

Global poverty

Living standards are also improving worldwide. Some 2.8 billion – almost half the world's population – were living on less than $2 a day in 1998.[24] The number of people living in extreme poverty worldwide increased between 1987 and 1990 from 1.2 to 1.3 billion, but decreased again to 1.2 billion – about one in five – in 1998.[25] However, the proportion of people worldwide living in extreme poverty (one 1985 dollar a day, which is the World Bank's reference point) decreased by 5 percentage points between 1990 and 1998, from 25 per cent to 20 per cent of the global population.[26] Between 1987 and 1998, the share of the population in developing and transition economies living on less than $1 a day fell from 28 per cent to 24 per cent.[27]

According to the UN, we have reduced poverty more in the last 50 years than in the last 500, and it has been reduced in practically every country.[28] Columbia University's Xavier Sala-i-Martin, commenting on a UNDP view that inequality is increasing between the richest and poorest countries, agrees that inequality has probably increased, on average, within countries, but observes that this varies from country to country. As for inequality across countries, Sala-I-Martin says: 'The UN misses an important point. If you measure incomes in terms of purchasing power rather than at market exchange rates, incomes are a lot more equal. When the UN says that the incomes of the richest 20 per cent were 30 times bigger than the incomes of the poorest 20 per cent in 1960, and

74 times bigger in 1997, it is using market exchange rates. In purchasing power terms, the corresponding ratios were 11 and 15. Despite the fall after 1980 (when the ratio was 16), the trend for the period as a whole is nonetheless up.'[29]

In India, for example, the average person's income in rupees in 2000 translated into just $460 per annum at the prevailing exchange rate. But because food, clothing, housing and other necessities are so much cheaper than in the USA, the same amount of rupees was equivalent to an American income of nearly $2,400. Similarly, the average Chinese income in 2000 was $840 at the official rate, but more than $3,900 in purchasing power.[30]

Fantastic progress has been made in reducing poverty in developing countries. During the last four decades, the social indicators have improved in all regions. In the past two decades, poverty has been drastically reduced in East Asia: from six out of ten living on under $1 a day in the mid-1970s, to two out of ten in the mid-1990s. There has also been a reduction in poverty during the last few years throughout most of southern Asia and parts of the Middle East, North Africa and Latin America.[31]

The UK-based Centre for Economic Policy Research, in a 2002 report, wrote: 'The increasing integration of the world's economies does not inevitably increase the inequality of incomes. The nineteenth century saw an explosion of inequality, but by the middle of the twentieth century it had stopped rising. The proportion of the world's population in absolute poverty is now lower than it has ever been.'[32]

Because of the concurrent population increase, the percentage of poor in the developing world has declined from 28.3 per cent in 1987 to 24 per cent in 1998. Indeed, although the total number of poor has remained about the same (1.2 billion), the proportion of poor people has been more than halved from around 50 per cent in 1950. Thus, over the past fifty years, some 3.4 billion more people have risen out of poverty. However, both the UN and the World Bank emphasise that there is a long way to go. The international development target is to halve the proportion of people living in extreme poverty and bring it down to around 12 per cent by 2015.[33] This goal is achievable.

As noted elsewhere, the worst problems are in Sub-Saharan Africa, where the number of people living in extreme poverty increased between 1987 and 1998 by 39 per cent. Sub-Saharan Africa's share of the population living in extreme poverty in the developing world increased from 18 per cent to 24 per cent over this period.[34]

The ratio of East Asian income to that of high-income OECD countries improved from one-tenth to nearly one-fifth over 1960 to 1998. In Latin

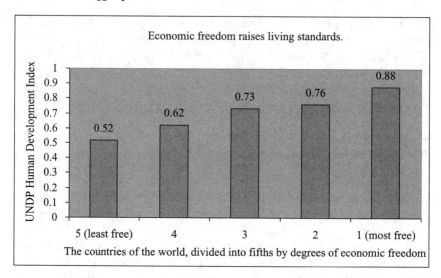

Figure 8. The relationship between economic freedom and the UNDP Human Development Index (Source: Gwartney and Lawson et al, 2001).

America and the Caribbean, this ratio remained roughly stable at one-fifth. Income in South Asia – after worsening in the 1960s and 1970s, then improving significantly in the 1980s and 1990s – remains about one-tenth of that in OECD countries. And in Sub-Saharan Africa, per capita income was around one-ninth of that in OECD countries in 1960 and had deteriorated to around one-eighteenth in 1998.[35]

We have accomplished a great deal over the past century. But our planet remains vulnerable. For example, the FAO estimates that approximately 50 per cent of major marine fish stocks are fished to their fishing capacity limit and some 18 per cent of those fish stocks are overexploited and have no potential for further increase.[36] The World Wide Fund for Nature has estimated that current fishing levels are at least 2.5 times the sustainable limit.[37] Industry observers like Thomas Kocherry, President of India's National Fishworkers' Forum, have blamed not just overfishing, but coastal aquaculture and industrial and domestic pollution.

Water – the world's key resource

One of the most serious challenges facing mankind is access to water. More than 96 per cent of all nations at present have sufficient water resources and, on all continents, water accessibility has increased per person. But our water consumption has almost quadrupled since 1940.[38] Population increases inevitably means more stress on water resources.

The major problem we currently face is water misallocation and wastage – and this occurs largely because water in many places is not well priced. This is particularly a problem for the poorest countries, which use most of their water for irrigation, in contrast to rich countries.[39] Despite these problems, the situation is improving, with the share of people in developing countries with access to water increasing from 30 per cent in 1970 to 80 per cent in 2000.

Water is the raw material of life, making up 75 per cent of our body mass. But of all the water on the planet, more than 97 per cent is salt water and less than 3 per cent is fresh. Of that 3 per cent, about 0.3 per cent is contained in lakes and rivers, with the polar ice caps, glaciers and permanent snow accounting for over 69 per cent, and 0.9 per cent is attributable to soil moisture, swamp water and permafrost. The remaining third of the world's freshwater comes from natural underground sources, groundwater.

The world has seen a sixfold increase in water usage since 1900.[40] 'The demand for fresh water increased between 1900 and 1995 at twice the population growth,' says Peter Gleick in *The World's Water 1998–1999: The Biennial Report in Freshwater Resources*. '[And] global population will increase from 6 billion to almost 8 billion within 25 years.'[41]

Fresh water on earth is stored as groundwater, and is vulnerable to pollution. The World Meteorological Organization (WMO) reports that one person in five does not have access to safe drinking water, and half the world's population does not have adequate sanitation.[42] Contributing to the problem, groundwater is being extracted for consumption at a faster rate than nature can replenish it. Gleick claims: 'There is no looming crisis, we *have* a crisis.'[43] The Worldwatch Institute [WI] suggests that stable world food supply is now dependent on an increasing global water deficit. A WI study estimates that 160 billion cubic metres of water annually are lost to thirsty cities and farms, which are not returning it to underground aquifiers.[44]

However, Julian L. Simon argues persuasively in his *The Ultimate Resource 2* that, given the vast volumes of the ocean, the only possible water problems are that (a) there is not enough water in a place where it is wanted at a given moment, and hence the price is too high; and (b) the available water is dirty. 'People "create" usable water, and there are large opportunities to discover and utilise new sources,' he says. 'Some additional sources are well known and already in partial use; transport by ship from one country to another, deeper wells, cleaning dirty water, towing icebergs to places where water is needed, and desalination. But there also are entirely new possibilities, about some of which there already are hints, and about others which – inevitably – nothing is known.'[45]

The major concerns, aside from pollution, are the losses caused by poor water management, uneconomic water pricing systems and hidden water subsidies, leading to inefficient consumption. For example:

- The poorest countries use 90 per cent of their water for irrigation, in comparison to 37 per cent in the rich countries.[46]
- Approximately 60–80 per cent of all water is wasted because of inefficient irrigation systems.[47]
- Manila, Philippines loses 58 per cent of its water because of its poor water distribution system, while Latin America loses on average 40 per cent.[48]

These are encouraging figures in that they indicate that the potential for savings through greater efficiencies is enormous. Worldwatch Institute says several studies have reported that a range of 30–90 per cent of water consumption could be saved at no additional costs to industry. Sandra Postel in *Pillar of Sand* says irrigation accounts for two-thirds of global use of fresh water, but that less than half the water actually reaches the roots of plants. Methods are needed to double the efficiency of water use, she says, citing several steps that are working. Supporting the findings of these studies, drip irrigation systems, practised in countries such as Israel, India, Jordan, Spain and the USA, have shown positive results with consistent reduction in water waste by 30–70 per cent while increasing yield by 20–90 per cent.

Rice farmers in an area of Malaysia increased water productivity 45 per cent by shoring up canals and switching from traditional transplanting methods to direct sowing of seed into the fields. Israel is now reusing 65 per cent of its domestic wastewater for crop production, freeing up fresh water for households and industries.[49]

The European Commission reports that water consumption in Madrid fell by 29 per cent between 1992 and 1994. Thus, 100 million cubic metres of water have been saved each year thanks to an intelligent use strategy. Losses in water distribution systems are estimated on average at 30 per cent throughout Europe and, in certain urban networks, may reach 70–80 per cent.[50]

As for pollution, according to the UN, 1 billion people lack access to safe water, and two out of three people will be living with water shortages

Table 2. *Estimates of global morbidity and mortality of water-related diseases (early 1990s)*

Disease	Morbidity (episodes/year or people infected)	Mortality (deaths/year)
Diarrhoeal diseases	1,000,000,000	3,300,000
Intestinal helminths	1,500,000,000 (people infected)	100,000
Schistosomiasis	200,000,000 (people infected)	200,000
Dracunculiasis	150,000 (in 1996)	–
Trachoma	150,000,000 (active cases)	–
Malaria	400,000,000	1,500,000
Dengue fever	1,750,000	20,000
Poliomyelitis	114,000	–
Trypanosomiasis	275,000	130,000
Bancroftian filariasis	72,800,000 (people infected)	–
Onchocerciasis	17,700,000 (people infected; 270,000 blind)	40,000 (mortality caused by blindness)
Total	3,342,789,000	5,290,000

by 2025.[51] That is if we do nothing. But the human experience is that policies adapt to new circumstances and information. The European Commission suggests that 20 per cent of all European Union surface water is seriously threatened with pollution and notes that the cost of supplying the EU with water almost doubled between 1990 and 1995 (from 12 to 20 billion euros).[52]

Living Water International (LWI), a US-based not-for-profit organisation, recently obtained financing from the US government-funded OPIC to acquire additional drilling equipment for its operations in Kenya. Since its inception, LWI Kenya has successfully drilled a total of seventy boreholes and rehabilitated twenty-five water systems. Today, over 150,000 more Kenyans are drinking clean, hygienic water throughout the country. The new equipment will allow the drilling of an additional twenty wells per year, at a cost of around $20,000 per well. The World Health Organization stated, 'At any given time 50 per cent of the population in developing countries is suffering from water-related diseases caused either by infection or indirectly by disease carrying organisms.'[53] About 5 million people die each year from water-related diseases (see Table 2).

Hans Zomer, in *the Politics of Water*, suggests the situation is even worse, asserting: 'Three-quarters of all diseases have to do with bad hygiene and unsafe water. There are truly water-borne diseases (such as diarrhoea, typhoid and cholera) and diseases related to water (such as malaria which is transmitted by mosquitoes that lay their eggs in water). Each year, 23 million people worldwide die of unsafe water. Diarrhoea alone kills more than 3 million people per year.'[54]

Pesticide pollution is a major concern worldwide. In many cases, the only guidance on how to use a potentially dangerous product comes from representatives of the pesticide companies, says Theodor Friedrich, of the Rome-based Food and Agriculture Organization's (FAO) agricultural engineering division. The agency provided these examples:[55]

- Malaysian spray operators have been poisoned because of the lack of training, badly maintained equipment and insufficient protective clothing.
- Colombian flower growers and orchard tenders in Brazil use ten times as much pesticide as necessary.
- Pakistani farmers waste about half their pesticides, which has led to groundwater pollution.
- High levels of pesticide residues are found in Indian crops.
- More than half the spraying equipment in Indonesia leaks.

But the knowledge that we *can* improve outcomes, given the will and the resources, is why there has been so much improvement at almost every level of human activity.

China, with its vast population, is a key area of concern, and faces major problems with industrial pollution, as well as upstream erosion, which has contributed to the silting up of such key rivers as the Yangtze River. The authorities do plan to spend $4.8 billion to prevent pollution on the Yangtze, where the giant Three Gorges Dam is being built to create the world's biggest hydroelectric station. However, the dam itself – which has forced the relocation of 1.13 million people – has drawn widespread criticism from environmental groups.[56]

And water has been a key source of international conflict over the centuries. Gleick compiled a water conflict chronology listing over sixty major conflicts concerning access to water during the past 500 years. They ranged from Leonardo da Vinci and Machiavelli planning to divert the Arno River away from Pisa during its conflict with Florence in 1503 to protests at the Roosevelt Roads Navy Base in Puerto Rico in 1999 against the US Navy's use of the Bianco River, and describes chronic water shortages involving conflicts in almost every region. Access to water is a key element in the ongoing Israeli–Palestinian struggle over settlements in the West Bank.[57] (See Water Conflict Chronology http://www.worldwater.org/conflict.htm.)

Water is receiving increasing attention from the World Bank and other donors as issues of rising demand, declining availability, pollution, and the need for conservation grow in urgency. Since 1993, the Bank has invested

$16 billion in water-related projects, with over 180 new operations costing $40 billion in eighty countries. The Bank's portfolio of water projects accounts for 14 per cent of Bank lending. Between 1985 and 1998 the Bank invested more than $33 billion in water-related projects.[58]

Can the international community act coherently? There are over twenty international agencies handling the issue of fresh water, which doesn't inspire confidence. However, progress is being made. The Thames, the Great Lakes, the Rhine and New York harbour are cleaner now than in past generations. According to Bjørn Lomborg's *The Skeptical Environmentalist*, the quantity of oil spilt fell from about 318,000 tons a year in the 1970s to just 110,000 tons in the 1990s.[59] New conventions are being drawn up. People do respond to crisis, eventually, forcing improvements by leaders who if they fail to respond are expendable at election time.

Julian Simon points out that, in a typical poor area in South Africa in the 1990s the average household spends about three full hours of labour each day hauling water from the source to the house in order to supply its water needs. In comparison, typical households in middle class areas can pay for a day's worth of water with the pay from perhaps one or two minutes of work. And the price of water brought to the house by a water carrier in poor areas of South Africa is perhaps twenty-five or thirty times the price of water in a modern middle class area in South Africa. This is how it also used to be only a century or so ago in what is now the rich world. The long-run trend, as with all other natural resources, has been towards a much greater abundance of water, rather than towards greater scarcity.[60]

The WTO has been working through its own approach on water, as well as on the environment. As Director-General, I was aware that the status of water in international economic law was becoming an increasingly controversial issue. It has two main components: first, the question of whether water, and in particular 'bulk water', can be considered as a 'product', and thus be subject to the disciplines of the GATT; second, the distribution of water and, consequently, the relevance of the General Agreement on Trade and Services (GATS) for this activity.

Water and the GATT

The question of whether bulk water can be traded and would be subject to international trade rules is relatively new and arose first under the NAFTA. While Canada owns large quantities of fresh water (and in fact is the main 'reservoir' of fresh water on the planet), some regions of the USA increasingly suffer from water scarcity. NAFTA sparked off a controversy as to whether Canada could be obliged to export water in large quantities and lose control over its water resources. This question has so far not been brought to a dispute, but it remains extremely sensitive.

No actual problem in relation with the export of bulk water has arisen under the GATT so far. Water did not seem to have been an issue as such, even when, during the Uruguay Round, contracting parties were discussing the status of natural resources. In fact, apart from the case of bottled mineral water, water has not been thought of as a tradable product, mainly because of technical problems: water is bulky, pervasive and cheap. However, increasing demand from 'thirsty' countries, associated with technical progress in the transport of water, may make this trade possible in the near future.

From a legal point of view, however, the questions to be examined under the GATT are similar to those under the NAFTA. First, it must be determined whether water can be considered a 'product'. If the answer to that question is affirmative, then water would be subjected to the disciplines of the GATT, in particular Article XI which prohibits export restrictions. The availability of possible exceptions allowing countries to limit or prohibit water export would also have to be examined.

Water and the GATS

For the time being, however, water seems to be more a concern of the GATS, and water-related issues have arisen here. Various proposals have been presented with a view to revising and updating the classification of so-called 'environmental services'; it is widely acknowledged that the current classification is obsolete. The most ambitious of these proposals comes from the European Community, which, as part of a new detailed classification of environmental services, proposes to include the distribution of water for human use (which would include water collection, purification and distribution services). Various Members, among them Canada, are opposed to the inclusion of water distribution in the classification of environmental services, on the ground that 'this related to the conservation of exhaustible natural resources and, therefore, should not be covered by the GATS'.[61] In fact, any kind of reference to 'water' appears to be politically unacceptable for a number of countries. Because the WTO is a member-driven organisation, it is unlikely to be ahead of the prevailing consensus.

However, water has become one of the 'favourite' themes, along with health, education and the environment, that NGOs have taken up to illustrate the 'threat' that the WTO/GATS may pose for public services.

The debate involves a range of questions related to the role of public services and tendencies towards privatisation, the protection of natural resources, the issue of water pricing, the right of access to potable water and the right to regulate.

In an attempt to respond to these attacks, I instructed the WTO Secretariat to fight back and we produced a publication *GATS Fact and Fiction*, which included a section entitled *The WTO is not after your water*. We explained that GATS does not require the privatisation or deregulation of any service, that a range of legitimate policy options are available with respect to water distribution, and that governments had the right to set levels of quality, safety, price and other policy objectives as they see fit. We also indicated that *no* Member has made GATS-specific commitments on water distribution so far.

The NGO Alliance for Democracy has expressed much concern about the implications of the GATS negotiations for water distribution services. It claims that progressive liberalisation under the GATS 'means moving towards privatisation of all services, including public services. It also means deregulation of services at the local state and national levels and subjecting them to the WTO's global rules for the benefit of transnational corporations.'

To put it as simply as possible, the WTO is not after your water. GATS does not require the privatisation or deregulation of any service. Any individual commitments would not affect the right of governments to set levels of quality, safety, price or any other policy objectives as they see fit, and the same regulations would apply to foreign suppliers as to nations. It is, of course, inconceivable that any government would agree to surrender the right to regulate water supplies, and WTO Members have not done so.

A theme of this book and a principle I believe in deeply is at work in the issue of water, as in so many of the other environmental and social outcomes discussed above. Given adequate information, political and economic markets work. The history of the past fifty years teaches us to be concerned, to take political action and that we can, if we have the collective will, solve almost any problem. Businesses globally see great opportunities and profits in solving this problem. Resources will be mobilised and drawn to water because nature, politics and commerce abhor a vacuum. The threat to our water supplies is at its highest now; if we act we can avert disaster further down the road. The evidence strongly suggests that access to water is ultimately an issue of political willpower, not declining resources, and that as usual the international community will respond to this problem a day late and a dollar short. But nonetheless a response is gathering momentum.

The WTO and the Environment

Overall, I side with those, like Lomborg, who argue that much of the criticism of the current state of the environment is alarmism. The best environmental outcomes have come about as a result of democracy, open markets, an active civil society and free media to keep politicians and business people honest, accountable and responsive. And they will continue to demand better outcomes from their leaders.

In so far as the WTO is concerned, the organisation has been portrayed as a monster by some extreme environmentalists. As is often the case, their criticisms are inaccurate. Consider the words of Michael M. Weinstein, in *Greens and Globalisation*. He writes: 'Remember all those protesters dressed up as sea turtles and carrying pictures of dolphins as they railed against the World Trade Organization in Seattle in 1999? And once again their target is a global bogeyman that the Humane Society of the United States has called "the single most destructive international organisation ever formed". But a close look at several recent rulings by the trade organisation suggests that the demonstrators' wrath may be misdirected: in fact, the free-trade group may be turning green.'[62]

Weinstein points out what other informed observers already knew: in crucial recent cases, the WTO has affirmed the right of countries to impose trade measures to protect the environment. He quotes John Jackson, a trade expert at the Georgetown University Law School, who has noted that in other words, environmental groups 'lost some battles, but won the war'.

In fact, the WTO's disputes system Appellate Body (AB) ruled against efforts by the USA to block imports of shrimp caught with nets that sweep up endangered sea turtles. The decision found that the environmental objective and nature of the US statute was compatible with the WTO, but that the way the regulation had been applied was a form of disguised trade restriction because it discriminated between some importers, and because the US import authorities did not leave exporters with enough flexibility to demonstrate that their way of fishing was sufficiently protective of turtles. The US revised its regulation, consulted with the main parties, settled with some, and increased the flexibility for exporters to prove their fishing methods were protective of turtles. The AB confirmed the new measure benefited from the environment justification, which allows members to give priority to environmental policies while requiring that, to the greatest extent possible, the market access rights of exporting countries are protected. In this case, as on other occasions, the protestors were ill-informed about the realities of international trade and the environment.

WANTED

HEAD OF THE WORLD TRADE ORGANIZATION

MIKE MOORE

For the wanton destruction of the world's forests, and the murder of countless endangered
species, also charged with supporting SLAVERY of under aged sweatshop laborers,
Head of a word wide syndicate bent on world domination.

Figure 9. Many environmentalists saw the WTO, personified by me, as
the enemy: for a while, they successfully demonised globalisation and
the WTO.

Weinstein adds: 'What would [the environmentalists] lose by declaring
victory, however limited? Perhaps part of the answer is that if the war
were perceived to be going their way, they might have trouble rallying the
troops in Quebec and keeping the pressure on.'

In fact, progress on environmental issues has been made in the WTO,
if not as much as I would like. At Doha, governments committed themselves to negotiations on the relationships between MEAs (Multilateral

Environment Agreements) and the WTO to ensure there are no contradictions, which could throw the world's trading systems into chaos.
Negotiations will also cover trade barriers to environmental goods and
services, with the aim of enhancing the mutual supportiveness of trade
and the environment.

Governments also agreed to give priority to the effect of environmental
measures on market access, and those situations in which the elimination
or reduction of trade restrictions and distortions would benefit trade, the
environment and development. Members are also working on labelling
requirements for environmental purposes, because many fear unilateral decisions on such issues as labelling could become disguised, even
targeted, protectionism.

Clearly, unless there is global action on the environment, there will be
local reaction, which could damage poorer countries.

Many developing countries are deeply suspicious of developed countries because they fear protectionist motives and point out that agricultural subsidies in OECD countries cost $1 billion a day and result in job
losses for poor countries, as well as pollution in rich countries due to
intensive, subsidised farming inputs, while massive subsidies for coal –
a great polluter – have slowed down investment in cleaner alternatives.
Fish subsidies by rich countries have a similar impact on the environment, another area of deep differences between governments that will be
addressed in the negotiations.

New Zealand Trade Negotiations Minister Jim Sutton charges:
'Globally the fisheries industry is hooked on subsidies. This distorts trade,
threatens fish stocks and impedes the development of poorer nations.'[63]
New Zealand officials estimate international fish subsidies at around $20
billion annually, or 20 per cent of global fisheries sales. New Zealand
Seafood Council General Manager Alistair MacFarlane commented:
'Most fishing subsidies go to fishing operators in the wealthy developed
countries of Europe, North America and North Asia. They are keeping
depleted and bankrupt domestic fisheries going to the point where some
are biologically collapsing. They also assist wealthy country fishing operators to shift to developing countries' fisheries, crowding out legitimate,
unsubsidised domestic operators who would otherwise be able to develop
those resources.'

There are some encouraging signs, however. The gutsy European
Fisheries Commissioner Franz Fischler in mid-2002 signalled a new
regime, telling Europe's 260,000 fishermen, 'We have never been so efficient at catching fish, but now we are overexploiting our oceans. Species
like cod and hake have been subjected to so much fishing that stocks are

near to collapse.' Fischler recommends cutting Europe's fleet by up to 40 per cent over time, phasing out aid now provided to modernise vessels and using the money to encourage fishermen to take up other jobs. He also proposed ending the system under which yearly catch quotas are politically decided every December, and replacing it with programmes lasting several years, which scientists say will protect stocks better. His moves have predictably encountered strong opposition from some European fishing nations.[64] A good result from the Doha Round would help drive these negotiations; globally, they are now on the agenda.

Some WTO Members believe environmental issues should not even be considered in the WTO, although we have a Committee on Trade and the Environment. But trade and the protection of the environment need not be in conflict and should be complementary. Some think that it is time for a new Global Environmental Agency, saying this is the missing link in the international architecture. Progress is being made: thirty years ago, no government had a Minister for the Environment; now most governments have a designated minister.

All serious research shows that poverty is the greatest threat to the environment. People don't live in polluted squalor by choice, nor do they trek miles to strip trees for charcoal by choice. There is a direct connection with rising living standards and better environmental outcomes. Higher education and living standards reduce birth rates. The same is true of the environment. Rich cities are cleaner than poor cities. Every time we lift people from poverty, we lift environmental outcomes.

Is economic growth, facilitated by trade, part of the problem, or part of the solution? Extremists argue that trade is bad for the environment. But there is no evidence that trade between nations is more environmentally damaging than trade within nations. One major reason why environmental protection is lagging in many countries is low incomes. Countries that live on the margin are simply unable to set aside resources for pollution abatement, or may not they think they should sacrifice their growth prospects to help solve global pollution problems, which they say in large part have been caused by the consuming lifestyle of richer countries.

If poverty is at the core of the problem, economic growth will be part of the solution, to the extent that it allows countries to shift gear from more immediate concerns to long-run sustainability issues. Indeed, at least *some* empirical evidence suggests that pollution increases at the early stages of development, but decreases after a certain income level has been reached, an observation known in academic circles as the Environmental Kuznets Curve.[65]

Efficiency is another word for conservation; efficiency comes from open markets and competition locked in by good governmental practices. Let us hope those who seek freedom to choose win through, not those who seek central controls to get desired results. History shows that the most polluted places and poorest people are those that have suffered from governments which tried to plan outcomes by central and government ownership, and that have suffered from fraud, the absence of democracy, accountability and the lack of an active, engaged civil society.

Part Two

From Seattle to Doha

6   Setback in Seattle

I had been approached several times over the years to consider being nominated as Director-General, even before there was a WTO. Back in the old days of the GATT I'd always refused, suggesting better people. I saw my own future in New Zealand politics. The people thought otherwise and although I'd come to within a few hundred votes and a handful of seats of winning the 1993 election, there's only one winner in first-past-the-post politics. I was replaced as Labour Leader and returned, grumpy, to the parliamentary back benches, but determined to do my duty.

A suggestion that I consider standing as a candidate to head the WTO came again in 1999, led by Ambassador Carlos de Perez del Castillo of Uruguay. I had strong support from Latin America and agricultural developing countries, so this time I expressed interest. Leaving New Zealand politics would be difficult as I had become something of an institution. But I also feared I was becoming institutionalised.

In parliamentary party politics, your opponents are in the other party, but your enemies are in your own. The New Zealand Conservative National Party Prime Minister Jenny Shipley was very supportive, as was Trade Minister Lockwood Smith and retired Trade Minister Philip Burdon.

I left home on a two-week trip to see where my support lay, which turned into a three-month odyssey. The toughest part physically? A non-stop series of flights from The Hague to London, Singapore, Sydney, Canberra, Sydney, Los Angeles, Miami, Buenos Aires and Montevideo in Uruguay, without stopping to sleep, meeting ministers in most cities.

The WTO's General Council, mainly ambassadors, had decided the selection would be based on three general criteria: volume of support (codeword for numbers); depth of support (codeword for trade weight); distribution of support (codeword for general geographic distribution of support). The process was overseen by two previous Chairmen of the Council, one from a developing country and one from a developed, Tanzania's Ali Said Mchumo and Switzerland's William Rossier.

The campaign turned very ugly as other nominees – good candidates all of them – fell out through lack of support. The choice finally came

Figure 10. New Zealand cartoonist Jim Hubbard saw me as a panda reaching for an elusive bamboo shoot in the form of the WTO and the key role France was to play in the leadership campaign: after a tough battle, I won the prize – only to find the real struggle was just beginning.

down to Dr Supachai Panitchpakdi of Thailand and myself. Supachai was an old colleague, but sometimes it's over-enthusiastic supporters in campaigns who take the battle to extremes. I could only laugh when a television personality in Thailand called on viewers to write my name on a piece of paper and pound it with a stone, the better to advance the prospects of their favourite son. Much more damaging, though, was learning from the Thai media – much to my surprise – not only that I had a brain tumour, but that I was a Labour union leader. Although both accusations were false, the latter was infinitely more dangerous, given the sensitivity of labour issues in the WTO. When protestors marched on the US embassy in Bangkok, it became very ugly.

The USA, Sweden, France, Germany and eventually most of the Europeans, Africans, South Americans, Economies in Transition and small island states in the Caribbean and Pacific indicated support. Some Asians privately supported me. The British, Dutch, Japanese and ASEAN were Supachai's main supporters. I was tarred as the American candidate, bringing my impartiality into question.

I was very happy to get support from Bill Clinton's Democratic administration. Originally they were divided, with the Treasury supporting

Supachai, and the US Trade Representative (USTR) and then the State Department backing me. Several Republican USTRs from earlier administrations also voiced direct and unpublicised support to those who matter. WTO Ambassador Rita Hayes from South Carolina, a skilful politician and diplomat, with strong contacts in the Senate and White House, became very supportive and a good friend. I believe I would not have gained either full US backing or the job without her.

However, I had been branded. I was never a Labour union *leader*. Rather I was a corporal in the movement who *wished* he *had* been a union leader, but my political life took a different road. I'm still described as a Union, US nominee. While that is literally true, I was never described as a Lesotho, Gabon, Mongolian, Papua New Guinea, French, Swedish, German or Uruguayan candidate, which was of course equally the case. Such is politics. But it didn't get my term off to a good start.

When the final decision was to be made, I found I'd won on all three criteria. I was never sure of the numbers, but knew I had the weight of support from the major trading nations and enjoyed better geographic support than Supachai. Had I lost, I'd have been on an economy flight home that night. My wife Yvonne and I had spent our modest savings. Then, to my surprise, WTO rules being what they are in what is, above all, a Member-driven institution, the minority vetoed the majority. If the campaign had not become so personal, I would not have been so determined to win. I guess that's the Irish in me. The atmosphere in Geneva was poisonous. This deadlock could have enabled a new compromise candidate, several of whom were waiting in the wings, to enter the ring.

I've been a politician since first getting elected to Parliament at the age of twenty-three. I have been deeply committed to the ideals of the multilateral trading regime for decades. Rather than having my opportunity to contribute, at a pivotal moment in the evolution of the global trading environment, written off completely, I cheerfully agreed to a slightly sordid deal to split the term with Supachai. Each of us agreed to take three years each.

The campaign was finally over. I'd won, but I was still of two minds. My party was going to win an election that year and I would be Foreign Minister. And being a New Zealand Foreign Minister is great: you have an opinion on everything and responsibility for nothing. We Kiwis have less than one per cent of the world's population, but a lot more than one per cent of the world's opinions.

I enjoyed a safe seat in Parliament. I liked my local constituents. But it was time to take on a new challenge. My duty was clear: ensure my local party had a good choice of candidates because the seat was not safe for a newcomer – which they did by choosing Clayton Cosgrove. I gave my last speech in Parliament and to the party caucus. My friends wanted the best for me, and my enemies wanted to see me go. For once, I was able to please everyone. At last, I enjoyed the total support of my party.

I left Parliament and New Zealand, ensuring my resignation was timed so I didn't double-dip salaries and that there wouldn't be a by-election just before a general election, which could have made my replacement vulnerable. As usual, I left Yvonne with all the problems of shifting base and trying to sell our home.

Alas, as I was soon to learn, the campaign compromise with Supachai caused resentment on all sides, costing the WTO several months of work that should have gone into Seattle preparations, and embittering ambassadors on all sides. There was a great difference between the promise of the WTO and the practice. The WTO usually does the right thing the wrong way, and the long way.

I arrived in Geneva a week before my contract started, stayed in a local hotel, and began to try and put things together for the WTO's now notorious Ministerial at Seattle in November 1999 – already scheduled for just a few weeks after my taking up office. My first step was to try and reach out to those who were my opponents. On the first day I rang the Thai Ambassador, suggesting an early meeting. He refused to meet me until the following week when I was formally the Director-General (DG). I told him: 'Fine, I will be able to fit you in, in a month's time.' He compromised, but said he wouldn't meet me in the DG's office. I agreed, but had to refuse his suggestion that I have a photograph taken with Supachai on my first day. There can be, I explained, only one DG at a time and I would be professional and ensure the transition, three years later, was clean, clear and proper; a duty I believe I carried out correctly and professionally.

Selecting my Deputy Directors-General (DDGs) was a revelation. Dozens of ambassadors wanted to press their candidates on me, which is fair enough, but exceedingly time consuming. How can you say 'No' to thirty ambassadors, many of whom say they have been instructed by their Presidents and Ministers to make a submission and push their favourite.

I was determined to have a balance and ensure that Africa had its first DDG. I think I selected a good team, with complementary skills and experiences. Andy Stoler from the USA was a tough, professional public servant, who got the most difficult work. He was to be the Minister of Finance. Every organisation needs a dedicated bastard, I told Andy, and that was his job. He also has a strong social conscience, which he diplomatically keeps well hidden. Paul-Henri Ravier is a classic French bureaucrat, in the best sense of the word, whose memos are masterpieces. I asked him to write me one-page notes, as though I was fourteen – he responded with missives that would have got through to a ten-year old. He intimately understood the myriad details that escaped me. Miguel Rodriguez Mendoza, a former Minister of State and President of the Institute of Foreign Trade for Venezuela, was also a technocrat who knew the subjects and had mastered the minutiae. And Ablassé Ouedraogo, a former Foreign Minister of Burkina Faso, had excellent contacts throughout Africa and access to the development agencies.

This proved invaluable in building coalitions and budgets, especially as I began to refocus the WTO to emphasise the Development Agenda.

Unfortunately, I didn't have time to bring the DDGs on board ahead of the Seattle conference. They had never met as a group until we assembled in the USA, and I was unable to lean on their strengths beforehand. Meanwhile, we negotiated towards destruction at the WTO headquarters. In Geneva, ambassadors are either at your throat or on their knees. At times the EU and the USA wouldn't return calls at ministerial level; hysteria grew and papers leaked – to my horror, diplomats or newspapers sometimes had them before they got to my desk.

To provide a flavour of the problems, a mini-Ministerial organised before my arrival in Geneva didn't even have an LDC representative. Ministers gave formal speeches, wasting time and locking in positions. I presented a possible Seattle declaration with a staggering thirty-two pages – three times the number of the Doha text – and seventy-nine numbered paragraphs, fifty-four of them within square brackets. Some thirty-seven alternative texts were set out and in some areas, such as implementation and agriculture, there were multiple alternatives for each part of the text. Markers were also left for the addition of other issues at a subsequent stage if necessary. Only twenty-five paragraphs were not within brackets or subject to alternative texts; a nightmare for over one hundred ministers to navigate under pressure in a few days.

I swore future mini-Ministerials must be representative and that there should be no formal speeches. At that conference, on three occasions I told ministers that without a change in mandates from ministers to ambassadors, this unworkable document would be arriving with all its contradictions and options in Seattle. Ministers just would not be able to bridge the differences. I even suggested to a couple of senior ministers we should consider postponing the conference. This was rejected. Some players later claimed I should have cancelled the conference, but of course under the WTO rules I did not have the power to do so without ministerial support. With hindsight, it was probably just as well. Seattle was a wakeup call for the WTO and we learned from the fiasco. Preparation for Doha, two years later, was the mirror opposite and was largely responsible for its success.

I flew to capitals like Tokyo, straight into meetings, often returning the same day. I couldn't shift ministers and ambassadors, many of whom assured me it would be all right on the day. I will also admit that I completely miscalled the willingness of some serious players, who I was told were playing 'chicken' with the process and would move at the last minute of the last hour of the last day, which had been the experience of previous Trade Round launches. There was enough blame for all of us to share, but as the Director-General, I accept the largest responsibility for failure, and for the costs of that failure to Members rich and poor.

I think it's generally accepted that Seattle was the worst-organised conference ever. Rooms were not soundproof. Phalanxes of large marines guarded VIPs, and feelings on all sides of the barricades were so bruised, polarised and untrusting that when interpretation facilities broke down for the African Ministers' caucus, there were wild claims that the CIA and the WTO staff pulled the plug.

Seattle is now recorded as a victory for the anti-globalisation movement. Nonsense. We didn't need their help to fail, it wasn't process or protest; we did it on our own. The situation wasn't ripe. The differences across the Atlantic and North/South were too large to bridge.

Riots erupted, tear gas flowed and tanks roamed the streets. Ministers were abused and some were violently attacked by people claiming to speak for democracy. This didn't help the humour or atmosphere. Protestors holding contradictory positions, from vegetarians to meat farmers and long-shoremen joined hands. At times, it looked the bar scene from *Star Wars*. Our opening was delayed for half a day with United Nations Secretary-General Kofi Annan imprisoned by demonstrators in a hotel across town, as was the US Secretary of State, Madeleine Albright. The situation became hysterical, with other agencies attacking our process, in embargoed statements, before the conference even began. Everyone got in a free kick. Why are WTO meetings so difficult? Labour, health and environment ministers meet all the time without much controversy. The answer is the contractually binding nature of our agreements. Grand resolutions and inspiring but meaningless declarations that will never be implemented come out of ministerials all the time. The WTO is different, because the negotiations are real, the results binding and enforceable.

I have a lasting memory of returning economy class in a flight across the USA and seeing some protesters in funny hats sitting behind some of our staff. I went to talk to our people to encourage them and perhaps to lay some guilt on those middle-class kids, saying how bad the result was, with the poor countries bound to lose out.

Figure 11. Seattle riot police use armoured cars to clear protestors: Seattle is now recorded as a victory for the anti-globalisation movement. In reality, we failed simply because governments couldn't agree. (Photograph by Robert Sorbo. Copyright Reuters 1999.)

When I turned to go, one protestor said to the other, 'Mike's travelling commercial, his aircraft must have broken down.' I didn't know whether to laugh or cry. But that conversation showed how much we had to do to explain what the WTO was really about.

Now we had to prepare a strategy for a successful Ministerial within two years. Trade Ministerial meetings had failed before – in Montreal and Brussels – but never before had it happened in such a spectacularly public and humiliating way. Many knowledgeable observers thought the multilateral system was doomed for at least a decade and some governments began to reassign senior staff for regional and bilateral work. I accepted the old Westminster theory of accountability: 'The result was not my fault, but it was my responsibility.'

But all was not lost. At the height of the protest and violence, a very gentle man came up, introduced himself as Minister Kamal from Qatar, and said his government would like to be considered as hosts for our next conference. I privately thought he must be mad, although I knew next time we needed a developing country host, and the idea of an Arab nation hosting a Trade Ministerial for the first time was attractive. I politely explained that choice of venue was the Members' decision, and that he should lobby for support. Others were expressing some interest.

But the Qataris quickly got the support of the G77 (established in 1967 to promote economic cooperation and greater influence in world affairs among developing countries) and some major trading partners and convinced potential rivals they had the numbers and support.

The myth now accepted as gospel is that this was a clever strategy staged by myself and the WTO to stop protests and hide from the outside world. It wasn't a conspiracy; I'm not that smart. The Qataris initiated, fought hard and won the dubious privilege of hosting the nightmare that WTO Ministerials had become.

7   Why the WTO matters

'Trade war looms,' is an all-too-frequent headline. Yet logically, it should read: 'No trade war: peace resumes, talks begin, panel established, WTO dispute system working.' For what makes the WTO unique in the international architecture is the binding nature of its disputes mechanism. I bet UN Secretary General Kofi Annan wishes he had binding dispute mechanisms to use in other areas of international disagreement.

It is an article of faith among opponents of the WTO that the system is 'undemocratic'. Critics such as Consumer International, in September 2001, claimed, 'The major reason for the disastrous outcome [i.e. Doha] was the manipulative and discriminatory process that has brought more shame to the WTO, its Secretariat and the major developed countries.'

The irony is that many of the things they do not like about the WTO stem from too much democracy, not too little. They want the WTO to introduce labour standards, protect animal rights, preserve the environment, watch over indigenous people, save the developing world from growth and capitalism, and a lengthening list of other goals – even when these goals are resisted by sovereign countries. They grasp that the dispute settlement system, and its threat of trade sanctions, gives the WTO unique power to impose policies on recalcitrant governments – if only the WTO could be made to exercise those powers.

Its very success makes it vulnerable. Critics ask why can we have a binding disputes mechanism in trade, and not in human rights, women's rights, indigenous, labour, migration rights, etc? Good questions. Yet many say the WTO is too powerful, then insist it take on wider powers and responsibilities, which would make the WTO or any international organisation even more powerful, even dangerous.

This myriad of issues is beyond the competence of an organisation with a staff of 560. Instead, governments might perhaps look at adopting similar binding disputes mechanisms to the International Labour Office (ILO), or the World Health Organization or the Commissioner for Human Rights with their thousands of staff, or one of the other institutions better funded and positioned to cope with the demands of these

Figure 12. One of the anti-WTO posters that circulated at Seattle.

issues. These are matters of jurisdiction, not principle. Other institutions have mandates in these areas. There is a need for a World Environment Agency armed with real teeth. And because of the compounding complexity of tax law and Internet-facilitated business transactions, there will soon be a need to multilateralise tax treaties. Perhaps we will have to create a new World Tax Organization, building on research done by the OECD Secretariat. Heaven forbid that the WTO be asked to take on this responsibility as well.

However, there is a sound argument for greater coherence between agencies. On issues such as ILO observerships to the WTO, I was disappointed we couldn't have developed better coherence on matters of mutual social concern, as many of the differences are about the jurisdiction of institutions not principles, but ministers' suspicions prevented us from moving forward. There are plenty of countries who call for labour issues to be in the ILO, not the WTO, then go up the hill from our Geneva headquarters to the ILO and oppose the same issues, or vice versa.

The undemocratic claim is based upon a basic fallacy. The WTO is not imposed on countries. Countries choose to belong to the organisation. No one is forced to sign our agreements. Each and every one of the WTO's rules is negotiated by Member governments, agreed by consensus, and ratified by parliaments. Countries choose to participate in an open, rules-based multilateral trading system for the simple reason that it is overwhelmingly in their interest to do so. The alternative is a less open, less prosperous, more uncertain world economy – an option few countries would willingly choose. It is difficult to conceive of a system that could be more democratic.

This explains the multilateral trading system's remarkable expansion, and why so many countries are queuing up to join. It began as the General Agreement on Tariffs and Trade (GATT) with just twenty-three Members in 1947. Today the WTO has 144 Members – including, most recently, China and Chinese Taipei – and this number could easily reach 170 or more within a decade. This also explains why Members have repeatedly agreed to widen and deepen the system's body of rules. The multilateral trading system was initially concerned mainly with trade in goods, and it was based not on a permanent organisation but on a provisional treaty, the GATT. By the end of the Uruguay Round in 1994, the system contained sweeping new rules for services, intellectual property, subsidies, textiles and agriculture. It was also established in 1995, on a firm institutional foundation, as the new WTO, with a strengthened mechanism for settling disputes, but without an increase in resources or much-needed internal reforms.

Nor is there any sign that the system has stopped moving forward. In the Doha Agenda, launched in November 2001, governments have agreed to expand the scope of existing agreements in key areas such as industrial goods, agriculture and services, and to try to build a framework of rules on issues of investment, competition policy, trade facilitation and government procurement. No other international body oversees rules that extend so widely around the world, or so deeply into the fabric of economies. Yet at the same time, no other body is as directly run by Member governments, or as firmly rooted in consensus decision-making and collective rule. The multilateral trading system works precisely because it is based on persuasion, not coercion – rules, not force.

Two fundamental concepts underpin the equal rights of WTO Members: non-discrimination and consensus decision-making. The principle of non-discrimination ensures that the WTO treats all Members alike, be they rich or poor, big or small, strong or weak. Central among the rules that underpin the principle of non-discrimination is the 'most favoured nation' obligation (which prevents WTO Members from treating products from one WTO Member better than those from another) and the 'National Treatment' rule (which obliges governments to treat like goods from foreign and domestic sources equally). Non-discrimination has been key to the multilateral trading system's success. Preferential trade blocs and alliances, by definition, exclude and marginalise non-member countries. This not only hurts the countries themselves, but can be harmful for the system as a whole. It is widely accepted that in the 1920s and 1930s competition and conflict amongst trade blocs was a major cause of global instability – paving the way for a descending spiral of tit-for-tat protectionism, the Great Depression.

The multilateral trading system was designed precisely to avoid a world of inward-looking, potentially hostile trade blocs and self-destructive factionalism. From a national perspective, the principle of non-discrimination has also allowed countries to liberalise their economies and integrate into the world trading system at their own pace. MFN and National Treatment do not demand 'harmonisation' towards universal norms or rules.

On the contrary, these rules were designed precisely to allow countries to maintain their own policy 'space', to set their own standards and priorities, so long as all economic actors – foreign and domestic – were treated equally. Non-discrimination has provided the essential underpinning for the huge expansion of global trade over the past half century, and for the broad political consensus to move the system forward into new sectors and wider responsibilities.

Non-discrimination has also enshrined universality as a central objective of the trading system. It is certainly one major reason why the GATT/WTO system has emerged, especially after the Cold War, as a major force for integrating developing and transition countries into the world economy.

Equally central to the multilateral trading system is the principle of consensus decision-making. Unlike other international agencies, the

WTO has no executive body with delegated authority to take decisions on behalf of Member governments. With a few limited exceptions, there are no provisions for majority or 'weighted' voting. And the small WTO Secretariat has only limited independent authority and initiative-taking rights, but no grants or loans to hand out, no licences to issue and no influence over individual countries' policies (although technical advice is offered, and some analytical comments are provided in regular trade policy reviews). In short, the WTO does not tell governments what to do. Governments tell the WTO.

All decisions – from the creation of the GATT to 2001's launch of the Doha Development Agenda – have been taken collectively by the Member governments themselves in the numerous councils and committees, the most important of which is the Ministerial Meeting. Each WTO Member has equal rights and an equal vote under the agreements. Because no decision is taken unless all Member governments agree, effectively every country – from the largest to the smallest – has the power of veto. Even the enforcement of rules is undertaken by the Members themselves under agreed procedures that they negotiated. Sometimes enforcement includes the threat of sanctions. But those sanctions are imposed by Members not by the organisation.

This is not to say that the day-to-day workings of the WTO are perfect. Far from it. One problem is that the system continues to rely on major new negotiating rounds – and 'package' deals – to create new rules or to clarify existing ones. This means that reforms to the system occur episodically and infrequently. Seven years elapsed between the end of the Tokyo Round and the beginning of the Uruguay Round; eight years between the Uruguay Round's completion and the launch of the Doha Development Agenda last November.

One reason for the successful launch at Doha was the series of important reforms to WTO decision-making processes since the failed launch of negotiations at the Seattle Ministerial in 1999. In Geneva and in consultations with ministers worldwide, thousand of hours were spent in plenary discussions and in meetings of heads of delegations. Every issue and every national position had been fully aired and explored before Doha. At the conference itself, every effort was made to keep ministers and delegations fully involved in the negotiations. The transparency and inclusiveness – which is to say the 'legitimacy' – of the process helps to explain why Member governments were more prepared and more willing to reach agreement.

Another challenge is that not all governments are equipped to participate in WTO processes as effectively as they would like – some countries, particularly LDCs, cannot even afford to maintain offices in Geneva. The scope, complexity and value of the WTO's legal system continues to expand. Much of the recent controversy about implementation of Uruguay Round commitments stemmed from the human and resource constraints faced by developing countries in adapting legislation to new obligations and building the infrastructure needed to implement them.

These constraints should concern every Member, not just the countries subject to them. As the WTO embarks on new negotiations and rule-making as a result of Doha, the system's future success will hinge directly on the ability of all Members to participate more fully in the process and to feel ownership of the outcome. That is why an increasingly important function of the WTO is technical assistance and capacity-building – helping transition, developing and least developed countries to integrate into the multilateral trading system and to participate fully in negotiations.

Another WTO goal is to help Member governments make better use of dispute settlement. The WTO system is not perfect; no system can be. Recognising this, the WTO's 144 member governments agreed at Doha that negotiations on improvements and clarifications of the existing disputes system should be considered.

It is good that nations continue to bring cases into the system; that's what the system is for. The relative de-politicisation of disputes by bringing them into the Disputes Settlements Understanding (DSU), coupled with the guarantee for developing countries that the rules are enforced against both big players and small, built credibility, which helped us get to the point of launching a new trade round. Only a tiny fraction of total world trade is affected by disputes. However, disputes such as the steel issue, which erupted in 2002 when the USA imposed new tariffs to protect its local steel industry, are very serious and, with other disputes, have the potential to poison the negotiating climate during the Round. But disputes have been managed during previous negotiating rounds, and at the time of writing, current disputes were being handled in a mature way. Perhaps they will even create a greater sense of urgency to finish the Round and get the job done.

Before 1995, under the GATT, panels which met to consider complaints published a report which was not binding. Now cases are heard by an independent panel, and dissatisfied Members can appeal to a higher authority, the Appellate Body, which rules. And that's final. With billions of dollars at stake and political prestige on the line, there has never been a hint of scandal or of national self-interest being considered by panellists who make these important decisions on cases brought to them by governments. This is a tribute to the WTO rules and to the culture that has developed over very many years of professionalism and public service.

It is always preferable that trading partners resolve disputes between themselves. Since the WTO came into being in 1995, nearly 250 complaints have been brought before the Disputes Settlements Body (DSB). Nearly forty complaints have been withdrawn before getting to the Panel stage, while slightly over half of all disputes brought forward are not pursued because consultations show that there is no serious problem, that the case is not strong enough, that the other side has already removed the alleged infringement or a settlement has been reached or is still pending.

The current WTO system is a structured process with clearly defined procedural stages. Panellists serve in their own individual capacities and cannot receive instructions from any government. The DSU thus provides an efficient, transparent and binding process, available to all Member governments.

Developing countries are increasingly active participants; in 2001 they filed about 80 per cent of all complaints, of which 20 per cent were against developed countries and the balance against developing countries. These figures show that, contrary to the widespread disinformation of the WTO's critics, the organisation provides justice for all countries and not just work for the rich and powerful. In 2001, there were twenty-three requests for consultations, nineteen from developing countries and six against developed countries. The WTO assists developing countries' dispute settlement needs. The WTO has expanded the rules of international trade manifold, compared to the GATT and created a new 'court' system with a possibility of appeal. Accordingly, legal advice in this sector is very expensive, creating considerable problems of access to justice for developing countries.

Developing countries can also draw on The Advisory Centre for WTO Law, which we established in 2001, which took an almost revolutionary step forward in international adjudication, by establishing itself as the first true centre for legal aid within the international legal system. The Advisory Centre was a response to international recognition of both the increased sophistication of the legal system and also of the court system in most countries, and certainly in developed countries, and increased costs of litigation, as well as continuing social inequality. Combined with the increased costs this made for a restriction of access to justice for large parts of the population, often precisely those social layers that were supposed to be supported by the new rules.

States banded together and created this new instrument, supported by a substantial guarantee fund, which makes subsidisation and the provision of high quality legal aid to states which need such help possible. Even this idea was opposed by some Members who said their politicians would be sensitive to claims that taxpayers' money was being used to take cases against local companies that helped generate those taxes. But it was a major step forward, an idea that will grow and become more important and better funded.

As always in the WTO, consensus must be reached to approve any changes. Assuming there is not to be a return to the old GATT-type system, as some Members have suggested, a number of ideas are in circulation. They include:

- completing the judicial character of the procedure, by making the Appellate Body (AB) into a permanent institution and turning the panels into semi-professional bodies
- providing Members with alternative dispute resolution mechanisms, also mentioned in the DSU, but so far under-utilised, such as mediation, conciliation and arbitration
- I'd be very cautious with this idea. I have mediated both successfully and unsuccessfully. Formalising a legal requirement would mean working in front of the media, with some countries calling for mediation and demanding to know why the other does not agree. In these cases, the DG should be heard but not seen
- reforming the remedies available. It has been observed that trade retaliation tends to be counter-productive, whereas trade compensation can be positive and trade-creating. At the moment, compensation can be rejected by 'winning' complainants, forcing recourse to retaliation. Compensation should, according to some observers, be made more attractive, by allowing the winner to insist upon the 'loser' lowering tariffs in a product area of their choice. Another option, not permitted under the current DSU, would be monetary compensation, i.e. cash payouts
- speeding up the process, which can take several years. Justice delayed can be justice denied.

Disputes arise when one Member claims that another has failed to live up to its obligations, but the challenging Member does not need to prove any special economic or legal interest to be authorised to initiate a complaint. It is up to the panel to find a resolution.

Trade sanctions, though often referred to in this context, actually play a limited role. Indeed, recourse to retaliation has rarely been required to enforce decisions. Of the cases filed, there have only been five instances where retaliation has been authorised, and only three occasions on which it was applied.

Joseph S. Nye, Jr. characterises the WTO system in his recent book *The Paradox of American Power* thus: 'While the WTO dispute settlement procedures intrude on domestic policy... a country can respond to domestic democratic process and reject a judgement if it is willing to pay carefully limited compensation to the trade partners injured by its actions. And if a country does defect from its trade agreements, the procedure limits the tit-for-tat downward spiral that so devastated the world economy in the 1930s... the procedure is like having a fuse in the electrical system of a house – better the fuse blows, than the house burns down.'[1]

This is a precious system, the jewel in the crown of multilateralism. However, it is vulnerable and can only thrive with the continued support of Member governments, who must be willing to abide by the rules they agreed upon. I suspect the next few years will see whether the system improves or becomes sidelined. What a cost to the world it would be if the system fell over by accident. We must never forget that one of the reasons the GATT/WTO was established was to prevent the rise of hostile trading blocs. That lesson from the 1930s has hopefully not been lost.

The fact remains that the multilateral trading system – for all its imperfections – gives even the smallest and poorest countries far greater leverage and security than they would ever have outside the system. Multilateral negotiations allow weaker countries to pool their collective influence and interests – as opposed to bilateral or even regional negotiations in which they have virtually no negotiating clout.

In the same way, a system which replaces the role of 'power' in international trade relations with the rule of 'law' is invariably to the advantage to the smallest and weakest countries. Under the WTO, small 'Davids' do take on and win against the 'Goliaths' of world trade. For example, the Costa Rica, USA, Ecuador, European Commission banana cross-retaliation ultimately favoured the poorer countries. Peru took on the EC and won in sardines, while the EC–India dispute over bed linen, which involved a challenge to an anti-dumping practice maintained for years by the big players, was eventually won by India. Costa Rica defeated the USA on an underwear case; New Zealand and Australia won on a lamb dispute.

The alternative is no rules and no impartial dispute settlement – a world where commercial relations are based on economic and political power alone, where small countries are at the mercy of the largest, the rule of the jungle. One definition of civilisation is the rule of law, not force. This is what the Age of Enlightenment taught us, and is best enshrined in the US Constitution, drawn as it was from the Bill of Rights, the Magna Carta and that body of ideals and common law built up over centuries.

Of all the international institutions, the WTO best lives up to this hope.

8   Forging a consensus

Looking at the WTO's remarkable progress from the setback in Seattle in November 1999 to the successful launch in November 2001 of the Doha Development Round, it is clear some observers still do not fully appreciate that the Organization's continuing efforts to encourage the reduction of trade barriers are not controlled by the executive writ of a few powerful nations.

The WTO's effectiveness is governed by the ability and willingness to forge a working consensus, of a diverse membership that runs the gamut from the poorest LDCs to economic superpowers. There is no equivalent to the UN Security Council; it's like trying to run a parliament with no parties, no whip, no speaker, no speaking limits and no majority voting system. It is consensus by exhaustion, with the DG's team relying on their diplomatic and political skills to manage and direct a wide diversity of cultures, personalities and ambitions into reaching an agreement that can be blocked at anytime by anyone.

We have 144 handbrakes and one accelerator, which can only be used by consensus. But every now and then a DG can push the accelerator and hope nobody notices. You have to encourage Members to allow you to step on the pedal, or look the other way. Sometimes it feels more like one of those old Laurel and Hardy movies, with the car out of control and the steering wheel coming off in your hands. I kept reading that I had the most powerful job in the world. That's just not true. It would have been a lot more fun if it were.

Through hard work, aggression and more than a little arrogance on my part, we have ensured that the WTO is now taken more seriously, that we are in the loop and are treated as an equal partner with the World Bank and the IMF. This coherence is necessary to deliver the outcomes that governments demand.

Those who accuse the WTO's more powerful members of riding roughshod over the less developed world have a limited grasp of the reality of international diplomacy within the WTO, especially given the surge in new members in recent years; over *eighty* new Members have joined since the launch of the Uruguay Round, mostly from the developed world or economies in transition. Those governments, ministers and ambassadors will not be bullied or bought. In fact, I spent more time with the ambassadors representing the LDCs – the Africa group and the African Caribbean Pacific group – than with the Quad (the USA, Canada, Japan and the EU)

There were many problems at Seattle. As explained, the preparatory process was not ideal, there wasn't enough time, not helped by the delay in appointing the DG. The Geneva based negotiations lacked sufficient transparency and failed to involve all WTO Members, nor were there effective systems in place to keep capitals and ministers fully engaged. Ministers in Seattle were asked to forge consensus in three days on issues that had eluded agreement by Geneva Ambassadors for many years.

But Seattle didn't fail because of process or protest; though these factors certainly didn't help. It failed because Members were too far apart on substantive issues. They disagreed on agriculture, labour and the environment, on competition and investment policy, on rules, on anti-dumping, tariff peaks and escalation, and on how to deal with developing countries' difficulties in implementing their Uruguay Round commitments.

The Uruquay Round was artificially concluded, leaving out a number of issues to be resolved later, the so-called implementation issues. That Round was finished because US legislation to facilitate the negotiations was expiring, ministers were exhausted, other options were being pursued, and because then DG Peter Sutherland's enormous political skills were able to bring the deal together. A WTO, diplomatic phrase 'constructive ambiguity' is sometimes necessary – as was to prove the case in Doha – allowing ministers to provide their own interpretation to their home audience and allow themselves space to keep negotiating.

Nor were the necessary strategic alliances sufficiently developed: we forgot that the objective was to launch a set of negotiations, not conclude them. The transatlantic divide was then as great as the North/South divide. Some ministers thought they were clever enough to 'stitch things up' at the last moment; they were wrong.

The Seattle Summit debacle was widely portrayed as a success for the anti-globalisation movement. In fact, it directly reflected the failure of the WTO's Members to forge a broad consensus ahead of this important meeting. Nonetheless, despite the temporary loss of momentum at Seattle, the rapid changes taking place in the global trading environment added urgency to the need for Members to agree upon and launch a new Trade Round.

Seattle created frustration and uncertainty. It also drove home some hard lessons. A second failure would have fatally weakened the WTO:

the question would have been posed whether it had become impossible, given the WTO's greatly expanded membership and the huge disparities among Members, to move the Organization forward through our consensus mechanism.

We resolved not to repeat the mistakes of Seattle in preparing for the Ministerial Meeting in Doha, Qatar, in November 2001. After a period of stocktaking and consultation, we devised a two-year strategy. And we succeeded: that meeting launched a new and substantive negotiating Trade Round – the first since the Uruguay Round in 1986.

Drawing up the road map

Several elements were key to this: accepting that not all critics were wrong; analysing what we had to do; and working through a deliberate, strategic roadmap week by week, issue by issue, to Doha. We needed to:
- rebuild confidence in the system
- ensure the successful launch of crucial mandated negotiations on agriculture and services
- address the difficulties of developing countries in implementing their Uruguay Round commitments
- ensure an inclusive and transparent preparatory process
- engage capitals and ministers, and ensure they built trust and relationships between each other
- enable more effective participation by Members, especially non-resident capitals
- inform key stakeholders of the potential benefits of a new Round and enlist their support
- develop coherence with other agencies
- develop a system of Champions in capitals with think tanks and in the media who could advance our common cause
- develop direct relationships with parliamentarians and their umbrella groups, as well as political internationals such as Socialist International, Democratic Union and Liberal International
- reorganise the secretariat to better focus on the issues at stake
- engage wider society and NGOs.

After Seattle, I could see how the deal could be done: I knew that the next twenty-four months would be a preparation for the last hundred hours of the Fifth Ministerial. I knew we had to have a Development Agenda which addressed developing country needs, thus widening the negotiating agenda for better trade-offs. I had spent my life working for the poor and the less well-off, so this was a comfortable fit and one reason why I wanted the job. I emphasised the importance of keeping the development dimension of the WTO at the core of any future work programme, by pushing to ensure adequate funding for technical and improved coherence among international organisations, so that developing country needs were better addressed. Members spent an enormous amount of time and effort on these development dimensions, something they should have done anyway.

High priority was given throughout the preparations to finding a base document for Doha that captured most concerns. Some ambassadors and officials in the secretariat – more attuned to the old GATT when a few developed countries really did call the shots – were dismissive of the development focus and questioned it. They hadn't learnt the lesson of Seattle, that the big guys on their own couldn't fix it on the day. Developing countries inspired me with their firm solidarity. They had their agenda and needed results.

I visited Africa six times in the build-up to Doha, and was the first to visit the Organization of African Unity, the African Caribbean Pacific group, as well as several of the developing countries. This approach was inevitably perceived as a confidence trick by some on both sides of the North/South debate, but was I believe a – and perhaps *the* – crucial element in launching the round. Some of the more extreme NGOs accused me of mounting a 'charm offensive' – something I doubt I'm capable of.

The reality was I both strongly believed in the moral need to address the development issues, and also saw that a deal would have to be done, based on identifying the key areas of self-interest on a broad enough basis to allow eventual trade-offs. Big countries also have needs. But there is a politically correct attitude within elements of the membership that says, because when major powers need something they are automatically wrong, that it is a trick by the rich to oppress the poor.

Yet some of these same critics are the first to complain if their developed country market's economy contracts and imports fall. The UN Conference on Trade and Development – and some poorest country ambassadors – have even had the nerve to call on major developed world nations to suffer some inflation on behalf of the developing world.

We started early and focused on restoring confidence. Almost thirty Members are non-resident, too small or too poor to have missions in Geneva. I hosted meetings, dinners and lunches with their representatives in Brussels and London, worked the phone directly to ministers and established 'Geneva Week', which brought senior officials from these smaller countries to Geneva to enable them better to participate and to widen the growing coalition of interests. Later, after Doha, this was to be mainstreamed into our annual budget and held twice a year.

Small details matter. We instituted a daily two-page news review of trade-related stories from the major newspapers worldwide, for distribution to non-residents. Most don't have the time to read the major newspapers, many can't afford the subscriptions. It was a good product that was so useful many smaller Geneva-based missions requested the same facility. After all important meetings, reports were drafted and distributed to these missions so that they could more easily report to their capitals. A very small initiative, but extremely helpful.

We pushed the installation of WTO reference centres in developing and least developed countries (106 in place by the end of 2001 as compared with 68 in 1999). Coherence was also stressed as we built closer cooperation with other international agencies, such as the World Bank and the IMF, to ensure consistency and coordination of development policies. This was, in the main, successful. UN Secretary General Kofi Annan never wavered and spoke strongly for a development round and for solidarity between agencies. From being the most alienated, these countries now see us as a champion to advance their needs in other international institutions.

In addition, we finally managed to launch the mandated negotiations on agriculture and services, a crucial component in any new Trade Round. Combined, these account for more than two-thirds of the world's economic output and employment. Advancing the highly sensitive agricultural negotiations to a point where Members were willing to recognise and accommodate each other's needs, and to make concessions to achieve consensus, was critical to our success at Doha.

Agriculture was always going to be a deal-maker or deal-breaker. The transatlantic divide was deep. North Asia was defensive; ministers could fall on this issue if they were seen to betray their powerful domestic rural interests. By making agriculture a development issue, we brought Africa, most of Asia and Latin America together on a common agenda. Research data explaining the gains to be made was made public by speeches and through media outlets, the cause of many complaints by some rich countries that I was biased. They were correct – I am.

I was frequently attacked by unnamed sources in the media for spending 80 per cent of my time on countries that accounted for less than 10 per cent of world trade. It was true – I did. Now I'm often accused by some critics of having betrayed the developing world at the behest of the rich countries. The rich countries certainly didn't see it that way. And neither did most of the developing world, many of whose members are far more concerned about being marginalised from world trade, than being crushed by it.

A dedicated process for addressing implementation-related issues left over from the Uruguay Round, the Implementation Review Mechanism, was established by the WTO's governing body, the General Council. Efforts to reach agreement on implementation issues intensified throughout 2001. Members were continually urged to demonstrate flexibility and realism to ensure that this complex and politically sensitive set of issues became a positive contributor to the Doha outcome, rather than a stumbling block.

Close attention was given to the external environment, with a view to building momentum. During the two-year period between the conferences, I personally drove the process, travelled over 625,000 km, visiting 182 cities and meeting with more than 300 ministers. Every week I rang ministers, and hosted and took part in many informal Ministerial Meetings. Mini-Ministerials in Mexico and Singapore, in particular, provided impetus and momentum. In these encounters, I signalled the urgent need both for active political involvement to allow for the necessary flexibility in negotiating mandates, and for close, continuous follow-up by ministers to ensure that this boost in political momentum carried through into action in Geneva and, ultimately, at Doha.

A turning-point for the process, and myself, was attending the G7 (plus Russia) Summit in Genoa. My old friend Renato Ruggiero, a past DG of the WTO, was by then Foreign Secretary of Italy, which was hosting the Summit. Renato ensured that the Trade Round was at the centre of their deliberations. The G7 wisely involved a number of senior and powerful African leaders and they supported our objectives. Making personal contacts with current world leaders made it easier for me to seek their personal intervention from time to time when we were in trouble, including at Doha. I also received a great deal of quiet support from Ruggiero and two other wise former WTO DGs, Arthur Dunkel and Peter Sutherland. I rang Sutherland every few weeks to bounce ideas off him.

Great care was taken to ensure that the preparatory process for Doha was inclusive, transparent and led by a 'bottom-up' approach. At the very start of the process, the 2001 General Council Chairman, Stuart Harbinson, Permanent Representative of Hong Kong, China, circulated a checklist of possible issues to be included on the Doha agenda. Stuart was brilliant throughout the lead-up and at Doha itself; able, patient, thorough, inclusive and professional. His eventual nomination by my successor Supachai as his new Chef de Cabinet was a wise decision.

One key lesson from Seattle was that the DG, the host Country Minister and the General Council Chairman have to work as one. At Seattle we didn't understand how fundamental to success it was to develop synergy and trust between those occupying these key roles, or to have the time to do so. Looking back, I think we didn't give Chairman Ali Said Mchumo adequate support. I ensured that the next chairman had an office near me. Some staff opposed this because in the past there had been tension between DGs and chairpersons, since the roles can be blurred, and personalities do count and sometimes clash. I ignored that advice and was blessed, in Stuart – as in Kre Bryn of Norway, his predecessor – with a chairman who was cooperative, smart and supportive of our wider goals.

The immediate focus of the chairman's process at this stage was to clarify and build towards agreement by Members on elements of the Doha agenda. This approach reflected the wishes of Members, as expressed during discussions, for an internally transparent, yet flexible and efficient process. A very important feature of the bottom-up approach was the 'proponent-driven' process, which placed the responsibility for bringing inputs into the General Council preparatory process with the proponents of particular issues.

It was the exact opposite of the Seattle process. That allowed everyone to have something on the agenda, then we needed a consensus to take an issue *off*. At Doha, proponents had to convince colleagues to get an issue *on* the agenda. As described, the Doha text was just one-third the size of that presented at Seattle, which came in at a whopping thirty-two pages.

I pressed for a 'reality check' by July 2001, to test Members' sentiment and ensure that the preparations for Doha were on course. Many Members thought we wouldn't make it. Later, some even strongly suggested I postpone the conference and blame it on security issues after the 9-11 horrors in New York. It was a high-risk strategy – basically all or nothing. I wanted a Round and pushed everyone to the edge.

Internal restructuring

Not all of our critics were wrong. Many of our problems were internal. The new WTO was launched with much fanfare at Marrakesh in 1995. But the new organisation was not substantially reformed given its new birth and greater responsibilities. Its staffing, resources and structures reflected the old GATT and not its new mandate, or the wider, broader membership.

Reforming multilateral agencies is much easier said than done, as I quickly discovered when I took up office. Here are some examples. When I arrived in Geneva, I wanted to have my four DDGs close by, on the same floor. I wanted to be able to drop in to their offices to seek advice. I'm used to a cabinet system and enjoy and benefit from a collective input. My DDGs had the skills, experience, knowledge and mastery of complicated details that I did not have at the time. A simple proposition, I thought.

What I learnt was instructive of the manner in which the WTO and international institutions operate.

The problem, I was solemnly advised, was that Andy Stoler, the US DDG, had a four-window office. If the others were to join us on our floor, they would have to suffer smaller, three-window offices. Given my New Zealand experience, where protocol doesn't exist, I couldn't take this advice seriously. Easy, I replied, let's paint over one of Andy's windows.

Staff scolded me, saying this was a very important issue; I wasn't taking this 'problem' seriously. It was pointed out that at another major institution in Geneva, a similar problem emerged with one DDG having a toilet and shower, a profound privilege that other DDGs in that organisation didn't share. 'Don't tell me,' I replied. 'They bricked out the toilet and shower to make them all equal!' 'Yes,' came the reply.

Then divisional staff responsible to DDGs lobbied, suggesting that they needed to be close to their respective DDGs, whom I, in vain, wanted to rename Executive Deputies, with Divisional Directors becoming Divisional Managers. Another clash of cultures. I lost. Round One to the bureaucrats and the system.

One of the great disappointments of failure in Seattle, and the need to focus on Doha, was that I didn't have the time to focus on the reforms I think are necessary inside the WTO. Which is not to denigrate the many fine and very professional staff who work at the WTO, which with some 560 employees is one of the smaller and, I'm told, one of the most efficient and effective of the multilateral agencies. I believe that's true, which is alarming when I look at other agencies with their thousands of staff and billion-dollar budgets, important mandates and responsibilities.

I believe one of the basic problems with the multilateral and intergovernmental institutions is the issue of tenure. We have total tenure and protection, which is of course a contradiction in an organisation dedicated to the proposition that protection is a bad idea. We have all the protection in the world for senior staff, much less for junior. The original idea of tenure was sound enough: to protect institutions from incoming regimes that may fill the place with nephews, cousins and all their own nationals. But it leaves senior management in the position where the only real sanction for poor performance is giving people less work to do.

Institutions change, their mandates change, their responsibilities evolve, yet the institutions can't change themselves to reflect this. For example, had we not launched the Round at Doha we should have sacked or suspended 30 per cent of our staff, because we wouldn't have needed them. But when we did launch the Doha Round, we then had to scramble to find the resources to implement the new agenda.

People are paid for their time put in on the job, not for performance, while many talented young people have to wait far too long for promotion because the senior ranks are blocked. The skills of being a specialist in one area are not always the same skills necessary to manage a division. I commissioned a management consultant to report on our structures; his conclusion confirmed my own instincts, that we had too many divisions.

My ambition was to move towards a system of a few super divisions, run by very competent managers employed on five-year contracts, who would be paid extra for performance. Those who wanted less responsibility for results could accept more security and less – though still very comfortable by private sector standards – conditions of employment.

The DG of the WTO has very few levers to pull. Other organisations have carried out some reforms by buying people out. They get funding for this by generous governments, or by reducing services to customers to do the job. One institution spent several million dollars to remove a deputy director, in order to replace that person with another who could serve that agency head's political ambitions. I could not and would not take that approach. We had twice as many divisions as we needed, greatly narrowing my options for staffing. In fact it did not take long for me to discover that the only real sanction I had on senior staff was to give them less work, for the same money. Which left me open on one occasion to being sued for 'loss of dignity'. Which happened, enabling those comfortable with the existing structure to argue that I should slow down the pace of reform.

In the end, I simply didn't have the time or resources to overcome bureaucratic resistance, while also trying to get the new Round launched. I was at least able to establish better reporting procedures, and professional annual review mechanisms so that we now have paper trails, so that staff who aren't up to it can be replaced, or at least don't get automatic pay rises. We didn't even have an anti-harassment policy.

I was surprised to learn that the twenty or so divisional directors – the number varied as we reorganised the Secretariat – didn't meet regularly as a group. I believe cross-cutting issues need to be discussed collectively; it gets better results and results in better team-building. I saw my DDGs as an 'inner cabinet'. I needed their insights, inputs and advice. Regular meetings of divisional directors and DDGs were held. Directors were instructed to report back to their staff; some even did.

I initiated meetings of all staff at stop-work meetings to cover housekeeping matters. Wanting to make savings and to be more prudent with resources, I cancelled my first-class travel 'privilege', preferring to travel business class so I could be with staff, and stopped staying in expensive hotels. I naively thought that if I showed prudence in my office, leading by example, I could make savings in other divisions, so I could redirect resources to serve Members and establish a reputation that would give us credibility in approaching Member governments for extra resources for the real work of the house. We did eventually get those extra resources, but only after Doha. In the run-up, I had to work the phones, pleading for $10,000 here and $15,000 there to fund confidence-building projects. Ministers and ambassadors kept publicly calling for more transparency and engagement with wider society, suggesting specific projects, and then denied us the resources to do the job. But even small changes are difficult to implement in institutions.

My talented counsellor from Malaysia had been told only a few years previously to go away, because the WTO didn't hire interns. The WTO's official web page said we had no interns. Yet I soon discovered there were dozens in the house. Ah, I was told, the lack of a transparent method for applying was to test interns' capacity to navigate through the system.

Total nonsense, of course. In reality, it was an old boys' network, with over 80 per cent of interns coming from developed countries when I arrived. It is human nature for people to employ those who look like them and went to the same universities. Now 80 per cent come from developing countries or economies in transition. I told divisional directors that this was an area where they could take risks. Of course an intern from Mali couldn't afford to come for an interview. Take a risk, I implored, these young people were worth a chance, and if we were wrong, the jobs only last a few months and the institution would recover. The system was working better near the end of my term, but every few months reminders still had to go out. I'm proud to note that the total number of nationalities represented in the Secretariat has increased from forty-eight in 1990 (twenty-two developed and twenty-six developing countries) to sixty-five by mid-2002 (twenty-six developed and thirty-nine developing countries).

One well-meaning staff member even hid boxes of letters from me because many were rude and abusive. How can you answer critics and improve your performance if you are isolated from criticism? Critics are also customers and these contacts afford an opportunity to reply, explain and try and win opponents over.

On the road to Doha, fortified by the cooperation and leadership of General Council Chairmen like Norway's Kre Bryn and Stuart Harbinson, the way in which business was conducted at the WTO's General Council was transformed over the two years. Without their commitment and drive, we would have failed. We had more full and informal meetings of our General Council than in the ten years previously, with proceedings becoming more transparent, open and participatory, and eventually even good-natured.

However, while this process worked better than before, it continued to impose a great cost in time, energy, resources and focus. The WTO still needs to fundamentally address its procedures and culture. We cannot keep extending our day by two hours every time we have a new issue, or want to admit a new Member. EU Commissioner Pascal Lamy described the WTO's functioning as 'medieval', after the Seattle debacle. I told him this was flattery, that we were Jurassic in managerial terms.

Widening and deepening contacts with civil society

Considerable efforts have been taken to improve the WTO's outreach activities with wider 'civil society'. In the brief two-year period between the tumultuous setback in Seattle, and the successful launch of the Doha Development Agenda, contact and positive dialogue with NGOs has intensified, as it has with other groups, such as trade unions, parliamentarians and the business community. Web pages were established targeted both at critics and at groups like parliamentarians who genuinely wanted information (see Chapter 13). The team did good work and the culture, while not changing, became more flexible in accepting that we are now all related to the wider world.

Significantly, during this period we also launched a series of initiatives to better inform and involve parliamentarians. I met them when they came to Geneva, and have appeared before twenty to thirty parliamentary committees, from the European Parliament to the House of Commons, to the US Ways and Means Committee. Appearing before congressional committees can be nerve-racking and I was frequently advised by my officials not to do so. It was always rewarding. I understood their problems. Imagine my surprise in Lesotho, when I thought I was to be cross-examined by a small committee and found myself addressing the entire parliament in special session, complete with a bewigged madam speaker.

This activity was new. More should be done, but the WTO's total budget is about the same as the World Bank's travel budget. But even this degree of dialogue was controversial and actively opposed by some Members, especially those with not very 'active' parliaments. It's an interesting fact that there is almost a direct relationship between ambassadors who call for more 'democracy' in the WTO, and their lack of democracy at home. By democracy, unfortunately, some simply mean that *they* want to be in control (see Chapter 15). A valid argument against such meetings is that they do not add much value if they just replicate the debate at home. If they simply provide opposition politicians with a platform to attack their ministers and governments, then it is of little use, except for a conflict-driven news-hungry media. Nonetheless, parliamentarians are the legitimate accountable representatives of civil society; in the end they have to ratify agreements reached in Geneva, and governments need congressional and parliamentary support to negotiate and, in most cases, to stay in power.

I pushed for the first-ever global parliamentary meeting on international trade. And I encouraged the Inter-Parliamentary Union (IPU) to hold serious seminars and workshop. But it was a hard message to get through. In an organisation that reflects 144 cultures and systems, and which relies on consensus for reaching decisions, some Members even complained about the hosting of a reception for the hundreds of parliamentarians who came to Geneva for the IPU workshops. I ignored them and introduced new techniques to communicate and involve political parties, politicians and party internationals.

Some ambassadors complained about communicating directly with the speaker of their parliaments. They gave up, knowing I was immovable and bullet-proof because I had a three-year term and couldn't be blackmailed. My own experience in securing election has resulted in proposals circulating to improve the process. In an earlier life, I opposed term limits for politicians. MPs are, after all, subject to due democratic process anyway. But I think that term limits are important for the heads of agencies. Otherwise the temptation to get re-elected by appeasing interest groups, or purchasing their support with taxpayers' money, creates a moral and political hazard.

Seattle buried the old GATT organisation; the WTO was born at Doha out of a long and dangerous pregnancy as we slowly reformed the institution leading up to Doha. The reforms we have been able to put in place were accomplished at a painfully, frustratingly slow pace. I believe we have not gone far enough and that more could be done. Proposals for further reform of the WTO are with the Committee on Budget, Finance and Administration, and hopefully my successor can carry this necessary work forward.

9   Denouement at Doha

Despite our much-enhanced preparation, the outcome of the Doha Ministerial Conference in November 2001 remained in doubt. While arguments in favour of launching a new Round appeared to be gaining ground – especially after the 9-11 terrorist attacks and the global economic slowdown – nothing concrete was agreed prior to the conference.

Given the international climate at the time, the fact the conference went ahead at all when a number of other international events were simply cancelled, was remarkable enough. Others copped out; we didn't. And there was a strong possibility up until the last moment that it would be cancelled. Rumours flew around Geneva; tensions were growing. I talked at length to Qatar Trade Minister Yousseff Kamal about the fact that some ministers were talking of not going to Doha because of the potential terrorist threat. Then, to my surprise and relief, a story appeared in the media that the Emir, while speaking to his old friend and business associate Vice President Dick Cheney, had been assured that the USA was definitely going to Doha. This was reiterated by President Bush at an APEC conference a few days later. Brilliant tactics by the Emir, I thought. Now everyone would follow the US lead. The scares resulted in a fall in the overall number of ministerial hangers-on attending, but that did us no harm at all.

As I flew into Doha, capital of the tiny emirate of Qatar (population 200,000 Qataris), over 600,000 guest workers from places like Pakistan, Afghanistan and India gave rise to serious security concerns, and some senior WTO staff, ambassadors and even ministers were openly predicting failure, with a few staff gleefully hoping for a bad result to reinforce personal, bureaucratic or national agendas. 'No' is the easiest, safest option, when you can't handle the substance of the issues, or your capital or cabinet is not engaged. It's hard to help someone who doesn't even know what they want.

Despite Kofi Annan's plea for coherence, some other UN Agencies took the populist line and attacked us. One agency, the Office of the High Commissioner for Human Rights produced a public report by 'experts', saying the WTO was a nightmare, without having met any WTO official and without coming into the building. Cheap shots were being fired everywhere. A few weeks before Doha, I was advised that a senior official from the UN Conference for Trade and Development was advising China not to join up. The continuing myth that the developing world had lost out during the Uruguay Round was irritating, especially when we were told by one ambassador that our proposed Doha Text set developing countries back a hundred years – especially when that accusation came from a country whose textile exports had gone up from under $100 million to $5 billion since the Uruguay Round. Tactical statements, not always meant as final positions, can look bad when they end up in the media and excite NGO opposition.

The opening ceremony took place on the evening of 9 November, with the substantive work getting underway the next day. Originally scheduled to close on the 13th as the conference got tougher, some tactically played for time and it looked as though we might not have time to conclude an agreement. Conference Chairman, Minister Kamal, extended proceedings for an extra day to enable us to finalise negotiations. (Yousseff, jokingly, privately offered to close the airport to stop people leaving because of a terrorist threat; I told him it wouldn't be necessary.)

In marked contrast to Seattle, the negotiating atmosphere was tense, but largely constructive. At Doha, ministers recognized that there was an urgent need for solidarity in the face of dangerous economic and political uncertainty. If my 650,000 km of travel, dozens of Ministerial Meetings, new negotiating strategies, better participation and transparency were appreciated as not just as a 'trick' to begin negotiations, and if we could prove the WTO had fundamentally changed, I believed we had a chance, that the risk was worth taking.

US Trade Representative (USTR) Bob Zoellick and the EU's Pascal Lamy worked tirelessly to contain their differences and refrain from raising the temperature, which was the direct opposite of pre-Seattle, where set positions were orchestrated through press statements. Both had known each other since serving as sherpas for high officials earlier in their careers, both had gone into the private sector and returned to public service, both were keen marathon runners, and they had over the years developed an excellent personal chemistry and mutual respect.

Their patience with each other and with me was heroic. Without their leadership we would have failed. Also key to the process was the appointment of a number of facilitators, drawn from a broad range of ministers, who played an essential role in the process. The Doha Ministerial Conference represented a watershed in the efforts to ensure transparency and inclusiveness. This included a consultation process by the facilitators, who reported back on their work to their constituencies and the

Figure 13. The Doha facilitators: we chose our facilitators with care, for their integrity, experience, commitment and balance. They hugely improved the transparency of the negotiations.

full Membership. This innovation was initiated at Seattle, but greatly improved upon at Doha. Another improvement was the specific allocation of two hours every day (morning and afternoon) when facilitators could report back and to allow regional and other groupings to meet and coordinate.

We chose our facilitators with care; for their integrity, experience, commitment and balance. No one complained about bias, which in itself was remarkable and a tribute to them as individuals, and to the care with which we assembled the team. At Seattle, they were chosen too late – in one negotiating subject I was refused by eight different ministers, until a minister finally accepted the responsibility to chair the group. The Doha facilitators were ministers of high quality and their appointments and integrity never questioned, unlike Seattle where excellent peoples' honour was frequently attacked.

Ever since Seattle I had believed the deal could be struck if the transatlantic relationship was repaired, and if the development dimensions were suitably addressed. Provided capacity-building commitments to developing countries were made, then Africa could join the Central and South Americans, so long as agriculture was suitably handled. In the last weeks before Doha it was apparent that if the EU waiver could be negotiated satisfactorily for developing African Carribbean and Pacific (ACP) countries, this would create constructive momentum. An excellent EU initiative, 'Anything but arms', a compromise called by its critics 'anything but farms', was quickly backed up by the USA's Growth and Opportunity Bill for African and Caribbean countries, and helped defuse tension, regain confidence and engage the weakest countries. Eventually, some twenty countries took unilateral action to open their markets and assist the poorest, the least developed countries.

However, in a consensus-driven organisation where every decision must be unanimous, it was still very difficult. Despite all this preparation, bitter differences remained. At one point before Doha, a paper began circulating entitled, *Ministerial Statement – Plan B*, which read: 'We the undersigned Nations confess our economic crimes against humanity, the planet, indeed the universe. We apologize and offer moral reparations. We note our commitment to common values of democracy, freedom and economic openness, but understanding that this is not enough, we apologize for our success in raising living standards and the creation of civil tolerance, therefore better social outcomes and announce that we are withdrawing from the WTO in shame and warmly recommend that the Nations who remain should make the WTO a sub-division of UNCTAD and suggest a working party of UNCTAD and the Human Rights Commission to establish the relationship between police excesses, poverty, debt, corruption, religious intolerance, trade and child labour and HIV AIDS. And, furthermore, resolve to establish a new trading group of the undersigned. We regret we speak for only 95 per cent of world trade.'

It was meant to be darkly humorous, but it contained an underlying truth. Why should the whole system stall for another decade if only a few countries stood out, some of them wanting a 'payout' that sometimes had nothing to do with a Trade Round?

Articles had begun to appear from conservative politicians and opinion leaders in the USA and Europe suggesting a NATO-plus-Japan trading arrangement, because the WTO was now unworkable. Regionalism was getting longer legs with members like Japan and Hong Kong–China, that had never struck regional or bilateral deals, in earnest talks. China, about to be gavelled in, was also in talks with Korea, Japan and ASEAN, about a free trade agreement. The multilateral system, not just a Round, was at stake.

The differences between Members in some areas, particularly agriculture, the environment, investment and competition, remained large, and trade-offs between issues that held the key to consensus were difficult to achieve. It was only right at the end of the conference that consensus on the final text was achieved. Tribute should be paid to our hosts the Qatari

Figure 14. A cartoon strip from a Qatari newspaper shows me as a sheriff with my posse in the Doha saloon.

Government, his Highness the Emir and especially Finance and Trade Minister Kamal, whose skills were deployed to great effect.

Led by the Emir, Qatar is playing a very smart game. Its neighbours are financial and sporting centres; Qatar seems to be positioning itself as a moderate, high-tech conference and cultural centre. The Emir is building up what I am told will be the leading museum of Islamic culture, to be housed in a stunning I. M. Pei-designed centre of Arab learning.

The conference facilities were excellent, and being able to hold everything in one building was a huge advantage, since it allowed us to waste less time and hold parallel meetings. It may be a developing country, but it set a benchmark of excellence in organisation, security and hospitality that would be hard to match. Which didn't stop either NGOs or some of our staff from complaining, even though facilities were infinitely better than what we had to deal with in Seattle, where there were no complaints about the host country. Daily briefings gave us a chance to assess the day and deal with any staffing issues and improve our performance and refine our strategies.

Hysteria broke out from time to time, with some senior staff failing to rise to the challenge of the problems that always crop up at such meetings. There was tension; several international conferences had been cancelled on security grounds and this was the first major event after 9-11. The day before the conference opened, rumours flew around the delegates when a gunman opened fire on the airport. This turned out to be, not a terrorist threat, but a deranged individual, who was killed by the Qatari forces.

Much of our translation work – everything has to be rendered in English, French and Spanish – had been subcontracted out as a cost-saving measure. We ended up producing over 3 million pieces of paper at Doha for delegations and NGOs. Which left us with a problem after 9-11, when we found ourselves with no moral or contractual leverage to persuade nervous translators into coming to an international conference in an Arab country. A week before the conference, we were desperately searching all over the world for translators and only just managed to get enough. Security was tight throughout the conference. Evacuation plans were readied, and beyond the horizon ships with military teams waited in case worst-case fears materialised. I offered staff the option of staying at home if they felt unsafe. A few did. We had to check our insurance and pension policies to make sure we were covered in the event of a terrorist attack. But where it mattered, at the heart of the negotiations and the substance of the issues, our staff performed superbly. They knew that if we failed, the WTO would have become about as relevant as the League of Nations.

Refining the process

In terms of process, Trade Ministerials have traditionally opened with a plenary in which each minister gives a five-minute speech. Horse-trading in Geneva and capitals on precedence for this formal ritual – mostly aimed at home-town constituents – often takes up days of ambassadorial time beforehand, and wastes precious hours at the actual Ministerial Conference. In practice, the big economies hog the cameras for the early part, then the DG and the Chairman leave the plenary and start the meeting proper, which needlessly offends the smaller players waiting their turn.

Host Minister Kamal was excellent: steady, humorous, sharp. His role was central and I will always be grateful to him. I told him that as DG I couldn't stop this process, but that if, as chair of the meeting, he wished, I could approach Members and get agreement so that we could run the plenary and the Ministerial effectively in parallel. He said yes, I did, and we proceeded on that basis, saving us at least five hours of negotiating time, by allowing each minister to go out, say his piece to camera for the record, then get back down to business. Ministers were pleased by the new process, oblivious to their ambassadors' extensive and irritating lobbying efforts in Geneva for prime-time speaking slots.

In the meeting proper, there were half a dozen key topics – and these were difficult issues. Yet whether it was agriculture, access to medicines, tariff peaks, or anti-dumping rules, the meeting was chaired and organised in such a fashion, and our report from Geneva was so close to what was acceptable, that on not one occasion was any minister stopped from speaking. I had expected that after say twenty or so speakers, the chair would have felt the need to then stop the meeting and ask the facilitators to meet key players and those with problems, and try and prepare a paper encapsulating the different views. But Kamal chaired the plenary meeting so well, the general mood was so good, and the basic paperwork prepared by Stuart Harbinson and our team was so close to the meeting's sentiment, that it was never necessary. Of course there were contrary views expressed, but we were able to continue with the understanding that the facilitators would talk to members informally to try and reach consensus.

This was reflected in the so-called 'Green Room' negotiations. The description originates in the WTO's Geneva headquarters, where there really is a meeting room known as the Green Room, into which the major players used to retire to broker deals. One of my failed innovations was to retitle it the Director-General's Conference Room, a title that was ignored. At every Ministerial, after everyone has expressed their view, facilitators and key representative ministers then get down to the nitty-gritty of negotiations in smaller groups, coming back to the Green Room for discussions on how each subject folded into the wider picture. These have often been, correctly in the past, criticised as being untransparent; as being an opportunity for the big players to bully the small; as being the scene of secret negotiations. The reality at Doha was that developing countries were always in the majority in the room, and could report back swiftly to their groupings.

There were twenty-two ministers present at the final negotiations through the night of 13–14 November, of whom six (27 per cent) were from developed countries, and sixteen (73 per cent) from developing countries. Geographically, the breakdown was seven from Africa (32 per cent), five from Asia (23 per cent), four from Latin America (18 per cent), with the minority from the 'west'. That is because I fought for and won the cross-section I wanted, with a majority of developing country friends I had made, whose interests I understood. My question was always, 'I know what you want; what do you need?'

Doha was the most inclusive and transparent Ministerial Conference the WTO ever held. On substantive talks (i.e. over and above the formal sessions of the conference), we held eleven informal meetings at Head-of-Delegation level (twenty-two hours); seven Conference Chairman's consultations (eighteen hours); forty-four Friends-of-Chair, or facilitators' consultations (ninety-five hours); and dozens of informal bilaterals with many ministers. I went three nights without sleep – just an occasional power nap and cold shower. This amounted to a total of sixty-two meetings consuming 136 hours (another innovation was holding the facilitators' meetings in parallel).

I insisted that there was always a majority of developing countries in the Green Room in Seattle too, although a few developing countries at that Ministerial chose to ignore this because alleged non-transparency played better in their home capitals. I remember watching a developing country minister giving a long interview on his cellphone to a reporter, complaining about the lack of transparency in the process – from *inside* the Green Room. There was never a time when the ministers from South Asia, who are most critical of the process, were not able to participate in Green Room negotiations. Hell, for two years, I could hardly go to the men's room without them! There were occasions when ambassadors from some countries forgot to tell their ministers that meetings were on because they wanted to be there, not their ministers – a capital offence in my political culture.

All the DDGs were deployed in Doha, unlike Seattle where they met for the first time. Small things matter. Paul-Henri Ravier pointed out the room assigned for the primary Green Room consultations was too large, and would have meant us needing to use microphones to communicate. He found a smaller, more comfortable, intimate, inclusive room and table; and kept the temperature very cold to keep people awake during the forthcoming marathon. 'Eat apples to stay awake,' someone else usefully advised.

I'm often asked what was the most important issue in reaching agreement at Doha. The answer is that it simply isn't that simple. There was no one overriding issue. As always in politics, a lot of it came down to personalities and chemistries; trade-offs and timetables.

On agriculture, we had been talking for years; in the end, as we argued over wording, it came down to a simple choice. I told the more protectionist countries: 'Do you want your agricultural subsidies to be phased out, or eliminated? It's got to be one or the other, or we won't get a Round.' They settled, sensibly, for phased out. And they acted with political courage, especially countries like Japan and South Korea, given their powerful domestic farming interests, where minister's political futures would be threatened in a negotiation. Without that commitment, there would have been no new Round; and there will be no final deal.

Some observers have suggested that the terror attacks of 9-11 were the key element. I do not agree. I think it helped focus minds on how costly a failure would be for international cooperation and the idea of the multilateral system. But without the other elements, we would not have made it. The time we put into constituency building over two years was essential. Our facilitators were well grounded and respected. We navigated the medicines and AIDS issues well, not helped by the fact that one minister from a large South American country was seeking his country's presidential nomination, and was running on this issue. The issue has everything: celebrities, multinationals, anti-Americanism, capitalism, simplistic slogans like 'People before profits' (whatever that means). It is a minefield, successfully navigated so far, but was not cleared before Doha.

The chemistry between Lamy and Zoellick was a major component. Had they not been prepared to move, and convince others of their sincerity, we would not have launched.

And had we not made development a core issue, had we not made a commitment to capacity-building to enable poor countries to help deal with old implementation issues and future negotiating needs, *by deeds* before Doha, I am convinced that the Round would never have got off the ground.

There were some who wanted all their concessions on implementation issues granted before agreeing to a Round; I've always argued that these issues should be tackled as part of the negotiating process. At Doha we agreed on 50 per cent of the implementation issues and left 50 per cent for future negotiation. Some say the wrong 50 per cent, but at Seattle we couldn't even reach agreement on a single one of the implementation agenda issues and grievances outstanding from the Uruguay Round.

It was touch and go right till the end. At one point, a concerned senior official from a major economy told me it was all over, that we would

fail, and commented that I didn't look worried. I replied that if worrying would work, I'd worry. Of course I was worried. At a tense moment when we were discussing the final draft and there will still major differences, a minister passed me a note with the word DOHA, a line through the 'h', to which he added: 'Dead On Arrival.'

The Green Room doesn't make decisions, but it can assemble the positions that could be finally acceptable. If the Green Room is representative enough, and the facilitators respected, then you can draft a document which the 140-plus membership might accept. Which we did. The facilitators pre-cooked understandings; then those understandings were folded into the wider deal so that everyone could see the trade-offs.

The clock was by then ticking. I knew the time would come when I had to threaten failure and disaster. At a critical point, I did just that. Then the facilitators rushed out to convince their various constituencies. The wise and experienced minister from Brazil, Celso Lafer, South Africa's Irwin, Egypt's Boutros-Ghali and Nigeria's Bello worked the African caucus. Kenyan Minister Biwott explained to the ACP caucus that the waiver decision was good news, and would be off the table without a wider agreement. I was able to move around friends and coalitions I had spent the previous two years cultivating, to point out where their interests were addressed.

Given that a small group, or technically any one Member, can stop progress and deny a consensus, these late-stage negotiations always provide an opportunity for someone to try and extract a special concession; to win under threat of total failure something they had been unable to achieve in Geneva or bilaterally. For some Members, this is their maximum point of leverage and power. There is something seriously wrong if we can reach a point every two years at a Ministerial when a single country can exert pressure over issues that haven't previously been resolved in the system. For smaller countries, regrettably that is sometimes the only time they can get the major powers to pay attention to their grievances. Predictably enough, in the last dramatic hours, one country wanted special consideration for their tuna industry from a fellow Member; another sought a few extra months' extension for their export zones. Given the emotion, inevitable rush, rumour, exhaustion and chaos of 140 ministers plus hundreds of advisers running everywhere, the potential for failure by mistake and last-minute misunderstanding is ever present. Historically, three Ministerials had failed to achieve their public objectives and collapsed. Fallout from Seattle still tainted the conference atmosphere.

We now had a document, the Doha Development Agenda. Would it float? The meeting convened and we held our breath. The first speakers were from Africa, who urged adoption. Minister Biwott, who spoke for

Figure 15. With Qatar Trade Minister Yousseff Kamal and Nigerian Trade Minister Mustafa Bello: Kamal was a magnificent chairman, while Bello and friends in developing countries led the charge in pushing for the new Development Agenda.

the ACP group and carried much weight with the developing world spoke early and in favour; it was looking good. After a dozen or so speakers, it became clear that only India and one Carribbean country had strong reservations. Other countries also had difficulties and could have joined them. I asked Minister Kamal to drag out the proceedings, and got some ministers to lengthen their speeches, while I quietly negotiated with those who still had difficulties accepting the document. Capitals were consulted. I thanked God for cellphones.

India had the most difficulties with the Doha text. It has suffered 400 years of British imperialism and 50 years of the London School of Economics; I sometimes wonder which has done it the most damage. India moved from the British Raj to the Permit Raj, as authors Daniel Yergin and Joseph Stanislaw have observed. People waited fifteen years to acquire a Diplomat car, a variation on an ancient Morris Oxford. Yet India's auto industry started out at the same time as Japan's. One businessman reported in the early days of the PC revolution that he had to visit the capital fifty times over a couple of years to get permission to import a computer. Now he owns one of the biggest high-tech companies in the world. Narayana Murthy founded Infosys – now one of the world's biggest software campus – with $250. India now supplies 30 per cent of the world's software engineers (there are 200,000 in Silicon Valley alone) and has a thriving software capital of its own in Bangalore.[1] But it has made more sensible and solid reforms in the last five years than in the previous fifty. I think India essentially wants to be left alone to carry out its reforms at its own speed; it certainly doesn't want the WTO or outside negotiations to force the pace. It was grappling with a coalition government comprising twenty-plus parties, and the political situation is always precarious. The challenge was to accommodate India and a few other like-minded countries' needs to ensure gridlock didn't deny the overwhelming majority of Members the benefits of a Round.

I once joked to Indian Trade Minister Maran that the basic difference between Indian and New Zealand negotiators was that when we get 30 per cent we tell our public we got 51 per cent. When they get 51 per cent, they tell their public they got 30 per cent. In fact, given India's agenda of blocking the introduction of labour, environment and other social issues into the WTO, and getting more time to focus on the 'New Issues', they have been very successful. Compare what the developed countries wanted in Seattle as opposed to what they got in Doha, from a developing country perspective. I am not saying either side is right or wrong, simply that India and its grouping did very well.

It is sometimes difficult for sophisticated economists and politicians to understand the deep historic and cultural problems some countries have with the idea of free trade. Some still equate it with their oppression from colonial days. It is a little over fifty years since Gandhi led a march across India in protest over the British salt tax. The calls for Indian independence was economic as well as political. Their word *Swadishi* embodies economic independence and self-reliance. Nationalism, the rejection of British goods and boycotts and the call to buy Indian products was part of that great cause. It is only a little over a century ago that Indians were forced to buy cotton fabrics made in Britain. Indians, who made their own fabrics, if caught, often had their thumbs cut off. India's share of the world textile market is now lower than it was 200 years ago. Gandhi talked of *Swadishi* as self-reliance, home and village production. Nehru saw self-reliance in heavy industry, mechanisation, electricity and was impressed on how quickly the Soviet Union had moved from feudal times to superpower status. Manmohan Singh, a courageous reforming Finance Minister, was also later to promote trade as self-reliance and aid as reliance. (I appointed him as one of my advisors.)

India remains cautious and suspicious, something I understand, and it speaks for many capitals, which do not have the strength or technical capacity to make their own case.

At Doha, in the early hours, eventually phone calls to capitals and prime ministers produced an overwhelming consensus to launch. In the end, Minister Kamal's summary – and a side letter to India which made clear that reaching an explicit consensus at the next Ministerial did not mean we had reached an agreement in the meantime on some of their issues of concern, won through. Semantics played a part: one minister had already told his parliament that he would never accept a Trade Round. But the deal was too good to refuse. I suggested we call it an agenda, not a Round. In the end, countries can't negotiate in public and deals can only be done on the spot, when the Members are together, and when there is a broad enough agenda to allow Members the freedom to go home and tell their home constituencies that, while they have given up something, they got something back.

Despite this, after Doha, some extremists, who ignored what ministers actually said, were still unhappy. They always will be. For the uncharitable, all interpretations are hostile. The World Development Movement alleged: '... and new evidence has emerged about the political pressure mounted on developing countries. There have been threats to cut off aid and end trade preferences, bribes and targeting of various WTO ambassadors for developing countries.'[2] José Bové complained: 'It is the worst agreement we could ever expect. It is a neo-colonial agreement. Doha has not taken Seattle into account. This agreement is conflict-carrying.' NGO activist Anuradha Mittal claimed: 'Doha was a defeat for democracy and developing countries, because of arm-twisting, blackmail and intimidation from the big trading powers.'[3] This is a cruel self-serving lie orchestrated by selfish observers and self-appointed critics who need to maintain the rage of their supporters to raise funds to stay in business and on the front pages.

Developing country ministers saw things differently. It was the Nigerian Trade Minister who led the charge in the final hours, urging acceptance of the package. Mustafa Bello said: 'Unlike in Seattle, Africa has been satisfied with all the stages in consultations and negotiating processes in Doha.' And I will never forget the face of the Brazilian minister, with tears streaming down his face, saying to me, 'At last, after thirty years, we have a mandate in agriculture to phase out subsidies and protections.' His country has 14 million hectares of land, which could feed the world without cutting down a tree.

One of the major problems of the way the world trading system currently operates is that it is perceived to be premised on a mercantilist approach, i.e. if I give up something to you, I want to get something back – in other words, horse-trading.

Former Mexican trade negotiator Luis F. de la Calle has observed: 'Negotiations in Geneva are often – or should I say, always – mercantilist in nature,' he told a WTO symposium in April 2002.[4] 'This, of course, means, in every decision taken, my gain is your loss. This applies to everything: from procedural details in the General Council to the trade-offs in a round of negotiations. That is why old Geneva hands keep an accurate tally of favours rendered and received.'

De la Calle added that the functioning of the WTO and the public perception of international trade would only change for the better once those involved got to grips with selling the real thing and forgetting about the export proxy. 'A trade is not a zero-sum game, for if it was, little benefit would derive from it, while the overwhelming empirical evidence is that trading nations do a lot better than others in the long term; and trade opening improves peoples' lives.'

De la Calle argues, as do many others, that the WTO's approach to trade negotiations is fundamentally mercantilistic: that negotiators seemingly behave as if exports are good and imports are bad. We need to remind ourselves that unilateral trade liberalisation is good in itself, and that if others do not reciprocate with their own reductions of trade barriers, there is a case for nations to unilaterally 'go alone'. Jagdish Bhagwati has argued this, not only by demonstrating that many countries worldwide have done so in recent years, but also by showing that even if others do not go with you in liberalising trade simultaneously, your unilateral lowering of trade barriers could, and often does, trigger subsequent liberalisation by others – what he calls 'sequential reciprocity'.[5]

Contradicting the notion that reciprocal bargaining is necessarily mercantilistic and therefore anti-trade, there remains an excellent case for reciprocal reduction of trade barriers, a practice embodied in GATT and WTO negotiations. Often, countries cannot make unilateral moves politically; reciprocity enables them to liberalise in these cases. Reciprocity enables politicians to mobilise the pro-trade groups, who will visibly profit from new export markets, to counter the anti-trade protectionist groups who typically oppose trade liberalisation. It is hard to imagine, for example, that the agriculture could have been brought into the trade agenda outside of the Uruguay Round with its built-in process of reciprocity.

Thus, in the Doha Agenda, a reduction of agricultural support by the major OECD countries could validate the gains from trade that countries like, say, Jamaica might reap by any liberalisation that they undertake in the context of the Round. In this way, multilateral liberalisation – using reciprocity as the fundamental negotiating tool – can and does lead to positive gains. This is the very antithesis of mercantilism.

We have, regrettably, so far failed to establish acceptance of the important idea that, if something is good for you, you should just go ahead and do it anyway, regardless of what your trading partners do. The evidence that free trade is good for countries is overwhelming. At Doha in November 2001, the majority of the WTO's membership recognized this; we successfully launched the first Trade Round since Uruguay in 1986.

10   Creating a 'World' Trade Organization

For me, China's accession to the WTO was more important than launching a new round of trade liberalisation. A failure at Doha, as we had in Seattle, would have been disastrous, but not fatal, though it could well have cost multilateralism a decade.

However, losing China after fifteen long years of negotiations, just before the generational change in China's leadership due in 2003, could have seriously impacted the reform process. Since Deng Xiaoping initiated the open door process in 1979, China has made astonishing progress in pushing through reforms to moribund state-owned enterprises, encouraging entrepreneurial activity and building the nation into a cost-efficient manufacturing powerhouse and quasi-capitalist society, lifting over 150 million people from extreme poverty in the past two decades.[1]

But while this process has successfully increased living standards and opened up society to new influences, it has also been a painful one for many of its people. Unrest in the countryside, as well as amongst new urban migrants and displaced workers, is regularly reported. For example, in an article describing a clan war involving home-made cannons that killed twelve people and destroyed sixty homes in Lanshan County, Hunan Province, *The New York Times*'s Erik Eckholm observed that the problems appeared to be most prevalent in the densely populated backwaters of central and southern China, where 'might makes right'. He quotes He Qinglian, an economist, in an essay on spreading lawlessness: 'In the contemporary Chinese countryside, traditional moral constraints no longer hold, and clan organisations and local criminal forces have come to fill the vacuum of power and authority.'[2]

Failure to persuade China to join the WTO and bring China on board as a fully responsible member of the international trading community would have had serious repercussions both internally and internationally. China's WTO entry, in the opinion of many observers, marked China's irreversible move towards market liberalisation and integration

Figure 16. With Chinese Trade Minister Shi Guangsheng and Qatari host minister Yousseff Kamal: a failure at Doha would have been disastrous, but losing China after fifteen long years of negotiations could have seriously impacted its reform process, as it went through a historic leadership and structural change. (Photograph courtesy of Agence France Presse.)

into the global economy, as well as formally acknowledging its status as an emerging global economic giant.

USTR Charlene Barshefsky and China's Foreign Trade Minister Shi Guangsheng had been wrestling with the delicate details for many years of the key US–China bilateral agreement that was one of the necessary precursors to accession. In all, thirty-seven countries negotiated bilateral agreements in order to ensure that China's accession to the multilateral system could take place. There was no doubt, throughout all of these negotiations, of the importance China placed, both politically and economically, on gaining accession. China's leaders, during many meetings, frequently stressed WTO entry was 'the biggest single economic step they had taken in fifty years'. Former European Union Trade Commissioner Sir Leon Brittan recently observed: 'In one of my meetings with [Premier] Zhu Rongji, he explained that everything we were asking the Chinese to do were things he wanted them to do anyway. If the Chinese didn't reach agreement with Europe and the US, they would still do them, but in their own time and in their own way.'[3]

And WTO Member governments showed sensitivity and flexibility in recognising that China – given its turbulent history, vast size and complexity, and history of state-ownership and control – would face difficulties in meeting its commitments. China, in turn, accepted a much more rigorous process of review and monitoring than other new Members.

China wanted firm international rules and a dispute system so that their exports and jobs were not vulnerable to *ad hoc* political decisions in their trading partners' capitals. They were also using the WTO system as a model to create a market economy based on property rights. Let no one doubt China's commitment on these issues; there are some 6,000 books about the intricacies of the WTO's rules in print, in Chinese, in China. And, undoubtedly, China's leaders hope to use the need to live up to their commitments as a lever against those resisting the reforms.

So the politics were complex. Indeed, just a few days before Doha, it looked like China might not go to the Ministerial because of problems with the sequencing of Chinese Taipei's membership. This difficult problem was quietly sorted out just in time.

Much has been written about the implications of this accession. The pressures on China from WTO membership will be considerable. Some 350 million farmers will lose their protected markets, as price controls are gradually lifted on a number of sensitive products such as rice, corn, and as global markets determine crop values.[4]

That China's two decades of economic reforms have created internal tensions is undeniable. In 1986, then Prime Minister Zhao Ziyang reportedly spelled out China's greatest challenge to an elite team of economists, bureaucrats and intellectuals, observing that, 'The government can control an impoverished China. But we must determine how the government can maintain stability, while growing China into a world power.'[5]

Stability, above all, has been the overwhelming obsession of Chinese leaders throughout the centuries. China's present strategy is working. The past fifteen years have seen 150 million people taken out of extreme poverty. It enjoys one of the highest rates of foreign direct investment in the world.[6] FDI in China is expected to reach an all-time high of some $47 billion in 2002, according to The State Development Planning Commission.[7] And of course a lot of those funds originated from or were channelled through Hong Kong–China and Chinese Taipei, or are parked there awaiting a suitable mainland destination. India, by comparison, received around one-tenth of that ($4 billion in FDI in 2001).

China had no workers in foreign-owned manufacturing in Mao's time, but by 1998 foreigners employed over 17 million workers, more workers than in France or Italy. These businesses accounted for 12 per cent of Chinese National Tax Income.[8]

The Chinese economy is expected to grow by about 7.4 per cent in 2002.[9] While economists sometimes dispute the exact degree of growth, the overall trend is clearly upwards. Since Deng's reforms in the late 1970s, GDP has increased at an average of almost 9 per cent a year.[10] China's share of world trade has doubled to 10 per cent in a generation. GDP per head has risen by 25 per cent to half the world's average. If China's GDP slows to a more reasonable 5.5 per cent, China's GDP could match that of the USA by 2015. China would then represent 17 per cent of the world's GDP. Around 10 per cent of China's people now own their own homes; newspapers in Hong Kong have been advertising apartments for sale – especially in Guangdong and Shanghai – for years. Although, in the early years, a number of Hong Kong and local mainland investors got burned by speculative developers, the trend towards private ownership is now firmly established in key Chinese urban centres.

China continues to grapple with the issue of banking sector reform; non-performing loans (NPLs) to essentially bankrupt state enterprises are estimated to account for around 40–50 per cent of the banking sector.[11] But mainland Chinese save almost 40 per cent of their earnings; there is a huge potential consumer market which is as yet still largely untapped.[12] By comparison, the US personal saving is approximately 5 per cent.[13]

Also a major factor in any analysis of China's ultimate economic weight in the world is the economic strength and interlocking networks of the widespread Chinese diaspora; almost 60 million Chinese live outside the mainland. The Chinese are only 4 per cent of Indonesia's population, but control an estimated 70 per cent of the economy.[14] An estimated 25 million Chinese live in Southeast Asia, making up 32 per cent of the population of Malaysia, five per cent in Thailand and one per cent in the Philippines. Their collective GNP has been estimated at $450 billion, which would make them, as a separate country, the world's ninth-biggest economy, according to figures quoted by Daniel Yergin and Joseph Stanislaw.[15]

Indeed, China is one of the great cradles of Asian civilisation. Chinese society was traditionally based on close and reciprocal family ties; although the Cultural Revolution and other excesses of the communist aberration damaged, it did not destroy these networks. And the traditional Confucian respect for learning travels well into a new economy based on ideas. It has been argued that the Chinese language itself has been a bar to progress – rote learning the 4,000-odd characters necessary to be reasonably well-read, does not necessarily provide the best basis for absorbing new knowledge. However, microchips may be helping solve that problem. Some observers predict that Chinese will be the most used language on the Internet within twenty years. The country already has 37.55 million Internet users (not to mention some 167 million mobile phone users, making it the leading world's mobile phone market).[16] It is perhaps no surprise that the best-selling book in China for four months was *How To Get Your Child into Harvard*. China is on the road back to economic greatness, something she enjoyed for thousands of years before the past couple of centuries.

Critics of China's accession have charged that China's human rights record and its relations with Chinese Taipei are grounds for keeping China out of the WTO. Thankfully, this has not been the view of our Member governments. Hong Kong democratic leader Martin Lee and politicians in Chinese Taipei publicly argued for the accession, while other well-meaning observers from afar said no. Even those governments critical of China in these areas made it clear that China's membership to the WTO should be decided on the basis of trade considerations. Those who opposed entry for political reasons failed to understand that bringing China more closely into the international community has heralded more positive developments in their areas of concern over the past two decades than in the previous century.

In joining an organisation that is based on binding rules, mutually agreed by consensus and enforceable through the dispute settlement system, China's leaders are locking into the multilateral system the economic reforms they have unilaterally put into place over more than twenty years. In doing so, China has accepted that openness – not only to goods and services, but also to people and ideas – is the best way to ensure a prosperous future for her citizens.

China's entry to the WTO will mean immense opportunities for businesses around the world. China was the world's fifth-leading importer last year, buying some $225.1 billion worth of foreign merchandise and $34.8 billion worth of services from foreign providers.[17]

Moreover, and equally importantly for both China and its trading partners, WTO entry in turn gives China much greater access to major markets in Europe and the USA. Many observers – especially amongst China's Asian trading rivals – believe that China has a lot less to fear from the world, than the world has from China. It is, as most business people are aware, very tough to out-produce local Chinese manufacturers in areas such as white goods and textiles.

China was the USA's fifth-largest supplier in 2000, according to US figures. In turn, China, Hong Kong–China and Chinese Taipei were all in the top ten export markets for the USA. Based on Chinese figures, after adjustment for re-exports through Hong Kong, the USA accounted for $71.4 billion of Chinese merchandise exports. The EU accounted for

$15.2 billion and Japan $16.3 billion. Together those three major markets accounted for almost 60 per cent (57.4%) of China's total exports.[18]

Beijing is, of course, aware of its neighbours' concerns, as the recent flurry of regional trade diplomacy indicates. It is pushing the case – and it's a plausible one – that China's economic growth will benefit the region. Impressive April trade statistics from South Korea, Singapore and Taiwan helped China make that point, showing exports to China contributing to a long-awaited rebound in each economy's exports, highlighting China's growing role as a buyer as well as a seller, reported the *Far Eastern Economic Review*.[19]

China showed great integrity during the Asian financial crisis by not devaluing its currency; as did the USA at that time by continuing to absorb many Asian exports, including steel, even though they could possibly have used WTO anti-surge safeguard provisions to keep them out. In a brave stand of economic statesmanship, then Treasury Secretary Bob Rubin took a long-term approach, fearful that the economic contagion, which was sweeping Asia, Latin America and Russia, could signal a new global recession.

A very modest surge in growth in, say, the USA or Europe, would reinforce the beneficial effects on China's society – and on China's millions of consumers – of the reform process.

Under its accession commitments, China's average bound tariff level for goods will fall to 8.9 per cent, ranging from 0 (zero) per cent – for many goods in the IT sector, toys, wood and paper products – to 50 per cent for just three tariff lines covering certain fertilisers. At the high end, the bound tariff rate for photographic film will come down from 55.7 per cent to 47 per cent, while the tariffs on passenger autos will come down from 50–60 per cent (61.7 per cent or 51.9 per cent) to 25 per cent.

Meanwhile, the average bound tariff on agricultural products will drop to 15 per cent. Within three years of accession, all enterprises will have the right to import and export all goods and trade them throughout China with limited exceptions.

China will eliminate dual-pricing practices. In banking, foreign financial institutions were permitted on accession to provide services in China without client restrictions for foreign currency business. For local currency business, within two years, foreign institutions will be able to provide services to Chinese enterprises, and within five years, to all Chinese clients.

China had, by the end of the first quarter 2002, reviewed more than 2,000 laws and regulations, and amended or abolished those that were inconsistent with its WTO obligations. The Ministry of Foreign Trade and Economic Cooperation, alone, had reviewed more than 1,400 laws and regulations, and has abolished half of them. In order to improve transparency, China has set up a WTO Notification and Inquiry Bureau in MOFTEC, which has so far responded to more than 300 queries from embassies, Chinese and foreign-funded companies and individuals.

China cut tariffs on some 5,300 imported items in January 2002, lowering them on average from 15 to 12 per cent. It has also removed non-tariff barriers on 238 product items.

There are some fears that China may wish – as have some other countries – to pursue a parallel trade strategy by seeking to form regional groupings. Beijing acceded to the Bangkok Agreement in April 2001, which offers preferential access to China for a number of smaller Asian countries. China also announced in November 2001 that it was negotiating to form a free-trade area with ASEAN within the next decade. It has also taken part in discussions on an ASEAN plus Three agreement, with Korea and Japan. However, much of this diplomatic drive in Asia seems to be aimed at shoring up rather neglected bilateral relations, as well as dispelling concerns that China's WTO membership will threaten regional economic interests.

And, of course, China has concerns of its own: about the extent to which domestic manufacturers and farmers will be affected by WTO entry; about the use of such trade rules as anti-dumping, countervailing and safeguards, as well as other issues.

Hugo Restall, in the *Wall Street Journal*, recently went so far as to suggest that the USA risked losing its status as the world's leading advocate for free trade. 'With its large market, China is in a great position to lead the developing countries in putting abuse of dumping and safeguard provisions high on the WTO agenda ... if the Bush administration doesn't get its act together, it could face the ignominity of finding itself in the diplomatic sights of a global free trade campaign led by Beijing.'[20]

As perhaps an indication of what is to come, in May 2002, two Chinese steel companies, Maanshan Iron and Steel and Weifang Steel Pipe Co., for the first time went through the entire legal process and won landmark anti-dumping cases in the USA, as opposed to having them dropped before they came to court. There are about 450 outstanding dumping investigations aimed at Chinese companies worldwide, including some 175 in the USA. In the past, Chinese firms have tended to take a rather passive attitude, partly because they doubted they would get a fair hearing in a foreign country and were reluctant to employ expensive foreign lawyers, according to a *Financial Times* report.[21] The US result was expected to embolden other Chinese groups to take a more proactive approach.

Many have asked me how China has behaved in Geneva. Certainly, the political sensitivities are considerable; its Hong Kong–China, China

Macau, Chinese Taipei and China. The use of proper terms is very important – it's the Representative from Chinese Taipei *not* the Ambassador. My diary once inadvertently recorded a meeting with Chinese Taipei's Ambassador, which caused some concern and was quickly corrected.

Is China living up to its obligations? I can answer that China, like other Members, will advance its self-interests. China so far has done so with dignity; its staff are professional and pleasant to work with. Where we had difficulties, such as selecting a new venue for the next Trade Ministerial, appointing chairpeople of negotiating committees and timetables – indeed on matters of process that some Members manipulate – when the issue was explained, China made its own views known and was open, honest and helpful.

We should bear in mind that the conditionality imposed on China is considerable. Members undergo a periodic Trade Policy Review (TPR) every two, four or six years, depending on the size of their trade. This TPR is not an 'enforcement' mechanism. China, as part of its accession conditions, has agreed to subject itself to an annual, ten-year long special Transitional Review Mechanism.

This mechanism comprises two parts: a review by sixteen subsidiary house bodies, followed by a separate review by our General Council, by 10 December each year. There were some concerns. China's difficulties have related, not to the substance of how initial reviews should be conducted, but rather to the forum where they should take place. However, some other delegations fear that our schedules do not allow such an end-of-year loading, and are pressing for more disclosure earlier in the year.

The WTO is all about process and consensus. This includes monitoring of Members through our various committees. And of course it also means that individual fellow Members can – if they feel it is necessary to defend their interests – ultimately bring a complaint against China into our disputes system. The important point is that China is now inside the system, not outside it. It is also worth noting that the WTO is in many ways a less confrontational and less formal organisation than the UN, and that it is inevitable that China will take a while to get to grips with the way the WTO does business.

Many millions of dollars have been sacrificed, in the pursuit of what author Joe Studwell has called 'The China dream – the elusive quest for the last great untapped market on earth.' Businessmen look above all for transparency from China – to doing business in a system where the rules are known, where there are no hidden pitfalls. I cannot guarantee that this will happen overnight. To expect significant progress in the first year of entry is, I think, unrealistic. But I can say that international businesses will increasingly have a far greater degree of certainty as to the rules of the game. Anyhow, China isn't the only untapped market. Markets are never finite. Assuming that South Asia and Africa had grown by as much as China (about 9.0 per cent per capita annually) and had experienced the same per centage reduction (about −15.0 percentage points) between 1900 and 2000, then the additional number of people lifted out of extreme poverty worldwide could have been over 200 million. At the same time, poverty rates in those regions would have fallen to levels similar to China in 1990 of around 30 per cent.[22]

China's accession constitutes a defining moment for the WTO and for the international economic, political and security arrangements that will influence our world in this century and beyond. After the horrific events in New York and Washington last year, multilateral cooperation is more important than ever before.

The leadership in Beijing faces problems of enormous difficulty, in a country that is awesomely complex to administer. China has made astounding progress. I have no doubt that it is doing everything in its power to meet its WTO commitments. I also believe we must continue to provide the leadership with all possible encouragement and support to do so.

The WTO is an instrument of peace in so far as it acts as a mechanism to facilitate greater understanding between China and her trading partners, including Chinese Taipei. Senior government officials in Chinese Taipei have said that Taipei will establish direct trade and transport links with China after each becomes a member of the WTO. Chen Shui-bian has announced he would allow private business groups to hold talks with mainland China on behalf of his government, to negotiate direct shipping, postal and travel links with the mainland.[23] The removal of these barriers could not help but foster closer cooperation and understanding between the two.

The WTO offers, as well, a forum in which disputes can be brought, argued and settled in a measured and equitable manner. In the past, trade disputes have had, in all parts of the world, a nasty tendency to flare into armed conflict. This becomes unnecessary when both parties know they will have a fair hearing in court. Such an international forum will help nurture stable relations between China and Chinese Taipei. The Taiwan straits are one of the hot points, and choke points, and have been the focus of much military attention. Mistakes can happen. Several times over the past decade, the world has held its breath as great battle fleets circled each other. Now business people on both sides are examining how to advance trade, investment and tourism. This has to be good for the peaceful evolution of the region.

For the WTO, the accession of China and Chinese Taipei is also a great step towards becoming a truly *world* organisation. Now that they have both become Members, the rules by which the great majority of global trade operates have been extended. Moreover, all of us will benefit by having officials from both places participate in the process of shaping new rules for the twenty-first century.

An angry left-wing Labour MP breathlessly burst into my office in the 1990s and, in an accusing manner, said, 'Look at this, the multinationals are closing their plants in Korea and Indonesia, and shifting to China because of lower wages.' 'Great,' I replied. 'I hope I live long enough to see wages in China rise so high that those jobs go to Ethiopia.' My colleague wasn't impressed with my response. But the process continues; in July 2002, Unilever announced that it was shifting some of its China production from Shanghai to cheaper parts of China inland, to trim costs in the competitive household product sector and meet stiff competition from both local and multinational players. The success of coastal China is moving inland; the system is working.

New members in the queue

Given the amount of abuse the WTO has encountered, it is surprising how many people want to join it. We had twenty-eight countries in the queue as of mid-2002. Why? I always joke that the only people who really value the WTO are those who aren't in it. The Albanian President once told me to tell the protestors that they should visit Albania so they could see at first hand what happens to closed societies.

I have dedicated more senior staff to the WTO's accessions division. In my time we have welcomed Lithuania, Oman, Jordan, Moldova, Albania, Estonia, Georgia and Croatia, as well as China and Chinese Taipei. Vanuatu has been formally accepted, but domestic politics, an election in 2002, stood in the way. This is unique – where a country was gavelled through, but the membership fees now stand as the only formal impediment.

There are still great holes in our world map. Saudi Arabia's accession, despite my best efforts, remains elusive and was my biggest disappointment in accessions, though some recent new initiatives and appointments may help. Prince Talal bin Abdul Aziz, one of King Fahd's half-brothers and a liberal reformer, told me it is fundamental for Saudi Arabia's future, its peace and progress, to join the WTO and to open its society. During a meeting he asked me whether joining the WTO may end up opening his society to other democratic influences. Picking my words carefully, I told him that other societies with distinctive cultures and histories have joined, many of Islamic heritage, adding that with or without the WTO, the information age and education makes people think and seek additional choices. 'Good,' he replied.

But we made progress in some troubled areas that are sorely in need of the boost that will come from full acceptance into the world's trading system. For me, one of the WTO's strengths is that it is able to help countries use trade to enhance security and reduce bilateral tensions. The Balkans and Central Asia haunt me. I returned from visits to these countries with a renewed sense of rage: there is no need for these countries to be poor. Their current plight is a direct result of tribalism and the horrors of a vengeance-driven concept of historical memory, as one of my heroes, ex-US Senator Daniel P. Moynihan warned in his book *Pandemonium: Ethnicity in International Politics*, which turned out to be sadly correct.[24]

I strongly believed the ex-Soviet colonies in Central Asia and the Balkan economies deserved more attention, and one of my last acts in 2002 was to organise a major Ministerial Meeting in Georgia with development banks, as well as various neighbours and other economies in transition that successfully completed the process, to motivate, explain and advance these accessions. I visited the Armenian President en route and later in Tblisi we were able to make progress on negotiating and navigating Armenia's accession, which has enormous political consequences for neighbouring Azerbaijan, which is also seeking membership, and with which it has very sensitive and serious differences. We were able to bring in representatives from Turkey, to talk with both parties and help move these accessions forward. Armenia should be admitted by 2003. I exceeded the WTO's mandate in missions to this region by widening the participants list. The Former Yugoslav Republic of Macedonia is almost there as well.

A similar mission was held for the Balkans in Croatia. At this meeting, a Serb minister from the former Yugoslavia visited Zagreb – a two-hour drive from Belgrade – for the first time in fifteen years and was able to meet his opposite number as well as the President and other cabinet ministers. We had people around the room who had been at loggerheads in a vicious civil war. I explained to them that one of the wonders of the WTO was that, for example, even when tensions between Pakistan and India were running high, both countries' representatives in the WTO worked as brothers to further their countries' mutual interests in textiles. Precisely because we are not the UN, with all the attendant focus and position-taking, we are often able make progress. I recalled a scene in Geneva when a beaming Balkans minister advised me with great pride he was taking their first case against a neighbour. This was a matter of celebration he said. Their landlocked Balkan country was bringing a dispute against its neighbour, which was preventing transportation of oil across its territory. Despite the history of recent sectarian carnage, they now have a non-violent place to work out their differences through legal procedures in the WTO.

Cambodia is also very close to joining. It is driven, focused and organised and has reaped the benefit of economic diagnosis and technical assistance, done as a beneficiary of the Integrated Framework, an excellent idea for inter-agency cooperation, which had gathered dust for years until I made it operational. My visit to Cambodia in early 2002 to accelerate its accession was one of the most moving experiences I've ever had. Pol Pot's regime was as bad as it gets. Creating the most extreme closed tribal society, he had killed millions by the end of his utopian reign of terror. By some reports, less than seventy university graduates survived in Cambodia.

And yet by 2002 patriotic young officials, mostly educated in the USA, Europe, Canada and Australia, all of whom had lost family members, had returned to rebuild their nation, knowing full well the dangers. One of their ministers told me he had lost seventy-five members of his family, murdered by the Khmer Rouge regime. Turning on television coverage of the Parliament, he pointed out Cabinet colleagues who were former Khmer. 'That man's a killer, so is that guy, and that guy,' he observed. I shook my head and told him he was a better man than me. I don't think I could work with people who killed my family. He was philosophical, telling me: 'We must be patriots, we can't govern alone. We would build a bridge, they would destroy it. If our country is to prosper and live we have to do this. Things will change.'

Their forgiveness and policies of reconciliation are awe-inspiring. I doubt if I could be so forgiving. Both sides realized that trials for war crimes and crimes against humanity, and western notions of justice or revenge, could ignite a further bloody civil war. Vietnam and the Republic of Yugoslavia are further away from accession, but both are within reach over the next few years.

But the reality is that for nations to join they must want it. They must be prepared to change laws in order to build and protect prosperity, and to maintain courts that can uphold agreements. For an organisation that is so widely condemned by outsiders, everyone wants its benefits. Membership is near universal, except for those rogue and failed states, who in the end will not give up economic freedom to their people, because they fear the political and social freedom that it unleashes and thus cannot sign up to the necessary rules. China has been an inspiration for many. It understood the benefits of the rule of law and the rejection of the central model of planning, took the tough decisions and has seen millions lifted out of extreme poverty.

Figure 17. President Putin showed an alarmingly detailed grasp of the WTO's costs, benefits and obligations. No one in the world at the moment has a better chance to change history. (Photograph courtesy of the Press service of the President of the Russian Federation)

The Ukraine was once the wheat basket of Europe and Vietnam was the rice basket of Southeast Asia. They could be again once their farmers are liberated to do what they do best and their countries build a democratic, legal and commercial infrastructure.

Russia remains the next great prize. I have met President Vladimir Putin on several occasions and he's well-briefed and fully understands the details and the implications. He was very frank: WTO membership is about binding rules, property rights, courts that work – he also sees external agreements as a way of stimulating domestic reform.

Accession would help clean up the corruption that comes from privilege and the absence of competition, and the WTO is therefore a target from some very powerful people who enjoy privilege and power in Russia. It's sad but not unexpected to witness the old communists join hands with the new phoney capitalists to stop competition and resist change.

Despite these problems, there are in Washington, Brussels and Moscow men with the horsepower, firepower and willpower to make this happen. Present energy prices are Russia's friend, so my hopes are high that it will get the economic growth it needs to move ahead. Working parties in Geneva are making solid progress. Accessions always come back to such core issues as agriculture, protected vested interests, energy costings, banking and insurance. I offended the Cairns Group a coalition of eighteen agricultural exporting countries who account for one-third of the world's agricultural exports by saying its ought not to be too tough on Russia's accession, and should think longer term. I was approached by a Cairns Group ambassador in Moscow, who said his country was dropping off bulk agriculture products into the market, so it was better not to have Russia in the system and building an effective agricultural system. I exploded. 'On that basis, your farmers would be better off if Japan was still in ruins and Antwerp still flooded.'

Some ask why Russia should get a better deal than China. I made a special visit to Beijing to promote Russia's accession and to enlist China's understanding. Chinese ministers joked that they have concerns that Russians don't understand capitalism. 'Yes,' I replied, 'too many ex-communists – you don't have that problem in China.' The Chinese delegation thought that this was one of the funniest things they had ever heard.

I can only hope that negotiators think in historic terms. It will be a victory if Russia is a member by the Mexico Ministerial in 2003; it will be a great failure if they are not members by the Sixth Ministerial in January 2005.

11 How the 'new issues' could strengthen the agenda

Much political play has been made of the so-called 'new' issues:
    competition policy
    trade facilitation
    trade and investment
    transparency in government procurement.
They are not new. Work on them has been under way for many years and was formally focused on at the Singapore Ministerial in 1996. However, resolving them remains difficult, and could be contentious; these issues have the potential to derail – or deepen – the Round.

The Trade Round is a single undertaking: nothing will be agreed until everything is agreed, which is an incentive for everyone to get the job done. The WTO simply offers opportunities to trade; what Members do with those opportunities is their own business. I tried and failed to broker the 'opt-in, opt-out' option on the new issues in the lead up to Doha. That would basically have meant countries agreeing not to oppose an agreement that included the new issues, but would have allowed individual countries who objected to opt in at a later date when they were ready and their institutions were in place. More to the point, some developing countries feared being singled out as falling short, since these areas are very much perceived by international investors as a good governance seal of approval. But the reality is that these nations are already at risk of investor isolation; investors go to where the rules are predictable and transparent and corruption is low.

The new issues are integral to a coherent Doha Development Agenda strategy. Consider: if we deal with tariff peaks and escalation, we open up investment opportunities in developing countries. For example, copper goes from Zambia to Japan in raw form because escalation in Japan protects domestic processing. If that escalation is removed, then value-added opportunities arise in Zambia. But to attract the needed FDI, Zambia would have to establish its credibility with foreign investors, by entering into a multilateral investment agreement. To prevent monopolies arising and to protect its own interests, it needs to look at competition policy.

To guard against problems of leakage and to ensure good governance, it needs to look at trade facilitation and transparency in government procurement. These are not, in the end, standalone issues.

We know that investment naturally seeks the safest place of best return. Those governments which remain unconvinced of this, or seek more stifling controls and restrictions, rather than setting up an enabling regime in which the rule of law is seen to operate freely, are punished. In those countries the state's GDP can actually shrink. This is perplexing for adherents of the old centralised economy school. But because of stifling rules, the black economy gets larger and government revenues fall. The more the restrictions and lack of transparency, the greater the perceived moral hazard and the less the revenues – a kind of Laffer's curve of diminishing returns, which some development experts have only just begun to discover. OECD governments are the most successful economically, because they are open and transparent; compare the percentage of the black economies in the OECD and non-OECD countries.

That's why, under the New Partnership for African Development (NEPAD), African leaders now have governance issues at the centre of their agenda.

At Doha, ministers nonetheless wisely agreed that work should continue on these issues. But they also agreed that creating developing country capacity to understand, develop policies based on national interest, and negotiate and implement the results of negotiations was a necessary ingredient for a successful conclusion of the Doha Development round. I hope governments can agree to formally negotiate further in Cancun, in September 2003. Agreement could bring significant benefits to both developed and developing countries.

I see no reason why developing countries that are not yet in a position to technically implement some of the requirements in these issues, should not participate fully in the negotiations, raise their objections and argue for their positions, but opt out of compliance until such time as they are ready – so long as they don't use them as an excuse to derail the Round. It may be argued that opt-in, opt-out is a violation of the MFN spirit, although we basically did the same thing with international telecommunications policy. I would suggest that special and differential treatment for one or two countries representing a fractional percentage of world trade and investment is probably not such a big deal. This may well be the solution arrived at for the next Ministerial in Cancun.

At Doha, we also agreed to negotiate on several other key issues, including access to medicines under the TRIPS agreement, which is also dealt with in this chapter. The environment is also on the table, as is an agreement to strive to improve our Disputes Settlement Understanding (see Chapter 7). In addition, in this chapter I raise the issue of why it is important that aviation and shipping be considered under the General Agreement on Trade in Services (GATS).

Competition policy

Contrary to the way it has sometimes been pictured in the NGO community, having a competition policy does *not* mean imposing *laissez-faire* capitalism. The opposite is the case; competition policy is a recognition that markets are not infallible and that appropriate regulatory policies are needed to ensure they work in ways that benefit the public at large, and not just producers.

Competition laws and policies provide the tools needed to deal with anti-competitive practices of enterprises, in the interests of consumers. Cartels (price-fixing agreements), anti-competitive mergers and abuses of dominant positions impose heavy costs on the economies of countries that lack effective tools to address them. Lack of such policies also allows protected vested interests, both commercial and political, to retain their privileged lucrative positions.

Judge Elbert Gary, the first chairman of US Steel, was – as Brink Lindsey points out – famous for holding weekly dinners with other steel executives to set prices. 'Gary defended this "cooperative plan" arguing that "the law does not compel competition; it only prohibits an agreement not to compete",' Lindsey writes. Some attitudes don't change.[1] President Theodore Roosevelt, as a pro-business Republican, attacked the great trusts. Sometimes governments must intervene to ensure that the market works. There is a difference between private enterprise and free enterprise.

Competition policy is an important aspect of pro-poor development. The need for effective competition policies in developing countries is recognised in the work of the WTO Working Group on the Interaction between Trade and Competition Policy over the past four years, and in the WTO Secretariat's work in cooperation with other inter-governmental organisations on the 'mainstreaming' of trade liberalisation and related policy reforms. In fact, some ninety to a hundred countries, including fifty or more developing countries, already have competition policies.

Competition policy is needed by poor countries because it: (a) provides tools to grapple with market restrictions that inhibit an efficient response to liberalisation, including the possibility of entry by new entrepreneurs; and (b) can address poor countries' continuing victimisation by international cartels and other anti-competitive practices.

A recent study for the World Bank found that international cartels have raised the cost of developing countries' imports by billions of dollars annually and, in several cases, have blocked entry into new markets by competing entrepreneurs from such countries.[2] This frequently results in a direct transfer of wealth from poorer to richer countries – a practical illustration of 'Robin Hood in reverse'.

Some believe that the need for WTO rules on competition policy has been supplanted by the newly established International Competition Network (ICN), an association of established antitrust agencies from the developed world along with a number of developing countries that was launched earlier in 2002. The ICN has a mandate to promote procedural and substantive convergence in competition law enforcement through inter-agency discussions. What the ICN cannot do – and is outside its mandate – is to manage the interface of competition policy with the multilateral trading system.

WTO rules on competition policy would *not* require the creation of an international competition agency, nor would they involve harmonisation of national approaches. Indeed, the imposition by the WTO of a 'one size fits all' approach to national competition legislation has rightly been rejected. WTO rule-making would focus, rather, on the adoption of broad principles relating to non-discrimination, transparency and procedural fairness in addition to the prohibition of private cartels. It would also encompass strengthened institution-building efforts for the benefit of poor countries and modalities for enhanced cooperation in the fight against anti-competitive practices that span the developed and the developing world.

Nonetheless, the critics are right that globalisation will not work to the benefit of citizens – particularly in the developing world – in the absence of rules and institutions that ensure fair competition and prevent exploitation of poor people by socially inefficient monopolies and private cartels. For example, those who believe in public health delivery should think forward a decade and consider the implications to health ministries' budgets when pharmaceutical industries merge and ministers must purchase from the Melbourne branch, not the Karachi office of the same company. Competition is hard enough to establish between companies, let alone within companies. And this is not just a developing country issue: most Western economies spend more of their health dollars in the last year of someone's life than all the other years put together. From 1989 to 1998, the amount spent on health expenditure of the OECD countries as a percentage of their GDP increased by approximately 15 per cent. In volume terms, the percentage increase in total healthcare expenditure of OECD countries from 1989 to 1998 is estimated to have increased by 2000 per cent.

Competition is a key issue with important implications; the cleansing power of transparency is undeniable. But the majority of the WTO's membership do not have domestic competition policies, making it difficult for them to even begin implementation, so institution- and capacity-building will be central to success in this area.

Trade and investment

In Doha, Ministers agreed to prepare for WTO negotiations on a multilateral framework covering long-term cross-border investment, particularly foreign direct investment (FDI). This is a subject that will require an explicit consensus to move to the next stage, and that decision will be one of the key issues for the 2003 Ministerial.

Attracting more FDI has become a key economic policy objective for many WTO Members, particularly developing countries, to help them integrate further and faster into the world economy. It brings an attractive foreign capital inflow, one that is comparatively stable, that has no fixed interest payments attached to it, and that contributes directly to productive investment. It also brings entrepreneurship, technology, managerial skills and marketing know-how – assets that are in short supply in many countries and difficult for them to acquire, yet which are vital to helping them raise productivity and accelerate their growth and development.

Broadening the multilateral system to cover foreign investment will help in achieving the WTO's core objectives – improving the allocation and use of resources worldwide and deepening the international division of labour. Foreign investment and trade are complementary. Host countries with open trade policies can hope to attract FDI that is highly competitive and that will help them develop export capacity. A liberal investment regime, that is transparent, non-discriminatory and relies on market forces, reinforces the benefits of a liberal trade regime. It will attract high-quality FDI, with state-of-the-art technology and know-how, which can make a crucial difference to the growth prospects of many WTO Member countries. Which country suffers from too much efficiently directed investment?

FDI has been growing much faster than trade, reaching a record flow of $1.3 trillion in 2000. Yet the bulk of this is still concentrated in the developed countries and a handful of the largest and most advanced developing countries. Others are failing to attract FDI in significant quantities to help supplement their domestic savings and meet their investment needs, despite having adopted in many cases more liberal investment regimes. Part of the explanation is that business still perceives the commercial risk involved to be too high, even in those countries that are actively pursuing bilateral investment treaties with their main partners.

The WTO can help correct this. A multilateral framework that brings greater transparency, stability and predictability to investment policymaking, underwritten by WTO rules, surveillance and dispute settlement arrangements, will help close the current gap between perceived and actual policy risk in the eyes of foreign investors, as it has done in the area of international trade. Lower policy risk means lower commercial risk, which means new, profitable investment opportunities and more investment overall. Further liberalisation of investment policies will reinforce this effect. The WTO cannot influence how FDI is distributed, any more than it can do so for trade flows. But the more FDI there is to go around, the more opportunity each country will have to attract a share of it.

Foreign investment should not only flow along bilateral channels; it should be encouraged to flow internationally, and be made more accessible to those developing and least developed countries most in need of it. However clean rules and transparency would cut out or limit the scope for corruption, which some politicians are reluctant to forgo.

Two groups seem to oppose an agreement on investment: rich country NGOs who talk of investment being a race to the bottom, and some in poor countries who cling to the notion that investment equals colonialism equals exploitation and the 'it's all an American plot' theorists. Unfortunately, this view is held strongest by some self-appointed spokespeople for the poor who live in rich countries. The truth is the opposite. Some 80 per cent of FDI by US manufacturing firms in 1998 went to other high wage countries like Britain, Canada, the Netherlands, Germany and Singapore. And the USA has itself over the last decade been the world's largest recipient of foreign investment.[3]

A better investment climate also increases domestic invstment and reduces capital flight, observes Peter Watson, CEO of the Overseas Private Investment Corporation, who quotes former ABB Chairman Percy Barnevik's comments that, while there are masses of potentially profitable projects in the developing countries, only a fraction of the available capital ends up there, and it is also extremely unevenly distributed. 'Indeed 12 major developing countries take 75 per cent, while 140 developing countries (including the poorest ones) share 5 per cent.' Barnevik asks: 'Why do various Arab funds invest in property in London and New York instead of in Egypt, Syria and the Gaza Strip? It is the investment climate.'[4]

In reality, US negotiators are at best lukewarm over an investment agreement. The strongest promoters are the EU, Japan and Switzerland. The US economic magnet doesn't need investment rules; the US attracts one-third of the world's FDI.[5] Meanwhile, FDI outflows from the USA in 1998 to the rest of the world were $133 billion, an increase of 500 per cent over a decade. The rate of outward bound FDI is greater than the rate of increase in trade and is greater than the rate of increase in world output.[6] Ironically, it is the investment-starved nations that need the very rules that many of them oppose for nationalistic political purposes. I've seen developing country ministers oppose even discussing the issue, and then leave to lead inward investment missions to New York and London. Again, we should look at the coherence the Doha Development Agenda offers in addressing these issues.

The mindset of developing countries against FDI has its origins in the fact that so much of it involves mineral and resource extraction, and as such is a bitter reminder of imperialist times. Their anger and fear can be better understood against this historic background. They also see richer countries operating by double standards – wanting to invest in their forests, but then putting tariff escalator clauses on to penalise local added value and local jobs. Equally bewildering is pressure from foreign investors who, once in a protected market, then seek protection from competition while they graze on the 'rents' such protection provides. The battle in Mexico between IBM, Hewlett Packard and Apple to enjoy the profits of protection is played out in many countries where 'first-in best-served' companies organise disparate coalitions of businesses, unions and local politicians, who band together in the name of sovereignty to prevent future liberalisation or competition. This was also true of small developed countries like New Zealand in the 1980s.

Negotiating a WTO investment agreement is not synonymous with surrendering national economic sovereignty to global capitalism. It's the opposite; it can preserve integrity and transparency, level the playing field, and could set acceptable rules of conduct for multinationals. The Ministerial mandate from Doha provides ample scope for provisions to be included in the eventual agreement that will respect host governments' right to regulate in the public interest and to pursue national development policies and objectives. The special development, trade and financial needs of developing and least developed countries are to be taken fully into account, and obligations and commitments are to be commensurate with these countries' individual needs and circumstances. However, it is one of the most confrontational of issues. Deeply felt views about sovereignty and commercial and political interests make it a minefield. But political appeasement to vested interests is surrender and economic death by instalment.

Transparency in government procurement

Governments, inter-governmental organisations and regional groupings around the world recognise the importance of promoting the basic principles of transparency and competition in this area. In the last two decades, many countries have set up or improved their domestic legal framework, often using the UN Commission on International Trade Law (UNCITRAL) Model Law. The World Bank and the regional development banks have not only been promoting the use of their guidelines for procurements related to projects funded by these agencies but have also been participating actively in legislative reform and institution-building efforts in a large number of developing countries. The Asia-Pacific Economic Cooperation (APEC) and the Free Trade Area of the Americas (FTAA) have been developing disciplines reflecting the core principles of transparency. The recognition of the economic importance of government procurement in trade relations also manifests itself in the recent surge of commitments related to government procurement in regional or bilateral agreements.

Governments have been aware of the importance of maintaining principles and disciplines in this area because of the substantial share of procurement in GDP. According to a recent OECD report, government procurement (excluding defence) is estimated to represent 7.6 per cent of the 1998 GDP (US$1,795 billion) for the OECD countries and 5.1 per cent (US$288 billion) for non-OECD countries – equivalent to 30 per cent of the world merchandise and commercial services exports in 1998. Other estimates made for the EC by the Commission (which include the procurement of public utilities) are rather higher, at some 14 per cent. Whatever is the correct figure, it is clear that, since more open and competitive government procurement procedures can often lead to savings of 20 per cent or more, there is very considerable benefit to be further reaped, especially in developing countries where government resources are scarce.

Government procurement is not new to the WTO. A plurilateral agreement, the Agreement on Government Procurement, in effect since 1981, contains rules on market access as well as transparency which are currently binding on twenty-seven WTO Members, with some fifteen others in the process of acceding to that Agreement. Moreover, the General Agreement on Trade in Services (GATS) incorporates provisions mandating multilateral negotiations in services.

The Doha Declaration reflects WTO Members' acceptance that there is a case for a multilateral agreement on transparency in government procurement because of the trade implications of government procurement practices, and the benefits of enhanced international cooperation in this area. The development dimension of procurement will be an important consideration in the negotiations, as they will take into account participants' development priorities, especially those of least developed country participants, and will be limited to the transparency aspects and therefore will not restrict the scope for countries to give preferences to domestic supplies and suppliers.

A WTO agreement laying down principles and disciplines in this area will underpin the domestic reforms that have been undertaken and would help guarantee the effective implementation of national legislation that has been drawn up recently in many developing countries and economies in transition. Many countries are not ready for serious negotiations. With some political parties raising their funds through 'friends' who seek government contracts, this area is a goldmine for the corrupt and is another good governance and development issue that needs to be faced.

Trade facilitation

In the area of trade facilitation, the Doha Ministerial introduced a new stage for WTO work. While the initial mandate restricted the Secretariat to undertaking 'exploratory and analytical work', the Doha declaration calls for the preparation of negotiations on this issue. The new mandate bears witness to Members' recognition that trade facilitation efforts need to be reinforced.

Increasing levels of trade liberalisation have become a worldwide reality. Successive GATT rounds significantly reduced traditional trade barriers, but serious practical obstacles in international trade remain. Traders from both the developed and the developing world have repeatedly pointed to the significant red tape that still exists in moving goods across borders. Documentation requirements frequently lack transparency, they are vastly duplicative and vary between countries.

Differing product standards, restrictive and non-transparent administrative regulations and border delays accounting for up to 20 per cent of the overall transport time hamper the integration into the global economy and threaten to undo some of the benefits of recent liberalisation efforts. Experience shows that the cost of complying with administrative procedures often exceeds the cost of duties to be paid. Recent studies indicate that the overall deadweight welfare loss caused by those inefficiencies amounts to $70 billion.

An Inter-American Bank study showed that a truck travelling through three South American countries spent 200 hours on the road, 100 hours of which were delays due to bureaucracy. It costs three times as much to move a container from some African countries to New York than from Hong Kong. APEC studies suggest facilitation gains would add 0.25 per cent to GNP. The small or new businessperson doesn't have the 'correct' contacts to push their case. The moral hazard created is dangerous to political life. Removing these hurdles is therefore a must to ensure the full realisation of negotiated trade benefits. In some countries, the richest civil servant in town is the customs officer. One ambassador told me the story in his country of a person who was offered a job in Customs and, on being told of the conditions and pay, asked, 'What? I get paid as well?'

Cutting the red tape will benefit both developing and developed countries by encouraging inward investment and trade growth. Facilitating trade means cheaper goods for producers, lower prices for consumers and a more cost-effective recovery of revenue. Experience shows that trade facilitation is not only compatible with revenue collection and enforcement, but even increases the achievement of those objectives. Simplified procedures lower trade transaction costs, improve the investment climate, foster competition and reduce corruption. They further help governments improve their administration, reduce operating costs and detect illicit transactions. Improved rules also help harness private sector support. Gains will be especially high for small and medium-sized enterprises and traders from developing countries, where difficulties created by opaque and cumbersome administrative burdens often keep them from engaging in trade at all.

Many countries have already recognised the numerous benefits of facilitating trade and are actively pursuing steps to facilitate import and export transactions. They see trade facilitation as a competitive advantage and are aware that the costs of non-participation will become increasingly burdensome in terms of lost investment and economic isolation.

As a key organisation for international trade, the WTO has a natural role in setting rules in this field. A rules-based approach will guarantee transparency and predictability for traders, ensure political commitment and steer reform in a consistent direction. A WTO framework would also ensure that regional initiatives develop in the same direction.

WTO rules are therefore necessary to secure many of the key benefits of trade facilitation. Only the WTO can assure the top-down approach required for thorough and lasting reform. At a time of economic turbulence, which has the potential to arouse protectionist sentiments, this is all the more important. If administrative and procedural obstacles risk subverting trade liberalisation, which we have worked so hard for in the WTO over the last fifty years, then the WTO should be part of any solution. Resolving this issue will be good for the taxpayer, consumer and honest businessperson, and bad for corrupt officials and politicians. This is a key development issue.

Access to medicines and TRIPS

On drugs patents and public health, a separate Ministerial Declaration at Doha stated that the WTO's Trade-Related Aspects of Intellectual Property Rights (TRIPS) Agreement 'does not and should not prevent Members from taking measures to protect public health', adding that it should be interpreted and implemented in a manner 'supportive of WTO Members' right to protect public health and, in particular, to promote access to medicines for all'.

This declaration was a shot in the arm for global efforts to address the public health problems afflicting many developing and least developed countries, especially those resulting from HIV/AIDS, tuberculosis, malaria and other epidemics.

With regard to the treatment and prevention of diseases, including HIV/AIDS and malaria, we should be supportive of the efforts for enhanced international assistance to developing countries, in particular through the adequate financing of the Global Fund. Attention can now focus on the key issues of funding and healthcare supply systems.

This aspect of the Doha Development Agenda was very much tailored to Africa's needs and it would be appropriate if – perhaps as part of the NEPAD initiative – the African countries play a key role in initiating and shaping the TRIPS Agreement and public health.

The Doha Declaration was designed to respond to the concerns that had been expressed about the possible implications of the TRIPS Agreement for access to drugs. The Declaration emphasises that the TRIPS Agreement does not, and should not, prevent Members from taking measures to protect public health. And it reaffirms the right of Members to use to the full the provisions of the TRIPS Agreement to provide flexibility for this purpose.

Second, the Declaration makes it clear that the TRIPS Agreement should be interpreted and implemented in a manner supportive of WTO Members' right to protect public health, thus providing important guidance to both individual Members and, in the event of disputes, WTO dispute settlement bodies.

Third, while maintaining Members' commitments in the TRIPS Agreement, the Declaration includes a number of important clarifications of some of the forms of flexibility available in it, in particular compulsory licensing and parallel importation. In addition, the Declaration provides for an extension until 2016 of the transition period for least developed countries in regard to the protection and enforcement of patents and undisclosed information with respect to pharmaceutical products.

The basic contradiction in this issue is that we all want investment into the next great plagues of our age, into AIDS and cancer and tuberculosis, because without investment there will be no cure. But once that cure is found, we want the product to be available immediately and as cheaply as possible. However, without protection for their patented results and a return on their investment, why should anyone invest? 'People before profits' is a good slogan. But if there is no protection of these property rights, then capital and investment will go to other areas offering better returns and less constraints.

It is my view that this issue can be settled fairly and that the international community should focus on other aspects, in particular funding, governance and healthcare supply systems, taking advantage of the momentum that has been built up behind the issue as a whole. When it comes to the relationship between health on the one hand and trade/ economic development on the other, expenditure on health not only yields benefits in its own right but is also one of the best investments in economic development. However, it is also important to recognize that economic development is important for health, because it provides the necessary resources. An open and predictable trading system is essential for economic development.

Aviation services

Although it's not one of the so-called 'new issues', an area that bears examining under the General Agreement on Trade in Services (GATS) is aviation and shipping. It is a little ironic that those sectors of the global economy that benefit most from the international trading system continue to work so hard to stay outside of this system and its rules.

Take aviation. It is difficult to find a services segment that benefits more from a smoothly functioning trading system. The sharp rise in merchandise trade over the past decade – up to $6.2 trillion in 2001 from $3.44 trillion in 1990 – has meant a greatly expanded air cargo business and indirectly has led to more air passengers seeking to buy and sell in foreign markets. The growth of services in the overall world economy is mirrored in international trade, with exports rising from $782.7 billion in 1990 to $1.44 trillion last year. Nearly a quarter of those exports were in the field of transportation. But the fact is that this important business remains largely outside the scope of WTO rules. It is time for that to change.

Inclusion of rules for international trade in services was one of the most important accomplishments achieved by trade negotiators in the last century. As the fastest growing segment of the international economy, the importance of services is beyond question. Companies in the services

sector employ more people in the industrial world than do their counter-
parts in manufacturing or agriculture. In many developing countries, the
percentage of jobs that are services related is rising rapidly.

For decades, services trade was not covered by any multilateral trade
agreements. The 1994 Uruguay Round agreement changed that when
governments agreed to establish the GATS, which has led to greater
foreign competition, a corresponding decline in monopoly power, an
increase in consumer choice and lower prices for services. This legal
framework of rules governing global trade in services has established a
predictable climate for investors, consumers and operators, facilitating
greater service sector investment, job creation and higher quality service.

Yet, although the GATS offers a wide framework and although governments have made a great many commitments to open their markets to
foreign suppliers, aviation has been exempted from the agreements. The
result has been a myriad of centrally planned arrangements, of either
a bilateral or plurilateral nature, which have ensured that competition
has been stunted, customer service eroded and the poorest countries
have been once again given short shrift.

The airline industry was once the most glamorous business in the
world. Today flying is a misery for many passengers – if they can afford
the price of ticket or convince airlines to serve their part of the world.
Many small island states in the Pacific and Caribbean have seen service
scaled back, while rates have risen to astronomical levels. When only one
airline services a small country they are at the mercy of big companies –
which are often state-owned and subsidised – when seeking to attract
tourists or export their products.

Even in the USA, the sharp contraction in the number of carriers has
resulted in some major cities finding themselves served by effectively only
one airline.

Today there are some 3,000 bilateral deals between countries which
determine the access airlines have to foreign markets. Oversight of these
agreements by the International Civil Aviation Organization has proven
a nightmare.

There are vast restrictions on foreign ownership, on route capacity and
on cabotage – the right for foreign carriers to fly between two points in the
same country and pick up passengers/cargo at that first point. The airline
industry is one in which companies need economies of scale to survive.
The drive for such economies has seen smaller carriers either swallowed
up by the big guys or forced into bankruptcy. Moreover, the barriers
to market entry for new carriers are high due to the costs associated
with launching an airline. For every EasyJet or Southwest Airlines that
succeeds, there are many more that fail.

The result is fewer carriers and deteriorating service, and frequent allegations of collusion on price setting. What we have now is an internationally inefficient, environmentally harmful system. The costs associated with being unable to collect or drop off passengers in places like Australia, the USA and Europe are astronomical. It's a disgrace that often in Latin America and Africa passengers must be routed to a neighbouring country via Miami or Paris or London.

Opening domestic markets to established foreign carriers would ensure greater service and more competition. The same principle holds for breaking up the duopolies in which international routes between two countries are served only by carriers from those two countries themselves. Foreign carriers bring experience in terms of safety, reliability and security. Yet the restrictions remain. It really is odd that perhaps the most global of industries should remain so protected domestically and even internationally. Let's hope an NGO will launch a campaign to alert the public and politicians to the environmental and developmental costs of the existing system.

Boutique markets exist and can thrive if the market is allowed to function. Why the controls and protectionism? Big countries and companies dominate and transport ministries are often captured by their airlines. In my day, the New Zealand Ministry of Transport was really the Ministry for Air New Zealand. When I was the Tourism Minister, looking at the wider picture, I found this was the greatest impediment to growth in what would become New Zealand's single biggest income earner.

Consumer tastes have changed in most areas of consumption. People view with distaste slave labour, unethical treatment of people and abuse of the environment. Nowhere is this more evident than in tourism, which is an area of enormous growth and future growth potential for developing and developed countries. Visitors no longer hunt with guns, but with cameras. Governments now realise that protecting our environment, forests, culture and history has a commercial as well as a moral value. Ecotourism is the growth market of the future and natural parks are becoming profit centres, not just worthy ideas. Sustainable development is an easy cliché for politicians to parrot and recycle, but in tourism it is brutally and obviously valid. The other WTO, the World Tourism Organization, has taken several important steps. These include:

- introduction of a Global Code of Ethics in 1999, endorsed by the UN Assembly, with a good base for fair trade tourism; and a Liberalisation Working Group
- appointment of a Special Advisor to the Secretary General on Trade in Tourism Services, with a pro-development, pro-sustainability track record

- establishment of a related strategy of Liberalisation with Human Face, profiling Developing State Needs and Sustainable Development in line with the Doha Agenda; and a 'White Paper' declaring its focus on developing state tourism, sustainability, fair market access, tourism trade support, analysis of linkages and leakages, adequate low priced air services etc.
- signature of a new accord with UNCTAD to link and accentuate work in this area. Starting with the joint launch at the World Summit on Sustainable Development (WSDD) of an 'out of the box' initiative ST–EP: (Sustainable Tourism – Eliminating Poverty) to catalyse new funding, research and practical, community-grounded action in this area; and to encourage positive public and private sector partnerships.

Success in using tourism to eliminate poverty is evident on any visit to a developing country. Handicrafts, music, culture and the experience of others' history is a powerful win–win situation for all. Both WTOs, given the mandate and leadership from capitals can advance this proposition.

Governments have opened their markets to foreign investment and the provision of services by foreign suppliers in so many other sectors, so why do such restrictions remain in aviation? There are a number of reasons for this. First is the concerns about national security, which have understandably heightened following the horrific events of 11 September. Second, there is a wish to ensure that service is provided to remote areas which may not be served by foreign carriers driven strictly by market forces. Third, there are worries that applying MFN, or non-discriminatory, treatment would be extremely difficult given the vast differences in development among WTO Member countries. Last, but by no means least, are the protectionist reasons – greater competition could mean fewer profits for domestic firms.

The national security issues are important, but WTO rules allow great scope for governments to implement whatever security measures they require. In terms of security and safety, remember that foreign airlines already call at airports and ports around the world. Increasing market access by extending the number of routes that could be served by foreigners should have no real impact on security.

In terms of providing service to remote areas, governments could subsidise carriers running such routes. The GATS has not, at present, developed rules for subsidies, but governments could certainly negotiate the inclusion of such support as part of any deal emerging in the Doha Development Agenda talks.

Addressing the MFN concerns is complicated as well, but again governments can choose to negotiate commitments in a variety of different ways, including plurilateral negotiations which would not cover all Member governments. This would create complexities elsewhere, including in the dispute settlement system, but such a system has been implemented before and no doubt will be again.

Lastly, WTO rules are flexible enough to provide temporary relief from competition to domestic manufacturing firms, and negotiations are underway to develop such safeguards for service companies as well. Temporary protection would enable industries to get back on their feet within an agreed timeframe, but is not an open-ended market share carve-out designed to protect inefficient carriers at great cost to consumers.

For too long, aviation has been less than a full participant in the global trading system – a beneficiary of expanding global trade but recalcitrant on accepting global rules that would provide greater certainty to customers and providers alike. The Doha Development Agenda provides a very good opportunity to address this. Yet there is a strange reluctance for countries to step up to the plate. National carriers are still seen as a symbol of political virility. I don't hold out too much hope for substantial progress in the Doha Agenda on this; perhaps it will have to wait for the Shanghai Round!

12   Why concluding the new Round is crucial

The best argument for concluding a new Round on time is the most obvious one: there is no better way to correct the imbalances and distortions in world trade, free it up, get products moving and help create the conditions for growth and more new jobs. It is undoubtedly true that the multilateral trading system can be greatly improved. It is also undeniable that the developing world would be much worse off without it. Many critics – and even some supporters – have spoken out about the inequities in the system, and they are right. Inequities do exist. Rich country agricultural subsidies deny millions of poor country farmers a livelihood; protective tariffs raise costs for poor consumers in rich countries, while protected farmers in the North undercut incomes for poorer producers in the South.

Which is precisely why we need to conclude a new Round of trade negotiations. There is no other way to change the rules of the WTO; no other way for developing countries to translate their interests and demands into real changes to the trading system, and no better opportunity for developing countries to use trade reform and capacity-building as tools of growth and poverty reduction.

Let us not forget what is at stake here:
- In economic terms, cutting barriers to trade in agriculture, manufacturing and services by a third would boost the world economy by US$613 billion. That's like adding an economy the size of Canada to the world economy.[1]
- Abolishing all trade barriers could boost global income by $US2.8 trillion and lift 320 million people out of poverty by 2015, according to the World Bank.[2]
- In development terms, the elimination of all tariff and non-tariff barriers could result in gains for developing countries of the order of $182 billion in the services sector, $162 billion in manufacturing and $32 billion in agriculture.[3]
- Callisto Madavo, Vice-President of the Africa Region at World Bank, states that the OECD agricultural subsidies, at approximately $300

Table 3. *UN Millennium Development Goals, 1990–2015*

1. Eradicate extreme poverty and hunger:
   - halve the proportion of people with less than one dollar a day
   - halve the proportion of people who suffer from hunger
2. Achieve universal primary education:
   - ensure that boys and girls alike complete primary schooling
3. Promote gender equality and empower women:
   - eliminate gender disparity at all levels of education
4. Reduce child mortality:
   - reduce by two-thirds the under-five mortality
5. Improve maternal health:
   - reduce the maternal mortality ratio
6. Combat HIV/AIDS, malaria and other diseases:
   - reverse the spread of HIV/AIDS
7. Ensure environmental sustainability:
   - integrate sustainable development into country policies and reverse loss of environment resources
   - halve the proportion of people without access to portable water
   - significantly improve the lives of at least 100 million slum dwellers
8. Develop a global partnership for development:
   - raise official development assistance
   - expand market access
   - encourage debt sustainability

billion annually, is equal to Africa's total GDP.[4] The Common Agricultural Policy continues to absorb around $46 billion per annum, or half the EU's budget. Kofi Annan wants $10 billion to fight AIDS per year, that's just twelve days of subsidies.

- Health and education are fundamental to any development programme. The cost of achieving the core UN Millennium Development Goal of universal primary education could be US$10 billion per year.[5] Yet developing countries would gain more than fifteen times this amount annually from further trade liberalisation.
- All of the UN Millennium Development goals – in health, education, poverty etc. – would require between $40 billion and $60 billion annually in additional aid[6] – just one-third the estimate of developing country gains from trade liberalisation.

2001 to 2002 was an outstanding period for the WTO, the most significant in our brief history. The WTO is no longer the old GATT with a few, symbolic gestures to the new global realities. It now better reflects the evolving needs of our wider membership; this is the legacy of Doha. However, our success at Doha, while important, will prove irrelevant unless we continue to get our core messages across to both governments and people worldwide; namely, that the multilateral trading system has been a huge plus to both the developing and the developed world.

The WTO's public campaign and political strategy to garner support for a new Round was difficult. Perception is reality in politics and many developing countries, stirred up by NGOs, had come to believe they had lost out during the Uruguay Round. We tried to kill the myth that developing countries were losing ground in the world trading system, and risked further impoverishment and marginalisation if a new Trade Round were to be launched. Like many myths, this one grew in authority and conviction, the further it departed from reality.

Developing countries are still being told that their share of world trade is declining; that their exports face the highest tariffs and most protected markets in the world; and that they lack the ability to influence or change a system that is inherently biased in favour of the rich and powerful. These powerful messages are repeated over and over again in the media by aggressive NGOs and, especially before Doha, by those who opposed a Round of any sort.

There is some truth in these arguments. But also a lot of myths. We owe it to developing countries – as well as to the WTO – to re-examine these in light of some facts. One fact is that developing countries are not losing out in world trade, despite what the WTO's critics say. The opposite is the case. Over the past decade, developing countries have consistently outperformed industrialised countries in terms of export growth – an average increase of almost 10 per cent a year, compared to 5 per cent for the industrialised countries. And trade among developing countries is growing more quickly than trade with the industrialised North.[7]

In 2001 alone, developing-country exports rose by 15 per cent – three times their GDP growth – the best rate of growth in five decades.[8] Even with the current global economic slowdown, developing countries are expected to show much stronger trade growth this year than the industrialised economies.

It is true these numbers demonstrate the average performance among developing countries; some are doing better, some worse. Even so, sweeping claims about poor-country 'marginalisation' distort what was really going on in world trade. For example, the forty-nine least developed countries saw the dollar value of their exports rise by 28 per cent in 2000 – some US$34 billion – the second year in a row where they exceeded the world average.[9] Bangladesh, Cambodia, Madagascar and Nepal all saw their exports soar in the 1990s – matching or even exceeding China's impressive performance.

The second claim – that rich-country markets are more closed and protected, while developing countries are being forced to open up – is also a distortion. It is certainly true that many developing-country exports continue to face significant barriers in rich country markets. Too often, the products in which developing countries are highly competitive are the very ones that confront the highest protection. These include not only agriculture exports, which often face insurmountable barriers, but also many industrial products such as textiles and clothing. These barriers – maintained by the world's richest countries against some of its poorest – are quite simply indefensible.

It is not true that industrialised countries are more closed or more protected than developing countries. The average bound tariff for the USA is just 3 per cent, for Europe it is 3.6, and for the industrialised countries as a whole it is under 4 per cent. In comparison, the average bound tariff for developing countries is over 12 per cent. And while developing countries slashed their tariffs by an impressive 20 per cent during the Uruguay Round, developed countries cut theirs by even more, almost 40 per cent.

However, that doesn't mean there aren't gross inequities. For example, taken in aggregate, US tariffs are indeed quite low. Last year, $18.6 billion in tariff revenues came from $1.32 trillion import revenues, an effective average tariff of 1.6 per cent (as opposed to the bound, or maximum, rate chargeable). But this is a little misleading. Tariffs are all but gone for two types of goods; sophisticated, high-tech manufactured goods such as semiconductors, computers and civil aircraft, and natural resources like oil, minerals and foods not grown in the USA, such as coffee and tea.

But as Edward Gresser, of the Progressive Policy Institute, points out, for many consumer products the situation is different, especially foods competing with US products and more especially clothing and shoes. These items now bring in half of all tariff revenue, even though they only account for 6.7 per cent of total merchandise imports. Also, tariffs are lowest on industrial supplies and luxury goods marketed to wealthy and middle-class families, and highest on cheaper goods that poor families buy. The EU and Japan are no better, and – as noted above – many developing countries impose even higher tariffs.

'The US tariff system... could have been maliciously designed as a burden for the poor,' says Gresser. 'And its consequences are at their worst for two sorts of people who least deserve them: single mothers in America, and workers in Cambodia, Bangladesh and other very poor Asian countries... Any tax that focuses, as tariffs do, on the necessities of life, will hit poor families harder than rich families.'[10]

Cambodia is a perfect example. Americans bought $942 million worth of goods such as T-shirts and baseball caps last year made by Cambodia's newly industrialising workforce; the buyers paid $150 million in tariffs. Thus Cambodians, with a per capita income of $260, face one of the highest effective rates in the world, at 15.8 per cent. Their industrialised neighbours in Singapore sold about $15 billion worth of semiconductors, surgical equipment and similar high-end goods. For this they were charged $96 million in tariffs, an effective rate of 0.6 per cent, about one-thirtieth the level of the Cambodians.[11]

Gresser cites another salient example: Mongolians and Norwegians both paid the USA about $23 million in tariffs last year. But Mongolia exported $143 million and Norway $5.2 billion, or forty times as much. In effect, Mongolians paid 16 cents to sell the USA a dollar's worth of sweaters and suits, while the Norwegians paid half a cent for every dollar's worth of gourmet smoked salmon, jet engine parts and North Sea crude oil. Bangladesh likewise pays more tariffs than France for one-fifteenth of the exports; Pakistanis pay four times more than Saudis for one-sixth the value of Saudi exports.[12]

Nonetheless, each year, developing countries claim a larger and larger share of the industrialised world's imports – from 15 per cent in 1990 to almost 25 per cent in 2000. Over half of Japan's manufactured imports now come from developing countries. For the USA, the share is 45 per cent and rising.[13] These trends do not reflect altruism of the industrialised countries so much as their self-interest – a realisation that imports from the developing world are key to low inflation, rising productivity and increased living standards.

But that same self-interest suggests that rich countries should be doing much more. Al From, CEO of the Democratic Leadership Council, notes: 'In 2000, tariffs stuck American consumers with an extra $20 billion on their bills – not to mention the higher prices domestic companies could get away with charging. But the tariff on clothes and shoes is the most outrageous, adding an average of almost 18 per cent to imports . . . It's estimated that in 2000 US consumers paid a whopping $21,000 in tariffs for every job on clothing and shoe production. But with proportionately more of their income needed to cover basic living costs, like clothing and shoes, poor people in effect paid the most to protect those jobs.'[14]

The principle of this short-term, self-destructive policy can be seen elsewhere – and not just in developing countries. Back in the early 1990s, for example, the USA imposed a 62.7 per cent import duty on imports from Japan of panel displays for laptops, with the consequence that Apple Computers abandoned plans to manufacture laptops in Fountain, Colorado, in favour of Cork, Ireland.[15] In the case of flat panel displays, imports were judged to be injuring an industry that didn't yet exist.

The third claim was that developing countries lack a voice and leverage in the WTO. How then to explain that so many 'development' issues were now at the top of the WTO's agenda? From being a fringe issue a generation ago, the debate over how to better integrate development priorities into the trading system has moved to the centre, and largely resulted in Doha launching a Development Round. Developing countries like India, Brazil and South Africa are in the forefront of countries defining the parameters of the WTO's future work programme – their ministers, ambassadors and officials are among the most effective and influential trade-policy practitioners in the world today.

Indeed, the important concept that a new Round of negotiations must be a 'Development Round' became universally espoused – from Kofi Annan (UN Secretary General), Jim Wolfensohn (President of the World Bank) and Horst Köhler (Managing Director of the IMF) to Clare Short (UK Minister of Development) and Lief Pedrovsky (the Swedish Trade Minister), who kept pushing European member states. Kofi Annan and Jim Wolfensohn were especially strong in supporting the launch of a new Round in the run-up both to Seattle and to Doha. All of this was evidence of a new, more assertive role for developing countries in the system, and of greater developed-country sensitivity to the needs of the poor; as South African Trade Minister Alec Erwin reiterated: 'It's about the customers of the future.'

Why? Because the WTO has emerged as one of the most important international institutions for development. Of course, we know that the requirements of developing countries in the area of WTO- or trade-related technical assistance extends well beyond what the WTO can and should provide. And we need to be absolutely clear on the limits of what the WTO can and cannot do with regard to the Doha Development Agenda. It is not for us to tell countries and companies to make T-shirts or shoes, build airports or seaports. It is true that over 10 per cent of our budget goes to the International Trade Centre, which exists to help businesses navigate through agreements and rules to get products to markets, and it does an excellent job. Other organisations can help with physical infrastructure. We can and do cooperate with other agencies. But we must stick to our core business which is trade liberalisation and rule-making. Implementing the Doha Development Agenda will bring down barriers to trade and strengthen the rules to provide more security so that people everywhere can benefit.

Developing countries already account for one-third of world trade, up from a fifth in the 1970s.[16] At current trends, their share will grow to well over half of world trade in the next twenty-five years – redrawing the economic map of the world in the process. They need stronger multilateral rules, not weaker ones; more trade liberalisation, not less. Already, a third of the cases before the WTO's dispute settlement body are brought by developing countries. They have gained significantly from trade liberalisation under the Uruguay Round and, according to one study, would realise some US$200 billion if remaining trade barriers were halved in a new Round. That is three times what the developing world receives in overseas aid; eight times what poor countries have so far been granted in debt relief.[17]

Of course, developing countries need not wait until the conclusion of the Doha Development Round to get results. South/south trade in the 1990s grew faster than world trade and now accounts for more than one-third of developing-country exports, or about US$650 billion. The World Bank reports that 70 per cent of the burden on developing countries' manufactured exports results from trade barriers of other developing countries. The quicker those walls come down, the quicker the returns to developing countries.

But all credit to the developing countries themselves, working under difficult conditions. Steps they have taken to open up their economies and encourage competition have created new incentives to find lower-cost inputs and to seek new markets abroad. Their embrace of technology has reduced communications and transportation costs, making it easier to access world markets. And their participation in unilateral, regional and multilateral liberalisation has contributed greatly to the growth of world trade and integration.

The biggest change is in attitudes. More and more, developing countries have come to see protectionism as a self-inflicted wound. It not only punishes consumers, grossly inflating the price they pay for necessities like food or clothing, but it also handicaps exporters and entrepreneurs, who can't hope to compete on world markets without access to world-priced inputs, efficient services and modern technology. Trade liberalisation is key to developing countries, not just because it opens markets, but, more importantly, because it makes their own economies stronger and more efficient. These are the customers of the future.

The Information Technology Association of America reported in 2002 that the IT market in the USA grew by one per cent in 2001, while it grew by 10 per cent in Brazil, India and China. Lifting living standards everywhere is good business for everyone. In Japan in the 1960s, consumers began acquiring refrigerators, washing machines and televisions; in the 1970s, cars, air conditioners, colour televisions and then embarked upon mass tourism. By the 1980s, eight of the ten largest banks were Japanese, and the Tokyo Stock Exchange was equal to the New York Stock Exchange. The Crown Prince pointed this out to me in a meeting in the 1980s. If they sold the Imperial Palace, he said, they could buy California. 'Why bother,' I replied, 'you own most of it now.' He thought that very amusing.

But it was a bubble which burst; now the new leadership is grappling with a 'lost decade', similar to the opportunities lost for a decade in Latin America. Prime Minister Koizumi's reforms have yet to be fully implemented. Plans to privatise the Japanese Postal Savings System, the world's biggest financial institution, with a value of $2 trillion, have encountered enormous resistance. Local postmasters are frequently the ruling Liberal Democratic Party's political eyes and ears. They know where the voters are.

But the new generation of young Japanese risk-takers and entrepreneurs are impatient and patriotic. They seek change, freedom and choice. The old iron triangle of bureaucracy, big business and old politicians is not attractive to those of the new generation I have met. They see a new Trade Round as forcing change in Japan, just as leaders from Albania to China and Russia see accession to the WTO as a way of locking in and further pursing domestic reforms.

A problem for many developing nations is that tariffs are still a major source of revenue. While the trade minister often sees and understands the opportunities of more open trade quite clearly, he is vetoed by his finance minister. I called together the OECD, the World Bank and the IMF, as well as representatives from the LDCs and the ACP (the Africa group in Geneva), to see how we could help build new, less porous and more efficient tax regimes.

I also put on the post-Doha agenda the need to put up 'restructuring resources' to try to avoid the crises that will come when special trade preferences held over from colonial times do eventually disappear. It is easy to imagine the anguish of a small Caribbean country, which relies on bananas for 90 per cent of its exports, looking at competition into its previously protected markets of products a quarter the price. Why wait for this to happen? We should be doing much more to help these countries diversify their product bases and improve their bureaucratic infrastructure now, a promise I made to some developing country ministers at Doha.

Defining and refining rules for trade – keeping the system relevant to a fast-changing world economy – will always be work-in-progress. Governments will never stop and say they have finished, that they are satisfied. The challenge is to secure balanced progress that reflects common interests; every deal is just yesterday's best compromise. We need to ensure that governments feel committed, not coerced. They have to see justice in the WTO agenda and national advantage in pursuing it.

But they must also be reminded of the achievements. More has been done to address poverty in these last fifty years than in the previous 500. Since 1960, child death rates have been halved in developing countries; malnutrition rates have declined by a third; access to safe water has improved dramatically, even if there are still gaping areas of need and concern.[18] While the current UN Millennium Declaration targets show that there is still a long way to go, and we need to keep in mind that trade is just one contributor to the progress that has been secured, we should not lose sight of the important role the multilateral trading system has played.

Nonetheless, what we actually achieved at Doha was a significant breakthrough.

Agriculture   In agriculture, developing countries stand to gain substantial commercial benefits under the negotiating mandate. Currently, according to Oxfam International, rich countries pay out nearly $1 billion a day to their farmers in agricultural subsidies.[19] Negotiations will open markets, and reduce, 'with a view to phasing out, all forms of export subsidies' and trade-distorting domestic farm support, while taking into account non-trade and development concerns, including through appropriate special and differential treatment in favour of developing countries (see Chapter 3).

Services   In services, liberalisation could mean gains of between 1.6 per cent of GDP (for India) to 4.2 per cent of GDP (for Thailand) if tariff equivalents of protection were cut by one-third in all countries, according to the World Bank.[20] Telecommunications, finance, transport and business services have many links to the rest of the economy and raise the productivity of many sectors. Under the Doha Development Agenda, special priority will be given to LDCs, and sufficient flexibility to developing countries. Negotiations will liberalize the entry of foreign services in as many domestic sectors as governments choose and make it easier to employ foreign workers on temporary contracts.

Implementation   In the preparations for Doha, implementation-related issues were a high priority for many developing countries. About half of the original ninety implementation issues raised were addressed by a separate Declaration adopted at Doha. Of particular note is the decision on the extension of exemptions for certain small developing countries, which allows a longer phase-out period for certain types of subsidies. The remaining issues will be addressed under the relevant negotiating mandates of the new work programme or in the standing WTO bodies on a priority basis. We couldn't agree to one single 'implementation' issue before and at Seattle.

Industrial goods   Market access for industrial goods is another immediate priority for developing countries. The negotiating mandate focuses on reducing or eliminating tariff peaks and escalation, in particular on products of export interest to developing countries, as well as on non-tariff barriers. Here too, the mandate states that 'the negotiations shall take fully into account the special needs and interests of developing and least-developed country participants'. Moreover, ministers agreed to capacity-building measures to assist least developed countries, and committed themselves to 'the objective of duty-free, quota-free market access for products originating from LDCs'. Three-quarters of the benefit of cuts to industrial tariffs will now go to developing countries.

But there is much to do to ensure that the next, Fifth Ministerial Conference, set down for Mexico in September 2003 is a success, and that the new Trade Round of negotiations is concluded within the tight three-year timeframe agreed by ministers in Doha – January 2005. The groundwork needed to make this possible has already been put in place.

In terms of the roadmap ahead I set a number of objectives, which I believe will facilitate Members' concluding their work on the Doha Development Agenda by the deadline. Key objectives include:

Maintaining transparency   The Doha success was built on a process that was transparent and inclusive. WTO Members share a collective responsibility to ensure that these principles are carried on and that all Members, large and small, are given every assistance to participate in our negotiations.

Reorganization   I reorganised the WTO Secretariat to reflect Doha's work priorities. New resources have also been directed towards mandated negotiations and work programmes, technical cooperation and capacity-building, accessions, coherence and outreach. Efficiency gains and cost savings were introduced. This reorganization has been supported by a budget for 2002 of 143 million Swiss francs, representing an increase of 6.75 per cent over 2001. No other institution has been so well supported by donors, reflecting the credibility we have won through our reforms and auditing and evaluation systems, which have ensured effective use of resources.

Technical assistance and capacity-building   For the first time, developing countries put conditionality on rich countries: unless capacity-building matches the ambitions of the Doha Agenda, especially in the so-called 'new areas', the momentum could be lost at the Mexico Ministerial. This must not happen. The Doha Development Agenda recognises that technical assistance and capacity-building are essential to help developing and least developed countries to implement WTO rules and obligations, to prepare for effective participation in the work of the WTO, and thus to benefit from the open, rules-based multilateral trading system. Members delivered on their promises through specially targeted extra-budgetary resources, such as the Doha Development Agenda Global Trust Fund; a proposed core budget of approximately US$9 million to provide secure and predictable resources to build capacity was more than doubled at a pledging conference.

Training   As well as doubling our in-house training capacity – effectively to its physical limits – we launched an innovative new programme. We know that a balanced, successful and timely outcome of the current round of WTO trade negotiations will depend on the active participation of all 144 of our WTO Member governments. One of the key success stories of the WTO has been the intensive twelve-week training courses that we run in Geneva for government officials. Building on cooperative arrangements with local universities in developing countries, we plan courses initially at Nairobi, Kenya, for English-speaking African countries, and in Casablanca, Morocco, for French-speaking African countries. The product, once proven, can quickly and cost-effectively move to other regions. Developing world ministers must have access to trained negotiators who understand the technical issues involved in the system, otherwise it is perfectly logical for them to say no or seek more time. One of my DDGs bet me we wouldn't get the pilot launched in 2002. Some staff opposed the idea, and bluntly undermined the concept. We succeeded; though not without resistance within and outside the WTO. World Bank Managing Director Jim Wolfensohn saved the day here, with resources just when they were urgently needed. I hope my successor can follow through on this initiative because it is a good product that can be franchised out to other regions. A number of other countries and institutions have already expressed interest.

Coherence   There is a multiplicity of international agencies and donor government instruments available for trade-related technical assistance and capacity-building. We had little enough coherence within the WTO, let alone with other agencies. Policies to ensure better coordination and to establish auditing and evaluation systems were put in place to avoid wasting donor resources and help us build donor credibility. The Secretariat provides a useful 'clearing-house' for WTO-related technical assistance, ensuring that both donors and recipients are promptly apprised of ongoing efforts to meet the requirements set out in the Doha Development Agenda.

Integrated Framework   The Integrated Framework, launched in 1996 to promote inter-agency coherence in LDCs, was essentially moribund, generating little more than travel points for officials. Ministers' instructions were ignored and belittled. Following a major inter-agency meeting I pushed for in early 2002, a pilot scheme was launched in Cambodia, Madagascar and Mauritania to reinvigorate the Integrated Framework. The pilot scheme is now being extended to eleven other countries. At that meeting, agency representatives recognised the urgency in enhancing linkages and improving coherence between the trade and development communities. They underscored the position that improved coherence was necessary to address the complex trade development concerns of the LDCs and the non-LDC low income economies.

Members' mandate   Distinct from WTO Secretariat actions are those which are rightfully within the prerogative of our Members. WTO is first and foremost a 'member-driven' organisation. We made a good start on the WTO's Doha Development Agenda. We had a new budget, a venue, a negotiating structure, chairpeople of negotiating committees and a formal plan for Members – a road map for ministers – in place within four months of the Doha launch, something the media suggested was not possible.

Trade Negotiations Committee (TNC)   The negotiating structure for the Doha Round is solidly in place, many months ahead of the timeframe it took us to get the Uruguay Round negotiating infrastructure set up. WTO Member governments assembled for the first meeting of the Trade Negotiations Committee (TNC) in January 2002, reaching broad agreement on the structure of the negotiations launched at Doha. They elected the WTO DG *ex officio* to chair the TNC. They also outlined the guidelines and procedures for the negotiations. In February 2002, Members agreed on the chairpersons of the various negotiating committees under the TNC. As agreed, the seven negotiating bodies – on agriculture, services, non-agricultural market access, rules, trade and environment, geographical indications for wines and spirits under the agreement on Trade-Related Intellectual Property and reform of the Dispute Settlement Understanding (DSU) – are now in place. Negotiations on agriculture, services, environment, TRIPS and the DSU reform are being conducted in Special Sessions of the regular committees

and councils where these issues are discussed. New negotiating groups have been created for negotiations in non-agricultural market access and rules. The TNC and all other negotiating bodies and groups will operate under the authority of the General Council, as mandated by ministers in Doha.

As the EU's Pascal Lamy noted: 'WTO Members in Geneva have taken the first, important, indeed necessary step toward implementing the negotiating mandate agreed in Doha. These decisions mean the WTO is now able to start the actual work of the negotiations.'[21]

The transition to the next DG, Dr Supachai, in September 2002, was handled professionally. I wanted a seamless transition and initiated regular briefings for him in 2002. I didn't want him or the system to suffer what I and the system went through in 1999. I wish him well. He's had three years to prepare himself and will inherit a stronger, more focused, better funded, more accountable WTO with a Development Agenda broad enough to accommodate the ambition of the membership and wide enough to get the trade-offs necessary for political success. The roadmap is there, the ministerial oversight programmes are in place. Success is never guaranteed, but, given strong leadership, the Round can conclude on time.

Storm clouds ahead

The path to Doha was a rocky one. Although I hope that concluding the Round will be a smoother process, I do not underestimate the difficulties of what remains to be resolved; that's why we never stopped for breath after Doha, pushing ahead with technical assistance, capacity-building and training, and locking down the details of the TNC as quickly as possible.

However, by mid-2002, there were already increasing signs of protectionism that may yet poison the new Round, triggered by the US decision to impose tariffs on its steel industry, which in turn set off a barrage of complaints from other steel-producing countries worldwide. Furthermore, the Farm Security and Rural Investment Act of 2002, also known as the US Farm Bill, was widely perceived globally as politically inspired and as undermining US credibility as a proponent of free trade. There were, of course, some observers who felt that the USA was 'crazy like a fox'; upping the ante, to give itself some negotiating points further down the road.

My concern over this was such that, unusually, I agreed to help draft and issue a joint statement with the World Bank's Jim Wolfensohn and IMF's Horst Kohler condemning protectionism in all forms.

Released during the May 2002 OECD ministers' meeting in Paris, the statement declared: 'Any increase in protectionism by any country is damaging. Such actions will hurt growth prospects where fostering growth is most essential. And they are sending the wrong signal, threatening to undermine the ability of governments everywhere to build support for market-oriented reforms. How can leaders in developing countries or in any capital argue for more open economies if leadership in this area is not forthcoming from wealthy nations? We remain confident that the commitments of Doha and Monterrey will carry us towards a world trading system that empowers the poor. But we must move beyond rhetoric, firmly resist protectionism, whatever its form or justification, and promote policies that foster growth and prosperity.'[22]

In terms of the Geneva process, I enjoined ministers that we cannot lose any further time on procedure, which was threatening in 2002 to bog down the negotiations. I stressed that participants needed to be much more forthcoming about their priorities. This is urgent so the negotiations can deepen and proceed on a basis of realism. As we moved towards the Mexico Ministerial, I emphasised that we need to see concrete proposals coming forward – otherwise we will be shadow-boxing until it is too late.

But of course Geneva does not operate in a vacuum. Nor can the WTO and its ambassadors insulate themselves from the wider global environment. Which is why I have pushed, at every possible opportunity, for the engagement of ministers in capitals.

There are some very black storm clouds on the economic horizon and hanging over the multilateral trading system – economic trends, the proliferation of disputes, the increasing domestic pressures for a return to protectionist measures. We need leadership and courage from ministers to improve the environment. We need their visible commitment to the negotiations and we need it now. We also need reassurance from the major players that they will ensure that the conflicts currently before them will not be allowed to undermine work towards a successful Round.

What are the necessary elements and dynamics that will help bring about a successful Round? At the May OECD, I told ministers: 'I encourage you to keep the blowtorch on your officials. This is the time to be reassessing your priorities and positions. This is the time to identify areas of flexibility. This is the time to be generating up and sending to Geneva your concrete negotiating proposals.'

But, in my view, the major challenge will be to keep all the players on board, all of the time. A Round will not succeed if it does not carry the support of the major traders – and I am thinking here particularly of the USA and the EU. Still, despite the negative climate in much of 2002, I think that the overall signs are encouraging. Both EU Commissioner Lamy and

USTR Zoellick played a central and proactive role in getting the negotiations off the ground and will continue their unique role. We need their coherent and credible leadership to conclude the round. The US government in July 2002 achieved a break-though in getting Trade Promotion Authority, the new fast-track legislation, through the Congress. President Bush and Zoellick put their reputations on the line over this, squeezing it through the US Congress by just one vote. It was a high-risk political strategy. Presidential prestige was on the line and President Bush showed great leadership there, succeeding where President Clinton had failed. This reflects the serious US commitment to these negotiations.

The May 2002 Asia-Pacific Economic Cooperation (APEC) forum, meeting in Puerto Vallarta, Mexico, saw APEC trade ministers personally commit to ensuring the completion of new global trade talks by the January 2005 deadline and reaffirm both their pledge to reject the use of protectionism and their commitment to abide by multilateral rules. They also agreed that the new round offered the best opportunity to address protectionism on a global basis.

Also encouraging were EU Agriculture Commissioner Franz Fischer's proposals, announced in July 2002, to reform the EU's Common Agriculture Policy (CAP), which, as noted above, swallows around $46 billion per annum, or half the EU's budget. European subsidies make food prices 44 per cent higher that they should be, according to OECD estimates. About 49 per cent of the EU's total budget goes to support farmers. And in most EU countries, and the USA, between 70 and 80 per cent of all subsidies go to the richest 20 per cent of their farmers. In *Open World*, Philippe Legrain quotes Patrick Messerlin's estimate that the cost of European protectionism comes to 7 per cent EU GDP – as much as Spain's annual economic output. 'Support for the farming industry costs an average family of four over $1,000 a year in higher taxes and prices – and doesn't even guarantee us safe food.'[23]

The EU is at last making changes. The enlargement to encompass Poland will blow out the budget. There are more farmers in Poland than the rest of Europe put together. The collectivised farming that was imposed in other parts of Eastern and Central Europe makes it easier to return from large inefficient state farms to viable farming units. Not so in Poland, where peasant farmers are still desperately trying to eke out a living on a few acres. The introduction of the common euro and the limits on deficit spending restrict governments from election-year payouts to farming sectors. The time is ripe for major reforms. These internal developments fold neatly into the Doha Agenda.

The latest proposals take on board, for the first time, the principle of supporting *farmers*, not *farming*, which, as a minister for trade from an agricultural country, I and others were putting to the Europeans nearly twenty years ago. But Europe and others in a similar situation can only make substantial reforms in the wider framework of trade-offs, which is where the WTO and the Doha Agenda comes in. That's another reason I am optimistic that the Round will succeed.

While the Round will undoubtedly help developing countries, it is also good for ordinary workers in the rich world. British Secretary of State for Trade and Industry Patricia Hewitt told Parliament before Doha that a successful Round would boost the income of the average household in the UK by £10 a week. When was the last time the unions secured a £10 a week pay increase for workers, after tax? Europeans pay over 40 per cent more for their food than they need to. Almost half the taxes they send to Brussels goes to make their food dearer. Rich countries will be big winners, enjoying the benefits of allowing them to cut taxes and redirecting resources into more efficient areas of the economy.

Equally, there is a need to keep developing-country Members engaged and actively participating. We have learned a lot since Seattle – that our processes need to be inclusive and that, with a much broader and more technically complex mandate, developing countries need assistance to understand the subjects and participate actively in negotiations. Provisions for technical assistance to developing countries run through virtually every section of the Doha Ministerial Declaration and they have been followed through by Members who have made substantial financial pledges for training and technical assistance activities. The WTO Secretariat is also upgrading its efforts to coordinate with other agencies whose job it is to build up the infrastructure and supply-side capacity of developing countries, so helping them reap the benefits of open markets.

Since Doha, we have established The Doha Development Fund to finance capacity-building, and funding is double what we anticipated: we have more than doubled our training facilities; set up two satellite courses with universities in Africa; established the negotiating structures and selected chairpersons; and we have confirmed Mexico as host to the fifth Ministerial Conference. Our deadlines are being met; the roadmap to success is in place. Cynics and critics said this would take years because that had been the historical experience. They were wrong. But observers should note that this is not a three-year negotiation. We've actually been negotiating for five years already; the 'new' issues aren't new at all. There is no reason not be on schedule in 2005.

At my last meeting of the TNC, I told ambassadors, only half-jokingly, that the next time they saw me I might be leading my own NGO demonstration outside the Mexico Ministerial with a large sign reading: 'Justice now, Finish the Round.'

A final – but crucial – element in the roadmap is getting out the right message to mobilise public support. I address in Chapter 13 the importance of engaging with wider civil society. We are now operating in a vastly different world and the case for free trade is far from won. Ministers and officials need to continue making the case for the multilateral trading system. Civil society needs to be sensitised to the potential benefits of a successful Round. We need particularly to show the developing world what is in this Round for them. Both governments and the business community can do a lot more to defend their system. The multilateral trading system and the system of rules it represents is a key mechanism for combating poverty, raising living standards and improving the human condition. It is not the only factor; but it is a major one and, more importantly, it is within our grasp.

Part Three

Citizens, corporates and a new deal for global governance

13   Engaging civil society

The WTO is one of the biggest crimes done against humanity in the name of corporate interests and super transnational profiteers. Global Exchange, 2001

I mean of course the industrial and financial transnational corporations for which the Bank, the Fund, the WTO, the OECD, etc. are merely fronts and servants (of globalisation).   Focus on the Global South/Walden Bello, 2000

Trade is the natural enemy of all violent passions. It loves moderation, delights in compromise and is most careful to avoid anger, making men inclined to liberty, but disinclined to revolution.   Alexis de Tocqueville

The WTO has been fiercely attacked by NGOs, most notoriously and successfully at its Seattle Ministerial Conference in 1999. It's not alone: all major political summits risk coming under siege by a variety of protestors sheltering under the umbrella of the anti-globalisation movement. Leaders now meet behind fortifications, like medieval kings.

Engagement by civil society in the political process is an essential element in creating and sustaining healthy participatory democracies. From the first democracy in Greece, philosophers promoted an engaged citizenry as a safeguard against tyrants. Political thinkers of all colours, including Hobbes and Kant, extolled its virtues. And of course both Marxists and fascists feared and sneered at its bourgeois tendencies.

This year, 2002, over 100 million Europeans went to the polls. Where were the extreme protestors and their agendas? Why didn't they set out their ideas directly in the democratic marketplace? Because they would not get public support. Many even disdain the parliamentary system, saying it is unrepresentative and corrupt, claiming that only they maintain the pure and uncontaminated truth. These extremists, who lay claim to follow the heritage of Gandhi and Martin Luther King, are really the descendants of strictly reactionary and even more utopian early fascists and Marxists. The last time the far left and far right held hands in the streets of Europe was to fight against decadent democracies in the 1930s.

De Tocqueville wrote frequently of his democratic American experience and the virtues of associations, clubs, groups and civil engagement. Civil society activists have played a key role in shaping the much improved and more free world in which we now live.

Our challenge is to bring wider civil society – not just NGOs, but parliamentarians, political internationals, trade unions, business representatives and individuals – into a productive dialogue on how the multilateral system can manage the impact of globalisation, not a shouting match across barbed wire barricades, dominated by unaccountable interest groups, competing for the most extreme headline.

Globalisation increases NGOs' reach

There is nothing new about such groups; many have changed the world for the better. The first transnational NGO was arguably the Anti-Slavery Society of 1839. An early and successful NGO was the International Committee of the Red Cross, which was established in 1864 by Henri Dunant, after his brutal experiences in the Battle of Solferino. NGOs have since exploded from about 32 in 1874 to 1,083 in 1914, to 13,000 in the 1990s, to an estimated 30,000 or more today, some of which – such as The World-Wide Fund for Nature – have larger budgets than some inter-governmental organisations (IGOs). The difference, obviously, is that globalisation itself has greatly increased the ability of NGOs to get their message across to the public.

Jagdish Bhagwati has observed that free trade is the target of a growing anti-capitalist and anti-globalisation agitation among the young that derives from what he calls 'the tyranny of the missing alternative'. Bhagwati notes, in *Free Trade Today:* 'The collapse of communism, the ideological system that rivalled capitalism, and the rise of Fukuyama-led triumphalism about markets and capitalists, have created an intolerable void among the idealist young whose social conscience is attuned to the conviction that capitalism is a source of injustice... The untutored conviction that markets and capitalism are to be equated with social injustice has fuelled the frustration that spills over into the street theatre stage against free trade and its principal institution, the World Trade Organization.'[1]

Most great and good social and political change has resulted from the mobilisation of public opinion; from the anti-slavery campaign to the anti-apartheid movement. However, street protest has also brought monsters to power, from Stalinist Russia to Nazi Germany. And we need to remain on guard against this extremist tendency. Molotov cocktail-throwers at the Prague meeting of the World Bank and the IMF insulted Czech President Vaclav Havel, a strong supporter of free trade, seemingly ignorant of the fact that he is a man of peace, poetry and democratic principles, who endured imprisonment for his ideals. He fought for their right to insult him, and he still does. In Seattle, protesters pushed the South African Trade Minister, Alec Erwin, a Marxist trade unionist who had been imprisoned for anti-apartheid campaigning, who now fights for free trade in agriculture, because he knows that this is the quickest way to get more jobs and revenues for his people.

Gerry Loughran, reporting on a May Day rally in London, observed: 'The protesters forced traffic to divert and hung posters from lamp-posts; "Blair, we won't go away," "Queen Mum Drop Dead" and "Reinvent Democracy"; then they daubed red paint over the statue of Sir Winston Churchill, Britain's honoured prime minister, and spattered graffiti on the Cenotaph in Whitehall, the monument which honours the dead of two world wars. The May Day action was the climax of a four-day protest against global capitalism which involved a self-styled "disorganisation" known as Reclaim the Streets, along with anarchists, ban-the-bombers, hippies, environmentalists, Kurds, Maoists, socialists and "situationists". One group sported red headbands with a redesigned Communist emblem – hammer and sickle with the addition of a machinegun'.[2]

But they can also be creative and funny. The Yes Men, a loose alliance of WTO opponents, in May 2002 succeeded in hoaxing a number of people with a false press release announcing the WTO's restructuring into the Trade Regulation Organization. They fooled not only Australia's Certified Public Accountants group, but a Canadian MP who was moved to raise the matter in his parliament.

This group passes my humour test, a necessary element in our rules of engagement. Those who cannot laugh at themselves and the occasional absurdity of the human condition and our contradictions, who think they alone have the answer, are usually humourless. Humour and irony are preconditions of democracy, open minds and open societies. It is the solemn duty of citizens to make fun of and question their leaders. We all know of the melancholy humour of Abraham Lincoln, the inspired, practised, 'spontaneous' wit of Winston Churchill. There aren't any compilations of Stalin, Hitler or Pol Pot's humorous asides, although underground black humour is a consistent, splendid subversive feature of those opposed to totalitarianism. Sometimes it's all the sane have to fight with.

Of course, humour doesn't always travel. A senior Chinese official, who in an earlier life was a Red Guard in Mao's destructive back-to-Marxist basics, which cost millions of lives, and now fights to engage his country fully in the world trading system, perplexed, once asked me: 'What did the signs at the demonstration mean which read "We are Wombles" or "Free Wimbledon!"?'

Figure 18. Powerful imagery: none of this is without some humour. I just wish I had the power I was always accused of having. (Photograph by Shaun Best. Copyright Reuters 2000.)

What has changed?

So who are these people, what do they stand for, and why is this happening?

The greatest change since my days as a trade minister in the 1980s is the explosion of NGOs, the huge increase in information flows and the intensification of interest in trade matters. For many ministers, negotiations at home with their congresses, their parliaments and their coalition partners are sometimes more complex and difficult than anything negotiated at Geneva or at Ministerials. Trade is the only policy area where the European Commission has total authority to negotiate, after consulting Member states; hopefully, this will soon be extended to European aviation policy. The EU Trade Commissioner has one of the toughest jobs in Europe. It doesn't help negotiations when politicians demonise the WTO, blaming it for all its woes, on issues unrelated to any agreement. That boxes officials into positions and makes future deals difficult. In one country where the government, or elements of it, have demonised the WTO, I was burnt in effigy in thirty cities simultaneously, which I considered quite an honour.

At least trade is no longer boring. In New Zealand, we couldn't get the public interested in the Uruguay Round, and the legislation passed quickly at night. By contrast, the New Zealand Parliament recently passed legislation to ratify a Singapore/New Zealand free-trade agreement, which represented about half a per cent of nothing. All hell broke loose with petitions, protests, public hearings and coalition partners threatening to quit and collapse the government.

The first Internet-fuelled, new age, global protest mobilisation was against the ill-fated OECD Multilateral Agreement on Investment (MAI) in 1998. The MAI's provisions were so innocuous that New Zealand, like many other countries, would not have had to change any of its existing legislation to comply. But by the time the anti-MAI campaign bit, people were convinced it was a global plot to privatise schools and hospitals, sell national parks and museums, and destroy the Treaty of Waitangi protections for indigenous Maori. A similar reaction was orchestrated worldwide, killing the initiative and forcing governments into a humiliating climb-down. It was an important lesson for us all. While the MAI campaign exploited anti-foreign-investment and anti-free-trade sentiment, it was, some observers argue, also an environmentalist campaign to secure within MAI rights to force foreign investors to implement tougher environmental polices than domestic ones. What the protestors couldn't achieve within their own domestic political system, they hoped to accomplish by using international treaties to force governments to implement the standards they sought.

The anti-globalisation movement is a unique umbrella, embracing a welter of often contradictory fellow-travellers. The Global Civil Society Year Book contains an interesting chapter by Helmut Anheier, Marlies Glasins and Mary Kaldor, which includes Table 4, breaking down civil society groups and positions.[3] I put myself into two rows of this table: as a supporter and as a reformer.

Table 4. *Typology of civil society group positions on globalisation*

	Types of actors	Position on globalisation	Position on plant biotechnology	Position on global finance	Position on humanitarian intervention
Supporters	Transnational business and their allies	Favour global capitalism and the spread of a global rule of law	Favour plant biotechnology developed by corporations, no restrictions necessary	Favour deregulation, free trade and free capital flows	Favour 'just wars' for human rights
Rejectionists	Anti-capitalist social movements; authoritarian states; nationalist and fundamentalist movements	Left oppose global capitalism; right and left want to preserve national sovereignty	Believe plant biotechnology is 'wrong' and 'dangerous' and should be abolished	Favour national protection of markets and control of capital flows. Radical rejectionists want overthrow of capitalism	Oppose all forms of armed intervention in other states. Intervention is imperialism or 'not our business'
Reformists	Most IGOs; many in international institutions; many social movements and networks	Aim to 'civilise' globalisation	Do not oppose technology as such, but call for labelling information and public participation in risk assessment; sharing of benefits	Want more social justice and stability. Favour reform of international economic institutions as well as specific proposals like debt relief or Tobin tax	Favour civil society intervention and international policing to enforce human rights
Alternatives	Grass roots groups; social movements; submerged networks	Want to opt out of globalisation	Want to live own lifestyle rejecting conventional agriculture and seeking isolation from GM food crops	Pursue an anti-corporate lifestyle, facilitate colourful protest, try to establish local alternative economies	Favour civil society intervention in conflicts but oppose use of military force

Source: Anheier, Glasius and Kaldov, 2001.

Figure 19. Protestors outside WTO headquarters in Geneva: many of these single-issue groups are more interested in publicity stunts to raise funds and enlist new members, than in serious dialogue. This is changing, but NGOs should have a voice, not a vote in the process. (Photograph by STR. Copyright Reuters 1999.)

The reality is that a new kind of international politics is emerging, its agenda set by organised, media-savvy groups of NGOs, activists and protestors, not just by politicians and bureaucrats. The drama is no longer played out only in meeting rooms and conference halls, but on the streets. And, in particular, power increasingly grows out of the zoom lens of a television camera. As Robert Conquest observed, on the breakup of the Soviet Union, 'The newer technologies had proved inimical to the system. The foreign radios broke the state's monopoly of news and opinion and showed many Russians that the official truths were untenable... When *glasnost* hit Russia's own television, the effect was stunning. The televised debates in the Supreme Soviet, with Andrei Sakharov standing up to Mikhail Gorbachev and speaking for democracy, resulted in factories everywhere closing down, with workers clustered round the sets.'[4]

It is obvious that made-for-television marches – still less mindless riots – are no substitute for rational political discourse. It is also a sad truth that as media attention inevitably subsides – in Somalia, on debt relief, or in Kosovo – so often does the public's interest. Moral outrage sometimes lasts only as long as the camera lingers. The demonstrators won the media battle at the G8 Summit in Genoa in 2001. However, it was a hollow victory; images of riot police and burning buildings dominated the evening news – not the leaders' progress on poverty, AIDS or development and trade. But the demonstrations and the cameras are not going to go away, nor should they. At a time when apathy and indifference characterises too many national elections in the democratic west, globalisation is emerging as the new flash point of popular politics.

Fuelling much of this NGO anger are perceptions of rich country, multinational dominance. When we have individuals who are worth more than countries, business is no longer as usual. In previous times, the British political classes contracted out licences to private companies like the East India Company, to conduct the imperial business and run armies, sanctified and blessed by Downing Street, at a pace suited to sailing vessel passages and protected by the might of the Royal Navy.

Times have changed. The information age is more transparent and immediate. Global brands may seem all-powerful, but brands are ultimately merely reputations, and the more global they are, the more highly vulnerable to attack. Many NGOs seem to feel that corporates are totally motivated by maximising returns to shareholders. And some NGOs have succeeded in many cases in hijacking the agenda. There have been some huge corporate PR disasters. Look at Monsanto's problems with genetically modified crops, or the pharmaceutical industries' astonishing decision to sue Nelson Mandela over HIV/AIDS on copyrights. Which marketing genius decided to sue the most beloved man on the planet?

Why do so few companies publicly support the WTO? Because they don't want to suffer the McDonalds syndrome and become symbolic targets, even though the International Labour Organization reports that it is the multinationals who offer better working conditions and lead the way for domestic manufacturers in areas such as footwear and apparel. The much-attacked Nike pays its workers in Vietnam five times the minimum wage, and in Indonesia three times the minimum wage.[5] In Vietnam, this is causing problems, as doctors leave hospitals and professors leave universities to work on the factory floor.

Our international organisations need greater transparency

So how should we respond to civil society's demand for greater engagement in the overwhelming issues of the day? I believe we need to welcome and open up the globalisation debate, not try to resist it. Organisations like the UN, the ILO, the WTO, the IMF and the World Bank do important work. And the decisions they take increasingly affect the lives of ordinary men and women. It is good that people want more information

and control, greater accountability and greater ownership. International organisations should welcome this scrutiny. It makes them stronger, less distant, more legitimate. Would there be as much progress on debt relief for poor countries were it not for the tireless campaigning of Jubilee 2000 and Bono? Would global warming be as high on the G8 agenda without environmentalists agitating, demonstrating and lobbying for reform?

At the WTO, we responded during my three-year tenure by greatly increasing our transparency and improving the quality of our dialogue with responsible members of civil society. Reinforcing those efforts, in late April/early May 2002, the WTO held a wide-ranging public symposium on the *Doha Development Agenda and Beyond*, in which, for the first time, representatives from civil society organised sessions on topics of their own choice. More than 600 participants took part in more than twenty different presentations and work sessions organised over two and a half days. This followed up on a WTO symposium on *Issues Confronting the World Trading System*, held in July 2001, which also attracted some 500 participants, who addressed some of the most contentious WTO issues.

Indeed, the Secretariat has been briefing registered NGOs after *all* major WTO meetings since the beginning of 2001. To improve transparency and allow wider participation, the briefing schedules are published on the website, which now averages some 19 million hits per month, representing some 600,000 regular users.

In fact, the Secretariat has run regular briefings for NGOs, as well as organizing workshops and symposia, since 1996, under a mandate from Members that was reaffirmed at Doha. But the WTO greatly accelerated its activities over the past three years. We introduced NGO lunch presentations to all Members and Observers, and participation by NGOs in technical seminars. We also now run familiarisation courses for those who want to do more than protest.

The WTO's *NGO Bulletin*, issued electronically since April 2000, provides a concise overview of these activities. Contrary to popular opinion, over 95 per cent of WTO documents are derestricted and downloadable from the website and the number is increasing. The WTO also has strong participation by NGOs who register at our Ministerial Conferences.

We are sometimes our own worst enemy. In June 2002, Member governments took a further step towards making the WTO more accountable, thanks to the drive of 2002 WTO General Council Chairman Sergio Marchi. After four years of often arduous negotiations, governments have agreed on new procedures which will accelerate the derestriction of official WTO documents. To this point, we hadn't done too badly. In 2001, for example, 65 per cent of the more than 21,000 WTO documents produced were available to the public – and placed on the official WTO website immediately after they were issued. Eventually, the rest of these documents become publicly available.

Now, thanks to the efforts of Member governments, documents which could include submissions by Member governments, Secretariat documents, minutes of meetings, negotiating documents pertaining to opening markets for goods and services and documents related to accessions will be publicly available far sooner than in the past. Governments have agreed to measures that will reduce the period of restriction on the remaining documents to an average of six to twelve weeks from the previous average of eight to nine months.

But we should demand equal transparency from our critics if they wish to formally participate. I've been a member of most good causes over the years. I've donated money and joined Greenpeace, Amnesty International, Beauty Without Cruelty and others. But I've never been invited to a meeting, asked my views or asked to vote on any of their positions. Recently I read an Amnesty statement, which attempted to justify the absurd situation where the USA was replaced on the Board of the Human Rights Commission, by citing the fact that the USA had laid landmines in Korea. Some of those countries re-elected dealt in body parts, and tortured dissidents. We should welcome the spotlight of scrutiny by informed NGOs. But there is no moral equivalence in these issues. These principles are black and white, not grey. There is such a thing as right and wrong.

Beware of intolerance

We should not tolerate intolerance. There is a world of difference between marching on parliaments, and shutting parliaments down. In Genoa, as elsewhere, rioters crossed that line. The masked stone-throwers who call for more transparency, the anti-globalisation protestors who claim to speak for 'the people' even as they attempt to sabotage international meetings, are not the new foot-soldiers for democracy. They are its antithesis. The new international order they say they want looks suspiciously like a much older disorder – intolerant, illiberal, reactionary.

The wilder elements of the NGO world seem more concerned with being fashionably antagonistic than seriously analytical; icon-worship and simplistic slogans too often prevail. Some examples: a recent fashion spread for the German magazine *Tussi-Deluxe*, recreated famous news photographs of the Marxist terrorist Baader-Meinhoff Gang, or Red Army Faction (RAF), estimated to have killed some 200 people from 1967 until formally claiming to have disbanded in 1998; also in Vogue, Baader T-shirts and other fashion accessories. Reported the *Financial*

Times: 'Andes Veiel, a documentary-maker, says: "For younger people, living in this period of globalisation when the individual is powerless, the RAF are the true heroes – they actually succeeded in achieving something".'[6]

There's nothing new here: Harold Laski, the UK Labour Party Chairman, praised Stalin's prisons as humane, while at the height of the Georgian's reign of terror, Fabian intellectuals Sidney and Beatrice Webb published a 1,000-page book in praise of the new Moscow man.

That the Soviet Union was a seductive model of development for recently liberated and new nations was understandable. It had, in a generation, catapulted itself from feudal society to the space age. One of the West's great mistakes of the twentieth century was to see communism behind almost every nationalistic instinct. While Beijing and Moscow artfully aligned themselves with liberation movements, the West was largely perceived to be fighting to hold on to imperial privileges, even though democratic socialist thinking, from Bevan to F. D. Roosevelt, argued for national independence, within a democratic, mixed economy framework.

Still, liberation chic meant that when millions were dying during China's Cultural Revolution, fashion-conscious politically correct leftists around the world wore Mao badges and quoted from his Little Red Book.

The information age is making it much harder for murderers to conceal their evils and public outrage forces politicians to respond. But the continuing level of wilful amnesia and ignorance is deeply worrying. Mao Zedong, Che Guevera, Fidel Castro and the like have long ago assumed poster-hero status amongst a generation which seems to have only the vaguest grasp of either their accomplishments or their excesses. Castro attended the GATT/WTO fiftieth anniversary ceremony in Geneva, and got longer and louder applause than Bill Clinton, as many ambassadors were pleased to remind me afterwards. Why would they do that? Because so many individuals and nations now define themselves in terms of how they respond to the USA. I find that shallow. The USA, like any other nation and its policies, can be right or wrong, principled and misguided. But if a small country gets it wrong, they are usually only a danger to themselves, whereas whatever the USA does impacts us all.

At the inauguration of Mexico's new President Vicente Fox in 2001, his predecessor Ernesto Zedillo (who I appointed to my advisor's group), was booed by members of his own party, precisely because he hadn't continued the Mexican tradition of rigging elections and instead had handed over power peacefully. By contrast, a string of pretty young female students sought out photo opportunities with Cuban dictator Fidel Castro, who also attended the ceremony. 'Why,' I asked one of them. 'Because he has done so much for the poor,' came the answer.

Does this sort of blind hero-worship of a leader who ruthlessly maintained absolute power, whilst impoverishing his people, really matter? I think it does. Especially when, by contrast, enlightened leaders such as Havel or Zedillo – whose remarkable economic reforms saw his country rise from the world's twenty-second-biggest to its eighth-biggest exporter – and who, more importantly, peacefully handed over power to his successor, are held in contempt by the ignorant and especially those who lost power through democratic change and don't like it.

Self-proclaimed intellectuals from the time of the French Revolution, through fascism and Marxism, have found ways of rationalising their support of tyrannical systems. The twentieth century saw this at its worst. To quote from Mark Lilla's book *The Reckless Mind – Intellectuals in Politics*: 'Socrates understands this. These intellectuals, though, lack his humility and pedagogic care; their reputations depend on exciting passions, not channelling them. Socrates suggests that such intellectuals play an important role in driving democracies toward tyranny by whipping the minds of the young into a frenzy, until some of them, perhaps the most brilliant and courageous, take the step from thought to action and try to realize their tyrannical ambitions in politics. Then, gratified to see their own ideas take effect, these intellectuals become the tyrant's servile flatterers, composing "hymns to tyranny" once he is in power.'[7]

Darrin M. McMahon, commenting on the left–right battles on US campuses in the 1960s, observes: 'While cultural conservatives attacked the allegedly monolithic power of the 1960s radicals, well ensconced and burrowing away in the nation's media and universities, the left countered with the fanatical spectre of the Christian fundamentalist, puritanical, out of touch with modern America, but dangerously close to ruling it nonetheless. If there was truth in either claim, there was far more falsehood. But this didn't prevent the two sides from hurling insults past one another with ever-increasing ferocity. For all its remove from reality, this invective had very real consequences in the political landscape.'[8]

Utopian idealism is blind. This is true of most revolutions and especially true of the ethical blindness to the excesses and failures of Marxism. No one risked their lives to escape from West Berlin to East Berlin. No one risks their lives to flee from Florida to Cuba. Apologists have even tried to rationalise the horrors of North Korea. 'But they are being reduced to cannibalism,' I protested to one New Zealand MP. 'That's just Chinese propaganda,' I was told.

There was no moral equivalence between the problems of the West and Eastern Europe. How there was ever a debate that puzzled me. To point this out during the days of the uprising of Solidarity in Poland earned the tag 'right-wronger', a deadly label domestically among Labour Party activists in New Zealand.

Wider debate can only benefit internationalism by demystifying globalisation. Better, more informed engagement, can lift discussion out of a virtual world of slogans and sound bites, and into the real world of difficult problems and tough choices. It educates, informs, forces people to think – and, in doing so, underscores the logic of a world of greater openness and cooperation. Without the freedom to express differences – as well as similarities – the concept of an open global society celebrating its differences is meaningless.

Who funds and supports the NGOs?

In many cases, these activists are pure lobbyists, paid for by special interests to promote and protect their narrow interests. They have always been with us, but now many masquerade as NGOs doing selfless public service.

Many NGOs, such as Oxfam, do good work and have distinct views on issues such as trade and globalisation. The World-Wide Fund for Nature (WWF) has been constructively engaged on a number of issues, such as fisheries. We need constructive critics, their ideas, idealism, alternatives and enthusiasm. I do not have any complaint about those who wish to form a group to argue a single issue. Where I do have a problem is in the way some NGOs engage – or fail to engage – with the organisations they criticise. On one especially busy day in Geneva, I had a packed diary, which included the US Secretary of Agriculture. That day, some NGO activists chose to handcuff themselves to the our railings. I said to one of them: 'If it's good enough for the Secretary of Agriculture to ask for an appointment to see me, why can't you?' The response: 'We don't want to talk to you, we'd rather rub a McDonalds in your face.'

On another occasion, activists from ATTAC organised a demonstration to clog up our switchboard by nuisance calls. I offered them a meeting, to fit into my schedule a couple of days later, the only slot I had available. But they were unable to respond with a yes or no at the time, and passed up the opportunity. Because, in my experience, many of these single-issue groups do not wish to engage in dialogue; many of them are more interested in publicity stunts to raise funds and enlist new members.

Many NGOs are funded by governments as an extension of their foreign policy or trade agenda, to buy and build political support back home. Alan Oxley, a former Australian Ambassador to the WTO, and academic, who has been researching NGO activity and funding for many years, makes the following points: 'One, the environmental movement is a core dynamic of the anti-globalisation movement and probably the leading public policy beneficiary of it. Two, the movement is substantially funded by aid and environment agencies in Europe and Canada and some foundations in the USA. Three, the EU is a significant funder; the effect, deliberate or not, is that this funding advances the EU environment agenda and tends to foster protectionist agendas.'[9]

Oxley also notes the reported funding of groups such as Public Citizen, and of support for the Seattle protests, by US textile billionaire Robert Milliken. 'I do not think the importance of the anti-NAFTA campaign in the USA and in Canada is to be underrated for the grafting of environment issues to protectionist issues. I think the strategy was to harness public sympathy for the environment, to protectionist interests, which did not enjoy much popular support. This legacy has been transferred to the overall global movement, fostered by the WWF, and enthusiastically adopted by Greenpeace and other hardline green groups. This protectionist ideology is now strong in the anti-globalisation movement. They have turned the WTO into public enemy number one of the anti-globalisation movement. This is understandable from groups with traditional hard left origins, but it has never been clear why WWF has been so active in this regard.'[10]

All of this is fine; but in many cases taxpayers' money is being used: NGO funding should be open, accountable and transparent. It isn't the WTO's or governments' role to determine whose views are legitimate; in a democracy, all views are legitimate. But we can determine how we engage and who we have as partners.

New rules of engagement needed

We need some new rules of engagement. We need to reach an understanding between civil society, international institutions and governments on a code of conduct. This code should require of NGOs the same critical elements that they demand of governments and agencies. It would include:

- rejection of violence
- transparency regarding their finances, their constitutions and their rules of decision-making
- a requirement to report to 'shareholders' and have annual meetings, as must public companies and political parties. This would protect the worthy so we can promote engagement with them and expose the others.

The code should also require governments, businesses, foundations and international institutions to be transparent about whom they fund and why. In return, NGOs should have a place to engage with the multilaterals and government agencies on a regular basis, where they can influence the debate and have their views taken into account. But they can't take part in the *decision-making* of the WTO – which represents governments – any more than they can sit at cabinet tables in Downing Street, the White House, or in the Japanese Diet.

Every few generations, a movement arises that creates a political market for itself by talking about a spiritual crisis in society. This historically has come from the right and the left. 'God is dead,' claimed Nietzsche. Marx and Engels wrote of their counter-revolution to the new Industrial age and its excesses in *The Communist Manifesto*, which advocates: 'Constant revolutionising of production, uninterrupted disturbance of all social conditions, everlasting uncertainty and agitation distinguish the bourgeois epoch from all earlier ones. If fixed, fast-frozen relationships, with their train of ancient and venerable prejudices and opinions, are swept away, all new formed ones become antiquated before they can ossify. All that is solid melts into air, all that is holy is profaned...'[11]

But activism is still better than some of the apathetic alternatives. Former US Secretary of Labour Robert Reich, in *I'll Be Short*, observed: 'The worst fate of all is resignation. Even if they acknowledge what's happening and don't try to escape from it, some people have grown cynical about the possibility of changing things for the better. Maybe they tried when they were younger and idealistic, but grew discouraged. Maybe they burnt out trying to make a difference. Or they concluded that the task is just too large, the regressive forces in society just too powerful. Others have simply given up on all forms of politics. They've decided politics is inherently corrupt.'[12] The idealism of the young is being largely alienated from conventional politics.

This is dangerous for democracy, because we need their enthusiasm and fresh thinking to invigorate our society and correct our mistakes. A living democracy needs citizens' involvement. Why should politicians, pollsters and policymakers target non-voters? And unfortunately, while it is the poor, ill-housed and abused who need political action the most, they are always the lowest percentage turnout of the vote. When more people watched the Superbowl than voted in the last election in the world's most powerful democracy, it's clear that many people have given up and don't think traditional politics can improve their life. 'Who cares?' they ask. 'Everytime we vote, we only get more politicians!'

What I characterise as the privatisation and democratisation of international diplomacy – by the new networks of NGOs and interest groups, democratised by the information explosion – is healthy; it's a positive development. It's good that international diplomacy is no longer practised by elites in their castles. NGOs should have a stake in the process – they have much to offer.

But this will always be a voice, not a vote, because ultimately multilateral decisions must be made, ratified and enforced by governments and parliaments, which are accountable to voters. But by their fundraising and media presence, smart NGOs influence those who do vote, and politicians know this. To disregard them is short-sighted, dangerous and irresponsible.

14   Corporate social responsibility

Global companies and their seemingly all-pervasive brands are frequently pilloried for cultural imperialism, corporate exploitation and multinational dominance. But there is nothing more vulnerable than a company's name and the valuable vault of credibility it has built up over many years and generations. The reason so much of corporate business keeps its head below the ramparts in the current anti-globalist environment is, of course, fear of triggering harassment by activist NGOs. A negative story can strip billions of dollars off a company's share value in minutes, hurting shareholders and employees. What is a brand but a reputation?

One of the paradoxes of the modern age is that, while global brands command immense trust, the companies that create and build them, do not, as authors Steve Hilton and Giles Gibbons have noted.[1] The challenge for corporates is to leverage the power of their brands for socially positive outcomes without damaging their profitability, and in doing so overcome some of the prevailing distrust of global business.

Global brands symbolise reliability in an age of scepticism. To put it simply, great brands become great global icons because, by and large, throughout the world, they have convinced consumers that they will deliver, more or less as advertised. When they don't deliver, they lose customers. When the same consumers' corrupt governments don't deliver, they can cling to power, usually by force. Unsurprisingly, in some countries, popular international brands are often considered to be more trustworthy than the local power elites or, unfortunately, local products.

The idea that multinationals are all-powerful behemoths, brainwashing minds through advertising and homogenising local cultures, is far from the truth in today's highly competitive global manufacturing and marketing environment. More to the point perhaps, there is not, as writers such as *No Logos'* Naomi Klein appear to believe, some sort of global corporate conspiracy to abuse human rights and the environment in pursuit of profit.[2] But there is a reluctance on the part of the global corporations to publicly defend their actions. Every great lie needs a little truth in it to be believed. However, with a globalised world, investigative journalists, NGOs and activist politicians on the prowl, businesses must be conducted ethically and transparently. Recall the Victorian cliché, 'My word is my bond.' In lieu of money, my word is my bond because it reflects and represents my reputation. Any short-termist can sell a car once; selling the next one is the real test.

It is worth noting a point Adair Turner, a former DG of the Confederation of British Industry, makes in his book *Just Capital*: 'Despite all the talk of globalisation, the vast majority of economic activity in rich countries is either not traded at all, or is traded with other countries of roughly equivalent income level and especially with countries that are geographically contiguous. The impact of trade with low income countries at the other end of the world on the macro economics of rich countries is massively overstated in populist accounts of globalisation. Imports of manufactured goods from low wage countries into developed economies account for only about 1–3 per cent of GDP and it is simply impossible for these imports to pose the threat to jobs and living standards which the conventional wisdom asserts.'[3]

Turner suggests that the confusion arises because of changing relative prices. Trade volumes rise faster than GDP, but the value of trade does not because the relative price of the goods and services traded keeps falling, relative to those that are not traded. 'In simple terms, the price of television sets, which are traded, keeps falling relative to the price of haircuts, which are not,' says Turner. 'That factor limits and may eventually reduce, the proportion of our economy which is traded.'

That is, the developed world is not generally – with the exception of some commodities – dependent upon the poor countries for markets. However, it is worth reiterating that many poor countries are hugely dependent upon the rich world, especially in agriculture. In fact, the agriculture sector is crucial for everyone's survival, and is by far the largest employer in the world, employing almost one-half of the world's workers. It is also one of the most dangerous sectors, with a high incidence of child and forced labour and environmental hazards. Marya Glass, Program Manager, Environment BSR, observes: 'For food and agriculture companies, the global marketplace has created increasingly complex supply chains, along with ever-more challenging demands from the world's stakeholder's communities.'[4]

Which is not to say that all corporates are perfect. There have been some egregious transgressions, and there are valid arguments against many global corporate practices. I believe that increased media and NGO scrutiny and consumer sophistication has greatly reduced such instances, and that the increasing emphasis on corporate social responsibility has heightened the awareness of companies both domestically and internationally.

This increasing civil society activity – though sometimes orchestrated to mischievous ends – is not fake; it reflects the growing public hunger in the West for involvement in these issues. The study *Stakeholder Dialogue: Consumer Attitudes* found the following:[5]

- 70 per cent of European Consumers say that a company's commitment to social responsibility is important when buying a product or service.
- One in five consumers would be very willing to pay more for products that are socially and environmentally responsible.
- The view 'the responsibility for addressing social issues lies increasingly with large companies, as well as the government' is held by two-thirds of European citizens, with greatest support in Switzerland, Spain and the Netherlands.
- The issues European consumers care about most are: (a) looking after employees and doing no wrong, and protecting the health and safety of workers; and (b) respecting human rights throughout company operations and the chain of suppliers (for example, not using child labour).
- The research strongly implies – in line with previous studies – that the public's key priority for companies is a demonstration of corporate citizenship rather than just charitable or community giving.
- The majority of the European public feel that a company's commitment to social responsibility is an important consideration when buying a product or service.
- In all of the twelve countries surveyed, over half the population believes a company's commitment to social responsibility is an important factor when making a purchase (the degree varies).

The difficulty is that even corporates that want to be socially and ethically responsible often don't know how to go about it. They are understandably wary of, on the one hand, throwing money at existing agencies or charities with sometimes dubious execution records or agendas; or, on the other, becoming too heavily involved in the delivery of services themselves to the detriment of their core business. Many are scared of getting involved at all, for fear of attracting activist attention. But appeasement in any form seldom works.

In my day, the running picket was a favourite union tactic to protest for higher wages and better conditions; these days, the tactic is just as likely to be mounted by protestors against McDonalds or Starbucks for allegedly displacing traditional farmers or exploiting third-world workers.

A significant role in corporate responsibility is likely to be played by the trade unions and pension funds. The California public servants, for example, have a $150 billion pension fund (CalPERS). Some 25 per cent

Figure 20. Police rain pepper spray on Seattle protestors: protest is healthy, differences are vital and I agreed with some of our critics. But at Seattle, the sworn objective of some was to stop ministers even meeting. This was dangerous and undemocratic. (Photograph by Andy Clark. Copyright Reuters 1999.)

of its investments are outside the USA; at one point their investment represented five per cent of the French stock market. Americans have some $11.5 trillion in pension funds, which are a key element in world capital flows. The economic implications are clear, but the social imperatives that drive trade unions, their growing concern about ethical, environmental and labour standards' issues, may well end up having more impact than well-meaning meetings about sustainable development. Imagine the dilemma in responding when protestors target trade union offices. Many unions and pension funds have anticipated this and are developing codes of ethics and standards for their investments.

Rather than focus on the negatives, however, I would like to explore ways in which we can use the undoubted power of global business to contribute towards better social outcomes. The MNCs are usually highly experienced at delivering goods and services in demanding environments. After all, if one of the few things that works in an isolated village in Africa is the Coke machine, perhaps we should be exploring ways to exploit the brand's marketing and distribution strengths. Instead, NGOs tend to abuse companies for doing basically what they are supposed to, which is make money for themselves, their shareholders and their employees, by providing services and products to customers.

But corporate social responsibility (CSR) is, for many participants, a sensitive area. Turner argues that it is a 'at best a cul de sac, at worst dangerous' to expect the good society to evolve because people in both their economic and political lives act in a good way, as opposed to this being brought about by laws, taxes and public expenditure producing a good result from largely self-interested actions. 'It sounds attractive to ask corporations to think through the wider social "balance sheet of gains and losses" but in practice it is an almost totally inoperable principle,' says Turner. 'Corporations can just about imperfectly identify the complex set of actions which will maximise their own profit within given constraints, but they are ill-equipped to calibrate the second and third and nth order social consequence of their actions and lack the legitimacy to make the trade-offs involved.'[6]

Critics like former OECD Chief Economist David Henderson[7] and the *Financial Times*'s Martin Wolf,[8] amongst others, have argued that CSR distorts the market by deflecting business from its primary goal of profit generation.

Henderson suggests: '...business organisations that have supported [CSR] have typically failed to contact or have even endorsed the arguments or demands of, anti-business activist groups. Their strategy is one of appeasement and accommodation. They show little awareness that the case for private business derives from its links with competition and economic freedom. They mistakenly identify defence of the market economy with more business, more popular and more respected.'[9]

In an interesting exchange at a forum held by the centre-left think tank IPPR, Wolf comments: 'Ill-defined, probably otiose, ineffective and dangerous – these are the adjectives I would use to describe, in turn, the notion of public interest, the adoption of CSR as a profit-maximising strategy, the acceptance of costly burdens by profit-seeking companies and the attempt to spread those burdens to competitors through regulation. If we want to pursue social goals, the right way is openly, through the political process where the pros and cons can be argued out explicitly. CSR will either achieve little or do harm. Which one it will be, I do not know. But I do know the right response is one of profound scepticism.'[10]

South African Finance Minister Trevor Manuel told the 2002 World Economic Forum in New York: 'Understanding the respective roles of governments and markets is vital to ensuring growth and poverty reduction. The role of business is to make a profit. The role of governments is to govern and to govern for all. Weak institutions hurt the poor especially, as much in failing to protect their civil rights as in failing to protect their economic interest. Growth with redistribution requires active engagement by government in all spheres. The creation of the legal and economic incentives that facilitate empowerment and growth – hard and soft infrastructure, from education and personal security to roads and regulatory authorities – is fundamental to poverty reduction.'[11]

It's interesting to note that, despite the perception that giant MNCs can evade taxes by transnational operations, in richer OECD countries, the contribution of corporate taxes to government revenues has remained about the same since the 1960s – around 8.8 per cent. 'Corporate taxes have fallen in many countries, but revenues have not, because a widening of the tax base has offset the fall in rates. As a share of GDP, taxes on company profits have steadily risen; from 2.2 per cent in 1965, to 2.4 per cent in 1980, 2.7 per cent in 1990 and 3.3 per cent in 1999,' reports Philippe Legrain. 'If businessmen are running the show, they are clearly masochists.'[12]

Focus on MNC revenues – and indeed on profit generation, important though it is – misses the point that the real power of these global corporations is in their enormous reach and in the mass public identification with their brands across cultures. There is no reason why we should not be encouraging companies at all levels to leverage their logo power to produce better social outcomes in the societies in which they operate.

Despite the opposition, the concept of CSR has gained a wide degree of support, and was given some added impetus by UN Secretary General Kofi Annan's Global Compact. Annan, commenting on poverty and good governance, said: 'Many business leaders still think these are problems for governments to solve and that business should concern itself with the bottom line. But most of them understand that in the long run the bottom line depends on economic and social conditions, as well as political stability. And increasing numbers are realising that they do not have to wait for governments to do the right thing – indeed that they cannot afford to. In many cases, governments only find the courage and resources to do the right thing when business takes the lead . . . Indeed, no one is better-placed than business leaders to refute the arguments of projectionists and penny-pinchers. They are the ones who can make the most persuasive case for opening the market of rich countries to labour-intensive products from poor ones and for an end to the farm export subsidies that make it impossible for farmers in poor countries to compete.'[13]

Of course, anti-globalists criticised this initiative as providing corporates with an excuse to shelter under the proposal without taking any concrete action, while ultraliberals saw it as an encroachment on pure capitalism.

But partnerships between business and social forces are beginning to emerge. WEF President Klaus Schwab has observed: 'In Davos, New York, the Bill and Melinda Gates Foundation pledged a further US$50 million for AIDS prevention in Africa, including US$20 million to fund a trial of promising microbicides that could offer women a breakthrough in protection against HIV/AIDS. Also, US Secretary of the Treasury Paul O'Neill accepted an invitation from Bono, the lead singer of U2, to travel to Africa, where Bono will show him first-hand the devastation caused by AIDS and other diseases. The member companies of the World Economic Forum's Global Health Initiative joined with international leaders to present an Executive Statement calling on business leaders to increase their advocacy efforts in the fight against HIV/AIDS, TB and malaria. In recognising the crucial role education plays in improving equity, South African President Thabo Mbeki announced that Microsoft will provide free software for all of South Africa's 32,000 government schools, and Jean-Marie Messier declared that Vivendi Universal will dedicate 20% of its philanthropic budget to projects related to bridging the digital divide.'[14]

The WEF's Global Corporate Citizenship programme aims to take into account different corporates' circumstances, while encouraging good social practices that are at the same time fundamental to their core business operations. Schwab is also, with his wife Hilde, behind the Schwab Foundation for Social Entrepreneurship, which he says aims to create 'a global community of outstanding social entrepreneurs to better tap into the dynamic body of knowledge generated by their practical approaches to solving social and economic problems.' The foundation seeks out and funds innovative and outstanding social entrepreneurs, like Fazle Abed's BRAC, the former Bangladesh Rural Advancement Committee, which mobilises the latent capacity of the poor to act in their own uplift through self-organisation. Its full-time staff of 26,000 has helped 3.8 million poor women establish 100,000 village groups. Its health programmes reach 10 million; its non-formal schools cater to 1.2 million children and its micro credit program has disbursed $1 billion in loans with a reported 98 per cent repayment rate.

Business must defend itself and take a lead role in staring down extreme NGO intimidation. I once upset some leftist colleagues in New Zealand by telling a trade union meeting that the movement shouldn't be attacking profits; members should be picketing companies that *lose* money. No job is safe if there are no profits.

The distrust of business has been compounded by the succession of massive corporate collapses in 2002, such as Enron and WorldCom. Adding to concern was what appeared to be complicity in dubious accounting practices by formerly respected firms such as Andersen (see Chapter 15). It is hard to put a price on this: one estimate – by the Brookings Institution, a think-tank in Washington DC – is that corporate scandals will cost the US economy $35 billion. That would shave 0.35% off US economic growth this year and would depress growth by up to 2.5% over the next ten years. $35 billion, which is a conservative estimate of the true cost of all these corporate scandals, is equivalent to the cost of a $10-a-barrel rise in the price of oil. The market meltdown of 2002, which eroded the pension funds of hundreds of thousands of Americans – as well as people worldwide who suffered from catastrophic share plunges – fuelled widespread unease. The point that stock prices had inflated greatly over the preceding years of boom times, and that there is no such thing as a free lunch, can justifiably be made to those individual investors who thought prices would only ever rise. But it is hard to blame workers, with funds trapped in now deflated pension funds, tell them that it was all their fault. Rules, laws and regulations are vital, but there are people who will break any laws; they are criminals, crooks and thieves; that's why we need prisons.

More to the point, there remains a strong conviction that it is only the workers and small shareholders who suffer, while executives can always sell out early for millions and get away with having their hands slapped. US economist Kevin Phillips has calculated that, while worker's wages in the USA roughly doubled (before inflation) in the two decades to 2000, the top ten CEOs' average earnings rose 4,300 per cent.[15] Or as mill worker Robert Hemsley put it, in an *International Herald Tribune* article: 'I imagine my concern about my company's share price is as great as my CEO's – a portion of my 401 (k) savings plan is in company stock. I recognise that my job depends upon my company making a profit. But I wonder if corporate executives appreciate the role workers play in their success. Free enterprise is a system of risks and rewards. As it now stands, employees suffer most of the risks, while executives enjoy most of the rewards.'[16]

That perception is widely shared, and is dangerous. Trust is a highly vulnerable commodity; easy to lose but sometimes impossible to recapture, as Andersen discovered in the aftermath of Enron. People need hope of better times to motivate them. Corporates need to be much more forward- and outward-looking in creating understanding of how business contributes to economic growth.

One interesting approach to this issue is detailed in *Good Business: Your World Needs You*. The authors, who consult to companies on CSR strategies, argue that in the current antiglobalist environment, it's not even enough for corporates to be socially responsible within their business.

'You need to demonstrate social leadership outside your business. It's not enough to change your company. You should use your company to change the world. That is the truly progressive course, and it is the way to persuade the world that you're truly responsible. Because leadership requires mass engagement; whereas responsibility can happily remain a well-kept secret and usually does.'[17]

Essentially, the authors suggest that major global companies should examine their operations for the myriad micro ways where they can make more of a difference than any pressure group or even many governments. They make a powerful argument – not for giving money to good causes – but for leveraging the power of their brands and operations to attract attention to positive messages in social and environmental areas. 'The way to be credible lies not in trying to *communicate* what you're doing in corporate social responsibility, but to actually *demonstrate* corporate social responsibility. And the beauty of it, is that by involving your customers in a direct way, it's more likely to help your business in a direct way.'

As noted earlier, one of the interesting points Hilton and Gibbons make is that there is a contradiction between the public's trust in the consistency, reliability and useful services of global brands, and its distrust of the corporations that produce them and of business in general. They attribute this largely to the generally anti-business message of much media coverage, both fictional and non-fictional.

An anti-globalisation, anti-growth activist – one of the 'back to the Middle Ages' advocates – once asked me: 'How do you fight poverty in a world that multiplies needs?' He was referring to the compounding and confusing materialism of the developed world. It's a good point. How many shoes can you wear; how big a house can you use; how many cars can you drive? I've never met anyone who said they have enough money.

But these debating points are usually only made by those who are already comfortable. They make little sense to the poor, unemployed or sick of the rich world. And fits of hand-wringing over consumerism are downright insulting to the millions whose lives are wretched, violent and brief. Those who want to halt world growth, now that the affluent countries are on top, infuriate leaders in the nations of the developing world. Equality of opportunity is a noble concept; unfortunately, there is something of a tendency for equal opportunists to achieve levelling down rather than up – an echo of the old adage that we are all equal in the party, except the party secretary. It's the road to Hell that's paved with good intentions, not the road to Heaven.

Among the many positive projects *Good Business* cites are Coca Cola's Valued Youth initiative, developed in partnership with local education boards, where troubled British fourteen-year-olds who are on the brink of being excluded from school are matched with younger children to teach them numeracy and literacy skills. 'It has a phenomenal success rate, with parents and teachers reporting transformed attitudes among the fourteen-year-olds as they learn a sense of responsibility. The essence of this project is that it works precisely because the Coca Cola brand is involved: because it's a brand that teenagers know and trust.'

They also, amongst other initiatives, cite the Mates condom band created by Virgin's Richard Branson as a way for business to respond to the looming AIDS crisis in the 1980s; a youth careers advisory service developed by BSkyB; a project to reduce bullying in school playgrounds in inner city London with Nike; and DaimlerChrysler and Richemont's Sport for Good program, which promotes neighbourhood renewal in Africa. They conclude with a simple test for every Chief Executive. 'Write down in one sentence your company's purpose. Does it capture your contribution to society? Do you have a social leadership program that uses every part of the corporate anatomy to bring that purpose alive? Could every employee and customer tell you what it is?'

Clearly, most CEOs could not pass this test. The potential for improving the world if they could is significant.

However, some CEOs and corporations do get it. Take John Browne, Group CEO of BP. Explaining his company's position during a lecture at Harvard, he said: 'We have to be transparent in reporting on our activities and finances, because where there is a dark corner there will be doubt... That transparency is part of the process of sound governance – with clear accountabilities, proper and effective controls, checks and balances and an explicit analysis and management of risks... Our approach, of course, is dictated by self-interest. Companies are not aid agencies or charities – and our purpose is simply to create future wealth on behalf of shareholders... To operate successfully companies need trust, and as the global marketplace changes, companies need to show that they can operate in complex areas. That is what the initiative of the global compact proposed by the UN is all about.'[18]

Rival petro giant Shell has been similarly proactive in recent years on these issues, adding side projects to its Malampya, Philippines, gas recovery project, which, for example, help develop local enterprises such as a fish farm; and included planting ten trees to replace every one felled in a combined job creation, environmental recovery programme where it had to reroute a pipeline. In Nigeria, a strict business ethics programme has seen nine employees dismissed and eight contractors removed after Shell companies in 2000 introduced a policy of encouraging staff and stakeholders to report unethical behaviour. Shell is also using its extensive network of some 2000 service stations in Sub-Saharan Africa to help fight the spread of HIV/AIDS. Stations display posters and provide information leaflets to customers, encouraging them to protect themselves against contracting HIV.[19]

Mining group Anglo American, South Africa's biggest employer, said in August 2002 that it would make AIDS drugs available to any of its 130,000 workers who needed them. 'The announcement – the first of its kind anywhere in the world – is a landmark not just for South African business but also for the continent. While the South African government remains hesitant about AIDS drugs, the private sector has acknowledged that only expensive and complicated treatment programmes for AIDS patients can prevent social and economic disaster in the region,' reported the *Financial Times*.[20]

Many of the arguments against CSR initiatives come down to the idea that they somehow distort or detract from the primary focus of the company, which is making money. Or that it will somehow require the imposition of a new regulatory layer on business.

I would agree that having too many rules, or creating institutions that have lives of their own, is as dangerous as not having any. Some of the new collectivists, having failed to control the nation state, are trying to impose globally what they failed so miserably to do locally because their command theories were too far left or right and did not work. The new democratic internationalism ought to be about standards and the rule of law, not controls. In other words, about ownership, property rights, rule of law, all the issues that are politely packaged in the politically correct slogan good governance.

What I am arguing for is the rather unfashionable – but none the less valid – axiom that virtue is its own best reward. Virtue used to be seen as a punishment; but virtue builds reputation, which is money in the bank of credibility. We are entering a millennium in which globalisation and ever greater competitiveness in terms of tax, interest and currency rates, are slowly exerting downward pressure on consumer prices as well as on national tax revenues in a rich world, where there are still major disparities. And, of course, the developing world faces even more immense challenges.

In an era where big business becomes ever more powerful and ever more capable of reducing its tax burden, I would argue that it has a moral social duty to take some responsibility for the wellbeing, not just of its shareholders and employers, but its wider community, if for no other reason than the self-interest that these represent its future employees and customers.

Large businesses now are in an analogous position to those nineteenth-century northern English factory owners who were spurred to personal philanthropy after realizing that wealth could not shield their workers and their own families from disease and death caused by unsanitary conditions. It was no use in Victorian England having the biggest mansion in the town if disease was brought into your home by servants, or if your mill-workers were too sick to work. These progressive Victorian liberals introduced municipal socialism, building public works, sewerage systems, roads and schools. This happened first at the local level, then the national, and gave Britain a huge competitive advantage in its imperial undertakings. Fit and educated workers were an economic as well as a social good. The same principal applies globally today.

There are public and global goods that the market cannot deliver. Great museums, art galleries, national parks, are probably not immediately profitable, but they make life beautiful and better. The state, institutions and global governance have a role; tax is the price you pay for civilisation. What has given government a bad name is corruption, short-termism and poor delivery systems. That is why public–private delivery systems are the way of the future, especially in countries without a mature, accountable, professional public service.

Capitalism changed dramatically in the early 1900s as a professional managerial class emerged, shareholdings widened, and great commercial families began to lose personal control of their empires. Capitalism is going through another extraordinary and evolutionary change. As I discuss in Chapter 16, company shareholding is becoming increasingly democratised through both individual and worker pension funds. More people now own shares in the USA than vote in presidential elections. The expected expansion of this trend, market volatility notwithstanding, will see increasing demands placed upon CEOs, directors and managers, to improve standards of corporate responsibility, ethical investment and greater accountability. We have seen how work, capitalism and ownership is fundamentally changing in the developed world. Now 10 per cent of the US work force is working for 1.5 million non-profit organisations.[21]

When the world's 200 biggest corporations have combined sales greater than the combined GNP of all but the ten biggest economies, this not only changes the way business is done, but how diplomacy and international governance is conducted.[22] I do not see corporates replacing governments. Nor do I see that there is any need for companies to sacrifice profits in seeking more enlightened ways of doing business. The irony is pointed out by Alan Shipman, in The Globalisation Myth: 'Far from being builders of a ruthless world market, multinationals are constantly trying to escape it, it has been governments that have promoted international integration in an effort to curb big corporational market power.'[23]

So much for the global capitalist/government conspiracy. Two cheers for a more enlightened age of corporate and global governance. There is no need for conflict between a world of rules and political responsibility, and enhanced individual and corporate social responsibility; these concepts can – and are – converging.

Pray for globalisation if you fear big business. Open trade forces competition and curbs monopolies and corporate giants by exposing them to competition. Take the global telecommunications industry; closed markets mean cosy, crony capitalism, with business purchasing privilege from politicians against the interests of workers and consumers. It is the absence of competition, not the size of business, that gives them their power.

15   Time to rethink global governance

Three-quarters of the flags, borders, anthems and monies represented at the United Nations today did not exist fifty years ago.[1] When the UN was founded in 1945, there were 51 member countries; now there are 190. So much for the predictions of the death of the nation state due to globalisation.

The Cold War is over, global economic integration is accelerating, and we now live in a world where a company like AOL-Time Warner can attain – and lose again in a matter of a year or so – a market value greater than the GNP of over 120 countries, including nations such as Norway, Finland, Colombia, Israel and New Zealand. Where upwards of 30,000 national NGOs utilise an ever-more pervasive media to spotlight corporate and political shortcomings and promote their agendas. Where borderless fanatics and terrorists threaten peaceful coexistence and economic security. Where diplomacy has gone from being the preserve of a ruling elite of kings, Kaisers and cardinals, to the point where a stateless pressure group can organise a ban on land mines, then enlist a sovereign power, Canada, to sponsor it through the multilateral system. In short, it is increasing privatisation and democratisation of diplomacy. This is good and it's getting better.

These trends are not unhealthy, even if they make the powerful uneasy. But they are testing the limits of international institutions and international conventions, which are now struggling to create a political roadmap; to find a legal and moral compass that can handle these new forces. While the global landscape has dramatically changed, the institutions serving the world have not. Leaders face the challenge of managing conflicts and challenges based on the Westphalian concept of the nation state, with global institutions that are unequipped to cope and often immobilised by procedures based on old realities. There are now dozens of international, inter-governmental agencies whose roles, agendas, even their locations, were often part and parcel of old Cold War priorities. Functions overlap, mandates conflict, objectives get blurred,

216

institutions have lives of their own and different systems of accountability or unaccountability to their owner governments.

My reforms at the WTO were focused in part on trying to address the real and perceived democratic deficit of this and other multilateral IGOs. This deficit is the fault of governments who devolve our global and regional responsibilities to institutions and treaties, without imposing corresponding accountability on the institutions, or adequate supervision by these governments and their parliaments. We must re-establish accountability and good governance in our global institutions by connecting better with governments, democratically elected representatives and wider civil society. We have begun; we now have to build upon those initiatives.

This is not to diminish the huge importance of the current international architecture. As Brink Lindsey observes: 'Postwar leaders were resolved not to repeat the mistakes of the past. At a terrible cost, they had rediscovered then long-neglected wisdom of Cobdenite liberalism – that free trade is vital to the preservation of world peace.'[2] Sir Henry Maine (1822–88) said, 'War appears as old as mankind, but peace is a modern invention.' Centuries ago Immanuel Kant wrote of a league of nations to ensure lasting peace.

Great leaders and enlightened thinkers were thinking about how to create the new structure even before the Second World War was over. The UN would be formed, to succeed where the League of Nations had failed. The seeds were sown and beginning to develop of the Marshall Plan, where, for the first time, a victor nation would help reconstruct vanquished countries and peoples, based on principles of democracy and open trade, the mirror opposite of the vicious Versailles Treaty.

Understanding that the Great Depression was made deeper, more prolonged and intractable because of trade protectionism, the leaders attempted to establish an International Trade Organization, later to be frustrated by the United States Congress. However, they did succeed in founding the General Agreement on Tariffs and Trade, or GATT, which eventually evolved into the WTO. The World Bank was to be a development bank, and the International Monetary Fund – originally to be the glue to hold together a financial system, based on gold, to maintain global stability – became a lender of last resort (though there remains debate within the Fund as to this), as well as an institution providing economic advice to nations.

This package of international mechanisms, infused with postwar optimism and idealism, was designed to create a coherent international architecture, providing security, support and encouragement to both developed and developing countries. This idealism was, alas, soon replaced by the frozen conflict of the Cold War. But despite all the imperfections of the existing international architecture, the world is better, safer and more secure because of its existence.

However, this architecture is now in its late middle age, and is urgently in need of a check-up, a blood transfusion and a reassessment of objectives. The world has dramatically changed, but while its institutions have expanded – sometimes to unmanageable proportions – they have not always remained focused on their customers. Food security was the issue in 1945, not food surpluses, free trade or genetic food modification. Fifty years ago no government had a Ministry of the Environment, now almost all do.

No single encyclopedia could store all the treaties, constitutions, bi-lateral and international agreements that have made the world safer and better over the past decades.

The nation state has often been a threat to liberty. Super states should be treated with even more caution. But no nation, or individual, can go it alone, nor should they. That's why governments contract out their responsibilities via international treaties and institutions. The real danger today in these institutions is the lack of accountability, ownership, scrutiny and political oversight. It is up to the owner governments to do more; it is dangerous to leave these problems to the institutions, their critics or supporters.

The Welsh socialist and visionary Aneurin Bevan warned in *In Place of Fear* of the need to '. . . guard against the old words, for the words persist when the reality that lay behind them has changed. It is inherent in our intellectual activity that we seek to imprison reality in our description of it. Soon, long before we realise it, it is we who become the prisoners of the prescription. From that point on, our ideas degenerate into a kind of folklore which we pass to each other, fondly thinking we are still talking of the reality around us.'[3]

There is no lack of reality; that's why leaders – from UN Secretary General Kofi Annan to British Prime Minister Tony Blair to French President Jacques Chirac – are increasingly calling for greater coher-ence between institutions, and for a fresh look at the international ar-chitecture. President Chirac has observed that as we move towards an increasingly multi-polar world, it is necessary to strengthen international institutions. 'We need rules and arbitrators . . . globalisation necessarily calls for a global response,' he has said. 'We must renew – and allocate sufficient financial resources to – the international system put in place in the wake of the Second World War.'[4]

So exactly what shape are we in? As the nation state arose, grew and gathered power and authority, conversely the empires of the soul, whose religious representatives took their seats behind the kings and princes in Europe, retreated. Ironically, in Europe it was a cardinal, Richelieu, who first advanced the proposition that national leaders must put the interests and wellbeing of the state and its furtherance in principle above even church interests. He was the powerful pioneer of the centralised control ethos that became the model for Europe, modern diplomacy and 'realism' balance of power theories, whose heirs run from Palmerston and Bismarck, to Teddy Roosevelt, Richard Nixon and Henry Kissinger.

Political realism and Wilsonian idealism

Hans Küng has commented on the current twin streams of geopolitical thought, 'political realism' personified in our time by the Nixon/Kissinger nexus, and the Wilsonian idealism of a world of laws, institutions, rules and treaties. 'The "idealists" should note that a complete subordination of politics to ethics does not do justice to the autonomy of politics and leads to irrationalism ... But the "realists" should not overlook the fact that a complete detachment of politics from ethics violates the universality of ethics and leads to amoralism. Values, ideals and criteria must not be neglected by politics. In the face of a largely individualistic and hedonistic society and a militarised foreign policy, there is a need for ethical responsibility.'[5]

The nation state itself is a reasonably new concept; philosophers, from the Kant of 'perpetual peace' to the Marx who wrote of the *Withering Away of the State* well before the evolution to the more recently fashionable Friedman–Thatcher–Reagan revolution, called for the removal of the state from people's lives. Marxists saw the individual being freed through common collective ownership. Friedmanites saw the individual being freed through the destruction of the collective impulse.

Lateral thinking is necessary; I applaud the move by the Archbishop of Canterbury to promote the exchanges of hundreds of devout young people from all religions to work in each other's mosques, synagogues and churches. We need much improved dialogue between civilisations and religions to create mutual understanding respect and peace. As Hans Küng presciently observed, before the events of 9-11: 'There will be no peace between the civilisations without a peace between the religions. And there will be no peace between the religions without a dialogue between the religions.'[6]

The tribal impulse

But despite such countervailing pulls and the onslaught of globalisation, the nation state not only survives, it is strengthening and increasing.

Tribalism is a powerful impulse and one consequence of globalisation has been to empower the viability and ability to secede of ever-smaller nation states. This is not a bad thing. Peter Drucker, in *Foreign Affairs*, notes: 'There is no other institution capable of political integration and effective membership in the world's political community. In all probability, therefore, the nation state will survive the globalisation of the economy and the information revolution that accompanies it. But it will be a greatly changed nation state, especially in domestic fiscal and monetary policies, foreign economic policies, control of international business, and perhaps in its conduct of war.'[7]

Hans Küng correctly observes: 'At the latest since the Second World War, despite all too manifest resistance, a new post-modern paradigm of politics is now slowly and laboriously becoming established, which is no longer Eurocentric, but polycentric, and which in a post-colonial and post-imperialistic way aims at truly united nations... there is a middle way between real politics and ideal politics. This is the way of a politics in the spirit of an ethic of responsibility.'[8]

Our problem is how to manage and deliver upon the expectations of the ever-increasing number of stakeholders on the global stage.

Greater coherence needed

Greater coherence amongst the numerous agencies that receive billions of taxpayer dollars would be a good start. National leaders are always calling for greater coherence, and they are right. A minister from a small Latin American country once told me how five different agencies simultaneously descended on his country to assist with customs problems.

Meeting frequently with the heads of other agencies, I understand how difficult these institutions are to manage. But this lack of coherence damages their collective credibility, frustrates their donors and owners and gives rise to public cynicism, despite the best efforts of leaders like UN Secretary General Kofi Annan, whose personal leadership of a Global Compact for Business and Civil Society, and a global trust fund to fight HIV/AIDS were lonely lamps of idealism and hope. They have yet to attract the support they deserve.

Agencies have different ways of selecting their chief executive, and even the Secretary General of the UN often doesn't have the power to impose change or discipline on the agencies he manages. The array of institutions is bewildering: within the UN systems of organisations alone there are 112 agencies (including the WTO, which has a special collaborative relationship with the UN, although it is not *per se* a UN organisation or agency). The International Labour Organization (ILO), the Food and

Agriculture Organizations of the United Nations (FAO) and the United Nations Children's Fund (UNICEF) alone employed 12,489 people, with total budgets of $2.09 billion, for the fiscal year 1998.

Trying to improve inter-agency coherence can be a dispiriting experience. In Geneva, I experienced many instances of how agencies can fail to work together, despite sharing in the same general and usually well-intentioned objectives. To take just one example, I discovered a real gap in agency coverage in Geneva – the nearly thirty countries that are too poor or small to have missions in Geneva. I initiated Geneva Week, where we paid for senior officials to come to Geneva for an annual briefing. To launch this, I had to ring around donor nations for $10,000 here, $30,000 there. But it achieved its initial objectives. Wanting to build it, I thought I could get other agencies to help in funding, since the week could logically cover their work as well. Foolish of me. Other than Kamal Idris of WIPO, and some help from Denis Belisle of the ITC, I was on my own.

I had initially approached the non-residents and asked what they wanted. Their advice was to establish a modest trust fund, which would return for their 'direction' about $1.4 million per annum. I set about to raise a trust fund. All hell immediately broke loose. Everyone wanted to be seen as filling this gap in the market. The African Caribbean Pacific group opened an office, the Agency for International Trade Information and Cooperation got new funding, and the Commonwealth threatened to put on new staff.

We have now funded the programme, twice yearly, out of the core WTO budget, which I see as progress, as well as setting up a Trust Fund to assist in technical assistance and capacity-building for these poorer countries. So ultimately the non-residents finished up much better-served, which is good. But they did so at a cost of many millions of dollars more from donors than they originally sought.

As lead agency, the WTO was able to resuscitate the neglected Integrated Framework (IF), which brought all the agencies together to mainstream poverty reduction programmes in a coherent manner, and has wider implications than just trade. Although the focus was to mainstream trade into domestic-economic planning, and get a coherent local policy within often competing government departments, the IF also focused the various agencies in a model of targeted measurable, accountable co-operation. Jim Wolfensohn and Horst Kohler were very supportive. It is usually not the heads of agencies who have 'turf' and policy problems, rather there are costly and indulgent jealousies at more junior levels (see Chapter 12). The IF is a good example of project-driven interagency coherence and could be a model for future cooperation. We all work better when we focus on specific projects.

In my experience, it's all too seldom about the customers or countries, it's about the expansion and power of the various institutions, whether in Geneva, Wellington or Washington DC.

One of Kofi Annan's most noteworthy initiatives was the 2002 Summit on Financing for Development, which produced the Monterrey Consensus. This stated: 'A universal, rules-based, open, non-discriminatory and equitable multilateral trading system, as well as meaningful trade liberalisation, can substantially stimulate development worldwide, benefiting countries at all stages of development. In that regard, we reaffirm our commitment to trade liberalisation and to ensure that trade plays its full part in promoting economic growth, employment and development for all. We thus welcome the decisions of the WTO to place the needs and interests of developing countries at the heart of its work programme, and commit ourselves to their implementation.'[9]

Monterrey was highly significant. For the first time, we were able to bring together at one event, not only more than fifty heads of state, but a stunning variety of senior ministers and officials with multidisciplinary skills from a broad range of north and south geographies, as well as the heads of all the key agencies charged with implementing donor agendas. Donors pledged a substantial increase in aid programmes.

By agreeing a consensus on the core world economic issue of our time, we have moved towards mainstreaming development in the economic strategies of the developed world. Monterrey also helped further the growing coherence that the agencies need to respond effectively to the needs of the developed world. We have buried the old aid versus trade argument. We need both; aid targeted at building public infrastructure to enjoy more trade in a win–win situation. Building an effective customs system, a non-porous tax base and effective, informed officials are as important as building dams, bridges and roads.

All the UN agency heads meet once a year under the chairmanship of Kofi Annan. I found these meetings very useful to work with other heads at building greater coherence into some of our programmes. We frequently saw more of each other outside Geneva than in. And it was fascinating to be briefed on their priorities in areas such as health and refugees in free-ranging and broad discussions.

But at one meeting, an agency head shocked me by stating: 'We are in a post-parliamentary, post-democratic age; nation states can't function any more, politicians are despised and people can't even be bothered to vote any more.' He went on to assert that the future of governance was with international organisations in partnership with NGOs representing civil society, bypassing politicians.

And of course many NGOs subscribe to and push this theory, it gives them power, status and resources. I told him I found such attitudes unhealthy and dangerous. I ventured that I was perhaps old-fashioned, but still believed in parliamentary democracy.

He was right in that there is a problem, but not about the solution. The difficulties are not usually at the national level. Effective democracy ends at the sovereign border; the difficulty is at the international level. Our so far elusive goal is to build democratic principles into global governance. Our interdependent world has yet to find the mechanism to integrate its common needs.

Involving all the stakeholders

Aside from the NGOs who draw so much attention – many of whom do very worthwhile work – a number of other parties are engaged in these issues, including many who are perceived as representing corporate interests (see Chapter 14). Outside the WTO, probably the least understood, well-known organisation on the globe is the World Economic Forum, based in Davos, Switzerland. It has been demonised as an exclusive club of the filthy rich, fatuous and famous, who plot in splendid isolation to shape a world in their image. Certainly it is elite: the elite of politics, business, NGOs, thinkers, personalities and Nobel prizewinners.

In response to its perceived 'globalisation agenda', it has even spawned an alternative Davos each year in Puerto Allegro, Brazil, which I see as healthy. And an interesting example of how the 'no logos' forces are quite comfortable and adept at co-opting others' brands for their own purposes. Incidentally, who put together the words Green and Peace? Who thought of the title and job description of an organisation called 'Friends of the Earth'? Brilliant marketing concepts, worthy of any Madison Avenue-advised multinational. Globalised NGOs opposing globalisation may seem a paradox, but that is the reality.

However, it might surprise both the Puerto Allegro summit and the WEF to realise how much they have in common. It's a sign of hope that dialogue can replace confrontation and reason replace righteous indignation.

The Monterrey Consensus, the Doha Development Round and Davos are all practical expressions of global idealism kept alive. As was Paul O'Neill's trip around Africa with Bono. This received some ridicule from inside-the-beltway commentators, but it showed courage and openness: perhaps reflecting the Treasury Secretary's roots in private enterprise rather than the bureaucracy. Such moves signal that progress is being made. But, given the present structure, can their bold ambitions be implemented?

Governments have a heavy responsibility to do better and provide leadership. We know that no one nation can enjoy clean air, run a tax system, cure AIDS or find political security on its own, without the cooperation of others. That's why we have the Law of the Sea, the Antarctic Agreement and hundreds of other international treaties and organisations. Nation states have correctly contracted this work out. But they have not expanded their political scrutiny of their institutions to hold them more accountable and transparent. These must be institutions of global governance, not global government.

People sense this loss of control and accountability. The explosion of NGOs reflects this (see Chapter 13). Monterrey was, incidentally, also significant because at this major summit, responsible NGOs were able to sit and share ideas at the same table, rather than shout at developed world officials across dividing barricades. This is rewarding for participants in the process and improves policy-making and outcomes – and easier to do when outcomes are not legally binding on governments.

Leaders and agency heads talk of conference fatigue and are becoming cynical about the setting of yet more global targets. No wonder. The G7 plus Russia meeting in Genoa, bringing together leaders and agency heads, including myself, Kofi Annan, Jim Wolfensohn and others, cost $100 million – much more than the WTO's total annual budget. The Doha conference was important; it launched a new Trade Round and brought China and Chinese Taipei into the WTO. Monterrey was vital: the USA pledged to increase its ODA by 50 per cent; it linked development, trade, overseas aid, investment and good governance.

The Johannesburg Earth Summit in September 2002 was important in bringing all these issues under the umbrella of sustainable development. But in assembling more than one hundred leaders and giving them five-minute speaking slots with thousands of journalists, NGOs and bureaucrats, such conferences are losing their lustre and utility.

Writing to my old friend Alec Irwin, the South African Trade Minister, to wish him well with his trade and environment agenda for the Johannesburg Summit, I joked that the conference was twice as large as Alexander's army and twice as dangerous. South Africa spent more than $50 million on the conference. Irwin later told reporters the ten-day summit had been too big and diffuse, and recommended that to make progress at a multilateral level, the world's leaders needed to consider tackling the issues of energy, trade and environment, with smaller, more focused groups. 'We were lucky to pull it off,' he said. 'It was a birth by fire for the new South Africa.'[10]

George Soros's most recent book put its finger on some uncomfortable realities. He bluntly notes an all too evident, but often understated, fact: 'Bad governments are a major source of poverty and misery in the world today. (Bad location is the other major source, but it is much harder to do anything about that.) Yet anti-globalisation activists have failed to give adequate weight in their advocacy to the harm done by bad governments.'[11] There aren't too many demonstrations outside the embassies of repressive governments from Eastern Europe, the Americas, Asia or Africa.

The New Partnership for Africa's Development (NEPAD) initiatives on governance and the creation of the African Union recognise this, though it makes for tough politics for progressive African leaders when the bad guys are in the room. But it is inspiring to listen to South Africa's President Mbeki or Nigeria's Olusegun Obasanjo and others urging that we go beyond the victim cult. Colonisation, slavery, imperialism were evils in their time. The West does carry guilt; in addition, because so many of the more recent failures of developing country policies can be traced to Marxism, an intrinsically European ideology. But as Churchill said: 'If we open a quarrel between the past and the present, we may lose the future.'

About the UN, Soros says: 'Its noble goals are expressed in the Preamble of the Charter, which is couched in terms of "We the People." But the Charter itself is based on the sovereignty of the member states, and the interests of the sovereign state do not necessarily coincide with the interests of the people who inhabit it. Many states are not democratic, and many inhabitants are not even citizens. As a result, the UN cannot possibly carry out the mission enunciated in the Preamble.'[12]

Soros has put his money where others mostly put their mouths, into directly assisting the building of democratic institutions on the ground, mainly in the economies in transition in the former Soviet bloc. Soros, through his foundation's networks, is spending $300–500 million annually in developing countries and economies in transition worldwide. And he has been creatively subversive: smuggling fax machines and photocopiers into the ex-Soviet colonies to boost the reach of civil society. He argues: 'In spite of its shortcomings, I am an ardent supporter of globalisation. I support it not only because of the extra wealth it produces, but even more because of the freedom it can offer. What I call a global open society could ensure a greater degree of freedom than any individual state. I consider the present arrangements, in which capital is free to move around, but social concerns receive short shrift, as a distorted form of a global open society.'[13]

He is not alone. A growing number of pro-free trade, pro-democracy, pro-good governance advocates are nonetheless uneasy about some aspects of globalisation. I share that unease. Unless it is answered, protectionist forces will regroup, which will be costly for everyone. Soros' manifesto calls for:[14]

'Institutional reforms in the following areas:

1 To contain the instability of financial markets;
2 To correct the built-in bias in our existing international trade and financial institutions (IFTIs) that favors the developed countries that largely control them;
3 To complement the World Trade Organization (WTO), which facilitates wealth creation, with similarly powerful international institutions devoted to other social goals, such as poverty reduction and the provision of public goods on a global scale; and
4 To improve the quality of public life in countries suffering from corrupt, repressive, or incompetent governments.'

The OECD was born out of the Marshall Plan; now it has 1500 people working for it. UNCTAD was supposed to be a conference, now it's an organisation. The WEF produces the World Competitiveness Report. Why isn't the OECD doing it? Because it would mean stepping on too many national sensitivities? What then should it be doing? These are core questions that need to be asked of all great international institutions about their original and future vision statements.

Increased donor conditionality is essential. We do need a world development bank, we do need an IMF; but mandates have to change. In many instances, the World Bank is simply rolling over bad money and there should be much more coherence between what the bank says and the IMF proposes. Their leaders know this, and the Wolfensen/Khol partnership gives rise to great hopes.

Democracy works because decision-makers are accountable, replaceable, expendable. As in any marketplace, there's always someone out there who's smarter, more ambitious, with a better idea or product, or who is more telegenic. Business, politicians, NGOs, trade unions, any form of leadership needs competition and rivals. The problem facing international institutions is that their accountability to governments is not often transparent, and deals between governments are compromises by their very nature. Any agreement is only yesterday's best endeavour. Trade-offs to make 'deals' must be private to governments, which can then sell the wider deals back home. Parliaments are televised, caucus and cabinet meetings will never be. Shareholder meetings are public events for business, unions and other players in civil society. Their board meetings can never be.

The hardest thing for a politician, business leader or institution is to say 'We got it wrong.' Political, social and economic markets are about confidence and reputations. Being imperfect, we do get it wrong, but that can be hard to say if you hope to maintain confidence in the marketplace. Accountability and transparency force corrections when people have information.

Whistle-blowers, the dissenting voice, media investigations are thus essential to correction. As Nobel prizewinner Joseph Stiglitz, past Chief Economist for the World Bank, notes in *Globalisation and its Discontents*, the institutions have sometimes been dead wrong.[15] He's right – billions of dollars were stolen in Russia and other economies in transition as a result of IMF policies in the late 1990s; Russians buying luxury houses with looted cash displaced Arab investors as premium buyers in London, generating a property boom.

Stiglitz writes: 'Not all the downsides of the Washington Consensus policies for the poor could have been foreseen, but by now they are clear...trade liberalisation *accompanied by high interest rates* is an almost certain recipe for job destruction and unemployment creation – at the expense of the poor. Financial market liberalisation *unaccompanied by an appropriate regulatory structure* is an almost certain recipe for economic instability – and may well lead to higher, not lower interest rates, making it harder for poor farmers to buy the seeds and fertilizer that can raise them above subsistence. Privatization, *unaccompanied by competition policies and oversight to ensure that monopoly powers are not abused*, can lead to higher, not lower, prices for consumers. Fiscal austerity, *pursued blindly*, in the wrong circumstances, can lead to high unemployment and a shredding of the social contract.' (*italics, Stiglitz*)

Crises are, by their immediate and urgent nature, desperate situations where decisions must be reached within hours and days on economies and societies threatened with collapse. The old joke in financial circles is that the only thing worse than the IMF coming in is when they don't. Battlefield surgery is always dangerous. As IMF Vice President Stanley Fischer has remarked: 'We are a bit like the doctor who visits and meets the patient, then gets the blame. The patient was already sick anyway.' It's easy to come up with a better answer with the luxury of distance from the field of war. Many books, scores of years after the event, have shown how Napoleon could have won at Waterloo – if only he'd had the benefit of the author's advice.

The Washington consensus must not be replaced by the anti-Washington consensus. Too often agencies have become the scapegoats for domestic shortcomings. Harold Wilson blamed the 'Gnomes of

Zurich' for his failures; some Asian governments blamed George Soros for the Asian Crisis.

Thinking back on the reforms in my own country, and the privatisations, so necessary to pay down debts, relieve a gigantic deficit and provide a more efficient domestic infrastructure and better allocation of resources, the absence of a competition policy was one of our biggest mistakes. The market *is* better equipped to get better outcomes, but privatisation at any cost costs a lot when – following noble, self-serving advice by rich countries and institutions – countries privatise telecommunications to one monopoly company, which can then charge what it likes, locking out the virtues of competition and shifting the social short-term cost of redundancies to the taxpayer. Then the sequence is wrong.

This did not happen in New Zealand to the same extent, but it is true of some developing countries and economies in transition. Food subsidies overall are counter-productive. Oil-rich countries that subsidise energy are fooling themselves and plundering their own resources. But what might be correct action for Europe, the USA or New Zealand is not always immediately correct for developing and vulnerable nations if social stability is to be maintained. What's the worst that can happen in New Zealand or France? Governments can fall, but no one really gets hurt, except for some bruised political egos. This is not true in more dangerous neighbourhoods, where failure can have lethal consequences.

The IMF's prescription, for example, in Indonesia to abolish food and kerosene subsidies, looked good on paper. But the impact on the poor was devastating. The riots, deaths and communal violence were predictable. Global economic policy must pay careful attention and focus on political social and ethnic stability. This is not to say we should do nothing; rather to look at *sequencing* before abruptly sentencing societies to violent disruption. Theories, beloved in the safety of marble institutional palaces, can have deadly implications for fragile societies. Radical reforms are frequently necessary, but without basic civil and political infrastructures, many recent reforms have allowed oligarchies to plunder economies as they moved from command systems to more open and free societies.

Pinochet in Chile overthrew the socialist democratically elected Allende. At the time, Allende was reported to have committed suicide – by shooting himself several times in the back, as was later revealed. Like most generals, Pinochet wanted to command the economy, but as that failed and unrest grew, even amongst his strongest supporters, he was given an ultimatum. He began to radically open up the Chilean economy, which eventually came to enjoy the highest growth rate in South America. His authoritarian government gave open markets a bad name for a decade at least, with the concepts of authoritarian political control and unfettered capitalism becoming linked, in some minds at least. Twenty years later, it bears an uncanny resemblance to China's reform process. An elected social democratic president from Allende's party is now carrying forward the same basic strategy with more effective social policies, protected human rights and less corrupt legal systems, with the military safely in their barracks.

By contrast, Bolivia's reforms were to become a model for the idea that democracies could open their markets without needing the force of a police state. Bolivia, the poorest South American country, has suffered 189 military coups in its modern history and saw inflation once peak at an astonishing 60,000 per cent per annum – prices were rising at 10 per cent every ten minutes. The government was spending thirty-six times more than it earned.[16]

In retrospect, it is surprising there hasn't been more violence and up-heaval in countries like Russia, where, as Stiglitz observes, radical reform failed. 'The devastation – the loss in GDP – was greater than Russia had suffered in World War II. In the period 1940–46 the Soviet Union indus-trial production fell 24 per cent. In the period 1990–99, Russian industrial production fell by almost 60 per cent – even greater than the fall in GDP (54 per cent). Those familiar with the history of the earlier transition in the Russian Revolution, *into* communism, could draw some comparisons between that socioeconomic trauma and the post-1989 transition: farm livestock decreased by half, investment in manufacturing came almost to a stop.'[17]

Life expectancy in Russia is now lower than in Indonesia or Egypt and death rates are higher than at the end of the Soviet era. But Russia was not a failure of markets, but of governance and government. The West was aware of the awesome strength of the Soviet military, but for decades underestimated its economic weakness. The Soviet Union was spending up to 50 per cent of GNP on defence, compared to 3–5 per cent in the West. If you gave the most efficient OECD factory one hundred points, its Soviet equivalent would rate ten. The Marxist line, 'to each according to his needs, from each according to their means' sounded seductive. In reality the old joke, 'We pretend to work, and they pretend to pay us' summed up the situation more accurately. Collapse was inevitable. But whereas if, say, Bulgaria collapses, the external consequences are rela-tively small, Russia is different. It has a massive nuclear capacity and its oil and gas plays a major role in the global energy market. Decision-makers have to take account of Russia. President Putin and the St Petersburg school of reformers are aware of the problems and are seeking to correct them. Yet another reason to think big about ensuring Russia's entry to the WTO.

According to a report by the Heritage Foundation, *The World Bank and Economic Growth, 50 Years of Failure*, of sixty-six less developed countries receiving money from the World Bank for more than twenty-five years, thirty-seven are no better off than they had been before they received their loan. Of these thirty-seven, twenty were actually worse off and of those twenty, eight had economies which had shrunk by at least 20 per cent since their first loan.[18] As Margaret Thatcher observed in her book *Statecraft:* 'No democratic government would have been re-elected if it turned in such a record. But although international institutions like the Bank may look all too like governments, they bear few similarities to democracies.' By no means all the blame can or should be laid on the World Bank of course; corruption, geographic conditions and location and myriad other factors are also involved. But past lack of accountability for programmes and short-term insistence by major shareholders for action to resolve immediate crises makes this work difficult to manage coherently. And is one reason why Bank President Jim Wolfensohn has heroically changed priorities and given new direction to the Bank.

The shock therapy advanced by theorists like Jeffrey Sachs, of a package of radical market reforms, had suggested short-term pain, unemployment, then recovery. It worked in Bolivia, less so in other places. It's interesting that in both South Korea and Poland, newly elected Nobel-winning Presidents had the initial support of the trade unions to manage the change. Spain and Portugal were led out of protectionist fascist-type government by enlightened socialist leaders. But governments that take on this challenge are politically doomed. I know; I was part of one. The reformers are associated with the pain, their successors with the results. Timing and sequencing is everything in politics, but there must be more to patriotic politics than winning elections.

The Solidarity trade union movement at its peak had 10 million members. Leader Lech Walesa became Poland's president and it won ninety-nine out of one hundred seats in parliament. The Soviet puppet communist bosses rang Mikhail Gorbachev and asked him what to do. Accept and announce the result he responded. Which was probably the most important and fateful phone call in history. It marked the end of communism and the beginning of the end of the Cold War. Before Solidarity, Polish shops were empty, mothers couldn't get milk for their children. Reforms more than doubled prices and people were hurt. The shipyard electrician who won the Nobel Prize and liberated his country, and was an inspiration for the liberation of half of Europe, at a subsequent election couldn't win two per cent of the vote. Shock therapy treatment is tough on the people and politicians of the time. But now Poland is progressing. The ex-communists have returned to power, but they are now pro-NATO, pro-EU membership and are not rolling back the reforms they opposed, nor are they strengthening the power of the state.

Horst Köhler, the new IMF Managing Director, stated on taking up his post: 'I will not have another Indonesia.' A painful lesson learnt. IMF First Deputy Managing Director Anne Kruger has publicly embraced some radical suggestions that only a few years ago were discounted, saying that perhaps, under certain conditions, government debt repayments could be temporarily suspended while negotiations take place on restructuring debt.[19] This would be a kind of international bankruptcy procedure.

It took centuries for the advanced economies to build up a core of domestic law. We are cautiously stumbling towards an international equivalent. It can only go so far. Those who see no need at all for an IMF or World Bank assert that these institutions create a moral hazard by their very existence. They are partly right about the moral hazard. But they are dangerously wrong about abolition offering a simple solution. Economic peacemakers and peacekeepers are as necessary as NATO and the UN. They offer last resort protection against domestic failure that impacts beyond national boundaries.

Some senior officials and think tanks are getting close to George Soros's ideas when they talk of empowering the IMF to issue SDR's – Special Drawing Rights – for financial emergencies. This would mean amending IMF articles and getting governments to commit more investment to the IMF. None of these policies will prevent financial crises for ever. Anymore than domestic bankruptcy laws outlaw company collapses. All politics is local and most economic policy outcomes are the result of political decision-making, which must balance domestic agendas. The question international agencies face is how to prevent local decisions badly made, contain them so they don't impact on others, then help rectify them.

What all this proves again is that when policy becomes ideology, then open, free dialogue and understandings of social and cultural historic prerogatives fly out the window. The principle of shoes is consistent, even if fashions in footwear change, but no one pair of shoes fits all. I suspect Lord Keynes, a founding father of the IMF, would have been puzzled, to say the least, about some of the prescriptions applied in the 1990s.

In the vacuum after the end of the Cold War, geo-economics for a time replaced geopolitics. Major powers wielded enormous political influence in institutions like the IMF and the World Bank. Loans to Russia were largely about bolstering Yeltsin and keeping the resurging communists out of power. In Indonesia, pressure went on to fuel reforms and force Suharto from power. Now observers are rethinking what was done, and asking whether there were better options available. This policy was prompted in part by concern over human rights issues and internationally reported revelations about the estimated $20 billion the Suharto family had allegedly diverted from the economy. Congress had been alerted to these issues by the NGOs and a concerned public through the media, which in turn forced the US President's hand.

One of the endearing features of the human species, in which I would bravely include politicians and economists, is our ability to fearless admit other people's mistakes. Still, this healthy hindsight makes us unique as a species; and it's a vital part of improving future perfomance. Stiglitz's book, like all such works – including even this one – is self-serving. It is a pity that the cheap shot Stiglitz took at the IMF's Stanley Fischer, a fine public servant, detracted from the important questions he raised. But the firestorm he has provoked is useful. When surgery is done on the battlefield, where options are narrow and decisions are made under pressure, some die on the operating table. Surprise-side economics are obviously dangerous. Have we learned anything from recent development history? Yes. Will future policies be based on our experience? I believe so.

All decisions are flawed, because people and information are imperfect, and the Bank and the Fund are only called upon when there is a failure of governance. The world would be a poorer place without these institutions. A world without the need for them would be truly wonderful – as would a world that did not need hospitals. The question is how do we keep people out of hospitals? So much surgery could be avoided if we lived healthier lives. Countries bent on economic suicide should not blame the doctor whose advice they have ignored.

Need for reform

There is a consensus that something must be done, some general agreement on what is needed, but no consensus on how we should go about it. Why? Because institutions cannot reform themselves. Two generations of institutional contamination and tenured self-interest ensure this deadlock continues. It's like asking the British House of Lords to reform itself.

Given all these challenges, contradictions and opportunities, I believe it is time for a small group of leaders to catalyse the issue of the democratic deficit in multilaterals; to seize it as an opportunity for progress, by beginning the reform and restructuring process. It is necessary to make institutions relevant and more legitimate; otherwise we risk further control of the agenda passing to some NGOs which – despite their claims to speak for the people – are largely unaccountable, except to themselves and their agendas, or as they would put it, their principles.

In mid-2002, I proposed to Kofi Annan that he should convene a panel of experts to examine how we can reform the system. Fifty-eight years ago, a small number of distinguished, principled people gathered in Bretton Woods, New Hampshire, to build the present international architecture. Their vision was born out of the nightmare of successive world wars and lessons from the Great Depression. The hotel still stands, little changed since it hosted that historic event. For once, there is a compelling argument that history should repeat itself. It is time for a new Bretton Woods conference. Where better to convene it?

We need to take a helicopter view of the issues, structures and objectives. Let's start with a clean piece of paper. I am proud of what I was able to accomplish at the WTO, in terms of organisational and operational changes, which I believe helped make it a more effective institution. But my time in Geneva, and a lifetime in domestic politics, has taught me that if you want gratitude get a dog; and if you want to be popular with staff and other agencies, then don't have too many new ideas. It's a poor bureaucrat who can't stall a good idea until its author is pleased to see it dead and buried. As Milton Friedman once said: 'Hell hath no fury like a bureaucrat scorned.'

Machievelli said that the reformer has for enemies all those who do well out of the old conditions, and as lukewarm supporters those who may do better out of new conditions and opportunities. I have an extensive background of public sector reform, but found international institutions to be considerably different. I have learnt that shortcuts take longer and that there is a difference between efficiency and effectiveness. I have some strong ideas on how this could be done, but, in my experience, reform fails if you signal your punches and don't build up constituencies for change.

We all could learn something from the example of Chinese poet Qu Yuan (c. 340–278 BCE) – a passionate opponent of corruption and mismanagement at court – whose patriotism led him to drown himself in frustration at his inability to save his beloved Chu state from Qin invaders and the corruption of his leaders. The story is commemorated in Chinese communities worldwide through the Dragon Boat races, which symbolise the search for Qu's body. But while the idea of Dragon Boat racing has been globalised, from Seattle to Wellington, few realise the genesis of this celebration of a great man's sacrifice. Perhaps we should suggest an alternative Nobel Prize for Good Governance, the Qu Yuan Award?

European Trade Commissioner Pascal Lamy has said of institutional reform that, first, it must be *transparent*; and second, it has to respect the good European principle of *subsidiarity*, by which we tackle subjects at the right level, only transferring to a higher body those questions which individuals, families, companies, villages, regions, nations cannot decide for themselves.

This is a promising basis on which to begin the debate. I am convinced that there is a compelling need for reform of the international architecture itself and the institutions within it, and that reform must be top-down. Political parties reform and reshape because they lose elections; businesses go bankrupt and start again, football teams lose and turn to new coaches, but institutions just keep on growing. When a new need emerges, the tendency has been to set up a new agency because the existing institution cannot do the job, rather than attempting to change and respond to the new mandate. A CEO is ultimately accountable to shareholders for success and failure, but in so far as restructuring is concerned, essentially only has to sell his strategy to the board. Their decision-making is considerably easier than trying to convince scores of member governments with conflicting agendas for change.

However, it is probably unrealistic to expect any group – however well-mandated – to impose discipline and change on the existing system without an enormous convergence of will on the part of the owner governments.

I do not underestimate or undervalue the depth of feeling of those protestors who wish to influence, or control, international institutions. I strongly believe – and have fought for – greater transparency about the workings of our institutions. I think a great deal of the basic misunderstandings about the alleged power and so-called hidden agendas of these organisations would be cleared up if wider civil society had a better grasp of how they actually work; the constraints under which they try to forge consensus, the very considerable challenge of building up infrastructure and honest institutions in the developing world; the good, the bad and the ugly of international diplomacy.

But I differ with many NGOs on how best to improve accountability. I believe that, in the first instance, we have a far more basic democratic need – to better reconnect ourselves to the owners of these institutions, the governments. While some governments are undemocratic, the vast majority are not, and an increasing number are elected. Most are more accountable and transparent than the demonstrators, who largely wield influence and exert power, without any need to demonstrate equal responsibility or do the hard work of seeking realistic sovereign country trade-offs between expenditures and priorities. The pie has to be divided up at some stage. And those are the difficult choices and hard work of governments.

A global democratic caucus

What should we do? I am not arguing for a global government, a dangerous concept that would set back the debate on global governance, because it would be misunderstood and seen as an attack on the nation state and is an unworkable utopian ideal.

Dozens of books, papers and speeches are being published about our new 'borderless' world. Many utopian academics are pursuing a general theme of contempt for the nation state. Debate is good, differences are healthy and necessary. But global government is a doomed and not a new ideal. No one can answer the simple question of constitution and representation; according to nations, people, proportionality to trade, population or what?

Would it be a true global democracy if India and China could outvote the world? Would it be a true global democracy if the microstates of the Pacific and the Caribbean could outvote Europe, China, the USA, India and Japan? This is where many suggest that democracy can be removed from states and the people and power planted in the hands of a globalised civil society and NGOs. *In Global Democracy*, Johan Galtung writes: 'States beware: as other key actors (NGOs, TNCs, LAs) catch the linkage between globalisation and democracy while states fail to do so, and the state system overdoes Westphalian sovereignty (350 years are enough!).' He and others speculate on one day bypassing the UN General Assembly, by a People's Assembly, directly elected. I find these arguments chilling.[20]

As Benjamin Barber observes in *Jihad vs. McWorld*: 'Specialists seem persuaded that to construct a new democracy, whether for Russia, Somalia, or for the whole planet, requires nothing more than the export of prefabricated constitutions and made-to-order parliamentary systems. Joshua Muravchik is a perfect exemplar, whose problems begin with the very title of his new book: *Exporting Democracy*. FedEx the Federalist Papers to Belorussia; send that multiparty system to Nigeria by parcel post; Email the Chinese the Bill of Rights; ship the UN a civilian-controlled, all-volunteer, obedient but conscience-sensitive peacekeeping force from a country with a high tolerance for casualties and no interest of its own . . . and in the flash of a laser beam: democracy. For global government, do exactly the same thing, globally. Not quite. Democracies are built slowly, culture by culture, each with its own strengths and needs, over centuries . . .'[21]

Nation-building, like bricklaying, is painstaking methodical work that requires a clear vision and plan, accepted and endorsed by the owners of the property.

But there are other initiatives that can work in parallel. Some thinkers have called for a global parliament. Richard Falk and Andrew Strauss have argued this case. They said: 'Citizens feeling unheard in the international system and often in their own domestic systems, have shown themselves willing to resort to increasingly destructive acts of violence. Setting up a global parliament is not as ambitious as it may sound. So as not to scare away national leaders, it could begin life as a largely advisory body. This is how its prototype, the European Union's directly elected European Parliament, began, Surely, with the power of popular sovereignty behind it, the Global Parliament, would, like the European Parliament, grow in power over time.'[22] This is debatable given the average 10 per cent lower turn-out in European Parliamentary elections than in national elections.[23]

The so-called Community of Democracies was advanced at a Warsaw conference in 2000 by Madeleine Albright. William Safire revisited this subject in a column in 2002 commenting on the expulsion of the USA from the Human Rights Commission. Rather than suspending US involvement in UN bodies, he suggested: 'A more creative reaction to the domination of the United Nations by dictatorships, oligarchies, and rogue nations, would be to breathe life into a parallel structure created with some fanfare, but largely forgotten, the Community of Democracies.'[24] Rather than being an alternative UN, this would create a democracy caucus within it, to promote human rights, transparency and the rule of law.

This idea has merit. But we need a voluntary global democratic caucus. This would not be directly elected, but made up of existing senior parliamentarians, serving in their national legislatures, who could form a caucus to provide the embryonic oversight of the international institutions, This democratic caucus could reach into their respective parliaments and congresses and bring into play a serious attempt to provide systematic oversight and begin to hold the great international institutions to democratic account – or at least under the eye of those who provide 90 per cent of the finance and represent over 90 per cent of world trade.

I am not arguing for a formal organisation – we have too many already. This democratic caucus meets now, very informally, in various fora around the world. I am arguing that we need, to a greater extent, to support both customers and owners to ensure that liberal democratic ideas prevail over the recalcitrance and self-interest of many of our tenured bureaucrats, those ambassadors and ministers who will leverage any situation for short-term mercantile gain, and the excesses and ignorance of the more extreme protestors.

I see this as not replacing national governments, but strengthening their surveillance and role in international institutions. A 'big fix' is utopian and unworkable. But a solid step can be made, rather than a great, but unworkable leap. Let's face it; although having parliamentarians assemble alongside the UN and other agencies could increase their accountability, there will never be an elected global government. Esperanto and Prohibition were probably good ideas too, but they didn't work either.

One reason I put so much effort into involving parliamentarians, congresses and ministers in the WTO – often against both bureaucratic and diplomatic resistance – was to address this democratic deficit and encourage greater national engagement with the WTO. I know that even if we conclude the Doha Development Round on time – which we can – it's difficult to believe that 144 parliaments, congresses, diets and dumas will find it easy to get the coalitions together to back the required ratification legislation. That is one reason why I started a 'bank' of politicians and champions of free trade, who can provide a counter-argument to the relentless anti-globalist campaigners. Ministers will be able to pull down from this bank of legislators, teams who could visit their parliamentary committees and share experiences and perhaps mould opinion. This will be important during the negotiations and more so when the deal is struck, given the complexity of the Doha Agenda and the changing configurations of congress and parliaments.

I advocated a democratic caucus to make existing institutions more workable, better focused and better led. J. F. Rischard, in his book *High Noon*, also offers an interesting approach; he identifies twenty major global problems and proposes a detailed twenty-year strategy to solve them. Rischard argues for creating a series of global projects based on the twenty most important issues for our progress – even survival – around what he calls Global Issues Networks. These would bring together governments, international civil society organisations and businesses to define each issue, establish a time frame, then throw back to governments the role of producing action.[25]

This action could be unilateral; perhaps a sponsor government would take the responsibility for a core global problem and use the available networks to prod and assist the established structures to respond better. This already happens. New Zealand, for example, took the lead two decades ago over the Law of the Sea, and was equally strong in pushing for what eventually became the Antarctic Treaty. More recently, action to ban landmines was initiated by an NGO, which advanced public opinion, then found a sponsor government, Canada, to push the case through the international system.

With a sponsor-led approach, there would be less likelihood of dumbing down solutions to the lowest common denominator or the slowest rogue state. Peer pressure, civil society oversight and political awareness could create an upward pressure to reach a global set of standards to deal with major issues, rather than the lowest common denominator results that sometimes come from the consensus systems of inter-governmental negotiations.

Rischard reminds us how, for example, the International Organization for Standardization has over the years pioneered norms and standards for thousands of products from condoms to credit cards with its ISO 9000 practices. This voluntary code is aspired to by both businesses and government organisations, because it gives their products and processes credibility and consistency. These ideas, refined and defined, could act as a spur to assist established institutions. The strength of such an approach is that it is problem/project driven, not powered by a jaded bureaucracy or tired structures. It has allowed the peaceful globalisation of many of the products we take for granted, creating savings and efficiencies without arousing the anger and compromises often engendered when governments negotiate.

The need for good governance is a cliché, but, like most clichés, based on a fundamental truth; progress is best achieved under conditions of freedom, democracy and the rule of law. The pillars of civilised progress can best be advanced by the strengthening of institutions that promote democratic political parties, open commerce, free and fair media, free trade unions and religious tolerance. For these freedoms to flourish, institutions need to be strengthened and sometimes even established, so they can operate in a transparent, effective manner. The conditions for progress include such basic elements of democratic society as proper customs systems, honest finance ministries, autonomous central banks.

In the current climate of opinion, political parties and politicians are increasingly distrusted and disliked. But strong, competitive, transparently run and accountable political parties are a necessity for democracy to function. This area is not promoted effectively by the international community, and certainly not by most NGOs, who see political parties as rivals as they trawl for committed, idealistic young activists. Political party membership is in decline; weak membership leads to weak decision-making.

As noted earlier, one of my innovations at the WTO was to encourage dialogue with and bring together such international party political organisations as Socialist International (represented in over fifty governments), the Democratic Union (representing conservative parties) and the Liberal International; the proposed Green International should also be part of this dialogue.

These groups are in broad agreement on the fundamentals of political life; that the peaceful transfer of power and accountable government, are good things. As umbrella groups, they could do a great deal to strengthen the building of democratic institutions. It would be a very positive move for these political internationals to cooperate, and for resources to be found to endow efforts to help create the socio-political infrastructure that helps build democratic infrastructures. Clean and transparent political parties are important to democratic economies. But no one speaks up for political parties and politicians. Sadly, the opposite is true: the media, many NGOs and much of the public hold politicians in contempt. And that is dangerous.

Although free trade and fair markets are very good things, they are not an end in themselves; it is not, as some free marketers seem to suggest, a case of abolishing all taxes and the role of government and thus ending poverty overnight. There are public goods – be it in heritage, health or housing for the poor – that the market on its own cannot provide. Justice systems, policing, defence and security are and must remain the basic responsibilities of the state.

Margaret Thatcher once famously claimed, 'There is no such thing as society.' I believe there is, and that it needs to be liberated, nurtured and protected. As we learnt from the great depression and world wars, we need economic and political safety nets and systems, not only to protect the poor and each of us from the other, but to preserve the market from itself. The open market on Monday can be a monopolised market by Friday, and then all the virtues of open markets are under siege. It is the natural tendency of business to seek more and bigger market share. That's why antitrust, competition, transparency policies are necessary. They act as a cleansing agent of good corporate administrative practice, illuminating, providing information for the system to work so it can continue to improve itself.

It's time also to celebrate and recognise that public service and bureaucracies are important to make society function. We have to convince citizens that public goods are better paid for together, because on our own we will never have the parks, the museums, the art galleries, clean air, education facilities or police necessary to make life worthy of its promise. These are things individuals, communities, corporations and nations must do together.

There are some fundamental values we should be fighting for. It's worth considering that, if we tried to introduce a Universal Declaration of

Human Rights now, it would take forever to pass in the UN. Yet this was a positive move, reinforced by the strong and confident position of the democratic west following the Second World War. The democracies were right about universal values: they are not a new form of imperialism. We should stop the cringing and become more assertive. Globalisation isn't responsible for all the ills of the world: a rules-based system to encourage free trade has improved prosperity worldwide and the institutions created after the war are important, useful and central to peace, prosperity and a better life for us all.

Technology has had a significant impact on global conflict. The information age has extended terrorists' reach, but it has also created the capacity for more effective responses, which offer the potential to reduce civilian casualties. War is the ultimate failure of politicians and diplomacy – an abomination always – but sometimes necessary. Over the years, the international community has developed some rules, standards and still-imperfect institutions to try to contain and manage conflicts. The Geneva Convention, the Red Cross societies, UN agencies to assist refugees, the International Court of Justice at the Hague can all help when the worst finally happens.

Democracies are always slow to act because they have processes and publics to consider. Dictators can be more decisive in the initial stages of war; democracies have to calculate the response of congress, pollsters, CNN, Civil Society and elections.

We can take some small comfort from the fact that war in some theatres is getting more effective, targeted and is now aimed by NATO and UN-sponsored responses at minimising what is euphemistically called collateral damage. The 9-11 terrorist attack was aimed at maximising civilian casualties; the US response was targeted at minimising civilian deaths.

David Halberstam, in his book *War in a Time of Peace,* writing of the planning in response to the invasion of Kuwait, observes that previously to secure a 90 per cent probability of having hit a target, the US had to drop some 9,000 bombs, involving 1,000 bombers and placing 10,000 men at risk. By contrast, with the new weaponry one plane flown by one man with one bomb could have the same level of probability, an improvement in effectiveness of approximately 10,000-fold.[26] (Which is not to say that mistakes do not happen; we are all at the mercy of the information available to us, but now civilian casualties are seen as horrific accidents, not used as deliberate targets.)

'What happened in Iraq was a precursor to the future. During the Gulf War, only about a third of the bombs were precision instruments, whereas two-thirds of the targets were hit by them.' The circle of bombing error had come down from 1,000 metres near the end of the Second World War, to 2 metres or even smaller. One military projection estimated that two squadrons of F-117s (a total of forty-eight Stealth fighters, not even the B-2 Stealth bombers soon to come) would have shut down the production of wartime Germany in approximately six weeks, instead of the three years it took. Some suggest that bombing Baghdad or Afghanistan is the same as the horrific attacks on 9-11. There is no moral equivalence. Bin Laden's attacks were aimed at maximising civilian casualties, whereas the coalitions' attacks against Milosevic and in the Gulf War were aimed at minimising civilian casualties.

The world will never be entirely safe; madmen like Milosovic and bin Laden will always exist. Neutralising them and bringing them to justice is the challenge. But others will appear and will have to be dealt with. Each time we learn and try to do better next time. For generations, foreign policy was based on non-interference in the affairs of other sovereign states. But now the civilised world sees and learns what's happening, often knowing more about the excesses in Rwanda, Cambodia or what was Yugoslavia, than their repressed and violated citizens. Freely available information about human rights violations and genocide in one country creates a demand in democracies, via outraged public opinion, for action, an answer and a result.

Terrorists aren't new, though the media provides an instant global stage for the few to hijack the many to demonstrate their atrocities. There is an interesting parallel here with piracy on the Barbary Coast in the early twentieth century, which helped lead the USA and President Teddy Roosevelt out of isolationism and into treaties and partnerships to fight and then civilise this menace. The media, hostage-taking and an outraged voting population was then also a spur to united action.

Bringing evil leaders to justice is only an important first step. They prosper in failing states. Nation- and institution-building, allowing commerce to flourish, building schools, hospitals and roads, is now accepted as the next phase of eliminating the conditions that allow extremists to flourish. This is true, whether in Yugoslavia or Afghanistan. The results have not been perfect, but this new direction is clear and appropriate. Hitting and running is no longer a good enough response to terrorists or dictators who threaten their neighbours as well as global tranquillity and progress.

The Marshall Plan worked when much more money had been spent in other continents, because there were institutions to build and resurrect. Nation-building is coming back into fashion. Remember Churchill's stirring speech in Fulton, Missouri, where he described an Iron Curtain descending across Europe from the Baltic to the Adriatic. In September 2002, seven ex-Soviet satellites from the Baltic to the Black Sea applied for membership of NATO – and this will happen. The story hardly rated front page coverage. The world has come a long way in a short time.

I am hopeful. It is impossible now to imagine a Europe-wide war. I hope I live long enough to see a free-trading and democratic Europe extending from the Atlantic to the Pacific Ocean. Britain is now united to Europe, not by its 400-year strategy of doing deals with the reigning second power in Europe, but by the EU and trade culture and the 'Chunnel' – itself an idea that goes back to Lloyd George's suggestion at the Versailles' negotiations (albeit that this had military connotations then). Anti-European feelings in the UK still run deep; a large minority still cling to the balance of power theories of British engagement in Europe, even if they can't articulate centuries of distrust, conflict and suspicion. Others have legitimate concerns over sovereignty and the reduction of Westminister's authority.

Equally, the predominance of US power and its perceived unilateralism will continue to arouse ire in the councils of Europe, not to mention the Middle East and many parts of Asia and Africa. This is inevitable and has been true of leading powers throughout history. The US economy is twice the size of its nearest economic rival Japan. The US government plans to spend more on defence in 2003 than the next fifteen to twenty biggest spending nations combined.[27]

The US remains the sole superpower; the complaint is that everyone needs to understand their politics, but they don't have to understand ours. The resentment is understandable. But as great powers go, the USA is arguably the most benign in history. Name another empire whose power has more often been directed towards transferring democratic ideals and accountability. Too many individuals and states defines themselves on how anti- or pro-American they can be, which is immature, dangerous and sometimes confuses US opinion-leaders.

H. W. Brands observes in *The Strange Death of American Liberalism* that from the Second World War until the 1970s, Americans trusted governments: Eisenhower's great public works, the interstate highway system, public universities, unemployment insurance, civil rights; JFK's New Frontier, then LBJ's Great Society. All of this contributed to a strong belief among the best and brightest that public service could deliver peace at home and abroad, in tandem with economic growth and social justice.[28]

Then came Vietnam, Watergate, high inflation and the collapse of LBJ's Great Society under the weight of its tax burden. Washington became seen as a venal place of self-interest, not of public service. The West has long lectured the world about the need for good governance; that domestic markets need competition, transparency and public investment in the intellectual infrastructure of health, transportation, communications, education, early and now for life. That workers need wages high enough to support retirement plans, further education and to support consumption, without borrowing too much. Now that successful, largely US, model is under attack.

The public humiliation and downright dishonesty of corporations who cooked their books, lied to shareholders, employees and consumers, revealed through 2001–2, introduced a new and dangerous element to anti-Americanism. The entire capitalist model, envied and exported from the USA, has taken a series of blows to its credibility. It will recover. The escalating exposés of corporate greed and chicanery will see Presidents, Congress and the guardians of the markets enter into a new phase of active regulation to clean up Wall Street and the corporate world.

Sarcastic comments from the developing world about the US corporate structure have inevitably surfaced, unsurprising given the lectures about good commercial governance delivered by the West to Asia, Mexico and Russia during their crises. President Bush is taking the lead, as he must. Domestic politics demands action because it is no longer about a few capitalists losing personal fortunes. It is about workers' pension plans, investor confidence and the need for the USA to remain attractive to investors; elections are about market corrections. Let us not forget that the USA is the engine room of the world economy, and remains a very prosperous place; 250,000 Americans have fortunes worth more than $10 million and about 10,000 Americans are worth more than $65 million according to *Forbes* magazine, which claims that the 400 richest Americans were ten times richer in the year 2000 than the 400 richest Americans in 1990, even though the economy was only twice as large. When the USA catches a cold, the rest of us get pneumonia.

The true genius of America is not just an incredible capacity for innovation and generating prosperity, but rather how rapidly circumstances change and how quickly leadership imposes reforms. One danger for the USA is of a regulatory overcorrection, that would make other investment destinations and currencies more attractive. We should get real. Dishonest people break laws; they broke the existing ones, they will break the new laws – that is what outlaws do. But to rebuild confidence, the public needs to see suitable punishment dealt out (see Chapter 14). Progress can best be made when problems are aired, debated and eventually corrected by governments taking action by legislation, or by democracy replacing those in power who just don't get it or fail to retain the electorate's confidence.

Joseph S. Nye commented recently: 'If America first makes an effort to consult others and try a multilateral approach, its occasional unilateral tactics are more likely to be forgiven. But if it succumbs to the unilateralist temptation too easily, it invites the criticism the Bush administration now faces. Moreover, America will often fail, because of the intrinsically multilateral nature of transnational issues in a global age, and there will be costly effects on US soft power. In general, even a superpower should follow the rule of thumb, "Try multilateralism first".'[29]

Bismarck once famously remarked that conducting foreign policy with principles would be like walking along a narrow forest path while carrying a long pole between one's teeth. Sometimes, I think, the smaller the country, the bigger the principles, because they don't have to carry the weight and eventual consequences of responsibilities.

The New Zealand Labour tradition I grew up in is purely Wilsonian, whereas the opposing conservative ethic has been that of dutiful colony, deft small partner to the powerful. Willy Brandt was rudely confronted by a strident leftist during a visit to my party caucus, who demanded of the great man that Germany kick out the Americans and their nuclear bases. He replied, rolling his eyes upwards, 'Oh, New Zealand, so lucky to be so far away. I have found that idealism increases in direct relationship to your distance from the problem.'

How does the Wilsonian idealist handle the following question? A fundamentalist-supported political party seeks election on the basis that, when elected, there will be no further elections and the state will no longer be secular, but based on their interpretation of the people's common faith? This has happened, is happening and will happen again. A minister in a Muslim country told me a story about an outside-directed religious protest about his government's moderate (i.e. by the critics' interpretation, decadent, impious) policies. The male protestors, dressed as women, were there to destabilise his country. 'What did you do?' I asked. 'We killed them all and sent their bodies back as a warning.' Life and politics can be brutal; not all societies have the luxury of liberal democratic choices.

There has never been a truly golden age for everyone, nor will there be. But we are entering an era of growing, robust, more transparent internationalism. Civilization and progress are – or should be – about ensuring steady improvements in people's lives. Globalisation, the information age, democratic space and freedoms of all types are growing. The nation state has gradually and often painfully evolved democratic values and safeguards. But there is as yet no accepted body of law, values and formal democratic controls, to manage globalisation. We are now in the process of wrestling with these issues and opportunities, and evolving answers.

The curse of short-termism

One of the curses of our age is short-termism – what the Cambridge historian Christopher Andrew aptly describes as Historical Attention Span Deficit Disorder. 'No previous period in recorded history has been so persuaded of the irrelevance of the past experience of the human race . . . the lack of a long-term historical perspective distorts our view of the future as well as our understanding of the past.'[30]

As noted earlier, one of the chronic problems of our age is a tendency for politicians to develop policies on the basis of focus groups, and to resort to spin-doctors to camouflage bad decisions. Spin-doctoring is by its very nature short-term, driven by the demands of the news cycle. Short-termism has many manifestations; from the countries that devalued in the 1960s and 1970s looking for a short-term gain in exports; to those which respond to domestic calls for protection with high tariffs to feed election cycle needs; to those who borrow to stoke consumption rather than build infrastructure and institutions; to companies that manipulate quarterly results for paper stock-market gains. Unions which demand pay increases that reward those with jobs at the expense of those without jobs; politicians who promise pension handouts when they know demographics make these unviable. Governments that run down their education systems and infrastructure pay later; business people who harvest in an unsustainable manner and pollute the environment. They all send the bill to the next generation.

We are going through a complex transformation in our world's history. What we are trying to do now at the international level is create a functioning system of checks and balances. But we sometimes forget it took the nation states centuries to evolve limitations on the power of the sovereign, accountable political and tax systems, reduce the excesses of the Industrial Revolution, build up trade unions, civil society and the checks, balances, freedom of the press and of information, to ensure it functioned. It still doesn't in many places.

The rights of man have been won by bloodshed and over many years. From the first signing of the Magna Carta in 1215 to British women getting the vote in 1924 took more than half a millennium of bloody wars and revolutions, and the reaction to this of Madame Guillotine's masters and the Russian Revolution, which shook the establishment to its roots. It took centuries to develop an effective public service which allowed the Age of Empire to explode over great distances and to function; then for a nation state to emerge and evolve that protected the people's rights and was not an instrument to oppress and exploit the citizenry by powerful elites. People sought protection from the state and the crown and slowly won this war, battle by battle.

In practice, the modern world began in 1776, when proud pioneers put pen to paper and drafted the US Constitution. Previously, patriotism was based on the nation state and the divine right of kings. Now, certain rights were to be held as self-evident. Patriotism was henceforth also to be about a set of principles and ideals that had universal application. The US Constitution embodied the best from the Age of Enlightenment. The people, not the kings, were to be the masters. In the famous Churchill speech in Missouri 1946, which has not enjoyed the same coverage as his warning about the Iron Curtain descending across Europe, he pointed out: 'We must never cease to proclaim in fearless tones the great principles of freedom and the rights of man which are the joint heritage of the English-speaking world and which through Magna Carta, the Bill of Rights, the Habeas Corpus, trial by jury and the English Common Law find their most famous expression in the American Declaration of Independence.'

There are many reasons for the American War of Independence, some romantically embellished over time. Trade played an important role. The British sought to protect their manufacturers and prevented the colonists from producing many products, including nails, and even hats. In London, Benjamin Franklin argued and asked whether it mattered if Englishmen on either side of the Atlantic produced the same product. Colonists were obliged to send their beavers to England to be processed and then purchase them back and pay tax over which they had no control. This became a classic case of trade diversion as the American 'English' sought control over sources for their imports, and finally rebelled so they could manage their own affairs.

A central theme of this book is democracy, the rule of law and property rights. Louis Menand reminds us in his book *The Metaphysical Club* that, for most of history, 'coercion is natural, freedom is artificial. Freedoms are socially engineered spaces where parties engaged in specific pursuits enjoy protection from parties that naturally seek to interfere in those pursuits. One person's freedom is therefore always another's restriction. Rights are created not for the good of individuals but for the good of society. Individual freedoms are manufactured to achieve group ends.'

The task is still not complete everywhere, but democracy is evolving and expanding. Central to this evolution is popular representation, universal enfranchisement, Bills of Rights, separation of powers, equality under the law, the right to industrial collective bargaining and to a trial by your peers. Systems to expose and regulate excessive political and commercial power are also necessary to act as a necessary balance. Countries with the most mature and sophisticated democratic instruments of public policy do the best.

It will take an enormous amount of patience, perseverance and people's will and faith, to ensure that the institutions we have created for global governance are open and also serve their owner government's needs, and through that their citizens' will. Constitutions are all very worthy, but they never stopped lynchings or the obstruction of people's rights. It took until the 1970s in the USA for African Americans to be fully enfranchised. Before then, they were subject to manifest injustices and indignities, including being subject to such unanswerably absurd questions as how many bubbles there were in a bar of soap, before they could vote. The Soviet constitution guaranteed every conceivable right, but was never implemented. There is still a hangover of these ideas in many countries, and in delegates' interventions in international institutions, with ringing rhetoric and meaningless statements of intent that can never be implemented or audited. Revolutionaries have now become resolutionaries.

Implementing bold ideals and protecting them from abuse at the national and international level is still a grand cause. And it won't be realised without permanent vigilance, focus and the active participation of leaders in politics, business and wider society.

The Industrial Revolution created new societies, nations and superpowers. The governmental machinery created in the eighteenth century couldn't cope and both reform and revolution were in the air. Parliamentary democracies adjusted – slowly, but they adjusted. Trade unions, suffragettes and other great movements for change, backed by progressive churches and political parties, sought to soften the excesses of the age. Lyndon Johnson used the willing political might of the AFL-CIO to press Congress to pass civil rights legislation. Without that determined NGO, the NAACP, would civil rights have been advanced in the USA? No. Many of these struggles were eventually won, though the appeal to the poor of both fascism and communism in the early twentieth century is easy to understand. Democracy had to evolve or die. It expired in many places and adjusted in others to the new conditions. So must our great multilateral institutions evolve, or they will be sidelined with the contempt they will deserve.

That's why the new internationalism holds so much hope. People worldwide are demanding more accountability and transparency from their leaders, in politics, business, sports, religion. NGOs hunt and haunt leaders. Journalists, raised in an age of cynicism and abuse of power, have exposed corruption in such once impregnable strongholds of piety as the

Olympics, FIFA, the churches and big business pin-up CEOs. This *can* be healthy. We live in an age of scepticism. Trust must be earned. But we must beware of betraying people's faith in institutions. It is much easier to raze the castle, than reconstruct a new architecture based on the wisdom of the founding fathers of Bretton Woods and on values that are now seen as beyond the experience of any one civilisation or continent, but truly universal.

Globalisation should not be idealised or demonised. There are the fundamentalist utopians who think the state, the market, their religion or whatever can solve everything. It's dangerous when free trade and the virtues of markets are lifted to a level of theology; no one single idea solves everything. The market is simply the most efficient and effective mechanism to create private wealth, from which governments can take a share to provide for public goods. Private and public goods should not be in conflict, but sometimes are, because of the conflicts between short- and long-termism discussed earlier.

Disease, terrorism, climate change and pollution don't respect lines on a map, nor do they bother to fill in customs forms or landing cards. We sink or swim together, our interdependence never so obvious and public in the history of our species.

By now you will have worked out that I am an incurable optimist. Think of five images that are etched into our recent historical memory. The brave young man standing in front of the tank in Tiananmen Square; the Berlin Wall coming down; Nelson Mandela's smile and victory dance upon liberation; the smiling eyes of those Afghan girls, free to go to school at last. And the queues of Zimbabweans, defying intimidation and corruption for hours in the sun for their chance to vote. As basic rights and instincts are reinforced around the globe, freedoms grow, and we are all better off and more secure.

16   Future challenges

When the Uruguay Round was launched, the Cold War imprisoned half the world in deep freeze, dictators monopolised power in most of Latin America, Eastern Europe and Africa, and Nelson Mandela, Vaclav Havel and Kim Dae Jung were oppressed dissidents. Such wonders – and horrors – as faxes, cellphones, the Internet and AIDS, were barely on the horizon. As we move towards concluding the first new Trade Round launched since then, we need to be aware we could be undone by fall-out from changes that we cannot yet envision. Failure to exercise our imaginations may leave us open to disaster.

Even the best minds can get the future badly wrong. Alexander Graham Bell thought the phonograph would be used mainly for recording and playing back wills. In the 1800s, economist Stanley Jevons predicted that Britain would be destroyed as a superpower because it would run out of coal. Thomas Malthus thought that rising populations would lead to mass famines, while Rachel Carson's *Silent Spring* predicted back in 1962 that manmade chemicals would wipe us all out within 20 years. *Science Digest* predicted a new Ice Age in the 1970s. Yet within a few years, equally reputable scientists were suggesting that we are more likely to end up in a global sauna. In 1980, acid rain was going to kill all the forests in Europe and North America. It didn't happen. Remember the Club of Rome predicting, in *The Limits to Growth* in 1972, that gold would be exhausted by 1981, tin by 1987, petroleum by 1992, and copper, lead and natural gas by 1993? We now have more copper than we can use, in the form of phone wires buried underground and close to redundant because of the invention of high-bandwidth fibre optic cable. And of course Bill Gates, the greatest technology strategist of the past century, famously initially failed to grasp the importance of the Internet.

A characteristic of all these mistaken projections, of course, is that people and governments responded to these dangers and change, embraced some aspects, rejected others, dealt with the downside, and ultimately absorbed new technologies, in the process reconfiguring the world. That process continues; I believe that globalisation, in tandem with a new

249

democratic internationalism, provides the world with its best hope for growth and security.

We've built up great international institutions. With all their imperfections, a world without them would be unmanageable and dangerous. There is always an industry of black armband wearers who will predict disaster. I believe they underestimate the intelligence and capacity of political and economic markets to correct failure once alerted to problems. We owe a duty of care even to false prophets, because they alert us to potential dangers. But while end-of-the-world doomsayers can carve out a higher profile than last century, thanks to the wonders of the Internet and the global media, we are nonetheless on the threshold of delivering longer and more sustained peace, longer and more sustained economic growth, and a fairer and better society.

Our great-grandparents would be astounded at the wonders of our world. In their time there were no aeroplanes, cars, computers or telecommunications. No one had ever heard a radio or seen a television show. Add to this refrigeration, power, air conditioning and central heating, instant hot water, space travel, automatic washing machines, dishwashers, microwaves and the vast cornucopia of other new products. Now the middle classes in the developed world enjoy a lifestyle that emperors in the past could not dream about. Meanwhile, the poor of the world can at least increasingly see, taste and aspire to those riches and are making their presence and their demands known.

But if we cannot know the future, we can see the shape of some of what is to come. Putting to one side such important macro issues as the geopolitics of China as the new superpower, Russia reintegrating into the world economy, poverty, and the political external and internal clash of civilisations and religions, there are some other key issues I believe will shape our world. These include emerging trends in biotechnology, population movement, the AIDS epidemic, health and ageing, and women's roles in society, all of which will have a profound impact on global policymaking.

The AIDS epidemic and the impact of ill health on society

The Rev. Thomas Malthus was dead wrong in his population predictions, though there are still echoes of that old hymn being hummed by some NGOs and professional scaremongers. The world is not going to become overrun with people we can't feed. But AIDS is threatening to undo decades of progress in increasing life expectancy in the developing world, and poses an enormous threat to social stability and economic growth prospects worldwide. The epidemic is real.

AIDS is the fourth biggest killer worldwide. Nearly 41 million people are infected with the AIDS virus worldwide, according to the US Agency for International Development (USAID). Since the epidemic was known, more than 60 million people have been infected by the virus.[1] UNAIDS/WHO reported that at the end of 2001, 40 million people are living with HIV/AIDS, a third of those are aged 15–24.

HIV/AIDS is predicted to cut life expectancy in South Africa to thirty-eight years. Some 30 per cent of South Africa's work force will be HIV positive by 2005, according to one estimate, by NMG Levy, a South African consultancy. However, the worst reported figures in Sub-Saharan Africa are in Botswana. Of its 1.7 million people, 38 per cent of the sexually active population between the ages of 15 and 49 are HIV positive. Between 1990 and 2000, life expectancy has dropped from sixty-four years to thirty-nine years. The country will have a lower life expectancy twenty-five years from now, than it did fifty years ago, according to Nicholas Eberstadt of the American Enterprise Institute. But, as their Health Minister Joy Phumaphi stressed to me, Botswana's figures are the highest in Africa because they admit the problem and have the best reporting system. Indeed, Botswana has one of the most effective public services in Africa.

The AIDS epidemic is not confined to Sub-Saharan Africa. A recent report published by UNAIDS/WHO states that Eastern Europe, especially the Russian Federation, has the steepest growth of HIV/AIDS infection in the world. In China, HIV/AIDS infection grew by 67.4 per cent in the first six months of 2001. At the end of 2000, 3.8 million people in India were living with HIV/AIDS, more than any other country with the exception of South Africa.[2] Cambodia reportedly now has 13,000 new full-blown AIDS cases a year with an estimated 250,000 sufferers in a country of 11.5 million; and the country's growing reputation as a sex tour destination, is only likely to make matters worse.[3]

Eun Jung Cahill Che, of the Children's Rights Program of the Hawaii Institute for Human Rights, gives a sense of the devastating impact of AIDS. Writing in the *International Herald Tribune* in 2002, Che noted that the millions of dead are not the only victims. 'Millions of children are left behind when their parents die. The US Census Bureau estimates that 15.6 million children were orphaned by the year 2000 in the 23 countries hardest hit by the virus. USAID projects that the number could reach 28 million worldwide by 2010. For children orphaned by AIDS, survival is uncertain at best. They are often stigmatized and isolated from society. Some studies suggest that orphans will eventually comprise up to a third of the population under age 15 in some countries.' Che adds that, because of its large population, Asia could have an even larger AIDS orphan problem than Sub-Saharan Africa, where orphans are often absorbed into an extended family of relatives.[4]

MIT's Juan Enriquez notes that in Zimbabwe businesses train three executives for each job because two may die of AIDS. A South African mining company reports that over 25 per cent of its is workforce infected; another company says the cost of their high rates of infection adds £8–10 to the cost of producing an ounce of gold.

But the world's health problems extend beyond AIDS. The report of the Commission on Macroeconomics and Health (CMH), chaired by Jeffrey Sachs, was published in December 2001. Commissioned by the Director General of the World Health Organisation, Dr Gro Harlem Brundtland, it addressed the magnitude of health issues and how they will impact the Millennium Development Goals. *Macroeconomics and Health: Investing in Health for Economic Development* stresses the longer-term losses to society through ill health. The report states that each life year is valued at around three times the person's annual earnings, reflecting the value of leisure time, market consumption, the pure longevity effect, and the pain and suffering associated with disease. A lost life at age twenty is by some estimates taken to be equal to a hundred times or more annual earnings.

'Whatever the precise numbers, the calculations remind us of something important,' the report states. 'When we assess the costs of a disease on society, we must ask, not only how the disease affects the level and growth of per capita GNP (for example by reducing worker productivity), but also how the disease affects the lifespan and lifetime earnings lost by society.'

The CMH report concludes that the resources and know-how exist to save millions of lives; that better health can be a major catalyst for economic development; and that a new 'health pact' between donors and recipients, and major new investment in health are needed to achieve this.[5]

With respect to HIV/AIDS, malaria and tuberculosis, effective intervention could save as many as 8 million lives annually by 2010, with many millions more relieved from disease and suffering and leading productive lives. According to information supplied to me by the pharmaceutical company Merck, a number of factors have caused an increase in malaria cases, including the increasing spread of populations across borders since South Africa held democratic elections in 1994, unusually heavy rainfall between 1997 and 2000, and the removal of DDT from malaria control programmes.[6]

But it will require a major commitment of energy and resources to make good these problems. For low-income countries, an incremental

Table 5. *Estimated incremental annual costing for required interventions for a range of illnesses ($ billion 2002)*

	2007	2015
HIV		
Prevention	6	8
Care of opportunistic infection	3	6
Highly active anti-retroviral therapy	5	8
Malaria		
Treatment	2	3
Prevention	0.5	1
Tuberculosis	0.5	1
Childhood-related illness		
Treatment	4	11
Immunisation	1	1
Maternity-related illness	4	5
Health system and other expenditures	31	50
Total	57	94
of which low-income countries	40	66

Source: WHO, 2002.

cost of $40 billion per year (at 2002 dollar costs) was estimated by 2007, rising to $66 billion per year by 2015. For middle-income countries with a GDP of less than $1,200 per capita per year, the comparable figures are $17 billion and $28 billion. The Commission estimated that the return on this investment of $66 billion in 2015 in low-income countries would be of the order of $360 billion annually from the effects of a healthier population on the economies of those countries. Each 10 per cent improvement in life expectancy is associated with an increase in economic growth of 0.3–0.4 per cent per year, assuming other growth factors remained constant.[7]

There are a number of coalitions and partnerships for coordinating technical approaches and ensuring access to medicines and other commodities, all of which will need reinforcing. The UN-sponsored Global Fund to Fight AIDS, Tuberculosis and Malaria will need to spend around $12 billion a year by 2015[8] – that's just twelve days of current OECD agricultural subsidies. The Fund's current total assets, as it began work in 2002, were just $2 billion. The Global Alliance for Vaccines and Immunisation will also need to develop sustainable funding levels. There are encouraging signs of the pharmaceutical industry responding, and some $2.5 billion has been donated through around fifty industry partnerships globally since 1998.[9] It is easy to see the connections between education and poverty. But leaders also need to take into account the connection between health and poverty; you can't learn if you are sick, and you can't earn effectively without appropriate education. Furthermore, in the developing world, children stay home from school and look after their parents, accelerating a vicious and deadly cycle of poverty and ignorance.

It was little wonder the whole issue of access to medicines threatened to break up the consensus at Doha. But skilful navigation of the issue before, during and after the Ministerial gives me hope that we can make progress. When Doctors without Borders, ministers and the pharmaceutical industry can all manage to agree, as they did at Doha, we must be heading in the right direction. The protestors outside my office moved in six months from saying 'WTO Kills' to 'Protect Rights to Medicines under the WTO Agreements.' For once, common sense prevailed. There are signs of hope; private and public resources are being mobilised, governments and corporates are beginning to cooperate and the wider public is demanding action.

Immigration and ageing

Alongside these grim facts, population demographics are changing, as a result of both ageing and immigration. Over the past century, the world's population has risen by 400 per cent. However, our environmental, water, military and political scenarios for steadily improving and sustainable outcomes have been based on an assumption of the continued expansion of a working population. Current demographic and migration trends call this belief into question, with observers such as Nicholas Eberstadt arguing that the progress of human development could be set back because of rapidly decreasing birthrates and declining lifespans.[10]

Despite the alarmism about globalisation, there were more people moving across borders a hundred years ago than there are today. In the second half of the nineteenth century and the early twentieth century, about 60 million people migrated from Europe to the New World.[11] Passports are, after all, a new invention, a century old.

Immigration is one of the world's oldest forms of technology transfer, German refugee contributions to the US nuclear and space programmes in the middle of the twentieth century being perhaps the best-known example. In my own country, New Zealand, the wine industry is based on Croatian immigrants; its dairy industry originated with Danish immigrants. I helped open up New Zealand's immigration programmes in the 1980s, on the basis that if we took in a Singaporean doctor, we were effectively bringing in half a million dollars of Singapore taxpayers' money. Nobody is a racist when they need a doctor. George Gershwin's remarkable opera Porgy and Bess reflected the affinity – born of tribal memories of oppression in Europe – of a Jewish composer with the oppression of a black underclass in America.

However, migration – or as they call it in WTO-speak, 'the movement of natural persons' – is now a supercharged political issue. There are two key elements here. One is the integration or assimilation into largely developed economies of poorer people seeking a better life. The concerns of the host country tend to centre on the fact that these are often not skilled migrants, but rather have been permitted entry to do the jobs that locals will no longer touch, and do not always integrate culturally.

The converse of this is the loss of educated or talented people from the developing world. And, of course, the same migrants can be involved on both sides of the argument; not every doctor gets to practice his or her chosen profession in a New World of choice. To cite just one of many possible examples, trained Filipina teachers with university degrees can make much more as maids in Hong Kong than working as educators back in the Philippines.

As a consequence, the political and social impact of immigrants – both legal and illegal – is now a major challenge for policymakers, as vividly seen in 2002 with the rise of anti-immigration politicians in such developed Western European centres as France and the assassination of Dutch anti-immigrant politician Pim Fortuyn. The controversy centres largely upon perceptions of job competition with domestic workers; that they are an economic and/or social drain on the host country, as well as charges that some immigrants are poorly integrated. People are not born racist; they are taught it around the kitchen table and in the playground.

Migration is a huge business, with remittances from migrant workers back home from their homes in rich countries reaching $80 billion plus globally, exceeding all overseas development assistance (ODA) of approximately $53.7 billion for 2000.[12] Not to mention the evil of professional people-trafficking by unscrupulous smugglers, shipping workers from such places as China and Africa to the Middle East, Europe and the USA, where they are often exploited to repay their 'entrance fee'.

A study conducted by the World Bank showed that remittances of selected African countries alone amounted to approximately $7.36 billion for 1999 (see Table 6). Some countries argue for the movement of people to be given the same rights as the movement of capital. This is a priority of some developing countries in the Doha Development Agenda, under the services negotiations. But when only nineteen countries have signed the UN High Commissioner for Human Rights' International Convention on the Protection of the Rights of all Migrant Workers and Members

Table 6. *African migrant workers' remittances in 1999*

Countries	Remittances, $ (million)
Algeria	942
Tunisia	761
Egypt	3,772
Eritrea	127
Seychelles	4
Comoros	12
Madagascar	7
Botswana	0.15
Lesotho	0.7
Namibia	6
Nigeria	1,301
Benin	73
Togo	0.03
Ghana	31
Niger	7
Burkina Faso	67
Guinea	6
Guinea-Bissau	1.8
Senegal	93
Cape Verde	69
Mali	84
Mauritania	1.8
Morocco	1,938

Note: Higher values than those indicated above can be expected due to the existence of internal money transfer networks.
Source: World Bank.

of their Families (of 1990), it's not likely we shall see dramatic change within the WTO, which does not have jurisdiction over the issue.

The larger question may be why the governments of poor countries would want a more open and rules-based international migration system. They risk losing their brightest and their best. What they gain in remittance income, they lose in talent that is difficult to train and retain. According to a 2001 International Organization for Migration estimate, 35 per cent of nationals with a university education, from twenty African countries, are now living abroad.

Asian migrant workers have grown from less than half a million in the 1970s, to an estimated 15 million today, according to the Asian Migrant Centre. Asian migrant workers, too, have become one of the most consistent sources to prop up weaker economies like the Philippines, Indonesia, Bangladesh and Sri Lanka – in the case of the Philippines this amounted to more than four times FDI in the late 1990s.[13]

The issue of immigration is of direct relevance – and indeed is to some extent fed by – the other major issue facing us in global demographics, that of the ageing developed world. There is still a perception that the world is at risk from population explosion. In fact, the key problem is one of age distribution. The population in developed countries is rapidly ageing, with seismic implications for pension plans and health costs.

In 1898, New Zealand created the second state pension system in the world after Bismark's, almost unnoticedly launching what has over the past century snowballed to become an funding minefield for developed world governments. New Zealand's original pension scheme covered less than 3 per cent of the population; in my lifetime that could balloon to 30 per cent. New Zealanders consume more taxpayer dollars in their last year of life through medical costs, than in all the preceding years. And when the grey group votes, the politicians cower, worldwide. The old vote, the young don't.

The proportion of people over sixty-five compared with those of working age, ranges from 20 to 30 per cent in almost all industrial countries, according to a recent *Financial Times* editorial comment.[14] It quotes OECD estimates that this dependency ratio will rise to roughly 40 per cent in the slowly ageing countries such as the USA, the UK and the Netherlands, and to about 50 per cent in the faster-ageing nations of Japan, Germany, France and Italy.

The Cato Institute's Brink Lindsey has written: 'Even with rising tax rates and declining returns, pay-as-you-go systems throughout the advanced nations are heading towards financial collapse . . . over the next 75 years, US Social Security's total un-funded liabilities have an estimated present value of $9 trillion – as compared to the current national debt of $5.7 trillion. In Germany and Japan, the current un-funded liabilities of the public pension system are well over 100 per cent of GDP; in France and Italy, they exceed 200 per cent.'[15]

He also notes that the trauma of ending the old command economies in the former Soviet bloc has added complications, with the drop in economic output and rise in unemployment dealing additional blows to system revenues in the east. 'By the mid-1990s the pension systems of the transitional economies were saddled with crippling high dependency rations,' says Lindsey, noting that, for example, in Poland pensioners totalled 61 per cent of active workers by 1996; in the Ukraine the figure was 68 per cent, and Bulgaria 79 per cent. Which meant raising contributions to punitive levels.

This problem hasn't exactly crept up on us. Back in the late 1970s, Peter Drucker, the management guru, had warned that if a clash between those receiving welfare and the people providing welfare to the state were to be decided by voting power, the older generation would win. He described a 'generation gap...between a developed and largely white world in which the increase in older surviving people is the main demographic phenomenon, and a less developed or underdeveloped world, largely non-white, where the basic phenomenon is the drop in infant mortality and the resulting explosive growth of young people (little trained and little skilled) to be fed and provided with jobs.'[16]

Take Japan, where current net migration levels are close to zero. Twenty years ago, Japan was the youngest society in the developed world; by 2005 it will be the oldest.[17] One quarter of all Japanese will be sixty-five or and over by 2015. To maintain total population size, Japan would have to import a long-term average of almost 350,000 newcomers a year for the next fifty years, and it would need nearly twice that number to keep its working age population from shrinking. Under the first contingency, over one-sixth of Japan's 2050 population would become descendants of present-day *gaijin* (foreigners); under the second contingency, that group would account for nearly one-third of Japan's total population. Neither scenario seems likely, given Japan's homogenous culture.

To prevent an eventual decline in the size of the fifteen to sixty-four grouping (often termed the 'working age' population), Europe's net migration will have to nearly quadruple to a long-term average of about 3.6 million a year. Migration of this magnitude would change the face of Europe: by 2050, under these two scenarios, the descendants of present-day non-Europeans will account for approximately 20–25 per cent of Europe's inhabitants.

The contrast with much of the developing world is marked. For instance, the twenty-two countries of the Arab League, accounting for 280 million people, have the largest proportion of young people in the world – 38 per cent of Arabs are under fourteen years of age – and it is estimated the population will top 400 million in twenty years.[18] In Saudi Arabia alone, some 65 per cent of the population is under twenty-five years. Muslims live predominantly in the developing world.

Consider: in 1999, the UN's State of World Population predicted that by 2050, 98 per cent of the growth in the world's population will occur in lesser developed regions, mainly Africa and Asia. Today, the UN reports that out of the 78 million people born into the world each year, 95 per cent live in the less developed region. The UN Development Programme (UNDP) states that 60 per cent of the world's population growth comes from just twelve countries, and at the top of the list are India, Pakistan and China. By 2016, it is projected that the population of India would exceed all of the more developed countries combined! In Italy, for example, birth rate is so low that the population could shrink by 16 million by 2050 according to one UN projection.[19]

The new demographics of age, gender, race and religion raise complex challenges in regions of stark and dangerous differences. This is true also of its most sophisticated and oldest democracies, from Holland to the USA. Within a generation, 'Anglos' will be in a minority against Hispanics, African Americans and Asians in California, Florida and Texas. No one can win the presidency unless they take two of those three key states.

Had the USSR not imploded, Russians would have become a minority within the wider USSR within a generation. The agony of Northern Ireland will take on a different complexion in a few years when Catholics may become the majority, according to some estimates by 2021.[20] Israelis will become a minority within a generation if Palestine does not become a separate state. The few 100,000 Palestinians who were forced out of their homes by the creation of Israel now number in the millions. Their right to return home is a sticking point in all negotiations about a peace plan. The present Jewish population of 4.2 million barely exceeds the total of 3.5 million Palestinians. By 2050, according to one estimate, the population living west of the Jordan River (inside the borders of the British mandate of Palestine, which included all of present Israel, the West Bank and Gaza) will be 80 per cent Palestinian and 20 per cent Jewish.[21]

In a speech to the Friends of Europe in February 2001, the EU Commissioner for the Internal Market and Taxation, Fritz Bolkenstein, said that in Europe the ratio of worker to pensioners will decline from 4:1 to less than 2:1 by 2040. He warned that if unfunded pension liabilities were shown up in national accounts of some member states, this would represent a debt of over 200 per cent of GDP.

The world's most populated country, China, faces an unintended consequence of its one child policy, a rapidly ageing population and a social security fund that is almost out of cash. The government asserts that China's total social welfare obligations are between $122 and 244 billion. Bank of China International says the total shortfall is around $850 million, others estimate it's closer to $1 trillion. By mid-year there was reported to be only $7 billion left in the fund.[22]

This all resembles nothing so much as a good old-fashioned Ponzi scam, whereby lucky early investors are paid out by the contributions seduced out of the next generation of unsuspecting suckers, until the entire pyramid topples over. Except that governments – and in some cases corporates – rather than escaping with the loot, have spent it to get re-elected.

It is worth noting, as Drucker points out, that through their pension funds, employees of US business today own at least 25 per cent of its equity capital. 'If "socialism" is defined as "ownership of the means of production by the workers" – and this is both the orthodox and the only rigorous definition – then the United States is the first truly "socialist" country.' The funds of the self-employed, of public employees, and of teachers own at least another 10 per cent, giving the workers of the USA ownership of more than one-third of the equity capital of US business, he adds.[23]

Of course, ownership does not necessarily equate to control, as recent corporate collapses, which have wiped out workers' savings, have demonstrated.

When I was in government in New Zealand, I tried for many years to encourage unions to organise their own pension fund schemes, but they resisted this, feeling that it was the state's role and that to take it over would weaken the role of the state in securing people's welfare. In the USA, the opposite sentiment has had wide currency.

Former US Senator Daniel P. Moynihan notes, for example, that 'In fairly short order [once ideas had crossed the Atlantic at the beginning of the twentieth century] workingman's compensation became near universal among the states, and the reformers now looked to universal health insurance, a logical follow-on. In a mode we have experienced in our time, this proved too much. Business grew nervous. The American Federation of Labour, led by Samuel Gompers, "joined his fellow members in impassioned opposition." Labor leaders of Gompers' generation looked with suspicion on government-provided benefits. They wanted trade unions to do that. World War I and its aftermath pretty much ended the era.'

As Drucker has noted, we could see a generation gap between the developed countries, where the increase in older surviving people is the main demographic phenomenon, and the developing countries, where the prevailing trend is the drop in infant mortality and the resulting explosive growth of young people. We know birth rates drop when living standards rise, as parents realise they no longer need large families to support them in old age. Lifting living standards produces better environmental, human rights and social outcomes. In turn, better educated and emancipated women assert greater ownership over reproduction.[24]

As developing country incomes rise, our very long-term future may see us facing up to a world with too few people, not too many.

The role of women

For centuries, societies denied their economies the full productive input of the female half of their population. Societies that deny themselves the skills of their women are writing off half their population as non-contributors. Those who refuse educational opportunities, based on where you live or who you are, not what you can be, pay a price.

Apart from the moral and ethical question of excluding people because of race, gender or age, equality is essentially a productive idea. High ideals are not incompatible with sound economic practice: they are frequently a precondition for social and economic progress.

In two decades in politics in the New Zealand Parliament, the greatest social change I saw was in the status of women. Women got the vote in New Zealand in 1893, a world first. Even so, twenty years ago, there were few women MPs. Now women represent about 30 per cent of MPs; indeed the last two New Zealand Prime Ministers have been women, as has the Chief Justice and the Head of State, or Governor-General under the Commonwealth system. Equal pay for equal work was established in the public sector in 1960; the private sector has seen the gap narrow, but it's still got a way to go.

When I was first elected, I'd meet women in my constituency office who had been thrown out of their homes by husbands with nothing. As they were not wage-earners, they couldn't legally claim a share of the estate; their contribution didn't count. We enacted law to ensure they received 50 per cent of the assets accrued while the marriage lasted. As in many other countries, these protections were subsequently extended to de facto relationships. After separation, women's incomes tend to go down and men's up, so that in some jurisdictions attempts are being made to push for a share of potential lost incomes, or a lien on future increased earnings of the ex-partner, given that women may have surrendered their earning potential while raising children.

These developments reflect societal changes that have taken place globally. We have observed in previous chapters the substantial progress that has been made in living standards worldwide. But poverty still exists, and its impact is most evident upon women and children.

For example:
- 70 per cent of the 1.2 billion people living in poverty are female
- estimates over a twenty-year period found the increase in numbers of poor rural women in forty-one developing countries to be 17 per cent higher than the increase in poor men
- there are twice as many women as men among the world's 900 million illiterates
- Half a million women die unnecessarily from pregnancy-related complications each year, the causes of which are exacerbated by issues of poverty and remoteness
- on average, women are paid 30–40 per cent less than men for comparable work

- in developing countries, only a tiny fraction of women hold real economic or political powers
- in twenty developing countries, under-five mortality was found to be greatest among women with no education, and in rural agricultural communities
- poor families tend to be larger than richer ones, which increases the reproductive and caring burden on women; adolescent pregnancy is higher in poor families
- while some 30 per cent of Saudi men are unemployed, the figure rises to 95 per cent for Saudi women, while an estimated two-thirds of Saudi women now aged between sixteen and thirty years of age cannot or will not marry.[25]

Despite these negative figures, women are making greater advances in employment, politics, business and education, than at any time in history. And, reaffirming the theme of this book, the best outcomes tend to be in democracies and in societies with open markets. These days, no democratic political party would dare face the electorate without a policy targeted at women. Just as very few countries do not have someone looking after the environment, so too most have someone who is responsible for Women's Affairs. In many advanced democracies, women now equal and in some cases outnumber men at universities. The new economy of services technology and information has seen female employment soar and now the OECD reports that young male unemployment outstrips female unemployment in eleven OECD countries.[26]

Even in largely Muslim Bangladesh, where women at the village level have traditionally been disadvantaged despite charismatic individuals from well-connected political families holding national political power, innovative banker Muhammad Yunus's experience suggests that small economic and social changes can significantly empower and motivate women. The founder of Grameen Bank, which grants micro loans to women who had no other access to capital, reports: 'In 1992, some four hundred Grameen borrowers were elected to union councils, and in 1996, Grameen borrowers led the way to an almost unthinkable feat – more women voted in the national election than men, which helped to nearly wipe a political party, that had taken positions against women's rights, out of Parliament.'

In the more developed world, women tend to live longer, creating a gender age gap that is under increasing scrutiny by pollsters and campaign managers. For example, in the USA, pre-war, the majority of women supported the Republicans. Voting patterns have since been reversed, with many more women supporting Democrats and men voting Republican.

Bill Clinton magnified that trend. If women alone had voted in the USA in 2000, Al Gore would have enjoyed a landslide.

Business Week's Gene Koretz reported the findings of economists Lena C. Edlund and Rohini Pande of Columbia University, who concluded that since the early 1960s, as the proportion of US marriages ending in divorce has risen to nearly 50 per cent and as more people have chosen to defer marriage or remain single, the unmarried share of the adult population has surged to 44 per cent. 'In the study, which appeared in *The Quarterly Journal of Economics*, Edlund and Pande relate this trend to the reversal in men's and women's party allegiances and the subsequent widening of the political gender gap. Arguing that the decline in marriage has tended to make men richer and women poorer, they find that states with rising divorce rates have seen a decline in support for Democrats among men and a marked rise in such support among women.'[27]

Francis Fukuyama, in *Our Posthuman Future*, suggests that, in part because more women in the growing elderly cohort will live to advanced ages than men, and in part because of a long-term sociological shift toward greater female political participation, elderly women will emerge as one of the most important blocs of voters courted by twenty-first century politicians.

'What this will mean for international politics is of course far from clear, but we do know on the basis of past experience that there are important differences in attitudes toward foreign policy and national security between women and men, and between older and younger voters,' says Fukuyama. In the case of American women, that is likely to translate into less support for US involvement in war, defence spending or the use of force abroad.

'Developed countries will face other obstacles to the use of force,' he adds. 'Elderly people, and particularly elderly women, are not the first to be called to serve in military organisations, so the pool of available military manpower will shrink. The willingness of people in such societies to tolerate battle casualties among their young may fall as well.' The result, he suggests, could be a world divided between a North whose political tone is set by elderly women, and a South driven by what Thomas Friedman labels 'super-empowered angry young men' such as those which carried out the 11 September attacks on the World Trade Center. 'Politicians will have to work within frameworks established by basic demographic facts, and one of those facts may be that many countries in the North will be both shrinking and aging.'[28]

Ownership, property rights, education, opportunity, access to capital, equality of opportunity all help create economic gains. The danger is that, when people for cultural or social reasons stubbornly refuse to be equal, the 'control freaks' move the argument from equality of opportunity to equality of outcome, which they try to engineer through legislative means. But if women are ever given the choices in controlled corrupt societies, that they have in free societies, there is hope. After all, polling and voting patterns show greater concern from women than men on issues such as the environment, equity, childcare, peace and development.

A greater role for women will help advance freedoms at an ever faster rate this century.

Genetics, biotechnology and the human genome

Churchill once said of the dangers of unregulated science, 'Scientists should be on tap, but not on top.' Implementing the Doha Development Agenda in a coherent way will help achieve that. Caution, prudent progress, national and international conventions and regulations and controls will be necessary as biotechnology and genomics research increasingly seeks commercial applications. Transparency, open debate, dialogue, more information and the engagement of wider society and its scientific, political, religious and business leaders will be vital for us to cope and turn this problem into an opportunity to lengthen life and improve its quality.

David Victor and C. Ford Runge suggest that the great promise of globalisation – that the benefits from free markets and market-driven innovation will lift incomes everywhere – will fail to be realised if the world's poorest and hungriest people do not share in the benefits of transgenic innovation. 'All this means that realizing the potential of agricultural biotechnology will require activist policy reform, not a laissez faire approach,' they write. 'Countries must tailor their regulations so as to minimize harm to trade while also responding to consumer concerns. They must recognize the weakness of international institutions in confronting politically popular regulations. They must increase public investment in agricultural development. And they must create intellectual property rules that encourage firms to both share and expand their intellectual property.'[29]

Dolly the Sheep notwithstanding, genetic engineering isn't new. Pekinese, Great Danes and the Old English Sheepdog are all the result of human intervention in the canine gene pool. Ancient paintings of sheep, cattle and deer show us how we have bred more efficient animals over the centuries. The same applies to agriculture. The original berry tomato was small and slightly poisonous; natural corn is the size of a dime. We now feed six times more people than 200 years ago. Without the advances of science, millions of people would have died from food shortages. Agricultural productivity has outstripped population growth and could explode further with freer trade.

There was an uproar at the Johannesburg Conference in Sustainable Development, when many NGOs opposed food aid that could have been genetically engineered. Millions of African lives could be saved with this food aid. The World Food Agency has been distributing such products for over seven years. The anti-biotech brigade suggests people should starve because the scientific jury is still out. Hundreds of millions now eat it, but this is part of a wider argument between the EU and the USA about the so-called precautionary principle that has raised its head in WTO negotiations. Some see this as protectionism in another guise because about eighty EU studies have failed to find a problem. Food aid causes other problems which I explain elsewhere (see Chapter 3) – over 36,000 jobs have been lost in Swaziland alone due to subsidised EU sugar, according to Action Aid, but that doesn't get the media attention of the GM issue.

In the 1960s, Norman Ernest Borlaug, the inventor of super-rice and super-wheat, saved millions of lives, winning the Nobel Prize for peace. Genetically modified food has the capacity to feed and save millions of lives. Recent famines in Africa have reshaped the 'Frankenfood' debate and forced a rethink. Yet at the Sustainable Development Conference in Johannesburg in September 2002, the politically correct, and politically gutless, won through. Genetically modified cotton, for example, now being utilised in India and China, is expected to fundamentally change the world's cotton market – it saves on fertiliser and pesticides. Given the recent uproar over genetically modified food, it would take a brave Nobel Committee to even consider Borlaug these days. Public concerns about food safety are growing, spurred by incidents such as BSC ('mad cow disease'), which of course had nothing to do with genetics as such, and outbreaks of foot and mouth disease.

But what is really different about today's genetic developments is the pace and degree of change. With the mapping of the human genome, research into DNA technology is exploding. Scientists assert, for example, that it will be possible to produce in animals a natural and inheritable immunity to certain diseases by utilising DNA technology. By implication, those changes can be extended to man. However, as Richard Lewontin pointed out in *The New York Review of Books*: '. . . the proportion of all the ill health and death in the US that stems from simple genetic disorders that are potentially curable by a "genetic fix" (of which we do not yet have a single successful example) is very small, as compared with what can be done by less damaging workplaces, less pollution and better nutrition.'[30]

The real concern is, of course, not about cloning Dolly the Sheep, but about redefining the DNA of Dolly's shepherd. Genetic engineering of the human race has mind-blowing implications. Francis Fukuyama's *Our Posthuman Future* asserts that the consequences of successfully cracking the human gene code will make the Internet and informatics boom look puny. Marry genetics and informatics, and we are truly looking at the creation of a different world, says Fukuyama.[31] These developments will change how we live, are born, our health, our weather and how the world functions. Which may be all too much for many people. Designer children? Factory farms? Tomatoes grown at the North Pole because a fish gene is spliced into the fruit? Umbilical cords (stem cell production units) harvested from grandchildren to save and extend the lives of grandparents? Human organs grown in animals? These issues are no longer the stuff of 1950s B movies, they are happening.

Juan Enriquez's *As the Future Catches You* argues that those who can 'speak' the language of genetics will acquire direct and deliberate control over all forms of life. But he observes that most countries and individuals remain illiterate and will be shut out from what is rapidly becoming the greatest single new driver of the global economy. Wealth will be more concentrated and those with knowledge to sell – both countries and individuals – will be the winners.

'Consider what will happen when: your genetic code can be digitally imprinted on an ID card and your insurance company and employer see that you are genetically disposed to, say heart disease; pharmaceutical products are developed so that you can eat genetically modified broccoli to protect yourself from cancer; cloning will be as common as *in vitro* fertilization and scientists can influence the genetic design not only of other species, but of your own children,' says Enriquez. But he warns: 'Lone individuals are giving birth to entire new industries that rapidly become bigger than the economies of most countries on earth, but create very few jobs.'[32]

Are we playing God, or do we do that anyway any time we transplant a heart or save a child with antibiotics? Dolly the Sheep resulted in uproar around the world. Would the public reaction be different if we cloned Polly the Panda? Science is moving faster than our moral, ethical, legal, political capacity to cope. Several nations have banned human cloning and stem cell research, which largely results in such research moving elsewhere. Some 150,000 people were employed in the USA on genomics by mid-2002, double the number five years previously.

We are, inevitably, haunted by echoes of the master-race theories that created such devastation in Europe last century. As Fukuyama writes: 'Hanging over the entire field of genetics has been the spectre of eugenics – that is, the deliberate breeding of people for certain heritable traits.' Fukuyama notes the term was coined by Charles Darwin's cousin Francis Galton and that in the late nineteenth and early twentieth centuries, state-sponsored eugenics programmes attracted surprisingly broad support, not just from right-wing racists and social Darwinists, but from such 'progressives' as the Fabian socialists Beatrice and Sidney Webb and George Bernard Shaw, the communists J. B. S. Haldane and J. D. Bernal, and the feminist and birth control proponent Margaret Sanger. Extreme left and right yet again finding common cause, because as usual they know what it best for us.

'The United States and other Western countries passed eugenics laws permitting the state to involuntarily sterilize people deemed "imbeciles" while encouraging people with desirable characteristics to have as many children as possible,' he says. The eugenics movement in the USA was effectively terminated following the revelation of the Nazi holocaust, and since then Europe has been effectively inoculated against any revival of eugenics and has, in fact, become inhospitable terrain for many forms of genetic research. However, Fukuyama notes that progressive, social democratic Scandinavia kept eugenics laws on the books until the 1960s.

A black market already exists in organ transplants. Even with bans on uncontrolled eugenics, a black market in recombinant DNA technology is sure to emerge. We must be wary. Science without morality, technology without humanity, business without honour, logic without faith, and government without compassion, all risk leading us towards a form of totalitarianism. The history of the past century shows us how easily tribes can be led astray by psychopathic leaders who burn books, kill sparrows and abuse their teachers in cultural revolutions.

As Matt Ridley concluded in *The Origins of Virtue*: 'The Hobbesian search for a perfect society ended therefore in the gas-chambers of Auschwitz, expressing not the human instinct for co-operation but the human instinct for genocidal tribalism, the Faustian bargain that comes, as we have seen, with groupishness.'[33]

Fukuyama suggests we are like the spectators at the Manhattan Project, watching in awe at the first nuclear bomb exploding. Excited, but frightened at what we might have unleashed. The parallel is a valid one: nuclear treaties have been drafted, international agencies and domestic controls, regulations and supervisory bodies established to ensure safety. And so far nuclear bombs have been used only twice and accidents have been very rare. Indeed, more people may have died from pollution generated by coal.

The dangers of unregulated experimentation are real. US National Medal of Science winner Robert A. Weinberg has observed: 'Most biologists regard reproductive cloning – a procedure used to produce an entire new organism from one cell of an adult – as riddled with problems. Why should we waste time agonising over something that is far removed from practical utility and may forever remain so?'[34]

The answer, suggests Weinberg, is that otherwise there may be an increasing move by commercially driven clone 'clowns' to bypass the established peer review process. Which in turn could undermine the credibility of other possibly useful developments, such as therapeutic cloning, using embryonic stem cells. 'Therapeutic cloning has the potential to revolutionise the treatment of a number of currently untreatable diseases, but it is only potential. Considerable research will be required to determine the technology's possibilities and limitations for treating patients.'

Keyhole surgery and the myriad of miracle drugs is only the beginning; in another half-century, today's surgical tools will seem as primitive as the use of bleeding cups 200 years ago. The scalpel will and is being replaced by laser surgery and injections by medicated patches. The military sponsored the Internet; now experiments with remote, computer-driven surgery so that doctors out of harm's way can operate on patients are rapidly approaching. What does this mean for local hospitals and ambulance attendants in the future? A surgeon safe in Paris or Boston could in future perhaps operate on a patient in a war zone thousands of miles away. Imagine the potential for mankind, especially those living in rural and isolated areas, when this technology comes on-stream. The beloved country hospital may be replaced with surgeons enjoying the good life in the cities, attending rural patient by the use of this new technology.

UNICEF reports that Vitamin A could reduce child mortality by between 25 per cent and 33 per cent, approximately 1–3 million lives, in many developing countries per year. Thus, splicing a 'Vitamin A' gene into rice could save millions of children's eyesight in the Third World. But businesses and politicians are reluctant to risk offending public opinion and the anti-GM forces are strong. Let us not forget that Galileo was exiled from Rome to his home near Florence for life because he said the Earth circled the Sun. Under the pressure of the Inquisition, he was forced to abjure his beliefs. Some of the most extreme environmentalists irrationally reject almost all elements of what the modern world can offer. The bottom line is that any civilisation that is afraid of science will ultimately be reduced to the realm of witchcraft.

Richard Lewontin observes that the eighteenth century theoreticians of representative democracy understood that an educated electorate was an underlying assumption of a well-functioning democratic state. 'But they could have had no conception of what such an education would entail two centuries later,' he writes. 'How is the democratic state to function if the mass of the citizens is dependent on the expert knowledge available only to a tiny elite, an elite that in its formation and direct economic interest comes to represent only a narrow sector of society?'[35]

I think we have proven that freely operating markets, good governance and transparent standards of integrity get better returns. When governments spend their income on guns and not children, on buying political power, and not on devolving that power to its legitimate owners, then the results are predictable.

One of the unfortunate byproducts of the 1980s and 1990s was the rejection of the idea of government. Government was 'the problem not the solution' became the cliché of the day. Like all slogans, this has some truth in it, but, carried to extremes, it undermines the lessons of history and the role governments have played in advancing civilisation and lifting living standards. Leadership does still matter. Only governments can fulfil certain functions of maintaining standards, setting rules of civil and commercial behaviour, and determining where social and civic investments should go. In developing countries and new world nations like my own, New Zealand, a government can be the best friend of the people, of business and of the young, if it keeps its hands largely to itself.

Lincoln did not call for the abolition of government, he called for the abolition of slavery. He talked of government by the people, of the people. Too much government is dangerous, but irresponsible governments which allow unregulated exploitation of human, social and environmental resources can trigger an overreaction. The absence of the rule of law is even more dangerous. The denial of the good governance principles we know are so essential for the good life if government, global or national, erodes public confidence; then all suffer.

Nowhere is this more evident than in the area of education and investment in human capital. In the old economy and the industrial age, production workers did routine work that didn't need high levels of creativity, flexibility or mobility of labour. The new economy demands exactly the opposite. Companies must innovate, create new products and ideas, and get their products and services to the marketplace faster, more efficiently and cheaper than their competitors. They must take risks, but not with their reputations. The responsibility for investing in human capital isn't just a government function, but that of every player: parents, society and business. Robert Reich, in his recent book *I'll Be Short*, reports on findings that companies which introduced formal employee training programmes experienced a 19 per cent larger rise in productivity than firms that did not train their workers.[36] Another report shows that raising the average education of a workforce by one year helps them become as much as 12 per cent more productive.

Reich concludes: 'The evidence is overwhelming that the sharper a person's skills, the higher that person's wages. Each year of education or job training after high school, whenever it occurs in the course of a career, increases average incomes by 6 to 12 per cent.' And what is true of the richest nations is also true of the poorest. Governments are necessary. Good choices on expenditures such as education make a crucial difference to our quality of life and our wider environment.

We must use diplomacy to provide the political and bureaucratic space and intellectual grace and space for information to flow freely, and allow leaders to create solutions and build constituencies to accept action. Leadership can no longer be imposed on citizens, except in times of great crisis or war. The great pyramid of science needs a wide base of support to gain height. Carl Sagan, in *The Demon-Haunted World: Science as a Candle in the Dark*, notes: 'The methods of science – with all its imperfections – can be used to improve social, political and economic systems.'[37]

Sagan concludes this book – an eloquent plea to overcome popular myths and superstitions – by saying: '[But] if the citizens are educated and form their own opinions, then those in power work for us. In every country we should be teaching our children the scientific method and the reasons for a Bill of Rights. With it comes a certain decency, humility and community spirit. In the demon-haunted world that we inhabit by virtue of being human, this may be all that stands between us and the enveloping darkness.'

Notes

CHAPTER 1

1. *The Economist,* quoted in Mike Moore. *Hard Labour.* 1987.
2. *The World Bank Development Report, 1997,* quoted in R. Douglas, R. Richardson, S. Robson. *New Directions for Public Policy. Spending Without Reform Commission on the Reform of Public Services, Interim Report.* 2002.
3. Don Brash. *New Zealand's Remarkable Reforms.* 1997.
4. Daniel Yergin and Joseph Stanislaw. *The Commanding Heights.* 1998.
5. Cordell Hull. *The Memoirs of Cordell Hull.* 1948.

CHAPTER 2

1. Francis Fukuyama. *The End of History and the Last Man.* 1993.
2. Vaclav Havel, quoted in *New York Times.* August 2000.
3. Antique Automobile Club of America. *Automotive History – A Chronological History.*
4. US Census and Statistics Bureau.
5. Geza Feketekuty. *The New Trade Agenda.* 1993.
6. C. Fred Bergstein, quoted in John H. Jackson. *The World Trading System. Law and Policy of International Economic Relations,* 2nd edn. 2002.
7. Philippe Legrain. *The Open World: The Truth About Globalisation.* 2002.
8. Peter F. Drucker. *Managing in a Time of Great Change.* 1995.
9. Friedman. *The Lexus and the Olive Tree: Understanding Globalisation.* 1999.
10. Kenneth Pomeranz and Steven Topik. *The World that Trade Created: Society, Culture and the World Economy: 1400 to the Present.* 1999.
11. David Voss. Geek Page – You Say You Want More Bandwidth? Solitons and the Erbium Gain Factor. *Wired Online.* 3 July 1995.
12. Nitin Desai. Redirecting globalisation for benefit of the masses. *Earth Times News.* 2 January 2001.
13. Phil Condit. Living in a changing, mobile world. Speech at the World Affairs Council of Orange County, California. 20 November 2000.
14. Peter Schwartz, Peter Leyden and Joel Hyatt. *The Long Boom: A Vision for the Coming Age of Prosperity.* 1999.
15. Friedman, 1999.
16. Juan Enriquez. *As the Future Catches You: How Genomics and Other Forces are Changing Your Life, Work, Health and Wealth.* 2001.

17. US Department of Statistics, Internet, 1998; Excerpts from President Bill Clinton's remarks to the Technology 98 Conference, 1998; The New Frontier, *WorldLink*, January/February 1998; Voss, 1995; Enriquez, 2001.
18. Enriquez, 2001.
19. Pomeranz and Topik, 1999.
20. Pomeranz and Topik, 1999.
21. *The Genocide of Native Americans: A Sociological View*; Jared Diamond, *Guns, Germs and People. A Short History of Everybody for the Last 13,000 Years*, 1998.
22. Douglas A. Irwin. *From Smoot-Hawley to Reciprocal Trade Agreements: Changing the Course of US Trade Policy in the 1930s*. 1997.
23. Charles Kindleberger. *The World in Depression 1929–1939*. 1986.
24. Pomeranz and Topik, 1999.
25. US Department of Agriculture, Economic Research Service. *Agriculture Resources and Environmental Indicators, 2000: Agricultural Productivity and Growth*. 2000.
26. Consuming Industries Trade Action Coalition. Study reveals that proposals for protecting US steel industry will cost consumers more than $2.89 billion annually (press release). 2001.
27. World Bank Policy Research Report. *Globalisation, Growth and Poverty: Building an Inclusive World Economy*. 2001.
28. Chinese Publishing House for Social Sciences and Documents. *Report on China's Population and Job Opportunity*. 2002.
29. Matthew J. Slaughter and Phillip Swagel. *Does Globalisation Lower Wages and Export Jobs?* 1997.
30. Joseph Yam, Chief Executive of Hong Kong Monetary Authority. Speech at the Crédit Suisse First Boston Asian Investment Conference. 29 March 1999.
31. Jason Booth. A new era: China joins the WTO: slowly Southeast Asia studies free trade. *The Wall Street Journal Europe*. 12–14 April 2002.
32. Record FDI expected in 2002. *Xinhua News Agency*. 4 December 2001.
33. Peter F. Drucker. *Managing for the Future: The 1990s and Beyond*. 1992.
34. Thomas L. Friedman. *Lexus and the Olive Tree: Understanding Globalisation*. 2000.
35. Joseph Yam, Chief Executive of the Hong Kong Authority. Risks and challenges in coping with international capital flows. Opening address at the Sixth Manila Framework Group Meeting. 20–21 March 2000.
36. Martin Wolf regards this comment as inaccurate in his commentary, *Countries still rule the world*, in *Financial Times*, 6 February 2002. He argues that proper comparison of countries' and corporations' sales figures would show that countries are bigger than corporations.
37. Enriquez, 2001.
38. Jon Jeter. Zambia pays heavy price as it courts Western markets. *International Herald Tribune*. 24 April 2002.
39. Jeter, 2002.
40. Economic Report of the President, USA. January 2001.
41. Anthony Spaeth. IDEAS/World Economic Forum @ the Web of Power. *Time*. 17 February 1997.
42. Drucker, 1995.

43. Environics International and World Economic Forum. *The World Economic Forum Poll: Global Public Opinion on Globalisation*. 2002.
44. Robert Conquest. *Reflections on a Ravaged Century*. 2001.
45. Scott M. Stanley. *What Really is the Divorce Rate?*
46. George A. Akerlof and Janet L. Yellen. *An Analysis of Out-of-Wedlock Births in the United States*. 1996.
47. Enriquez, 2001.

CHAPTER 3

1. Can Manufacturers Institute. *Cans: A Visual History*.
2. Much of the information on sugar in this chapter was drawn from Pomeranz and Topik, 1999.
3. Pomeranz and Topik, 1999.
4. Pomeranz and Topik, 1999.
5. Brent Borrell and David Pearce. *Sugar: The Taste Test of Trade Liberalisation*. 1999.
6. Douglas A. Irwin. *The Case for Free Trade*. 2002.
7. Irwin, 2002.
8. Bruce Vaughan, Chairman of The Global Alliance for Sugar Trade Reform and Liberalisation. Speech to the Cairns Group Ministers. 10 October 2000.
9. Robin Klay. *Free Trade a Sweeter Deal for Everyone*. 2002.
10. Mark Vaile, Minister for Trade. Speech to the IFAP Family Farmers' Summit on International Trade. 29 November 1999.
11. Mary Jordan. A revolution in the fields as Cuba turns from sugar. *International Herald Tribune*. 30 July 2002.

CHAPTER 4

1. John Stuart Mill. *Principles of Political Economy with some of their Applications to Social Philosophy*. 1909.
2. Matt Ridley. *The Origins of Virtue: Human Instincts and the Evolution of Cooperation*. 1997.
3. Hans Küng. *A Global Ethic for Global Politics and Economics*. 1997.
4. Adam Smith. *The Wealth of Nations*. 1776.
5. Adam Smith. *The Theory of Moral Sentiments*. 1759.
6. Hernando de Soto. *The Mystery of Capital: Why Capitalism Triumphs in the West and Fails Everywhere Else*. 2001.
7. Peter Watson. *The Economic Arsenal in the War Against Terrorism*. 2002.
8. De Soto, 2001.
9. Brink Lindsey. *Against the Dead Hand: The Uncertain Struggle for Global Capitalism*. 2002.
10. Lindsey, 2002.
11. Lindsey, 2002.
12. Muhammad Yunus. *Banker to the Poor: Micro-Lending and the Battle Against World Poverty*. 1999.
13. Isaiah Berlin. *Freedom and Its Betrayal: Six Enemies of Human Liberty*. 2002.
14. Plato. *The Republic*. 360 BCE.

15. Jean Jacques Rousseau. *The Social Contract*. 1762.
16. Robert Putnam. *Making Democracy Work: Civic Traditions in Modern Italy*. 1993.
17. Lawrence E. Mitchell. *Corporate Irresponsibility: America's Newest Export*. 2001.
18. Charles Darwin. 1882.
19. Alexis de Tocqueville. *Democracy in America*. 1835.
20. Putnam, 1993.
21. Bill Moyers. *Bill Moyers Reports: Trading Democracy*. 2002.
22. Ralph Nader. PBS interview.
23. George Orwell. 1984. 1954.
24. De Tocqueville, 1835.
25. Mill, 1909.
26. John Blundell. *Waging the War of Ideas*. 2001.
27. Roland Vaubel. *The Centralisation of Western Europe: The Common Market, Political Integration and Democracy*. 1995.

CHAPTER 5

1. Ian Hart. *Floating Down the River: The River Thames – Its Pollution and Clean Up*. 2002.
2. Department of Computer Science, University of Exeter. *Running Water: Then and Now*. 1996.
3. Ian Hart, 2002.
4. US Environmental Protection Agency (EPA). *National Air Quality and Trends Report 1997*. 1998.
5. Freedom House. *Democracy's Century: A Survey of Global Political Change in the Twentieth Century*. 1999.
6. Bjørn Lomborg. *The Skeptical Environmentalist: Measuring the Real State of the World*. 2001.
7. United Nations Development Program (UNDP). *Making New Technologies Work for Human Development*. 2001.
8. UN. *UN Population Information Network*. 2001.
9. International Labor Organization (ILO). *Life at Work in the Information Economy*. 2001.
10. World Bank. *World Development Indicators 2001*. 2001.
11. UNDP, 2001.
12. IMF/OECD/UN/World Bank. *Better World for All. Progress towards the International Development Goals*. 2000.
13. UNAIDS. *AIDS Epidemic Update*. 1999.
14. Lomborg, 2001.
15. World Food Summit (WFS). *World Food Summit: Technical Background Documents*. 1996.
16. WFS, 1996.
17. Food and Agriculture Organization (FAO), *Food Supply Situation and Crop Prospects in Sub-Saharan Africa*, 1996; FAO, *The Sixth World Food Survey*, 1996; FAO, *The State of Food and Agriculture*, 1997; FAO, *The State of Food Insecurity in the World 1999*, 1999; FAO, *The State of Food Insecurity in the World 2000*, 2000.

18. FAO, 2000.
19. Per Pinstrup-Andersen, Rajul Pandya-Lorch and Mark W. Rosegrant, *The World Food Situation: Recent Developments, Emerging Issues, and Long-Term Prospects*, 1997; Rip Landes, Paul Westcott and John Wainio, *International Agriculture Baseline Projections to 2005*, 1997; USDA, *Production Database from March 2000*, 2000.
20. Johan Norberg. *In Defence of Global Capitalism.* 2001.
21. Amartya Sen. *Development as Freedom.* 1999.
22. IMF/OECD/UN/World Bank, 2000.
23. World Bank, 2001.
24. World Bank, 2001.
25. International Bank for Reconstruction and Development (IBRD)/World Bank. *Global Economic Prospects and the Developing Countries.* 2001.
26. IMF/OECD/UN/World Bank, 2000.
27. World Bank. *Attacking Poverty.* 2001.
28. UNDP. *Human Development Report 1997.* 1997.
29. Xavier Sala-I-Martin. *The Disturbing 'Rise' of Global Economic Inequality.* 2002.
30. World Bank. *World Development Report 2002.* 2002.
31. World Bank. *World Development Indicators 1998.* 1998.
32. Centre for Economic Policy Research. *Making Sense of Globalisation: A Guide to the Economic Issues.* 2002.
33. Lomborg, 2001.
34. IBRD/World Bank. *Global Economic Prospects and the Developing Countries.* 2001.
35. UNDP, 2001.
36. Food and Agriculture Organization (FAO). Fisheries home page.
37. World Wildlife Fund for Nature. WWF welcomes fishing nation's action on subsidies (press release). 1999.
38. World Bank. *World Development Report 1992: Development and Environment.* 1992.
39. World Bank, 1992.
40. World Meteorological Organization (WMO). *Ground Water: The Invisible Resource.* 1998.
41. Peter H. Gleick. *The World's Water 1998–1999: The Biennial Report on Fresh-water Resources.* 1998.
42. WMO, 1998.
43. Gleick, 1998.
44. US Water News Online. Report says overpumping keeps world food supply stable. September 1999.
45. Julian L. Simon. *The Ultimate Resource 2.* 1996.
46. World Bank, 1992.
47. UNICEF. *The Progress of Nations: Water and Sanitation Commentary.* 1997.
48. John Briscoe. Financing water and sanitation services: the old and new challenges. Keynote address to The World Congress of the International Water Supply Association. 1995.
49. Sandra Postel. *Pillar of Sand: Can the Irrigation Miracle Last?* 1997.
50. Europa. *European Research in Action: Water: A Vital Resource Under Threat.* 2002.

51. Kofi Annan. Speech delivered on World Water Day. 22 March 2002.
52. Europa, 2002.
53. World Health Organization (WHO). *Water and Sanitation: Fact Sheet.* 1996.
54. Hans Zomer. *The Politics of Water.* 1998.
55. US Water News Online. UN Agency reports pesticides pollution and poisoning worldwide. June 1997.
56. US Water News Online. China to invest in pollution prevention on 3 gorges. January 2002.
57. Gleick, 1998.
58. The World Bank Group. Managing world's water resources requires partnership innovations (news release). 18 March 1999.
59. Lomborg, 2001.
60. Simon, 1996.
61. WTO. S/CSC/M/18/Rev.1. 24 April 2001.
62. Michael M. Weinstein. *Greens and Globalisation: Declaring Defeat in the Face of Victory. New York Times.* 22 April 2001.
63. Dow Jones. New Zealand government favors cuts to international fish subsidies. 6 May 2002.
64. Franz Fischler, Member of the European Commission Responsible for Agriculture, Rural Development and Fisheries. Speech. 2002.
65. James Andreoni and Arik Levinson. *The Simple Analytics of the Environmental Kuznets Curve.* 2000.

CHAPTER 7

1. Joseph Nye. *The Paradox of American Power.* 2002.

CHAPTER 9

1. Daniel Yergin and Joseph Stanislaw. *The Commanding Heights.* 1998.
2. Barry Coates, Director of the World Development Movement. Comment on the WTO Ministerial Meeting in Doha. 12 November 2001.
3. Walden Bello and Anuradha Mittal. *The Meaning of Doha: Focus on the Global South and Food First.* 2001.
4. Luis F. de la Calle, Public Strategies Inc. The Functioning of the World Trade Organization. 2002.
5. Jagdish Bhagwati, *Free Trade Today,* 2002; Jagdish Bhagwati (ed.), *Going Alone: The Case for Relaxed Reciprocity in Freeing Trade.* 2002.

CHAPTER 10

1. World Bank. *Disparities in China: Sharing Rising Incomes.* 1997.
2. Erik Eckholm. China's countryside sees increase in lawlessness. *New York Times.* 30 May 2002.
3. Leon Brittain. A practical view of economics. *Far Eastern Economic Review.* 23 May 2002.

4. Thomas Crompton. As China rises, some will ask: will it stumble? *International Herald Tribune*. 18 December 2001.
5. Crompton, 2001.
6. Jason Booth. A new era: China joins the WTO: slowly Southeast Asia studies free trade. *The Wall Street Journal Europe*. 12–14 April 2002.
7. Record FDI expected in 2002. *Xinhua News Agency*. 4 December 2001.
8. Tom Korski. Bureau of Natural Affairs. 1998.
9. Asian Development Bank, *Asian Development Outlook 2002*, 2002; International Monetary Fund, *World Economic Outlook 2002*, 2002.
10. United Nations/World Bank. Millennium Development Goals: Poverty 2000.
11. Gordon Chang. The big four banks head toward collapse. *International Herald Tribune*. 2 April 2002.
12. The bottomline. *Asiaweek*. 20 October, 2000.
13. US Bureau of Economic Analysis.
14. Mangai Balasegaram. Analysis: South-East Asia's Chinese. *BBC News*. 29 August 2001.
15. Daniel Yergin and Joseph Stanislaw. *The Commanding Heights*. 1998.
16. *ZDNet UK*. Nua Internet Surveys.
17. WTO Secretariat.
18. UNSD Comtrade database; WTO Secretariat.
19. Susan Lawrence. China–ASEAN trade: enough for everyone. *Far Eastern Economic Review*. 13 June 2002.
20. Hugo Restall. Commentary on trade. *The Wall Street Journal*. 10 April 2002.
21. James Kyunge. Chinese steel groups win US dumping case. *Financial Times*. 30 May 2002.
22. Calculation based on World Bank. *World Development Report statistics*.
23. *Taiwan, China to talk on links*. Financial Times. May 2002.
24. Daniel P. Moynihan. *Pandemonium: Ethnicity in International Relations*. 1994.

CHAPTER 11

1. Brink Lindsey. *Against the Dead Hand: The Uncertain Struggle for Global Capitalism*. 2002.
2. Margaret C. Levenstein and Valerie Suslow. *Private International Cartels and Their Effect on Developing Countries*. 2001.
3. Daniel T. Griswold. *WTO Report Card: America's Economic Stake in Open Trade*. 2000.
4. Peter S. Watson. *The Economic Arsenal Against Terrorism*. 2002.
5. Stephen Brooks and William Wohlforth. American primacy in perspective *Foreign Affairs*. July/August 2002.
6. *Report of the President 2000*. 2000.

CHAPTER 12

1. Drisilla K. Brown, Alan V. Deardorff and Robert M. Stern. CGE modeling and analysis of multilateral and regional negotiating options. In Robert M. Stern (ed.) *Issues and Options for US Trade Policies*. 2001.

2. World Bank. *Global Economic Prospects 2002: Making Trade Work for the World's Poor*. 2001.
3. Stern (ed.), 2001.
4. Callisto Madavo, Vice President of the Africa Region at World Bank. HIPC and beyond: challenges for Africa. Speech delivered at the European Union Parliament. 13 September 2001.
5. Shantayanan Devarajan, Margaret J. Miller and Eric V. Swanson. *Development Goals: History, Prospects and Costs*. World Bank Policy Research Working Paper. 2002.
6. Devarajan, Miller and Swanson, 2002.
7. WTO. *Annual Report 2001*. 2001a.
8. WTO. *International Trade Statistics 2001*. 2001b.
9. WTO, 2001b.
10. Edward Gresser. *Hidden Tax on the Poor: The Case for Reforming US Tariff Policy*. Progressive Policy Institute Policy Report. 25 March 2002.
11. Gresser, 2002.
12. Gresser, 2002.
13. WTO, 2001a.
14. Al From. America by the numbers: how tariffs hurt the working poor. *New Democrats Online*. 25 January 2002.
15. Bryan T. Johnson. Laptops: US pulls plug on a domestic industry. *Wall Street Journal*. August 1992.
16. WTO, 2001a.
17. Joseph Francois. *The Next WTO Round: North–South Stakes in New Market Access Negotiations*. 2001.
18. Bjørn Lomborg. *The Skeptical Environmentalist: Measuring the Real State of the World*. 2001.
19. Oxfam International. *Rigged Rules and Double Standards: Trade, Globalisation and Fight Against Poverty*. 2002.
20. World Bank, 2001.
21. Pascal Lamy, EU Trade Commissioner. Comment at a WTO Session. February 2002.
22. Horst Köhler (IMF), Mike Moore (WTO) and James Wolfensohn (World Bank). Joint note on Doha Development Agenda at OECD ministers meeting in Paris. 17 May 2002.
23. Philippe Legrain. *Open World: The Truth about Globalisation*. 2002.

CHAPTER 13

1. Jagdish Bhagwati. *Free Trade Today*. 2002.
2. Gerry Loughran. Of thuggery and ungrateful youth. *Daily Nation*. 14 May 2000.
3. Helmut Anheier, Marlies Glasius and Mary Kaldor (eds.). *Global Civil Society 2001*. 2001.
4. Robert Conquest. *Reflections on a Ravaged Century*. 1999.
5. Liza Featherson and Doug Henwood. Clothes encounters: activists and economists clash over sweatshops. *Lingua Franca*. March 2001.

6. Annabel Hobley. Red Army fashion is the height of terrorist chic. *Financial Times*. June 2002.
7. Mark Lilla. *The Reckless Mind – Intellectuals in Politics*. 2001.
8. Darrin M. McMahon. *Enemies of the Enlightenment: The French Counter-Enlightment and the Making of Modernity*. 2002.
9. Alan Oxley. Communication with the author. 18 August 2002.
10. Oxley, 2002.
11. Karl Marx and Friedrich Engels. *The Communist Manifesto*. 1847.
12. Robert Reich. *I'll Be Short*. 2002.

CHAPTER 14

1. Steve Hilton and Giles Gibbons. *Good Business: Your World Needs You*. 2002.
2. Naomi Klein. *No Logos*. 2000.
3. Adair Turner. *Just Capital: The Liberal Economy*. 2001.
4. Marya Glass. *Food and Agriculture: At the Crossroads of Corporate Social Responsibility*. 2002.
5. Market and Opinion Research International (MORI). *Stakeholder Dialogue: Consumer Attitudes*. 2000.
6. Turner, 2001.
7. David Henderson. *Misguided Virtue: False Notions of Corporate Social Responsibility*. 2001.
8. Martin Wolf. Sleepwalking with the enemy. *Financial Times*. 16 May 2001.
9. Hendersen, 2001.
10. IPPR. Ella Joseph and John Parkinson, *Confronting the critics*; Responses from Will Hutton and Martin Wolf. January 2002.
11. World Economic Forum (WEF). *Global Agenda Monitor*. 2002.
12. Philipp Legrain. Open World: The Truth about Globalisation. 2002.
13. Kofi Annan. Companies must take lead to ensure globalisation benefits many. *Financial Times*. 4 February 2002.
14. WEF, 2002.
15. Kevin Phillips, quoted by Colin James. The gangster capitalism spectre that stalks the parties. *New Zealand Herald*. 2 July 2002.
16. Robert Hemsley. Executives need employees. *International Herald Tribune*. 24 July 2002.
17. Hilton and Gibbons, 2002.
18. John Browne, Group CEO, BP. Leading toward a better world? The role of multinational corporations on the economic and social developments of poor countries. Speech delivered at Harvard. 3 April 2002.
19. *The Shell Report 2001: People, Planet and Profits*. 2002.
20. James Lamont and Geoff Dyer. Anglo's initiative. *Financial Times*. 8 August 2002.
21. *Newsweek*. September 2002.
22. Sarah Andersen and John Cavanagh. *The Rise of Corporate Global Power*. 4 December 2000.
23. Alan Shipman. The Globalisation Myth. 2002.

CHAPTER 15

1. Juan Enriquez. *As the Future Catches You: How Genomics and Other Forces are Changing Your Life, Work, Health and Wealth.* 2001.
2. Brink Lindsey. *Against the Dead Hand: The Uncertain Struggle for Global Capitalism.* 2002.
3. Aneurin Bevan. *In Place of Fear.* 1952.
4. Jacques Chirac, President of the Republic of France. Speech at the Conference of the Institut Francais des Relations Internationales. 4 November 1999.
5. Hans Küng. *A Global Ethic for Global Politics and Economics.* 1997.
6. Küng, 1997.
7. Peter Drucker. The global economy and the nation state. *Foreign Affairs.* 1997.
8. Küng, 1997.
9. United Nations. *Draft Outcome of the International Conference on Financing for Development.* 1 March 2002.
10. J. Lamout. Earth summit was 'birth by fire'. *Financial Times.* 6 September 2002.
11. George Soros. *George Soros on Globalisation.* 2002.
12. Soros, 2002.
13. Soros, 2002.
14. Soros, 2002.
15. Joseph Stiglitz. *Globalisation and its Discontents.* 2002.
16. Daniel Yergin and Joseph Stanislaw. *The Commanding Heights.* 1998.
17. Stiglitz, 2002.
18. Heritage Foundation. *The World Bank and Economic Growth, 50 Years of Failure.* 1966.
19. Kenneth W. Dam. *The Rules of the Global Game: A New Look at US International Policy-Making.* 2001.
20. Barry Holden (ed.). *Global Democracy: Key Debates.* 2000.
21. Benjamin R. Barber. *Jihad vs. McWorld. Terrorism's Challenge to Democracy.* 2001.
22. Richard Falk and Andrew Strauss. Next, a global parliament. *International Herald Tribune.* 19 April 2002.
23. David Jesuit. *Political Participation in National and European Parliamentary Elections in Western Europe: Does the Regional Context Matter?* Paper delivered at the International Sociological Association at Nuffield College, Oxford, England. 11–13 April 2002.
24. William Safire. Needed: freedom's caucus. *International Herald Tribune.* 31 May 2001.
25. J. F. Rischard. *High Noon: 20 Global Problems, 20 Years to Solve Them.* 2002.
26. David Halberstam. *War in a Time of Peace.* 2001.
27. International Institute for Strategic Studies. *The Military Balance 1999/2000.* 1999.
28. H. W. Brands. *The Strange Death of American Liberalism.* 2001.
29. Joseph S. Nye. Unilateralism vs. multilateralism. *International Herald Tribune.* 13 June 2002.

30. Christopher Andrews. Foreword to A. G. Hopkins (ed.) *Globalisation in World History*. 2002.

CHAPTER 16

1. World Bank. *Education and HIV/AIDS: A Window of Hope*. 2002.
2. UNAIDS and WHO, *AIDS Epidemic Update*, December 2001; Nicol Degli Innocenti, Survey: Botswana: virus hits at the country's life force, *Financial Times*, 26 September 2001.
3. James Pringle. Cambodia's new agony: an AIDS epidemic. *International Herald Tribune*. 12 June 2002.
4. Eun Jung Cahill Che. AIDS orphans by the millions. *International Herald Tribune*. 17 April 2002.
5. World Health Organization. *Macroeconomics and Health: Investing in Health for Economic Development*. 2001.
6. Merck. Background briefing paper. 2002.
7. World Health Organization. *Implementation of the Millennium Declaration: Treatment and Prevention of Diseases, including HIV/AIDS and Malaria*. Note from the Director-General. 2002.
8. Shantayanan de Devarajan, Margaret J. Miller and Eric V. Swanson. *Development Goals: History, Prospects and Costs. World Bank Policy Research Working Paper*. 2002.
9. Merck, 2002.
10. Nichlolas Eberstadt. The population implosion. *Foreign Policy*. March/April 2002.
11. Richard Baldwin and Philippe Martin, *Two Waves of Globalisation: Superficial Similarities, Fundamental Differences, NBER Working Paper*, 1999; Andrés Solimano, *International Migration and the Global Economic Order: An Overview, World Bank Working Paper*, 2001; A. G. Hopkins (ed.), *Globalisation in World History*. 2002.
12. OECD. *ODA Steady in 2000: Other Flows* Decline. 2001.
13. Asian Migrant Centre. *Asian Migrant Yearbook*. 1999.
14. The wages of longevity, editorial comment. *Financial Times*. 11 May 2002.
15. Brink Lindsey. *Against the Dead Hand: The Uncertain Struggle for Global Capitalism*. 2002.
16. Peter Drucker. *The Pension Fund Revolution*. 1976.
17. Peter G. Peterson. *Gray Dawn: How the Coming of Age Wave Will Transform America – and the World*. 2000.
18. Arab Human Development Report. Self-doomed to failure. *The Economist*. 6 July 2002.
19. Anthony Browne. Special report: race in Britain. The last days of a white world. *Guardian*. 3 September 2000.
20. *Political Demography in Northern Ireland*. 2001.
21. Andrew Killgore. *Washington Report on Middle East Affairs*. June 2000.
22. Gordon Chang. *The pension money is running out. International Herald Tribune*. 18 July 2002.
23. Drucker, 1976.

24. Drucker, 1976.
25. Eric Rouleau. Trouble in the Kingdom. *Foreign Affairs*. July/August 2002.
26. Peter Schwartz, Peter Leyden and Joel Hyatt. *The Long Boom: A Vision for the Coming of Age of Prosperity*. 1999.
27. Gene Koretz. Economic trends: divorce and women voters. *Business Week Online*. 11 March 2002.
28. Francis Fukuyuma. *Our Posthuman Future: Consequences of the Biotechnology Revolution*. 2002.
29. David Victor and C. Ford Runge. Farming the genetic frontier. *Foreign Affairs*. May/June 2002.
30. Richard Lewontin. *The New York Review of Books: The Politics of Science*. 9 May 2002.
31. Fukuyuma, 2002.
32. Juan Enriquez. *As the Future Catches You: How Genomics and Other Forces are Changing Your Life, Work, Health and Wealth*. 2001.
33. Matt Ridley. *The Origins of Virtue: Human Instincts and the Evolution of Cooperation*. 1997.
34. Robert A. Weinberg. Of clones and clowns. *The Atlantic Monthly*. June 2002.
35. Lewontin, 2002.
36. Robert Reich. *I'll Be Short*. 2002.
37. Carl Sagan. *The Demon-Haunted World: Science as a Candle in the Dark*. 1995.

Index

ENDGAME SERIES

Novels:
The Calling
Sky Key
Rules of the Game

Digital Novellas:
Endgame: The Training Diaries Volume 1: Origins
Endgame: The Training Diaries Volume 2: Descendant
Endgame: The Training Diaries Volume 3: Existence
Endgame: The Zero Line Chronicles Volume 1: Incite
Endgame: The Zero Line Chronicles Volume 2: Feed
Endgame: The Zero Line Chronicles Volume 3: Reap

Novella Collections:
Endgame: The Complete Training Diaries
Endgame: The Complete Zero Line Chronicles

This book is a puzzle.
Decipher, decode, and interpret.
Search and seek.
If you're worthy, you will find.

RULES OF THE GAME
AN ENDGAME NOVEL

JAMES FREY
AND
NILS JOHNSON-SHELTON

HARPER
An Imprint of HarperCollinsPublishers

Rules of the Game: An Endgame Novel

Copyright © 2016 by Third Floor Fun, LLC.

Puzzle hunt experience by Futuruption LLC.

Additional character icon design by John Taylor Dismukes Assoc.,

a Division of Capstone Studios, Inc.

All rights reserved. Printed in the United States of America. No part of this book may be used or reproduced in any manner whatsoever without written permission except in the case of brief quotations embodied in critical articles and reviews.

For information address HarperCollins Children's Books, a division of HarperCollins Publishers, 195 Broadway, New York, NY 10007.

www.epicreads.com

Library of Congress Control Number: 2016952952

ISBN 978-0-06-233264-6 — ISBN 978-0-06-256191-6 (intl ed)

16 17 18 19 20 PC/LSCH 10 9 8 7 6 5 4 3 2 1

First Edition

KEPLER 22B

Ansible chamber on board the Seedrak Sare'en, active geosynchronous orbit above the Martian North Pole

kepler 22b sits in a shiny chair in the center of a black, low-ceilinged room. His seven-fingered hands are woven together, his platinum hair bound into a perfect sphere perched on top of his head. He reviews the report he is about to give over the ansible to his conclave, many light years away. The game taking place on the blue-and-white planet in the next orbit has experienced hitches and unforeseen developments, but it progresses nonetheless. Most of what has transpired is not terribly worrying, with the notable exception of the destruction of one of Earth's 12 great monuments. This was the one that belonged to the La Tène Celts, the one called Stonehenge, and it is now utterly gone and useless. kepler 22b is deeply disturbed by this. At least one of these ancient structures—ones that were erected many millennia ago, when his people walked alongside the young humans of Earth—at least one is required to finish Endgame.

And this, more than anything, is what he wishes to see happen.

For a Player to win.

A Player.

He turns his attention from the report to a transmission hologram projected into the air not far from his face. A dim real-time blip moves over the map of a city on the Indian subcontinent. A Player. Judging by the speed, he uses some kind of vehicle.

This Player is not the one that kepler 22b expects to win, but it is the one he has been most curious about.

He is a shrewd and incautious Player.

Unpredictable. Excitable. Merciless.

1

He is the Shang, An Liu.

And kepler 22b would continue to watch but then the ansible hums and the hologram flicks off and the room fills with pitch blackness and the temperature drops to -60 degrees Fahrenheit. Moments later the blackness pricks with drifting motes of light and the room glows bright and there they are, their projections surrounding him on all sides.

The conclave.

kepler 22b would prefer to watch the Shang, but he cannot.

It is time to give his report.

AN LIU

Beck Bagan, Ballygunge, Kolkata, India

The Shang.

SHIVER.

blink.

SHIVER.

An Liu rides a Suzuki GSX-R1000, trying to gain speed but getting thwarted by the Kolkatan throng.

He twists the grips. The wheels spin over the uneven pavement.

No helmet, teeth gritting, lungs burning, eyes like slits. Chiyoko's remnants press into his chest. Next to the necklace of his beloved is a SIG 226 and a small collection of custom-made grenades. All of these are hidden from view by a cotton shirt.

He pushes north for South Park Street Cemetery. Pushes, pushes, pushes.

The cemetery. It is where he is. One of the Players who Chiyoko had nicked with a tracker. One of the Players that An is now tracking.

The cemetery is where he will find the Nabataean. Maccabee Adlai. Who has Earth Key and Sky Key. Who is winning.

Or believes he is winning.

Because there is a difference between these.

If An gets there soon, there will certainly be a difference.

If An gets there, Maccabee will not be winning. Not at all.

He will be dead.

And An is less than two kilometers away.

So close.

But the streets are full. Kolkata has poured her citizens out of doors this evening, all of them clamoring for information, for loved ones, for a decent cell signal. An dodges businessmen and spice wallahs, brightly dressed women and stray dogs, crying children and stalled Ambassador taxis, rickshaws with reed-thin men pulling their carriages along haphazard streets like fish working upstream. He curls the bike around an oblivious Brahman bull. Some people get in An's way. These either get nudged by the bike or get a swift kick from An's foot.

Out of *SHIVERSHIVER* out of the way.

In his wake are screams and bruises and cursing and shaking fists.

There are no cops. Not a single officer of the law.

Is it because the world is on the cusp of lawlessness?

Is it because of Abaddon, even now, before it has struck?

Could it be?

Yes.

An smiles.

Yes, Chiyoko. The end is near.

Two large men appear at the intersection of Lower Range Road and Circus Avenue. They point and shout. They recognize him. They saw his video—everyone in the world has seen his video by now—and they want to stop him. They may try to *kill* him, which An finds preposterous. He revs the bike and people scatter, but the men hold strong and lock arms.

Fools.

An rides straight for them, through them, knocking them aside and running over one, tearing skin from an arm. The men yell and one produces an ancient-looking pistol from nowhere. He pulls the trigger, but instead of firing properly it explodes in his hands.

He falls, screaming.

The gun was faulty. Old. Broken.

Like this BLINKBLINKBLINK this world.

An might feel sorry for the man and his mangled hand, but he is the Shang and he doesn't care. He jams the throttle and rises out of the

4

saddle and weaves the bike's rear wheel back and forth and scuttles away, one of the men screaming as his leg is momentarily caught under the rubber and made bloody and raw.

An's smile grows.

He leaves the men behind. Passes a barbershop, a sweetshop, a mobile phone shop, an electronics shop crowded with people. On the screens in the windows of this store An catches the image of kepler 22b.

The alien outed himself when he gave his announcement about Sky Key. kepler 22b began to show his true colors. Endgame is real for everyone now. It is real for rich people and poor people, the powerful and the impotent. The brutal and the kind. Everyone.

And An loves it.

Now the whole world knows that the first two keys are together. That Maccabee has them. That Endgame continues despite some of the other Players' misguided attempts to stop it. That it continues despite fear and hope and murder and even love.

Best of all, kepler 22b told the people of Earth that Abaddon can't be stopped. That the giant asteroid will fall in less than three days and there is nothing anyone can do about it.

That millions will die.

An loves it.

The bike churns. The street widens. The crowds part and An moves a little faster, up to 60 kph now. He glances at Chiyoko's watch. Sees the tracker's display screened over the numbers.

Blip-blip.

There. Maccabee Adlai.

So *BLINK* so *SHIVER* so close.

So close that An can smell them.

An screams across Shakespeare Sarani Road and goes two more blocks and spins northwest on Park Street. He looks at the watch again and sees it.

Blip-blip.

Blip-blip.

5

Only blocks away.
BLINKshiver
Chiyoko Played for life.
SHIVERblink
But I
SHIVER
I Play for death.

SARAH ALOPAY, JAGO TLALOC, AISLING KOPP, POP KOPP, GREG JORDAN, GRIFFIN MARRS

The Depths, सूर्य को अन्तिम रेज, *Valley of Eternal Life, Sikkim, India*

"Everybody chill the fuck out!" a man yells. He's mid-40s, weathered, drenched in sweat, a little chubby. He stands in the middle of the hallway that is crowded with Players and their friends.

Sarah and Jago are at the far end, their backs to an open doorway. The Donghu, the Harappan, the Nabataean, and both Earth Key and Sky Key were in the room beyond the doorway not minutes before. Baitsakhan was very alive and very intent on killing Shari Chopra out of a psychotic sense of revenge, but Maccabee felt sorry for the Harappan, and he stopped the Donghu. He was about to take sole possession of both Earth Key and Sky Key when Sarah and Jago surged into the room. As Baitsakhan lay dying, the Olmec jumped forward and attacked Maccabee, and while the fight was close, Jago won. Sarah had a chance to kill Little Alice Chopra, the girl who is Sky Key, a death that should have put a stop to Endgame.

But Sarah couldn't do it.

And Jago couldn't do it either.

Aisling's squad arrived moments after the fight ended. The Celt had a chance to kill Sky Key too, and she tried to take a shot with her sniper rifle, but at the last moment Sky Key reached out and touched Earth Key and in a flash of light the little girl disappeared, taking an unconscious Maccabee with her, and the mutilated body of Baitsakhan as well.

The only living person left in that room is Shari Chopra, knocked out, with a large lump on her head courtesy of Maccabee. He could have killed her too but, perhaps out of mercy or righteousness or empathy, Maccabee let her live.

Where Maccabee and the keys are now, none of them know. It could be that they went to Bolivia, or to the bottom of the ocean, or are in an Endgame-finishing audience with kepler 22b himself.

All that is left here, in the routed Harappan fortress carved out of the Sikkimese Himalayas, are these Players and Aisling's friends.

All that is left is their fear and their anger and their confusion.

And their guns.

Most of which are pointed at one another.

"Just chill out," the man implores again. "No one else has to die today," he says.

You might, Sarah thinks, her pistol trained on the man's throat. Sarah refused to kill the Chopra girl, but she wouldn't think twice about shooting this man, or the people with him, if it means escape.

The man steps around Aisling, places a hand on the barrel of her rifle, forces it down two inches. It's now aimed at Sarah's chest rather than her forehead. The man's other hand is empty and palm forward. His eyes are wide and pleading. His breath quick.

A peacemaker, Sarah thinks.

The man licks his lips.

Sarah says, "I'll chill out when none of you are standing in our way." Her voice is calm. Sarah notices that Aisling Kopp is flushed. She has a smear of blood on her skin—maybe hers, but probably not.

Blood. And sweat. And grime.

Aisling asks, "Where's Sky Key?"

Sarah's gun is light. One bullet. Maybe two.

"Move out of our way," Jago insists. His pistol is aimed at Aisling's head. Aisling looks different from when he last saw her. Older, harder, sadder. They must all appear so. Endgame was simpler in the early stages, before any of the keys had been recovered. Now it is vastly more complicated.

"We're not going anywhere," Aisling says, her eyes not moving from

Sarah's. "Not until we find out where Sky Key is."

Sarah says, "Well, she's not here."

Shoot her! Sarah orders herself. *Do it!*

But she doesn't.

She can't.

Aisling tried to do what Sarah couldn't. She tried to kill the little girl. Aisling tried to stop Endgame.

Which means that Aisling and her friends can't be all bad.

Sarah glances at the other men in the room, the ones who haven't spoken. One is old but formidable-looking, an eye clouded and white. Maybe a former La Tène Player. The other is middle-aged, a contemporary of the Peacemaker. He has a bandanna tied over his head, wears round eyeglasses, and is strapped with a heavy-looking pack spilling with communications equipment. He also carries a sniper rifle, which he doesn't bother to aim at anyone. Instead, he reaches into his shirt pocket and pulls out a hand-rolled cigarette. He puts it in his mouth but doesn't light it.

Both men look spent.

Long day, Sarah thinks.

Long week.

Long fucking life.

Sarah figures she could jump backward and fire simultaneously, killing Peacemaker. Aisling would instantly return fire, but since Peacemaker has his hand parked on her rifle, this shot would miss. Jago would kill Aisling. Then they would finish the old Celt and the hippie walkie-talkie. Provided no one else is hidden nearby, she and Jago could let their guard down and fall into each other's arms and exhale. They could walk out unscathed. They could continue their mission to stop Endgame. Sarah puts their chances of killing these four people at 60 or 65 percent. Not bad odds, but not great.

"Don't do it," Peacemaker says, as if he can read Sarah's thoughts.

"Why not?" she asks.

"Just hear me out." He glances at Aisling. "Please."

"Here it comes," the man with the cigarette mumbles, breaking his silence. The old man with the white eye stays mum, his gaze dancing from person to person.

The man says, "My name is Greg Jordan. I'm a retired, twenty-plus-year vet of the CIA. I'm associates—no, *friends*—with Aisling here. I know all about Endgame. Maybe more than any of you know about it, believe it or not." He glances at Aisling. "More than I've been letting on," he says apologetically. Aisling's left eye twitches. The old man exhales loudly. "Anyway, I've seen my share of Mexican standoffs, and this qualifies big time. One wrong move and we all die in this hallway pretty easily. Like I said, no one else has to die today. A lot of people already have." Sarah doesn't know what he's talking about. She doesn't know that Aisling and Greg and the other two men—and also a woman, now dead, named Bridget McCloskey—spent the previous day marching into the mountains and killing everyone they met. Killing, killing, killing. By the end of the day many, many Harappan were dead. Well over 50.

Too many.

The man sighs. "Let's not add to the body count."

Aisling's shoulders slump, her burgeoning guilt palpable. Greg Jordan's words so far make some sense. Bullets remain in chambers. Feet remain planted on the ground. Sarah's and Jago's faces say, *Go on.*

Greg Jordan continues. "I'm going to go out on a limb and say that I think we can *all* be friends. I think we all want the same thing— namely, to put a stop to this madness. Am I right? Whadya say, guys? Friends? At least until we've had a few minutes to chat and are out of this Himalayan fortress?"

Pause.

Then Jago whispers, "Screw these guys, Sarah."

And a part of Sarah is inclined to agree, but before she does anything rash Aisling asks, "Why didn't you kill her, Sarah? Why couldn't you do it?" As she speaks she lets her rifle fall to her side. Aisling is now completely defenseless, and that counts for something.

The Celt steps past Greg Jordan. "Why?" she repeats, staring intently at Sarah, her voice barely above a whisper.

Aisling wants the game to end badly. She wants to stop it. She wants to save lives.

Just like Sarah and Jago do.

Sarah's forearm pounds, reminding her that in the fight with Maccabee and Baitsakhan she suffered a gunshot wound that needs attention. Her head spins a little. Her grip on the pistol loosens. "I know I should have . . ."

"Damn right you should have," Aisling says.

"I wanted it to stop. I *needed* it to stop."

"Then you should have pulled the trigger!"

"You're . . . you're right. But I needed it to stop," Sarah repeats.

"It's not going to stop until that girl is dead," Aisling points out.

"That's not what I mean," Sarah says, her voice dropping half an octave. "I want Endgame to stop too, Aisling, but I needed—what did you say, Greg? Madness? I needed the madness to stop. The madness in my head. If I'd pulled that trigger, then it would've . . . it would've . . ."

"Destroyed you," Jago says, also letting down his guard a little. "I also tried, Celt. I couldn't do it. It may have been selfish, but I think Sarah was right not to kill Sky Key. She was a child. A baby. Whatever happens, she was right."

Aisling sighs. "Fuck." No one speaks for a moment. "I get it. Truth is, I was praying the whole way up here that I wouldn't have to do it up close and personal. That I'd have a clear and long shot with this." She jostles her rifle and peers around Sarah into the dark room at the end of the hall. "But I guess I missed, right?"

Sarah nods. "She's gone. She was repeating 'Earth Key' over and over and I think she touched it and—"

Jago clicks his tongue. "Poof."

"What do you mean, 'poof'?" Jordan asks.

"They just disappeared," Sarah says. "It's not that crazy when you consider that about thirty minutes ago Jago and I and the other two Players were in Bolivia."

"Bullshit," Aisling says.

"What, you didn't teleport here too?" Jago asks, trying to make a joke, even while he still aims at Aisling's temple.

Aisling doesn't care anymore. It's not the first time someone's aimed a gun at her and it won't be the last. "No, we didn't teleport," Aisling says. "Just good old-fashioned planes, trains, and automobiles . . . and feet. Lots of feet."

"But Sky Key—she *is* gone, right?" Jordan asks.

Sarah nods. "Her mother's in there, though."

Aisling double-takes and tries to peer into the room. "Who—Chopra?"

"Yeah," Sarah says.

"Alive?" Aisling asks, her voice a little too desperate.

"*Sí,*" Jago answers.

"Shit," Jordan says. "That's not good."

"Why not?" Sarah asks.

Aisling says, "We uh . . . we just killed her entire family."

"*¿Que?*" Jago says.

"This is a Harappan stronghold," the old man explains from the back of the room, pride lacing his words. "Except it wasn't strong enough."

"She's not going to like me too much when she wakes up," Aisling says. "I wouldn't like me, either."

"Shit," Sarah says.

"*Sí. Mierda.*"

"We should kill her," the old man says.

But Aisling raises a hand. "No. Jordan's right. It's been too much today. Marrs"—Sarah and Jago realize that Aisling is talking to the man with the walkie-talkie—"you can keep her all Sleeping Beauty, right?"

"Sure, no problem," Marrs answers, his voice nasal and high-pitched.

Jordan says, "Hey, we all sound cool. We're cool, right?"

"Cool*er*," Sarah says. But she gets where he's going and lowers her gun. Jago does the same.

Aisling lays her rifle on the floor. "Listen, Sarah, Jago. I'm done Playing. I thought for a while that I would try to win, but there's no winning here. We're all losers—maybe the one who wins will end up being the biggest loser of all. Who wants the right to live on Earth if it's ugly and dying and full of misery? Not me."

"Not me either," Sarah says, thinking again of how she set the whole thing in motion when she took Earth Key at Stonehenge.

Thinking again of Christopher and her guilt.

Aisling drifts toward Sarah, holding out her hand. "When me and Jordan and Marrs teamed up I told them that if we couldn't win Endgame then we would try to find like-minded Players. We'd give them the option of teaming up with us so we could stop this whole fucking mess. For instance, if I ever find Hilal, I want to fight with him. He was right, way back at the Calling. We should have worked together then. Hopefully it's not too late to work together now."

Sarah steps closer but doesn't take Aisling's hand. "How do we know we can trust you?"

Aisling frowns, the corner of her mouth turning up. "You don't know. Not yet."

"Trust must be earned," Sarah says, as if she's quoting something out of a training manual.

Aisling nods. She's heard that. They all have. "That's right. But you can have some faith. I didn't shoot you when I tried to kill Sky Key. I didn't shoot you in the back in Italy when I had the chance, though I arguably should have. Pop over there certainly thinks so." The old man grunts. "And a few days ago I thought the same thing. But maybe I didn't do it so we could meet right now. Maybe I didn't because the three of us aren't done yet. What will be will be, right?"

"*Sí.* What will be will be," Jago mutters.

Aisling says, "If we try to stop this thing together, really try, then I won't hurt you. None of these guys will. You have my word."

Sarah cradles her injured left arm. She stares at Jago and tilts her head. Suddenly all she wants is to fall asleep in Jago's arms. She can tell that he wants the same thing. He snaps off a quick nod. Sarah leans into his body.

"Okay, Aisling Kopp," Jago says for them. He puts out his hand and takes the Celt's. "We'll put our faith in you, and you will do the same with us. We'll kill Endgame. Together. But one of my many questions can't wait."

Aisling smiles. It's as if a gust of air has blown into the hallway. Sarah feels it too, and relief washes over her. No more fighting on this day. Jordan makes a low whistle and Marrs lights his cigarette. He crosses the hallway, mumbling something about checking on Shari Chopra as he passes Sarah and Jago. The only one who stays on edge is the old man.

Aisling ignores him and gives her full attention to her new allies. Maybe her new friends. "What question is that, Jago Tlaloc?"

"If Sky Key survived and we missed our chance, then how do we go about stopping Endgame now?"

Aisling looks to Jordan. "I'm guessing that's where you come in, isn't it?"

Jordan shrugs. "Yeah."

Aisling sighs. "I know you've been holding something back since the day we met, Jordan. So, you ready to get on the level here?"

Marrs laughs loudly from the next room. Jordan straightens. He says, "Friends, it's time you met Stella Vyctory."

$$ds^2 = -c^2dt^2 + dl^2 + (k^2 + l^2)(d\theta^2 + \sin^2\theta\, d\phi^2).$$

MACCABEE ADLAI, LITTLE ALICE CHOPRA

South Park Street Cemetery, Kolkata, India

Maccabee thumbs a Zippo lighter. The flame pops and flickers. They are in a small and pitch-black chamber, one that Maccabee doesn't recognize. Apparently, Maccabee has been teleported somewhere beyond his control yet again.

He lowers the flame and there, yes, is Sky Key. She trembles before him. Big eyes, beautiful dark hair. Fists balled at her chest. A terrified child.

All the girl can manage is, "Y-y-y-y-y-you."

"My name is Maccabee Adlai. I'm a Player, like your mother." His words are muffled, his voice twangy from the beating he took from Jago Tlaloc before he woke up here in the darkness. He reaches up and shifts his jaw back into place with a loud *snap!*

"Y-y-y-y-you."

His whole body hurts, especially his groin, the pit of his stomach, his left pinkie, and his jaw. The pinkie is bent completely backward. At least he has his ring. He flips the ring's lid shut so the poisoned needle is covered, then he cracks his finger straight by pushing it against his thigh. A line of pain shoots up his arm and into his neck. The finger won't bend at the knuckles, but it's not sticking out at an odd angle anymore.

When I do win this thing there'll hardly be any of me left, he thinks.

"Y-y-y-y-you," the girl says again.

He moves toward her. She recoils. Color drains from her face. She can't be older than three. So young. So innocent. So undeserving of what's happened to her.

The game is bullshit, Shari Chopra said. And in that moment Maccabee agreed with her. He realizes that this sentiment was probably the one that saved Shari's life—the one that prompted him to knock her out instead of gun her down. Looking at Alice now, he doesn't regret this decision.

So young.

"Your mother lives," Maccabee says. "I saved her from a bad person. He came for her and I . . . I stopped him." He almost said *killed*, but that would be inappropriate, wouldn't it? With a child? He says, "She lives, but she's not here—wherever we are."

"Y-y-y-y-you," she repeats, her eyes widening.

Maccabee shuffles forward another foot, his chin tucked to his chest, the back of his head grazing the stone ceiling. The air is damp. The only sound is their breath. Maccabee wiggles his fingers at her, the unmoving pinkie like a stick growing out of his hand. "It's okay, sweetie. I won't hurt you. I promised your mother I wouldn't and I meant it." He stumbles over something. Looks down. A clump of cloth.

"Y-y-y-y-you. From my dream. You-you-you *hurt* people. . . ."

"I won't hurt you," he repeats. He lowers the lighter and pushes the thing on the ground with his foot. It's heavy. He looks. A limb. A leg. A hole burned in the cargo pocket on the thigh. He sweeps the Zippo through the air, illuminating the blood-spattered face of Baitsakhan, his eyes vacant and staring, slack-jawed, the throat torn open by the bionic hand that still clutches the cervical section of his own spine. Baitsakhan.

Take.

Kill.

. . .

Lose.

His Endgame is over.

Good riddance.

Maccabee spits on the floor as the girl gasps and points. "No! Not you! *Him! He* is the one! *He* took Mama's finger! *He* hurt people! *He* is the one! *He* is the one!"

Maccabee kicks the Donghu's body so that it flips facedown. He steps between Sky Key and Baitsakhan. She shouldn't see that. No child should see that.

"It's okay. You're okay. He can't hurt you."

"Mama."

"He can't hurt her either. Not anymore."

Maccabee is suddenly afraid that Shari also made the trip to wherever they are. And the Olmec too, and maybe the Cahokian. He spins, searching the rest of the chamber, but no one is there. It is just him and Sky Key and—

"Earth Key!" he says.

WHERE IS IT?

The girl shudders. She jumps up and then her body stiffens as if she's possessed. Her right hand falls to her side, her left hand juts out, palm up. Maccabee leans closer. She doesn't move. It's like her fear has been spirited away and replaced with emptiness. *Shock,* Maccabee thinks. *Or maybe a force more powerful.*

He peers into her hand. A little ball. Earth Key.

He swipes it from her. Her eyebrow twitches but otherwise she's expressionless.

"I'll keep that." He slips it into a zippered pocket on his vest and pats it.

"Earth Key," she says.

"That's right," he says. He inspects the small room. *Where the hell are we?* The floor is earth, everything else is featureless stone. There are no windows, no doors. No way in or out. As he looks around he runs a hand over his torso, checking to see what he's got to work with. No guns, but he has his smartphone, a pack of gum, and his ancient Nabataean blade.

A wave of pain crashes over him as the adrenaline fades from his system. He realizes that everything that's happened recently—finding Sarah and Jago in Bolivia, tracking them through the Tiwanaku ruins, getting teleported somewhere through that ancient portal, fighting, killing, fighting some more, and then getting knocked clean out by the live-wire Olmec, who is 20 or 30 kilos *lighter* than him, and then getting teleported yet again—all of that probably happened in only the last couple hours.

He needs rest. Soon.

"Earth Key says that . . ." the girl says in a monotone.

His pant leg vibrates.

". . . says that one is coming."

It vibrates violently. He touches his leg—*the tracker orb!*

Another Player!

He looks left and right and up and down and can't figure out where to go. Is another Player going to appear in this small room? Is he going to have to fight with a broken-down body in this box? This, this—sarcophagus?

He whips around, the lighter's flame blows out. He thumbs the flint. *Flick, flick, flick*—the sparks don't take. But in the total darkness something catches his eye. Right before his face. A thin white line. He follows it, tracing a faint square on the ceiling. He stuffs the lighter in a pocket and places both hands on the stone overhead and pushes. It's heavy and he strains and grunts as his panting mingles with the scraping sound of rock on rock. An opening. Light. Hot air pours into the small room as he gets his fingers around the edge of the six-centimeter-wide slab, heaving it away. He gets on his tiptoes and looks over the edge.

They are in a hole in the ground. The hole is covered by a pillared gothic cupola like one that might cover a grave or a monument. A point of orange light from a streetlamp somewhere, the muted glow of dusk in the sky beyond the cupola, the black boughs of leafy trees hanging over everything like a curtain. A dove coos and then flaps away. The muted jostle of a city—traffic, AC hum, voices—in the near distance.

Maccabee grabs Sky Key and pushes her out of the hole. He jumps out. They're in the middle of a vast cemetery from a bygone era, every grave marker grand and significant and carved from stone—domed Victorian tombs that must hold entire families, and seven-meter-tall obelisks and basalt pedestals that weigh thousands of kilos. Many are covered in moss and lichen and all are splotchily weatherworn. Plants grow in every available nook and patch—grasses, palms, hardwoods, weeds, sprawling banyan trees with their air roots diving down to the ground here and there. It's one of the most impressive cemeteries Maccabee has ever seen.

Sky Key steps onto the path, her arms glued to her sides, her legs moving like a robot's. She's completely zoned out but manages to say, "One is coming. He is close."

Maccabee gets out the orb with his right hand and pulls his knife with his left. His unbending pinkie sticks out. As when Alice Ulapala closed in on his hideout in Berlin, the orb simply glows its warning, not giving any intelligence as to who is coming or from which direction.

Maccabee knows that for the first time in his life he is going to have to run. He's too hurt and too unarmed and too disoriented and too vulnerable with Sky Key to stand his ground.

He stuffs the orb in a pocket and snags the girl, tucking her under his arm like a parcel.

He takes off along a dirt path, the cemetery dark and claustrophobic, until the trees and massive graves give way to an open area. A three-meter-high stone wall rises in front of them, plain concrete buildings beyond it on the street side.

Where the hell am I? This doesn't look like Peru or Bolivia at all. Or even South America!

He goes to the solid wall, peers left then right. It's rough enough to scale, but not while carrying Sky Key. He turns left and trots along, keeping the wall on his right. The orb in his pocket has calmed a little, so maybe whoever's coming got thrown off the trail.

Sky Key weighs about 15 kilos. He holds her sideways, her head forward and her legs flopping behind him. It's like he's carrying a life-sized toddler doll.

Near the interior corner of the wall Maccabee comes across a cache of gravediggers' tools: a shovel stuck in a pile of sand, a pickax, a coil of sturdy rope. He carefully puts down Sky Key and cuts a four-meter length of rope. He lashes it around his waist and shoulders and then works Sky Key onto his back and loops the rope under her butt and twice over her back. He pulls her tight, tying a hitch in the X of rope that crosses his chest. She's secure in this makeshift child carrier, and he has the use of both hands. He feels her quick breath on his neck. She remains zoned out, likely from the trauma of being taken from her mama, and from coming into contact with Earth Key.

He wants to climb the wall and get out onto the street of whatever city he's in, but the wall is smoother here and there's nothing for him to grab. He's about to double back to where he can climb but then freezes. The rope! The pickax!

He ties the rope to the wooden handle and hurls the pickax over the wall, creating a kind of grappling hook. He gives it a hard tug and it holds. He places his feet on the wall and starts up.

But then, at the same instant, the orb in his pocket jostles like a tiny earthquake, and Sky Key shakes off her zombie-like state and grabs a handful of his hair and yanks it. He loses his footing and swings a half meter to the side. The air cracks around him. A chunk of wall explodes next to his face, followed by a pistol report.

"He's here," Sky Key says.

Maccabee dives behind a stone grave marker as three more rounds tear by them, each barely missing. Maccabee kicks the shovel into the air and snatches it. He spins to his right, but Sky Key yanks his hair again and says, "Other way."

That would take them across the line of fire, but Maccabee trusts her. He quickly guesses that the male Player must be the Shang, An Liu. Marcus and Baits are dead, Jago's with Sarah, and Hilal is probably recovering from his wounds back in Ethiopia.

And if it is Liu, then he's probably got some bombs.

That means that Maccabee has to *MOVE!*

He takes a shovelful of sand and throws it into the air, creating a smokescreen, and sprints behind it. He hears a muted clunk, and he spins around a thick tree trunk and throws his hands over Sky Key's head and *boom!* An explosion from where they just were, debris showering all around, leaves whipping along on the shock wave, bits of wood and rock pinging here and there. It was a small explosion but big enough to have hurt them if he hadn't moved.

"Turn right here," the girl says calmly.

He's blind in this place and his body aches from everything that's happened but she *did* save them, so he listens.

"Left here. Straight. Left. Left. Straight. Right. Left, left, left."

He follows every instruction, even if it feels like they're going in circles. They bob and weave, pivot and fly. They're narrowly missed by several more shots and one more small explosion. She's transforming the dense cemetery into a maze, and it's working. Somehow she knows where An is. Maccabee realizes that this girl, at least in this moment, is vastly superior to the mysterious orb that he's been using to track the Players.

Finally they round a black stone block and find an arched break in the wall big enough for a car. Two small buildings flanking it are painted pink. A wrought-iron fence is on the far side. Past that a wide street, cars moving along, a late-model motorcycle parked on the curb.

The exit. It's 10 meters away, a straight shot. But those 10 meters are completely exposed.

"It's too far," Maccabee says. The orb in his pocket moves back and forth so fast he's afraid it's going to jump out. "He'll kill us."

Sky Key scratches the side of his neck. "Here," she says.

"I see the exit, but it's too far!"

They don't have more than a few seconds. She scratches harder, begins to claw at his flesh. "Here!" she whispers into his ear.

Then Maccabee understands. Something is in his neck: *a tracker*. One that An and who knows how many other Players have been using to follow him!

He whips up his knife and expertly carves a lump of skin from his neck. He's careful not to nick anything important or shred a muscle or tendon. The pain isn't too bad, but there's a lot of blood.

"That's it," the girl says.

Maccabee pulls the knife away and stares into the lump of flesh and, yes, there it is. A small black blob.

He balls up the flesh and chucks it away. The bloody projectile sails over a gravestone and disappears. He gets ready to run, but the girl digs a nail into this latest wound and whispers, "Wait."

He stifles a cry and does what he's told. One second. Two. Three.

"Now. Straight."

He drops the shovel and runs as fast as he can for the exit. No shots come. They were waiting for An to take the bait of the discarded tracker, and apparently he did.

The exit gets closer and closer and they're going to make it. A person walks by outside, a woman wearing an orange sari. A bus drives past and Maccabee sees a cigarette ad on the side. The writing is Hindi.

India. We're in India.

They're going to make it. The orb in his pocket is going crazy now. He reaches down to secure it but then it pops out and he skids to a stop.

"Leave it!" the girl says.

Maccabee backtracks, the orb glowing bright and yellow and bouncing around on the ground like a living thing.

"No!" she says.

Something catches Maccabee's eye. There, on the path, is An Liu, a dark pistol in his fist. He hasn't seen them yet, he's swinging back and forth and Maccabee almost has the orb but then—too late. An Liu locks onto Maccabee and Maccabee dives sideways and the orb glows so bright that its light eats up the wall and the path and An too. Shots come but all miss since An is blinded by the light and can't see Maccabee anymore.

"Leave it! I am using it! Go!" the girl implores.

Once again he does what he's told. He vaults toward the street. He sees the motorcycle and breaks open its ignition switch and hot-wires it in the blink of an eye. He jumps on. It zings to life and they take off, fast. The light from the orb chokes out everything for 20 meters now and people on the street are yelling, pointing, running.

"I am using it," the girl repeats in a soft voice, her head slumping onto Maccabee's shoulder. "I am using it." Her body feels limp. She is exhausted too.

A block later the light gives way to a high-pitched whine and then it's snuffed out and then—*FFFUHWHAM!*—the entire street puffs up in a ball of smoke. Maccabee dips the bike around a corner, its rear wheel skidding and his foot planting on the ground as a pivot. Bits of buildings and cars and trees whip through the air at their backs.

The girl passes out, the Indian city is a blur, and for the moment An Liu is no longer hunting them.

For the first time in his life Maccabee ran from a fight. And it worked. With the help of this small, remarkable, maybe possessed Sky Key, it worked.

I won't let anyone hurt you, he thinks.

And he means it.

AN LIU

South Park Street Cemetery, Kolkata, India

An kneels. He shakes his head, trying to get it clear.

Almost got them.

SHIVER.

Almost.

BLINK.

That was a big blast.

An had thrown a grenade into the light at the last second, but that explosion was from something else. The Nabataean must have planted that glowing thing and set it off in order to create some space and some time. It was successful. The Nabataean is gone now. With the first two keys.

Gone.

BLINK.

An peeks under his shirt at the Chiyoko necklace. Like everything around him it's covered in a fine dust. He pulls the necklace over his head and shakes it gently, wipes it with his fingertips, blows on it. When it's reasonably clean he slips it back on.

He brushes himself off, finds his SIG. He loads a new magazine. Sirens in the distance.

Shivershiver.

The world knows about Endgame, and Abaddon is coming, but the law isn't all the way gone. Not yet.

He trots to the exit. The Nabataean is gone, and An's bike is gone too. An spits, the stream thick with black ash.

The Nabataean is gone.

AISLING KOPP, GREG JORDAN, GRIFFIN MARRS, POP KOPP, SARAH ALOPAY, JAGO TLALOC, SHARI CHOPRA

Heading south along the Teesta River near Mangan, Sikkim, India

Aisling looks over her shoulder into the back of the jeep. Shari Chopra slumps in her seat, an IV bag pinned above the window, a tube running into a spike in the back of her hand. Dripping into that line on a regulator is a small dose of BZD, keeping her good and asleep for as long as necessary. All the way to Thailand, where Jordan is taking them and where Stella Vyctory awaits.

The jeep bumps along the road, mountains looming all around. Aisling thinks about Shari. After the standoff with Sarah and Jago, Aisling followed Marrs into the deepest chamber of the Harappan fortress and saw the raven-haired mother of Sky Key, alive and more-or-less well. This is a wrinkle that has Aisling feeling very conflicted. On one hand, Aisling suspects that Shari is one of the decent Players, one who doesn't deserve a meaningless death at the hand of a psychopathic Player. She's glad that Baitsakhan and Maccabee didn't kill her. But on the other hand, as far as Shari's concerned, Aisling probably *is* that psychopathic Player. If it weren't for Aisling, Shari's family would be alive. Sure, her daughter would probably still have been taken by the Nabataean, but all the Harappan who'd taken refuge in the mountains would be breathing if it weren't for Aisling and her ragtag death squad.

Aisling tries to reason out of this by blaming Endgame for what happened—Aisling didn't make Shari's daughter one of the fucking keys, Endgame did. Aisling was only doing what she thought she had to do to stop Endgame, and Shari, for her part, was only doing what any mother would do.

All of which makes Aisling want to stop Endgame—and punish the Makers, especially kepler 22b—all the more.

Aisling knows in her bones that when Shari wakes up she won't be in a very forgiving mood. All Shari will want is revenge, and Aisling knows that revenge is a soul-gnashing affliction that operates completely outside the realm of logic. Sure, Aisling could wave her hands at Chopra and plead for reason, insisting that Endgame killed all of Chopra's people, but Aisling also knows that's bullshit. *She* killed those people, along with Jordan and Pop and the rest of her team. And for better or worse, Chopra is now slumped behind Aisling in the jeep.

Jordan drives, Aisling wedged between him and Marrs in the front seat. Whenever Jordan shifts gears he reaches between Aisling's legs. He half apologizes each time until Aisling tells him to shut up. He does. Sarah's in the middle of the backseat, between Shari and Jago, her body folded awkwardly into Jago's lap, her injured arm, which Aisling patched up, bent into a sling. Jago is awake and mostly silent. His hand rests on top of Sarah's head, his fingers entwined in her hair. He's said very little, but when he does speak he's been even-tempered and friendly.

Pop is a different story.

He's in the wayback, jigsawed into the gear they couldn't leave behind—mainly guns and a mobile satellite uplink that Marrs uses for internet access. Pop has not said a single word since they forged this latest alliance. He hasn't asked about Sky Key or spoken to Sarah or Jago at all. He hasn't said if he's on board with the plan to meet Stella, and he hasn't said he's against it.

To Aisling, his silence is the same as a full-throated scream. She knows that Pop hates the course they're charting. It goes against every one of his beliefs. It is not what Endgame is meant to be.

Aisling is not sure how she's going to handle Pop, but she knows that it will fall on her to handle him when the time comes.

The others don't seem as concerned. Especially Jordan and Marrs. Ever since getting into the jeep, Marrs has been tearing around the internet, going from news sites to encrypted government forums to deep-web hovels full of rumor and intrigue, providing an account of recent world events and bantering with Jordan on pretty much every point.

"The space agencies have been scrambling since the kepler's announcement. At the moment, NASA's got Abaddon falling in the North Atlantic," Marrs says in his nasal monotone. "South of Halifax. Gonna wipe out a lot of land. A *lot*."

"Fucking hell," Jordan says. "What's DC doing?"

"Moving. Lock, stock, and barrel. Looks like to Colorado."

"NORAD?"

"Naturally. Gold's going through the roof, New York's under martial law but seems pretty tame. Boston is coming apart at the seams, though. One of the New England Patriots did a murder-suicide with his wife and kids—dog too."

"Any flags on other Players?" Jordan asks.

"There's some indication that the Shang is in Kolkata, but it's pretty tenuous, and my Bengali is shit. No sign of the Nabataean yet. Oh— and looks like someone's destroying monuments."

"Besides Stonehenge?" Jordan asks incredulously.

"Yeah. This morning while we were trekking from the fortress, a group of nongovernmental operators that remains anonymous, at least to our guys, blew up the ziggurat at Chogha Zanbil. That was the Sumerian one."

"Stella won't like that."

"No, she won't," Marrs says.

Jordan whips the jeep around a slow-moving truck, guiding them into oncoming traffic, which is de rigueur for India. A motor scooter buzzes out of the way into the shoulder and passes them.

"What the hell are you guys talking about?" Jago demands.

Aisling nods. "Yeah, what *are* you talking about?"

"Your line has a monument that is more sacred than any other—right, Aisling?" Jordan asks.

"Jordan, you know it was Stonehenge." *Asshole,* Aisling thinks.

Jordan says, "And you, Tlaloc?"

"We do. It's on the Yucatán Peninsula in Mexico."

"La Venta," Marrs says.

Jago looks a little surprised, and thinks that maybe these guys really do know more than he thought they could about Endgame. "*Sí.* That's what we call it."

Jordan asks, "And your girlfriend?"

"I wouldn't know," Jago says. He's lying, though. He knows the exact location of the prime Cahokian monument. It's called Monks Mound, and it's in southern Illinois, not far from St. Louis, Missouri. He knows this because it's where the Cahokian Rebellion of 1613 occurred. The rebellion that the Olmec oracle, Aucapoma Huayna, told him all about. The rebellion that branded the Cahokians as unworthy of winning Endgame, which was precisely why Aucapoma had implored Jago to end his alliance with Sarah Alopay. No, more than that—the Cahokians were so dangerous that Aucapoma had ordered Jago to *kill* Sarah so he could prove to the Makers that he'd not been poisoned by the Cahokian Player.

Too late for that.

As much as he might want, Jago isn't about to start talking about all of this. It would be too revealing, too . . . *complicating.* So he plays dumb, and they believe him.

"Well, her line has one," Marrs says. "Called Monks Mound. Big tourist attraction now, kinda like Stonehenge but not as well-known."

"Never heard of it," Jago says.

"I have," Aisling says. "Used to be the center of some huge Native American city."

"Once upon a time it was the largest city in all of the Americas, long before any Europeans outside of Vikings even knew about the New World," Jordan says.

"All right," Jago says, "but why are these places so important to finishing Endgame?"

"What he said," Aisling adds, sticking a thumb in Jago's direction.

"I'm going to let Stella fill you in on the details," Jordan says as he works the jeep through a series of accordion-like turns, "but we're certain that Sun Key is hidden in one of them."

Jago leans forward, nearly pushing Sarah's head off his leg. "No shit?"

"No shit," Marrs says. "And if they all get toasted before the Player with the first two keys finds it, well . . ."

"No one will be able to win," Aisling says.

"Bingo," Jordan says.

"Who *is* this Stella woman?" Aisling asks.

"You'll find out soon enough," Jordan says.

Jago leans back in his seat, resettling Sarah's head across his thigh. "Whoever she is, you've gotten my attention, Mr. Jordan. I look forward to meeting her."

"I can promise that the feeling is mutual. She has been waiting to meet you—*all* of you—for a very, very long time."

SARAH ALOPAY, JAGO TLALOC

Heading south along the Teesta River near Mangan, Sikkim, India

Sarah is not asleep. She hasn't slept at all. And while Jago has been friendly with the others, and truly does want to meet this Stella Vyctory, he's not convinced. Not by a long shot.

Sarah slumps across Jago's lap, her hand resting under her hair and on Jago's thigh. She taps out messages to him in Morse code, and he answers in the same code by squeezing her scalp so softly that the movement can only be felt by her and not seen by anyone else.

Their conversation has been long and a little testy, and it revolves around one question, which in this moment Sarah asks for the seventh time: *Should we really trust these people?*

And Jago answers, *We have to for now. If what Jordan says is true, then maybe we now know of another way to stop this thing. Even if Abaddon hits, and the world is changed, we might have a way to prevent a Player from winning. And if Jordan isn't right, it seems that these people really do want the same thing. They can help us, Sarah. We can help them.*

Help us so that we can stay together.

Yes. So that we can stay together.

We stick with them, then.

Yes.

All right, she taps. *I only wish . . .*

What?

I wish we were alone, Feo. I wish it were just you and me.

This is the first time she's said it all day.

And Jago squeezes back, *I do too, Sarah. I do too.*

33

HILAL IBN ISA AL-SALT

Ayutthaya, Thailand

Hilal is also headed to Stella Vyctory, except he is much, much closer.
He hustles out of the Phra Nakhon Provincial Railway Station, turning
this way and that, slicing through a mass of people. He went directly
from the Bangkok airport, where he last spoke to Stella, to the central
Bangkok train station. He got on the first train to Ayutthaya and now he
makes his way on foot to Stella, who is a short four kilometers away.
He goes south from the station through a platoon of food carts,
smelling fried things and salty things and sweet things. Squid,
mushrooms, pork, onions, garlic, sugar, basil, citrus, peanuts. His large
rucksack claps his shoulders as he jogs. It contains his twin machetes,
a change of clothing, a first aid kit for his wounds, the device from
the ark (which has ceased working since the kepler's announcement),
and the incomprehensible book he took from Wayland Vyctory's hotel
suite in Las Vegas.

A few blocks from the station a large group of worshippers blocks the
street and forces him to detour into the Wat Pichai Songkram temple
complex. Monks are everywhere. Bald and saffron-robed and busy.
Devotees wearing conical shade hats and carrying parasols surround
the holy men, pleading for mercy and praying to Lord Buddha. Hilal
does the same in his mind as he rushes past the gilt icon covered in
marigolds and lotus blossoms and surrounded by a pyre of incense. He
searches for a way out of the complex so he can pick up the pace again
and get to Stella as soon as possible.

After a minute he finds himself on the banks of the Pa Sak River. He
turns south and resumes running. Longtail boats ply the cloudy water

and schools of huge catfish boil to the surface to eat bread being thrown by children. It is nice to see young people doing everyday things, to witness innocence.

It is also nice to feel the sun.

He is afraid that, thanks to the impact winter that is likely to shroud the skies after Abaddon, sunlight will be something of a luxury soon.

He is very afraid of this.

He tilts his disfigured face to our star as his feet carry him toward Stella.

The sun. Earth's life force. The photons that bounce off his skin and everything else around him left the solar surface eight minutes and 20 seconds ago. Eight minutes and 20 seconds! They hurtled through the void of space and entered the atmosphere and made a beeline for this spot, right here, on Earth, in the continent called Asia, in the country called Thailand, in the city called Ayutthaya, onto the man and Endgame Player named Hilal ibn Isa al-Salt. A great cosmic accident that happens over and over and over again to everything the sun's light touches. Over and over and over again.

Stella.

He quickens his pace.

Stella. Her name means "star," like the sun.

May she give us light, Hilal thinks.

He turns east onto the wide Rojana Road. He jogs now, passes car dealerships and beauty salons and tourist offices and convenience stores and Thai motorcycle cops in brown uniforms who give him suspicious looks but who don't do anything. He passes a two-story stupa right in the middle of the six-lane road. He passes a group of teenage boys loitering on souped-up scooters, smoking filterless cigarettes, whistling at girls, laughing.

Hilal slows to a brisk walk when he sees these young men. Four of them wear makeshift masks of a face that everyone has seen and everyone has memorized and everyone is confused by and many are terrified by.

The pale face of kepler 22b.

There were Meteor Kids throwing raves and partying after the twelve meteors that announced Endgame, and now there are kepler Kids.

The teens are loud as Hilal approaches, but when they notice him the silence hits. They see his scarred face and his discolored eyes and his lack of hair and his missing ear. Two of the kids pull the masks from the tops of their heads and over their faces, as if to hide.

Hilal doesn't break stride. *"Krap,"* he says, dipping his chin and raising his hand.

None of them say anything in return.

He resumes running. Another kilometer and he reaches the Classic Kameo Hotel, a collection of glass and cement blocks, all white and modern and clean. Hilal imagines it caters to upscale tourists and Asian businessmen.

This is where he will find Stella.

He goes inside. The air conditioning slaps him in the face. He moves through it, crossing his arms for warmth. Nice lobby, big chairs, front desk, clerk, elevator, hallway, room.

Its number is 702. He is about to knock when he is overcome with nerves. He is going to see her again. Stella. The woman who beat him in a fight, who helped him, who claimed Wayland Vyctory as her father. Hilal trusted her in Las Vegas, and he trusts her still, but now that he is on the edge of whatever comes next in Endgame he pauses. Breathes.

Knocks.

He hears the soft pad of footsteps on the far side of the door. The world turns some more.

The door opens. The woman smiles.

"Hilal," Stella says. "Come in. It is so good to see you again."

AN LIU

Shang Safe House, Unnamed Street off Ahiripukur Second Lane, Ballygunge, Kolkata, India

An walks from the cemetery back to his safe house. He walks briskly, angry and red-eyed and oblivious to the world around him.

He had them. The Nabataean and Sky Key and Earth Key too. Right in his sights. He had them and his shots missed and they *outplayed* him! And they got away.

They are gone.

"Gone, Chiyoko, gone! How could I let it happen?" he curses *BLINKshiverBLINK* he curses himself as he marches through the choked streets, and when he finally reaches the secluded side entrance of his hideout his emotions are a tempest.

He opens the door and bolts it shut from the inside and punches a code into the security system. He stalks toward the bathroom, stripping off his clothes as he moves, letting his garments fall to the floor in heaps. He rants the whole way. "I had"—*BLINKBLINK*—"I had them! I could have killed"—*shiverBLINK*—"killed"—*shivershivershiver*—"killed"—*BLINK*—"them." *SHIVERshiver*. "Could have"—*SHIVERshiver*—"Could have"—*SHIVERshiver*—"Could have stuffed a grenade in his mouth and stepped back and laughed and watched the whole thing burn!" *BLINK.* "No"—*BLINK*—"No"—*BLINK*—"No"—*BLINK*—"No winner could be"—*shiverSHIVERshiver*—"no winner could be"—*BLINKBLINKBLINKBLINKshiverBLINKBLINK*—"No winner could *be!*"

He's in the bathroom and naked except for Chiyoko's necklace. He puts his hands to it but they shake too much. She can't calm him right now, she can't, and he lets go of the necklace because he's shaking so much

37

that he's afraid he'll break it, that he'll *hurt* her, and he raises his arm and bites it and clamps down, gnashes, grinds. It hurts and stings and a little blood comes and he stops shaking. He turns on the hot water tap, and his hands calm. He removes Chiyoko and sets her gingerly on the edge of the sink and steps through the curtain and into the stall. It is scalding and his skin turns red and he winces and holds his breath from the shock of the temperature.

He calms some more. His arm throbs. He ducks his stubbly head under the water stream. It burns.

"The world would have gotten what it deserves," An says.

And in that moment there is a small sound deep in his mind and he knows it is her and she's trying to speak to him but he can't hear. He strains and concentrates but he can't hear her.

"What it deserves. All because of me."

He feels better. He washes, dries, cleans the necklace, gets dressed, eats, and then moves to a control room and settles down. He checks the tracking program that marks the Olmec's position, and then turns on several monitors at once and watches the news.

The news. The news. The news. It is glorious and beautiful and amazing.

BBC, CNN International, Al Jazeera, Fox News, TASS, France 24, CCTV. Fear is rampant. Martial law in every Western country. Police forces thinning out as their members flee to be with family. Full military battalions being repositioned to minimum safe distances. Nuclear energy facilities being put on lockdown. Chemical plants following emergency shutdown protocols. Municipal airspaces the world over thick with helicopters and drones. Astronauts and cosmonauts on the International Space Station initiating emergency sequences and preparing for a prolonged isolation from Mission Control. The destruction of the ancient monuments of Stonehenge and Chogha Zanbil—the former of principal importance to the La Tène Celts, the latter equally as essential to the Sumerian line. No one knows who is obliterating them, or if they do know, no one is telling. Are other such monuments slated for destruction as well? Will those belonging to the Olmec, the Cahokian, the Nabataean, the Harappan, the Shang, and all the others be destroyed in time? Is the kepler destroying them? A consortium of the world's militaries? Some group as yet unknown? An is unsure. He watches a dozen segments about the alien called kepler 22b. Interviews with people who revere him or hate him or want to befriend him or kill him. People who want to subjugate themselves to him. People who want to enslave him. But mostly people who want to run away from him, even if there is nowhere *to* run.

Don't tell the leaders of the world that, though. Don't tell the rich. An watches stories about presidents and prime ministers and scientists and educators and MPs and the wealthy, all fleeing, all bunkering, all burying themselves. Trying to disappear. Everyone else looting or taping up windows or trying to get inland and for the most part failing. Shoot-outs on clogged highways up and down the American East Coast. Throngs of people at churches and mosques and temples and synagogues praying to their gods. The Vatican, the Dome of the Rock, the Western Wall—all three so crowded that worshippers at each are being trampled and crushed.

An falls asleep to this beautiful chaotic dance at around three in the morning.

He wakes 2.4 hours later. The television screens are still full of fear and confusion and questions. When will Abaddon hit? How big is it and what's it made of and how many will die?

And some answers.

Abaddon is a dense nickel-and-iron meteor that will strike soon on the edge of the Nova Scotia shelf, 300 kilometers south of Halifax. The asteroid is spherical with a diameter of just under three kilometers. It will punch a hole in the atmosphere and the sky will light up, snuffing out the sun's light. The initial blast will vaporize everything around it and underneath it and over it for hundreds of miles. The impact will trigger a massive earthquake to ripple across the globe, which will even be felt on the other side of the world. After the quake comes the airborne shock wave, destroying everything for hundreds and hundreds of miles. And last but certainly not least will be the tsunamis, affecting every North Atlantic city from San Juan to Washington, DC, to Lisbon to Dakar.

In the hours and days that follow, the secondary effects of Abaddon will wreak havoc over the entire planet. These are less certain. They could include eruptions of long-dormant volcanoes as they are shaken from their slumbers. The Big Island of Hawaii could crack and calve a huge section into the Pacific, causing massive tsunamis up and down the Pacific Rim. Acid rain could fall everywhere, but especially within a few thousand miles of the crater, poisoning the sea and all drinking water in the vicinity. Electrical storms and hurricanes could whip up and ravage the land and sea around the crater.

An flips through the channels. There will be tornadoes, floods, landslides, ash, fear, depravation, suffering, death. There will be firestorms. Impact winters. No more internet in a lot of places. No more air travel for a long time. And on and on and on and, yes, soon, very soon, a lot of things are going to die.

At around six in the morning the first report of a visual comes on air. Spotted in the sky over the South Pacific. A dark speck skirting across the sun's disc. A video plays on CNN International in a GIF loop: fishermen in small wooden boats hoisting Mylar-covered binoculars to the sky. They're surrounded by blue water and white sand and green trees and the sky as clear as ever, and the men point and scream and yell.

That's when everyone knows that it's really true.

That's when An knows it's not a dream.

It's better than a dream.

He will miss the internet, though. Sorely.

An turns from the news and hops up and moves. He needs to get back on the road, to get out of this city before it goes completely insane. The asteroid will hit on the far side of the globe, but he wants to be in the countryside for Abaddon, not in Kolkata or anywhere like it.

He has a quick breakfast of fish cakes and warm Coke. In the garage he loads his bulletproof Land Rover Defender with his go box and the cans of extra gasoline and his guns and bombs and Nobuyuki Takeda's katana and the other box too, the precious box that contains the vest should he ever need it. The 20-kilo suicide vest that is his fail-safe. By 9:13 he is ready to go.

But now that he's sitting in his Defender and looking at the monitors that show what's happening outside his safe house, he's a little worried.

An didn't expect this.

Not at all.

Hundreds of people choke the alleyway outside. All men. All crammed into the narrow street that is his Defender's sole egress. They sit on the ground, lean against walls, mill around. Someone must have followed him from the cemetery and called their friends, and then they called friends, and *they* called friends. The men have sticks and pipes and machetes and a few have semiautomatic rifles. Some have dogs on ropes. Many are shirtless and rail thin and wear the ubiquitous loose cotton pants seen all over India. Some carry placards. Most of these are in Bengali or Hindi, which An can't read, but some are in English. They say, WE SEE YOU! and BROTHERHOOD OF MAN! and EARTH IS OURS! and NO TO ENDGAME! NO TO THE PLAYERS! NO TO KEPLER 22B! More than a few have blood smeared over their faces and arms. Blood from chickens or goats or dogs, sacrificed in ceremonies at local temples.

An understands. These men know who he is—the Shang, An Liu, Player of Endgame—and they want his pain. His life. His blood.

He understands perfectly.

BLINKshiverBLINK.

An pounds something into a laptop mounted in the center of the car. He hits enter. Like all Shang safe houses, this one is wired to blow, and blow dirty, irradiating this section of Kolkata. But the bomb will only detonate when his system detects that he and his vehicle have reached a safe distance.

He flicks the laptop closed.

"Are you ready, Chiyoko?"

And then he hears a small sound deep in his mind.

"Chi"—*BLINK*—"Chi"—*SHIVER*—"Chiyoko?"

The sound grows a little louder, like a hum in the distance.

"Are you ready?"

SHIVERSHIVERSHIVER.

And then—*I am*, she says in the voice she never had.

The quality of her voice doesn't surprise him. Calm but firm. It is her. It is perfectly, succinctly, fully her.

He's been expecting her.

He says, "You are always ready and I love you for it."

An taps a button and the garage doors crack open.

"I love you." An repeats. And she says it too, at the exact same moment, his voice mingling and weaving with hers.

He smiles.

Chiyoko and An. The Mu and the Shang.

They are the same.

The mob outside stirs and crackles.

Those who were sitting stand.

He hits the button again and the doors swing wide. A Kalashnikov fires. Shots explode across the Defender's bulletproof windshield.

BLINK. SHIVER.

He flips the key in the ignition. The engine comes to life. He jams the gas and the engine roars. The men howl and gesticulate, wave their arms and sticks and their ridiculous placards, as if An cares for any of what they have to say.

This is not a protest, it is a war.

And he will fight it with his beloved.

SARAH ALOPAY, JAGO TLALOC

Gulfstream G650, Bogdogra Airport, Siliguri, West Bengal, India

Sarah and Jago recline in very comfortable seats in Jordan's very comfortable private jet trying to figure out what to do. It took them a long time to get down from the Himalayas, and now they're stuck waiting for permission to take off.

The wait is agonizing.

Aisling and Jordan are in the cockpit going through preflight stuff. Marrs is outside dealing with airport personnel. Pop sits in a seat alone near the bulkhead, staring out the window, his rocky knuckles white with tension. Shari is unconscious in the rear of the plane, already seat-belted in place, an IV bag hanging from the overhead compartment. Her chest rises and falls evenly.

Sarah is envious of Shari. Being knocked out would quell the hate and guilt and doubt and fear roiling inside her. Being knocked out would quiet her mind, her soul.

She leans into Jago's side and whispers, "I wish we were fighting, Feo. Right now. I wish we were moving—*Playing.*"

"I know," he says. "Me too."

Action or oblivion, she thinks. *Those are the only options right now.*

Aisling emerges from the cockpit, interrupting Sarah's train of thought.

"How long till we're outta here?" Jago asks.

Aisling drops into the nearest seat. She reaches for her Falcata and lays it over her thighs. She runs her fingertips over the sword.

"At least an hour," she says. "Maybe less if Marrs can bribe the right air traffic controller. But for the moment we're holding." She pulls a stone

43

from a pocket and runs it over her blade's edge. It's razor sharp and doesn't need the attention, but she needs something to do.

Also restless, Sarah thinks.

Sarah straightens and asks, "All right if Jago and I take over the lav for a little while?"

Jago snickers.

"Really?" Aisling's eyebrows spring upward. "Now?"

Jago flashes his glittery smile and strokes Sarah's knee. "*Sí.* No time like the present, *¿sabes?*"

Sarah jabs him with her elbow. "Don't listen to him. Jago picked up a dye kit back in Peru. I'm gonna be raven-haired from now on. Since Liu's video came out and we can all be made, I don't want to take any chances."

He runs his fingers through his platinum hair. "I'm sure you couldn't tell, Aisling, but I'm not a natural blond."

Aisling shakes her head and tilts the blade in her lap, eyeing a miniscule nick. "Go for it. It's all yours."

Sarah and Jago move to the rear of the plane. The lavatory is very nice. There's space between the toilet and the sink, and the sink is normal-sized, not a tiny bowl wedged into the corner. The towels are real, the toilet paper plush and soft.

Jago closes the door behind them. He helps Sarah out of her shirt, being careful with her wounded arm. She leans over the basin, face down, and Jago washes her hair using a plastic cup and the liquid soap on the counter.

"Rosemary," Sarah says. "And lemon. Smells nice."

"Mmm," Jago says. He massages her scalp, rinsing out the soap. He runs his fingers along her nape and lets them trail down her back and over the band of her sports bra.

"Give me a towel," she says.

He does.

She wraps it around her head and stands. They're face-to-face. Her bra brushes his shirt and a shot of electricity races up her back. She smiles. "Can you dry my hair?" she asks.

"*Sí.*"

But instead he immediately leans forward and they kiss. She holds his head tightly between her strong hands and pulls him closer.

And they kiss.

And kiss.

They stop.

She sits on the closed toilet seat. He dries her hair. She brushes it, working through the tangles, while he preps the dye. When she's done brushing, Jago separates her hair into sections and fastens a towel over her bare shoulders. He puts on latex gloves and gets to work, moving methodically from the back of her head and over the crown.

"Feels good, Feo."

"I know." He pushes his leg into hers in a show of affection. She pushes back. "I'm glad we're alive," he whispers.

"Me too. We shouldn't be, though."

Jago pauses so she can speak.

"Baitsakhan had us dead to rights back in the Harappan fortress," she explains. "You were out and I was pretending to be. He had the opportunity, the motive, and the gun. Would've taken a second. *Pop, pop.*"

Jago's hands resume working. "Why didn't he?"

"Who knows. Arrogance? He was messed up from the teleportation? Who cares?"

The plane's hydraulics and servos make some preflight music. Jordan says over the PA, "Just got word that we're close, amigos."

Sarah looks up at Jago, his ugly scar, his stern eyes. "Know what we should do, Feo? Steal a plane first chance we get," she jokes. "Run away and make babies and teach them how to fight and survive and love."

"Sounds great."

"It will be."

They both chuckle at the impossibility of all that.

They are silent for a while.

"If we want to do that someday—and I do—then we really need to stop Endgame," Jago says seriously.

"Yes, we do."

"And you think these people will show us how?"

Sarah shrugs. "I hope so." Then, very quietly, as if she's worried they're being listened to, she says, "Do you believe Aisling? Do you trust her people?"

Jago shrugs. "They haven't tried to kill us."

"No. And I guess we haven't tried to kill them, so we're even there."

"True." He removes some clips from her hair, places them carefully in the sink.

"Okay. Done." He drapes another towel over her. He opens the door and angles his head into the cabin. "Sarah, I have to tell you something."

Sarah frowns, takes his hand, and he leads her to the closest pair of empty seats. Aisling is near the front, sitting next to Pop in silence. Shari is across the aisle, the closed window shade by her shoulder illuminated by the dawn's early light.

Sarah laces her fingers into Jago's. "What is it, Feo?"

"I couldn't tell you before. It was too much. It was Aucapoma Huayna. My line's elder. She told me that . . . she told me that you needed to die."

Sarah releases Jago's hand. *"What?"*

Aisling turns to look at them for a brief moment. Sarah and Jago lower their voices.

"And she said that I was the one who had to do it."

Sarah clenches his hand tightly, painfully. "Why would she say that?"

Jago looks her directly in the eye, not wavering, not showing any signs of being dishonest. He wants her to hear. He needs her to. "It had something to do with your line. She said the Makers would never allow the Cahokians to win, nor would they allow my line to win so long as I walked alongside or Played with you."

Sarah winces. "That's nonsense."

"She said your line did something extraordinary. She said that back in

46

the sixteen hundreds the Cahokians actually *fought* the Makers!"

Sarah shakes her head. "What do you mean?"

"According to her, before the very last group of Makers left Earth—back in 1613—They asked the Cahokians to fulfill an old bargain. You had to give up a thousand young people in a grand and final sacrifice, I guess for Them to take with them on their ships."

"And?"

"And your people *refused*. She said that by then the Cahokians understood that the Makers were mortal and that they appeared to be godlike simply because they possessed more knowledge and technology than humans. She said your people fought, using an old Maker weapon against Them, and that as a last resort the battlefield was iced from orbiting ships, killing everyone there, Maker soldiers included."

"A Maker weapon?"

"Yes. And she said your line received *more* punishment. She said you were made to forget your rebellion and much of your ancient past, even the original name of your line. 'Cahokian' is apparently what you've called yourself since this battle. Before that you were known as something else."

Marrs bounds back into the plane and closes the door behind him. He plants his hands on the bulkhead and leans forward. "Buckle up. We're flying in five."

Sarah pulls the seat belt over her lap. "I don't know what you're talking about," she says a little more loudly as the plane's engines come to life. "The Cahokians have plenty of documents going way past 1613. I've seen them. We have plenty of language and knowledge, Jago. Plenty of *history*. And I have never heard anything like what you're describing—"

Jago raises a hand. "I'm merely telling you what she said. It's been eating at me. Obviously I'm not going to kill you, Sarah. And obviously I don't care what the Makers think or want for themselves. I want you, and I want to stay alive, and to save my family if I can, as fucked up as they are. I want to fight—and fight hard—for what's right." He shrugs as the plane lurches backward. "Who knows," he says. "Maybe she didn't expect me to kill you. Maybe she wanted me to doubt you—doubt *us*—so that I'd leave you at my parents' estate. So *they* could deal with you."

"We're number one for takeoff," Jordan announces on the PA. The plane pulls around a turn and jerks to a stop. "Flight attendants, cross-check, and all the rest. Sit down and do a crossword."

Aisling peers around the edge of her seat at Sarah, smiling at Jordan's lame joke.

Sarah smiles back, not letting her expression relay the seriousness of the conversation she's having with Jago.

"You didn't let me finish," Sarah says, thankful for the sudden hiss of the engines as the jet throttles down the runway. "I don't know about this battle, but I *do* know about the weapon. I've never seen it, of course. No Cahokian Player has since—get this—*1614*. But I know where it's hidden."

"Where?"

"A little south of Monks Mound. The Cahokian monument Marrs was talking about earlier."

"A place that someone, for some reason, might try to destroy."

Sarah shakes her head decisively. The plane jostles through a small cloud, sunlight lancing the cabin as soon as they clear it. "Maybe, Feo. But not if we can get there first."

AN LIU

Shang Safe House, Unnamed Street off Ahiripukur Second Lane, Ballygunge, Kolkata, India

An Liu's Defender moves into the daylight to meet the mob. His Beretta ARX 160, specially modified with a powered picatinny rail, fires through a slot below the windshield. The report is loud inside the vehicle and he likes it. The bullets sail into the crowd. The casings pitter onto his lap. A few men are hit. They dive and scatter to the side but the mob doesn't dissipate. He gives the rifle four more long bursts, swinging it side to side. Red sprays of blood and small clouds of dust as bodies fall and feet scamper. An puts the car in second and lets out the clutch, and the Defender jumps forward. Another volley. He hopes the men will thin enough for him to escape to the wider street at the end of the alleyway.

And for a moment this is exactly what happens. But then the men yell and turn back all at once like a school of fish, surging toward his car. They throw rocks and pipes, and the soldiers with rifles fire at will. These projectiles bounce off his car without causing any real damage, but now things are about to get trickier.

They're blocking his escape.

He'll have to run them down like dogs.

Which is fine with him.

An yanks his rifle into the interior, the flap under the windshield closing immediately. He flips open a panel on the dashboard. Two covered switches and a pistol grip with a trigger are built into the console. He snaps open the switch covers. Presses the left button. It glows red. He takes the grip and angles it up and pulls the trigger. A white arc traces from the front of the car, the projectile rainbowing over the crowd, sailing 30, 40, 50 meters before hitting the ground at the end of the alley and detonating. The air there turns orange and black as the grenade does its job.

An feels giddy.

He slams the clutch, puts the car in the third, and grinds forward.

He meets the men. The sound is sickening, lovely, unusual. Yells of defiance turn to screams of pain and terror, but still the men press in on him. The Defender rides over a body. Faces mash into his windows, their flesh going flat and pink and brown and white against the glass. A pair of men grabs the door handles and tries in vain to work them open. The car slows a little. An drops it into second gear. The men beat the car and grab at it and jump on top of it. The car rocks side to side as An jogs the wheel, pinning men on the sides between the car and buildings, blood smearing across the hood and then the windshield. Some men with the kepler masks get caught and crumple under the rear wheels. The car is a four-wheel-drive beast. He lets out a little laugh. He flicks the wipers. Bad idea—the blood smears and obscures his view. The car moves forward more slowly now, the men treating it like a drum, but it's useless. It's too heavy for them to topple and they can't get in or breach its armor. An is sure that he'll make it out and get away.

But then a giant man jumps from a low building onto the hood. He turns and sits on the roof, facing out, his feet planted wide. An peers through the arcs of blood swiped across the glass and sees that he's almost reached the street where the grenade went off. A burned-out car, a few bodies, a dying cow. A strangely dressed woman—cropped hair, a stick tied to her back—darts across the street. A matted stray dog limps from left to right. The grenade cleared a path and if he can get there then he should be able to gain some speed and get away and then, once he's three kilometers distant, *poof!* His bomb will detonate and that will be the end of the mob and the end of this safe house and the end of this dank little corner of Kolkata, India.

But then, *BAM!* An is rattled. The man on the hood has swung a heavy maul into the windshield. The bulletproof glass holds. The men outside whoop and yell and—*blink SHIVERSHIVERblink*—An's heart nearly stops as a trio of men heave a thick metal bar across the end of the alleyway and bolt it into place. It's a meter off the ground, and there's no way he'll be able to drive over it.

An pulls the car to within five meters of the barricade and stops. *SHIVERSHIVERSHIVERblinkSHIVER*.

"This can't be it, Chiyoko, can it? Do we abandon the car?" He turns left and right and looks into the cargo area for ideas. His equipment, his weapons, the sword. His vest.

It would be a waste to use that now.

The street.

The barricade.

"We have to at least try."

BAM! The maul again and the car shakes.

BAM! Again. A small spiderweb in the glass. A chink in the armor.

An puts the car in reverse and guns it. The mauler falls onto his hands and knees, his weapon sliding off the hood to the ground. The mob at the back folds under the car as it rides over them. More mashing. More popping. The mauler looks over his shoulder, stares right at An. Anger, menace, stupidity. An slams the brake and the mauler slides up the hood and into the windshield, his legs bunching under him. An grabs the rifle and sticks it back into the hinged flap, and he fires directly into the mauler's thigh and buttocks. The mauler rolls to the side in agony. An puts the car in first and it jumps forward and the mauler tumbles off the hood.

Clutch, second, gas, clutch, third, gas. He's up to 55 kph in no time, the men flying away from the car, gunshots hitting the rear window. He takes the wheel with both *blinkblinkblink* both hands and peers at the barricade. Will it hold? Will it buckle? Will he make it?

An squints, readying for impact. And then—what is that? A head sailing through the air?

Whatever it is, it rolls under the barricade, and then another head-like ball, and then, at the last second before impact, the barricade is unlocked and the grille slams into it and the bar swings violently away and into the street. He hits the brakes. The car swerves and stops. The street ahead is clear enough for him to complete his getaway. But before he leaves he looks back down the alley, full of bodies living and dying and dead. What is left of the mob comes for him.

But another comes for him too. The woman with the cropped hair. She's wiry and fast and strong. A stick—no, a *sword*—in her hand. And her face.

Her face.

It looks like Chiyoko's, except 20 or 30 years older.

SHIVERSHIVERSHIVERSHIVERSHIVERblinkblinkblinkblinkSHIVERblink SHIVERSHIVERSHIVER SHIVERSHIVERblinkblinkblinkblinkSHIVERblink SHIVERSHIVERSHIVERSHIVERSHIVERblinkblinkblinkblinkSHIVER blink BAM! BAM! BAM!

"Go, go, go!" the woman yells in Mandarin. She stands on the running board, right next to An on the outside of the car, slapping her hand on the roof. "Go! They'll kill us!"

"Who are you?"

"I am Nori Ko. I am Mu. I knew Chiyoko. I can help you. Now, *we have to go!*"

And An's heart fills and he feels light and free and he wonders how many has he killed today and how many more will die when the bomb goes off and *ChiyokoChiyokoChiyokoNoriKoNoriKoChiyoko* and he feels free and light and An's heart fills.

He drives. Half a kilometer later he stops. He lets her in. "Watch," he says, and she says nothing. He drives some more and a short while later the sky behind them lights up, and they are free.

MACCABEE ADLAI, LITTLE ALICE CHOPRA

Road SH 2, Joypur Forest, West Bengal, India

Maccabee runs a straight razor over his bare scalp. He swishes the blade in a copper bowl half-filled with a stew of water and black stubble and soap. Next to the bowl is a pair of scissors covered by a pile of thick hair. He squints at his reflection in a clouded mirror that's propped against the wall. He's never shaved his head before and he likes the way it feels. The smoothness, the lightness. Also, with his bruises and his crooked nose and his physique, the baldness makes him look like a real badass.

Which of course he is.

"What do you think, Sky Key?"

The girl sits next to him. She leans into his side. Her body is warm, and he feels comforted by it. He wonders if she is comforted in turn. Probably not.

Her legs are tucked up and her arms are wrapped over her knees. She doesn't answer his question. He briefly touches her hair. It's thick and soft, the hair of a girl who's been well cared for.

If he's going to get her to the end, he'll have to take good care of her too. He passes her a bowl of rice and lentils, a stiff circle of dal balanced on top. "Here. Have some more food."

She digs in with her bare hands and eats. Her appetite is strong and, so far, insatiable.

They are in an abandoned roadside hut 130 kilometers west and north of Kolkata. It's midmorning. The landscape outside is lush and verdant. Jungle surrounds the hut, but fields of jute and potatoes lie less than a kilometer to the north. Sporadic cars and buses pass on the road, but other than that there are no signs of people here.

Which is good. Early that morning he and Sky Key wandered through a shopping center west of Kolkata buying supplies. Rice, soap, candles, batteries, towels, a sewing kit, a small butane camp stove with a liter of fuel. Baby wipes, pull-up diapers for Sky Key to sleep in, a blanket, and three changes of clothing for the girl. He also lucked into finding one of those cloth child carriers that straps over the shoulders and holds the kid tightly on the back. At a pharmacy he bought generic ibuprofen, amoxicillin, Cipro, zolpidem, and a small first aid kit with an extra bottle of iodine. Back at the hotel he packed all of this into a new knapsack as well as into the stolen Suzuki's touring panniers, one of which blessedly contained a SIG 226 and two magazines.

The same kind of gun An Liu had fired at them back in the cemetery. It was then that he realized he'd had the good fortune to steal An Liu's bike.

He checked the SIG's decocker and stuffed it into the top of his pants. Throughout the morning he'd dealt with merchants and for the most part they were nice to him. He had to pay a small fortune for everything, though—prices were going through the roof under the threat of Abaddon, even here on the other side of the world where the effects of the asteroid would be less urgent. The fact that he wasn't Indian didn't make things any cheaper. Regardless, none of the shopkeepers recognized him as a Player, which was fortunate.

But then they stopped for breakfast at a dosa stall, and as they sat at a plastic picnic table the owner turned up the news on the small television mounted over the counter. He gabbed on in Bengali with one of his workers, no doubt talking about all the craziness happening in the world, while stills from An Liu's video clicked past one by one on the screen. And that's when Maccabee saw his own face, clear as day. He didn't worry about it at first. He was banged up from all the fights he'd been through and he didn't think that the shop owner was paying close enough attention to make the connection. But he was. He turned on Maccabee and Sky Key in a flash, pointed a finger, started yelling.

Maccabee stood, his mouth half-full of curried potatoes, and hoisted up the girl. The man stepped around the counter with a long kitchen knife. Maccabee backed away, swallowed his food, lifted his shirt to reveal the butt of the pistol, and said, "You don't need to get hurt, my friend. None of us do."

Stunned, the man quieted for a few moments as Maccabee and Sky Key left. He resumed yelling as soon as they were out on the street, and people began gawking, but the pair made it onto the bike in front of the hotel and Maccabee got Sky Key into the child carrier and they whisked out of there.

They rode all morning, stopping once to buy some rice and lentils at a food stall. Not long ago he caught sight of this hut flickering through the trees. Sky Key had been squirming for the previous 10 kilometers, and Maccabee had to piss, so he pulled over. He hid the bike in the bush and crept toward the corrugated metal building, the SIG pistol in hand. The hut was empty of people. It contained some basic items like bowls and a mirror and a few bedrolls and a low table. Maccabee figured it was a crash pad for itinerant farmhands, but it didn't look like it had been used in a while.

They went in and he fed Sky Key some already cooked rice and lentils that came in simple plastic bags. Then he got going with the scissors and the straight razor. And now he is done. It isn't a perfect disguise, but he doesn't look anything like he did in the video.

It will do.

"Well, I like it," Maccabee says of his new look.

Sky Key chews and manages a grunt. One of the first noises she's made all morning.

Maccabee scoots over so that he's sitting opposite the girl. A warm breeze pushes through the windows. The leaves outside rustle, a tree trunk creaks.

So young, he thinks.

Too young.

He dips his fingers into the bowl of rice and lentils and takes a handful in the Indian fashion and brings it to his lips. For food purchased from a roadside hawker, it's surprisingly good.

Sky Key's face is wind worn and streaked with grime. He reaches across the bowl and uses his thumb to wipe her cheek. She doesn't move away. Her eyes are locked forward, staring at Maccabee's chest.

"I'll steal a car soon. You shouldn't ride like that. Too exposed."

She chews. Stares. Swallows.

"Good," she says, breaking her silence since the day before.

"So you *are* going to talk?" he says, trying to sound kind.

"I don't like it. The motorbike."

"We'll get rid of it then."

"Good," she repeats. She takes another mouthful of food.

"The problem is—once we get a car, where do we go?"

She doesn't say anything.

"I mean, we should probably wait out the impact before we keep going," he says, thinking out loud more than talking to her. "But where will we be safe? And how will we find Sun Key?"

"We'll be safe, Uncle," she announces emphatically.

He frowns.

She takes another bite of food in her fingertips, pushes it into her mouth.

Strange girl, he thinks.

"Please, call me Maccabee. Or Mac."

"All right, Uncle," she says, as if she's agreeing to a different request.

He ignores it. "How do you know we'll be safe?"

The girl swallows her food before answering. "The Makers won't destroy me or Earth Key. Mama said. The bad thing will happen far from here. From me. From who is with me. What we need to be afraid of are the others. Like the man from yesterday. That's what Mama said too."

"Your mama," he says slowly.

"Yes. Thank you for killing the bad man, Uncle," she says in a smaller than usual voice. "Thank you."

Very strange girl, he thinks as pangs of guilt shudder through him. Baitsakhan was absolutely bad, but that didn't make Maccabee a saint. Not by a long shot. After all, he nearly killed Shari Chopra too.

But he didn't. And this girl, she does not need to know otherwise.

"You're . . . welcome," he says. He wonders if she's always spoken beyond her years. He wonders if touching Earth Key made her this way, or if she was like this before.

He can't know that she was.

That Little Alice was always precocious, always special.

He says, "All right, let's assume we are safe from the asteroid. I still don't know where to go. How do I win? Where *is* Sun Key?"

She chews. Swallows. Then she sticks out her arm and points a few degrees south of due east. "I know, Uncle."

Maccabee frowns. "You *know*?"

"Two two dot two three four. Six eight dot nine six two."

He gets his smartphone, launches Google Maps, and punches in the coordinates. A pin over water pops up, a short distance from the coast of the western Indian port city of Dwarka. He shows it to Sky Key.

"This? Is this where we'll find Sun Key?"

The girl nods.

"It's not that far at all!"

Giddiness wells in his heart and works into his throat.

"Yes, Uncle. Sun Key is there."

"You're certain?"

"Yes."

He fumbles with the smartphone and his smile grows. Two thousand four hundred thirty-four kilometers. Thirty-six or 37 hours of driving. Maybe faster if he can find a plane to steal.

He can win Endgame, he can guarantee the survival of the Nabataean line after the cataclysm, he can see the new Earth and live on it until he is old and frail. Maybe he *can* save this young girl and fulfill the promise he made to her mother.

Maybe he can win *and* right some wrongs.

He jumps to his feet, intent on going outside and flagging down the next decent-looking car that comes along the road and carjacking it. He can hardly contain himself. "Sky Key, this is amazing!"

"I know, Uncle." The girl takes another bite. "They call me Little Alice."

"I could win, Alice! *The Nabataeans could win!*"

She chews. Swallows. "I know."

AN LIU, NORI KO

HP Petrol Pump, Baba Lokenath Service Station off SH 2, Joypur Jungle, West Bengal, India

An's heart is full.

After the explosion Nori Ko moved to the Defender's backseat. She said in Mandarin, "Drive west."

He did.

He watched the road slip under the car and continue to unfurl before them and he watched her in the rearview mirror and he watched the road and he watched her. The road and her. Road and her. He did not speak. He did not need words. He did not speak for over three hours. She did not bother him with words either.

Chiyoko would have done the same.

ChiyokoChiyokoNoriKoChiyoko.

Now they've stopped to refuel. He's outside. She's in the car, her head propped against the far window. He's in the stifling heat, a gas pump in his hand. The paved highway lies to the north. A few kilometers earlier they entered a jungle reserve and now trees rise all around, making the air a couple of degrees cooler than it is out by the open fields of jute and corn. Behind the filling station is a low concrete building, a white bull lolling under a jackfruit tree, its leafy boughs heavy with oblong fruit. Aside from the attendant in the air-conditioned booth, no people are around.

An finishes and pays and gets in and drives.

"West?" he asks.

"West."

He merges onto State Highway 2, headed for Bishnupur. They drive through the jungle. An doesn't see any buildings or signs of people except for the road they're on and a brief glimpse of a derelict metal hut hiding behind the trees. He thinks nothing of it.

After another quarter hour, An says, "I'm ready"—*blink*—"I'm ready"—*blink*—"I'm ready to talk." *SHIVER*. "We have to talk."

"We do," Nori Ko says. She moves An's rifle from the front passenger seat and climbs forward. "You have questions."

An nods. "Why did you find me?"

"I found you because I also loved Chiyoko."

His skin crawls at hearing another person say her name. Even this one, who comes from her stock and looks so much like her. He's reminded of the British interrogator on the destroyer who insisted on saying it. That one who wielded the name like a blade. Drove it into An's ears and twisted it. An almost tells his new ally that she should not say Chiyoko's name either, but he knows he doesn't have the right. Whoever Nori Ko is, she was someone to Chiyoko. That counts for something.

"Chiyoko," Nori Ko says quietly.

Yes, it counts for something. But . . .

The name is mine now, he thinks. *Chiyoko. Chiyoko Takeda.* My *name.*

Nori Ko reaches across the inside of the car, her fingers yearning for the necklace that hangs around An's neck, breaking his train of thought.

SHIVER.

He moves away from her.

"It's okay," she says. "I want to touch her. Like you do."

BLINKSHIVERBLINK.

She touches the necklace. After a moment Nori Ko returns her hands to her lap. Her fingertips rub together, the residue of Chiyoko on them. "I *love* her," Nori Ko clarifies. "After what happened I couldn't sit idly by. That's why I found you."

"After what happened?"

"I am Mu. A high member of the training council. I know much about Endgame." She pauses, and then says quietly, "I saw a recording of your conversation with Nobuyuki. I saw how you killed him."

SHIVERSHIVER.

"Yes, I saw it, Shang. There was a black box containing surveillance recordings that survived the fire in Naha. I heard what you said, what he said. I thought Nobuyuki was unfair to you. Under no circumstances would he have allowed you to Play for the Mu, but I thought it not right of him to test you like that."

"He deserved what he got," An says.

"No, he did not."

SHIVER.

She says, "You didn't need to honor his request for Chiyoko's remains. You did not have to respect Nobuyuki the way you respected Chiyoko. But for that same reason, you should have spared him. Not for his sake, but for hers. Killing him dishonored Chiyoko, An. As well as yourself. It did nothing to tarnish the honor of Nobuyuki Takeda."

BLINKBLINK.

Her voice is cold.

SHIVERBLINKblink.

"You speak like him," An finally says.

"I *can* speak like him. But I am not him."

An wrings the wheel in his hands. His knuckles whiten. He pushes the gas a little more. The car accelerates.

Her voice is cold.

Her words cut.

"I loved Nobuyuki too," she says. "But don't worry, I'm not interested in honor like he was. I'm not here to punish you for his death." The thought of this woman punishing him almost makes An laugh.

She continues. "I chose you precisely because I've seen what you're capable of."

Death, he thinks. *She wants death.*

"What were you to her?" An asks.

"A trainer. Bladed arts, karate, acrobatics, evasion, disguise. She was my best student. I've never met anyone faster or more ruthless. She was—"

"She should not have died."

"No. She shouldn't have."

Silence. One kilometer. Two.

"You love her," An says. "I love her. This doesn't explain why you're here."

"Because I want the same thing you want."

"And that is?" He's glad to be wearing Chiyoko right now. She gives him strength. Allows him to speak without too many glitches or tics. So glad.

She is like you, love, Chiyoko says to him.

Nori Ko says, "What you want is as plain as the nose on your face, An Liu. Love multiplied by death—by *murder*—has only one solution."

Pause.

"Revenge," An says.

"Revenge," Nori Ko says.

More silence. The sky is bright. They pass a multicolored Tata truck laden with rebar.

She doesn't lie, love, Chiyoko says. *Her anger makes her strong.*

I know, An thinks. *It is the same with me.* Chiyoko doesn't say anything to this.

"How did you find me?" An asks.

"I've been on your trail since Naha. I was going to approach you the other day, right after you arrived in Kolkata, but then Endgame caught us by surprise, didn't it?"

"It did. Things happened quickly. Very quickly. We were so close."

"To Adlai?"

We were so close to killing the Nabataean, love, Chiyoko reminds him.

He nods. "Yes. We were *very* close," An says to Chiyoko and Nori Ko.

Nori Ko ignores An's use of the first person plural and says, "I tried to reach the cemetery, but I was too late to help you. Believe me, I would have."

An thinks of what she did to the mob in Ballygunge. He says, "I believe you."

"Good."

Silence again. They pass roadside things. A group of women in bright clothing, a flock of pigeons rising from the treetops, a road crew patching potholes in the oncoming lane.

The other side of the world faces the apocalypse, but in India life goes on.

"What do you think of when you think of revenge, An?"

"Blood. Ashes. Swollen things."

Nori Ko shakes her head. "No. I mean, *who* do you think of?"

The answer is quick. "The Cahokian. The Olmec. They were there when she died. If they hadn't been, she would've lived."

A brief silence before Nori Ko intones, "Then I want their deaths too, An Liu."

SHIVERshiverSHIVERshiverSHIVERshiver.

"But tell me, An Liu—is there someone else you want dead?"

The car jounces over a bump. Neither speaks for a moment. He looks at the instrument panel. The Defender whips along at 123 kph. The engine hums at 2,900 rpms. It is 37 degrees Celsius outside.

"Yes," he answers.

Nori Ko says, "The kepler."

An nods. "Him. *It.*"

Nori Ko grunts. "I'm also in the mood for his blood. And I will see that you have it. That we both have it."

An says, "You're not like Chiyoko."

"I'm older than she was. Age does things to a person, and people who know of Endgame age even faster and in different ways." She waves her hand as if to bat away a fly or an unpleasant memory. "I had ideals once, if that's what you mean."

BLINKshiverblink.

"It is."

"I've learned a lot about Endgame over the years, An. From a lot of different people, not all of them Mu. Not all of them *wanting* Endgame the way the Players did. My ideals, such as they were, suffered the more that I learned." Pause. "They were dashed for good when Chiyoko was killed."

Hearing her name again hurts. *She shouldn't say it,* he thinks.
Chiyoko whispers, *It's all right. She will help you. Don't be hard on her. She will help you. She will help us.*

An shakes his head—not a tic, just a hard shake to quiet her voice, which echoes in his brain.

A car appears in the rearview mirror, driving very fast.

"So tell me—where *are* we headed, Mu Nori Ko?"

"You've been watching the news?"

"Yes."

"And seen that someone's destroying monuments from Maker-human antiquity?"

"Yes. Do you know who?"

"I have a hunch, but that's not important. What *is* important is that we get to the next closest monument—which happens to be the Harappan one in western India. Odds are that is where the Nabataean is taking the first two keys. It is where he thinks he will win."

"Where exactly?"

"A sunken temple near the Gujarati town of Dwarka."

An jams the brakes and holds the wheel tightly and Nori Ko braces herself on the dashboard and the tires squeal and they come to a lurching halt.

The car that is driving fast so fast overtakes them. A small late-model sedan, one driver, bald and in a hurry. No passengers. The driver looks nothing like Maccabee and there is no one else in the car so An doesn't pay it any mind. Everyone drives like a speed demon in India anyway.

"Why is Adlai going there?" he asks urgently. "Is it because of Sun Key?"

"Yes."

"Is it there?"

"I don't know for sure."

"But you think it's at one of these monuments? The ones that are being destroyed?"

"Yes. It is. Although I don't know which one."

He pauses. Squints. The car disappears around the next turn. He says, "Then Sun Key could also be at the Mu monument? Or the Cahokian? Or the Olmec? Or—the *Shang*?"

"Yes. It could."

An puts the car back in gear, whips the wheel around, pulls a tight U-turn, and heads back in the direction from which they came, going fast fast fast.

"What are you doing?" Nori Ko demands.

BlinkSHIVERSHIVERblinkBLINKBLINKSHIVERshiverBLINK.

She reaches out and puts a hand on his arm. He yanks it away.

China, Chiyoko says.

Yes, he answers.

"The Nabataean could already be halfway to Dwarka!" Nori Ko protests.

"I know. And if he's lucky enough to find Sun Key there, then he's already won, and we are already too late," An says through clenched teeth. "Nothing we do will matter. We need to get the keys to see the kepler face-to-face. If he wins, then we will have lost our chance to meet and then kill the Maker. *But . . .*"

And then Nori Ko understands. "The pyramid of Emperor Zhao."

"Yes. We start at the Shang monument. If Dwarka doesn't have Sun Key—and the odds are decent that it won't—then Adlai will go to the next closest monument. *Mine.*"

"China," Nori Ko says. Accepting. Approving.

"Yes. We're going home," he says, thinking of all the things he hated about it, of all the pain he endured during his training, of all the suffering. "My hellish home."

SHARI CHOPRA

Mercedes Sprinter Van, Ayutthaya, Thailand

Shari Chopra is not in her home, although that is where she would rather be more than anything. In her home, smelling cooking food, watching her child run through the garden, holding her husband's hand.

But her husband is dead.

She is not home, but she is awake, and none of the others know it yet. Her eyes remain closed but her reawakening senses tell her much. She is bound, in the rear of a vehicle, probably a van.

She came around 15 minutes ago. She's been counting slowly in her mind, partly to keep calm and focused, partly not to cry out for her daughter, partly to get her bearings. She pictures the numbers instead of saying them in her mind. Some of the numbers are made of green leaves, some are simple lines like the strokes of pen on paper, some are made of sticks, some are made of blood.

Shari is careful that none of these images remind her of Little Alice. No peacock feathers, no pakoras, no toys, no numbers scrawled in crayon by a child's hand. Of course Little Alice is there in Shari's memory. She always is. But right now, in order to keep up her subterfuge, Shari has shifted Little Alice to the wings of her consciousness. Because if she brought her to center stage now it would be too painful and dangerous.

She counts.

984.

985.

987.

No. I skipped one.

986.

She is still groggy.

She hears the voices of others talking. She hears Aisling Kopp and Jago Tlaloc and Sarah Alopay. She remembers each of their voices from the Calling. She remembers their accents. She remembers the sharp and tinny edge of Jago's voice, the throaty innocence of Sarah's, the sanguine twang of Aisling's.

Aisling Kopp. The Celt. The Player who killed the Harappan.

The Player who Shari will kill someday in turn. Hopefully sooner than later.

My enemies.

987.

988.

989.

My enemies are so close.

There are other voices she doesn't recognize. Two men. Middle-aged. And a third man behind her in the van who doesn't speak, but whose breath is plain and audible. He has a rattle deep in his throat.

Perhaps he sleeps. Perhaps he's angry. Perhaps he too is a prisoner.

The vehicle comes to a stop. Everyone but the silent man gets out.

The air wafting into the van is hot and humid. They're not in the mountains anymore. The voices talk outside. "*This* is the place?" "Where is she?" "Are you sure your friend will help us?" "Will she be able to stop Endgame?"

Yes, yes, yes, yes, one of the unknown men answers.

They move out of earshot.

Shari considers opening her eyes now, springing to action, getting revenge.

But she stays. She is bound and she can't trust her body yet, its responsiveness, its strength. She doesn't know where she is or why these three Players are together and not trying to kill one another. Have they called a truce? Have they come to an understanding, like she and Alice Ulapala did? Are they working together? She doesn't know.

She stays. She needs to be sure that if revenge is the tonic she seeks, she will get it.

The others move back into earshot and then climb into the van and restart the engine. None talk. Shari feels the tension between them.

Did one mention trying to stop Endgame?

Yes. One did.

Is that possible?

She wants to serve her revenge, but she also wants to sate her curiosity over what these people are up to.

She stays.

She stays.

Most of all she wants to live, and acting now would not guarantee that. She *has* to live if there is any chance that Little Alice is safe.

The van moves forward. Makes a tight turn, rides over a bump in the pavement, and feels as though it moves inside. The ground pitches downward five or six degrees. They drive for several minutes, making twisting turns like one would in a multistory garage. Then the ground levels and they stop.

She counts.

1,009.

1,010.

1,011.

Doors open. People get out. "Don't forget the Harappan," one of the men says. Jago Tlaloc grunts as he works Shari out of her seat and heaves her over his shoulder. A shot of pain in her side. She wants to call out but she doesn't.

She welcomes the pain.

It means she is alive.

That her senses are returning.

By the sound she can tell that they move into a hard-walled room. The smell of food, spicy and oily and salty and peppery and doughy and fresh. Her stomach turns. She hopes it won't call out and grumble.

She counts.

She concentrates on severing the connection between her gut and her woken brain.

She counts.

Jago places her on a chair. She keeps her body limp. He props her up. The zip ties on her wrists, which are not terribly tight, dig at her flesh. Her legs are not bound.

If it comes to it, she can run.

She counts.

Some eat. The three Players sound unsure of why they're here. They talk in short bursts, their tension palpable. They're waiting for someone. Someone Shari has never heard of.

Someone named Stella Vyctory.

She counts.

1,050, made of white feathers.

1,051, made of water droplets suspended in space.

Please live, Shari thinks. *Let my child live.*

1,052, made of blood and bones.

AISLING KOPP, SARAH ALOPAY, JAGO TLALOC, SHARI CHOPRA, HILAL IBN ISA AL-SALT, STELLA VYCTORY, POP KOPP, GREG JORDAN, GRIFFIN MARS

Bunker beneath Classic Kameo Hotel and Serviced Apartments, Ayutthaya, Thailand

They are assembled in a brightly lit conference room 103 feet underground. Its northern and southern walls are made of concrete, the eastern and western ones of thick structural glass, each with a high-tech sliding door set in it. At the moment, both of these doors are closed.

Beyond the westernmost glass door is a large garage containing a late model Mercedes sedan and a Sprinter Van that they drove here in from the airstrip northeast of town. The van was courtesy of Stella Vyctory, and it's full of weapons and supplies and a cooler of ice-cold Cokes, and they are thankful for all of it. Especially the Cokes.

Behind the vehicles is a steep driveway that leads to the surface. The only other obvious way in or out of the bunker is a stairway behind a metal door just outside the easternmost glass partition. This stairway, Jordan says, is the one that Stella will use to join them from the hotel above.

She is almost here.

As they wait they sit around a large teak table set with food, though only Jordan and Marrs bother to eat. The others are clearly anxious. Jago has ejected the magazine from a new Glock 20 and plays with the slide. Sarah and Aisling, who also have new pistols from the van, are motionless. Aisling watches Shari. Shari, who everyone assumes is unconscious, keeps her eyes shut and tries to keep her mind calm. And then the doorway swings open and Stella appears. She is Caucasian, tall, dark-haired, muscular, confident, late 20s or early 30s, and she strides into the conference room accompanied by a dark-skinned man whose face has recently been hideously burned, his hands clasped easily at his waist. He wears loose cotton clothing and carries a heavy rucksack by the shoulder straps at his side. Stella is dressed in black jeans and a gray V-neck T-shirt and dark running shoes. She has no jewelry and no visible weapons. The man with her also does not appear to be armed.

Jordan rises to greet Stella, grabbing her by the shoulders and pulling her into a hearty hug. "It's good to see you again," he says. "I'm sorry we parted ways for a while."

She shrugs it off. "It's good to see you too, Greg." Then she gently pushes him aside and says to the room, "I am *so* glad to see you. I've been waiting my entire life to be in a room full of Endgame Players." The relief and joy and gratitude in her voice are palpable and a little infectious.

A good first impression, Sarah thinks.

Aisling and Jago think the same.

Shari thinks, *Where am I? Who is this new stranger? Is she an enemy too?*

Stella addresses each of them individually. "Aisling . . . Sarah . . . Jago. Thank you for agreeing to trust Greg. I know it hasn't been easy. I'm sorry you couldn't kill the little girl that is Sky Key, as terrible as that sounds. I'm sorry you couldn't stop the Nabataean from taking her."

Little Alice is alive!

Little Alice is alive!

Little Alice is alive!

Shari wants to scream for joy and relief, but her training controls her body, not permitting her to move even a centimeter. Her chest doesn't heave, her fingers don't twitch, her eyelids don't flutter.

Little Alice is alive, Shari thinks.

And then something terrible strikes her: *Could it be that my captors and these strangers are also my . . . my friends? That like me, they know that Endgame is amoral? That it is wrong?* Her stomach turns at this thought and it takes all her concentration not to vomit all over her lap.

"And you must be Mr. Kopp," Stella says, interrupting Shari's train of thought.

Pop, at the far end of the table and half turned away from Stella, grunts disapprovingly.

So that's the silent one, Shari thinks. *A line member of Aisling's. He must have been with her in the mountains.*

He also will have to die for what happened to my line.

And then Stella says, "And Shari Chopra is here too. I'm happy to see her."

How does she know all of our names?

Stella continues, "But does she need to be kept unconsc—"

She's cut off as Aisling and Sarah blurt in perfect unison, "Who the *hell* are you?"

The two Players look at each other and almost smile.

Shari thinks, *Yes. Who?*

Stella makes a small curtsy. "Well, as Greg has told you, my name is Stella Vyctory. And I am very interested in Endgame."

"Why?" Jago demands. "You're no Player."

"What line are you with?" Aisling asks.

And Sarah says, "How do you know *anything* about Endgame?"

Stella pats the air in front of her. "I promise, I'll tell you everything the more we get to know one another. But we're short on time, so for now I'll say that my adoptive father taught me about Endgame. He wasn't with any of the lines, but—"

"Your father?" Sarah says.

"Why isn't he here?" Jago asks.

And Aisling says, "I trust Jordan, but how do I know I can trust you?"

"Please," Stella pleads. "You *can* trust me. You *must* if we are going to stop Endgame. I can tell you how."

"The prophecies say nothing about non-Players intervening," Sarah says. "Least of all to stop Endgame."

Stella shakes her head. "No. They don't. But the prophesies are false. And the rules—"

"The rules of the game have changed," Jago says gravely.

"That's right, Jago Tlaloc," Stella says.

"Or rather, there are no rules," Aisling reminds them. "That's what kepler 22b said. If we really are going to stop Endgame, then I guess we're finally going to have to embrace that, completely."

"I understand your concern, Sarah," Stella says. "If I were in any of your shoes I wouldn't trust me at first either. And after what I tell you about my father I would probably trust me even less."

Jago leans forward. "And that is?"

"My father knew a lot about the Makers. More than any of the lines do, more than *all* of the lines put together. He knew a lot because, well, because he was one of *Them*."

What? Shari thinks.

Looks of doubt dominate the Players' faces.

"It's true," Jordan says quietly.

Pop grunts again, barely masking his dislike for Jordan or Stella or anything either has to say.

Finally Sarah says, "So—you're a Maker too?"

And in case the answer is yes, Jago quietly slides the magazine back into his Glock and gets ready to fire.

Stella stays cool. She keeps her eyes locked on Sarah. "Absolutely not. All I want is to stop Endgame."

The man with the terrible burns steps forward. "I beg you, my fellow Players. Listen. Ms. Vyctory is sincere. I trust her completely. I implore you to do the same."

Sarah claps her hand over her mouth.

Jago blurts, *"Aksumite?"*

"What . . . what happened?" Aisling asks.

Shari yearns to open her eyes, to see what is so disturbing about Hilal ibn Isa al-Salt. She wants to see the Player who revealed the location and identity of her daughter, the man who enabled the decimation of her line.

She wants to see him and she wants to kill him.

Hilal says, "I was attacked by the Donghu and the Nabataean after the Calling. Sadly, both survived."

"One's dead now," Sarah whispers. "Baitsakhan. Jago and I saw his body."

Goose bumps rise on Shari's nape and along her forearms at the mention of the Donghu's name. She hopes no one notices.

"I am glad he is dead, at least," Hilal says. "But I am also ashamed to say that I am sorry the girl lived."

"I couldn't do it," Sarah says after a moment. "She was so young. So vulnerable. It was too much."

"I couldn't either," Jago says quietly.

Hilal sighs. "I do not think I could have done it myself."

They are *friends*, Shari realizes. *They are my enemies* and *my friends. Hilal and Aisling too. Or if not friends they are at least human beings, like I am. Like we are.* Once more she pushes back the urge to retch.

Hilal looks to Stella. "May I?"

Stella nods, holding up a hand for Hilal to speak.

"If you remember, in China I asked us to pause before we began to Play. I asked that we pool our knowledge of Endgame and work together. I ask you now to do the same. Everything I have learned since Endgame began has led me to believe that it is an evil endeavor, one that we and our forebears have been tricked into preparing for and prosecuting. This is our chance to make amends, not only for ourselves, but for our lines. I do not know the motivations of the kepler and nor does Ms. Vyctory, but if we can stop Endgame from progressing any further, then that is a good thing for the world. I for one wish never to see the Maker again, unless I am looking down on his death mask." He clears his throat. "Barring a miracle, Abaddon will arrive on the other side of the globe in a matter of hours. It will kill untold millions and will make the world a hard place in which to live for a very long time. Be that as it may, we *can* live in it—together. But first we must put aside the prejudices, hate, and myopia of our separate heritages so that we can fight back—*together.*"

There is a long pause. The lights flicker. Stella frowns briefly before deciding it's nothing.

"What do you want us to do?" Jago finally asks.

Stella places her hands firmly on the table and leans forward. "We must find Sun Key before either the Nabataean or the Shang does. As Greg has told you, I know that Sun Key is hidden at one of twelve ancient monuments scattered across the world. As you know, two have already been destroyed."

"You know who's doing this?" Aisling asks.

Stella nods. "They are a brotherhood as old as the lines—maybe older. And its members work against us. Luckily, this brotherhood also works against the Makers, otherwise we'd be totally fucked. Unluckily, in addition to destroying your lines' most sacred monuments, they're also trying to destroy *me*. And if you accept my help, they will also try to destroy you."

"But who *are* they?" Jago asks.

"That's simple. They're people loyal to—"

A snappy hiss followed by a small biting sound and Stella Vyctory gasps. She brings her hands from the table to her throat. Hilal reaches over and grabs her arm to steady her, but her breath cuts short and the veins in her temple pop and the capillaries around her nose darken and her eyes bulge and water. She doesn't look afraid or angry so much as disappointed and sad.

"Pop!" Aisling yells, spinning to her grandfather.

Stella's knees buckle. Hilal catches her, supporting her full weight, while everyone else stands at once. Pop spits a metal tube from his mouth and it clinks onto the table. He's standing too, one hand a fist and the other reaching for the pistol resting on his hip. "Blasphemy!" he hisses as he backpedals, Aisling quickly advancing on him. She has her sheathed

77

Falcata in her hands and she whips it at her grandfather, simultaneously knocking his hand from his gun and the gun off his belt. The lights flicker again, plunging the room into complete darkness for nearly a second, which feels like an eternity. When they come back on, Sarah and Jago look all around, trying to make sense of what's happened, their shoulders touching as they guard each other before helping anyone else. Hilal stands over Stella, cradling her head. Jordan is on her other side, gripping her arm and cursing. Stella sputters and begins to turn pale green. Shari risks half opening an eye to witness all of this. No one notices. Marrs has his pistol up and he's pointing it at Pop.

He shoots as Pop surges toward Aisling. The shot misses. "Traitor!" Pop yells, raising his arms and crashing forward to head-butt Aisling. She's shocked by this attack but her training kicks in and she moves by rote, grabbing one of Pop's wrists and pirouetting around him and twisting his arm painfully. His knees crumple. With his free hand he reaches for a long knife on his thigh. Aisling mashes her foot on top of his hand, and it crunches to the floor. The knife comes free, Aisling flicks it with her foot, and it slides across the room.

Aisling doesn't notice that it stops at Shari Chopra's feet.

"Christ, Pop!" Aisling exclaims.

Marrs takes careful aim now. He has a bead on Pop, except that the line of fire goes right through Aisling's thigh. Still, he doesn't hesitate. He pulls the trigger.

But he does not see Jordan sliding around the table, his eyes wild. He tackles Marrs full-tilt and the second shot rings out as the slug bounces off the floor next to Aisling's leg and embeds in the underside of the table.

Jordan says, "Damn it, Marrs! Not like this!"

Marrs protests but Jordan is much stronger and better trained for this sort of thing, and he brings his friend and colleague under control.

At the same time Aisling says, "Someone help me!"

Jordan eyes a bag on the table. "There's a tranq in there, Jago. Brought it for Shari. Use it!"

Jago glances at Sarah. "Go on," she whispers. Jago jumps onto the table and runs over it, grabbing the bag as he moves.

He reaches Aisling in seconds. She's grinding her knee into her grandfather's back, his vertebrae cracking audibly. Aisling looks up to call for help again, but Jago's right there, a syringe aimed for exposed flesh. He puts it in Pop's neck and presses the plunger and Pop Kopp relaxes.

"Christ, Pop," Aisling repeats in a whisper. "Why the fuck did you do that?"

Pop passes out.

She stands and looks across the room. Hilal is on one knee now, Stella Vyctory draped over his thigh, her arms hanging limp and lifeless at her sides, her legs crossed under her hips at an uncomfortable angle. The bright fletching of a small dart sticks out of the center of her throat. Her face and neck are coated in saliva and mucus as these stream out of her mouth and nose. Her chest rises and falls quickly, a few bubbles forming on her swollen lips, and then this stops.

Stella Vyctory is dead.

Then the lights flicker once more and a sound like an explosion rattles down the tunnel that leads to the surface and the lights go out for good. All that is left is blackness and the sudden silence and the uncertainty. Hilal says, his voice now hard and bitter, "It is too late. They have found us—*together.*"

SHARI CHOPRA, HILAL IBN ISA AL-SALT, AISLING KOPP, SARAH ALOPAY, JAGO TLALOC, POP KOPP, GREG JORDAN, GRIFFIN MARS

Bunker beneath Classic Kameo Hotel and Serviced Apartments, Ayutthaya, Thailand

Shari doesn't hesitate. She can't think about whoever it is that's coming for them. Because she's *not* one of them. She is the Harappan, and her daughter is out there somewhere. And in order to get to her Shari needs to be free.

She slides out of her chair and feels around on the floor, her fingertips searching, and she finds it. Pop Kopp's blade. She snags it and flips it around and slips it carefully between her bound wrists and then snaps the blade up, cutting the zip tie that binds her hands together.

The zip tie falls to the ground. She bites the blade between her teeth like a pirate and hunkers down and waits for her chance to run.

A flashlight's white beam pierces the dark. It belongs to Sarah. The beam skirts around the room as she asks, "Who's coming, Hilal?"

"The people destroying the monuments. The people who want—*wanted*—to kill Stella," Hilal explains, Sarah's light illuminating the side of his face and that of a very dead Stella Vyctory.

While they talk Shari takes advantage of the flashlight's shifting ambient light to get her bearings. Aisling stands over her grandfather, near the sliding door that leads to the cars. Shari'll need one of those to escape. This door opens as Jago slips into the garage. She moves her eyes over the floor, searching for Pop's gun, and yes—there it is—a shadowy lump near the same sliding door.

Jago bounds back into the room. "People are coming down the ramp.

They're trying to be quiet but I can hear them."

Sarah racks her pistol and moves toward Jago. "I'm coming. We'll cover the tunnel. Won't let anyone down it alive."

"Good," Jordan says through clenched teeth. "Go!"

Sarah sprints out of the room, brushing past Aisling.

Marrs uses the hem of his T-shirt to clean off Stella's face. "Goddamn it, why did your grandfather do this?"

Aisling flicks on a flashlight and watches Marrs wipe the corners of Stella's eyes, her mouth, the bridge of her nose. "I should have known better. I should have left Pop in the van," she says.

"I want to know too," Jordan says. "Stella is like—*was* like . . ." He trails off. Their grief and confusion is cut short by the sound of two gun reports from the tunnel.

"Now is not the time, my friends," Hilal says.

Jordan straightens. "No. It isn't."

Aisling shakes off what Pop has done and forces herself to concentrate. "We need to get out of here. The stairs!"

Jordan points at the van in the garage. "But all those guns. All those supplies."

"There are more where they came from," Hilal says, unzipping the top of his rucksack. He reaches in and draws out a single machete, the word *LOVE* engraved on its hilt. "Stella briefed me after I arrived last night. She has another supply cache here in Thailand, though it is a few hours away."

"She also brief you on who exactly these people *are*, Hilal?" Aisling asks, taking a few steps away from her unconscious grandfather.

Shari senses an opening. She creeps toward the cars. Another flashlight goes on, this one belonging to Marrs. Hilal says, "They are people loyal to her adoptive father—to the man named Wayland Vyctory."

"The hotel guy?" Aisling asks incredulously.

"The same," Hilal answers.

Aisling doesn't understand. Everyone has heard of Wayland Vyctory—

everyone in America at least. He's one of the richest and most successful men in Las Vegas. His business is casinos and showgirls and five-star restaurants and golf courses, not Endgame. She says, "Why the hell would a hotel billionaire have anything to do with End—"

But she's cut off by another loud blast, this one much, much closer. The whole bunker flashes brightly, and the glass doors on the eastern side of the conference room push in with the shock wave but don't break. Jordan runs to a keypad by the glass doors and enters a code. Behind the doors is a cloud of white billowing smoke. This cloud lights with muzzle flash as hidden shooters let loose with semiautomatic rifles. Jordan winces as the shots strike the bulletproof partition and bounce away next to his face and chest. He hits enter. The doors lock shut. They are safe from the men coming down the stairs, at least for a few moments.

Aisling leaves her grandfather and joins Jordan, Marrs, and Hilal. This is Shari's chance. She doesn't wait. She's in the middle of the action but everyone is preoccupied. She slips across the floor. She takes the gun and stuffs it in her waist and hooks her hands under Pop's shoulders and drags him toward the vehicles. She works quickly, silently, reaching the Mercedes in under 20 seconds. There's enough light from the flashlights for her to operate. She opens the passenger door quietly and gets in the Mercedes and drags Pop into it. She slides over the center console, working Pop into the passenger seat. Once he's in she pulls the door shut, locks it, and gets belted into the driver's seat.

She runs her hands over the steering column and yes, there is the key. The van's on her left, Sarah and Jago out of sight on the far side. The others are in the conference room on her right. There's a concrete wall directly in front of the car. The only way out is the way they came in: the tunnel.

She looks over her shoulder at it. Lights dance some distance up the ramp. A man appears around the corner, his rifle up, and Jago and Sarah fire on him. He falls and rolls down the incline.

They are coming.

She can't think about this shitty situation they're in.

She has to act.

Shari takes a deep breath. She'll take the tunnel. She'll run over whoever she finds in it, probably taking fire the whole way. She hopes the car is bulletproof. She expects it is but won't know until someone's shooting at her. She grips the wheel with one hand and holds the other over the ignition and takes a deep breath and gets ready to turn the key.

She just waits for the right moment.

Meanwhile, Aisling, Hilal, and Jordan stand shoulder to shoulder as four men—tall and athletic in head-to-toe tactical gear, their faces covered by helmets and goggles—emerge from the cloud obscuring the stairwell. They move into position, only a few feet from Aisling and Jordan and Hilal, behind the locked and very well armored glass door. They open two duffel bags containing explosives and detonators and get to work.

One of the men flips up his goggles. Jordan shines a light on his face. The man blinks. His skin is pale and his eyes are set a little wider than they should be. His mouth is open, and Hilal can plainly see that he has no tongue.

A mute. Like Wayland's guards in Las Vegas.

"Nethinim," Hilal says quietly.

"Shit," Jordan says.

Hilal twirls his machete. "They are not so tough. I took down two in Las Vegas. But when those doors open we cannot wait. We must strike at once."

Aisling doesn't have a clue what they're talking about, but now isn't the time to ask.

"We can take them," Aisling says.

"We *will* take them," Hilal says.

"Maybe we won't have to," Jordan says. He spins to Marrs, Stella draped over his shoulder. "Get her to the van, Marrs. See if there's another way out of here. Stella wouldn't blind alley herself like this."

Marrs answers by double-timing it to the Sprinter. He's so shocked to be carrying the dead body of Stella Vyctory, and the darkness is so complete, that he doesn't notice Shari or Pop is gone. He walks around the sedan and doesn't see Shari sitting in the driver's seat, staring at him hard, waiting for the moment to make her run for it.

Marrs opens the van's side door and gently lays Stella across the backseat. Then he jumps in and fires up a laptop mounted on the dashboard. He pounds the keyboard furiously, trying to access the bunker's security system to see if it will divulge any of its secrets.

In the conference room Aisling, Hilal, and Jordan watch one of their ambushers spray aerated C4 on the glass door in a starlike pattern. Another points a rifle at them, its muzzle dancing between their heads, a smile on his face.

Jordan sticks up a meaty middle finger at him before saying, "I'm sure we can take these guys, but I think we should get in the van too. It's our best cover. It's bullet- and bomb-proof and full of guns." Jordan takes a half step toward the garage. "Come on!"

The beam of Jordan's light bounces between Aisling and Hilal's faces. Aisling looks ready to follow Jordan, but Hilal is less certain. It's hard to read his expression because of his injuries.

After a beat, Hilal says, "You are right." He picks up his rucksack and swings it over his shoulders. He hasn't told them what else is in this bag of his—the Maker book from Wayland Vyctory's hotel suite. He hasn't told them how important it could turn out to be, and how essential it is that Wayland's Nethinim do not, under any circumstances, regain possession of this book.

Hilal holds out a hand for Aisling. "We should fight these men on our terms, not theirs. Come, Aisling Kopp."

Aisling doesn't need to hold his hand or anyone else's. She bats it away and takes the lead, running toward the garage, but at the far end of the table she stops short. "Give me a hand with Pop, will you? Wait. What the—?"

Hilal continues for the van while Jordan bumps into her. "What is it?" Aisling points at the floor. "Where the hell is he? Marrs!" she yells. "Did you get Pop?"

"No!" Marrs answers from the van.

"What the fuck?" Aisling says, moving the flashlight all over the ground. "He was knocked out." And then she remembers.

Shari.

The beam of light whips to Shari sitting in her chair.

Except that now it is empty.

Jordan grabs her roughly by the arm and tugs her toward the van. "Come on, Aisling! We don't have time!"

But Aisling ignores him. She shines the light here and here and here. The cut zip tie. Pop's missing gun. A scuff mark on the floor leading to the cars.

She raises the light and shines it directly at the Mercedes sedan, a circle of white light on the dark window. On the other side of that window is Pop, slumped in the passenger seat. And next to him, gripping the wheel and staring murderously at Aisling, is Shari Chopra.

"No!" Aisling yells, wriggling free of Jordan's grasp. She is about to sprint for the car and save Pop but at that very moment Aisling and Jordan are lifted off their feet and sent sailing through the air. They slam painfully into the side of the sedan. The men have blown open the glass door at the far end of the conference room. The blast is large and deafening, its shock wave rattling around the bunker with great force. Both vehicles rock, and inside the sedan Shari braces herself and catches the sun visor, knocking it open. Something falls into her lap. She shakes off the ringing in her ears and reaches between her legs and picks up a small remote with two buttons. One green, one red. The blast also knocks Sarah and Jago off their feet, but they're the farthest from the explosion so they don't suffer too much. They dive into the van as Marrs starts the engine, steeling himself for a rough drive back up the tunnel and through who knows how many enemies.

"Come on, Aisling!" Hilal yells.

Jordan scrambles to his feet, his ears stuffed by a high-pitched whine, grabbing Aisling. Gunfire *rat-a-tats* from the tunnel. Shari turns on her car's engine. Marrs revs the van. Aisling follows Jordan reluctantly— she so badly wants to get Pop away from Shari. Jordan and Aisling move between the vehicles and now Aisling is less than a foot from Shari, the sedan's closed door between them. Aisling reaches for the door handle and yanks it but it's no use.

Locked.

Shari eyes Aisling contemptuously, shaking her head. *He's mine*, Shari mouths.

More gunfire, this time on their other flank from the men who've breached the conference room. Bullets zing off the armor and whiz past Aisling. Jordan yanks her hard as slugs crackle all around and then she's inside and the door's closed and she's safe.

Everyone is out of breath. "I couldn't find anything," Marrs says, pointing at the laptop. "We're trapped."

The pitter of bullets bounce off the outside of the vehicles like frantic music. Aisling stares at Shari. Marrs stares at Jordan. Jordan stares at Stella's feet hanging off the backseat, the shock of her death grabbing him. Sarah and Jago stare at each other, holding hands. Hilal says, "What now?"

Shari remembers the object that fell in her lap. She takes it back up. Green button. Red button.

She picks red.

As soon as she pushes it the concrete wall in front of the vehicles slides down in a flash, revealing a subterranean road wide enough for two cars.

Again, Shari doesn't hesitate. She jams the gas and squeals away, her car's high beams illuminating a long, straight tunnel.

"Go, go, go!" Jordan shouts.

Marrs punches it too, fishtailing into the void, the red taillights of Shari's much-faster car already receding into the distance.

Shari is so happy she doesn't know what to do except drive as fast as she can. She knows the others are behind her, but so what? This car has 280 kph on the speedometer. Even if they've also escaped, she'll surely outrun them.

Then, to see what happens, she presses the green button.

She can't see from her vantage point and distance, but the door that so serendipitously opened for them closes, sealing the men hunting them into the bunker.

And then the bunker and the hidden tunnel and the ground shake and shake and shake.

The men aren't hunting them anymore.

The men are dead.

All of them—Shari, Aisling, Jordan, Marrs, Hilal, Sarah, Jago—are in disbelief. They escaped an ambush. They made it out and they are not being chased anymore.

Shari thinks, *I'll find you*, meri jaan.

And Aisling thinks, *Fuck, fuck, fuck.*

Please don't kill him.

Fuck. Fuck!

SHARI CHOPRA, POP KOPP

Subterranean tunnel, Ayutthaya, Thailand

Shari drives like a hellcat, one eye on the road and one eye on the unconscious man bouncing in the passenger seat. She drives with one hand on the wheel and her other hand on the knife she took from the floor.

"I know what you did," she says to Pop, thinking of all the Harappan he helped to kill. All of them so beautiful and true and loyal.

Paru and Ana and Pravheet and Peetee and Varj and Ghar and Brundini and Boort and Helena.

Shari remembers the hate that filled her heart when Helena died. When the Celt said to her, truthfully, that they were both already in hell.

Yes, this is hell.

She looks at the man. "I know what you did."

The road curves left. She handles it expertly.

"I should kill you right now."

She holds the knife to his throat.

She rounds a wide turn and the lights of the van disappear behind the curving wall.

She pushes the blade forward and it touches his neck and makes a thin depression. The man's skin is wrinkled and loose and it folds over the metal a little.

The wrinkles make her think of Jovinderpihainu.

Shari wonders if Jov was killed too. Perhaps not. There could have been survivors at the Harappan fortress, people who hid and waited and lived. Jov could have done this. If Jov—all 94 years of him—was anything, he was a survivor.

What would you do in my place, Jov? she wonders.

The road straightens and a few moments later the van's lights appear behind her.

She looks at the instrument panel. They have traveled 0.9 kilometers. The car is humming nicely at 126 kph.

She thinks, *Jov would spare him. Vengeance doesn't run in his blood, certainly not when there is a chance to be strategic. I must be strategic to have the best chance of finding Little Alice.*

She slowly pulls the knife away from his neck and then stabs it onto the dashboard out of frustration and anger and grief, above everything grief.

I can't kill you.

The headlights reveal a change in the road ahead.

A fork.

She hits the brake. The car stops. She looks to Pop. She grabs the knife's handle again, its blade a good four centimeters in the leather and plastic console.

"I should kill you right now," she says one last time.

The van gets closer. She doesn't want to see them. She picks a passage and guns the engine again, taking the left-hand tunnel. When the van reaches the fork, it follows.

I can't kill you.

I have to hold the hate back. I have to let it go as much as I can.

MACCABEE ADLAI, LITTLE ALICE CHOPRA

Unnamed road near Shree Dwarkadhish Temple, Dwarka, Gujarat, India

Little Alice is strapped to Maccabee's back in the child carrier. Men all around yell and throw up their hands and warble in half a dozen languages, a mélange of Gujarati and Hindi and English and Urdu and Punjabi. Maccabee and Little Alice get swept up and are funneled through an alley of concrete buildings. A 2,000-year-old Hindu temple is on their right, its main feature a towering cone of carved stone, weather-beaten and grandiose. A multicolored flag stands at attention in the stiff wind coming off the Indian Ocean only a stone's throw to the west.

They turn a corner and the alley opens onto the ghat, a concrete walkway with stairs leading down to the Gomti River. It's low tide so the river is in retreat, exposing sand and silt mixed with refuse, the water's dark surface a few more meters away. The far bank is also man-made but looks more industrial. A few people are scattered here and there on its rocky slope.

The walkway here is narrow and crowded, however. Everyone is turned to the southwest, to where the river ends and the Indian Ocean begins. Many either talk into cell phones or hold them up to take pictures or shoot video.

Maccabee shoves his way to the top of the steps. He stops next to a man nearly his height wearing a perfectly tailored western business suit. Maccabee's briefly envious of the clothing. He misses the way a good suit feels, the way a perfect shirt hugs his shoulders and arms, the touch of fine cotton and wool against his skin.

He misses the order and neatness of the world before Endgame. Splotches of sweat stain the neck of the man's yellow dress shirt.

Maccabee asks, "What's happened?"

The man looks him up and down. His nose wrinkles at the sight of Maccabee's bald head and his busted nose and the black rings under his eyes, but mostly at the small Indian child fastened to his back, her head peeking over the top of Maccabee's shoulder. "There was a large blast not far off the coast," he answers. "Some think it was a small meteoric companion to Abaddon, but rather one falling on this side of the globe," he says with a poetic lilt. He points. "Do you see that?"

A dense swarm of dive-bombing seabirds confettis the air less than a kilometer away.

"Yeah."

"It was there. The birds are picking off chum, it seems."

Maccabee peers at the birds.

Little Alice says, "That's where it is. The underwater temple. Two two dot two three four. Six eight dot nine six two."

The businessman squints at Little Alice. "What did she say?" He leans close to her. "How old are you, pakora? Two? Three?"

She shakes her head furiously. "Not *pakora*. Only Mama calls me that."

Maccabee angles her away from the man, but he persists. "Where *is* your mama? Is this your child, my boy?"

Little Alice says, "Two two dot two three four. Six eight dot nine six two."

"Thank you, sir," Maccabee says, shuffling away. The man reaches for Maccabee and asks again how old Little Alice is, but the crowd closes around the man and he doesn't follow.

A little farther on Maccabee stops next to a slight man sitting on a burly friend's shoulders. The man on top presses a worn brass telescope to his eye. Maccabee holds up his hand. "Mind if I have a look?"

The man barks at Maccabee in a language he doesn't understand.

"Friend, I *need* to have a look," Maccabee says forcefully in English. "I'll give it back."

The little man protests again but hands it over and then cups his hands over his eyes to ward off the sun. The larger man stares at Maccabee's profile.

Maccabee holds the glass to his eye with both hands.

Little Alice says, "Two two dot two three four. Six eight dot nine six two."

"Quiet, sweetie," Maccabee says. "I'm trying to see if another Player beat us here," he says quietly.

He doesn't see how it would be possible, but maybe An Liu, or a different Player altogether, knows that this is where Sun Key is. Maybe someone has narrowly beat him to it.

He scans the sky and finds the birds. White gulls and dark cormorants and masked boobies teeming as one. He moves the telescope to the water's surface, which is roiled by the wind but otherwise unexceptional. The crowd hoots and ahs.

Little Alice bats the telescope. "Look, Uncle."

He pulls the telescope away and sees a large, dark object rising vertically above the birds. Maccabee recognizes it immediately as a medium-sized four-rotor drone. It shoots up 30 or 40 meters and stops, tilting into the stiff wind in order to stay in place. He peers through the telescope and catches sight of the thing before it zips away, moving toward the shore.

The little man shakes his hand for the telescope. The larger man nudges Maccabee's shoulder. Little Alice says, "Two two dot two three four. Six eight dot nine six two." Everyone but Maccabee watches the drone. He looks to the ocean again.

And then the ground shakes violently.

The crowd crouches all at once, but not Maccabee. He merely winces and turns his head. Little Alice barely flinches at all.

"Two two dot two three four! Six eight dot nine six two!"

An explosion much larger than the previous one has just detonated under the water. A thick column of water grows skyward, instantly rising 50, 75, 100 meters. Many of the birds are swallowed by it, the rest are scattered and cast away. A halo of water rises next, ringing the bottom of the column, and almost immediately afterward black spikes of debris arc through the foam. It reminds Maccabee of a grand fireworks display, but far more impressive, as this is not a show of light but an explosion moving weight and mass, displacing anything near it. Within a few seconds the crowd is pelted by debris, some chunks as big as a fist slamming here and there. Maccabee deftly unfastens Little Alice's carrier and swings her into his arms, shielding her with his body. The crowd panics. Feet and legs and hands push on Maccabee, but he is like a rock. The bombardment doesn't last long, and when it's over he asks, "Are you all right?"

"Two two dot two three four. Six eight dot nine six two," Little Alice says.

"Yeah, you're all right."

The crowd thins out quickly. A few people lie on the ground, moaning and bloodied. Little Alice points. Maccabee sees it. The drone is headed back out to the water. It flew in to take cover, and now it's returning to the site of the explosion. He shifts Little Alice into his left arm and lifts the telescope. "It's taking readings," he says frantically. "Little Alice—do you think Sun Key is . . . gone?"

Before she can answer, the telescope's owner appears and tugs at Maccabee's shirt. The man holds out his hand.

Maccabee shakes his head. "Not now, friend. I'm keeping it."

The large companion steps next to the small man, a toothless grin on his face. Maccabee knows that look. The man likes a good fight.

So does Maccabee, but these two aren't worth the trouble. He stashes the telescope in a pocket and whips out the SIG, leveling it on the little man's face. "I said I'm keeping it. Move along. Now!"

The men backpedal. *"Acha, acha, acha,"* they say. They head back to the streets of Dwarka and disappear.

Maccabee reholsters the gun and returns to the telescope. The drone makes the blast site. For a minute or two it zips there and there and there, rising and lowering and rising. It finishes its work and begins the short trip back to the city, again headed directly toward the river. "Someone's running that thing. Someone close by." He scans the tops of the buildings and the length of the ghat but doesn't spot anyone suspicious. "Tell me it isn't gone, Little Alice."

"The place where it was is gone," the girl says slowly.

"What?" he demands. "You mean . . . ?"

"We have to leave here, Uncle."

"But how will I win if—"

"Move, Uncle!" the girl yelps, and Maccabee gets an overwhelming sensation of something bearing down on him. He dives to the steps of the ghat, being careful not to land on Little Alice, and a chunk of concrete explodes less than a meter above them. He rolls onto his back, the edges of the stairs digging into his spine, as the report sounds in his ears. In his periphery he sees the drone coming in low, and on the far bank he sees two things and knows instantly what they are. The long line of an RC antenna and the glint of a sniper's scope. He makes them for 120 meters. A very long shot for a pistol. He's flat on his back, Little Alice lying across his chest. He sights over Little Alice's head and down his arm with the SIG. He throws his left arm over Little Alice, who at this moment is his human shield, a situation he can't abide. He pulls the trigger on the shooter, three times quick, making micro adjustments for recoil and the wind coming from the ocean. The glint of the sniper scope blinks out and a dark figure pops up and falls sideways. Hit. The one with the RC controller moves quickly for cover and Maccabee fires twice more, striking the hip and the flesh above it. The person falls and disappears behind the opposite embankment.

He zips the gun left and right, searching for others, but finds none. "You okay, sweetie?"

Little Alice dips her chin. Her hands are cupped over her ears. She's shaking.

"I'm sorry," he says. "But you're okay?"

"Yes, Uncle."

"Who the hell was that?" Maccabee was listening to the news as they tore across India, and he heard all about the other monuments. He says, "First Stonehenge, then Chogha Zanbil, now Dwarka. Who's destroying these places? Not the kepler. Not another Player. Right?"

"Look, Uncle." She points at the drone, hovering practically overhead, 30 or so meters away. Maccabee pops up and aims. "Cover your ears again."

She does. He fires twice. The casings bounce off the concrete. Two rotors are hit, and the thing loses altitude. Half a minute later it hits the walkway along the ghat, now absent of any other people. He works Little Alice into the back carrier and goes to the drone. It whines like a winged housefly bouncing on a stone floor. He stomps out the other rotors. He flips it over and sees the camera and the sensors and the portable drive hooked into the frame. He unplugs the drive, pries it free, and slips it into a pocket. "Maybe this will have some answers." He looks back to the ocean. The water churns from the explosion. It was massive. Waves wash into the river's mouth like a fast moving tide. "It's gone," he whispers. "Isn't it?"

How will I win?

"Yes. The temple is gone, Uncle . . . But Sun Key . . . Sun Key." She is quiet for a moment. Her eyes flutter as if she's been struck with some new information. She points to the northwest and says, "Three four dot three six two two six. One zero eight dot six four zero two six two."

"I don't understand, Alice." Maccabee frowns.

"Three four dot three six two two six. One zero eight dot six four zero two six two."

"Are you saying it—it moved?"

"Yes, Uncle. Three four dot three six two two six. One zero eight dot six four zero two six two."

"That's in . . ." He runs through the basic coordinate system seared into his brain. "That's in China, Alice. Near Xi'an."

"Three four dot three six two two six. One zero eight dot six four zero two six two."

Maccabee nods. "Xi'an. We're going back to where it all started."

AN LIU, NORI KO

Nathula Border Crossing Station, India-China Border, Sikkim, India

Nori Ko bribed their way up to Nathula, one of three overland trading posts on the Sino-Indian border. At over 4,300 meters it is extremely remote, with the mountain state of Sikkim on the Indian side and, after the trip down the Himalayas, the Tibetan Plateau on the Chinese side. The land around is desolate and rocky and steep and tufted by rough alpine grass. It is a little past noon, and the gray sky hangs low. The air is damp and cool and very out of place for midsummer.

Legally only Indian citizens are allowed this close to the crossing, requiring a permit and registration with the Indian Army. But legal concerns have "gone the way of Abaddon," as Nori Ko put it aptly after bribing the last soldier with a measly 10 American dollars and a cheap ballpoint pen. The soldier assured them there were no more men at the gates.

No more Indian men, anyway.

They've stopped a few jagged switchbacks below the pass. The mountains' teeth disappear into the clouds. Weatherworn prayer flags whip in the wind on plastic poles.

Nori Ko lights a Golden Bat cigarette. Her window is rolled down and she props her elbow on the edge of the door. "This place is too far-flung for people to care about now," she says, staring at the tidy red-roofed administrative buildings surrounding the pass.

An strokes Chiyoko's hair. "I would love to see a place where people *do* care," he says. "I would love to see New York City. It must be terrifying. It must be beautiful."

She blows a stream of smoke. The wind catches it and takes it out of the car, away from his nose and his senses. An is happy for this. He does not like the smell or taste or the sight of cigarettes. His father smoked them. His uncles.

The men who hurt him.

Who broke him.

The men who put their cigarettes out on his skin.

The men who singed him and burned him and scarred him with joy and glee.

She is not one of these men so he lets her smoke.

She says, "Trust me, An. You don't want to be in New York City right now. It must be hell on earth."

"But I want to see hell, Mu. Like a God would see it. Like a Maker."

"Like a devil."

"Yes. Like a devil. I want to smell it. Hear it. Touch it."

Pause.

A gust of sweet air slices into the car.

"Let's go," Nori Ko says, changing the subject. She points the cigarette's ember up the road. An puts the car in gear and after a few meters she adds, "I know what I see in you, An Liu—opportunity. But sometimes I'm not sure what Chiyoko saw."

An whips his head to his passenger, about to spit, *Don't say her name! It's my name now!*

But instead *shiverBLINKshivershiverblinkshiverBLINKBLINKblinkSHIVER SHIVERSHIVERblinkBLINKSHIVERblink—*

Nori Ko snags the wheel with one hand and slaps him hard across the cheek with the other. "Snap out of it, An!" she says, the cigarette dancing between her lips.

He does. He pushes the brake. The car stops again. His cheek stings. It feels good. He takes the necklace in both hands and brings it to his face and buries his nose in it. There is so little of her smell remaining that it might as well be odorless, but it does the trick. His body quiets. His heart pounds.

"She didn't see me like that," An says. "She never saw that. I was whole around her. I was . . . better."

Nori Ko takes a deep drag and flicks the hot filter out the window. She almost says, *So she pitied you,* but thinks better of it.

Instead she says, "Chiyoko eschewed relationships—mutes tend to do that—but she always liked a project."

An tightens his grip on the wheel. It's all he can do not to lash out at this woman. He could kill her, but he needs her.

For now.

Thankfully Chiyoko says, *I love your vulnerability, An. I love your broken heart. I love your buried tenderness, like you showed me on our one night together. I love that you're a Player, like me, but one completely unlike me. I love you because I shouldn't. Because it is impossible.*

He loves the sound of her voice. Why couldn't she have shared it with him when she was *BLINK* alive?

"That's not how it was," An says after a few moments. He will not share these feelings with Nori Ko. They are too personal, too revealing. He says, "I was not a project. She loves—loved—me, Nori Ko. That's all you need to know."

Nori Ko releases the steering wheel. "Well, love *is* mysterious." Pause. "Sorry. I'm just on edge. You might want the world to end but, believe it or not, I prefer if it didn't." She lights another cigarette. "Nothing I can do about Abaddon now. Nothing except make sure that kepler bastard dies one way or another."

"Yes."

"Let's both shut up for a while and get to China."

"Yes."

He resumes driving. As they wind up the mountainside Chiyoko says over and over, *China. You're going home. China. You're going home. China. You're going home.* Her voice is soft and flowing and sweet. Like the water in the painting that used to hang in her room in Naha.

You're going home.

The road squeezes between a set of buildings and these give way to walls that rise on either side, hemming them in. The trade route is literally a passageway cut from the mountain pass. A tall white gate hangs between the walls like a curtain. Above the gate is a red sign with white lettering in Chinese and English. Both read NATHULA BUSINESS CHANNEL FOR CHINA-INDIA BORDER TRADE.

And now there *is* a man. A solitary Chinese soldier on the far side of the gate, parading back and forth. He has the dark green uniform and the wide-topped green military cap with the red band and the stiff black visor and the red star on front. His breath is visible in the cool air.

A bolt-action service rifle leans on his shoulder. His feet go high, he spins, he paces, his feet go high, he spins, he paces. Repeat.

The Defender is plain for him to see, but he doesn't acknowledge it. He just keeps pacing.

"I'll handle this," An says. He opens the door, pulling the Mu katana from under the driver's seat.

"You won't need that. He's a boy," Nori Ko says.

An pauses before closing the door. "Some would say the same of me."

She gives him a look that says, *You have a point,* but doesn't speak.

An's feet and legs move in hurried, stabbing steps. His shoulders hunch around his chest. His eyes stare at the ground. He holds the sword in his left hand. He pulls the hood of his thick sweatshirt over his bald head, now speckled with black stubble.

He stops at the gate. The soldier really is a boy. All of 15 or 16. The uniform barely fits him. It's cuffed at the ankles and the wrists, and the hat is too big.

He continues to pace.

"Open the gate, soldier," An orders.

The boy passes less than a meter in front of him. The gate—easily climbed, and so porous that it would serve as more of a channel than a barrier to a sword or any other slender weapon—remains closed. The soldier remains silent.

He paces left to right, hits his spot, spins on his heel, and paces back. An unsheathes the katana and slides it through the gate, blocking the boy soldier's path. He stops. He has pale skin and rosy cheeks from the chill. An guesses by his features that he is ethnically Han. Black peach fuzz lines his upper lip.

"Open the gate," An says. "This is not a request."

"I know who you are," the boy says, his Mandarin thick with a Qinghai accent. "My father showed me. You're the Shang. You're in Endgame."

"Who's your father?"

"My father's dead."

"So is mine."

"He sent me up here before he died. To do his job when he no longer could. To protect the homeland from . . ."

This boy isn't even an official soldier. He's a pretender. A misguided patriot. "Open the gate. I won't say it again."

The boy half spins and brings the rifle to firing position, aiming for An's chest. An hears the door of the Defender click open behind him, but he doesn't look. Nori Ko is undoubtedly aiming a Beretta at this child.

But his old rifle is rock steady. "You're calm. It's impressive," An says.

The boy moves the muzzle from An to Nori Ko.

An pulls the sword back half a meter and angles the tip so that it presses the flesh of the boy's stomach. It does not cut. Not yet.

"Keep the rifle on her. Put it on me again and you're dead. Like your father."

The boy doesn't move.

"She's Japanese. You know what they did to us in the war, yes?" An says, trying to stoke his nationalistic ire. An doesn't want Nori Ko to die, but he's curious to see what this one might do.

He does nothing. The rifle stays.

"What are they saying about me?" An asks.

The boy doesn't speak.

An pushes the sword forward a centimeter. It effortlessly slides through the first layer of the uniform.

The boy says, "The government says you should be killed on sight, but the generals say you should be captured. Some people say you are a monster. Others say you will save all of China from Abaddon's coming winter."

"What do *you* say? What did your *father* say?"

He says nothing.

"Answer. I am a Player of Endgame, and I am coming home. You can facilitate that, or you can die."

The boy shakes his head ever so slightly. "You can't come home. No one can. Father said. 'The borders are sealed. No one is allowed in or out. Guard them, son. Keep them.' The border is sealed."

No it isn't, An thinks. He thrusts the sword forward in a flash. The hilt's hand guard clanks into the metal gate. The boy lurches forward. He convulses and squeezes off a round, but the slug hits the pavement and bounces away harmlessly. The blade juts out of the boy's back and drips thick blood. An slides his hand through the gate and lifts a small box off the boy's belt. He pulls the sword free. The boy crumples to his knees. Blood pools on his lips. "The border is sealed," the boy says before pitching onto his side.

An presses the button on the box. The gate creaks and clatters as it slides open.

"No it isn't."

An goes back to the car. His steps curt. His shoulders slumped. His sword dripping. He wipes a flat side of the blade on his palm, transferring some of the blood to his skin. The liquid is warm and comforting, like an old glove.

Nori Ko utters her disbelief in Japanese. An can't understand her exact words but he doesn't need to and he doesn't care.

Chiyoko says, *China. You're going home.*

An smiles.

He is glad to be going home with blood on his hands.

SHARI CHOPRA, AISLING KOPP, HILAL IBN ISA AL-SALT, SARAH ALOPAY, JAGO TLALOC, POP KOPP, GREG JORDAN, GRIFFIN MARRS

En route to hidden airstrip, Thailand

Shari emerges from the escape tunnel six klicks north of the hotel. It opens onto a paved road hidden between a pair of jute fields. She drives fast for a few minutes, wanting nothing more than to drive and keep driving. Away from the people behind her. Toward her daughter.

But where *is* Little Alice?

She looks from the road to Pop to the road to Pop. *I didn't kill him because it was the strategic thing to do. The strategic thing. What else would be strategic?*

She's so far in front of the van now that she can't see it in the rearview mirror, but she knows they're following her.

She knows they might have information about Little Alice.

Much as she hates it, she knows she could use their help.

She slams the brakes, coming to a screeching halt on the side of the road. She exits the car and stalks to the passenger door and opens it. She takes Pop by the collar and pulls him out, letting him fall onto the ground in a heap. She goes to the back of the car and sits on the trunk and waits, reminding herself every few moments that not killing Pop Kopp is the smart thing to do.

Even if she wants to do the not-smart thing very, very badly.

The van appears in the distance. It is not being pursued. Shari can see that they're several kilometers west of Ayutthaya now, a tendril of smoke rising above the city's skyline. This must have been where the hotel was. Where the people hunting Stella were.

The van is closer.

Little Alice. You're doing this for her.

Closer.

Close.

Here.

Shari pops off the trunk as the Sprinter screeches to a halt in the middle of the road. Before the van comes to a complete stop Aisling opens her door and jumps out.

"Where is he?" Aisling demands, jogging to a stop a few meters away from Shari.

"He's fine," Shari says.

Aisling marches toward her. "But *where*?"

Shari points toward the front of the car. Aisling stops for a moment, glaring at Shari. Shari glares straight back. "I'm telling you, he's fine."

"He better be," Marrs says from inside the van. "Because I'm going to fucking kill him."

Aisling shoots Marrs an angry look before checking on Pop. He's been dragged into the dirt and there's a bloody nick on his neck, but Shari's telling the truth. Aisling props Pop into a more comfortable-looking position and slowly walks back to the Harappan, eyeing her warily.

"Listen, Shari," Aisling says, intending to offer some explanation as to why so many Harappan had to die.

But Shari's head twitches. "No. *You* listen. There are things I need to say to you." She points at the van. "You too, al-Salt. All of you, in fact." The van's doors open and everyone files out. Hilal takes a spot next to Aisling. His head held high but his eyes forlorn and contrite. Jordan and Marrs stand behind them, their faces red with anger over Stella's death and shame over the death of Shari's family. Sarah and Jago, sensing this has little to do with them, stand off to the side.

Shari asks, "First—are we being followed?"

"I don't think so," Marrs says.

"Did you set that bomb off?" Jago asks.

"Yes," Shari says. "I found a remote detonator in the car. I got lucky."

"You mean *we* got lucky," Sarah points out.

"Yes," Shari says reluctantly. "We did. But that's not what I want to talk about. I want to talk about what I heard in that place. What I heard this Stella say. I want to talk about *you*." She bites her lower lip. "I want to kill you," she says, squinting at Aisling. "For what you did to my family and what you wanted to do to my daughter."

Aisling takes a breath to speak but Shari cuts her off again. "No. Don't talk. I can't hear your voice anymore. It's too painful. The same goes for you, Aksumite."

Hilal nods. Aisling is stock-still.

"I know Endgame is amoral," Shari says. "I know that the Makers are amoral. I know it must be stopped. I think I knew this the moment I understood who—*what*—my daughter is. My child, Little Alice. She is the *only* reason I didn't kill your line member, Aisling. The only reason I have not tried to kill you right here and now."

"Can I ask something?" Sarah says.

"Yes."

"What if we were to help you? What if we promised to help you find your daughter? Would you help us? Because I think we're going to need all the help we can get."

"Sarah speaks for me as well," Jago says. "I'm truly sorry we intended to kill your child. But you heard us. We couldn't do it. We wouldn't."

"I think I speak for Aisling and Hilal too," Sarah says. "And for these men. Their names are Greg Jordan and Griffin Marrs."

Smart of her to name them. Humanizes them, Shari thinks.

"I'll consider it," Shari says slowly. "But Hilal, I have a question. You said Stella had another supply cache in—we're in Thailand, right?"

"We are," Hilal says. "And yes, she does. At an airstrip in the north. This place is at least three hours away."

Shari bites her lip again. "All right. Then let's go. I'll follow you. And I'll think about your offer while we drive. Is this acceptable?"

"Sounds good to me," Sarah says.

"Me as well," Hilal says. The others nod silently.

After a moment Shari says, "If I do agree, I'll have two conditions. First is that if we split up I cannot go with Aisling or her men. You have hurt me too much. Second is that we make saving my daughter a priority. We don't place it above stopping Endgame, but we do place it above everything else, including our own lives. Little Alice is special, and if this world is to survive I believe it will need her. If you think that's a bunch of nonsense, then at least agree to this condition because of what you've done. You owe me at least this much." She takes a deep breath. "Little Alice is three years old. Every child who survives Abaddon will inherit this world. But it will be *hers*." She points to the sky. "Not the Makers'." She pats her chest. "Not mine." She points at them. "Not yours." She lets her hand fall to her side. "If I agree, then I ask you to help me deliver it to her."

Afternoon crickets in the brown field. The growl of a generator in the distance. The smell of a brush fire upwind.

Defying Shari's order for silence, Aisling says, "I swear I will help you, Shari Chopra." But her voice is so low and so small and so heartfelt that they all understand that she's really saying, "I'm sorry. So sorry." Jordan and Marrs swear it next, their voices equally contrite, before helping Aisling retrieve Pop. They take him to the van and put him in the back and then get in themselves.

Sarah and Jago promise their help and also go back to the Sprinter. Finally, Hilal says defiantly, "I swear she will live. On my life."

Then he climbs into the van and closes the door.

They move out, Shari following them alone in the car.

Hilal is wrong. It takes them *five* hours to get to Stella's airstrip. They loop west toward Sai Yok National Park, then head north on small roads through hilly jungles. Jordan insists on this circuitous route to make sure no one follows them. They eventually link up with a main road in Tak and head north-northeast for Lampang, turning west again before reaching the city center and then leaving it to detour deep into the jungle.

As they drive Hilal briefs them on Stella's plan. He says that the airstrip has three Bombardier Global 8000 jets, each modified for extended range and equipped with enough food, weapons, and supplies to last them weeks. "She wanted us to form three teams that would go out into the world in search of Sun Key. Stella and I were to be one such team. We were to go to the Koori monument in Australia and then to the Mu monument in the South China Sea."

"I assume Sarah and I would be another?" Jago says.

"Naturally. She wanted you to go to the Cahokian and Olmec monuments. You know where these are, yes?"

"Of course," Sarah says.

"*Sí.* I know La Venta. *No problema.*"

Hilal points to the sky, which is now clear and dark, a few stars here and there. "What *will* be a problem for you is Abaddon. It is due to hit very soon. Your side of the world will be very . . ."

"Different," Sarah says dejectedly.

"Yes. Your lines' monuments, even though they are thousands of miles from where the asteroid is supposed to hit, may not survive."

"One way to find out," Jago says. "We go to them."

Hilal strokes his arm—the same arm that's wrapped with the wooden ouroboros from his fight with Wayland Vyctory back in Las Vegas—and shrugs.

Sarah gets the impression he's not telling them something.

Before Sarah can ask what this is, Aisling says, "And what about us? Obviously we're not heading to my line's monument, since Stonehenge is long gone."

Hilal tilts his head. "Stella suggested the Donghu monument in Mongolia followed by the Shang one in China."

"I'm game, Hilal, but by my count you're leaving four out," Jordan says. "The Nabataean, Minoan, and Harappan monuments—and *yours.*"

Hilal holds up a finger. "You are right, Mr. Jordan. I can assure you that the Aksumite monument has already been searched and is being guarded by my master and our line members. Sun Key is not there.

Categorically. And Wayland's people will not be able to breach it or destroy it."

"And the other three?" Sarah asks.

"We will be in contact as we finish searching these places, and will decide who will go to them after this first phase. With any luck, we may not have to. Hopefully we will have found Sun Key and thereby prevented Adlai or Liu from winning."

"About that," Aisling says. "Based on the way it's gone so far, I'm pretty sure we can agree that the Shang isn't interested in winning."

"So you would consider him an ally?" Hilal asks incredulously.

Aisling shakes her head vehemently. "Fuck no. He's got his own agenda, whatever that is. I'm only saying I don't think he wants to *win*. That doesn't mean he wants to stop Adlai from winning or stop Endgame or make sure the Makers don't get whatever it is they want. It simply means that, well, he's unpredictable."

"Honey," Sarah says, "we're all unpredictable at this point."

"True," Aisling says with a snicker.

"We're almost there, guys," Marrs says from the wheel. "Another klick or two up this road, if your coordinates are right, Hilal."

The van dips through a large bump in the road as Hilal says, "They are correct, Mr. Marrs."

They fall into silence for this last leg of their trip. The road they're on is not much more than a dirt track, and the jungle is tight on all sides, including overhead. Each of them is preoccupied with what's coming—the concerted search for Sun Key, yes, but also the impact of Abaddon. How will it alter their world? They know it will be big, but will they feel it on this side of the planet? Will it be a geologic-level extinction event like the one that killed the dinosaurs 65 million years ago? Will the entire planet be shrouded in darkness for months or years, or will they be spared an impact winter? Will all the plants and all the animals that depend on them die? If the sun is blotted out, how long will it be until they can stand on the earth and look up and see the life-giving solar disk again?

And what of humanity? Will nearly everyone die, as promised by the Makers? If Adlai manages to win, will his line really be the only one to survive? How will the Makers ensure that everyone else perishes? None of them can answer these questions. No amount of training or studying has changed this fact. All they can do now is act, and do this in good faith, with hope in their hearts. The truth is that no matter what the prophecies say, life must be lived to be experienced. The rules of the game may have changed, but this rule is immutable.

Time will tell.

What will be will be.

Shari thinks of these things too as she follows the van into the jungle. She doesn't know the details of their plan, but she does know that the reckoning promised by the Makers is imminent.

Finally, at a little after midnight, they stop at a chain-link fence running right through the jungle's undergrowth. Shari watches as Hilal jumps out of the van and moves to a kiosk hidden under a thick-trunked tree. A few red lights flicker here and there and then the fence starts to slide open. Hilal—stark-looking in the halogen glow of her sedan's headlights—gives Shari a little salute.

She doesn't salute back.

He wouldn't have been able to see her anyway.

As Shari follows the van through the gate she notices several guns mounted on swivel turrets and a few cameras here and there. She concludes—rightly—that when the gate closes behind her, the perimeter of this hidden airstrip will be guarded by a computerized sentinel system.

Shari follows the van down the length of a smooth runway. It is well hidden. Nearly the entire length of the strip is covered by jungle canopy, with an opening in the trees at one end for takeoffs and landings.

They stop near three private jets parked on the side of the tarmac. Shari stays behind the wheel while the others get out and form a semicircle near her car. They're waiting for her.

"My enemies are my friends. For now. My enemies are my friends," she repeats, trying to convince herself. "I'll use them to get Little Alice. Then . . . then I don't know."

She gets out and joins them. They stand in silence for a moment.

Friends.

Enemies.

No. The Maker is the enemy right now.

"Well?" Sarah asks. "You in?"

"Yes," Shari says. "I'm in."

They will leave at first light.

Right after Abaddon falls into the ocean on the other side of the world. But they don't talk about Abaddon. It's too much. They can't.

Instead they get ready, spending the night taking care of business.

They clean off Stella's body and dress her in fresh clothes and bind her in a stark-white sheet from one of the airplanes. Hilal wraps a bullet and the red bloom of a local flower he does not know the name of in a piece of cloth and tucks this package into Stella's rigor-mortised hand.

They bury her in an unmarked grave under a tall rubber tree, Jordan and Marrs pushing back tears, Hilal giving a brief but heartfelt eulogy for this remarkable woman he knew for less than a week.

They swear to be true to her memory by doing everything in their power to stop Endgame.

They also check weapons, go through preflight routines on the planes, establish channels of communication. They charge satellite phones and radios, and Marrs sets up an encrypted closed channel designated Alpha Romeo Five Seven. They agree on check-in times over the coming days. Jordan shares a string of clandestine clearance codes used by spy planes so that they can safely navigate restricted airspaces. Aisling and Marrs tend to Pop, placing him safely in the plane, binding his wrists and ankles and hooking him up with the same IV cocktail they had in Shari to keep him unconscious and harmless.

Most importantly they bring Shari up to speed on their plan. They ask her who she'd like to go with and, to their surprise, she chooses Hilal. "It can't be Aisling," she reasons, "and I think Sarah and Jago should go to their places alone. That leaves you, Aksumite."

"I happily accept," Hilal says.

"I can't say the same. But I won't try to kill you. I promise you that."

"Understood. And all the same, I am pleased."

At around four in the morning Sarah and Jago gather wood from the jungle and make a fire. Hilal and Shari join them, while Aisling, Jordan, and Marrs retire to their plane for some much-needed rest.

Sarah, Jago, Hilal, and Shari pass the rest of the night talking. Each tells of where they've been, who they've fought, who they've lost. Shari is reluctant to speak at first, but Sarah moves next to her and puts an arm over her shoulders and says, "It's okay. We want to hear." Shari takes a breath to speak but instead of words come tears, fast and hard, and for eight solid minutes she bawls and shakes and clings to Sarah because Sarah is the only one there is and she needs to cling to someone.

When she's done crying she says weakly, "I can't talk about them, my family. So let me speak about Big Alice Ulapala."

She tells them about seeing Alice on the bus after the Calling, about how Shari delivered a baby right there, about how Alice helped. She told them about Alice's special connection to Shari and about a thing Big Alice called the Dreaming. She told about how Big Alice rescued her from the Donghu, and about how Big Alice had also figured out that Little Alice was Sky Key.

She said, "I don't know how she died, but Big Alice shouldn't have. She should be here now, with us. She would have wanted to stop all this needless suffering too, I think."

The other Players believe her.

When she's finished, Sarah and Jago speak about how they escaped the Calling and decided to Play together, about meeting Chiyoko and watching her free Christopher from Maccabee and Baitsakhan, about Stonehenge and An Liu, and of course about Renzo. Jago briefly eulogizes his friend, pointing out that both he and Sarah would be dead if it weren't for him.

As if waiting his turn, Hilal goes last. He speaks carefully about his belief in the goodness of man, and about how he came to realize that there's something wrong with Endgame. He talks about the Ark of the Covenant and Master Eben and the men who perished when the ark was opened. He talks about the device he found in the ark. He talks about meeting Stella, and how he came to believe her. He talks about how he confronted and killed her father, Wayland Vyctory, an ancient alien also known as Ea.

And, at long last, he tells them about the book. "According to Stella, it is ten thousand years old at least, and is one of a very few artifacts here on Earth that came from the Makers' home planet."

"Will it help us?" Sarah asks.

"It already has," Hilal says, before remembering that Shari is sitting right here. He looks down to the ground and says, "I used it to discover . . . to figure out why your daughter is important to Endgame." An awkward silence drifts over the fire. It cracks and glows. The creatures of the jungle click and whoop, and the birds call and sing, as the sky brightens with the dawn.

"Let me show it to you," Hilal says. He goes to his plane and comes back with a large silver tome held out in both hands. He sits on the ground and places it on his lap. He traces his dark fingers over the fine cover, pointing out a coin-sized glyph tucked into the lower left corner. A pair of snakes twisted in a figure eight and devouring each other, set over an eye shape inside a circle.

"The mark of Endgame," he says.

Then he opens the book and beckons them to come and look.

Sarah and Jago move to either side of him while Shari stands off a little. She's not sure she wants to see the thing that exposed her child and her family to ruin. In her mind it is evil and not to be trusted.

But she *is* curious.

Hilal leafs through the book's vellum-like pages. They see diagrams of ancient monuments, an alphabet of lines and dots, pages full of things that appear to be mathematical formulas, constellations and spirals and webs of complex systems that describe who-knows-what. They see long passages of indecipherable glyphs. They see graphs and line plots and sweeping arcs that describe orbits or light-year parabolas through time and space. They see a few things they recognize—monuments, details from stones and hieroglyphs, shapes like pyramids and obelisks and spheres laced with coordinate systems.

But mostly it is mystifying.

As they peruse the book's pages Jago asks, "Stella could read this?"

Hilal shakes his head. "No. Hardly at all."

"But you read part of it, right? To figure out what Sky Key was?" Sarah asks.

"Correct. The device I told you about translated that section, and only that section, when I pointed it at the book."

"The device that's busted now," Jago says.

"Unfortunately."

Sarah puts a finger on a passage. "And this is Maker language?"

"Yes. It is."

"And it's about Endgame?"

"That and much more, I would presume," Hilal says.

"So it *could* help us—if we could figure out what it says?" Sarah asks again.

"Yes. Do you have an idea of how we may accomplish this?"

She shakes her head. "No, I'm just thinking out loud."

"It's useless, then," Jago says.

And here Hilal holds up a finger. "Ah. It is not at all useless. Look."

He flips to a section at the back of the book and then goes through it page by page until he stops. He plants a forefinger in the middle of the page. "Do you recognize this drawing, Sarah?"

She leans closer. The jungle animals continue their dawn symphony all around.

"Well, it's a little different—less eroded, newer looking—but I think it's Monks Mound."

"That is correct." He flips a few more pages. "And here is my line's monument—the Temple of Yeha." It is a stonework tower with an ornate, pyramidal roof.

He flips through more pages. They recognize the monuments for the Olmec, Nabataean, and Minoan lines, and they see other, unknown monuments for the other lines. After looking at one that looks more like a garden than a building, Hilal stops. The drawing on this page has been blotted out by an orderly series of lines.

"What's that?" Jago asks.

"That was Stonehenge. As soon as it was destroyed, this page flickered and changed into what you see now." He flips to another. "This was the Sumerian monument. It also was snuffed out the moment Wayland's people destroyed it. This is a living book. Somehow connected to Earth's innate energy. Even if we cannot understand its words, it is useful, Jago Tlaloc. It will tell us what monuments survive Abaddon, and which may fall to further destruction at the hands of Wayland's brotherhood."

"Good for preventing wild goose chases," Sarah says.

"I have not heard that expression before, but if I understand, yes. No wild gooses."

Shari leans closer too. "Where's the Harappan monument?"

Hilal flips through a few more pages. "Dwarka, of course. It is the last one. Here—oh!"

He stops on another page that has been crossed out and effectively erased.

Shari's shoulders slump. "I've lost that too, it seems."

Hilal glances at her sideways. "Yes. I am sorry for this as well. Wayland's men continue their work, apparently."

"We'll have to be ready for them as we look for Sun Key, won't we?" Sarah asks.

"*Sí. Muy listo,*" Jago confirms. He likes the idea of fighting. In fact, he *loves* the idea of fighting.

He's tired of talking.

He imagines the same is true for Sarah.

Shari sits back down. Jago takes the book from Hilal and pulls it into his lap and he and Sarah look through more of its strange pages. Hilal sits and looks at the sky. The morning is here now, the sky clear and bright.

He wonders what the sky looks like under threat of Abaddon. Black. Red. Torn asunder.

On fire.

And then, at that very moment, all the birds and insects and small creatures go silent, as if a predator has drawn too close. Sarah looks at her watch. Jago closes his eyes. Shari hums a prayer to herself.

The silence is deafening.

A barely perceptible tremor shakes their bodies.

A piece of wood topples over in the fire.

"That was it," Sarah says. "That was Abaddon."

"*Sí.*"

A bird of prey screeches in the jungle.

Hilal says, "It is a new and terrible world."

And the second angel blew his trumpet,
and something like a great mountain, burning with fire,
was thrown into the sea.

AN LIU, NORI KO

Provincial Road 204 near Wakang, China

An Liu and Nori Ko wind their way out of the Himalayas, catching glimpses of the Tibetan Plateau between peaks and valleys. The geography they're headed toward is limitless and barren. Sky and land, sky and land, sky and land.

An loves its emptiness.

Nori Ko has on a pair of headphones and fiddles with the dials of a field radio. She searches the Chinese state-run media for any news of Abaddon, but it's useless. Most of what she finds are stations playing nationalistic songs on a loop or news programs discussing air quality and water rationing in the western half of the country. China has sealed her borders, restricted her airspace, and declared martial law in many cities until the post-impact dust clears.

"It's like they're plugging their ears and singing la-la-la!" Nori Ko says. "They're treating Abaddon like it's a Western problem that the East can simply ride out."

"They'll be"—*SHIVERblinkblink*—"They'll be"—*BLINKblink*—"They're wrong."

"I hope they're not. But yes—they're wrong."

She rolls down her window. The air is warming as the sun rises and they lose elevation.

They round a turn in the mountains and the land below opens up. Tan and brown and gray and as wide and limitless as the sea. *I could stay here,* An thinks.

I know, Chiyoko says. *We could.*

He bites his lip, trying hard not to converse with her out loud. It's not easy. Because as far as he's concerned, she's here.

Next to him.

With him.

Always.

If anyone bothered us we could kill them, he says to her in his mind.

Yes, love. We could do that. Chiyoko's voice is supple and inviting. *We could be alone. We could be . . .*

Happy, he thinks, finishing her thought. *No people, no trouble. I could stay right here if I didn't have to kill the Players who killed you. If I didn't have to kill the kepler.*

I know, love.

But I do.

I know, love.

ShiverBLINKBLINKBLINK

"I do," he says out loud.

"What was that?" Nori Ko asks, pushing the headphones from her ear.

"Hmm? Oh." He sweeps a hand over the dashboard, indicating the landscape. "Was only saying I do like this place. So empty."

"Ah," Nori Ko says. "It's very—" She cuts herself short. "The channel went dead." She spins the dial this way and that, searching more. She finds nothing at first, but then hears a few stunned voices in the studio, a producer saying, "No, no! Play the anthem!" Followed by the first bars of "March of the Volunteers."

"I think . . . I think it's happened, An," she says.

"Good," he says.

And he means it.

MACCABEE ADLAI, LITTLE ALICE CHOPRA

Hotel Shivam, Railway Station Road, Dwarka, India

Maccabee and Little Alice are in a dark hotel room in central Dwarka. Maccabee sits on the foot of the bed. Little Alice is curled up, her back pressed to his thigh, her chest rising and falling in sleep. He rests a hand on her shoulder. He watches the news on NDTV, which is about to air a live broadcast from the Indian prime minister.

The screen shows nothing more than the NDTV logo. It dips to black and the Indian governmental seal fades up. Three clocks pop up in the corner. The first reads GMT 02:26:08. The second reads IST 07:56:08. The third reads simply PA 0000 00:00:00.

The clocks tick.

Then a crackle and some voices and yes.

Here he is, in a spare wooden chair against a patterned backdrop. He looks straight into the camera and begins speaking. "Friends, Indians, fellow humans. Abaddon is down."

The clock labeled PA begins to count forward. Maccabee understands. Post-Abaddon.

A new age of human existence on planet Earth.

Little Alice tosses in her sleep, her lips part, her eyes dart back and forth beneath her eyelids. Maccabee mutes the television and shakes her gently. "Come on, sweetie."

Her eyes bat open. Wet and dark.

He says, "We have to leave. Now. If we're lucky, we'll get to China before any of the others."

She rubs her eyes. "Okay, Uncle." She takes one of his large hands. She smiles. The smile of someone decades older. He can't help but marvel at this small creature yet again.

This Sky Key that he will give to the kepler.

And when he does this, he will break his promise to Shari that he would take care of her.

Because the kepler will most likely take her. And then, who knows what he will do with the child?

Maccabee turns away. He can't look her in her eyes.

She doesn't seem to notice his remorse. She squeezes his hand and says, "Yes." And then, "Let's go."

AISLING KOPP, SHARI CHOPRA, HILAL IBN ISA AL-SALT, SARAH ALOPAY, JAGO TLALOC, GREG JORDAN, GRIFFIN MARRS

Hidden airstrip west of Lampang, Thailand

Aisling is woken by the staccato burst of small arms coming from the jungle, followed immediately by the wail of an air horn echoing through the trees.

She pops out of her very nice bed on the very nice plane that Stella left for her and runs to the door near the cockpit. She leans out and sees the others—Hilal, Sarah, Jago, and Shari—standing at attention around a small campfire.

Another burst of gunfire.

"What was that?" Aisling yells to the others.

"The security system has been activated," Hilal exclaims. "Wayland's men must have followed us. It is time to fly. *Now.*"

Jago kicks out the campfire as the others move toward their planes, their weapons already drawn, their feet already running, their brains already coursing with adrenaline.

Aisling spins inside her plane and yanks the door shut. Jordan appears right next to her as Marrs whisks past a slumbering Pop, moving into the cockpit.

"Go time," Aisling says.

"Good," Jordan says, his eyebrows drawn across his forehead in a grave and unwavering line.

Outside, Jago and Sarah sprint side by side, Sarah pulling ahead with each step. She bounds up their plane's steps and pirouettes into the

124

cockpit, Jago right behind her. He shuts the door and seals it and joins her at the controls.

Shari follows Hilal into their plane and both plop into the flight seats, Shari in the copilot chair.

Aisling sits next to Marrs in the cockpit of her plane and pulls on the headphones. "We're ready," she says. Their plane is first in line. Marrs is already pulling it onto the runway.

"You are clear, Aisling," Hilal says. "We will talk to you at the first check-in in twenty-four hours."

"Roger that, Hilal. Good luck."

"And to you."

Aisling peers out the window and sees Sarah at the controls of her plane, her hand whipping off a quick salute. Aisling returns the gesture as Marrs pushes the throttle. Their jet wash obliterates what's left of the small campfire as the plane hurtles forward, the jungle canopy rushing overhead like an inky blur. At the midway point Aisling sees the gate they drove through the night before, its sentinel system going full bore, the swivel-mounted rifles flashing and spraying bright casings onto the ground. As they pass, there's an explosion that takes out one of the guns, but it doesn't matter to Aisling or Marrs or Jordan because a few seconds later the canopy breaks open to reveal the blue sky. As they hit 128 knots Marrs pulls the stick and the nose tilts up and they shoot through a hole in the jungle and they're free.

Sarah spins up her engines and says, "Ready to fly—copy back, Hilal. You first or us?"

"You first, Sarah," he says, and she can't help but think that even now Hilal's manners are impeccable. "Get on your heading as soon as possible."

Jago takes the controls and the engines hum and their plane rounds onto the runway, the ribbon of concrete laid before them. He engages the throttle and the aircraft jolts forward. As they zip past the break in the trees that leads to the road they see lots of muzzle flashes and another explosion and Sarah catches sight of two men cutting a hole in the wire fence, each working fast with bolt cutters.

Sarah yells into her headset, "Hilal, the gunmen are going to make the runway! I repeat, *they are going to make the runway*!"

Before the trees break overhead Jago pulls up on the flight controls. Their jet spits out of the fringe of leaves hanging over the open end of the runway. As soon as they're over the jungle they bank hard to starboard. And then Jago pulls up and punches the throttle and they climb fast on a steep angle and they're free too.

But the last plane—Hilal's—is not.

Shari yanks off her headset. "Get us airborne, Hilal, but don't go full speed until I give you the all clear." She clicks out of her seat belt and stands up.

"Where are you—"

"Fly the plane, Hilal!"

Shari exits the cockpit and heads to the storeroom in the tail section, going right for the guns. She grabs a stock M4 with an extended clip and an undermounted M203 grenade launcher preloaded not with incendiaries but with smokers.

Then she bounds back to the front of the plane and does something very inadvisable for taking off.

She opens the door.

It flops open below her, the steps on the inside of the doorway leading to the ground below.

"What are you doing?" Hilal asks as warning lights ping across the flight console.

"Making sure we get out of here," Shari says, pulling the cockpit door shut so she can concentrate better. "Just fly!" she commands.

Hilal yells something in a language she's never heard, but he listens. The plane lurches forward and begins its turn onto the runway. Shari drops to the floor, a gust of warm morning air coating her face. She peers down the runway and sees the fire and the outlines of three men—no, four—taking cover near the gate. She smells the cordite from the firefight. She braces her feet against the bulkhead and quickly fires the grenade launcher. *Fwomp! Fwomp!* The projectiles travel on low arcs before hitting halfway down the runway, exploding in a dense blue haze that instantly obscures the gate.

"Go!" she yells, but Hilal doesn't need to be told. The plane surges, the bottom of the door scrapes noisily along the concrete, sparks flying. They take fire, but due to the smoke and their rapid acceleration, these shots all miss to the aft of the tail. As they trundle down the runway, her hair stiffening in the wind, her eyes squinting and watering, Shari pulls the assault rifle into her shoulder. She lays down cover fire as the plane goes faster, faster, faster, the blue smokescreen getting closer, closer, closer, and then they are through it. The men stand and Shari holds her breath as she fires three-shot bursts, her body pivoting as the plane passes her targets. Seven quick bursts, four of them finding their targets. Two heads, one chest, one leg. All four men fall and the one with the leg injury screams but she can't hear because the wind is so strong now.

After a few more seconds the trees give way to the sky and Hilal pulls up. A few stray shots come from behind them as one of the survivors fires, blindly and pointlessly.

Shari carefully gets to her feet, bracing herself in the galley as air whips around her and screams in her ears. She grabs the top of the door's handrail and pulls with all her might, but it's useless. The force of the air holds it open and she can't get it to close.

She picks up the closest handset. "I can't shut it!" she yells.

Hilal says something but she can't understand him over the deafening whine of the wind.

"What?" she asks.

He says it again and then the plane accelerates and jerks violently to port and before Shari can get ahold of something she's falling over and cradling her head and she feels momentarily weightless. Her shoulder mashes into something hard and her rifle flies out the open door and to the greenery below. The plane straightens and she looks up but instead of the ceiling she sees the floor and she understands. They're inverted, flying in an arc. The door remains open and she's not sure what Hilal is doing or if they've been hit and he's lost control of the plane, but before she can think about any of this the plane flops over and is suddenly right-side up. The door obeys the laws of physics and hinges shut with a loud *clap* and Shari doesn't waste a second as she springs to her feet and grabs the lever and pushes it hard into the closed position.

Shari spits hair out of her mouth. Her shoulder stings. She smiles.

"It worked?" Hilal asks from behind the cockpit door.

"Yes, Hilal!"

She falls to her bottom and sits there and begins to laugh. The plane pitches up and accelerates more.

It worked.

They are free too.

They can Play the way they want.

They can go and find Little Alice Chopra.

51.397742, 84.676206[i]

KEPLER 22B

Ansible chamber on board Seedrak Sare'en, active geosynchronous orbit above the Martian North Pole

He sits in the chair again. The dark room pinpricks to life and grows incredibly cold, then glows brightly. His brothers and sisters on the Heedrak mother ship, more than 600 light-years away, surround him on all sides.

Five men, six women.

The 11 members of the conclave speak as one entity. Sentences start in one mouth and are finished in another. This is the way his people communicate when they are near one another. Unfortunately, the ansible transmits sight and sound but not thought, so in this chamber it's like receiving only part of what's being said. This cuts in their direction too—they cannot hear his thoughts either, and all struggle against this.

He takes their voices in—drinks in their tones and timbres—as they go around the room with their obligatory salutations. Their speech—low resonant warbles punctuated by high-pitched coos and rhythmic clicks—is like music in his ears. It is far more gracious than Earth humanspeak, and he is eager for the day when he can sit among his own kind and be woven into discussions with both thought *and* vocalization. His Nethinim are serviceable telepaths, and he has had many fine conversations with them, but as mutes they lack the ability to convey nuance and feeling through their voices. Conversing in one mode—either purely through speech, as with the conclave, or purely through thought, as with his Nethinim—is like speaking with half his vocabulary.

Once the salutations are over, they turn to the business at hand.

The conclave says, "Give us the news, Sare'en Gamerunner."

"The asteroid has impacted," he says. "The Nabataean Player is close to presenting the three keys at the Shang monument. We are confident that completion of this game is imminent." He speaks in the first person plural, as is their custom.

"Were any primary monuments destroyed after impact?"

"Unluckily, the Minoan was lost to a stray bolide accompanying Abaddon, and there are some fluctuations at the Olmec monument. We are monitoring this. We may lose it as well."

"Pity. But we merely need one for the game to end. What of the other Players?"

"Most have banded. It is our belief that they wish to stop Endgame from progressing. The Shang Plays, though. He alone chases the Nabataean Player in pursuit of the keys."

"Have we considered direct intervention?"

"We have not as yet, but it is an option."

"We may order you to pursue this option. Tell us, who is destroying the monuments?"

"This is our main concern, Heedrak. They are people loyal to the old member of our race. The one we abandoned so long ago."

"Ea?"

"Yes."

"But you previously reported that the Aksumite killed him."

"We did, and this is true. But his brotherhood lives on. And they are not pleased. As you know, Ea did not wish for Endgame to occur. His loyalists are trying to carry on in his absence. They are trying, in their own crude way, to stop what has begun."

"This brotherhood cannot succeed. Are we tracking them?"

"Yes, but Abaddon has severely stressed Earth's surveillance systems. We will not be able to follow their movements as easily. Having said that, we surmised that after destroying the Harappan monument they were on course for the Donghu monument."

"We are concerned."

"We are as well."

"We have a notion. We encourage you to follow it."

"What is this notion?"

"It would require two things. The first is that we channel Sky Key as soon as we can. In order to help speed the Nabataean along."

"And the second?"

"That the Nethinim on your Seedrak descend to the surface for a brief time."

"To do what?"

"To stop this brotherhood."

"They can go to Mongolia and do this as soon as our session ends."

kepler 22b half rises out of his chair.

"Wait. One Nethinim can do this in Mongolia. The other one *must* go to the Cahokian monument."

kepler 22b sits back down. He frowns. "Why?"

"We left an object there a long time ago. We have never told you about it. You need to know about it now, though. This thing could be dangerous to us."

kepler 22b leans forward, intrigued. "I am listening," he says, intentionally using the first person to indicate his high level of interest. "Please. Do go on."

MACCABEE ADLAI, LITTLE ALICE CHOPRA

Boeing 737, en route from Ahmedabad to Xi'an, China, crossing 90° E

Maccabee sits in a first class seat, Little Alice awake and silent next to him, in an otherwise empty Air China 737. There were precious few flights after the impact, but he'd found one persuadable Chinese pilot in Ahmedabad willing to take them to Xi'an, and all Maccabee had had to give him was $300,000 worth of gold.

A bargain, if it will guarantee that he wins Endgame.

They fly north and east. A laptop sits on the large fold-out table afforded to all first class passengers. Little Alice's hand rests on his thigh. His hand rests on hers.

This tenderness almost makes him sick. He hasn't spent more than a few days with this girl, but she is so fragile, and the forces that have made her important to Endgame seem so craven, that he cannot help but care for her.

And he thinks that, despite everything, she cares for him too.

What will be will be.

Maccabee opens and closes a few windows on his laptop. The hard drive he took from the drone in Dwarka is hooked up to it. He looks from the girl to the clock in the corner of the computer screen and then out the window. The flight is halfway over. They have crossed the Himalayas.

The sky outside is unlike any he's seen. They're cruising at over 40,000 feet. Sooty, gray clouds are everywhere. The dark blue arc of the upper atmosphere stretches above the aircraft, but the horizon is an odd gradient that, moving from top to bottom, goes from blue to white to brown to orange to the gray floor of the clouds. The air is thick and poisonous looking.

This is the first sign he has seen of Abaddon.

Soon, he assumes, soot will blanket the earth. Winter will come, and it will stay for a long time.

But he is not too concerned about this. He's too excited. He can barely contain his anticipation. His happiness.

He is so close to winning.

He turns back to the computer. He types away. He's accessed the innards of the drive, finding curious things. Vestiges of names and organizations. Instructions. Locations. Timelines. Names. Ea. Rima. Stella. Lists of coordinate locations. An organization called the Brotherhood of the Snake.

"Who are they?" he wonders out loud, not expecting Little Alice to say anything.

But she does. "They are people who want to stop Endgame. Who want to stop us."

"That's why they blew up the Harappan temple?"

"Yes. And no."

"I don't understand. Sun Key was there, wasn't it?"

"It would have been if you'd reached the temple's star chamber, but as you didn't, it was not there. Sun Key is safe."

"How do you know this, Little Alice?"

"I am not Little Alice. Not right now. I am kepler 22b."

"*kepler 22b?*"

Her face snaps to him and her black eyebrows rise but otherwise she maintains her blank expression. "Yes. And no. I am mostly Little Alice, daughter of the Harappan Player. But I can also speak as kepler 22b at certain locations on Earth. We are riding along the ninetieth eastern meridian right now. This is one such location, Nabataean."

Maccabee's heart quickens. "Where are we going?"

"The girl knows all of the locations where we can conclude Endgame. The next closest is near Xi'an, China."

"Sun Key will be there?"

"Yes. Sun Key is always moving, Player. It is not merely one thing, and not merely in one place."

"It has a quantum component?"

"You will find out when you reach Emperor Zhao's burial temple, Nabataean."

"It'll materialize when I get there, then?"

Little Alice/kepler 22b tilts her head. "In a manner of speaking. Patience, Nabataean. Endgame is the puzzle of life, and the reason for death. You will see when you reach the Shang temple."

Pause.

Maccabee asks, "Will other Players be there?"

Sky Key frowns as if she's trying to peer through a mist. "Uncertain. But you should be prepared."

Maccabee actually laughs at this one. "I *am* a Player of Endgame," he says by way of explanation.

"Good."

"One more question."

"Yes?"

"The girl—what'll happen to her? Will you . . . hurt her?"

"No."

Maccabee breathes a sigh of relief. "I'm glad for that at lea—"

But Little Alice/kepler 22b cuts him off. "Her death will be painless, Nabataean. In fact, she'll barely be aware of it at all."

Maccabee expertly hides his emotions—shock, anger, disgust, guilt—when he says, "Good."

"You are moving off the meridian, Nabataean. Do not tarry when you land. Go to the temple. Find the star chamber within. Call to me and claim your prize. Win Endgame. For you and for your line."

And then the plane bumps over a patch of rough air and Little Alice's face goes slack and she blinks four times. Her head cocks to the side. Maccabee holds his steely expression, afraid that the Maker can still see him. He only relaxes when Alice says, "What is it, Uncle?"

kepler 22b is gone.

"Nothing, Alice." He turns away in shame and reaches for a bag of chips. "Hungry?"

She shakes her head. "No. Thirsty."

"Let me get you something." He stands and walks past her. "What do you want?"

"Chai if they have it."

She wraps her arms around a pillow. Her wrists are chubby with baby fat. He smiles weakly. "I'm sure they do. I'll make it special for you."

"Thank you, Uncle."

He walks to the galley. He has never felt more empty or full of self-hate in his life.

I am sorry, Shari Chopra. I lied.

I cannot protect your daughter. Not from him.

Not at the end.

This is Endgame.

AN LIU, NORI KO

G310 National Road, 313 km west of Xi'an, China

Nori Ko drives.

An Liu lies in the rear seat, keeping out of sight.

He cradles his Beretta rifle and Nobuyuki's katana. His fingertips grace Chiyoko's hair.

It's midday but the sky is dark and covered with ponderous clouds.

Light rain lashes the windshield. The wipers dance. The tires hiss.

BLINKSHIVERBLINK.

"How will I find your murderers now, Chiyoko?" He whispers so that Nori Ko won't hear.

Patience, Chiyoko answers. *They will show themselves.*

He stares at the watch on his wrist. The same one that used to belong to Chiyoko. The blip-blip marking Jago Tlaloc was there two days earlier. But as he and Nori Ko drove through the bleak desert of western China, as the Olmec moved over northern Saskatchewan, he disappeared in a poof and hasn't come back.

Dead? Crashed? Shot down? Did he finally remove the tracker? He better not be dead. I need to be the one to kill him.

He isn't, love.

"He better not be."

"What's that?" Nori Ko asks, an unlit Golden Bat cigarette dangling from her lips. She knows by now that An hates the smoke, so she's refrained from lighting up.

"Nothing," he says.

"You said *some*thing."

"I said that Maccabee better not"—*blinkBLINKshiver*—"better not get there before us."

Nori Ko swipes at a phone mounted on the dashboard. A map pops up, tracking their location faithfully. She smiles, pleased that things still function on this side of the planet. Abaddon triggered a few serious earthquakes on the Kazakh border, but they didn't buckle or rend any of the roads An and Nori Ko have taken. She can only imagine what's happened in the United States—did the San Andreas finally trip? Did the Mid-Atlantic Ridge buckle and rage? Is the rain falling there poisonous and acidic? She doesn't know and she doesn't want to know.

Because that side of the world is screwed.

They've driven nonstop since Kolkata, taking turns in six-hour shifts. The car stinks of body odor and socks and empty food containers. She inhales sharply, enjoying the sweet smell of the unlit cigarette below her nostrils. "We'll find out about the Nabataean soon enough. Less than four hours to go."

"Good," An says. He runs a finger over Chiyoko's hair, and then over the cool metal of his rifle's receiver.

Patience, love, Chiyoko says again.

They drive in silence. An listens to the rain and the wind. He listens to his heartbeat. He listens to Chiyoko hum a traditional Japanese song he can't recall ever hearing before. When she is finished he whispers, "That was nice."

Thank you.

Nori Ko says, "I have a question."

"Yes?"

"If—*when*—we get the three keys and you see the Maker again, how are you planning on killing it?"

An doesn't hesitate to answer. "You've noticed the metal box in the back?"

"Yes."

"It has a suicide vest in it."

"Dirty?"

"More." *BLINKSHIVERBLINKBLINK.* "Nuclear."

"Ah. The Maker shouldn't be able to survive a point-blank explosion that big."

"No. Even I have faith in some things."

"The Church of Immaculate Demolition."

An cracks a smile but doesn't laugh. "That's right. I Play for death."

"And I do too," she says.

"I know," he says.

They don't talk for a quarter hour. The road is mostly straight here, but then they round a turn and Nori Ko taps the brakes. "Shit. Checkpoint. About half a kilometer."

An thrusts his head next to hers. "How many?"

Nori Ko squints. "Four cars. At least as many officers."

"Police or army?"

"Looks like police." She downshifts the Defender. "You'll have to hide under something."

An climbs into the passenger seat. "No, I won't." He counts five—no, six—officers. All standing around in slick rain gear. They look bored. One is on a radio. Two others smoke, their hands cupped over the orange ends of their cigarettes. One officer looks up, throws his cigarette to the ground, moves to the center of the road. Waves a hand back and forth demonstratively.

An flips open the panel on the dashboard that hides the car's grenade launcher. He presses the left button and slides his fingers over the pistol grip. He grabs the steering wheel with his other hand and jerks it from Nori Ko.

"Hey!" she protests. The car snaps left. An pulls the trigger. He releases the wheel as a white arc traces forward, the projectile clanking into one of the police cars and then rolling in a tight spiral on the pavement. The cops scatter as they anticipate the explosion, but the one in the middle of the road plants his legs and draws his pistol and begins firing.

"Speed up," An says calmly, the slugs glancing off the bulletproof glass, none of them hitting the wipers that swish back and forth.

Nori Ko does as she's told.

The grenade goes off. But it doesn't explode in a ball of fire like the one in Kolkata. Instead it lights up brightly and falls open and the police cars' twirling cherry lights go out. In fact, all of the cars' lights go out— the white headlamps, the red taillights, the yellow parking lights.

"EMP?" Nori Ko asks.

An doesn't say anything, but Nori Ko sees his head snap in the affirmative.

Nori Ko chuckles. "I suppose they won't be calling for backup, then."

"No," An says. "They won't."

The police peek from behind cover. The Defender isn't more than 100 meters away.

An opens his window. Air rushes in. "Slow down," he says over the sound of the wet road.

He casually hoists the Beretta to his shoulder and sticks it outside. Rain splashes onto the weapon and his arm. He aims quickly and pulls the trigger. A casing sails into his lap, a police officer twirls and falls, the back of his head gone. The cop in the center of the road adjusts his aim to get a bead on An, but Nori Ko turns slightly so the front of the car shields the Shang. An fires three more times at the scrambling officers, and three more officers die. The only cops left are the one in the road and another who's abandoning her post, running as fast as she can south across a field of waist-high grass.

"Stop," An says.

Nori Ko hits the brakes. The Defender swings 90 degrees, rocking to a halt and straddling the centerline of the road. The officer fires at will, aiming directly for Nori Ko's stoic face. He empties his magazine into the glass, not understanding why his bullets aren't doing anything.

Nori Ko almost feels sorry for him.

An exits on the sheltered side of the Defender, rifle in hand. He drops to the ground and, shooting below the undercarriage, lets off a burst. The bullets hit the man above his feet. He falls into a heap, screaming, reaching for his shredded ankles. His hands come up soaking red. Nori Ko shakes her head.

What a Player, she thinks.

An swings his rifle to the field. The fleeing officer is about 50 meters away, the swaying grass above her hips. A torso and a head and pumping fists bobbing up and down, up and down. Alive and scared. *Fool,* An thinks. *She should drop and hide among the greenery.* But fear clouds her mind and she runs instead. He flips open the scope's covers. Sights through it. Tucks the rifle into his shoulder. She moves in and out of the crosshair. He exhales.

Let her go, Chiyoko says.

A *SHIVER* rattles his stomach but doesn't rise into his arms or hands. His eye is unblinking. He presses the trigger. The officer is thrown forward with the shot. A bloody mist pops in the rain like a firework and then is washed away.

No one gets away, An thinks.

He turns to the downed officer in the road. Walks forward. Nori Ko puts the Defender in first and creeps along. An reaches the officer, a fresh-faced young man not much older than he is. The officer's mouth is drawn shut in a tight line. His eyes are red and full of anger. His eyelashes are clumped together from rain and tears. The man spits, but the gob of phlegm misses An's pant leg and lands in a puddle. An smiles. He places the muzzle on the man's forehead. The skin turns pink around the metal. Water runs down the barrel and onto flesh.

"You!" the man says.

"Yes."

Nori Ko honks the horn. "Come on!" she calls from inside the Defender.

"They'll find you," the man says.

"No, they won't."

"I see you. Someone else will too. They'll find you and—"

The final shot rings over the countryside.

Nori Ko honks again.

An gets in and they leave.

Nori Ko wants to light the cigarette, and badly. *Screw it,* she thinks. She digs in her pocket and pulls out a lighter and flicks it on and holds it to her sweet-smelling Golden Bat. Her cheeks glow orange. She smokes noisily, making a show of enjoying it.

"Open your window," An says, but Nori Ko already is. Fresh air whisks the smoke away.

"Can we take back roads to Zhao's pyramid?" An asks, releasing the Beretta's magazine and checking it.

"I think so," Nori Ko answers, swiping at her phone's map once more, trying to hide that her hand is shaking.

"Good." An opens the glove compartment and takes out a box of ammunition. He snaps new rounds into the cartridge one at a time. *Click, click, click.*

"I don't want any more of that today." He holds a single brass-colored round between his thumb and forefinger. "I want to save these for the Nabataean."

He pushes it into place.

Click.

"He better not be there before us, Nori Ko."

And she understands perfectly. *Because if he is, then An Liu is going to try to kill me too.*

She takes another pull off the cigarette. She blows the blue smoke out of the side of her mouth, aiming it at An.

She says, "Don't worry. He won't be."

SARAH ALOPAY, JAGO TLALOC

En route to Monks Mound, Collinsville, Illinois, United States

Sarah and Jago fly out of Thailand on an initial heading of 009° 35' 26". After double-checking to make sure their plane didn't get hit during takeoff, they spoke to Hilal and Shari and Aisling to make sure they got away safely too. They did. They synchronized their watches to Zulu time and reiterated when they would check back in. They wished one another good luck and said good-bye and that was it.

For at least the next two or three days, Sarah and Jago will be on their own.

And they couldn't be happier.

They pass over Laos, China, Mongolia, Russia. The Asian air is empty of other aircraft and, in the immediate aftermath of Abaddon, still normal-looking. They enjoy clear skies and unlimited visibility. They encounter very little turbulence and virtually no communication from ground controllers, all of whom accept Jordan's top-secret clearance codes without question.

Their heading turns easterly as nighttime settles in. They trace over the Arctic Ocean and see signs of life on the surface below—the orange twinkle of far-flung Siberian settlements and the white glow of ships plying the cold, dark waters. Signs that things perhaps are not so bad on the surface below.

Both Players remember that night at the Calling, when kepler 22b showed them an image of a scarred and ravaged Earth, promising that this was what their planet would look like at the conclusion of Endgame. And both Players think: *Maybe, just maybe, Abaddon won't be that bad. Maybe the kepler was wrong.*

The plane's navigation system works as it's meant to—meaning that the GPS satellites orbiting 20,000 miles above Earth haven't been swept away by the asteroid—so nine hours into the flight they activate the autopilot and go to the spacious cabin. The chairs are huge. The tables are wide. The bathroom is stately, there's no other word for it. And, best of all, there's a bed.

Sarah is exhausted and teeming with nerves, but she also wants to feel what it's like to forget. Jago wants it too. They stand shoulder to shoulder and hand in hand, staring at the bedcovers for a few moments.

"Action or oblivion," she whispers, lacing her fingers into his. "Those are the only things I want now, Jago. To stop Endgame, or to have my memory wiped clean."

He wraps an arm over her shoulder. His lips touch the curl of her ear as he whispers, "I could say maybe the cheesiest bedroom line ever right now, Alopay."

"What's that?" she asks coyly.

"I can't. It would ruin the mood, what little there is."

He helps her out of her shirt and peels her legs out of her jeans and she sighs when he inexplicably fumbles with her bra's clasp and then he takes off his own clothing eagerly and clumsily and she sees how young he really is, how young she is, how for all their experience—with each other, and Jago's with other women, and hers with Christopher—even with all they know about the world and their bodies and their physical limits, she sees and she feels and she knows just how young they are, and how foolish. While he's on top of her, being careful of her arm, and deliberate with his movements, while she's enjoying the attention and the sensation and fulfillment of her immediate desire, she realizes why it is that the Players are required to be young. Until then she thought it was so they could have long leaderships as they helped to guide and repopulate a broken planet, but the real reason must be because only young people are so sure of themselves and so willfully foolish. *Especially* the young Players of Endgame, who are taught from the beginning that they're special—no, *unique*—as if all of their received wisdom and training could wring their foolishness out of them. But now Sarah sees that really, it's their foolishness that is exactly what's being counted upon by the perpetrators of Endgame. She wonders if the Makers were likewise as foolish at some point in their cognitive development. She wonders if true wisdom runs through their veins now. Because for all of her own foolishness— which led her to kill Christopher, which allowed her to believe that she was responsible for finding Earth Key, which drove her so quickly into Jago's arms—she also sees in her heart some wisdom. Baitsakhan, he was foolish. But he was also 13. Jago, Hilal, Aisling, Shari—probably Chiyoko too—these are not foolish people. Not necessarily wise, but not *only* foolish, and each of them is proof that the Makers have miscalculated.

Maybe they should have started Endgame sooner.

She wonders if kepler 22b thinks something similar. She wonders if he might possibly be *worried* about whether Endgame will go the way he wants it to go.

These thoughts fly through her mind in rapid succession, but then she refocuses on Jago. She kisses him fully and clumsily and tugs at his lower lip with her teeth. Jago, who is so humanly unpretty and so strong and also so tender. He kisses back, and keeps moving, and within moments she's gone.

There it is.

Oblivion.

Sweet, sweet oblivion.

She stays gone—*they* stay gone—until they're finished. Probably not more than a few minutes, but while they're there it feels stretched out and all-encompassing and timeless.

Afterward she pulls a sheet over their bodies and she falls into a deep sleep. She's shaken awake as the plane passes through some rough chop and Jago sits bolt upright.

She rubs her eyes. "How long was I out?"

"Not very long. Maybe an hour."

"You sleep at all?"

"Mmm, no." The plane flies smoothly again and he lies back down.

"Mainly I was doing more cheesy things."

"Like?"

"Watching you."

"Creepy."

"*Sí.*"

Pause.

"What were you going to say before?"

"*¿Cuándo?*"

"Before. The bedroom line."

"Ah. I was going to say, 'I can give you action *and* oblivion, Sarah Alopay.'"

"*Super* creepy!"

He shrugs. "Would've said it in Spanish at least. '*Yo puedo dar acción* y *olvido.*' Everything sounds better in Spanish."

She pushes her hip into his thigh. "Yeah, it does."

The plane jostles again but this time it doesn't stop. Jago bounds out of bed in a T-shirt and underwear and zips to the cockpit. Sarah goes to the bathroom. She has to hold onto the handle as she pees. She removes a robe from a hook and pulls it over her shoulders, keeping her injured arm underneath the plush terrycloth. She works her way through the cabin, her good hand grasping for things to help her stay upright. When she reaches the cockpit she plops into the copilot chair and buckles in, shoulder belts included.

What emerges in the distance is bewildering.

They're well over 3,000 miles away from the eastern United States, but it doesn't matter.

It's there.

Abaddon *is* as bad as kepler 22b said it would be.

There is no horizon in the east. The entire expanse from top to bottom is black, like a hole punched through the sky and earth. The only light comes from high-altitude lightning flashing constantly and everywhere over the reaches of Canada, and while it's a ways off, they're going to be flying through this storm soon.

"It's going to get rough," Jago says, flicking switches and punching commands into the touch screen, disabling the autopilot.

"I know. We can handle it."

For the next several hours they fly through or over a succession of terrible storms, each growing in intensity. They stay in the cockpit and don't sleep as they white-knuckle it across Canada. Somewhere over Saskatchewan they lose contact with the external GPS systems and are forced to fly by instruments alone, hoping that by the time they reach the small airport Hilal marked for them, everything will be working again, otherwise they're not sure they'll be able to find it. As they cross the US border they manage to reconnect to the satellites overhead, but for the rest of the flight this connection remains erratic and unreliable. They get a few automated pings from ground control systems in North Dakota, and they answer these with Jordan's codes, but otherwise they have no indication that anyone on the ground is tracking or even aware of them.

Dawn arrives but the sun does not. The sky barely brightens. A little light leaks through the gas and ash directly overhead, but otherwise it's as if the world has been dipped in smoky ink. Sarah expected the eastern side of the country to be like this but not the western too, and for a while neither she nor Jago can figure out why it's happening. The jet stream should be blowing everything Abaddon has kicked up over the Atlantic, not over the plains.

And then, somewhere over Nebraska, they understand.

The plane flies into a pocket of decent visibility, and when they look west they see the contours of a massive plume of ash, several hundred miles across, billowing from the Rockies like it's being vented from the depths of hell. The plume rises so high that it looks as if it reaches into space itself. Every now and then crooked streaks of blue and purple lightning web through it, or the plume glows with a fiery orange light that's quickly snuffed out.

"The Yellowstone Caldera," Sarah says. "It blew. Jesus Christ, it fucking blew." She turns to Jago, her face pale. "My family's down there somewhere, Feo."

"Countless other families are relying on us right now, Sarah."

She ignores this. "I want to see them."

"You can't. Not yet."

She almost protests—they went to his family, didn't they?—but he's right. They can't take a detour. *Action or oblivion,* she thinks. *Running to Mom and Dad is neither.*

"All right, but I *do* want to see them eventually."

Jago can't argue with that.

Her thoughts of home are interrupted when their visibility returns to zero and they slam into a wall of turbulent air that lasts the rest of Nebraska. The jostling reaches a crescendo over a corner of Kansas that throws the plane 20 feet in all directions over several minutes. The air settles again over Missouri, which they pass over at a relatively low 25,000 feet, flying under a high-altitude storm and over a low-slung bank of ash carried on the wind. Not since the far north of Canada have they seen the ground. As they approach the small Creve Coeur Airport near St. Louis, Jago puts the plane into a virtual dive to get below 2,000 feet, trying to keep the engine intakes from jamming full of particulate. Communication with the GPS system is blessedly functioning and they find the airport—really nothing more than a runway and an array of private hangars—to be completely empty. They touch down at a little after 11 a.m. local time, and as they taxi to the hangar Hilal marked for them, the plane's tires cut through a thin layer of Yellowstone ash that coats everything. The windshield wipers swish back and forth, pushing the stuff to the side and making streaks on the glass. The sun is nearly at its zenith, but the sky is stuck in a constant state of dusky twilight, and with the exception of the airstrip's emergency lighting, including that on the runway, nearly all power in the area appears to be out.

After a couple hours spent getting the plane inside and packing bags with weapons and supplies and changing clothes and putting on respirators and goggles and firing up a vintage Harley-Davidson XLS Roadster, they hit the road.

They don't bother with helmets.

No point. Not like anyone's going to pull them over and write them a ticket.

There are hardly any vehicles moving around. Sarah guesses that the blast from Abaddon, while devastating to large areas of the eastern seaboard, had the added effect of washing at least half of the country in a giant electromagnetic pulse, frying nearly every circuit east of the Mississippi. And she is correct. This is why no one's out driving around—their cars simply don't work. The motorcycle works because its engine is purely mechanical—including its kick-starter. As they take their ride and begin to get a ground's-eye view of what Abaddon has wrought—even over a thousand miles away way from the point of impact—it dawns on Sarah that if people could go somewhere, they wouldn't know where *to* go. Most of them must be holed up at home, taking stock of food, water, batteries, fuel, clothing, pets, livestock, and, this being America, guns and ammunition. People are hunkering down and waiting, trying to get news from the radio or neighbors or whatever authority figure they can find.

People are *scared*.

Sitting on the back of the bike and using a paper map, Sarah navigates them around St. Louis to the north, crossing the Mississippi River on a completely dead I-270, which cuts over Chouteau Island. The four-lane highway is peppered with derelict cars, abandoned right where they died. Many have their doors open. Many overflow with personal items and things that will soon be thought of as supplies.

Might as well be zombies out here, she thinks as they motor over the short causeway into Illinois.

After a short ride on the Illinois side Sarah squeezes Jago with her legs and they exit the highway, taking local roads that wind east and south.

Monks Mound is very close. She sees it on the map, but more than that she feels it in her skin.

They turn onto Horseshoe Lake Road. Jago goes right down the double yellow line. No cars, abandoned or otherwise. A wall of hardwoods and power lines on their right. A grass tract on their left abutted by a line of modest two-story homes. A few people run into their houses when they hear the prattle of the motorcycle engine. One man doesn't run. He has a long hunting rifle, the butt parked on his hip. He waves them down. Jago brakes to a stop.

Sarah pulls the respirator from her face. "Need any help, mister?" she yells.

"Sure I do! Can you clear the skies and turn the power back on?"

"Wish I could."

"Yeah, well . . . I was flagging you 'cause you probably shouldn't go that way, less you want trouble."

Sarah runs a finger over her map, scanning it for the name of a nearby town. "Unfortunately we have to go that way. Got a big sister over in Shiloh with two little ones," Sarah lies. "Haven't heard from her since before. Need to make sure they're all right."

"I hear you, then. You know where all this ash is coming from, by the way? Ain't nothing on the radio. Can't be that Abaddon, can it?"

"Nah. I heard that Yellowstone blew up. Abaddon probably triggered it or something. There's a huge volcano under there."

"Yellowstone? Old Faithful Yellowstone?"

"That's the one."

He runs a hand through his hair a couple times, clearly distressed. "Goddamn. I mean, I know this is Illinois and all, but we ain't in Kansas anymore, are we, miss?"

Sarah nearly laughs. She's happy to be home, if only for a short visit. "No, we're not."

Jago says quietly, "What's he mean?"

"I'll explain later," Sarah says.

The man says, "Well, be careful out there, you two." He leans to the side and squints, eyeing the pistols on their waists and the rifle-shaped duffels strapped to their bike. He says something to himself that Sarah can't hear, but she can read his lips: "Looks like you're being careful."

"We will, mister. You too."

They wave to one another and Sarah and Jago take off.

But not more than half a mile away they stop again.

A black Ford police cruiser is ditched on the right side of the road. Its front doors and trunk are open. The communications console mounted to the dashboard is shot to pieces, probably by a shotgun blast. But far more disturbing is the taut rope that leads from under the car's rear bumper, angling toward the crossbeam of a nearby telephone pole, and over it, to the lifeless body of a uniformed cop hanged 15 feet above. They can't see his face. He's missing his shoes, and a black sock is bunched around the arch of his right foot. His gun holster is empty. His hands are purple. One is clenched in a fist.

Jago bounds off the bike to inspect the car. Sarah slides forward in the saddle and draws her pistol. *"Nada,"* Jago says. "Weapons are gone. Handcuffs, ammo, pepper spray, all of it."

She stares at the dead man. "Bad omen, huh?"

"Bad for him, anyway."

"Yeah. We should cut him down."

Jago rummages through the trunk. "There's a tarp in here. We could cover him, no?"

They work together to get him on the ground and laid out and covered at the base of the telephone pole, which takes on the double purpose of a grave marker. Sarah makes sure to close his swollen and bloodshot eyes before laying the tarp over him. She lays stones around its edge to keep the wind from blowing it off. She says a quiet prayer for him in her old Cahokian tongue.

They carry on.

They turn right onto Bruns Road, a meager strip of frost-heaved asphalt, and head south. The land is flat and dark, the road straight. The soybean plants on either side of the road are, like everything, covered in a thin layer of volcanic ash. They pass a farmhouse and a huge willow tree. They turn right onto another farm road and then left. The land begins to roll. More trees. Sarah looks at her map. Closer now. The road passes over I-55/I-70. They see more abandoned vehicles on the highway. One car creeps along in the distance, its yellow hazards flashing and its headlights cutting eerie beams through the dusty air.

A scavenger who, like them, lucked into finding a functioning vehicle. Sarah looks to her left. If her memory serves her, it should be there. And yes, over the tops of a stand of trees she makes it out. A flat-topped earthen pyramid covered in grass, about 92 feet high and 951 feet long. Sarah knows from her studies that it's also 836 feet across, meaning that at its base it's a little larger than the Great Pyramid of Giza.

Jago banks the bike onto Collinsville Road. And then they slow down abruptly.

Yes, Monks Mound is there, waiting for them. Maybe Sun Key is hidden in its depths. Maybe not. And to the south is the Maker weapon Sarah wants to find.

But first they have to deal with the danger that the nice man warned them about.

Sarah twirls her finger next to Jago's face, asking if he wants to turn around to avoid trouble.

He answers by gunning the throttle and rushing toward it.

A hundred yards later he pulls to a stop, the bike angled across the road at 45 degrees. He cuts the engine and kicks down the stand. Neither gets off.

They stare straight ahead.

"This is gonna get ugly, Feo."

"*Sí*. Stay sharp."

"You know me."

Eight motorcycles are pulled to the edge of the fields. As many men in leather vests and dirty jeans and dark leather boots are nearby. A car, apparently still functioning, is hemmed in by the bikers. One bike has a pair of black boots tied to the bitch bar. An argument is well underway.

"Hey!" a towering man built like a castle yells to Sarah and Jago when he notices them. He points. "Whose bike's that?"

"Ours, amigo," Jago says through his respirator.

"I ain't your friend." The biker walks toward them to get a better look at the Harley. "And that ain't gonna be yours for much longer, hombre. Like the look of that gas mask too."

"*Es bueno,*" Jago concedes.

Sarah gets off and rests her good hand on her pistol. "Not to point out the obvious, but by my count each of you already has a bike. How do you plan on taking ours also? You use some pixie biker dust to ride two at once?" While she talks she peeks past the biker at the car. It's an early 2000s silver Ford Taurus, a lot like the one they keep at her family's Niobrara River compound in western Nebraska. This one is dinged up badly, as if it's taken a few direct hits with baseball bats or, as is more likely, falling debris. It has no plates. There appears to be a single occupant, a driver, probably male. She can't tell if he's speaking to the bikers surrounding him, but she can tell that he's locked himself in and that the bikers are growing frustrated.

"Hey, Curly," the large biker shouts over his shoulder, "we got us some more smart-asses."

Curly leans from behind a man much bigger than him and says, "Who's that, Misty?"

Misty? Sarah thinks.

Jago laughs quietly.

"These two. Got a nice ride. Eighty-something XLS." Curly gives the giant an order and extracts himself from the car situation. Curly isn't much taller than five feet. He's as thin as rope and moves like it too, in a loose, boneless gait. He carries what is clearly the hanged police officer's shotgun in his left hand and in his right a buck knife, which he twirls expertly.

"Howdy, travelers. Name's Curly. And you are?" He addresses Jago.
Jago shrugs. He slouches nonchalantly in the saddle. "*Sólo hablo un poco de inglés*. Sorry." He makes a point of rolling his *R*s.

"We're just passing through," Sarah answers for them.

Curly turns to her. "Friend's a spic, eh? Guess I'm talking to you then." He spits a thin stream of clear saliva onto the road. "Maybe you are passing through, miss. But it'd have to be after we make a little trade. You give us that bike, and I'll let you keep your pretty little face. I assume there's a pretty face under all that. Best offer you're gonna get today, I'm sorry to say."

Sarah's eyes are hidden behind her goggles, so Curly can't tell that she isn't bothering to look at him while he talks. Instead, she watches the giant brandish a tire iron in the background. "Last warning!" he yells to the man in the car, his voice a high-pitched whine that completely contradicts his stature.

Sarah points. "Can we help you with anything back there, Curly?"

Curly half glances over his shoulder. "That? Nah. Nice motorist got lost and needs some directions. Funny thing is, he won't take 'em." He spits again. "Can you believe what the world's come to? Aliens on TV, killer asteroids, teenage assassins playing some kind of apocalypse game, and now this guy who won't talk sense with us simple road warriors. Folks are losing their minds these days. Along with lots of other things."

"And here you are to shepherd them to sunnier pastures," Sarah says, raising the riding goggles onto her forehead. "Figuratively speaking, of course."

Curly raises an eyebrow. "I like that. Mind if I use it? In the future like?"

"It's all yours."

"Say, you *are* pretty. Pretty eyes, anyway."

Sarah fakes sounding scared when she says, "Thanks."

"Speaking of using something that isn't mine . . ." He raises the shotgun and rests it across his right forearm. "Sorry for pointing this at you, miss, but I can see you're armed, so—nothing personal."

155

Sarah holds up her hands. "All right, all right." She nods at Jago. He puts his hands up too. "The bike's all yours. I'm just going to take the key out of the ignition. So I can slide it over to you. Cool?"

"Cool." Curly tilts toward the other biker without taking his eyes off them. "I like this one, Misty."

"Me too."

Sarah pulls out the key and wraps her gloved fingers around it. The giant raises the tire iron and takes a step away from the Taurus's passenger-side window. She sees the driver's eyes in the rearview mirror, wide and intense and, oddly, looking straight at her instead of at the man who's about to attack his car. Sarah waits for the right moment, and then instead of sliding the key to Curly she tosses it directly at him.

He fumbles as he instinctively tries to catch it with his knife hand. He fails. At the exact moment that the key hits the ground, the giant smashes the glass and it shatters and rains down onto the pavement. Misty glances at Curly. Jago jumps backward off the bike and draws his blade in one motion. The giant leans into the car and, to his surprise and Sarah's as well, he is *pulled* halfway inside. Something causes the back of his leather vest to tent upward and then it quickly falls, and the giant's legs lift off the ground and shudder and shake. He's dead, his nervous system just doesn't know it yet.

Meanwhile, away from the car, Sarah drops and rolls, her bad arm stinging, as Jago flings his knife, hitting Curly square in the neck. Curly twists away and squeezes the shotgun's trigger, but the blast sprays harmlessly into the air. Curly drops in a heap. The men around the car hoot and yell, and Sarah hears more glass breaking and a lot of cursing from the bikers and she pops up right in front of Misty with a short knife in her hand. He swings a meaty paw in her direction but she ducks under it and jams her fist toward his neck, catching it full bore with the blade. It sinks in four inches, severing everything Misty needs to eat, breathe, and deliver blood to his brain. Sarah whisks the knife free. Misty falls to his knees and brings his hands to his throat and blood spills over them.

Sarah and Jago rush toward the car and draw their pistols. The five bikers on the driver's side have retreated a few steps and hold up their guns. Not aware of what's happening with Sarah and Jago, they fire freely at the car, peppering its side with bullets and, unfortunately for them, masking the sound of the shots that are simultaneously being fired in their direction. Within three seconds Sarah and Jago hit each biker in his unprotected head—they're not wearing helmets either, not that it would matter—the last two facing them, their eyes full of disbelief and a little bit of terror.

Keeping their guns in the ready position, Sarah and Jago advance on the car, Sarah in the lead and Jago half a step behind her. His gun dances from biker to biker, making sure they're well and truly down. Holes perforate the car's side panels and the glass is broken and scattered on the pavement and the seats inside. The giant's head lies across the center console. It took a few shots and it does not look pretty or very head-like. Both tires on this side are flat. The air reeks of cordite. The driver's seat back is fully reclined. A large black mound of cloth takes up what's left of the rear seat.

There's no sign of the driver.

Sarah looks at Jago quizzically.

Where could he be?

But before Jago says anything a voice from under the black mound says, "Sarah?"

She knows that voice. She'd know it if it were whispering under the screams of thousands.

"D-dad?"

The black mound, a bundled pair of ballistic vests, is pushed away. And jutting above these is the beaming face of Simon Alopay.

KEPLER 22B

Teletrans chamber on board Seedrak Sare'en, active geosynchronous orbit above the Martian North Pole

His large hands are immersed in plasmastone—a molten rock-like substance—all the way to his forearms. A three-dimensional map of Earth spins before him, midair. The two Nethinim are at the far end of the room, occupying the transpots. Each has a svelte pack with supplies strapped to his back and each is dressed in a paper-thin jumpsuit that bends and reflects all light, rendering the Nethinim virtually invisible. These suits extend over their long hands and fingers, and are pulled tightly over their heads and silvery hair. A see-through flap can be pulled down to cover their faces, but these are up for now. He looks at their faces. The trace of their braided hair moving back from their foreheads. Their flaring nostrils. Their obedient eyes. He makes final adjustments with his fingers in the plasmastone.

Go, he telesays.

He twists his arms, the far end of the room grows unspeakably frigid, the portals open, shimmery yet dark, like the one that took them to the Great White Pyramid for the Calling. Their suits activate, and the Nethinim all but disappear, their faces floating seven feet above the ground.

Return as soon as you've achieved your objective, he telesays.

Each nods.

Each takes a step backward.

And each disappears completely from the room, and the ship that sits idly in space.

AISLING KOPP, GREG JORDAN, GRIFFIN MARRS

Approaching 45.1646, 98.3167, Govi-Altai Province, Mongolia

"Bum-fuck nowheresville," Jordan says, his feet packing the loose earth one step at a time, his gaze wandering over the high Mongolian desert. "Yeah," Aisling mutters. "This place is *dead*."

More than anything it reminds her of pictures of Mars she's seen over the years—the planet, not her adopted CIA case officer. She suspects that the sloping land in this part of Mongolia is carpeted in stout green grasses at the end of the wet season—and she sees little clumps of dried plant life here and there to support this—but right now it's reddish-whitish-grayish dirt and pebbles and rocks that culminate in a range of stark but beautiful mountains in the near distance. Nowheresville, like Jordan said.

Yet, here they are. While Sarah and Jago and Hilal and Shari are all airborne, Aisling and her team have already touched down in Mongolia and are hoofing it to the Donghu monument to search for Sun Key.

The flight from Thailand took a few hours. It was completely uneventful. There was no turbulence, no sign of Abaddon's aftermath, no problem with ground control systems. The only rough things were landing the plane, which they had to do on a long flat expanse of desert a few miles south of a mountain range, and this hike they've embarked upon to get to the target hidden in said mountain range. Oh, and dealing with Pop.

Aisling had Marrs wake him up before they shoved off. She expected Pop to be groggy and disoriented, but as soon as his eyes opened he pulled at his restraints and his neck muscles trussed his skin and he screamed through his teeth, "Traitor! Traitor! Traitor!"

"Pop!"

"Traitor!" he shouted, picking up right where he'd left off in the bunker in Ayutthaya.

"Hit him with another dose, Marrs," Aisling said quietly. Marrs did and Pop's eyes flagged and his neck relaxed and he slouched. "Shesatraitor, Ais. Donbeonetoo. Dontrussherfriends."

Aisling took one of his hands. "I have to. It's the only way to stop Endgame. Won't you help us?" And then more quietly, "Won't you help me?"

He blinked before saying no.

Aisling hung her head. "I want you to help me, Pop," she said quietly.

"No."

"What else would you have me do?"

"Win."

She looked at the top of Pop's head. Thin white hair, tan scalp, age spots.

"Enough of that already, Pop. Abaddon hit. Our home is probably gone. Shit, all of New York City is probably gone. Who knows how many are dead. No one's winning this thing . . . except maybe the kepler."

"Win. win . . . er try to beat tha Maker but on yer own."

She shook her head and held out her hand. "I'll take it," she said to Marrs. He passed her the syringe that was plugged into Pop's IV. She cradled it in her fingers.

"I know wha yer doin, Ais. Why yer doin it."

"No, you don't, Pop." She put her thumb over the plunger. "I'm doing this for everyone. But mostly I'm doing it for you and for Dad. For Declan."

"Fugh me and fugh Declan. Whadideeno?"

She pushed the plunger all the way in. "He knew more than either of us. I'll see you later, Pop. Sweet dreams."

"Fugh Declan an fugh yoo . . ." And then he was gone once more.

They left him belted down in the plane and took off on foot.

According to Hilal, the Donghu monument is located in a cave at

45.1646, 98.3167, 4.3 miles from where they landed. They walked uphill over mostly open land, and then through a crooked arroyo leading up the mountain like a witch's finger. Aisling enjoys the movement, the sweat, the dry and fresh air in her lungs. She enjoys the desolation, too. The sky is grayish blue, undoubtedly filling with some of the ash and gas and water vapor that Abaddon has thrown to the heavens. On the ground there are no scampering animals, no yurts, no horses or riders, and absolutely no regular people trying to figure out what to do after the impact. No people at all as far as she can tell.

It occurs to Aisling that the men and women who live nomadically in this place—including Baitsakhan's line members—might not be affected by Abaddon at all. They're resourceful, they know hardship and deprivation, and they have a long and unbroken history of survival in a harsh environment. So long as Abaddon doesn't completely cover the sky in clouds for years, these Mongolians and others like them across the Eurasian Steppe and down into the 'Stans should be fine.

After about an hour she stops and checks the GPS. "Got a mile left. How do you think we should approach? If Wayland's men are bent on destroying these places, we have to assume they could be here too."

She glances across the otherworldly landscape.

Jordan points. "Get on that knoll and see what you can see through the scopes. I'll cover."

"Got it," Aisling says.

She and Marrs drop their packs and scramble up a rocky hill. Aisling sights through her sniper's scope as Marrs works with the range finder and his GPS, scouring the mountainside for the cave's exact position. It takes a few minutes, but then he says, "There. A little to your left . . . two degrees higher . . . That's it."

Aisling peers at Marrs's spot. It doesn't look like much. A fold in the side of the rock face about 10 feet above a shallow canyon floor. Marrs says, "A little farther up the canyon are some steps cut from the stone. They're kind of worn, but they're definitely steps."

"Oh, yeah. I see them." Aisling brings her eye away from the scope. "Doesn't look like anyone's there."

"No."

"Guess there's only one way to find out, huh?"

"Yep."

They keep walking.

They make the cave in under an hour, encountering nothing but more rock and dust and the cool air rolling down the mountainside. In spite of the emptiness Aisling scans the surrounding country the whole time, looking for movement, tracks in the dirt, reflections, any pattern that's out of the ordinary. She sees none. But she knows how easy it would be to camouflage oneself in this place.

Too easy.

Before taking the steps up to a ledge-like path, Aisling pops two canisters of tear gas into the cave mouth—a rough and low semicircle whose sides curve inward like an old man's toothless mouth. The gas pours out of the cave and into it at the same time, the canisters hissing.

No one screams, no one runs out.

Aisling pulls on a gas mask. "All right, let's go." She leads them up the steps, a beige FN SCAR pulled to her shoulder. She walks along the narrow ledge, scanning the walls, the ground, the cave's entrance. Something catches her eye. A bright silver hairline near her feet.

She drops to one knee. Jordan stands over her. "What is it?"

Aisling runs her fingers over the dirt. "I swear I saw something," she says. "Trip wire, maybe."

"Where?"

"Right—there!"

It flashes again. It's curled over the ground, not more than a few inches long. "Not a trip wire. Looks like . . . hair." She picks it up and inspects it. "It *is* hair. *Silver* hair."

Jordan pokes his rifle into the cave.

Aisling stands. "The kepler has silver hair," she says slowly.

Neither Jordan nor Marrs says anything to that. None of them want to run into the alien prematurely.

Aisling stands. "Stay loose and let's move."

She ducks into the entrance, which is less than five feet high. Jordan comes next and then Marrs. They walk through the tear gas in an awkward semicrouch for 15 feet before the cave opens up. Light here is scant, so they flip down the goggles on their helmets and activate their night vision.

The chamber is large and round. There are no prehistoric paintings like in the cave in Italy, no signs of previous occupants like a fire pit or footprints, and no seven-foot-tall aliens waiting for them.

It's just a cave.

Except for the perfect and narrow rectangle cut from the stone 34 feet away.

Aisling hoists her rifle and walks to it carefully, testing each step before putting her weight down, eyeing the ground for booby traps or wires.

She reaches the doorway. The ground slopes sharply on the other side through a passage that's the exact dimensions of the door—8 feet high and 2.5 feet wide. Her eyes run up one side, over the top, and down the other. And there, near the ground, she sees two things that nearly stop her heart.

She kneels. Brushes away a pile of dirt collected in the corner.

And yes. There. A small rune of two snakes twisted together, devouring the other's tail.

"The mark of Endgame. Like on Hilal's book," Aisling says. She points at the other thing. The faintest outline of a shoe print. "Looks like we might not be alone after all."

"Let me see," Jordan says.

They switch places while Aisling scans the rest of the floor inside the chamber. "I don't see any others. Whoever it was was good at erasing tracks. No sweep marks . . . no telltale craters or anything."

"Maybe it was a ghost," Marrs says.

"Maybe," Jordan says.

Aisling pushes forward and disappears through the doorway. This time Marrs is second, and Jordan covers the rear.

Down, down, down, 50 feet, 100, 150. As they descend the air gets cooler and damper. The sounds change, as if the walls are sponges soaking up noise.

At the bottom the tunnel makes an abrupt left turn. Aisling stops. She pulls a small pen-sized periscope from her breast pocket and slides it past the edge of the wall. She looks inside.

The tunnel goes a few more paces and then opens into a hard-angled room. It appears empty.

She stashes the periscope and brings the rifle back up and turns the corner. She steps carefully, never letting her heels touch the ground. She checks her corners. Clear. She steps forward again.

Jordan squeezes her shoulder. She stops. It is very cold here, and the night vision shows that the room is somehow illuminated. She risks flipping her goggles up, and yes, the room's walls glow with a faint blue phosphorescent light. There's a round, bowl-shaped depression in the center of the room, its surface covered with shiny metallic leaf. She pulls out a flashlight and shines its white beam into the bowl.

Gold.

They split up and look around.

The room is shaped like a six-pointed star, with one of the inward-facing points blunt and flat. Another doorway—a portal, it appears—is surrounded by more mysterious glyphs, though she recognizes some as Egyptian and Sumerian and an old version of her line's written language as well. She runs her hands over these. Her breath hangs thick in the air. This portal reminds her exactly of the one set into the Great White Pyramid in the Qin Lin Mountains.

She touches the jet-black stone in the middle of the doorway, half expecting her hand to pass through it.

But it doesn't.

It's rock hard and freezing and her hand recoils from the cold.

"What do you think? Twenty degrees in here? Less?" Aisling asks.

But no one answers. Marrs is too busy searching the opposite side of the room and Jordan inches toward something tucked into one of the corners.

"Come here," he whispers, his voice slithering around in a bit of acoustic gymnastics. "You should see this."

Jordan stares at four tubelike objects. They're the size of people and they're stacked like logs, one on top of the other.

"Holy shit," Aisling says. She tiptoes past him. She shivers. The air near the tubes is well below zero. "kepler 22b stacked us up in these shroud things at the pagoda in Xi'an. He's been here recently."

"What're you talking about?" Jordan asks.

Using the muzzle of her rifle Aisling catches the edge of the nearest tube and lifts it away. The other side of the material is covered with a dark, glittering surface, like a star-filled night sky. Inside the tube is the face of a corpse, his skin blue and pale, his eye sockets large and set farther apart than most people's.

"That looks like one of the guys who stormed Stella's bunker," Aisling says.

Jordan slips the knife between the man's lips and pries his jaw open. He has no tongue.

"A Nethinim. Definitely one of Wayland's guards." Jordan peels back more of the shroud. The man is dressed in full tactical gear, his hands resting on the receiver of a Bushmaster ACR.

"I meant to ask before—why do they not exactly look . . . human?"

"They are human, but Wayland messed with their genetics to make them appear more like Makers. These men were here to destroy this place, Aisling. Like they destroyed Stonehenge and the other monuments too."

"To wit," Marrs says from across the room. "Check it out."

Aisling and Jordan quickly cross the chamber to find Marrs tucked into a star-point near the portal. He's hunched over something, his rifle slung at his side, his hands working in front of him.

"What is it?" Aisling asks, her eyes glancing all around nervously.

"A bomb," Marrs says casually.

"What?"

"Don't worry. It's been disarmed. Strange design. Looks like PETN is the main explosive, but I haven't seen one configured like this before. And here—" He points at a metal panel on the side.

The same glyph that marked the threshold in the room above.

Jordan points at the bomb. "So 22b came down here from wherever he is, killed Wayland's guys, and broke up their bomb. I thought he was only supposed to come back to wrap up Endgame?"

"He was," Aisling says. "Apparently the rules of the game have changed for him too."

Marrs stands and faces them. "Why would he do any of that? Seems risky."

"Because Sun Key is here?" Jordan asks.

Aisling shakes her head slowly. "I don't know. It doesn't look like it. Maybe he took it with him?"

"But why go through the trouble is what I mean," Marrs says.

"It's like Stella and Hilal said—one of these places has Sun Key, therefore 22b can't sit on his thumbs while they're getting blown up by a band of Maker-looking humans loyal to Stella's dead father. So he decided to come here and put a stop to it."

Marrs snaps his fingers. "Aisling—what if Endgame has run so far off the rails for him that he's getting *nervous*?"

This feels like a revelation. Aisling says excitedly, "Yeah . . . What if he feels squeezed by Wayland's demolition crew on one side and us on the other? What if he thinks Endgame won't have a winner, and for some reason that's not acceptable? He could be out there doing whatever it takes to make sure Maccabee is crowned the winner, since Maccabee is the only one interested in winning the way he's supposed to. 22b could be bringing Maccabee Sun Key *right now*, killing whichever other Player he comes across along the way, killing Wayland's men too, interfering even more than he did when—"

Her jaw drops open.

"What?" Jordan asks.

"Fuck."

"What?"

"What if 22b finds our plane? What if he finds Pop? I thought he was safe out there, but . . ."

Aisling doesn't wait. She bolts out of the chamber, Jordan and Marrs following. Up, up, up through the tunnel, outside, off the ledge, double-timing it down the arroyo toward the plane. Aisling is in much better shape and she wants to get her legs into a dead run and Jordan yells, "Go!" and she takes off and within 15 minutes she's not much more than a speck to Jordan and Marrs.

Her pack digs at her shoulders and bounces painfully on the base of her back. Her rifle is heavy and after an hour and 20 minutes her arms are leaden and she has to slow down, but she's a lot closer. She stops for a moment behind a boulder and checks the GPS: 0.74 miles to the plane.

Have a look first, Ais. Fools rush in.

She gets on top of the boulder and surveys the flat section of desert where they landed. The scope zips over the Bombardier and her nerves ease up. It's there. It isn't a smoldering pile of scrap metal. She moves the scope back and finds it and zeroes in.

And then her heart nearly jumps out of her chest and through her shirt.

The plane is where they left it. It's not engulfed in flames. Its tires are fully inflated. Its door is closed.

But its wings are lying on the ground. They have been cut off clean and neat by who knows what and they are lying on the ground.

Aisling spits a string of curses. She puts her eye back to the socket and looks everywhere for 22b but sees no sign of anything. She scans and scans and scans.

She slides down the boulder and paces and breathes and tries to calm her heart and finally after 15 minutes she hears the noisy footsteps of

Jordan and Marrs approaching. She tells them the news.

"And Pop?" Jordan asks, badly concealing his disappointment at losing the plane.

"Don't know," Aisling says, her voice shaking. "I've been waiting for you before going down there. I think you should stay here and cover with the long guns. I'll go alone. You can run if things go south."

Marrs quickly says, "Not alone, Aisling." Jordan charges a round into his rifle in agreement.

She doesn't argue. They strip their gear to the essentials and a few minutes later, as the sun begins to cradle into the horizon, they take off.

They triple-time, guns up the whole way. When they're 500 feet from the plane they fan out, Aisling in the center and Jordan and Marrs 30 feet on either side. She moves up a little so they form a three-point wedge. She looks and looks in the late evening twilight.

Nothing.

They reach the plane. Aisling's heart has never beaten so fast. Marrs gawks at the wings, thinking, *It's as if lasers cut them.*

Aisling indicates the plane's door with her rifle, signaling that she'll cover Jordan while he opens it.

Jordan nods. Marrs moves into a cover position too. The door swings down and the stairs fold out.

More nothing.

Aisling forces her legs forward, her heart in her throat, and bounds silently up the stairs and clears the cockpit and pivots into the cabin.

Empty.

Empty except for Pop Kopp. She slides to him, checking behind seats. Clear. She kneels next to him. Feels his arm. Warm. The pulse is there. His breath is good. Yes, he's against everything she's trying to do in Endgame, but he's alive, and that's what matters.

She goes back to the door. "He's all right," she says.

A chill wind blows from the south.

Marrs says, "Good."

And then it gets very cold and a ring-shaped pulse tears the air between the three of them and it hits Marrs in a millisecond and he gets pushed back a few feet as if he's been punched in the chest and then he kind of disappears, leaving a few shreds of cloth and metal and probably skin too but no blood, and all of these pieces blow away and are gone.

Aisling and Jordan fire at will at the spot where the pulse came from. The rounds bounce away and some seem to be absorbed into the air itself, or the dirt, or the rocks, Aisling can't really tell. She breathes out and sees her breath in the chilly air and Jordan shouts, "Fire in the hole!" and he pumps out one, two, three grenades from his launcher, and somehow all three are caught by a huge invisible hand, and they explode, and Aisling hears the explosions, but it's like they went off miles away or underwater, and she can't see them. Not at all.

And then another pulse, this one aimed at Jordan, who fires a fourth grenade at the same moment, and this one does explode as expected and Aisling is thrown backward into the plane and she can't see what's happening to Jordan, if he was vaporized too or blown up or knocked on his ass like her. She kicks her feet in front of her and scoots backward. Her back hits the far side of the cabin and the open door is in front of her and her heart booms all over now, in her temples and toes and armpits. The air shimmers and her feet are like ice and only then does she realize that 22b is invisible and right in front of her! She presses the trigger and holds it down and the bullets simply hit 22b and slide around him and continue off into space, as if he's Teflon coated.

Her magazine is empty. Her trigger finger aches. Firing the grenade would be suicidal.

But if she's going to die anyway, she might as well try to kill this fucker too.

She applies pressure to the grenade's trigger as the pale face of an alien—not 22b, but one of his kind—appears in front of her like a phantom. And before she can squeeze all the way, the world goes light and dark simultaneously and she's gone.

All she's aware of in that last moment is the cold.

The terrible, terrible, freezing cold.

19h 16m 52.2s[ii]

HILAL IBN ISA AL-SALT, SHARI CHOPRA

Approaching -21.6268, 129.6625, Yuendumu Hinterland, Northern Territory, Australia

Hilal and Shari walk southeast through the red sand grassland of the Australian outback. Nighttime. No people. No moon. No breeze. They weave through stands of mulga trees and creep around mounds of grassy spinifex, some of which look like earthbound corals. They walk silently, listening to the clicks and coos of insects and bats and other small animals plying the night for food and shelter.

The stars are out, and they are brilliant. The duo's eyes have adjusted from the inside of the plane, which they left 4.7 kilometers to the north, and the starlight is all they need.

Hilal has been to the southern hemisphere many times—to the bush of Zimbabwe and Mozambique and Botswana—but he has never seen stars like this.

He would talk to Shari about the stars if she had not ordered him to be silent before they set out for the ancient Koori monument. "I am angry beyond angry at you, Aksumite."

He did not argue with her. If he were in her position it would take every ounce of his will not to slaughter him where he stands.

But the stars. If he could talk he would point out Achernar, a few degrees above the horizon, the final star in the wandering constellation of Eridanus. Next to it, rising from the earth itself, the Phoenix takes wing. And to their right is Acrux, the bright white star that anchors the Southern Cross. From this constellation he arches his head back and follows the glowing swath of innumerable pinpricks and pink and blue and yellow clouds that stitch the heart of the Milky

Way together. There is the Centaur, and Lupus the hound, and Norma and Circinus and Ara, and directly overhead are Scorpius and the archer, Sagittarius. Between these are the thickest and brightest star clouds, marking the center of our galaxy, 26,092 light-years away. If he were speaking to his companion he would spin around and point his machetes toward Vega, which glows brightly, even through the Abaddon dust that begins to sully the northern and western skies. This star belongs to the constellation Lyra, and flying next to it is the long-necked swan, Cygnus.

He would talk about all of them.

Of course Shari is probably equally enthralled and knowledgeable. Maybe she looks up and places her departed loved ones among the stars. Certainly she hopes that she can save her Little Alice from returning to these stars.

For that is where they will ultimately return, just as it is from where they ultimately came.

To the stars. From the stars. Like every atom of every thing.

Shari is 10 paces in front of him and she comes to a sudden stop. Hilal cocks an ear but only hears the same thriving nocturnal buzz of the bush that has accompanied them since the plane.

Before leaving their Bombardier Global 8000, they consulted Wayland's book to see if any ancient monuments had been destroyed or otherwise affected by Abaddon. The book showed that the Olmec monument had indeed been damaged, as well as the Minoan monument, which was curious since it was so far from the impact zone. Hilal reasoned that perhaps Wayland's brotherhood had reached it and converted it to ruins.

Shari didn't appear to care.

"All I want is to see my daughter and hold her in my arms."

Again, Hilal could not argue with that.

But he is not thinking about that right now. He wonders what Shari senses as they stand stock-still in the Australian outback. She carries a holstered Glock 20 and pistol-grip Mossberg 500 Cruiser tactical shotgun. Hilal clutches a suppressed Colt M4 Commando in his right hand and the machete named *LOVE* in his left. The other machete is sheathed on his hip. He also carries Wayland's book in his pack. It is too precious to leave anywhere.

Shari kneels and runs her fingers over the dirt. She inches forward without standing. Hilal doesn't move. The ground underfoot slopes toward a dense thicket of wanderrie wattle that they can't see past. Shari points at the ground, running her finger in a straight line.

Hilal sees it. Two grooves etched in the parched dirt, joining in a point at Shari's feet. The grooves run as straight as arrows, the angle between them appearing to be exactly 60 degrees. Inside these lines is the gnarled and dense shrub, outside is sand and earth.

"It is in there," Hilal whispers. "We need to find the entrance."

Shari holds out her shotgun, indicating that she wants Hilal to take the lead. He does this without thinking twice. He knows that a large part of Shari wants him dead, and he will not fault her at all if she decides to strike him down.

He will accept it as a price paid.

But she does not strike him down.

He walks due south, toward the Large Magellanic Cloud seeping over the horizon like a milk stain. The two Players curve around the edge of dense wattle. Hilal sees that the grooves in the ground depict a star, such as one would find on the Seal of Solomon, roughly 30 meters in diameter. As they reach the northern side of this star the earth rises on their left to head height, forming an amphitheater for the star shape, and when they reach the northern star-point they find a low but clear path through the plantlike wall.

They will have to crawl.

Hilal takes off his pack and disappears into the thicket. Shari follows him immediately.

Half a minute later they emerge not in a star-shaped interior, but in a 15-meter circle created by the foliage. They stand on the edge of this circle, shoulder to shoulder, and Hilal is almost afraid to step forward.

Both he and Shari know that they are in a sacred place.
Luckily, they appear to be the only ones there. No members of Wayland's brotherhood. No Koori men and women guarding it. Strangely, the sounds of the outback that were so present outside the thicket are nonexistent here. The breeze that brushed over their faces from the west is gone. The fine sand underfoot is pebble- and rock-free and has recently been swept by a rake, making a pattern of centimeter-wide concentric circles whose center is the ancient and gnarled trunk of a dead tree. This rises two meters from a bowl-shaped depression. The inside of the bowl appears to be coated in a metallic substance.

"This is the place Stella told me about," Hilal whispers. He steps forward. The ridges and valleys of the circles drawn in the ground are flattened and rearranged into a bootprint. Hilal adjusts his grip on the machete named *LOVE*. Shari stays rooted to her spot.

A sudden sound overhead, like the wind has picked up. The air grows perceptibly colder. A dark flicker like a bird taking wing at eye-level. Hilal raises his machete and wheels, and Shari spins in a semicircle, flashing her shotgun, but both are caught off guard as the bush itself comes to life.

Hilal is grabbed at each wrist and his arms are yanked outward, like Christ on the cross. He tries to kick, but a snare has jumped from the dirt and encircled his ankles. Strong hands twist his weapons backward, forcing him to release them. His other machete is lifted out of its sheath, and just like that he is unarmed. He is bound, his back brushing up against the coarse leaves of the shrub.

He would call out to warn Shari, but he can see that she is already similarly incapacitated.

All of this happens in less than three seconds, and all of it without a sound save that of a few rustling branches and their leaves.

Hilal feels a warm breath on his neck. A blade—one of his own—flashes below his face and he feels the hairline metallic edge grace his Adam's apple.

"Wait," Hilal says.

The metal pushes into his flesh.

"Kill me if you must, but please spare the other. Shari Chopra is her name. The Harappan. She was friends with Alice Ulapala, your line member. Shari is mother to Sky Key. She deserves the chance to see her daughter again."

The metal pushes in more. Hilal feels a bead of warm blood trickle down his neck and settle in his suprasternal notch.

"Stop," a raspy female voice says.

The blade is removed. Hilal would fall if the hands restraining him did not prop him up.

A diminutive elderly woman in jeans and a dark windbreaker stands next to the tree trunk, her hands thrust into her jacket's pockets. Her head is wrapped in a white bandanna, her face is pudgy and round, its skin crumpled, her nose turnip-like, her eyes bright and beady. Flanking her are two large figures, presumably men, dressed head to toe in branches and leaves. They look like living bushes. Hilal scans the circle and now understands that the entire interior was lined with these unspeaking sentinels. Three stand around him, and two around Shari, who kneels on his right, her arms also pulled wide, a knifepoint dimpling her temple.

The old woman waves at Shari. "Easy," she says. The knife retreats.

"Show me Chopra's face," the old woman says with a broad Australian accent.

A light shines on Shari. She blinks.

"That's her." The woman pokes out her blunt chin. The light goes off. "I seen you in the Dreaming. Seen your daughter too," the old Koori says. "Been watching yours since Alice zoned in on her. I seen both you and your daughter when Alice died."

"Where is Little Alice?" Shari demands.

"Dunno. Wish I did. Truly."

Pause.

"I was there," Shari says slowly. "In that dream. I saw Alice die, too."

"That's the Dreaming all right. You and yours were there like me. Difference was I went there on purpose, whereas you two ended up there on account of, I'm thinking what I'll call your *innate* abilities. That or luck."

"It is never auspicious to see a friend die," Shari says as much to herself as to the old woman.

"Good words," the elder says approvingly.

Shari shakes her head. "You've seen me before, then?"

"Yeah."

"I haven't seen you, though."

"Nope."

Shari says, "I . . . don't understand . . ."

"You tried to save Alice from that little Donghu brute—remember that?"

"When I saw her die?"

"That's right, Shari. But while it looked and felt like a dream, it also happened to be—"

"Real," Shari says, her eyes cast to the ground.

"Yeah," the old woman says, her voice low and sad.

"I'm sorry. I tried—"

"Weren't nothing you could do. Me neither. We were like ghosts. That's the Dreaming for you."

"I would have helped her if I could," Shari says quietly.

"And me too. Like I said, that's the Dreaming for you."

Hilal says, "Madam, I am sure that I do not understand any of this."

The old woman says, "No, you wouldn't."

"She's related to Alice," Shari explains to Hilal. "I'm guessing."

"You're guessing right."

Shari continues, "Alice and I had a connection. I can't explain it, but it was there. It was real."

Hilal says, "I see. Madam, may I ask your name?"

"Sure you could *ask*." She snickers. "Don't have to answer, though.

But since Alice and Shari were mates, I'll tell ya. Name's Jenny. Jenny Ulapala. Gram to Alice, among a couple dozen others. Elder scion of the Koori line, even out here in Yuendumu, where our Warlpiri sisters and brothers keep themselves and the land."

"My name is Hilal ibn Isa al-Salt, the—"

"I know—the Aksumite. And she's the Harappan. The one who lost her daughter for no damn good reason that I can fathom."

"Don't kill me, Mrs. Ulapala," Shari says a little out of the blue.

"Not planning on it," Jenny says.

The guards release Shari's restraints. The knife that was pressed to her head disappears into a sheath.

The old woman says, "Not sure about you, though. What do you say, Shari?"

Hilal's heart skips a beat. Shari has found a new ally. She might not need him anymore.

Hilal would plead for mercy, but he knows it would be unbecoming. He also understands that, from Shari's perspective, he more than deserves her wrath. He was the one who revealed her line's secret fortress to the other Players, who used that information to kill nearly all of them.

"He . . ." Shari says. "He . . . I want him dead."

"All right," the old woman says.

The blade returns to Hilal's neck and presses into the nick that was made moments before. More blood trickles down his skin.

He closes his eyes. He does not want death, but he will accept it.

"But you should not kill him," Shari says at the last moment.

Hilal's eyes shoot open, Jenny flicks her hand, the knife moves away, his life is spared.

For now.

"I suppose I will need all the help I can get to see my daughter again," Shari explains. "I would rather use your guilt to that end, Hilal, than succumb to base revenge."

Hilal lets out a quiet sigh of relief. "Understood. And I am grateful, Shari."

A moment passes. The stars turn.

Jenny says, "I'm curious. Abaddon is down. My Player is gone. Why are the two of you here, together?"

"Because we have seen enough of Endgame," Shari says. "We do not want it anymore. The lines don't deserve it, and the people of Earth don't deserve it either."

"And we are here because we want to find her daughter," Hilal says with as much sincerity—because he *is* sincere—as he can muster. "We want to stop Endgame, Mrs. Ulapala. Shari and the Cahokian and the Olmec and the La Tène want this as well. We are working together. We do not Play for what the Makers wanted us to Play for. Not anymore."

Jenny frowns but she has clearly listened carefully. "What do you Play for, then?"

"Many have gone to the stars today," Hilal says. "I do not know the magnitude of Abaddon's destruction, but I feel that it is great. Now we Play to save lives. To prevent more from returning to the stars. Together we can achieve this. We have power and we have knowledge. We even have something that belonged to the Makers."

"Whachya mean?"

"It is in my pack," Hilal says.

"He's telling the truth," Shari says.

"If there's something in your pack you'll have to get it yourself, Aksumite." One of his machetes whips down on the cord around his left wrist and it is free. A guard gingerly holds open his pack at arm's length. "No malarkey," Jenny says. Hilal feels the cold ring of a gun barrel pressed to the back of his head, behind where his ear used to be. "None," Hilal says. "I swear it."

He reaches, feels the cold edge of the book, and slowly pulls it free. "It is merely a book. A Maker book from the first days. I invite you to inspect it." He holds it by one of the covers and lets it fall open. "It is harmless."

Jenny leans forward. "Bring it here."

The guard drops the pack, takes the book, and walks to Jenny. The gun stays pressed to Hilal's head. His skin warms the metal.

The guard holds the book open in both hands. Jenny turns its pages slowly. She leans forward. Squints. Shines a light on it. After a few moments she glares at Hilal. "Where did you get this?"

"From a man named Wayland Vyctory."

Jenny grunts. Hilal guesses that she knows who this man is. "You read this book already?" Jenny asks.

"What? No," Hilal says. "I cannot."

"And you, Shari?"

Shari shakes her head.

"Can *you*?" Hilal asks.

Jenny takes the book from the guard and shoos him aside. She continues to leaf through the pages. "You have all heard of the Mu, have you not?"

"Of course," Hilal says. "Their Player was exemplary by all accounts."

"They like to claim their line's the first, only 'tain't true. Oh, their line is old—going back twenty, twenty-five thousand years and more than any of yours. But my line, *we're* the oldest. My people been walking these lands on foot and in the Dreaming for forty, fifty, sixty thousand years. That's when the Baiame—the Makers—first came down and met with *us. We're* the original line. We just don't like to brag about it."

"Chiyoko did not brag," Hilal points out.

Jenny says, "Good on her . . ." Uneasy silence falls as Jenny continues to peruse the pages. "Flames above, do you know what this is, Players?"

"What?" Shari asks.

Jenny smirks. "It's an instruction manual. Called *Domination*, roughly translated. Here are some section headings, and these are only guesses, because their language is very odd: 'Explaining Flight to Earth Beings,' 'Modern Deification,' 'Images and Idols,' 'Metals Primer,' 'Genetic Lines of Establishment,' 'Fear for the Sake of Good.' It goes on and on."

Hilal brims with excitement. That there is a person alive who can decipher this text is magnificent.

He can tell by her voice that Shari feels the same. "Mrs. Ulapala," she says respectfully, urgently, "*will you help us?*"

Jenny closes the book and tucks it under her arm casually. She takes a step back. "Let 'em go, boys. Keep their weapons. One false move and kill, no questions."

Their bindings come free, the gun is removed from Hilal's head. Shari is pulled to her feet. Jenny retreats another step into the shadow of the old tree trunk.

"What're you here to do?"

"Try to find Sun Key before the Nabataean does," Shari says.

"He alone Plays the way the Makers want," Hilal says. "He has the first two keys. He is close to winning."

Jenny nods slowly. "I know. I seen as much in the Dreaming. It's why we're here guarding this place now. To make sure the Nabataean didn't claim his prize."

"We're also here to save my child," Shari says, her voice measured and firm.

Jenny smacks her lips. "There are no guarantees there, Shari. Like any of us, your daughter could die a thousand different ways in the next day or week. But I am glad to hear you're lookin' for her. Big Alice would be glad too."

"Thank you," Shari says.

Jenny's shoulders slacken. "Too much violence these days, if you ask me. Since I got properly old I kinda soured on Endgame. I been telling the Koori about it for a while, but I've always been a bit of an odd bird." The bush-covered guards retreat to the edge of the circle as if on cue and seem to disappear. "Listen, now. I have a proposition like. And it will require a thing much more hard to come by than violence."

"Trust," Hilal says.

Jenny dips her head in his direction. "Trust, Aksumite. Line to line,

182

human to human." Then, her head slowly turns to Shari. "And, most importantly, mother to mother."

The stars turn overhead. The Milky Way pulses with an untold amount of life, even if it is cold and distant and unobservable. Hilal can feel it.

"I'll help you. And together we'll try to Dream Little Alice Chopra right on back into her mother's arms."

The air grows warmer, and Hilal again hears the breeze, where before he heard nothing of the world.

Jenny grins kindly at Shari. The old woman only has a few teeth left.

"We'll get you your girl, mum," Jenny says. "Promise."

SARAH ALOPAY, JAGO TLALOC, SIMON ALOPAY

Monks Mound, Collinsville, Illinois, United States

Sarah holds on to her father so, so tightly. She can't breathe. Excitement. Relief. The improbable—no, the *impossible*—good fortune of crossing paths with him.

And judging by how tightly Simon holds on to her, he feels exactly the same way.

After several moments Jago clears his throat. Sarah eases up on her embrace and Simon pulls away from his daughter, holds her by the shoulders. Jago looks this way and that, watching for any movement on the horizon, his gun reloaded and ready.

"What did you do to your hair?" Simon whispers, staring into his daughter's eyes.

"Disguise. After the Shang showed us in his video."

"Of course. With Abaddon and Yellowstone and everything else, I'd actually forgotten about that video."

"It's all kind of overwhelming, isn't it?"

"I can't imagine what it's like back east," Simon says.

"Me either. Don't want to, frankly."

"It is hell, we all know it," Jago interjects.

Simon's gaze shifts to Jago. His eyebrows scrunch. "And you are?"

"Jago Tlaloc. The Olmec. Sarah's . . . friend."

Simon steps back defensively and puts a hand on a black pistol holstered to his hip. Jago doesn't flinch. Sarah claps her hand on top of Simon's gun hand, squeezes his knuckles. "It's all right. He *is* my friend. He's saved my life more than once. He's here to help."

Simon's eyes dart back and forth—Sarah, Jago, Sarah, Jago—as he tries to decipher what's happening. "Why are you *here*?" Simon asks Sarah. "Do you have the keys? Are you ready to end it?"

"No. It's a long story, but basically we're here because we need to find the third key. According to some people who seem to know, it could be hiding in there." She points at the grass-covered hill that is Monks Mound.

"Sun Key's in there?" Simon says. "I've been in there a hundred times. Sun Key is not in there."

"We still have to look," Sarah says. "If we have any chance of stopping Endgame then we have to find it. It's the best chance we have at surviving. And by 'we' I mean humanity, Dad. All of us. You. Me. Jago. Pricks like these," she motions to the bikers littered around their feet.

"Mom . . ." Her face goes white.

"She's fine, Sarah."

"Omaha?" she asks.

"No. The farm. She's there with your uncles and Aunt Millicent and also a few neighbors from home. We couldn't leave them behind to fend for themselves. We brought the Smithsons and the Nixes and the—"

"Vanderkamps?" she asks, a big part of her hoping he'll say, *No, not the Vanderkamps.*

"Yeah, the Vanderkamps too," Simon says. "I thought they would hole up at one of their ranches, but they didn't want to be alone. Especially not after, well . . ."

"What?"

"It's Christopher. He . . . disappeared. Not long after you left. I'm sorry, Sarah."

She falters. Jago reaches out and touches her arm.

I'm going to have to tell them. His parents. I'm going to have to tell them what I did to their son.

"I'm sorry," Simon repeats. He can tell something isn't right, but he doesn't press.

"It's okay," Sarah says.

186

Jago peers to the east. "A car's coming. We should move."

"Yeah, of course." She holds out her hands. "Dad, will you come with us? Will you help?"

"Search the mound for Sun Key?" he asks.

"Yes," she says. "But before that, we need to do something else."

"Sarah, come *on*," Jago says urgently. He points through the haze. A pair of bright halogen lights is headed right for them, but not with any apparent urgency. "Probably nothing to worry about, but we *are* standing in the middle of a murder scene. No point in asking for more trouble."

"Agreed. We didn't come here to kill people," she says, as much to herself as to Jago. *That was so easy,* she thinks of killing the bikers. *Too easy. If I really am going to get back my humanity, I need to work harder at sparing people. Even people like these.* Especially *people like these.*

"Are our line members at the welcome center?" Sarah asks her father.

"No. I told them to be with their families before the impact. I told them I was on my way here and that they weren't needed anymore."

"Good," Sarah says. "Get the bike, Jago." He pivots and runs to the Harley. "Let me help you with your passenger, Dad."

She moves around the Taurus and takes one of the giant's ankles with her good hand. Simon takes the other. They heave in unison, pulling hard on over 270 pounds of dead weight. But Sarah and her father are strong, and they get the giant out of the car. What's left of his head makes a sickening *smack-pop-hiss* when it hits the pavement.

Jago pulls up next to them. "Go to the welcome center," Sarah shouts over the bike's engine, indicating a building off the main road to the south. Jago guns the bike and leaves them. Simon slips around the front of the car and gets behind the wheel while Sarah climbs into the backseat, where the seats are blood-free.

"We're going to stop Endgame, Dad." She speaks quickly, hoping Simon won't interrupt her. "We're working with other Players and some CIA guys. A woman named Stella Vyctory was helping us too, but she was killed. The Makers may have been gods to us once, but not anymore. They're frauds. Maybe we all are."

She takes a breath and holds it. *Here it comes.* She expects him to rail against her, to remind her of their history, of her training, of the honor of being named and molded into a Player, of her dead brother, of her dead friends, of her destroyed school, of the old stories and the rituals and the rites and *ahama muhu gobekli mu, ahaman jeje, ahaman kerma.*

And while she waits for it she remembers what she said on that commencement stage in the sun, right before the meteors came, when she was still young and innocent as well.

I choose to be the person that I want to be, she'd said. Those words felt so meaningless after finding Earth Key, and then again so true as she chose not to kill Sky Key.

What a fucking ride it's been, she thinks, waiting for Simon to light into her.

Except he doesn't.

She looks in the rearview mirror and finds her father's eyes. He looks at her, not the road. Jago banks the bike into a parking lot in front of them. Simon blinks. He follows the Harley.

Sarah leans into the front half of the car. "Dad, why are *you* here?"

"Because I'm scared, Sarah."

"Of what?"

"Maybe of what you're hinting at."

"The Makers . . ."

Simon shrugs. "At the worst, yes. But also of people. Of uncertainty. Of *that.*" He tilts his head to the east, to Abaddon. "Let's not kid ourselves. None of us ever thought we'd see it. No Player or trainer really does, and now that I *have* seen it I understand why we thought we never would."

He pulls next to Jago in a handicap spot right next to the entrance. Jago is already off the bike and stalking to the welcome center, gun up, to clear it of anyone else who might be hanging around.

A crack of bright lightning near the mound. A loud clap of thunder shakes the car. A gust of cold wind.

Simon runs his hands nervously over the top of the steering wheel.

"Why am I here? Because once Abaddon happened all I could think of was keeping what's left of my family and my friends safe, and—" The corners of his mouth crumple. His eyes well. "You look so much older, Sarah."

She touches his cheek. "You too, Dad."

"Grown-up, huh?"

"I guess. Mostly just fucking exhausted, mentally and physically."

"Me too. Maybe that's all it means to be grown-up."

Pause.

"I'm so glad I found you," Simon says. "Me and your mother, not an hour has passed since you've left that we haven't spoken of you. We think about you always. Hoped you were alive, hoped you were Playing, or at least surviving."

"You trained me well."

"I know. Now I understand why. It wasn't because I wanted Endgame or even cared for the prophecy, if you can believe it. It was because I wanted to protect you. You'd been chosen and I wanted to give you the tools you'd need to survive, whether the prophecy came true or not. But lucky us . . ."

"Yeah, lucky us."

Jago emerges from the welcome center, giving a thumbs-up.

Simon grabs one of Sarah's hands. "I came here to get the weapon, Sarah. The one the stories tell of, the one the Makers gave us and showed us how to use. If I'm going to continue to protect the ones I love, then your mom and I thought we should have it."

"No shit," Sarah says.

Simon doesn't understand.

"I'm not being flip, Dad. The weapon? That's why we're here too. If we're going to ever cross paths with a Maker—and before this thing is through, we might—then we want it too."

Simon smiles wanly. "I really *did* train you well."

Jago raps a knuckle on the passenger window. Simon rolls it down.

Jago leans in. "Done catching up?"

"More or less," Sarah says.

Jago looks at Simon. "You going to help us, Señor Alopay?"

Simon reaches for Sarah's shoulder and kneads it lovingly.

His thin smile melts away as his eyes darken. "Let's get our gun."

Event 17[iii]

AISLING KOPP, POP KOPP, KEPLER 22B

Seedrak Sare'en, active geosynchronous orbit above the Martian North Pole

Ssssssup!

Aisling can't see but she can hear.

Her head swims, her eyes flutter, her quads twitch, her fingers clench into fists. She feels light and upside-down and twisted and her stomach turns and she strains forward to let it out but her entire body—stretched long from head to toe, her arms pressed to her sides—is locked in place.

The vomit comes anyway. Her last meal and some cashew nuts and water and bile. Mostly bile. The vomit doesn't fall onto her shirt or her shoes or across her face. It doesn't linger on her lips, she doesn't have to lick it away, it doesn't get stuck in her nose or entangled in her hair. She realizes that that sucking sound has whisked the vomit away. She realizes that her face is covered with something—a mask, a skin, a device, she's not sure what. She tries to turn her head but can't. She tries to move her legs but can't. She tries to scream but can't. The intent is there, the neurons are firing, the synapses are transmitting, the axons and dendrites are twinkling, the brain is converting her disorientation into fear, but there is no release, no flight, no fight.

Because she can't.

There is only her body, and her clouded mind, and the darkness, and her fear.

And more bile.

Ssssssup!

Gone.

An electric pulse shoots through her body, from bottom to top. She senses it most in her toes and behind her knees and under her triceps and at the base of her neck and then at the tip of her tongue. In a fit of synesthesia she experiences the pulse as color and taste. Blue at first, bursting and bright, imploding from the edge and flying toward the center and consuming everything. The blue spikes with fingers of red then purple then orange and then a blob of green that eats all the other colors away. While these kaleidoscope through her visual cortex, her taste buds are subjected to an onslaught of milky sweetness, to the point of being disgusting, and she retches again and vomits whatever might be left in her stomach into the tube.

Sssssssup.

She flicks her tongue and finds that it's blocked by something, that it can't reach her teeth or her gums, and in this instant she realizes that a tube has been inserted into her mouth, and her tongue is inside the tube. She swallows and feels an extension of the tube in her throat. And then a thought forms—the first not dedicated to her body or her senses or to her primal fear.

Where am I?

For some indeterminate amount of time she is unsure. She remembers Mongolia perfectly—Marrs's vaporization, Jordan's last volley, the cool face of the kepler who wasn't 22b, the frigid air that enveloped her— but there is nothing after that. She is a prisoner, of that she has no doubt, but where, and what exactly, is her cell?

An inkling of an answer comes when she finally discerns something. Several feet from her face the light changes, and she makes out the hazy contours of a ceiling. It is curved and reflective and liquidy. Wisps of white and yellow trace across it, and a tuft of red and a fun-house mirror blob of blue. A reflection. She squints through the film covering her face and understands that the red is her hair, and the tube is her body, shrink-wrapped in an unknown material.

She tries to move again but can't. It's not so much that she's being restrained as it is that her body simply doesn't work. Her toes and her tongue and her eyeballs in their sockets can move when she wills them to, but none very well.

She strains to look in as many directions as possible. She eventually sees that another form is some distance to her left, topped by white instead of red. This must be Pop. Her fear is nearly all-consuming, tinged with a small offering of relief in this moment. She is not completely alone. Pop is not dead. Or if he is, his body is intact. *Maybe I am dead,* she half thinks. *Certainly as good as dead.*

There is nothing else. Seconds or minutes or hours or days pass. She can't tell. The slivers of color on the ceiling change now and then, like a psychedelic dream. Something shoots through the tube and passes tastelessly over her tongue and passes directly into her stomach. Food. The electrical pulses tickling her body come and go. She is powerless, and afraid, but she settles into her predicament as best she can. What else can she do?

She drifts here and there and in and out and then . . .

Then . . .

Then . . .

Her eyes tear up and shoot open and in front of her is not the ceiling or the wall but the unmistakable face of kepler 22b, lithe and blue and cold.

The alien busies its hands over her body, tending to unseen controls. His dark eyes are blank, his mouth slightly agape. She tries to make a noise but it's useless. kepler 22b certainly doesn't make any noises.

He does whatever he does and lifts away, apparently satisfied. Aisling's mind begins to cloud again. She's been injected with something. The sickly sweet taste returns. kepler 22b spins away and speaks—no, he doesn't speak, he thinks. Aisling can hear his words not as language but as ideas, clear and completely comprehensible.

She is strong, and the grandfather holds on. Both survived the transport. We hope the other two will survive as well. We hope we can retrieve our weapon.

It cannot hurt that we have more Player-hostages, Nethinim. More will be better.

SARAH ALOPAY, JAGO TLALOC, SIMON ALOPAY

Monks Mound, Collinsville, Illinois, United States

Sarah and Jago follow Simon along the groomed walking paths that loop around the smaller hillocks south of Monks Mound, and then beat a track through a stand of leafy hardwoods. Each wears a respirator and goggles and carries a compact M4—Jago's with an M203 grenade launcher—and a blade.

Simon consults a small laminated map the size of a credit card. Although it's midday it looks and feels like a cloudy evening, one where a storm is on the horizon or has just passed. And while they know the sun is high overhead, the yellow disc is blotted out by the ash and gas choking the atmosphere. The lights of houses and buildings in the middle distance are extinguished, the power still out. People are somewhere out there, huddled inside and confused, but for now these three Endgamers are alone.

Sarah is glad for that. She's had enough of other people for one day. They head south for half a mile and hit the Conway rail tracks running east to west. No train cars block their path. They skirt over the steel bands and leave the boundary of the state park, jogging over an open and rough field, the settled Yellowstone ash padding their footfalls. They don't speak. Jago watches the countryside like a hawk, and Sarah watches Jago. She trusts him to safeguard them, but she's not sure what he might say about this Cahokian rebellion that the Olmec elder told him about. She hopes he says nothing. They're here to do a job, not to talk fuzzy ancient history.

They pass a few squat maples and round some overgrown bluffs that belonged to the ancient pre-Columbian city that once flourished on this Mississippian flood plain. Taken with Monks Mound, the 109 mounds of this city formed the heart of a thriving Mesoamerican metropolis that was as large and populous as any in the Americas, from the Bering Strait to Cape Horn. In fact, the city that grew around the mounds, with as many as 40,000 people at its height, was *the* largest city in North American history until Philadelphia surpassed it in the mid-1780s, long after any cultural trace of the Cahokian people had disappeared from the record books.

Long after their line's secrets were moved and dispersed and hidden from the prying eyes of Europeans and other Native American clans. Long after the Cahokians retreated in order to stay better prepared for Endgame.

"A little over half the mounds are in the state park," Simon says, pulling to a stop in a patch of thigh-high switch grass. He turns in a semicircle and tucks his map into a breast pocket. His voice is muffled and hollowed out by his respirator. "The rest are scattered. The one we're looking for is so eroded that you wouldn't recognize it as anything significant." He slides a metal bracelet down his arm, folding his hand through its circle and yanking it off. He swings it in an arc, like he's using it to dowse for water.

A dirty drizzle falls, a chill wind blows from the north. Rain streaks their goggles and clothing. Sarah shivers as the wind touches an exposed section of her neck. Another lightning strike near Monks Mound. They swing around to look, but it's lightning, nothing more. Simon resumes his search for the hidden mound. He walks slowly, heel to toe, measuring distance. The bracelet guides him.

Sarah and Jago inch along a few paces behind. Out of the blue, Jago says, "Obviously Sarah's told me of this weapon, Señor Alopay. But I'm very curious."

"Yes?" Simon says, concentrating on his search.

Shit, Sarah thinks. The tops of the trees on the other side of the tracks bend and sway in their direction. The drizzle turns to light rain. She unclips a ball cap from her belt and puts it on over her raven-dyed hair, pulling the brim tight to the goggles to keep them dry. *Please don't say it,* she thinks.

"What does it do exactly?" Jago asks. "And why did your line hide it? Why not keep it and use it? That's what the Olmec line would've done if we'd been given such a gift."

Simon pauses. He tilts toward Jago. "Our people buried it because it's powerful, Jago Tlaloc. The books say that it can light the heavens, and that it can kill Makers. Did my people ever try to do that? Not to my knowledge. To be honest, I don't know if it's real, or if it'll work. It's been buried for a long time. As to *why* we hid it, I assume it was because my ancestors were afraid of it. It is a weapon that belonged to Them. And the Makers were to be feared. Surely your people share this fear."

Jago says, "Of course. But how did the Cahokians get it in the first place? Did they steal it?"

Sarah reaches up and flicks the back of Jago's ear. He flinches and gives her a look that says, *Okay, okay!*

Simon stops again. "All I know is that it's supposed to be buried ... here!" Simon does a little prestidigitation with the metal ring, and right before their eyes it's standing on its narrow edge in the palm of his hand, as if propped up by invisible forces.

He goes on one knee and works his fingers through the thick grass, parting it like hair. "Help me look," Simon says. "The marker's an oblong stone in the shape of an eye and about the size of a fist. This ring is a kind of key. It will open any important chamber in this ancient city. This one, and the one up there." He tips his head toward Monks Mound to the north.

Sarah gets on the ground several feet away from Simon. Jago picks a spot and does the same. Sarah's goggles are fogging, so she lifts them from her eyes and pulls them over the top of her hat. She works the fingers of her good hand through the grass and over the dirt.

They search for a couple minutes with no luck.

Jago straightens, scanning their surroundings. No sign of anyone. Just more dirty rain, probably acidic and toxic, and more cold air blowing in from the north. "You sure it's here, señor?"

"I'm sure," Simon says. "When I lapsed, my father brought me to this very spot and showed me the rock. He didn't know much about the weapon either, except that it was buried and that it should only be unearthed in extreme circumstances."

"You mean if Endgame actually began," Sarah says.

"That was the gist of it, yeah. We saw the rock and went back to the park. Had a picnic by the train tracks. Counted empty coal cars as they lumbered by, headed back to West Virginia."

Sarah crawls forward and is surprised when her left knee digs into something hard. She moves over and uses her hands and, yes. "Here!" she says.

A black and smooth stone—completely out of place in this non-volcanic part of the world—shaped like an Egyptian hieroglyphic eye.

"That's it!" Simon exclaims. He puts the bracelet next to the stone and works his fingers around its edges and pries it free. The dirt underneath is wet and buggy, worms corkscrew and writhe as they dive into the safety of the earth. Simon ignores them and digs in, pushing the dirt away and severing some unlucky worms with his fingernails. After a minute another hunk of sleek black rock is revealed at the bottom of a 12-inch hole. The rain intensifies. The ash coating everything washes from the leaves and the grass and their clothing. The water also helps Simon clean off the rock, and now Sarah sees that in its surface is a rounded indentation about two inches deep.

An indentation that is a perfect match for the bracelet.

Simon fits the bracelet into the slot. It slides into place and he wraps his fingers around it and turns it 37 degrees. A click and a hiss. He lets go and pulls away.

But nothing happens.

A flicker in Sarah's periphery and she hoists her rifle reflexively, aiming north toward the tracks and beyond at the rain-lashed trees.

"What is it?" Simon and Jago ask.

Sarah squints through the rain. "Thought I saw something but it's . . . Eh, it's only the wind in the trees."

They return their attention to the vessel peeking from the ground. Jago says, "Why isn't—" but is cut short by a rumble underfoot. All three dance defensively. Sarah and Jago think anxiously of Stonehenge, of how it morphed and grew around them after the disk activated the monument, of how Chiyoko was crushed by accident.

But this time nothing so dramatic happens. The rumbling lasts a few moments and instead of a glass-and-stone monstrosity rising from the ground it is nothing more than a simple black pillar, seven feet tall and three feet in diameter, the bracelet rooted to the top.

From where they stand the thing appears solid, with no recess or door that might hold this ancient weapon.

Simon walks around the pillar, letting his fingertips trail over its glassy surface. When he gets to the far side his eyes widen and he makes a sound that's equal parts relief and wonder.

Sarah and Jago join him. The pillar has a recess covered by a clear glass panel. Simon touches this and it swings open, revealing a fist-sized metal object shaped like a lump of malformed clay. The only indication that it might have any purpose are three finger-sized holes running through one side and a cradle for a thumb on its top.

Simon takes it, carefully inserting his fingers through the holes. It fits in his hand perfectly.

"It looks like a paperweight, not a death ray," Jago says.

Simon points the thing away from the Players and angles it toward the ground and taps his thumb into the cradle, expecting it to act as a switch or trigger. But nothing happens.

Jago shrugs and reaches on top of the pillar, popping out the bracelet. "We got it, whatever it is," he says dismissively. "Now let's look for Sun Key and get out of here. We need to check in with the others soon, Sarah."

As he speaks the spindle of stone drops back underground.

Sarah is about to agree with Jago when the air gets very cold. An invisible presence brushes past her, and Simon twists violently and is thrown to the ground, the Maker "weapon" is knocked out of his grip and tumbles into the grass. Jago and Sarah lift their rifles but don't know where—or what—to shoot. They twirl and search and Sarah calls out, "Dad!" and Simon moans and Jago shouts, "There!"

Sarah looks, not knowing what to expect, and Jago taps his trigger, firing three shots. The space between them ripples and then darkens and a thing like a net appears from nowhere and catches Jago's bullets. It surges toward him and then sucks up his arms and his chest and his face. His skin turns blue and within a fraction of a second his entire body is wrapped in this gossamer shroud and he's unconscious and teetering to the ground like a falling tree.

The Maker! Sarah thinks desperately.

Simon moans again, straining toward Sarah.

She dives sideways as another net-shroud hurtles overhead, missing her by inches. She skids over the dirt, her respirator catching the ground and twisting uncomfortably around to the side of her head and crunching her ear. She sees the clump of metal less than a foot away and scrambles toward it. She gets it, her fingers fit perfectly, her thumb grows almost unbearably hot as it settles into the imprint. Her arm locks at the elbow and her shoulder feels like it's being used as a pincushion by a thousand needles. Her bad arm, tied to her stomach in a sling, aches. She rolls onto her back and points the weapon defensively, sighting along her arm. She blinks at the thing in her hand. It isn't a little mound of metal anymore but an elongated spike extending from the pinkie side of her hand for about three feet. Despite its sudden length it's featherlight. The air shimmers and another net-shroud opens from a small point above her and spreads into the air like an ink stain. She squeezes her entire hand around the weapon and keeps her eyes open and thinks of what she wants it to do—reveal the Maker and cut it down—and the spike glows yellow and gray and a thin disk of light appears from the tip. It flashes for a millisecond, a blade of light extending to the clouds and beyond. The net-shroud is shredded into a thousand pieces. It blows away on the wind. And behind that, about seven feet above the ground, a melon-sized object flips through the air and thumps onto the ground close to Sarah's feet.

A form appears before her in streaks. Whatever it's using for camouflage fritters and malfunctions. She sees a body, skinny and pale, headless and falling. When it hits the ground it's completely visible, and she knows for certain that it's dead.

"YEAH! *Yeah!* Fuck you!" she spits. "Fuuuuuuuuuhuuuuuck yoooooouuu!"

She sits up hastily and yanks her bad hand from the sling and tears the respirator and goggles and cap from her head. She zips the weapon all around, getting to her knees, covering every angle while she looks for another target, but there isn't one and the thing in her hands is already morphing back to its innocuous state.

She pants, her breath quickened by adrenaline and joy and disbelief but mostly joy.

I killed him.

I killed kepler 22b.

She lets out a laugh, full and hearty, and crawls to Jago. She tugs at the shroud, which is bitterly cold to the touch. It crinkles and cracks as she frees him from it, and as soon as he's out his eyes flutter and he's back with her.

She wraps her arms around him and kisses his face all over: his lips his scar the bridge of his nose his blinking eyes. They embrace awkwardly on the ground, the weapon that is very much a weapon there in her hand.

The rain falls ever harder. She doesn't care.

"I killed him," she whispers, her lips on the soft skin of his ear. "I killed him, Jago."

He smiles, but his eyes dart to the side. "And your father?"

Sarah peers over Jago's shoulder. Simon works his way onto his elbows as he gets his bearings. "He looks fine."

Sarah kisses Jago one more time, a smile plastered to her face. She jumps up and bounds to Simon. He *is* fine. He laughs. They hug. They regroup over the next several minutes, drink water and check their guns. They are entranced by the alien body and its severed head. Sarah and Jago argue about whether it is actually kepler 22b—it doesn't look exactly the same—but Simon giddily asks, "Does it really matter?"

No, it really doesn't.

They have the weapon. And it works, and it can kill Makers.

They take the alien head, slipping it into a plastic bag and tucking this into Jago's large pack. They firebomb the body with an incendiary grenade, making sure it burns, and as the fire rages at their backs they return north, a sense of victory in their throats. Within the hour they enter the Cahokian monument and find the central star chamber and search for Sun Key. It isn't there. Simon is convinced. They will have to move on and search the next monument. They leave and go up, up, up, outside and to the vehicles. Sarah and her father get in the old Taurus, bloodstained and bullet-riddled. Jago gets on the Harley.

They go back to the plane. They will talk to the other Players. Get new orders. Maybe rendezvous with them somewhere else. Maybe head to La Venta, as planned.

Or I can go home and see Mom, Sarah thinks as they board the plane after refueling. And as it hurtles up the runway and bumps into the air, Jago at the controls, her head resting on her father's shoulder in the main cabin, her good hand holding his hand, she says quietly, "Or I can go home . . ."

Within minutes she is asleep, the smell of Simon's hair in her nose, dreaming of what could be.

AN LIU, NORI KO

Approaching 34.36226, 108.640262, Huzhucun, China

Nori Ko turns off an empty six-lane highway, bouncing the Defender
onto a dirt service road. Both roads cut through flat farmland, the
fields green with corn and soybeans and potatoes. To the east and
south is the semi-industrial sprawl of Xi'an—water towers and a tangle
of wires over electrical substations and soulless buildings and tall
concrete chimneys spewing smoke and steam.

Countering these, and watching over the farmland like half-asleep
dragons, are the pyramids. Unlike the hidden Great White Pyramid,
these structures sit out in the open. There are dozens scattered around
Xi'an, making this area a vast graveyard for China's ancient emperors.
The tomb that An Liu and Nori Ko are headed to belongs to a Han
emperor named Zhao, who only lived until the age of 20 and ruled
for a mere 13 years between 87 and 74 BCE. At least this is the
pyramid's nominal purpose. Its other purpose, and one that is much
more important than that of resting place for a forgotten child-king,
concerns Endgame.

Nori Ko drives a few hundred meters north to the nearby pyramid,
although it doesn't look like much of one anymore. It's more like
a slump-backed hill, crisscrossed with worn footpaths through
clumps of wild grass. The site is culturally significant, and technically
protected by the Chinese government, but there is no welcome center,
no ropes cordoning it off, no formal parking lot for visitors. Instead
there's a shabby patch of open dirt at the western base of the hill
littered with plastic bottles and bags and food wrappers. A cornfield
full of leafy stalks grows right next to the hill.

No other cars are here, and An is glad for it. He almost says as much to Chiyoko, who speaks often now, saying annoying things like *Stay* and *Honor life* and *Let it be* and then things that contradict these niceties like *No quarter* and *Take the keys* and *Seek blood, love. Seek blood for me.*

An *SHIVERblink* An *SHIVERSHIVER* An and Nori Ko exit the Defender.

He bites his lower lip in order to keep quiet. He wants to talk to Chiyoko, but he knows that doing so would make Nori Ko ask questions.

He glimpses his reflection in a car window. His stubbly head, his tattooed tear, his deep-set and sleepless eyes, his thin purple lips. *We're nearly there, Chiyoko,* he thinks.

She doesn't respond.

He checks his weapons and his supplies. He checks his string of homemade bombs. He slings Nobuyuki's katana over his shoulder. Nori Ko's movements mirror his. She clicks metal on guns and sheathes blades and makes sure that clothing is not loose. Her face is hard and cold. He has grown used to her over the course of their drive from India, and while it hasn't been more than a few days he's already begun to take her for granted.

"I am glad Chiyoko sent you to me, Nori Ko," An says.

Nori Ko pauses. This is the first time An has said something that sounds grateful, even kind. She smiles a little as she says, "I'm glad too." She slaps a magazine into her rifle and snaps the charger. "Now let's go get those keys." She winks and spins away from the car and slams the door.

She leads, he follows. They pass a tidy shrine at the base of the pyramid, a small plaque inside naming Emperor Zhao and giving the years of his truncated reign. A bouquet of wilted flowers and the butt ends of a few sticks of burned incense are inside, no doubt left by some superstitious farmer who believes in the grace or ire of local spirits. An and Nori Ko march up the dirt track. An notices for the first time that the northern face of the hill is covered in a stand of dark pagoda trees. A perfect place to hide an entrance to this forgotten relic from another age.

It's a short climb—the hill is only 30 meters high—and Nori Ko reaches the summit first.

But when she does she freezes and drops to the ground, swinging her rifle in a 45-degree arc. An checks their flanks. A truck cruising north on the wide highway to the west, and another ancient pyramid rises over the farmland another mile past that.

He gets on his belly and military crawls behind Nori Ko. "What?" he whispers.

"There's a car parked at the bottom of the opposite slope."

"People?"

She shakes her head.

An slithers next to her and peers over the lip of the hill. The car is a dark-blue late-model Fulwin, unremarkable in every way except that it's shiny and not road-worn. "Rental," he says. "From the airport." He points to the northeast.

"Let's move," Nori Ko says. "Crossing cover, four meters apart. I'll lead. I know where the entrance is. No more talking."

SHIVERBLINKSHIVERbilnkblinkSHIVER.

Nori Ko rises to a crouch and points her rifle to the trees. An rises too. They move forward until they're a few meters apart. He angles his rifle so it covers her front and she points hers so that it covers his. If someone pops out and tries to surprise Nori Ko, An will kill him. If someone tries to surprise An, Nori Ko will kill him.

BLINKshivershiver.

An sees movement and he swings his weapon in her direction, his finger hovering over the trigger but not firing. Nori Ko mistakes this motion, thinking for a brief moment that he's aiming at her, and she also swings her rifle in his direction, momentarily sighting him before tipping her Beretta to the ground and mouthing, *Sorry.*

Blinkblinkblink.

A squirrel chitters and spirals around a trunk and then disappears into the branches above. An follows it with his weapon and then repositions to cover Nori Ko. He takes a step forward. She mouths another apology and they continue to advance.

They walk downhill now, weaving through trees. After 10 meters Nori Ko puts up a fist and both stop in their tracks. They're on the edge of a patch of grass, a large tree blocking An's line of sight. Nori Ko signals him to stay put. She slips into the trees and he catches slivers of her as she flits around, clearing in every direction with her rifle.

Nori Ko reappears, her gun pointed down and held tight to her chest, her face wrinkled with concern. She motions him closer.

He stalks to her. A curved obsidian spur rises from the clearing to waist height. Broken and discarded earth is thrown to the side as if the stone has grown up from the ground below. An cranes his neck and sees that one side is cut away, revealing a hole big enough to slip into. "There're stairs," she says cautiously. "I'm sorry, An. But I think the Nabataean is already here."

An shudders, he quakes, his knees begin to falter, his head begins to pound, but through the riot of his body he hears her voice:

It's all right, love.

SHIVERshiverSHIVERshiver

It's all right, love.

blinkblink BLINKblink

It's all right.

shiverBLINK

Love.

An bites the side of his tongue. The tics stop. His eyes water. The pain feels good. "It's not all right, An," he says.

Nori Ko regards him with a confused look and says nothing. She doesn't like the tics or the fact that he's speaking to himself.

SHIVERblinkblink.

You can still kill him, love.

shiver.

Move! Chiyoko implores.

"It's all right," he says calmly. He looks to the sky, the tops of the trees silhouetted against it like spear points. "He hasn't won yet. We would know."

"Okay, but let's find out for sure," Nori Ko says.

An hoists his rifle and brushes past her. "You can still kill him," he says.

"Good," Nori Ko says. "But won't *you* kill him?"

"Yes. That's what I meant." He steps around the stone and into the ground. Nori Ko follows.

And then he says, "You can still kill him, love."

Nori Ko doesn't know what to think of that. Is he coming undone, now that they're so close to the end?

She very much hopes that he is not.

She needs him. He needs her.

He can't come undone.

Not yet.

KEPLER 22B

Teletrans chamber on board Seedrak Sare'en, active geosynchronous orbit above the Martian North Pole

He stands alone in the room, staring at the blank archway of transpot 2. One Nethinim is dead—*dead!*—and the other is safe in stasis. The La Tène and her grandfather are interned and semistasised. He wanted to bring back the Cahokian and the Olmec too as extra insurance, but they remain free on Earth.

But worse than this—much, much worse—they have the weapon.

"More Players would have been better," he says. "But no matter. We have one. And we may not require her in the end."

Because here, twinkling in the darkness of the transpot, he sees the form of the person he waits for.

The Nabataean. With the first two keys, and on the verge of discovering the third. He is entering the Shang monument's star chamber.

kepler 22b has not felt such excitement since he first arrived in the quadrant over 15,000 Earth years ago. Since he saw the lush sweep of the blue planet and the barren expanse of the red one.

It is nearly over.

A winner approaches, and in a few moments, kepler 22b will crown him.

Crown him with the prize of death.

HILAL IBN ISA AL-SALT, SHARI CHOPRA, JENNY ULAPALA

-21.6268, 129.6625, Yuendumu Hinterland, Northern Territory, Australia

Hilal and Shari stand shoulder to shoulder at the heart of the Koori monument. It is evening. The sky is dark. It is less than 24 hours since they met Jenny Ulapala but it might as well be weeks. Jenny likes them, and while they've not yet had their weapons returned, they like Jenny. Jenny and Shari and Hilal have spent the better part of the last 20 hours in a simple hut immersed in Wayland's book, deciphering as much as Jenny can about this last stage of Endgame. It hasn't been easy. The book is organized in a manner that defies logic, so her understanding of the specifics of Endgame is incomplete, but nonetheless it is greater than it was the day before.

They have learned many things.

First, Jenny confirmed that at least one of these twelve ancient monuments is needed to finish Endgame, as Stella believed. But Jenny also learned that in the hearts of these monuments are "star chambers," which serve a secondary and, especially in the old days when Maker ships orbited Earth by the hundreds, essential purpose. They were transportation hubs.

The Makers had a technology with an unpronounceable name that harnessed something they called "Earth's intrinsic energy lines," Jenny explained early that morning. "These are the same things we use to work through the Dreaming. We use the Dreaming in spiritual or mental capacities, not in physical ones. But the Makers—They *can* use this energy to get about."

Jenny learned that while They had flying machines that could travel at great speeds and deliver material around the globe in the days of human prehistory, the Makers preferred to get around using their teleporters. There were many hundreds of these all around Earth in the old days—in places like the pagoda in Xi'an and at the Gateway of the Sun in Bolivia and in the Depths of the Harappan fortress—but these portals just linked places on Earth.

They did not posses the ability to move Makers to and from orbit.

"But the portals in the star chambers of the world's most ancient monuments *did* possess this ability. And they still do today," Jenny said.

After breakfast Jenny kept reading the book, Hilal and Shari helping her to take notes. Their other discoveries were far-ranging, concerning things as varied as gold extraction, genetic modification, neuropathology, advanced bioengineering, religious indoctrination, and, of course, the implementation and execution of the thing the Players have always known as Endgame.

Jenny needs more time—months or perhaps years—to fully understand why it's happening and how, but after a few hours she was convinced that the ultimate goal of Endgame as espoused by the Makers and accepted by the lines was false.

As Hilal observed, "Endgame is merely another tool designed to exert control over an alien race. *Us*. It is coercive in nature, designed to get us to act against our best interests."

"The Makers are like bloody politicians, then," Shari quipped.

Jenny chuckled at that one.

As the sky darkened that afternoon, the sun hidden behind gathering clouds, Jenny said, "Here's what we're looking for." She stabbed a section of the book. Hilal and Shari huddled closer to her. "It's about the keys."

"Does it say anything about my daughter?"

"It says her genetic code contains something essential to finishing Endgame. Seems like they hid some bit of information in the lines' genes, and that certain children are born with the section of code they need. Your Alice, unfortunately, has that running around her little system."

Shari said, "We *need* to get her, Mrs. Ulapala."

"Call me Jenny, mum."

"All right, Jenny."

"We will get her, Shari. A promise is a promise," Hilal said. "But I want to know, Master Ulapala: What about the third key?"

"It's all right here," Jenny said. "And it's simple as simple can be, Aksumite. It's you. Or Shari. Or one of your mates—Jago or Sarah or Aisling. Or Adlai."

"Sun Key is a Player?" Shari asked urgently.

"It's the Player who's got the first two keys. There's also a code in your genome, one you all got. That's why Players are chosen. You don't have this code, you can't Play. Anyway, when it's all said and done this code links with Sky Key's, and when these are combined with Earth Key in one of these star chambers, then the Maker gets whatever it is he wants out of Endgame."

"I wish we knew what exactly that was," Hilal said.

"And me too. This book'll show us sooner or later. Need more time to study it is all. But right now we got to act. Sky Key is in grave danger, mum."

Shari frowned. "More than we already know her to be in?"

"Yeah. Says here that at the end, she'll die," Jenny said. "Player will too."

Shari clapped Jenny's wizened hand. *"Jenny."* That was all she said.

Jenny nodded. "I know, mum. We'll save her. And I got an idea how. Bit risky, but I think we can use the Dreaming to figure out when Little Alice comes into one of these star chambers. Once we see her I open the portal at the Koori monument—I've done this before, but I was always too scared to go through since I didn't know where it let out. But now I do. You can stay in the Dreaming and hold the connection to Little Alice while Hilal and some of my Koori mates go and whisk her away. We get her here, I close the portal right quick on our end, and that's it. Endgame over—or effectively over, anyway."

"We can define what it means to win," Hilal said.

"That's right," Jenny said.

"Is it safe?" Shari asked.

"That I don't know, mum. We definitely need to try it first. Don't want to hurt your girl out of rash stupidity."

And so here they are, back at the heart of the Koori monument, doing a trial run of a Sky Key rescue mission.

Now Jenny and Shari sit cross-legged near the tree in the middle of the circle. The Koori guards stand at intervals around the circle.

Hilal watches and waits.

"Ready, mum?" Jenny asks Shari.

"Ready."

"Take my hand and close your eyes and follow my lead," the old woman says.

Shari does.

"You see your girl, don't jump, understand? You're just a passenger for now."

"I understand."

Jenny squeezes Shari's hand. "It's going to be fine." Shari nods nervously. Over her shoulder Jenny says, "Hilal, when the connection is solid I'll come out and we'll test the door. Shari, you stay in the Dreaming. Your presence will hold our connection to the other portal in place."

"I'll try," Shari says.

"It'll be easy for you. You'll see when you're there, mum. You've already done it in your dreams, you just didn't know it."

"All right. Let's give it a go."

Jenny clicks her tongue. "Close your eyes now, mum. Here comes the Dreaming."

SHARI CHOPRA

With those words her world goes dark and silent. It is not so much dreamlike as it's simply no longer there, like any person experiences as she gives way to sleep and is not yet delivered to her dreams, whether these end up being banal, strange or, as it often happens, simply forgotten.

Time does not exist. Space does not exist. The desire to see her daughter, the wreckage of Endgame, the vast Australian desert beyond her physical body—none of these exist.

In many ways she does not exist.

She spends some time here. Seconds or hours—she doesn't know and she doesn't care.

But then, after an interval, a form comes to her through the darkness. The form is small and her steps are childlike and her hair is dark and straight. Shari can't see her face, but she knows who it is. She would know who it is from any distance by the way she swings her arms and stands on her toes when she walks. It is Little Alice Chopra.

She seems to walk to her forever, never getting closer or bigger, yet increasing in presence. The front of her body and her face are cast in shadow, and Shari reaches out and calls for her but the girl doesn't do anything. She just keeps walking easily toward her mother.

When the little girl finally comes into view Shari is shocked to find that it's not Little Alice but Jenny Ulapala. The old woman holds out both hands. Shari is overcome with sadness, and then fear, and then she remembers why she's here. Where *here* is.

"The Dreaming," she says.

"Stay with me, mum," Jenny says. "Don't act. Follow."

Shari takes her hand and they walk, side by side, over the darkness. The ground beneath is not hard or soft. The air is not cold or warm. The void is not limitless or pressing in on them. Jenny swings her hand joyfully, and Shari can't help but swing it too, like a child would do with her mother or father.

Like Little Alice would do.

Eventually they come to the circle of dirt and shrubs in the desert, the same one their physical bodies occupy. It's early evening. They keep walking, getting incrementally closer to the tree and the portal carved in its trunk. Hilal and the guards are nowhere to be seen.

"Will it work?" Shari asks, her lips and tongue tingling, her voice echoing through her skull.

"Quiet, mum," Jenny answers.

Shari becomes aware of a shade passing next to her, or perhaps also following. It's tall, substantial, and with a head of twirling black hair. Whenever she looks directly at it, it disappears, but she doesn't need to see it to know who it is. Shari's just happy she's here, in some form. It's Big Alice.

And she has something to say.

"They're all behind you, Shari. You won't see 'em, you can't, but they're all here. An unending parade." At that moment Jenny and Shari reach the tree in the Dreaming, and the space in the doorway shimmers and turns black like ink. Jenny squeezes Shari's hand reassuringly. Alice says, "All of 'em. Jamal and Paru leading the line, back through the centuries. They're all smiling, Shari. The entire line. *Your* line. All of 'em."

Shari's heart fills, and her gut empties of sadness, and she smiles with them.

"They're all here, mate. They're all here."

HILAL IBN ISA AL-SALT, SHARI CHOPRA, JENNY ULAPALA

-21.6268, 129.6625, Yuendumu Hinterland, Northern Territory, Australia

"By the Makers," Hilal says, staring at the portal. It changes before his eyes. It reminds him of the door in the pyramid at the Calling, except that this one is darker and not reflective. It is black and empty save for the faint twinkling of lights like those of intermittent stars.

"Wait here, mum," Jenny whispers to Shari. "Stay present and hold the link."

Shari doesn't speak.

Jenny releases her hand and rises, her old body creaking upright. She walks halfway to Hilal.

Jenny says, "Time to see if this portal links with another star chamber. You have the markers?"

Hilal holds up a pair of flat red stones the size of large coins. Both come from this patch of Australian desert, and both are easily spotted. They walk to the tree together. Jenny says, "I'm going back to Shari for a sec. The link to the other portal is there, but it's like on old window jammed in its frame. Needs unsticking before it's all the way open."

"When will I know?"

"You'll know." She sits back on the ground gingerly and takes Shari's hand.

Hilal watches as Jenny's eyes roll forward, revealing the whites, and then her lids flutter shut. For several moments nothing happens. The portal stays dark and inky and Shari and Jenny remain motionless and silent.

But then the surface of the portal changes again. Hints of faint blue light stream from it, and a line here and there like the edge of a wall, and a shiny thing set in the ground on the other side like a large salad bowl. It is a star-shaped room, and he knows that it is real and right there, even if it is thousands of miles away.

"Now!" Jenny blurts.

Hilal hurls one of the stones at the portal. Its surface ripples exactly like when a rock disturbs a glassy lake, but the stone sails through to the other side. It slides over the floor, dipping into the bowl and shooting into the air on the far side, finally stopping in one of the room's pointed corners.

"It worked!" Hilal says.

"I see it, Aksumite," Jenny says. "We should be able to cross in either direction when the time comes."

Shari grunts. Hilal assumes she is speaking in the Dreaming but is unable to make the words here in the world.

But then an epiphany. The world includes the Dreaming. This is so spiritually pleasing that he cannot help but smile. Whatever has happened with Abaddon, this world remains, and it is wondrous.

"We're gonna try another chamber, Hilal. Gotta make sure we can get to wherever Little Alice shows up."

"Understood, Master Ulapala."

Jenny hums a low tune. Hilal watches the image of the room recede and fall out of focus and disappear, the surface turning placid and black once more.

"It'll take a while to navigate through the Dreaming," Jenny whispers.

"I will wait," Hilal says excitedly. "With pleasure."

MACCABEE ADLAI, LITTLE ALICE CHOPRA

34.36226, 108.640262, Huzhucun, China

Maccabee and Little Alice descend a narrow spiral staircase carved from a tube of slick black stone. The staircase is less than a meter wide, forcing Maccabee to angle sideways. Little Alice, who becomes more afraid and unsure the deeper they go, holds his hand. The cramped tube, along with Little Alice's increasingly tentative steps, causes them to move slowly. Maccabee's pistol is in his right hand. He has a blade on his hip and the poison ring on his pinkie. Earth Key sits securely in the zippered pocket of an ill-fitting windbreaker he bought at the Ahmedabad airport. Between his teeth he holds a cheap and weak-beamed flashlight, also bought at the airport. Its batteries are already failing.

These are the things he carries to the end.

These are the things he carries to win.

These are the things he carries to meet kepler 22b, and to see how this girl will die.

He squeezes Little Alice's hand. She squeezes back.

"I'm scared, Uncle."

"Don't be, sweetie," he lies, his brow covered in a cold sweat.

He feels awful. He feels sick. He feels elated. He feels nervous.

He feels.

After 21 minutes and three seconds of descent the ground levels and the tube opens into a room. The air is a few degrees below freezing. He zips his jacket to his neck.

The walls glow, and his breath visibly plays in the flashlight's beam. He pinches his teeth and the light clicks off. Little Alice shivers.

"We're here," she says.

"We are."

The room is high ceilinged, its hard-angled walls laid out in the shape of a six-pointed star. At the far end of the room, blunting one of the in-facing points, is a tall and slender alcove, its edge surrounded by glittering runes, a few of which he recognizes. The interior of the alcove is jet black and liquefied, a limitless pool set on end. In the floor in the middle of the room is a gilt, bowl-shaped depression.

Maccabee steps forward, but Little Alice clutches his leg and won't budge. "I'm scared," she repeats.

"It's all right," he says.

"I . . ."

"Yes?"

"I want my mama," she says weakly.

For a moment he can't move. He swallows hard. If he were her, he would want his mama too.

KEPLER 22B

Teletrans chamber on board Seedrak Sare'en, active geosynchronous orbit above the Martian North Pole

kepler 22b hears this conversation from his ship above the red planet. He sees the girl. Knows her fear. It is real and well-founded. He almost steps through to reveal himself in this moment, to speak, but he wants them to come closer. There can be no doubt that this Player will claim his prize.

None.

He wants them to come closer.

AN LIU, NORI KO, MACCABEE ADLAI, LITTLE ALICE CHOPRA

34.36226, 108.640262, Huzhucun, China

An Liu moves quickly but silently. Maccabee is close. The girl is too. He can smell both.

Don't rush to the kepler, love. Have patience.

BLINK

Quiet!

SHIVER

They'll hear you!

SHIVERSHIVERBLINKBLINKSHIVER.

Patience. Don't hurt the girl.

They'll hear you!

He bites the edge of his tongue so hard that the tips of his teeth meet and grate. His eyes water. He wants Chiyoko to shut up, to let him work.

To let him kill.

But she won't.

Don't hurt the girl, she insists again, not hearing An's thoughts. *You'll need her if you want to kill the kepler! Don't hurt her!*

He moves, one foot grapevining after the other, one after the other, in the utter darkness. Nori Ko has fallen farther behind.

"Shush!" he hisses.

Spill Adlai's blood, not hers!

"SHUSH!"

He stops. That was too loud. He waits for a response from below, hears nothing. Nori Ko comes to his shoulder. She nudges him with her knee.

They have been descending for nearly 10 minutes. He estimates that they're more than 100 meters underground, the air getting colder and colder as they go.

He cocks an ear to the darkness. No sound from Maccabee. The hole must be that much deeper.

ShivershiverBLINKshiverBLINKBLINKblink.

An releases his rifle's hand guard and takes one of Chiyoko's shriveled ears and slips it between his lips.

It tastes like paper.

SHIVERblink.

Like nothing.

blink.

But it works.

She is quiet.

He moves his feet, faster now.

Much faster.

"It's all right," Maccabee whispers. He kneels before Little Alice, holding her gently by the shoulders.

"I want my mama."

Maccabee looks at her feet. He's too ashamed to meet her gaze. "When we're done here, I'll take you to her," he lies again. "We'll find her and I'll take you to her. I promise."

"After you win?"

"Yes. After I win."

"Promise?"

If she's going to die, he doesn't want her to be stressed. It should be peaceful. Painless.

Like the Maker promised it would be.

Maccabee raises his face and stares at her intently, tenderly. "I swear it." The sincerity in his voice surprises even him.

You fucking monster, he thinks.

Little Alice blinks. "Okay." She peeks into the middle of the room. "Okay."

Maccabee runs the back of his hand over her cheek. "Do you know what to do over there?"

"Yes, Uncle."

"Show me. The sooner we're done, the sooner we can see your mama."

"Okay."

She walks to the bowl in the middle of the floor. He follows, unzipping the pocket that contains Earth Key. He wraps his fingers around the small stone ball, its surface unusually warm, and pulls it free.

I am going to win, he thinks, he rationalizes.

Little Alice stops at the edge of the depression, her toes hanging over it. She holds out her hand. Her small body shakes.

"Okay," she says. "Give me your hand, Uncle. Give me Earth Key."

KEPLER 22B

Teletrans chamber on board Seedrak Sare'en, active geosynchronous orbit above the Martian North Pole

kepler 22b steps to the edge of the transpot. He pulls his cloak of armor around his body. He slips the hood over the topknot perched on his head. The hood's edges adhere to his cheeks and then grow and meet, covering his face.

Endgame is over, and he is glad for it.

He takes a breath. It is slightly tentative, shaky.

What is this odd feeling? The one he hasn't had in such a long time?

Ah, yes.

Nervousness.

Slowly, he steps forward.

HILAL IBN ISA AL-SALT, SHARI CHOPRA, JENNY ULAPALA

-21.6268, 129.6625, Yuendumu Hinterland, Northern Territory, Australia

Hilal watches as Jenny and Shari work through the Dreaming.

He watches the portal.

After a while the black surface changes, as before. A line here, a line there, the faint light.

He starts to see another room.

And then Shari screams. Jenny throws both arms around her, half pinning her to the ground.

Hilal squints at the image in the portal.

The room pulls into focus.

This room is not empty like the other one. In the middle stands Maccabee Adlai, and clinging to his leg is Little Alice Chopra! The Nabataean is seconds away from winning!

"Do you see kepler 22b?" Hilal asks desperately.

"No!" Jenny shouts. "But—"

"The Shang!" Hilal yelps, pointing past Maccabee. "There is the Shang!"

AN LIU, MACCABEE ADLAI, LITTLE ALICE CHOPRA

34.36226, 108.640262, Huzhucun, China

An reaches the bottom of the steps. He is as silent and cold as the air enveloping him. Nori Ko could not keep up with his pace, and she is at least a minute behind.

The Nabataean and Sky Key stand in the middle of the room. Adlai looks shorter than An remembers, but then An notices that Adlai is in a small hole in the ground. On the far side of the room is a dark doorway, its surface black and opaque. An calmly adjusts his aim for the back of Adlai's neck, right below the skull. He puts the slightest pressure on the trigger. A couple more millimeters and the Nabataean's spine will explode and his throat will collapse and his face will be torn away and flung into the star-shaped room and he will be instantaneously killed.

Sky Key says, "There, Uncle!" She points. An can't help but look. A play of light on the far side of the room causes him to ease off the trigger. The blackness in the doorway stirs, like an invisible stick has swirled its surface, and near the floor An sees something foot-shaped begin to step out of it.

HILAL IBN ISA AL-SALT, SHARI CHOPRA, JENNY ULAPALA

-21.6268, 129.6625, Yuendumu Hinterland, Northern Territory, Australia

"Gun!" Jenny orders. "Give Hilal his blades!"

Shari writhes and calls out for Little Alice, her eyes shut, her hands outstretched, her legs kicking.

Hilal sees Maccabee and Sky Key and An, but none of these people appear to see him. If he can make it to the star chamber on the other side of the portal he will have the element of surprise.

He skids to a stop in front the threshold. A Koori guard throws a pistol at him and Hilal snatches it from the air. He tucks it under his chin and holds out both hands as his machetes arrive, *LOVE* in his right hand and *HATE* in his left. He hastily slips one under his belt and takes the gun.

"Go!" Jenny yells. "Go and get her!"

AN LIU, MACCABEE ADLAI, LITTLE ALICE CHOPRA

34.36226, 108.640262, Huzhucun, China

The kepler! Chiyoko screams. *Stop him, An! Adlai will win if you don't. Stop him now!*

An releases his Beretta. It falls to his chest, making a muffled sound. Maccabee hears this and he whips around. In a single motion An yanks a ball from the strand of explosives hung around his body and slings it through the room. It arcs over Maccabee, who stabs one of his massive hands into the air, missing it by a few centimeters. Maccabee drops to the ground, covering Little Alice with his arms, shielding her with his broad shoulders and back.

The tiny bomb lands in the middle of the archway on the far side of the room.

It is rigged to explode on impact.

And it does precisely that.

HILAL IBN ISA AL-SALT, SHARI CHOPRA, JENNY ULAPALA

-21.6268, 129.6625, Yuendumu Hinterland, Northern Territory, Australia

Just as Hilal steps through the portal, its surface crackles and shivers and the room on the other side shatters and snaps. The blackness returns and he almost slams headlong into it, but someone strong snatches his belt and twists him to the side and he whiplashes into the tree trunk, mashing his cheek on its rough bark.

The person holding him is Jenny Ulapala.

"It's no good. There was a blast. You go through that now and you'll end up in the void, Aksumite." She winks. "Trust me."

He does.

"Shari," he says.

Shari lies on the ground, her eyes blinking, her stomach spasming in fits of sadness and pain.

"I pulled her out of the Dreaming," Jenny says.

"I saw her!" Shari wails.

"You did," Jenny says gently.

"Why couldn't we save her?"

"You saw," Jenny says.

"The Shang," Hilal says quietly.

"Shut up, Hilal!" Shari spits through her tears. "I saw her. *You saw her.* I was so close I could smell her hair, her skin."

Hilal casts his eyes to the ground.

"You couldn't smell her, mum," Jenny says, trying to calm her. "Those were your memories. They get tied up with what you experience in the Dreaming. She was there but you weren't. Not really. Not in body."

"I could smell her," Shari insists, her tongue razor sharp.

A moment. The hiss and whorl of the wind. Crickets. A snapping branch.

"What happened?" Hilal asks.

"An Liu threw one of his bombs," Shari whispers. "The Maker was coming. An stopped him."

"Shari, that's good," Jenny says. "It means the game ain't over. It means your daughter lives."

"No it isn't! I don't have her!" She points at the blank portal in the tree trunk. "One of them has her! Or one of them is killing her! Or . . . or . . ."

"Easy, mum," Jenny says. "The Maker doesn't have her. That's what counts."

Another moment.

Jenny starts to speak again but Shari raises a hand. She gathers herself, sits and wipes her eyes with the back of her hand. "The explosion was concentrated," she says quietly. "Adlai smothered her. They were alive when you pulled me out, Jenny. I saw. Adlai was rising to fight, and Alice . . . she was curled up. Like a little bug. Like a cat. Curled up and scared."

"So she does live," Hilal says, trying to sound encouraging. He moves toward Shari. "Until it is proved otherwise, that is what is true."

"Hilal's right," Jenny says.

The sky is dark and featureless. The clouds cover the stars, the same that were so brilliant the night before.

"She lives!" Hilal insists. "And if I must die to deliver her safely into your arms, then I will." He gets on his knees right next to her. He stretches his fingers for her arm but doesn't touch. "Our plan will work. All we have to do is execute it again. She lives!" he repeats like a refrain, like a prayer. "You *will* see her alive again, Shari Chopra. This I swear."

AN LIU, MACCABEE ADLAI, LITTLE ALICE CHOPRA, NORI KO

34.36226, 108.640262, Huzhucun, China

The portal is destroyed.

Little Alice cowers as Maccabee rushes An Liu. Maccabee's gun rises. He pulls the trigger, aiming for An's chest. The shot echoes harshly throughout the room. An is felled by the force of the first shot and twists into the entryway, disappearing for a moment.

Maccabee is there in a flash. An's chest heaves, his hands clutch at his throat. The shot hit armor and he gasps for air. Maccabee reaches down and grabs An's rifle strap. He yanks the gun awkwardly around An's side where it's impossible for him to reach it.

But An has other things.

Like a sword.

It flashes and cuts across the muzzle of Maccabee's pistol, slamming it to the wall and crunching the Nabataean's knuckles into the stone entryway. The pistol fires uncontrollably as it's knocked free. The slug hits the stone and bounces around but doesn't hit anyone. An draws a deep breath and holds it so he doesn't have to fuss with his struggling lungs. He bounces to his feet. Maccabee, relieved of his pistol, backpedals as the tip of An's sword zips past Maccabee's face. Maccabee draws a tactical knife, double-edged with a hilt.

The Nabataean parries the sword with the knife, catching the edge with the hilt and pushing the sword away. The knife might be short next to the sword, but Maccabee's superior strength more than makes up for it.

They parry and attack and counterattack for a few seconds as each sets his feet. An exhales and surges forward and Maccabee leans to his left to avoid An's steel. He stabs for An's exposed neck and is certain he'll strike but then An steps into the bowl in the middle of the room and shrinks by a foot. The knife scratches the top of An's head, but it doesn't draw much more than a few drops of blood.

Where is Sky Key? Maccabee thinks. She was in the bowl, terrified and curled up like an insect, but now she's gone. *Did the Maker get her? Is she safe?*

Maccabee slices his knife down hard, cutting An's rifle strap. He grips the side of the stock and pulls it free, but An zips a backhand at the weakest section of the gun, where the receiver meets the barrel. The rifle is actually cut in two. The top half twirls away and the bottom half falls to their feet as Maccabee folds himself backward like a circus acrobat, narrowly avoiding the rest of the blade. An sets his feet and grips the sword two-handed and is about to smash it into Maccabee's leg when another shot rings in their ears, a bullet grazing the Shang's ear and causing his strike to miss. Maccabee clambers to his feet. Both Players search desperately for the shooter, and both are shocked to see Little Alice Chopra clutching Maccabee's pistol like a giant deadly toy. An is between the girl and the Nabataean. She aims at An again and pulls the trigger, pulls it pulls it pulls it. She fires all the bullets left in the gun, and all miss badly, the recoil nearly knocking her over. The gun clicks. Empty. An runs toward her, Maccabee follows, yelling, "Leave her alone!"

Chiyoko yells, *Don't hurt her, love!*

An can't help himself. Not now. Sky Key is going to get hurt.

She's going to die.

An reaches the girl—terrified and crying and shaking so badly she can barely hold the gun—in less than two seconds. Maccabee is right behind him but he'll be too late. An is going to strike.

But before he can, An's face lights in pain and the world goes silver and then black.

Maccabee skids to a stop. An's knocked halfway across the room, hit hard in the head with the butt of a rifle. He splays across the floor, flat on his back. A woman steps from the entryway behind Little Alice, and also behind the rifle that knocked An Liu to the floor.

Maccabee has never seen the woman before, but there is no doubt that she resembles the Mu, Chiyoko Takeda.

Maccabee holds out his hand to Little Alice. "Come here." The girl sprints to him, slams into his leg, grabs it, digs her nails into his pants, his flesh. His hand clutches the top of her head, his fingers in her hair.

He can smell it. Rich and sweet and powdery, like a baby's.

"I want my mama," she says.

"I know, sweetie," he says.

He gently—lovingly—squeezes her scalp.

"I'm sorry," she says.

He thinks, *No, I'm the one who's sorry.*

The woman steps all the way into the room. She's three meters away, her rifle tucked to her shoulder. Her eye is in the sight. Her finger is on the trigger. It is aimed for Maccabee's crooked and bruised nose.

Maccabee smooths Alice's hair. He tilts his head in An's direction. The rifle moves incrementally. "Don't let him hurt—"

His back goes straight as a board. His neck snaps. He falls.

He doesn't hear Little Alice cry out. He doesn't feel any pain.

He didn't even hear the shot.

KEPLER 22B

Teletrans chamber on board Seedrak Sare'en, active geosynchronous orbit above the Martian North Pole

Transpot 2 ripples and shatters like broken glass, blasting debris into the teletrans chamber and throwing kepler 22b to the floor. He became aware of the Shang at the last moment, when it was too late to stop him from detonating a bomb inside the star chamber of the Shang monument.

kepler 22b scrambles backward. His armor protected him and he is uninjured, but transpot 2 is plainly damaged beyond repair. He jumps to his feet and rips off his hood. He hastens past the holographic map of Earth. He stops in front of transpot 1 and sinks his arms into the plasmastone control panel. It shouldn't take more than a few seconds to link transpot 1 to the portal in Xi'an. His fingers dance furiously and the liquidy stone grows over his bare arms and past his elbows. His eyes flit between transpot 1 and the map, transpot 1 and the map, and yes, there, he sees the link and yes, transpot 1 is powered up and yes, there, it is activated!

He can go to the Nabataean! He can still finish Endgame!

His eyes rest on the empty space of the transpot, expecting it to fill from the edges with the dark medium that will enable him to move instantly to Earth's surface.

But the dark medium does not appear.

His fingers work faster, and his mind too, and the transpot lights around the edge. He checks and double-checks the switches and connections and they're all correct but nothing happens.

He swings to the map. The dot marking the Shang monument changes color, indicating that the portal in that room so far away—that room that contains the three keys—is no longer functional. It is utterly destroyed.

He will have to wait until a Player gets the keys to a different star chamber now.

He will have to simply wait.

Unless he can finish Endgame on his own!

He tears his hands from the plasmastone quickly, peeling a thin layer of skin from his forearms. He curses aloud and stomps from the room, crossing the ship's hallway and entering the medbay where the La Tènes are interned. He rips the Player free from a web of wires and bindings, checks her consciousness level, yanks the mask from her face, pulls out the tubes that snake around her mouth and down her throat to her stomach and her lungs. She remains unconscious but her body reflexively gasps for oxygen, of which there is little on the Seedrak. He pulls a bag from the wall and slips it over her head, and it filters the nitrogen- and methane-laden air. She breathes. He drops her on the floor and takes a storage shroud from a far corner and wraps her body in it.

He picks her up with one arm and moves back to the teletrans room. He looks at the map. He has a Player. All he needs is Earth Key and Sky Key, and in order to get these he has to make a guess as to which monument they will show up at next.

He must decide correctly. If he doesn't, all could be lost.

He considers the situation carefully. The Shang has probably already killed the Nabataean, so Liu now has Earth Key and Sky Key. kepler 22b knows that the Shang loved the Mu. He knows that Liu is as sentimental as he is disturbed. Which means that if An Liu has any choice in the matter, and is resourceful enough to figure it out, he will take the keys to the Mu monument located at 24.43161, 123.01314.

kepler 22b has decided.

He shoves his free hand into the plasmastone of transpot 1 and reconfigures its connections.

He will go to the Mu monument.

He will go to the undersea temple of Yonaguni.

AN LIU, NORI KO, LITTLE ALICE CHOPRA

34.36226, 108.640262, Huzhucun, China

"Come on. Wake up."

Nori Ko nudges An with her foot. She holds her rifle in one hand and Sky Key in the other. The girl slumps over Nori Ko's shoulder, her face nestled in her neck, her arm jutting out at an odd angle. Nori Ko injected the girl with a very small dose of Demerol from her field kit. The girl was beside herself with fear and anxiety over losing the Nabataean and who knows what else.

"Wake up, An," Nori Ko repeats.

An rolls onto his side.

"There you are. Come on."

He moans. His hands rise to his face, they rub his skin and eyes. A red welt grows over his left eyebrow and cheek where Nori Ko struck him.

"Wha-what . . ."

"The Nabataean is dead."

An cranes his neck and squints at Maccabee Adlai. "How?"

Nori Ko pats her rifle. "Don't know why you bothered with the sword."

An pushes to a sit. He drapes his arms over his knees. His head hangs between them.

You should thank her, love, Chiyoko says.

SHIVERSHIVERSHIVER. His head quakes like a madman's. *SHIVERSHIVERSHIVER.*

Quiet! he thinks.

You should thank her for saving the girl. You were being rash, and foolish, Chiyoko says. *Thank her.*

239

BlinkSHIVERblink.

An's head snaps up. "Thank you, Nori Ko." His eyes point to Sky Key. "I wasn't right in the head. You've seen me when I'm fighting. You understand."

Good, Chiyoko says.

"I couldn't have done any of this without you. I wouldn't be here without you. Thank you." He says it because he needs Nori Ko, but he also says it because it's true.

Nori Ko reaches down and offers a hand. "I understand. Players are made to kill. You most of all."

"Yes." She pulls him up. He presses a thumb into one of his nostrils, shutting one side tight. He exhales sharply through his nose, a bloody ball of phlegm smacking Maccabee's leg. "You check him?" An asks. "He's dead."

"Is he rigged to blow if he dies?"

"No. Are you?" she asks, half joking.

"Not right now," he says seriously.

An doesn't notice Nori Ko roll her eyes. "He doesn't have any explosives of any kind," she says.

"And Earth Key?"

"Here."

Nori Ko holds out a fist. An cradles his hand underneath it. She unfurls her fingers and a stone ball drops into his palm.

"It's so . . . small."

"I'm sure that's what the others thought too."

An zips it into a pocket. He picks up Nobuyuki's sword and sheathes it, saying, "I didn't shoot him because the Maker was coming." *Blinkshiver.* "I couldn't let that happen."

"What do you mean?" Nori Ko asks urgently. "Did you *see* the Maker?"

An points at the cracked stones around the portal. "I did. He was stepping through there. It was like a doorway to wherever he is hiding. I greeted him with fire, but I don't think he was hurt."

Nori Ko reaches for him. He flinches a little when her hand comes to

240

rest on his shoulder. "We *will* have our revenge, An."

"That's all that matters."

"Nothing else," she says.

He fingers the necklace of hair and flesh. Points his chin at the girl.

"What did you do to her?"

"Drugged. She was hysterical. She seemed to . . . care for the Nabataean. She didn't want him to die."

Do not scare her again, love, Chiyoko chides.

"I'll try," he says.

Nori Ko frowns. "What's that?"

BLINKshiverSHIVER.

"Nothing. Thinking out loud. The Cahokian," he says, getting to the point. "The Olmec. They're next." Nori Ko nods. An unclips a bomb from his vest. Presses a few buttons and then places it carefully in the middle of Maccabee Adlai's stomach.

"One hour until this explodes," he explains. "No Maker will come here again." He pushes past Nori Ko and the girl and steps through the exit. "No one will ever come here again."

SARAH ALOPAY, JAGO TLALOC, SIMON ALOPAY

Famoso Airfield, Bakersfield, California, United States

"Hey there, sweetheart."

Sarah opens her eyes. Simon stands over her, kneading her shoulder gently.

"What happened?"

"You fell asleep."

She sits. "Shit." She rubs her face. "Been doing that a lot lately."

"That's what Jago said. He also said you went a few days with hardly any sleep at all in Peru, when his parents took you captive, so it's not very surprising."

"He told you about that, huh?"

"He did."

Sarah glances around the inside of the plane. "Where's Jago, anyway?"

"Outside. Trying to convince Rodney Q and Hibbert not to kill him," Simon jokes.

Sarah knows both men well. They're Cahokian trainers, one specializing in extreme survival skills and the other in metallurgy and demolitions.

Sarah rises to her feet. "So we're in Nebraska?" she asks. "We're home?"

She's excited to see Olowa, to hold her hand, to tell her she that she loves her, face-to-face.

"No," Simon says. "We're in Bakersfield, California. The West Coast is a mess—earthquakes rippling up and down the San Andreas Fault since the impact—but the power grid, along with radio communications, GPS, and various satellite feeds, are working here."

Sarah frowns. "What do you mean, we're in California?"

"We couldn't risk flying home. Yellowstone's still erupting and there's too much debris to risk it. I drove to Illinois, you know."

"Then we should have driven back!" Sarah says.

"I'm sorry, Sarah. But you couldn't abandon this plane. You know that. So long as you can find fuel, it will get you anywhere in the world."

"Not anywhere," Sarah points out.

Simon squeezes her arm gently. "We're not going to stop Endgame in Nebraska, Sarah. Jago explained what's happened. All of it. He convinced me. To be honest, it wasn't that hard."

"*All* of it?"

"All of it. Including the Cahokian Rebellion."

"You sound like . . . you already knew about it."

"I've known about it for a long time, and I would have told you too after you aged out. But I couldn't while you were training. If Endgame actually happened to you then you couldn't begin with doubt in your heart. Yeah, I knew about our rebellion, but I also believed there was a chance that the prophecy was true. It was a teeny chance, but it meant you could win, and it mean that we might be able to live a long life—together. All of the Cahokians. Or, as many of us as possible . . ."

He trails off and looks at the floor. She knows he's thinking about Tate, because that's who she's thinking of too.

"Dad . . ."

Tears fill Simon's eyes. "I miss him."

Sarah's grief catches in her throat. She wipes her nose with her arm. "Me too," she manages to say.

Pause.

"I should have told you, Sarah. I understand that now, and I'm sorry."

"It's okay, Dad. I'm sorry too."

"For what? I'm proud of you. *So* proud."

You shouldn't be, she thinks, the image of Christopher's face hanging in the air next to her father.

Simon continues, "If you'd known about the rebellion you wouldn't have been able to stop Endgame from starting, Sarah."

243

She shrugs. "Maybe. I could've blown myself up at the Calling, along with every other Player and maybe kepler 22b too. That might have stopped it. It would have saved him, if nothing else, the big idiot."

"What're you talking about?"

"I—" Sarah says, but is cut short as Jago bounds into the cabin.

"Sarah—Jordan's on the radio. Hilal and Shari should be on soon too. We need to talk to them." Jago holds out his hand. Her gaze lingers on her father—she wants to tell him that she killed Christopher, she *needs* to tell him, but not right now. She grips Jago's strong fingers.

"Come on," Jago says, a smile creasing his scar.

Sarah glances at her father once more as Jago pulls her away.

Simon follows, still wondering what it is that Sarah needs to say.

GREG JORDAN

Govi-Altai Province, Mongolia

"This is Charlie Echo One, on secure channel Alpha Romeo Five Seven, over. Repeat, Charlie Echo One, over."

He clicks the transmitter and waits. Silence. He's in the cockpit of the de-winged Bombardier, his face bruised, his nose broken. Breathing hurts. Badly. The explosion from his grenade as it met the alien's projectile threw him at least 20 feet over the rocky Mongolian terrain. He has at least one cracked rib on his right side, and what feels like two or three on the left below his shoulder blade. He has a long abrasion up the back of his right arm and a golf ball–sized lump on the back of his head, and his neck is so strained that he can't tuck his chin to his chest. He was unconscious well into the night of the attack, and barely able to move the whole next day. It took him an hour to get to his hands and knees and crawl the 50-odd feet to the plane. Once inside he drank water and ate some crackers and threw up and ate some more crackers and began treating his wounds. He tried hard not to fall asleep, since he was positive he'd been concussed.

Whatever. He's the lucky one. Because he's alive. He's here.

"Charlie Echo One, on secure channel Alpha Romeo Five Seven, over. Repeat, Charlie Echo One, over."

He takes a breath—or tries to—and is stopped dead by the pain stabbing his side. "Fuck," he whispers. He spits into a paper cup from the galley. The saliva has trails of blood in it, which is an improvement. It's a lot less than when he first came around, shivering in the twilight. His spit then was dark purple and thick. He was afraid he was bleeding internally, but since then it's let up.

The lucky one.

A crackle on the radio. Jordan clicks his transmitter again. "Charlie Echo One, copy back, over?"

"This is Oscar Kilo Fifteen. I read you." Jago. "We have company?"

"Negative," Jordan says. "Maintain silence for third party, copy back."

"Copy that. I'll get the other," Jago says, referring to Sarah.

Jordan is glad that at least one other group lives, especially the one that had to go back to America and so close to the impact zone. He takes three tiny sips from a plastic water bottle and waits. He wonders how much he should say. What he should reveal about his situation, about Marrs and Aisling and Pop, in case the Makers are listening. They must be listening.

He doesn't have long to contemplate his options. Hilal's voice pops over the radio, crackling with urgency. "This is Tango Lima One. Is anyone there?"

"Oscar Kilo Fifteen, checking in," Sarah says.

"Charlie Echo One, checking in," Jordan says.

"Excellent," Hilal says. "Tell us your status."

Sarah says, "Objective complete. Near West Coast of US. Ready to move to the next monument."

Jordan says, "Objective complete." He pauses.

Hilal says, "Objective changed on our end, but the results are positive. We have some news regarding—"

"I gotta say something," Jordan interrupts.

Hilal says, "As do I, Charlie Echo One. Please, listen—"

"I'm sure your shit is urgent too, but my news is probably more urgent. We were attacked. By one of Them. Marrs was killed. Our plane is disabled. I should have been killed too but . . . got lucky." He spits into the cup. He hasn't spoken so much since coming around, and every word hurts. "Didn't see what happened to Aisling. She's either dead or . . . she's not here, whatever happened to her. Pop isn't either. No sign of them."

"He took them." It's Shari. "He must have. If what we learned about Sun Key is true, then he needs one of us to finish the game. He took her!"

Jordan turns his ear to the speaker and raises an eyebrow. "What do you mean? What have you learned?"

"One attacked us too," Sarah says before Shari or Hilal can explain about meeting Jenny Ulapala and her being able to read the Maker's book.

"*What?*" Shari asks.

"We were ambushed near our objective. The Maker nearly got us, but we . . ." Sarah pauses. "We fought back. We survived."

"How the fu—" Jordan starts, remembering the invisible and bulletproof force that waylaid them, the thing that obliterated Marrs where he stood, the giant unseen hand that caught three grenades and let them explode in its grasp as if they were popping balloons. But then he thinks better of it. If Sarah and Jago have some way of fighting the Makers, best not to talk about it over the radio.

Hilal says, "Charlie Echo One, please reconfirm: You cannot travel?"

"That's right. Might as well be on the moon. But I'm safe. Have food, water, medicine, shelter, and power. I'll be fine till you can circle back."

"And you, Oscar Kilo Fifteen?"

"Mobile and ready. We can go wherever you think we should go," Jago says. "You were going to tell us something important about Sun Key?"

"Yes," Hilal says, "but I think it better to discuss in person, in case this channel is compromised. Shari is transmitting coordinates now. I will meet you at this rendezvous ASAP. If you arrive first, please encamp at the airport. Once we are together we will move to the next monument in force."

"Roger that," Sarah says. "We'll see you there."

Hilal says, "Safe travels, Players. I will see you soon. I want to hear how you killed the Maker."

"I wanna hear that too," Jordan chimes. "But until you can tell me face-to-face, get out there and fucking kick ass, Players. For Marrs, for McCloskey, for the Harappan, for everyone. For Stella. For Aisling. Just fucking kick ass. This is Charlie Echo One, out."

AN LIU, NORI KO, LITTLE ALICE CHOPRA

Private plane holding area, Xianyang International Airport, Xi'an, China

An sits at the controls of his modified Y-12E, a laptop on his thighs, his fingers stabbing the keys. The turboprop is dormant but otherwise fueled, its course charted, its occupants ready for take off. It originally flew maritime surveillance for China Flying Dragon Aviation out of Harbin in Heilongjiang, but it has belonged to the Shang line for as long as An remembers. Of all the planes and helicopters he's flown, real or in simulation, An's logged more hours on his precious and reliable Y-12E than any other.

Over 992 hours, to be exact.

All he needs is a few more hours.

Except that he and Nori Ko and Sky Key can't take off. They can't fly to Yonaguni and to the Mu monument—which is also where the Olmec appears to be headed. When they left the Shang pyramid An checked Chiyoko's tracking watch, and there, to his delight and surprise, was the blip-blip marking Jago Tlaloc. He hadn't died. Not yet. The fool hadn't figured out that he'd been tagged way back at the Calling. Now he is over halfway across the Pacific, on a heading that will soon cross the Japanese island of Yonaguni. The place where, if they could only get airborne, the Olmec will find nothing but death.

But An and Nori Ko and Sky Key can't fly to Yonaguni because the military clearance codes An's relied on for so many years aren't working. Air traffic over China and Taiwan, which they'll have to fly over to reach Yonaguni, has been severely restricted since Abaddon.

BLINKSHIVERBLINKBLINKSHIVER.

He raps his knuckles on his temple three times. Pain shoots down the side of his head and through his jaw. The pain is good. The tics subside. He's been trying to hack through a back door of Beijing's aviation administration so they can cross China with no questions asked.

"How's it going?" Nori Ko asks from the cabin. She's working a computer too while monitoring Sky Key.

An yells, "This last encryption is challenging." *SHIVER.* "How about you?"

"I spoke with my brother Tsuro in Yonaguni," she says, her voice getting closer. She appears behind him and leans into the cockpit. "I'm glad the Mu planted him there so long ago. He's going to help us out."

"I'm glad he's there too," An says.

"Tsuro filed the request for emergency medical supplies with the trans-Asian relief agency. I sent you the doc number with our mocked-up manifest. That's the one you should use with Beijing. As far as anyone knows we're flush with gauze, iodine, and IV bags, not sniper rifles, explosives, and a nuclear suicide vest."

"Okay"—*blink*—"I"—*shiver*—"I"—*SHIVER*—"I got it. Good work."

"Thanks. I also told Tsuro that if any of the others get there before us then he needs to stall them."

"With any"—*blinkBLINK*—"with any"—*SHIVERshiver*—"with any luck that won't happen."

"Yeah. With any luck," Nori Ko says.

An shudders visibly. He holds his fingers out over the laptop, obviously trying to keep them from shaking.

"Hey, you okay?" Nori Ko asks.

"Y-"—*blink*—"Y-"—*BLINK*—"Yes."

He lowers his fingers to the keyboard and punches away.

"All right." Nori Ko points at the navigation computer. "What's the Olmec's ETA?"

"Less than six hours," An says. Nori Ko watches as windows on his computer screen open and close, open and close.

"Get us airborne, An."

"I'm trying."

Nori Ko turns back to the cabin.

Get us in the sky, love.

"I'm trying, Chiyoko."

Nori Ko freezes. "What?"

"I said, I'm trying."

SARAH ALOPAY, JAGO TLALOC, SIMON ALOPAY

Bombardier Global 8000, 590 miles northeast of Yonaguni, Japan

Sarah Alopay pinches her nose and blows out her ears. They squeak and pop but she doesn't care. They're too close for her to care.

She and Simon sit at a shiny walnut table. A bowl that's bolted to the edge of the table near the window holds the unremarkable-looking Maker weapon and a pack of Trident gum. Jago flies the plane at a level and smooth 42,000 feet. They picked up the two Cahokian trainers, Hibbert and Rodney Q, for added muscle. Both are sacked out in the plane's bedroom, sleeping in all of their gear like good soldiers always do. Sarah's injured arm is out of its sling, her elbow extended on the table. She grips a bright tennis ball, releases, grips, releases. Her arm's getting better. It's far from healed, but it can handle some light duty. She plans on keeping it out of the sling for this next mission. With any luck, their *last* mission.

Simon hits redial on his satellite phone's keypad. The phone works— he's placed random test calls to several numbers in the eastern hemisphere—but it hasn't been able to reach the Alopay compound in Nebraska. He's tried 74 times on this long flight, and 74 times he has received the automated message of a nice-sounding lady saying, "Inmarsat cannot place the call as dialed. We apologize for any inconvenience. Please try again."

But then, as Jago announces they're beginning the descent into Yonaguni, Simon's face lights up. Sarah releases the tennis ball. It makes a little spiral on the tabletop before rolling into her lap. She catches it with her thighs. "What?" she asks.

Simon hits the speakerphone button and holds up the receiver.

Ring.

Silence.

Ring.

Silence.

Ri—

"Hello?"

"Mom?" Sarah says. *"Olowa?"* her father says at the same instant.

"Sarah! Oh my goodness, Sarah! Is that really you?"

"It's me, Mom!" Her eyes meet Simon's. "It's us!"

For a few minutes they fawn over each other, talking love and loss and how Sarah and Simon found each other and what's been happening in Nebraska. Olowa and the others can't go aboveground on account of the air quality, but the bunker is warm and the power works fine. Olowa's rationing their supplies, and while she has more people to care for than she expected ("Eleven of us!"), they're good for at least five weeks. Olowa explains that she had to repair a relay to the phone's antenna and that was why they hadn't been able to get through.

"But we're fine, sweetie. How're—goodness, how're *you*?"

"She's good, Ole. She has a new boyfriend," Simon jokes.

"Dad!"

"And guess what. He's a Player!"

"Dad!"

"All right, all right," her father says.

"Who is he, Sarah?" her mother asks.

"It's not important."

"Sure it is."

Sarah shrugs. "His name's Jago. He's the Olmec."

"And he has diamond studs set in his top incisors," Simon adds.

"What?" Olowa asks.

"It's true," Simon says. "He's good for her, though. They've saved each other multiple times, apparently."

Her mother says, "Tell me as much as you can. How *are* you doing?"

Sarah sighs. "I've been better, Mom. I miss school and soccer and worrying about college. I miss being normal—or pretending to be normal. Jago and I have talked about it a lot. As he's pointed out, those days are gone. Actually, he maintains they were never really here. That I was always not normal. I still miss them, though."

"I miss all that too."

"But I'm alive. I guess, all things considered, I'm good. I can't tell you how happy I am Dad's here."

Simon takes Sarah's hand. Jago walks out of the cockpit to use the bathroom before landing, ignorant that they've been talking about him. Simon motions for Jago to wake up the Cahokian men. Jago nods and disappears to the rear of the plane.

When he passes them again a minute later, Simon joins him to help with landing the plane, and also so Sarah and Olowa can be alone. Sarah gives her mom the quick version of all that's happened, leaving out certain things intentionally in case the kepler's listening. She doesn't mention the Maker weapon, or anything about their plans to stop the aliens, but she does talk generally about how hard the road's been, and about finding Earth Key and losing it, and seeing Sky Key, and lastly about killing. "It's been so easy, Mom. Too easy. That's basically why I lost it after Stonehenge," she says, not mentioning Christopher.

She can't bring herself to say his name.

"Oh, Sarah," Olowa says. But her voice sounds strange. On their own the words mean, *I'm so sorry,* but the way Olowa says them it sounds more like, *You're strong. So* be *strong, Sarah.*

And then it spills out of her like a flood. She tells everything that happened right after leaving Omaha. She tells about how Christopher followed her and about how she fell in love with Jago as if they'd known each other for months or even years. She talks about feeling out of touch with herself, about how at her worst moments she's had no idea who she is. She tells her mother about how when she drove out of London she nearly had a nervous breakdown in the car, screaming and crying at the top of her lungs without being aware of it. She talks about how easy it's been to move and Play and kill, and to hurt people, including herself. About how easy it's been to deliver and receive pain, and bear it, except for one kind of pain that's been impossible to carry. And she still can't say what it is. She can't say the words to her mother—the woman who gave birth to her and taught her so much about life and love, and yes, also about blood and how to make it flow.

She can't say, *I killed Christopher.*

What she does say is, "Endgame's fucked me up, Mom. Really badly. I probably should have killed that little girl. Sky Key. But I couldn't. I . . . I couldn't. Not after . . ."

She can't say it.

"Stop, sweetie. Nothing could have prevented Abaddon."

"How do you know?" Sarah takes the tennis ball in her fingers. Squeezes. Releases. Squeezes. The ball caves and breaks and pops. The connection over the phone crackles. "Mom? You there?"

"I'm here."

"How do you know?" Sarah asks again, pleading.

"Listen—Abaddon's here, so there's no point in second-guessing. Nothing could have prevented it. It was too big. The Maker has too much power."

"But what if he doesn't have that much power? What if he's as desperate as we are? What if I hadn't gotten Earth Key? What if I hadn't . . ."

She can't.

"You don't have to say it, sweetie."

"Say what?"

"I know Christopher's dead. As soon as you said his name, I knew."

"Mom, I . . . I . ."

"I know you killed him."

Silence.

"How?"

"I'm your mother, Sarah. No one knows you better than I do, whether you like it or not."

"Ten minutes to touchdown," Jago announces over the comm.

Sarah hears Hibbert say something to Rodney Q from the bedroom.

"You have to go," Olowa says.

"Yeah. But I need to tell you what happened, right now. I might not get another chance."

"I already know, sweetie."

"Mom, I'm a monster!" Sarah whispers, her lips practically pressed to the receiver.

"You're not, Sarah! Oh, honey . . . Don't you see what Christopher *really* did?"

"He didn't *do* anything, Mom. That's what's so messed up. He saw what I'd become and he wanted to die. He said he loved me, and sure, he meant it, but in the end that didn't count for shit. I still pulled the trigger. Christopher fought to stay with me after the Calling, even after he'd met Jago and seen that we were, I don't know—*together*. He fought hard to be at my side and help me. But in the end he couldn't, Mom. And I killed him for it." Sarah's ashamed over the bitterness of her words, but they ring true. Until this moment she never realized how angry she was at Christopher for following her, for loving her, for standing there and staring at her and taking it as she killed him.

For judging her.

"You're wrong, sweetie. Christopher did do something."

"What?"

"He saved your life, Sarah. And now you have to keep on living. For him."

The plane bumps through some clouds.

Olowa continues, "That's what I'm going to tell his parents, too. That he died so that you could live. That's not a lie. I'm going to tell them that you were with him when he died, and that you tried to save him but couldn't. Christopher is a hero, Sarah. You are too. If you and your friends succeed, then you'll all be heroes. Endgame could have gone a million different ways, but in *this* Endgame? Christopher, for all his faults, may be the biggest hero of all."

Several moments of silence. Sarah stares out the window at heavy clouds. The water below is dark. She does not see any land. "Jesus, Mom."

"Jesus has nothing to do with any of this."

"No. I mean I think you're right."

"Of course I'm right, sweetie. I already told you: I'm your mother."

Sarah chuckles.

"I know you don't like killing, Sarah. You're not supposed to. You're human. But you're good at it. Your friends are good at it. And before this ends, you're going to have to do it again—maybe more than once. So don't beat yourself up. Forgive yourself. Christopher saved your life. End of story. Now go out there and save what's left of our lives, before it's too late."

The plane thumps as the landing gear folds out.

"I will, Mom. Thank you."

"Thank me when you see me."

"All right. I love you."

"I love you too, sweetie. And I always will, no matter what."

HILAL IBN ISA AL-SALT

Bombardier Global 8000, 488 miles south-southwest of Yonaguni, Japan

Hilal checks the navigation system. He's got 51 minutes left. Sarah and Jago, based on their last check-in, should touch down in 10 minutes. He works the radio controls. Gets the right channel and clicks on.

"This is Tango Lima One for Oscar Kilo Fifteen, over."

Nothing.

"Tango Lima One for Oscar Kilo Fifteen, over."

Static and then, "Tango Lima One, we read you, over." It's Jago.

"What is your ETA?"

"Nine minutes, seven seconds. Should have visual once we get under cloud cover."

"Understood. I am right behind you. A little more than forty minutes out."

"Roger, Tango Lima One. Any intel?" Jago asks.

"I spoke with the regional air director ten minutes ago. A man named Tsuro Masaka. I pretended to be an American and gave my name as Harold Dickey. He does not know we will be armed, so be prepared to subdue if you deem it appropriate. For explanation, tell him we are working on a joint US–Japanese top-secret mission in response to Abaddon."

"*Entiendo*. Anything else?"

"Yonaguni is a small island. Masaka confirmed that no one has been coming or going for the last sixty-five hours. I have checked the manifests online and can confirm that this is accurate. Masaka made it sound like the place is virtually deserted."

"So no Shang bogey?"

"Affirmative. If Liu is coming here too, then we have beat him."

"*Excelente.* Oscar Kilo Fifteen, out."

SARAH ALOPAY, JAGO TLALOC, SIMON ALOPAY

Yonaguni Airport, Yonaguni, Japan

Jago cycles down the engines. The airport outside is not much more than a few buildings pushed against a single runway, the East China Sea lapping at its long northern fringe. There's a small and empty hangar to the west and an Erector set–like radio tower to the east. A few single-engine Cessnas are mothballed nearby, their windows blocked off and dirty. The buildings are unassuming and tidy. In fact, there's no sign of anyone until a small man swings open a glass door and walks toward them. He smiles broadly, his hand raised in greeting. An orange bag is slung over his shoulder, and he wears an army-green T-shirt with a line drawing of the most venerable and loved Jedi of all time. The caption reads in English, *My Yoda Shirt, This Is.*

Jago slides open the window. "Hey there."

"Hello!" the man announces happily in English. "You are Mr. Dickey's friends?"

"That's right! Name's Feo."

"Wonderful, Feo! Welcome to Yonaguni!"

Jago claps the window shut. "That's our guy."

Simon says, "I'll send Rodney Q and Hibbert out to clear."

"Good idea," Sarah says.

They move to the cabin. The Cahokian trainers pop up from their seats, a Colt pistol snapped to each of their hips, an M4 in each of their hands. Rodney Q has a black bandanna tied loosely around his neck and Hibbert chews a big wad of pink bubble gum.

Hibbert says, "What's the word, Sarah?"

"Go out there, introduce yourself, and report back. Don't tell him why we're armed."

Hibbert nods. "Gun's the only reason he'll need," he says brusquely.

"If we're clear then start unloading. We'll move out as soon as Hilal gets here."

"Got it."

Jago throws the latch on the door and pushes it out. The stairs fold quietly to the ground. The outside temperature is warm, the air humid. The sun hides behind the clouds of ash that now cover the entire globe. Rodney Q—six foot four, 240 pounds—ducks through the opening and steps down. Hibbert, who's much shorter and lighter, follows him.

"Oh, hello," the man calls out from below. "Mr. Dickey didn't say anything about"—he swallows—"guns."

"Sorry," Rodney Q grunts, not sounding at all sorry. Masaka shuffles to the side as Rodney Q sets foot on the ground, looking this way and that.

Hibbert looks Masaka directly in the eye and says, "Don't move, please." He's not pointing his gun at Masaka, but it's clearly a threat barely concealed as an order.

Masaka stammers, "I-I'm s-sorry, sir, but—"

"And with respect, be quiet," Hibbert adds in flawless Japanese.

Masaka shuts up.

Sarah watches from the shadows inside the doorway as Rodney Q expertly skirts around the man, checking the buildings and the corners. He disappears to circle the plane. She looks past the airport. Lush trees line the road. Mount Urabe rises to the south. A white horse lazes in a field in the distance.

After a minute Rodney Q reappears. "We're good."

Masaka shifts from foot to foot, his hands joined nervously at his waist.

Hibbert moves to the side of the plane. The cargo door thumps open.

Sarah leans halfway out the door. "Thanks, Rodney. Sorry if this comes as a surprise, Mr. Masaka," she says to the unfortunate man. "We mean you no harm." He blinks but doesn't speak. She turns back inside, facing Jago and Simon. "Ready?"

"More than ready," Jago says, smiling broadly.

Sarah smiles back. "Me too."

Jago takes her arm. "You look different, Alopay. Lighter. Easier."

"I *feel* lighter, Feo. And you know? I feel confident too. I'm glad we decided to work with the others."

"Me too."

"And Dad, having you here is . . . it's good for me. Talking to Mom—that was *really* good. Thanks for making it happen."

Hibbert calls for some help with a heavy case. "I'll go," Simon says. He pushes past the Players and walks down the steps and disappears around the side of the plane.

Jago gives Sarah a full kiss on the lips. His breath is terrible. He turns aside and bounds down the stairs.

Sarah moves to the top step and inhales sharply. The air is salty and sweet and fresh. Earth is injured, but it is not destroyed or broken.

Earth won't *be* broken.

It can't be.

She thinks of Christopher. Of what she did. Of what *he* did.

She's not broken, either.

She can't be.

Jago waves to her. She moves forward.

And then the air cracks, and Jago's head pops sideways, and blood and brains splatter over his shirt and the stair's handrails, and she barely makes out the suppressed hiss of a rifle's report as it slithers down from the mountainside.

"Sarah!" Simon yells.

She leaps down the remaining steps, already drawing her pistol, already running as fast as she can.

The air cracks. Her eyes don't work. Her ears don't work. Her legs don't work. The world disappears.

She was wrong.

It *is* broken.

Like Maccabee before her, she never got a chance to hear the shot.

AN LIU, NORI KO, LITTLE ALICE CHOPRA

Northern foothills of Mount Urabe, Yonaguni, Japan

A white horse bolts across the field below, the hooves like miniature thunder.

Thank you, love, Chiyoko says breathlessly.

They are the sweetest words An has ever heard.

"I told you I'd"—*blinkSHIVERblink*—"I told you I'd kill them."

Thank you.

Nori Ko peers up down right left through the range finder. Tsuro waves a hand in their direction, giving them a thumbs-up. "That was some exceptional shooting, An," she says. "Five shots, five kills. Four of them in motion." She checks the time in the range finder's HUD. "In under eight seconds."

Compliment her, Chiyoko says.

An pulls his eye from the scope and angles the rifle into the air. "I couldn't have"—*blink*—"I couldn't have done it without you, Nori Ko. Or your brother down"—*SHIVER*—"your brother down"—*BLINKSHIVER*—"your brother."

"Tsuro's been waiting a long time to help me," she says.

They'd landed less than an hour before the Cahokian and the Olmec and rushed to get their gear into a Mitsubishi Montero and up to this position south and west of the airport, leaving Tsuro to deal with An's Y-12E. While they prepared for the kill shots he single-handedly moved the plane to the back of the hangar and out of sight.

An moves from his position on top of a grassy bluff and twists to Sky Key. She's drugged and sleeping, propped against Nori Ko's pack.

Keep moving, Chiyoko says.

"I don't want"—*BLINK*—"I don't want to wait for the others, Nori Ko. Waiting for"—*BLINKBLINK*—"for this Dickey person is too"—*SHIVERblinkSHIVER*—"too unpredictable."

"Agreed." She stows the range finder in her pack, careful not to disturb the girl. "Tsuro will handle them." She taps her watch. "Besides, we have to kill 22b, and time's ticking away."

An leans his jet-black JS 7.62 rifle against a rock and checks his vest. He fumbles with his shirt buttons, his eyes blinking and blinking and blinking, his shoulder muscles twitching. He finally gets the shirt open and tugs at the vest's straps one more time, making sure they're secure. It presses into his skin, constricting his rib cage painfully. It's heavy—nearly 20 kilos—but it feels oddly comforting, like a snug blanket.

"You all right, An? Your tics are getting worse."

He's fine, Chiyoko says.

Except An is the one who speaks these words.

"What do you mean, 'he'?" Nori Ko asks.

An straightens. He buttons his shirt back up. He looks Nori Ko in the eye.

Don't tell her about me, Chiyoko says.

"I mean I'm fine," An says. "It's an old trick. When my body does this, sometimes I pretend it belongs to someone else—therefore 'he.' It helps me get a handle on everything." This is a lie, but a good one. And it works because, by luck, his body is composed and under control as he speaks.

He pushes a few buttons on a custom keypad strapped to his wrist. A light on the pad flashes three times and then glows red. "It's armed. I'm ready."

He snags the sniper rifle and an ammunition satchel and heads to the Montero, leaving Nori Ko to deal with the large pack and Sky Key. She gathers both, cradling Sky Key like a baby. The girl stirs as Nori Ko flops her into the backseat. Nori Ko takes Sky Key's chin and peels open an eyelid. Her pupils are wide and dilated. They flutter toward her nose. She's completely out. Nori Ko gets in the passenger seat and An puts the car in gear and they move.

They wind over a dirt track, heading east and south, until they link up with the main road over Mount Urabe. An drives very fast. The landscape is open and lush, with fields of hay and young wheat and dense stands of trees along the mountain's ridgelines. As they make their way back downhill toward a small marina on the southern side of the island, Nori Ko gets out her phone and makes a call.

It barely rings before she starts talking. She speaks for a few minutes in rushed Japanese. An can't understand a word of it. As soon as she hangs up An says, "Your brother again?"

"Yes. Everything's ready. We'll have to dive with tanks, but it's not deep. And we've got a full mask for the child, so we can keep her unconscious." She glances at Sky Key. "We should be inside the Mu monument within the hour." They approach a T intersection. "Go left." He tears around the corner, the Montero fishtailing.

An presses the gas more. The car accelerates. They are nearly there.

HILAL IBN ISA AL-SALT

Bombardier Global 8000, landing at Yonaguni Airport, Yonaguni, Japan

Hilal brings the plane in smooth and easy. He watches out the right side of the cockpit window as he taxis, the plane bouncing over the tarmac. He sees the other plane, but he does not see the others.

A few minutes later, as he brings the plane to a stop, Hilal sees a small Japanese man in a T-shirt and jeans maneuvering a large and laden luggage cart to one side of the receiving area. Sarah and Jago's plane is closed up and in good shape, if a little dirty and worn for having flown through what must have been an airborne hell over Canada and the United States.

Hilal cycles down the engines. The man waves at him gleefully, and then mimes opening the window. Hilal obliges.

"Mr. Dickey?" the man yells in perfect English.

"That's right," Hilal says, maintaining his American accent. "Mr. Masaka?"

"One and the same!"

"Did my friends arrive?"

"Yes!" He points over his shoulder. "They're inside, trying to enjoy some tea. They are very impatient for you to arrive, though."

"I'm sure. I'll be right out."

Hilal unbuckles and moves to the cabin. He slings on his pack. It holds a satellite phone he can use to call Jenny and Shari back in Australia, some food and water, and a pair of night-vision goggles. He pulls on shoulder webbing with extra magazines for his rifle and slings a leather belt around his waist, his machetes on either hip. Finally he snags a matte black HK416 and turns to the door.

Hilal, merely out of habit, toggles his 416 to fire.

He releases the latch and the door swings out and the warm sea air rushes in. It is sweet and heavy, and Hilal likes it.

Masaka lets out a gasp. "Oh my," he says, clapping a hand over his mouth. Hilal knows that this is a reaction to the wounds on his head and face.

Hilal reaches the tarmac and bows. "Mr. Masaka. I apologize for my appearance. I know it is unsettling. And thank you for allowing my friends and me to land."

"Of course . . ."

"We are not here to hurt you. Quite the contrary. I am sure my friends told you something similar."

"Yes—they did."

"How long since they arrived?"

"About thirty minutes," Masaka says, unable to pry his eyes from Hilal's face.

"Good. And you say they are inside?"

"Yes, over there, behind that door." He spins and points at the nearest building. "They're eager to see you."

"And I them." Hilal starts to walk toward the building when Masaka slaps his forehead.

"Goodness! I nearly forgot my manners. Please, one moment." He takes a half step back. "Your friend Sarah asked me to do this!"

"And that is?"

"Tea! She liked my tea so much she asked me to bring you some. I have some right here!" He points at a lacquered tray resting on the edge of the luggage rack. "Please. It's tradition!"

Hilal shrugs. "All right."

Masaka shuffles to the tray and picks it up, careful not to spill anything. In seconds he's standing before Hilal. "I'm sorry if this is strange. You are visitors, and I pride myself on welcoming visitors properly." He holds up the enamel tray, a pair of jade-colored cups on it. Steam swirls above them. As he draws closer Hilal's nose is greeted with the subtle but intoxicating odor of earth, cut grass, roasted grains, and a bite of acid that tickles his nostrils.

"It does smell good," Hilal admits.

"It's my own special blend," Masaka says.

Hilal takes the cup closest to Tsuro. Masaka takes the other. The tray falls to his side. They raise their cups. A stiff breeze blows over the airport from the west, whipping around Sarah and Jago's plane. It pushes away the smell of the tea and replaces it with the smell of trees and fresh water on concrete, like after a squall.

"*Kampai,*" Masaka says.

"*Kampai,*" Hilal echoes, but not very enthusiastically. He slowly raises the cup to his lips.

But then Hilal notices that the concrete around the other plane is shiny and wet, while the plane itself is utterly dry.

Hilal's eyes drift to the base of the luggage cart. He freezes.

A single drop of dark liquid falls from the cart and plops onto the ground.

Blood.

Hilal drops his cup. It shatters on the concrete, the piping tea splattering his pant cuffs and shoes.

Masaka says, "What's the matter, Mr. Dickey?"

Hilal steps back and points his rifle at Masaka's neck. "What is on that cart?"

"Luggage," Masaka says nervously. "Please, have I offended you? I apologize! Your friends—I can bring them out right now. Please!"

"You will do nothing of the sort," Hilal says, dispensing with the American accent. "I warn you, and only this one time. Do not move."

But Masaka does move. He leaps directly sideways, slipping out of the rifle's line of fire. Instead of tracking him Hilal twirls the rifle and swings for Masaka's head. The strike misses as Masaka swipes the tray—its edge honed and sharp—at Hilal's neck. Hilal bends away to avoid it, simultaneously swinging a foot at Masaka's exposed rib cage. He lets out a whelp, and Hilal sidesteps him with lightning quickness and snaps the rifle across the backs of Masaka's knees. The man buckles and falls. In a quick motion Hilal takes the machete named *LOVE* and, keeping it in its sheath, brings it to Masaka's neck and holds it there, pressing it into his Adam's apple.

Hilal checks their surroundings. No other people are around, hostile or otherwise. He prays that Masaka is working alone, or Hilal may already be as good as dead.

Hilal drags Masaka to the side of the cart, and he sees what is behind the high stack of bags.

A blue tarp quickly rolled and tucked over a misshapen lump the size of a large animal.

But Hilal knows that it does not conceal an animal.

He applies more pressure to Masaka's neck. The man gasps. Using the muzzle of his rifle Hilal raises a corner of the tarp and then whips the whole thing off. It flies open on the breeze.

Five bodies. All dead courtesy of medium-caliber head shots. Three men he has never seen before, although it is hard to make out their faces on account of their wounds.

And piled on top of these figures, her right arm thrown haphazardly over the narrow part of his waist, are Sarah Alopay and Jago Tlaloc. Both killed by sniper fire. Hilal checks around one last time, concludes that Masaka simply lured the Players and their associates into the open, where they were killed from a distance, and then dealt with their bodies. Hilal reasons that if the sniper were still out there, then he would already be dead.

Meaning he is safe. At least for the moment.

Masaka tries to speak but Hilal pulls *LOVE*'s scabbard so hard into his throat that he can't breathe. Hilal needs to find something before he deals with this little man. If Sarah and Jago really do have a weapon that can kill a Maker then he needs to take it from them. Hilal quickly frisks the Olmec. He does the same to Sarah, moving up from the feet. He finds a strange object in a pocket—a lump of metal that fits perfectly in his hand. It looks completely nonthreatening, but there's something about its heft and shape that makes him think this is it. He looks at the fallen Players one last time.

Lost comrades.

Heroes.

He says a low prayer in Amharic and pulls the tarp over them.

Their Endgame is over.

He pulls Masaka to his feet and drags him back out on the tarmac and then under the wing and fuselage of the plane, giving himself some cover. He forces Masaka to his knees and unsheathes *LOVE* and points it at the man's face. "Put your hands on your head, Mr. Masaka."

He does as he is told.

Hilal can tell from how he served the tea, and from the tilt of his shoulders, that Masaka is left-handed.

"Hold out your left hand, Mr. Masaka."

He protests in Japanese.

"Your head or your hand, Mr. Masaka. Choose now."

"Okay, okay!" Masaka says. He sticks out his left arm.

"Fan your fingers."

Masaka does.

Hilal rests *LOVE*'s edge on the base of his pinkie. "Who are you working with?" he demands.

Masaka says something else in Japanese, almost certainly a string of curses.

Hilal pushes down on *LOVE* and the pinkie comes free. The man calls out and tries to pull his altered hand close to his body but Hilal quickly reaches out and grabs Masaka's ring finger. He holds the hand in place and calmly lowers the blade to the skin.

"Speak," Hilal says.

"Fuck you," Masaka says in English.

Hilal cuts off this finger too. He drops it near the pinkie and grabs the middle finger. Blood is all over both of their hands now.

"Speak," Hilal says.

"I won't," Masaka blabs.

The finger is getting slippery, Hilal can't hold on. So he takes his wrist and slides his machete up Tsuro's arm, stopping at his shoulder.

"Do not test me."

"All right, all right! It was my sister!"

"Who is your sister?"

"She is Mu."

"You are *Mu*?"

"Yes."

"Your Player died a long time ago," Hilal says, not understanding.

"Fuck you," the man says again.

"Who is your sister?" Hilal demands.

Masaka doesn't speak.

Hilal thinks he understands. "You are working for revenge, yes? This is the best explanation I can come up with."

"Fuck. You."

"Last chance," Hilal says, pressing the edge of the machete into Masaka's flesh. "Who is your sister and is she alone?"

"I am Mu. My blood is Mu. I am Mu." He spits. A ball of phlegm hits Hilal's foot.

Hilal doesn't flinch.

Instead he raises the machete a few inches and then whips it down. Blood spurts everywhere. Hilal drops the arm. Masaka screams. Hilal moves the tip of his blade to Masaka's neck. "Mr. Masaka, time is my enemy right now. Tell me if your sister is alone."

Masaka quickly goes into shock. Hilal knows he doesn't feel any pain. The adrenaline won't let him.

"Answer me."

"Sh-Shang. The Shang."

"And they are where?"

"Marina. South side of island. Please."

Shock is a wonderful truth serum, Hilal thinks.

Hilal steps back three paces. Takes up his rifle. Points it. Fires one single shot. Masaka slumps forward.

Hilal wipes his machete on Masaka's pants and sheathes it. "This was unexpected," he says out loud.

Hilal hooks his fingers under Masaka's belt and lifts him by his pelvis. He takes the severed arm. He hustles to the luggage cart and puts Masaka on top of the pile of bodies, checking his pockets first and finding his car keys.

He decides to burn all of them.

He works quickly to douse the impromptu pyre with aviation fuel and when he's done he takes a lighter and sets it off.

He leaves the airport and gets in Masaka's Toyota hatchback and takes off. As the little car winds up the mountain and away from the water he uses the phone to call Jenny. It rings once before she answers with a curt, "Yeah."

"Go to the Dreaming now," Hilal says. "Find the Mu monument and open your portal. It will happen quickly, one way or another. The Shang will be there. He has the keys. And he has an accomplice. A Mu."

"Blimey," Jenny says.

"I know. I am on my way now. Send the signal when you see me in the star chamber. Then I will move in and save Little Alice. Tell Shari I will bring her daughter."

"I will, mate," Jenny says. "Godspeed."

"And to you, Master Ulapala. Godspeed to us all."

Four and Six and Eight and Twelve and Twenty[iv]

AN LIU, NORI KO, LITTLE ALICE CHOPRA

24.43161, 123.01314, near Yonaguni, Japan

Nori Ko dives off the small fishing boat anchored directly over the sunken Mu monument. She takes her pack and a flare gun and has a bright nylon line tied to her waist. She does not wear a wetsuit. The water is warm and pleasant and bright blue. She swims down seven meters, kicks hard with her fins, her arms at her sides. She blows out her ears three times. Bubbles rise around her face and carbonate her loose hair. On her left is a sprawling stepped pyramid that's been hidden under the waves for thousands upon thousands of years, its provenance and purpose an eternal mystery to the tourists and locals who've dived it over the years.

A pyramid of Mu.

She reaches a shelf, the blue deepening into darkness on her right. She twists under an outcropping and behind a huge frond of fan coral. Yes. There, like a mouth before her, is the dark entryway. She ties off the nylon line, its other end secured to the boat bouncing on the surface. She lights a flare and holds it before her, the black stone twinkling with orange and pink and white. She hits a wall and looks up and sees the square mirror of an air pocket a meter overhead. She detaches her weight belt and kicks twice. She emerges into a dry room, its stale air trapped inside the structure for thousands of years. She tosses the flare into the room before jumping into the water and swimming back down. She tests the nylon line. It holds. She aims the flare gun at the surface, making sure to avoid the hull of the small boat, and fires.

It shoots upward in a burst of bubbles and explodes, looking like a deformed firework from under the waves.

She swims back to the room and pulls herself into it. She lights three more flares and tosses each to a different corner. The room is rectangular, and she knows from a previous Mu mission that it's three meters wide and 4.854 meters long. A slender and tall doorway sits in the western wall. This leads to a shaft that angles downward for several meters and opens into another rectangular room. This second room is as far as she got when she last came here. If she's to go any farther today—and she hopes she will—it will be into uncharted territory. While she waits for An she unpacks the bag and checks their swords and their guns and takes what is hers.

A plume of bubbles disturbs the patch of water five minutes later. An and Sky Key appear simultaneously. The Shang Player holds up the girl and Nori Ko takes her and places her gently on top of her empty pack. She slips off the girl's specialized mask with sealed auto-equalizing ear covers and smooths Sky Key's wet face and dark hair, the skin around her chin and under her ears creased and reddened from the mask. The girl stirs and moans, but she doesn't wake.

Go easy now, love, Chiyoko tells An as he watches the other two.

He *BLINK* he slips *SHIVERSHIVERSHIVER* he slips out of his scuba gear and strips to *BLINKblinkshiver* to his underwear. He opens a large dry bag and pulls out the Chiyoko necklace and Earth Key *BLINKBLINK* and the vest and the wrist pad and a dry set of cotton clothes that are like pajamas. He brings Chiyoko over his head and smells her hair and kisses her ear. He slips Earth Key into a Velcro pocket and then puts his arms through the vest and pulls the straps extra tight against his rib cage. He slips the wrist pad over his left forearm and puts on the clothing that conceals the bulky explosive he will deliver to the kepler. He passes Nori Ko and the girl without talking, slings the strap of his ARX 160 over his shoulder. He picks up *BLINKBLINK* Nobuyuki's *SHIVERblink* Nobuyuki's katana and straps it to his back, its hilt jutting above his head.

You are ready, love.

"Ready," he says, staring at Sky Key while addressing Nori Ko.

Nori Ko stares at An in the eerie light, his deep-set eyes like black coals, his body practically glowing with vengeance, and wonders briefly if she's made a mistake.

But only briefly.

For the thing about An that frightens her most is exactly what draws her to him.

He is a killer first. And in this terrible game, killers win.

She throws An a flare. He catches it nimbly. She picks up the girl and pulls her to her chest. Sky Key's head flops onto Nori Ko's shoulder. The girl remains utterly unconscious. She will not witness her end, and Nori Ko is thankful for it.

She *is* a child, after all.

"Through there," she says, indicating the doorway. "You first."

An goes to the door and disappears through it. Nori Ko hustles after him, and after eight minutes of a corkscrewing descent they turn a sharp corner and practically stumble into the next room. Its proportions are the same as the one above, but it's twice as large. A butcher block of a table carved from the black rock, its edges straight and true, sits in the middle of the room. At the far end is another doorway, its stone door sealed shut.

The keys will open it, love, Chiyoko says.

"The keys"—*BLINKshiverBLINK*—"the keys will do it."

"Are you sure?" Nori Ko asks.

"Give me the girl," An says.

Nori Ko holds her out. An takes her in his arms. He carries her to the closed door. The girl is heavy. Earth Key is heavy in his pocket. He is heavy and getting heavier.

And then—

KEPLER 22B

24.43161, 123.01314, near Yonaguni, Japan

His eyes pop open, black slits set against his mother-of-pearl skin. A grating sound, stone sliding on stone, from not very far above.

It is time.

The old temple moves. In a few minutes its uppermost promontory will be visible to the world above the waves, a rectilinear pillar of sea-worn stone, wet and encrusted with bivalves and corals and anemones.

Like Stonehenge before it, this ancient monument has awoken.

He must prepare for the Player.

He steps from his spot and glides to the room's center. He folds in half at the waist and places the tips of his seven-fingered hands around the periphery of the gilt bowl set in the floor. The metallic surface swirls with dark colors and glimpses of the cosmos and an occasional beam of escaped light that lances to the ceiling.

He pulls his hands away, careful not to let any part of his body touch the inner bowl.

It is ready for the keys.

He moves to the portal. He places his right hand on the stone doorjamb and this liquefies and he thrusts his hand forward. He moves his fingers in the plasmastone, so cold to the touch for not having been used for thousands and thousands of years. The blank interior of the portal shimmers and blackens and he leans forward to make sure the link is open. His head appears, millions of miles away, in the teletrans room of his ship. He pulls his head back, and he is wholly in the Mu star chamber.

He swipes a finger across a sensor in the sleeve of his armor and a projectile weapon swings over his right hand. He adjusts its shot from the default wide scatter to pinpoint-thin.

He waits. The grating above continues. He scans the room one last time, moving clockwise from his left. There is the La Tène, should he need her, the living code embedded in her genes. There is the door leading up. There is the bowl in the middle of the room. The walls glow blue. But what's this? He squints. He quickly crosses the room into the farthest star point and peers down. Something he didn't see before.

A round red stone.

A stone that shouldn't be here.

He picks it up and smells it. The grating sound stops. The pebble smells distinct and he places it immediately.

It is from Australia. From near the Koori monument in the hinterland. He glances over his shoulder. The stone was exactly opposite the portal. It was thrown into the room from the Koori monument!

He drops the stone and thrusts his left hand back into the plasmastone, fine-tuning its settings. He knows that Players have moved around the world with these portals, he assumed by happenstance like when some went from Bolivia to the Himalayas, but the presence of this telltale pebble means that at least one of them has learned how to *use* the portals. This Player has not connected to this portal yet, but he assumes that he or she is trying to make a connection.

After another few moments he pulls his hand from the plasmastone and tosses the rock at the inky black of the portal. The rock bounces away and lands at his feet. Then he sticks out his hand, and it passes effortlessly through the frigid void and into his ship.

The test is satisfactory. Only he can pass now, in either direction. No one else will be able to use it to escape or to come here.

He spins back to the middle of the room and waits.

AN LIU, NORI KO, LITTLE ALICE CHOPRA

24.43161, 123.01314, near Yonaguni, Japan

An Liu and Nori Ko plant their feet as the ground shifts and turns. The sound of grinding stone is deafening, and even with no external point of reference, An senses that the room is rising through the water.

It's happening again, love, Chiyoko says. *Like when I died.*

"What's this?" Nori Ko yells. She stumbles and grabs the corner of the carved table, which is attached to the ground.

"The"—*BLINKshiver*—"the"—*SHIVERSHIVER*—"it's changing. Stonehenge did it"—*BLINKBLINKblink*—"did it too."

It means we're on the right track, love, Chiyoko says.

"I"—*BLINK*—"I know."

It means we can go the rest alone, Chiyoko says.

"I know."

Sky Key grows more restless as the room shifts and twists like a Tilt-A-Whirl, but after a few frenzied minutes it's finished.

Silence reigns.

A gust of cold air spills into the room. Sky Key's eyes flutter. She points.

"Earth Sky Sun," she says quietly.

An follows the girl's finger. The doorway is open. Another narrow passageway descending into darkness. An pushes his head into it, and his breath rises visibly around his face.

"Earth Sky Sun," Sky Key repeats.

An plops the girl onto the floor roughly.

"Hey!" Nori Ko says. "No need for—"

She's cut off as An whips his rifle into his hands and sights Nori Ko's face.

Blink.

No. Let her go! Chiyoko implores.

Except An says these words too.

BLINKBLINKBLINKBLINK.

Nori Ko raises her hands defensively.

And she finally understands.

Nori Ko says, "Listen to her, An. Chiyoko loves you."

"N-n-n-no," he says. "Thank you for"—*BLINKblinkBLINK*—"for getting me"—*SHIVERSHIVER*—"getting me here, but—"

Nori Ko cuts him off. "I can help. I'll make sure no one comes after you, An."

Let her go, Chiyoko says.

"I—I—I—I—I d-d-don't know," An stammers. "You should"—*SHIVERblinkblink*—"you should die."

Why? Chiyoko asks.

But before An can explain that it's because they all have to die and that he has to be the one to kill them, Nori Ko says, "I understand what you are, An. It's why I picked you. You're Death! Let me guard you so you can give this to the Maker, and find it for yourself. Let me help you. Let me help Chiyoko. Please!"

BLINKBLINKSHIVERshivershiverBLINK.

"Earth Sky Sun Key," the girl says.

BLINK.

Listen to her, love. Go to the kepler. Avenge me, Chiyoko says. *Now!*

BBBBBLINK. BBBBBLINK. BBBBBBBBBLINK.

His hands shake. The rifle lowers a few inches. Nori Ko considers diving behind the stone table, but while An's tics give her a chance they also show how on edge he is, how unpredictable.

She stays rooted to the spot.

SHSHSHSHSHIVER. SHIVER. SHSHSHSHShiver.

Noises echo from the passageway leading up and out of the monument. The hiss of crashing waves, a *clunk-clunk* like a metal container repeatedly bring struck like a drum, and there, right there

for a moment—the sound of a man saying, "Faith."

"More are coming!" Nori Ko says urgently.

"Earth Sky Sun," the girl says loudly.

An nudges her with his thigh. "Shh."

Let her go.

BBBBBBBBBBBBLINK. SHSHSHSHSHSHSHSHSHSHIVER.

The Beretta falls to his side. "Okay. Keep me"—*BLINK*—"keep me safe, Nori Ko. Keep her"—*SHIVER*—"her"—*blinkblinkblink*—"her"—*SHIVERSHIVERBLINKblink*—"her"—*SHIVERBLINKBLINK*—"Chiyoko safe too."

Without saying another word he grabs Sky Key by the shirt collar and half carries, half drags her out of the room and into the darkness, the girl gurgling and moaning. The last thing Nori Ko sees or hears of either is the red glow from An's wrist pad, the one indicating that his nuclear vest is well and armed.

Nori Ko takes three breaths and centers herself. She draws her sword with her right hand, grips her rifle with her left. She leans against the table and drops behind it, completely hidden from whoever is coming from above.

HILAL IBN ISA AL-SALT

24.43161, 123.01314, near Yonaguni, Japan

Hilal grips a rope that's secured to his Zodiac's bow and manages to stay on the planking. The water churns as a twisting, telescoping pillar of stone rises from the waves. When it stops it juts four meters above the surface like a small lighthouse.

The dive boat that he's lashed his Zodiac to—the same boat that An and his Mu accomplice used to reach this same point—clanks against the stone rhythmically. A huge fan coral is flopped over its side, holding the boat in place. An opening large enough for a person appears on the side of the rock.

This is it.

Hilal reaches into his pocket and threads his fingers through the holes on the lump of metal. Again it does nothing. But again he is certain that somehow, some way, it will work when needed.

"I must have faith," he says.

He checks his machetes one last time and his HK416 rifle and steps off the boat and through the opening, his faith helping him take each step forward as he moves toward the end.

Reality is a dream.[v]

SHARI CHOPRA, JENNY ULAPALA

"The Dreaming," Shari says.

Their physical bodies are in Australia's Yuendumu Hinterland, but their spiritual bodies are here, in the shared void.

Shari holds Jenny's hand in both realms. In Australia they sit side by side on the red earth, knees touching. In the Dreaming they walk briskly through nothingness, have been walking for what could be fractions of a second or hours. Their arms swing with purpose, their thighs occasionally brush against each other. Shari can see forever in every direction, but wherever she looks there is nothing to see.

"When?" Shari asks.

"Soon, mum."

They are alone this time. Big Alice is not there whispering that the Harappan are at Shari's back, waving their hands, mouthing her name, pushing her forward, ever forward.

A blue glow appears in the distance. Jenny guides them toward it. She says, "I'll stay with you when we get there, mum. But when Hilal arrives and it's time for him to bring your daughter through the portal, I'll have to leave you to signal him. Otherwise he won't know we're ready for him. You gotta stay centered and quiet in the Dreaming until Hilal's crossed with your girl, and you gotta stay calm. No matter what you see happening there, you stay calm or we could lose the connection and any chance of getting them back. You understand, yeah?"

The light grows brighter.

"I understand, Jenny."

"Good. No more talking. No more spoken thought. Silence, mental and otherwise. This is gonna be the hardest meditation you've ever done, 'cause every fiber of your being is gonna tell you to move and act on behalf of your child. You can't do none of that. Help her by being there and nothing else. If the Maker gets tipped to our presence he'll shut the door to us and we'll be good and screwed."

"I understand."

"Be nothing, like a stone on the floor, like the floor itself. You are the foundation."

To acknowledge her, Shari squeezes Jenny's hand, in this world and in that one. Here and there. Everywhere and nowhere.

They continue.

Brighter.

Brighter.

Brighter.

They see the room now, star shaped and glowing and prepared. They can't see the Maker anywhere but they can feel his presence.

He waits. He hides.

Jenny freezes near the portal. Shari does too.

Little Alice is not there yet. But—

Aisling Kopp *is* there, her unconscious face and bright-red hair peeking above the edge of a silken shroud.

Shari wants to know how this happened, but she can't speak. She can't think. She closes her eyes in the Dreaming and breathes breathes breathes.

Nothing.

Nothing.

Nothing.

Nothing is what will save them now.

NORI KO

24.43161, 123.01314, near Yonaguni, Japan

The man's voice above has been silent since she first heard it. If he's coming to her—and he must be—then he's keeping quiet. Nori Ko's repositioned herself in the passageway that An and Sky Key disappeared through, prone and propped on her elbows, her rifle covering the door on the far side of the room. The air falls around her like a frigid blanket. She mashes her teeth to keep them from chattering. The room beyond is pitch-black. She lies motionless in a void, waiting, her only window on the visible world a night vision–equipped riflescope. She keeps her eye pressed to this. She sights along the edge of the table and up to the door. Since she is a few short meters from her target she can't fit more than half the door in the field of vision. To keep sharp and ready she shifts the rifle every three seconds. Up and down and up and down and up and down.

The man—and whoever is with him, for he might not be alone—will round the final corner and appear and she will wait for the right moment and she will cut them down.

The doorway remains black and empty for four minutes.

Five.

Six.

Seven.

Eight.

This is how long it took her and An and Sky Key to get here from the room above.

Somewhere below, An is closer to meeting the Maker.

And Chiyoko too—or what is left of her. Around his neck, in his mind.

In his dark heart.

Nine minutes.

Up and down and up and down and up and down.

Up and down.

HILAL IBN ISA AL-SALT, NORI KO

24.43161, 123.01314, near Yonaguni, Japan

Hilal keeps his rifle up one-handed, the mysterious weapon ready in the other hand. His night-vision goggles are flipped over his face. He moves methodically through the dark and the cold.

After seven minutes of steady, twisting descent, Hilal stops.

The passageway ends less than a meter away. Hilal makes out the long wall of a room. If he hadn't been moving so slowly he would have poured into it. Who knows what might be waiting for him on the far side.

He moves his rifle aside and inspects the floor, looking for trip wires. Nothing. He checks the edges of the doorway for sensors. Nothing.

He stands there for several seconds, thinking about what to do.

About what he *must* do.

Faith, he says to himself.

He kneels and readies the rifle. He will roll forward and to the right, hoping to find something to hide behind.

He counts.

One.

Two.

Three.

The tip of Nori Ko's nose feels like an icicle.

She moves the rifle up and down and up and down.

Up.

Down.

Up.

A figure rolls from the doorway. She presses and holds the trigger, pushing the rifle against the recoil and adjusting to hit the target on the floor. Modified for full auto, the rifle sprays bullets into the room, muzzle flash strobe-lighting the contours of her head and shoulders and the stone walls. The figure disappears behind the end of the table. She's not sure if she scored a hit. She releases the trigger. The last few shell casings tinkle onto the floor. Her ears ring. She parks her rifle, aiming for the end of the table, painfully aware that she cannot simultaneously sight the door.

If there is more than one of them, she is done for.

She slides the gun back to the base of the door, then to the top of it, then to the table. She draws this little triangle for five full seconds, which feels like five minutes. She hears a child's wail from somewhere deep in the ancient building. She draws the triangle again. Again. Again.

Maybe she's gotten lucky. Maybe there's only one.

Movement. The figure that tumbled into the room sticks a rifle around the table's corner. They fire simultaneously. The shots being fired at her miss, but her shots hit, and a man's voice calls out in pain and his rifle drops to the floor with a clank.

She shoots this and it slides out of reach.

Then she sights the top of the door, the bottom, the table. The triangle again.

The table.

The bottom of the door.

The top.

Again.

Then she hears a sound like an arc of electricity and sees a blinding yellow light and she rolls defensively to the side, wedging between the floor and the wall. The flash zips past her in a millisecond and catches her ARX 160 right down the middle, cutting the scope and both receivers clean in half. This energy projectile burns the flesh on the back of her trigger hand, and although her eyes are shut it's so bright that all she sees is orange and red.

But the flash is gone as fast as it arrived, and the sound too. There's the smell of burned flesh and of what she swears is molten metal.

But she can't be sure because now, with the light lingering in her eyes and her night-vision scope ruined, she's completely blind.

She hops to her feet, draws a long tactical knife, steps gingerly into the room. She swings the knife here and there, here and there.

"Come on!" she blurts, defying the darkness. *"Come on!"*

Hilal twiddles the fingers of his right hand. It was rattled badly when the 416 was shot from his grip and it tingles like when a cricket batsman gets a curving pitch near the hands.

But this sensation is nothing next to what is happening in his left hand.

As soon as his rifle was hit the lump of metal came to life, as if it knew he was in imminent danger and its services were needed.

His arm went as straight as a board, locking at the elbow, as a long spike grew from the pinkie side of the piece of metal, extending for a little over a meter. As soon as this happened his hand felt as if it was joined with the metal, and his thumb found the socket, and he pressed it. His arm lit up with a jolt of energy as a bright disc flew from the tip of the spike, careening across the room in a flash and hitting his adversary.

But this shot did not kill her.

Now he takes more careful aim. He peers at this woman for a brief moment. If she had night vision before she does not now, as she stands before him swiping randomly at the air. She is undoubtedly the Mu that Masaka told him about, as she looks very much like an older version of Chiyoko Takeda. Hilal can only guess why this person is helping the Shang, and he is too pressed for time to consider it for very long.

He presses his thumb into the trigger again. The room flashes yellow once more and the weapon fires its energy disk and the air crackles with electricity and two thumps.

Hilal looks to the far side of the room. Two halves of a person lie on the floor, the contacted flesh and innards cauterized and popping-hissing.

A child wails from deeper down in this ancient monument.

"Sky Key!" he hisses.

He stoops and runs his fingers over his 416. The magazine was knocked free and the mag well is dented and misshapen. It is useless. He straightens. Draws *HATE* in his right hand and keeps this amazing Maker weapon ready in his left.

He steps past the cleaved body and through the doorway and slips silently into the darkness and the cold that lies below.

AN LIU, LITTLE ALICE CHOPRA

24.43161, 123.01314, near Yonaguni, Japan

Keep going, love. BlinkSHIVERSHIVERblinkblinkblinkshiverBLINKBLINK SHIVERSHIVERSHIVER BLINKSHIVERSHIVERShivershiverBLINK.
An *blink* An *blink* An drags an increasingly conscious Sky *SHIVER* Sky Key down *blink* down *SHIVER* down.
The air is cold *shiver* cold *blinkblink* cold *blink* it's freezing. A faint glow grows below. His vest feels like it weighs *shivershiver* weighs 200 kilos not *blink* not *BLINK* not 20.
Walk, love. Next foot, next foot, next foot. Move. Move!
She encourages him, speaks to him without any *blink* any hitches. No tics in her *shiver* in her voice.
She is pure. In his mind. In his heart.
The pure part of him.
SHIVERSHIVERSHIVERblinkblink. SHIVERblinkshiver.
He's so anxious *blink* so shaken *shiver* so *blinkblink* so ticking he can't *blinkblinkblink* can't talk to her *SHIVERSHIVER* either out loud or *blinkblink* or in his mind.
His mind.
His heart.
His mind.
His black heart.
Chiyoko.
Chiyoko.
BLINKSHIVERBLINK.
He tightens his grip on the girl's collar, catching a clump of *blinkshiver* a clump of hair. The follicles *blinkblink* snap-snap-snap out of her skin.

She yelps and wails and starts speaking in Hindi or Bengali, whatever it is he can't *blinkshiverSHIVERblink* he can't understand a word. She kicks and swings her arms and An gives her a hard shake but this only *blinkshiverSHIVERblink* it only makes her more upset.

She wails again.

Gunfire, and lots of it, echoes from above and beats *blink* beats *shiver* beats on his ears.

A brief silence then another burst, followed by a loud *zzzuuppp!* like a shot of electricity.

Then silence.

Sky Key cries again.

SHIVERSHIVERSHIVERBLINKBLINKSHIVER.

Keep moving, love. Don't fail now.

The child writhes and spits. Nori Ko says something above. Another *zzzzuuup!* and then silence.

Don't hurt the girl.

He can't *blinkblink* can't help himself. He shoves his rifle around to his back and yanks up Sky Key and *shivershiver* wraps both arms around her. Her back presses into his chest. He claps a hand over her mouth. She bites the web of skin between his thumb and forefinger and yells out once again.

"Ack!" he blurts. He works his fingers under her *blinkblink* under her chin and claps her mouth shut and holds it this way. He stops walking.

BLINKSHIVERBLINK.

He works his other hand over *blinkblinkSHIVERSHIVER* over the girl's nose, pinching it shut.

She needs to live, An! Don't!

Sky Key kicks her short legs into An's gut and pelvis. She gets him in the groin and he bends over to help relieve the pain, crooking her body in his. She tries to move her head side to side but she isn't strong enough. She keeps kicking, kicking.

Don't.

SHIVERSHIVERSHIVERSHIVER.

Her kicks die down. Her head stops straining. He releases her nose.
Holds his hand under it.

The warmth of her breath coats the top of his hand.

She lives. She is unconscious again.

BLINKBLINKBLINK.

Good, love. Now. Go!

He cradles the girl. His vest is so heavy, and so ready, and the release of
death is so near.

He is so happy.

Walk.

Next foot *SHIVER* next foot *blink* next foot. Down down down.

The blue glow gets brighter.

BLINKSHIVERBLINK.

Closer.

Brighter.

Colder.

BLINKSHIVERBLINK.

Closer.

Brighter.

Colder.

He takes one more step and stops.

The star chamber. The tics are gone. The girl shudders as if disturbed
by a bad dream.

We are here, love.

SHARI CHOPRA, JENNY ULAPALA

Shari sees Little Alice's shaking body in the Shang's hands. Shari can't think she can't yell she can't call out she can't reach she can't act she can't feel she has to repress it all she is powerless she is powerless she is powerless and she has to embrace the powerlessness.

Jenny stands next to her, they both see, they both let what they see pass through them, as if each were an unthinking camera, nothing more than a lens to an observer's eye.

They both see the Shang step forward and look around and stop.

They both hear him say, "I am here, kepler 22b. I have the keys. I claim my prize as winner of Endgame. Show yourself."

AN LIU, KEPLER 22B, LITTLE ALICE CHOPRA, JENNY ULAPALA, SHARI CHOPRA

Star chamber, 24.43161, 123.01314, near Yonaguni, Japan

The Maker moves and the air shimmies and wrinkles and he appears, as if stepping from a rend in space itself.

Welcome, An Liu, Shang Player of the 377th line of humanity.

An's right hand touches the pad on his left wrist. Both are obscured from the Maker by the drape of Sky Key's clothing.

An sneers at the kepler. He would enjoy seeing him suffer, but he senses that any hesitation will make it more likely that he will not succeed in killing him.

I can almost touch you, love. Come to me, Chiyoko says.

I am, he thinks.

He smiles at the Maker. "Thank you, kepler 22b." His finger finds the detonator button. The vest feels light, airy, already like it is igniting moving in and out at the same time, taking him with it and everything around him, warming his flesh and spirit.

I am coming.

He says, "But my name is not An Liu. My name is Death."

He presses the button.

And nothing happens.

He presses it again.

Nothing.

He drops the girl. She lands awkwardly at his feet and bounces. She groans. Her mouth moves, eyes flutter.

She is in pain.

· · ·

Shari closes her eyes in the Dreaming. She can't look. She will keep the connection to this place by imagining Little Alice, as she was in the yard in Gangtok, chasing Tarki through the brush, as she passed through the kitchen while Shari cooked, as she rode on Jamal's broad shoulders, as she sat in Jovinderpihainu's lap and smiled at his wrinkled face. She imagines these things without putting words to them. By filling her spirit these images help keep her rooted in the nothingness of the Dreaming. It is the practice of her meditation turned on its head and writ out as large as it can be: find timelessness *solely* by being in the present, hold nothingness *solely* by accepting everything.

Little Alice is already with her.

She always has been.

Thank you for not harming the second key, An Liu.

An desperately jams his finger onto the wrist pad. He presses the detonator, presses, presses. Nothing. He pulls back his sleeve and sees that the red arming light is extinguished.

He looks to the kepler's pale face. An is slack-jawed, eyes widened.

Oh, the bomb would kill me and stop what I am here to do. But the detonator will not work so long as I am alive and close to it. You simply cannot kill me, An Liu.

Move, love!

An drops and rolls over the girl, coming up a meter closer to the Maker, the rifle that was slung behind his back in his hands. He fires. The bullets sail into the alien and hit him and bend around his clothing and his neck and his face. The slugs bury themselves in the stone beyond the Maker, producing a cloud of blue dust as a drifting backdrop.

Although the bullets do nothing, An keeps firing. His teeth grind. Tears stream from the corners of his eyes.

The magazine is empty. The gun bolt *click-click-click-click-click*s. An releases the magazine and flips it and shoves it back in and he is about to resume shooting when the Maker raises his arm and points his fist at An. A pulse of invisible energy, like a gust of concentrated wind, lifts An from his feet into the air, throwing him against the doorway he and Sky Key entered through. He would sail through it except that now it's shut by an invisible barrier.

I said nothing will work, Shang.

An's entire body aches. He jumps to his feet and draws Nobuyuki's sword and rushes to the Maker. He leaps over the girl, who was unaffected by the Maker's blast, and arrives in front of the alien in less than three seconds, the sword driving at his long neck.

It slams into the Maker, who smiles.

Who laughs.

The sword's sharpened edge does nothing either.

Enough.

kepler 22b takes An by the neck and lifts him off his feet and holds him at arm's length. An kicks, swings the sword helplessly. The alien's hand is so cold it burns An's skin, which bunches below his jawline, turning blue and white. An tries to curse the alien but he can't make a sound. His lips turn purple. His eyes redden and bulge from their sockets. He can't breathe.

You don't need to kill him, love. Come to me anyway. Die and come to me anyway.

No! An thinks. *Death!*

I hear your thoughts, you know. I hear the thoughts of everyone in this room. You, the girl, the dead Mu who lives in your twisted mind. I hear the thoughts of the Aksumite, who will arrive at the doorway in a few seconds.

Death!

No, Shang. Not for you. I was going to kill you when I used your body to finish Endgame, but now I see that you don't deserve death. Life, Shang! That is what you despise and that is what you shall have. That is what you deserve. But . . . time is precious, so . . .

He lifts the rail-thin Player another foot. He holds out his free hand

and opens it and one of the Shang's pockets vibrates and jostles and Earth Key strains at the cloth and shoots out, settling in the Maker's hand. Then he hurtles the Shang to the right and into one of the star-point recesses. An Liu bangs his head against the stone and crumples into it, alone and silent and completely unconscious.

We can talk about life later.

He glances at the La Tène.

I do not need your body to finish Endgame anyway, An Liu.

He drifts toward Sky Key, dropping Earth Key into the bowl in the middle of the room. It rattles and bounces and settles in the lowest part, waiting to be joined by the girl and the Player.

He reaches Sky Key and bends and picks her up. Her back goes as straight as a board as his frigid hands touch her and she screams. She screams and screams and screams.

This noise should shake Shari Chopra from her meditation within a meditation, but it does not. Instead, when the screams drift into her awareness she sees a playful Little Alice on a swing set, pealing with shrill delight, smiling, filled with life and joy and happiness.

She sees her as she should be.

As she is, always, in Shari's heart.

HILAL IBN ISA AL-SALT, LITTLE ALICE CHOPRA, KEPLER 22B

Star chamber, 24.43161, 123.01314, near Yonaguni, Japan

Hilal stops shy of the door. The Maker stands not three meters away. He holds the girl. He stares at Hilal, black-eyed and smug.

Hello, Aksumite.

Hilal raises the weapon. "Good-bye."

He angles the weapon so that it will strike kepler 22b and not Little Alice. He drops his thumb into the trigger and squeezes. His arm lights in pain and the weapon glows and the disk shoots forward, the light consuming Hilal and the door between them and kepler 22b.

But instead of relieving the alien of his head, the blast hits the invisible shield suspended between them and it explodes and dissipates and throws Hilal violently backward into darkness.

Fool.

kepler 22b places the girl in the bowl with Earth Key. As soon as Sky Key comes in contact with the bowl she stops screaming, becoming quiet and peaceful.

The end won't hurt. kepler 22b didn't lie to the Nabataean about that. All he needs now is the third and final key.

A Player.

All he needs is the La Tène.

JENNY ULAPALA

Very quietly, very discreetly, very gently, Jenny says, "Hell with this. I'm old anyway."

She releases Shari's hand in the Dreaming, keeps ahold of it in the physical realm back in Australia.

She drifts into the center of the star chamber, hovering over Little Alice. She watches the Maker unwrap the redheaded Player named Aisling Kopp. The Maker remains unaware of Jenny and Shari. He cannot see them. He is so sure of himself.

Too sure of himself.

Jenny turns away from the Maker and faces the limitless psychic void of the Dreaming. She leaves the room and Shari and the felled Players and moves to the great line that feeds and serves the Dreaming and which is always there just beyond perception. She gives herself to it. The world of her ancestors grows and surges and glows to life around her. She sees those she knew in the flesh and those she met in the Dreaming and those she only ever heard of. She sees the great expanse of the desert and the ancient trees and the mountains and valleys of her native land but also all of Earth, rivers of ice and pinnacles of stone and teeming jungles and voluminous life-giving seas and molten iron and nickel and black storms laced with electricity and power and windswept dunes as high as skyscrapers and deep caves dripping with mineral water and the depths of the oceans black and cold yet full of life and orange pluming vents bubbling up from the center of the ancient planet, every inch as ancient as the Maker's home world, every inch as complete and wondrous and and and otherworldly, right here. Earth.

Home.

Home to life and death and the Dreaming. Because Jenny knows heaven isn't up there in the stars—it's right here, on Earth and of it. And salvation is coming.

"Hey!" she calls into the Dreaming, and the lands and seas and peaks and glaciers and drifting treetops fill and overfill with faces and shoulders and arms and fists.

"Come on now. Jenny Ulapala needs you."

And they silently raise their fists in unison, millions and billions of the dead and gone in the Dreaming. Her army. Their army. Ours. Greater than any otherwise assembled on this planet or any other at this time or any other.

She turns her back on humanity.

Not to forsake it.

But to lead it.

She takes one step back from the void and toward the Maker.

And there, next to her, comes Big Alice.

"Oi, Jenny."

"Alice," Jenny smiles.

"Baiame fucked up good, yeah?"

"How so?"

"They shouldn'ta shown us how to go walkabout in the After-After like this. It was foolish."

Jenny is so pleased. She sights the head of the Maker in the room back in the physical world. "It was."

Big Alice points at Sky Key, at the doorway blocking a stirring Hilal ibn Isa al-Salt. "Time we show him how powerful we've become."

"Quiet now, Alice."

"You got it, Gram."

Jenny marches into the star chamber. The Maker carries the La Tène, naked and pale and asleep and breathing shallowly, in his arms. Shari remains calm and connected. She holds the connection in spite of everything. Jenny concentrates her mind to a point and aims this at the door. She could strike the Maker, but the weapon that will *definitely* kill him lies outside the room, in Hilal's hand.

Jenny is ready. Before she launches forward she whistles at the Maker. He finally sees them.

And he is aghast.

How?

"You made a mistake. We all do."

And before he has a chance to say anything else, she carries herself forward with the psychic weight of all that's behind her and materializes in the star chamber and smashes into the barrier that seals off Hilal and the weapon that can slay their common enemy.

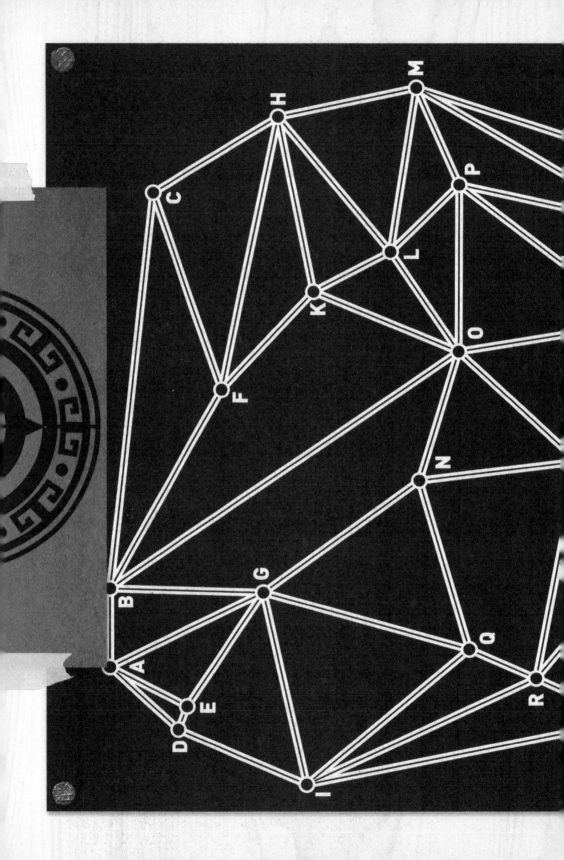

HILAL IBN ISA AL-SALT, LITTLE ALICE CHOPRA, JENNY ULAPALA, KEPLER 22B, AISLING KOPP

Star chamber, 24.43161, 123.01314, near Yonaguni, Japan

"Now!" Jenny yells as she appears as if from nowhere and flies over Hilal and collapses behind him.

Hilal lies on the ground, his limbs akimbo. He twists and aims and though he's groggy and his vision is imperfect and cloudy he holds up the weapon. The Maker drops the La Tène and raises his own gun and Hilal squeezes and squeezes and squeezes and the first shot meets a shot fired by the kepler and these cancel each other out but the next shot and the next and the next all launch from Hilal's hand and fire into the room and Hilal feels the power and his arms tingle and he sees the light in his eyes and there is a loud noise and then a louder one and a deep and clamorous scream and then—

Silence.

Hilal sits bolt upright. He blinks. He is surrounded by pitch blackness. He feels around the floor and finds what he's looking for. Night vision. He slips the goggles over his head and presses the button and, thank the stars, they work.

Jenny is under him. He gently shakes her by the shoulders. She moans. She is alive. He takes her face in his hands, pinching her pockmarked cheeks, moving her head, slapping her lightly. "Master Ulapala. Master Ulapala."

"Uhn . . . Oh . . ."

"Wake up, Master Ulapala!"

"Hilal?"

"Yes," he says, full of disbelief. "How did you . . . ? You did not come through the portal . . . you just appeared in thin air . . ."

"It was a trick I never tried before. I'll tell you about it later."

"Are you all right?"

"Did we?"

"Yes. I mean, I think so."

Jenny strains to look past Hilal but winces. "Ah. My leg. I think it's broken."

Hilal pushes aside a pile of rubble. The old woman's ankle is bent at a strange angle. "This will hurt," he says, "but I have to check."

"Yeah, all right."

He runs his hand along her leg, feeling for bone or blood.

"It is not compound. You will be fine."

"Hilal. You gotta go check on . . ."

He stands. "Yes. I know. I will be right back, Master Ulapala. Do not move."

"Not going anywhere," she says.

Hilal moves into the star chamber, listening to the aches and pains of his own body.

"Uncle?" Little Alice says.

She sits cross-legged on the floor, Earth Key in her hand. Hilal rushes to her.

"Hello there. I am a friend of your mother's."

"Another?" Little Alice says. "So was Maccabee."

Hilal won't argue with her, not now. First he has to know: "Where is the Maker?"

"What?"

"The Maker."

She points directly to her left. "There, Uncle."

Hilal spins and looks and

And

Yes

The Maker is cut into at least three pieces. He is as dead as he will ever be. And Hilal looks past the Maker and sees Aisling, naked and her skin very pale in the strange green hue of the night vision, but breathing.

They did it.

They did it.

"Wait here, Alice," Hilal says.

He goes to the portal that will lead them back to Australia and to safety. It is not black and inky but bright. He pulls off the goggles and sees the red earth of the outback on the far side casting its daylight into the room. The Koori guards stand alert and shocked. They're waving their arms at him and gesturing for him to cross over. At their feet is Shari Chopra, sitting on the ground, eyes closed and entranced, holding her meditative place in the Dreaming, keeping the portal open.

He holds up a finger. "I am coming, brothers," he says. "*We* are coming."

He backtracks to Jenny. Alice says, "Uncle," but he says, "One moment. You will be with your mother soon. I promise."

"I know, Uncle, but—"

"One moment," he says, so full of joy and triumph and relief.

He reaches Jenny and pulls her arm over his broad shoulders and picks her up. "We did it," he says. "You did it."

Jenny blinks. "Really, mate?"

He laughs. "Yes, Master Ulapala. Really."

"Stop calling me that. I mean it."

He laughs again. "All right, Master Jenny," he says, his teeth gleaming in a broad smile.

"And Little Alice?"

"Come."

He puts his other arm around her waist and they walk slowly to Little Alice and stop in front of her.

"Auntie," Alice says.

"Little Alice," Jenny says quietly, holding out her hand.

Alice takes it and stands. "I'm hungry," she says.

Jenny and Hilal laugh. "I am too, sweets," Jenny says. "Starved, actually."

Together they move toward the portal.

"Uncle," Alice says.

"We're almost there."

"Auntie."

"I'll cross with you and then come back for Aisling," Hilal says.

And then they reach the doorway that will transport them away from here, but when they try to move through it they are blocked.

Jenny slaps a hand on the image of the outback in front of them, but hits what feels like a sheet of glass. She slaps it again. Hilal whispers, "No!"

Jenny punches it. Glances around the room at the Maker's body and blurts, "He sealed it!"

"Can you take us back the way you came?" Hilal asks.

"Can't. That was a one-way trip," Jenny says.

"We will have to leave the way I came then," Hilal says, thinking how long it will take and how much effort. Thinking of how distraught Shari will be to have to wait that much longer to have her child in her arms.

"Uncle," Alice says. "Auntie."

Both look at the girl. "What is it?" they ask together.

She points to her left. "Him. There."

Their heads whip to where she points. And then they see. They were so excited about the death of the kepler, and the end of Endgame, that they had forgotten.

An Liu.

He is motionless and wedged into a corner and completely nonthreatening.

Hilal says, "He cannot hurt you anymore, Little Alice."

"I know," the girl says. "But look. His arm."

Hilal squints at the Shang and there—yes—a flashing red light.

"Wait here," Hilal says, propping Jenny against the shuttered portal.

Hilal bounds to An, reaching him in seconds. He takes his arm. Sees the wrist pad, the buttons, the notations in Chinese and English.

He pats down An's body and feels the bulk and grabs his shirt and tears it open. The nylon the straps the wires the explosives.

Not C4.

Not TNT.

Not PETN.

Hilal is not sure what it is, but given what he knows about An Liu, he knows it is worse than any of these other options.

The red light flashes faster.

And faster.

He quickly inspects the wiring. There are too many for him to disarm it, and he does not have tools to work with anyway.

He stands.

"What is it?" Jenny asks.

"Bomb!" he yells, running to them. "There is no timer readout, but it is armed."

"What kind?" Jenny asks.

"I do not know. Probably a small nuclear device."

Jenny's eyes widen. "We need to get through this portal!"

"I know!"

Hilal zips around the room looking for something anything something.

Jenny runs her hands up and down the blocked portal, tries to ignore the people on the other side, her guards and the call of the Outback, the proximity of safety.

"Auntie," Alice says.

"Not now, honey," Jenny says.

"There," Alice says, ignoring her.

She points at the stone to the side of the doorway. Jenny runs her hands up to it and—yes!—when her fingers touch it, it liquefies and she pushes her hands into the stone. She doesn't know what it is, but inside she feels buttons and switches and sliders. "Hilal, I think . . ." She moves her fingers, twists her arm, pushes it in deeper. "I think . . ." Hilal appears at her side. "This is the lock," Jenny says.

"Can you open it?"

"Maybe?" she says unconvincingly.

Hilal looks at the Shang. The red light blinks faster. "Hurry."

Jenny turns her hand again and there is a click from inside the stone and Hilal reaches for Australia but no, it is still sealed off.

"Bugger!" Jenny says.

"What?"

"I can't . . . I think it scanned my hand. And you know, I ain't got Maker mitts, so . . ." She pulls out her arm with a painful-sounding *pop*.

Hilal turns a tight circle. The light blinks faster. Faster.

"Uncle."

"Not now. I am trying to think."

Little Alice doesn't say anything else. She just tugs hard at Hilal's *HATE* machete and he actually lets it go and the small girl drags it scraping across the floor to the Maker. Hilal and Jenny watch her with perplexed looks as she stops by his pale torso and struggles to lift the blade.

"His hand, Hilal!" Jenny blurts. "Get his bloody hand!"

Hilal leaps to Alice in a single bound and snags *HATE*. He peels back

313

the Maker's armored sleeve and lifts his blade high and snaps it down
and he drops the metal and replaces this with frozen Maker flesh.
He snags the girl around the waist and bounces back to the portal,
giving Jenny the limb. She jams it into the stone and it melts again
and there is another click and a hiss and the warm dry Australian air
hits their faces. Hilal thrusts Alice through the portal as the guards
rush to them. They take the girl and help Jenny through. Hilal steps
through too when he remembers Aisling. He pivots, catches sight of
An's red light flashing so fast it's practically solid. He stumbles and falls
over Aisling and picks her up and jumps back to the portal. He passes
Aisling through to a Koori guard, the surface twinkling and snapping
with electricity, and then he jumps in, through space and time and
into another part of the known world.

Little Alice runs to her mother and wraps her arms around her neck,
but Shari is so far away that she doesn't notice. Hilal tries to get
everyone away from the portal, away from the path of the coming
blast. The guards move Jenny and Aisling and themselves. Hilal comes
back to pick up Shari and the girl, and as he leans over them Shari's
nostrils twitch with the scent of her daughter's hair and her eyes shoot
open and the portal flashes white for a fraction of a second before
being snuffed out and sealed with the blackness of dark stone.

Shari is awake, free of the Dreaming. The connection is lost. The portal
is closed.

They are safe.

Hilal collapses onto the ground, panting and sweating. He sits slump-
backed, staring at what's in front of him.

He laughs. Deep and throaty.

He laughs at it.

At the kissing, loving, fawning, pawing, desperately grateful lives of a
mother and a child, brought together for good and at last.

Come to me, love.

An blinks. He can't move. His body is broken and pain-ridden. Like it has always been, in one way or another.

Come to me.

He watches the others. The red light illuminates his face and the tattoo tear under his eye. He watches them take the Maker hand and use it in some way he can't understand. Watches the second key leave, and he doesn't care. He watches them escape.

"He's"—*blink*—"he's"—*SHIVER*—"he's"—*BLINKBLINK*—"he's gone, Chiyoko." *BLINKSHIVERSHIVERBLINK.* "He's dead."

I know. I saw it.

BLINKBLINKblink.

"I didn't kill him."

They Played for life.

"They did," An says.

In your way, you did too.

He watches Hilal almost leave and then return and trip over Aisling Kopp and then pick her up.

"No," An says.

Yes.

"No."

Hilal passes Aisling through the doorway, and then he jumps after her and is gone.

Only An is left.

He manages to bring his hand to his neck. He finds her dark hair with his fingers. He caresses it.

The red light is nearly solid.

"No."

Yes, love.

"I didn't Play for life."

Yes, you did.

He grips the necklace tightly.

"I Played for you."

And then a bright light, the brightest the whitest the hottest he has ever known.

And then nothing.

Live blindly and upon the hour. The Lord,
Who was the Future, died full long ago.
Knowledge which is the Past is folly. Go,
Poor child, and be not to thyself abhorred.
Around thine earth sun-wingèd winds do blow
And planets roll; a meteor draws his sword;
The rainbow breaks his seven-coloured chord
And the long strips of river-silver flow:
Awake! Give thyself to the lovely hours.
Drinking their lips, catch thou the dream in flight
About their fragile hairs' aërial gold.
Thou art divine, thou livest,—as of old
Apollo springing naked to the light,
And all his island shivered into flowers.

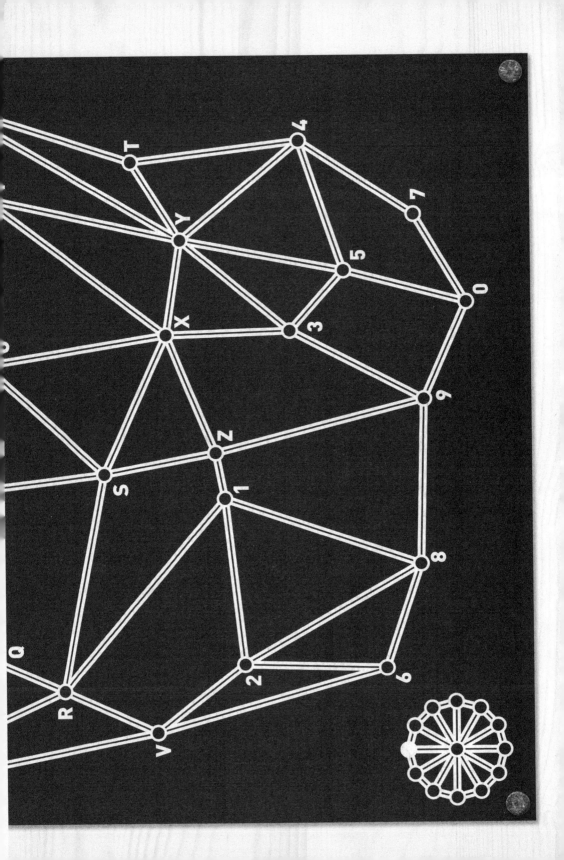

23 MONTHS, 5 DAYS LATER

Below Mercator Station, Palisades, New York, United States

Aisling and Hilal walk in the dawn twilight up a single-track dirt path. The Hudson River lies at their back, gray and flat and wide and silent but flowing powerfully toward the Atlantic Ocean, several miles to the south.

With the exception of a pair of four-inch folding knives, neither Aisling nor Hilal is armed.

Both like it that way.

They walk without urgency along the switchback trail that leads to a series of ladders and lifts plying the vertical cliff face up to the heart of Mercator Station. Their lungs and legs work against gravity. Though it's August, a summer chill is in the air and, as always in this part of the world, the sky is hung with gray clouds. These aren't very ominous, though—worldwide, but especially near the Impact Zone, the storms subsided significantly about nine weeks ago—so the two former Players haven't bothered with rain gear for their morning hike.

The basic geography of this area is mostly unchanged PA. The 200-million-year-old basalt cliffs that rise like a wall on the western shore of the river were unaffected by the impact. Being that old, and that durable, gives a thing a good measure of staying power.

These cliffs are the bones of this ancient valley—one that predates the existence of all sentient life in the Milky Way, including that of the Makers, by over 150 million years—and they loom now before Aisling and Hilal. They are dark and glistening, and while it isn't raining, the two Players still hear small gurgles of water moving all around them and under their feet, making its way down into the river and, soon enough, to the ocean itself.

But if the bones of the world survived here (and they categorically did *not* survive in the Crater Zone), the skin of the world did not.

The ecosystem here has simply been reset.

On that day nearly two years ago, everything was either burned away or torn from the ground and carried on the shock wave to the vast Debris Wall to the south and east. The force of the blast was so strong that even this wide fluvial rift did not catch any detritus, and it was laid bare. Out in the open, where Aisling and Hilal are right now, it's not much different than it was in the immediate aftermath of Abaddon. Not a single beam of direct sunlight has penetrated the clouds since then, and so the entire landscape is denuded and brown or black or gray. All that remains is dirt and rock, and all that grows are mushrooms.

Hilal stops and inspects one of these, bulbous and priapic, with a bright orange top. Aisling walked right by it without noticing. He stoops, unfolds his knife, and pokes the fungus. *"Amanita caesarea,"* he says quietly. "A young one."

Aisling stops and turns. "Hmm?"

"This mushroom." He cuts it quickly at the stem and slips it into a plastic collection bag. "Childress will like to see it, I am sure," he says.

"Childress would like to see a turd so long as it was growing out of the ground," Aisling points out.

Hilal simply smiles, tucks the bagged mushroom into a pocket, and stands back up. "Your phone is buzzing," he says.

Aisling looks left and right and pats her pockets. "Goddamn it, where—?" She finds her phone and slips it out and quizzically looks at the number display before shrugging and pressing it to her ear. "This is Aisling," she says curtly. A slight frown gives way to a smile as she says, "Oh hey, Jenny."

They talk.

At this moment Jenny is in Kazakhstan with Greg Jordan. They're preparing to board a brand-new Titan XA1 rocket carrying the final payload to an orbiting ship that will, in two weeks' time, embark on a three-year voyage to Mars. Their mission: to serve as the resident Maker and Endgame experts for an international team tasked with retrieving kepler 22b's ship for research and development purposes. And also, Aisling hopes, to retrieve the body of Pop Kopp so that he can be brought home and laid to rest.

Aisling grins broadly at some joke Jenny makes, the purple mark on Aisling's left cheek expanding as it curves from the corner of her eye down to her jaw. This is the last visible remnant of her time spent in 22b's ship, although she has no shortage of more personal and emotional remnants.

She has nightmares once a week or more. And Hilal hears about each one, writing down the details, keeping a log, trying to help Aisling understand them and get past them.

The women continue to talk. Hilal moves up the trail, patting Aisling's arm as he passes. She winks playfully. The cool air rises around his shoulders and neck from the Hudson River below. He makes three sharp turns, going higher up to Mercator, until Aisling's voice isn't more than a murmur fading into the background.

He stops. He is at least 15 meters higher than Aisling here, and the view is completely unobstructed. Boats and barges and ferries ply the water to the south. Above Manhattan, along the tops of the cliffs on the eastern bank, are newly built towers of steel topped with red blinking lights, and at their feet are lines of semipermanent buildings. Some of these are half-domed and green, others are not much more than white rectilinear trailers. These kinds of structures line the horizon to the north as far as the eye can see. Almost directly above Hilal a system of cables spans the river, and Hilal spies the sodium-orange lights illuminating the cabin of the cable car on the far side. Dark silhouettes of men or women are in it, preparing for the first crossing of the day. Above the car is the domed and pinnacled complex that is Van Houten Station, sister to Mercator, which is behind Hilal and just out of view over the lip of the Palisades. Aisling and Hilal—and Shari and Little Alice too—live in Mercator, along with 1,845 other men and women. Shari and Aisling and Hilal are true friends now—thanks mostly to Little Alice, but also to hours of counseling and a desire to set an example for the world by healing the rift that the Makers tore between them. If the lines can come together and heal, then the people of the world can too, and while Earth and its nations have not been transformed into a nirvana, they have made great if imperfect strides toward it.

Hilal and the others are here to lend their hands at righting what was put so wrong. The mission of everyone working here is twofold. The first is to terraform this area of the ruined Impact Zone. Under each dome grows a thriving ecosystem of young forests and wetlands and meadows that will, when the sun returns, be uncovered and set free onto the land. Second is to oversee the final stages of rubble remediation of the city that was once called New York but that is now, at least unofficially, called Phoenix East. This will be the first city to rise PA, a beachhead for the New New World, one born of defiance and determination and cooperation and goodwill. And preparing the land to build it anew has required a lot of work. While most of the structures in the five boroughs of New York were torn from the ground and flung into the Debris Wall, many, many metric tons of infrastructure remained underground, all of which had to be dealt with and, in most cases, dug up and removed.

Soon, as Jenny begins her journey to the Red Planet, 58 heads of state will travel here from all corners of the world to cut a ribbon on the New Jersey side of the New George Washington Bridge. Hilal and Aisling and Shari and Little Alice will be at the US president's side, and on that day the rebuilding will begin in earnest.

The cables twang overhead. Hilal squints. The cable car dips out and moves over the water.

The clouds, usually uniformly gray like an unending blanket, are graded and defined, like a bunch of dark cotton balls.

Aisling calls for him and waves. She's done talking to Jenny. He rubs his arm below the wooden ring he wears around his bicep. The ouroboros. A symbol of violence and all that they fought against, but also a symbol of rebirth.

All that they fight *for*.

Aisling walks toward him, wending up the path.

His pocket vibrates. He retrieves his phone and looks at the display.

Little Alice has texted him. *Come up, Uncle. I want to show you what I made this morning.*

He writes, *10 minutes.*

The wind picks up.

His phone buzzes again. *I can see you. Look up.*

He glances over his shoulder. Thirty meters above, leaning between the steel bars of the railings, is Little Alice. She's five years old now and taller than any child her age. She leans out farther than Hilal likes, but she is young and excitable and Hilal is certain that Shari is a few feet behind her, calm and attentive. Understandably, Shari hardly ever leaves Little Alice alone.

Little Alice waves fiercely. Hilal waves back.

The wind whistles down the valley as a bright flash, yellow and orange, slices the air. It hits the wet basalt cliff a few meters below Little Alice's feet. The girl pulls from between the railings and jumps up and down and points to the sky in the east. Hilal can't hear her, but he knows Little Alice is ecstatic, and that Shari must be ecstatic too.

Hilal swings around. Aisling is less than a meter away, and she too stares to the east, slack-shouldered and awestruck.

The clouds have broken, and there, filtering through a hole, are three long spears of dawn sunlight.

"Holy shit, Hilal," Aisling says.

"Yes," he says.

A loud air horn goes off at Mercator, and seconds later another horn answers from Van Houten, then smaller horns echo up and down the valley from substations and garden domes and mess halls and office blocks and dormitories.

Hilal bounds down to Aisling and wraps an arm around her shoulders.

The sun stays.

The wind blows.

The clouds move.

The sun disappears.

The horns blare on nonetheless.

"That was beautiful," Aisling says.

"Yes."

"We're actually going to make it, aren't we?"

Hilal looks Aisling directly in her eyes. His skin hideous and scarred. Hers porcelain and clear but marked. Both marked by Endgame.

"Yes," he says.

And then together: "Yes."

(Endnotes)

i   http://goo.gl/afsgAT

ii   http://goo.gl/D4hJFC

iii   https://goo.gl/b1GIbn

iv   http://goo.gl/SGdRu8

v   http://goo.gl/jHDVwM

KEEP READING FOR A SNEAK PEEK AT:

ENDGAME

THE FUGITIVE ARCHIVES
VOLUME 1: PROJECT BERLIN

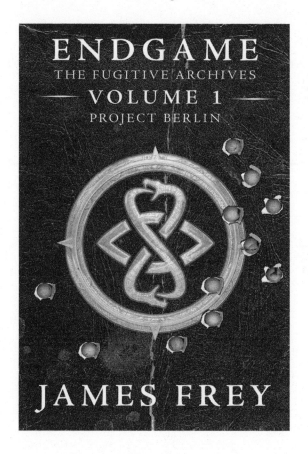

CHAPTER I

Boone
December 24, 1948

"How you doing, Peterson?" Driscoll asks as we descend through the thick fog. "You look a little green. Do me a favor and try not to lose your lunch all over my plane, okay?"

The C-54, buffeted by a crosswind, shakes fiercely, rattling us like peas in a can. It's been like this the whole flight. Driscoll grins at me. My name isn't Peterson, but he doesn't know that. He also doesn't know that I've been in far more nerve-racking situations than a rough approach. I may look like any other 19-year-old GI, but I'm far more than that.

"Last time I flew over Berlin, I was *dropping* eggs on their heads," Driscoll continues, shouting to be heard above the roar of the engines. "Now I'm bringing them eggs for their breakfast." His joke about the bombing raids that destroyed huge parts of the city during the last days of the war isn't funny. I smile anyway. I need him to think I'm just one of the guys, at least for a little longer.

The truth is, I *am* a little bit nervous. I've been training for war since I was a kid. I've been through more than Driscoll and all the other soldiers on the plane ever saw in boot camp. But this is my biggest mission yet. A lot is riding on it. And yet I don't even know exactly what it's about.

I know the basics. I've got to find a man and get him out of Berlin. I know his name and his suspected location. And I know that if he won't come with me, or if someone else gets to him first, I have to kill him. A simple plan. That's why I know there's more to it than the council has told me. For some reason they don't want me to know the details

1

of why this man is so important, which means they don't want anyone *else* to have that information either. If I get captured, my enemies can try as hard as they want to get me to talk, but I can't tell them what I don't know. Not that I would talk anyway. I'd never do anything to jeopardize the safety of my line. The council knows that, so it bothers me a little bit that they're taking this precaution. More than a little bit, if I'm honest. This is the first time since I became the Cahokian Player that they've kept me in the dark about something. I don't like the feeling.

I push that irritation from my mind as the Tempelhof airstrip appears—seemingly out of nowhere—and meets the wheels of the plane. The rumbling intensifies, shaking my bones, and I hang on as Driscoll applies the brakes. Through the cockpit windows I see groups of children standing on top of piles of debris that line the runway. They wave at us, grinning and clapping their hands.

"Look at that," Driscoll says. "It's like we're Santa Claus."

In a way, we are. After all, it's Christmas Eve. And along with the ten tons of eggs, milk, meat, flour, and other basic supplies in our hold, we're bringing bags of wrapped gifts to hand out to the people of the city. Chocolate bars for the kids. Cigarettes for the men. Perfume for the women. The war ended in 1945, but more than three years later, Berlin is still trying to recover. And since the Soviets cut off all sea and land access to the city's western zone earlier in the year, life has gotten even harder.

Thankfully, the airlift organized by the American, French, and British militaries has been successful in bringing supplies to the city. It's also provided me with a handy way inside. Posing as an American soldier has been easy enough. There are so many young men being assigned to the dozens of daily airlift flights coming out of Rhein-Main Air Base that no one notices one more. All I had to do was put on a uniform and start helping load the plane.

When the Skymaster comes to a stop, we reverse the process begun three hours earlier, transferring everything in our cargo area onto the trucks that pull up one after the other.

"Nobody disappear!" Driscoll shouts as we launch into action. "General Tunner's orders! We get this stuff off, turn around, and land back in Frankfurt in time for eggnog and cookies!"

The airlift is a well-oiled machine. Planes land at two-minute intervals, and the total time from unloading to takeoff is 25 minutes. Everything moves like clockwork, and everyone has a job to do. I can't make a break for the main terminal or someone is bound to notice the missing pair of hands. But when we're almost finished, one of the mobile coffee trucks arrives filled with pretty German girls who hand out drinks and smiles, and I take the opportunity to slip away while the others are distracted. I don't look back, and nobody calls Peterson's name. Even when they finally notice he's gone, it won't matter, as the United States Army has no record of him anyway.

Once I'm away from the airport, I make my way into Berlin. In an attempt to maintain a balance of power, the city has been divided into four sectors, each one controlled by one of the Allied superpowers: Great Britain, France, the United States, and the Soviet Union. In reality, though, it's become the Soviets on one side and everyone else on the other. Fortunately, Tempelhof is in the American sector, and a GI walking through the streets is a common sight. I'd prefer to be dressed like a civilian, but at least wearing a uniform means that nobody questions me. And in case they do, all my identity papers carry the name of Alan Peterson.

It's early evening, a little past seven, and already dark. A light snow is falling. And even though the streets are dotted with rubble—some of the buildings I pass have shattered windows and walls that have crumbled, so you can see into living rooms and kitchens still filled with furniture—it somehow manages to feel like Christmas. There are wreaths on some of the doors, and trees decorated with ornaments are visible in the parlors of some of the houses. The shops I pass don't have much displayed in their windows, but signs reading FRÖHLICHE WEIHNACHTEN are taped to the glass.

Bells chime, and when I turn a corner, I see people walking into a church. The inside is lit by candles, and the sound of a carol being played on an organ floats from the open doorway. This makes me think of my own family back in Illinois. It's just after noon there, and I know my mother is getting ready for the Christmas Eve gathering. She's been cooking all day. The Tom and Jerry bowl and glasses that only come out once a year are set out on the sideboard. She's probably already hung the stockings from the mantel over the fireplace, one for each kid, arranged in order from youngest to oldest: Marnie, Evan, Lily, Ella, Peter, me, and Jackson. In the morning, the stockings will all be filled to overflowing. Even mine, although I won't be there to open it. And even Jackson's, although it's been three years since he died. The people of Berlin aren't the only ones who've lost something to the war. I hurry by the church, clearing my mind by focusing on the address the council gave me. I memorized it, as well as the best route to reach it. Writing things down is risky. As my father told me repeatedly when I started my Player training, the brain is the only notebook nobody can steal.

It takes me another 20 minutes to find the house. It's in a section of the city that was hit hard by the Allied bombing, one of a row of connected brick town homes. Most of the buildings are empty, uninhabitable because of the damage. This one looks empty too. Most of the windows are boarded up, and the front door has an official notice on it warning people not to enter due to unsafe conditions. But looks can be deceiving. Just because you can't see somebody, it doesn't mean nobody is there. Sometimes, you just have to look harder.

I don't announce myself by knocking on the front door. This isn't a social call. Instead, I go into the bombed-out house next door, climb the stairs to the third floor, and step through a shattered window onto a narrow ledge that runs along the front of the whole row of houses. I press myself against what's left of the wall and slowly move one foot at a time toward the house next door. If anyone notices me, maybe they'll just think I'm Saint Nicholas coming to deliver presents.

When I reach the closest window of the target house, I pause beside it and look inside. The bedroom behind the cracked, dirty glass is empty. When I push on the window frame, the window slides up. I slip inside, turn on the small flashlight I carry in my pocket, and look around. It's just as cold in here as it is outside, and I can see my breath. There's no heat. But coal is in short supply, and no one is supposed to be living here anyway, so this might not mean anything. More telling is that everything in the room is covered with a thick layer of dust. No one has been here in a long time.

Then I notice the footprints. They start just outside the door, run along a hallway, and disappear down a flight of stairs. A faint glow emanates from the second floor. Someone is here after all. I creep to the end of the hall and pause. I can hear voices. There are two speakers, a man and what sounds like a younger woman.

This is a problem. There's supposed to be only one person here. A man. I haven't seen him yet, but even if the man I hear talking is the one I'm after, who is the girl? Is she a wife? A daughter? Something else? I need to get a look at them.

I draw my M1911 standard-issue military pistol and walk down the stairs. It's not my weapon of choice, but it's what Private Peterson would carry, and nobody would think twice about me having it, so it's what I've got. The voices grow louder as I descend. When I reach the landing, I pause. The speakers are in a room just to my left.

"I wish Oskar and Rutger were here with us," the man says.

"You know how Oskar is," the young woman says. "He didn't want to risk anyone following us to you."

"I think everyone must have forgotten about me by now," says the man.

"Still, he's right to be cautious. I worry about you making visits here."

"Perhaps it's time for you to leave," the girl says. "You've shut yourself up in here long enough. Pass the duty on to someone else. Oskar and I—"

"Lottie, please," the man interrupts. "How many times have we talked about this? I cannot leave."

"You mean you will not," says Lottie. "Do you want to spend the rest of your life here?"

"I'm already a dead man. Remember?"

The man's words chill me. What does he mean? And who is this girl? Maybe it doesn't matter. Maybe I'm better off if I don't know who Lottie is. I know from experience that it's easier to kill someone when you know nothing about her.

"Let's not discuss it further," the man says. "It's Christmas Eve. Play something for me. You know I always love to hear you play."

A moment later, I hear the sound of a piano. It's badly out of tune, but the melody is familiar. "Silent Night." The girl begins to sing, and the man joins in.

I risk moving closer and looking through the doorway. Inside the room, a scraggly pine tree stands in front of a boarded-up window, its branches hung with silver tinsel and a handful of colorful glass balls. The piano is against a wall, with the young woman seated at it. The man stands beside her. Both of them are wearing long, thick coats.

I recognize the man from the photo the council showed me. It's Evrard Sauer. I'm in the right place. But the council said nothing about the girl. Now I have to decide what to do about her. My orders were to leave no witnesses, which gives me only one option. I know what I should do—what I've agreed to do for my council and my line—but the thought of actually doing it doesn't sit right with me. The girl is simply in the wrong place at the wrong time. I hate to make her pay for that with her life.

They finish singing, and the man takes something from the pocket of his coat. It's a present wrapped in newspaper and tied with plain white string. He hands it to the girl, who carefully opens it. A happy smile spreads across her face.

"Toffees!" she says. "Wherever did you get them?"

She doesn't wait for an answer before taking one of the candies from the box and unwrapping it, the cellophane crackling in her fumbling fingers. She puts the toffee in her mouth and sucks on it, her eyes closed. I don't think I've ever seen someone enjoy a piece of candy so much.

She opens her eyes and reaches into her own pocket. She takes out a package, this one wrapped in brown butcher paper. She gives it to the man. He opens it and holds up a red knitted scarf.

"I unraveled one of my sweaters for the yarn," the girl says, sounding embarrassed. "Wool is still rationed."

"It's beautiful," the man assures her as he wraps it around his neck. "Thank you."

The girl turns back to the piano and begins to play again. This time the song is "O Tannenbaum."

I've obviously interrupted their Christmas Eve celebration. And if I do what I've been instructed to do, I'm about to make it a whole lot worse. I still feel like something is off, but there's no time to contact my council for further advice, so I have to make a choice based on the available information and what I've been told. That means completing the mission according to plan.

I accept the reality of my situation, even though I don't like it, and prepare to act. Then the sound of a door being kicked open comes from the first floor. Wood splinters. Heavy footsteps pound up the stairs. The man and the young woman stop singing and look at each other. I have just enough time to dart back to the stairwell before three figures burst onto the landing. Two of them have guns drawn.

"Evrard Sauer," one of them, a man, says. "You are under arrest for collaborating with the National Socialist German Workers' Party." He's speaking in German, but with a heavy Russian accent. And although he's used the more formal name for them, I know he's just accused Sauer of working with the Nazis.

"Who are you?" the girl asks.

"Be still, Lottie," says Sauer. "Do as you're told."

His voice is quiet, sad. As if he has feared this moment for a long time. I huddle on the stairs, my pistol at the ready. Besides the two men, there is a woman in the room. She stands slightly behind the men, her hands in her pockets. As I lean forward for a better look, my foot presses against the floorboards, making a faint creaking sound. I see her tense. She turns her head toward the stairwell, and for a moment I think she's seen me. But I can't look away. She's younger than I thought. My age. And beautiful. She has long dark hair and dark eyes, and for a second I'm sure that I've seen her before. Then it hits me— she looks like Wonder Woman from the comic books my sister Lily loves so much. I find myself frozen in place.

Then she turns away, and it's as if a switch has been turned off and I can breathe again. I blend into the shadows, my finger on the trigger of my gun in case I need to use it. I know I *will* need to use it. I can't let these people take Sauer. I think I know who they are. MGB. Russian intelligence. And apparently they want him because of his association with the Nazis. What he did for them, I don't know. Just as I don't know why he's so important to my council. What I do know is that I can't let them leave with him.

"If you come quietly, there will be no problems," the first man says. Sauer nods. He motions to Lottie, who stands up.

It's time. I start to raise my pistol, aiming it at one of the Soviet agents. Before I can fire, the woman draws her hand from her pocket. She's holding a Tokarev TT-33. There are two shots, and her companions collapse to the floor. She lowers the gun.

"You have a choice," she says to Sauer and Lottie. "Come with me and live, or join them."

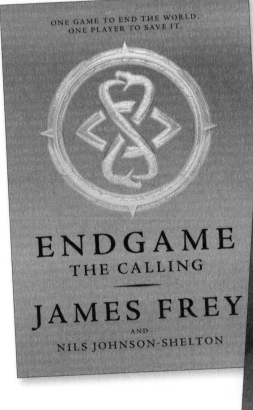